Massively Multiplayer Game Development 2

Massively Multiplayer Game Development 2

Edited by Thor Alexander

CHARLES RIVER MEDIA, INC.

Hingham, Massachusetts

Cover Design: Tyler Creative
Cover Image: © Sony Online Entertainment. Reprinted with permission.

CHARLES RIVER MEDIA
25 Thomson Place
Boston, MA 02210
617-757-7900
617-757-7969 (FAX)
crm.info@thomson.com
www.charlesriver.com

This book is printed on acid-free paper.

Thor Alexander. *Massively Multiplayer Game Development 2.*
ISBN-13: 978-1-58450-390-3
ISBN-10: 1-58450-390-4

All brand names and product names mentioned in this book are trademarks or service marks of their respective companies. Any omission or misuse (of any kind) of service marks or trademarks should not be regarded as intent to infringe on the property of others. The publisher recognizes and respects all marks used by companies, manufacturers, and developers as a means to distinguish their products.

Library of Congress Cataloging-in-Publication Data
Massively multiplayer game development 2 / edited by Thor Alexander.
    p. cm.
Includes bibliographical references and index.
ISBN 1-58450-390-4 (hardcover : alk. paper)
1. Computer games—Programming. I. Alexander, Thor, 1968-
QA76.76.C672A4283 2005
794.8'1526—dc22
                                    2004030997

Printed in the United States of America
07 7 6 5 4 3 2

CHARLES RIVER MEDIA titles are available for site license or bulk purchase by institutions, user groups, corporations, etc. For additional information, please contact the Special Sales Department at 800-347-7707.

Contents

SECTION 1 MASSIVELY MULTIPLAYER DESIGN TECHNIQUES 1

Acknowledgments

First, I want to extend my deepest appreciation to the contributors whose hard work made this book possible, and the contributors of the first MMP book who blazed the trail for others to follow.

Second, I want to extend a very special thank you to the following people who have personally encouraged or inspired me throughout my life to chase down my dreams and fulfill them: Jimmy Monson, Marcia Prescott, Diane Pavlik, Steve Lindquist, Gary Moore, Andy Anderson, Jodie Norton, Scott Thomson, Tony Rocco Castellani, Phil Bailey, Lauren Winters, Debbie Schneider, John Rooney, Missy Henrickson, Kelly DeCook, Mark and Kelly Cussans, Andy and Sara Lynch, Buck and Dawn Andrews, Ryan Stoddard, Scott Wescott, Dan "Neller" Heller, Dmo Betts, The Aiello Brothers, Eddie Hamaty, Carl "SSCGBB" Jacobs, Anne Bowers, Scot Barnes, Jose Cayao Jr., Reza Beha, Phil Dawdy, Melanie Rogers, Howard Jones, and last but far from least, Aimee Noel Vladic.

Next, I want to thank all of the great and talented people with whom I have had the pleasure of working with over the years in this wacky business that we call the *game industry*, especially John Donham, Rob Martyn, Phil Gorrow, Andy Hollis, Erick Hackenburg, Craig Alexander, Rade Stojsavljevic, Adam Isgreen, Aaron Cohen, Debbie Johnson, David Yee and the EnB team, Rick Hall, Gordon Walton, Jeff Anderson, Richard Garriott, Drew Markham, Greg Goodrich, Mal Blackwell, Alex Mayberry, Corky Lehmkuhl, Max Yoshikawa, Starr Long, Jeremy Gaffney, and the UO2 Team.

Finally, I want to like to thank über-publisher Jenifer Niles for all of her help with and support of this book series.

Foreword

Gordon Walton
Sony Online Entertainment

In the fall of 1977, my life was ruined when I was exposed to my first multiplayer online computer game. That game was *Empire* on the Plato system. *Empire* was a graphical *Star Trek* game where several dozen people battled it out with and against others for control of the universe playing on the Federation, Klingon, Orion, or Romulan sides. It was played on a graphical terminal with a monochrome plasma screen over a modem to a CDC mainframe at the University of Illinois at Urbana. It was awesome, and I spent over 100 hours playing it before moving on to the other single-player and online games that the Plato system supported.

Perhaps calling my life "ruined" is an overstatement, but I have certainly found it near impossible to hold a "real" job since then and have spent almost all the intervening years working on computer games in some capacity. For years, I designed and built standalone games, since multiplayer gaming wasn't really very commercial yet. However, I never forgot how cool playing with and against other people was. With the rise of the online services like CompuServe, Genie, and later Quantum Link/ AOL, there suddenly was a small but growing market for online games. With the explosion of the Internet from 1995 onward, suddenly massively multiplayer gaming became much more widespread.

In early 1995, I had the opportunity to join Kesmai Corporation. John Taylor and Kelton Flinn founded the company and had been making massively multiplayer (MMP) online games commercially for over 13 years by then. They had recently been acquired by NewsCorp and were expanding rapidly. John and Kelton brought me in as their studio manager and proceeded to teach me about the design, development, and business of MMP online gaming.

Boy, did I have a lot to learn! So many of the lessons of standalone game design were totally inappropriate for online games. Huge amounts of work had to go into facilitating communication and community for players. You had to think about the server and the client, about latency of response and race conditions, and 99% uptime and maintainable code were requirements. It was a new and very complex world indeed. Making games had always been hard, but this was impossibly hard, and since I love a challenge I really loved the process of making games in this medium.

However, that was only the start of my obsession with online gaming. I started to learn about game communities. I had been participating in online communities since about 1981, first on dial-in BBSs, then on Bix, CompuServe, Genie, and AOL. Therefore, I had some familiarity with how people might act online, especially if they were passionate about the subject matter of the forum. However, I was not prepared for how important an online game was for many of our players. They had passion that was the square of anything I had seen before. They weren't playing the games, they were living a big part of their social lives within them. They were expressing themselves in ways impossible in their day-to-day life. Experiencing this and seeing it in action across several games made me realize we were inventing an entirely new entertainment medium—and I was hooked! Not since those first experiences playing on Plato and then owning my very first microcomputer and making games in the late 1970s through the mid 1980s had I been this excited. I had that feeling again that what I was doing might just change the world.

Before I had been at Kesmai a year, my life had changed because I was committed to working only in the MMP gaming medium for the rest of my career. It was the one place in gaming where the rules were still being written, and the opportunity to change the world was the greatest.

MMP online gaming is a new and unique entertainment medium. Most importantly, it can engage and touch people emotionally like no other entertainment medium to date. First, it is interactive, which means the players control their own experience. They decide what to do to derive entertainment from the work. Next, it is an entertainment medium that includes other people who play with or against you within the game environment. While there can be game-directed entities within the world, real people are interacting with you also. Most games are always available, meaning you can play when you want to, not just at set times. Your persona within the game world persists over time, and the world itself may have changes to it to be persistent as well. As a player, you have anonymity, meaning that while other players may know your in-game persona they do not have access to who you are in real life. Most of these games require teamwork (playing with others) to overcome challenges within the environment.

This alchemy of elements produces a unique entertainment experience that meets a need of modern society that is largely unfulfilled. For eons, humans have lived in relatively small groups with tight social bonds. They knew the dozens of people who lived around them pretty intimately. Today, because of the evening news, most people are conditioned to avoid getting involved with their neighbors. It is a rare person who knows the first names of all the people who live on the eight compass points from his or her home. Whereas for almost all of human history this has been the norm, I assert that this has left most people in our urban societies with a huge socialization deficit. We know something is missing, but not exactly what it is.

Our medium allows people to preserve their anonymity while satisfying their unmet socialization needs in an extremely safe environment. This is why we see so many people who start an MMP game become so deeply engaged, even if they were not a hardcore gamer prior to that time.

This medium is tremendously powerful since we are tapping into fundamental human desires and needs. We should approach our work with wonder, awe, and some sense of caution. As my friend Jonathan Baron is fond of saying, "The human heart can't distinguish virtual feelings from real ones." The emotions we tap into and the effect we have on our players are real. Therefore, it is incumbent on us to be good stewards of our players' experience in these worlds given the depth at which we engage their feelings. What we do and how we do it matters!

I'm pretty sure that we are nowhere near reaching competence at this aspect of our medium, much less mastery. This is why I remain so excited to be involved in this work, as we are still discovering what works best. This is an important book for our medium in that it shares the experience of so many professionals within the business, allowing us to capitalize on their successes while avoiding their failures.

What the Future Holds

There is a degree of pessimism among game developers about this MMP online medium. Several projects have dramatically underperformed and many more have never made it to launch. Frankly, we haven't innovated very quickly, and many games have failed to learn from the MMP games that came before them. Consequently, many of the games in progress are copies of games that have already been successful, without any significant innovation to distinguish them.

However, I remain completely optimistic. It is the nature of entertainment to be highly Darwinian, meaning that we need to have a fair amount of failure in the process of discovering new and exciting directions. Repeated failures serve to drive the lessons home more effectively. Moreover, the occasional brilliant success, in addition to driving far too many clones, will help spark someone to try something even more outrageous in a future title.

My only advice to those of you involved in the creation of this medium is to educate yourselves as much as humanly possible. Don't just read all the books and articles out there (although that is a great start). Play many of the live games, and play them as a player, not just as a professional game developer. Play them long enough to master them (which can be 2 to 12 months depending on the game) so that you end up getting a full experience. Learn as much as you can about sociology, politics, history, game theory, and networking (the human kind). Throw in some viral marketing, management, and of course all forms of standalone computer gaming. Then work on understanding the human condition and all the other entertainment mediums. I know I'm recommending a lot of study, but the innovation that moves our medium forward will come from such people. And I for one am sure that significant innovation is coming before another decade passes.

I am expecting MMP games to surpass standalone gaming in importance as an entertainment medium in my lifetime. I believe it is inevitable and that the last 25 years or so have been a historical anomaly fostered by the lack of connections between computers during the 1970s through 1990s. Gaming is inherently social and there were relatively few examples of standalone gaming prior to the introduction of the personal computer. Now that almost all computers have connectivity, I fully expect gaming to be dominated by online gaming, and MMP online gaming to be the most important segment of online gaming. I hope you join us in creating the future of the MMP online medium.

Who Are These Authors?

All the authors of this book are dedicated professionals in the business of making MMP games. I have worked with most of them, and as a group, they are incredibly smart, totally committed, and really nice people to boot! You can't go wrong reading what they have to say, and if you have a better way to handle anything covered in the book, please submit it for the next edition. No one knows all the best ways to make and run an MMP game, and even if they think they do, larger scales and evolving consumer tastes will assure that more experimentation, learning, and optimization will need to occur.

What Is This Book About?

This book exists to help anyone who is interested in creating MMP games. We want the medium to evolve, and the best way for that to happen is for knowledge to be shared. The lessons learned about what has worked and what has failed is critical to accelerating that evolutionary process. It happens far too slowly naturally, and this book is an accelerated way to acquire key pieces of knowledge about making and running MMP online games. If you work with people who haven't read it, make sure they get a copy and do so. Everyone involved with this book wants you to make a successful online game that pushes the medium forward. So get busy!

Preface

Thor Alexander

Welcome to *Massively Multiplayer Game Development 2*.

This book is a comprehensive and insightful anthology of articles from the developers of the most successful and anticipated massively multiplayer (MMP) games, including *EverQuest*, *Ultima Online*, *The Sims Online*, *Second Life*, *Asheron's Call*, *Star Wars Galaxies*, and more. Within these pages, you will find a wealth of unique and rare knowledge acquired in the trenches of MMP and online game development by some of the online game industry's best and brightest developers.

Intended Audience—Not Just for Programmers!

Although this book is patterned after the successful *Game Programming Gems* series of books, also published by Charles River Media, it strives to appeal to a wider audience. While programmers will find a multitude of technical *gems* within these pages, designers and producers will also find many articles quite readable and informative without all of the technical terminology found in most programming books. Customer support representatives will find articles in several sections that will prove to be an invaluable resource of knowledge that they would be hard pressed to find elsewhere.

How to Read This Book

There are two suggested ways to read this book:

Hunt-and-peck: Skip through and read what you find interesting.
Cover-to-cover: This could take a while, so keep your bookmark handy.

Hunt-and-Peck

Hunt-and-peck is the recommended method. Most of the articles are meant to be bite-sized and digested in one sitting. Their self-contained nature allows them to be read out of order without regard for the articles that precede them.

Cover-to-Cover

Anthology works such as this are not written by a single author, and the individual articles are meant to be complete in themselves if read in a standalone fashion. However, all of the articles share common subject matter and have an interconnected focus. The sections and the articles within them are laid out in a manner that lends itself to being read in order if so desired.

The "Big" Idea

Information wants to be free! Ideas are easy. It is the *execution* of those ideas that produces great games. By sharing this knowledge with you, the reader, it is the express wish of this author that this book will help foster an atmosphere of collaboration and cooperation between MMP and online game developers.

About the Cover

EverQuest II from
Sony Online Entertainment

EverQuest is the king of North American MMP games, and its sequel is targeted to build on that success and introduce the world of *Norath* to an even wider audience.

Special thanks to John Donham and the crew at SOE for getting us permission to use this image.

Contributor Bios

Thor Alexander—Hard Coded Games

editor@hardcodedgames.com

Thor Alexander has been working in the game industry for 12 years as a designer, engineer, and entrepreneur. He has held lead design and senior programming positions at Electronic Arts, Microsoft, and Xatrix Entertainment, and is a founding member of Asgard Interactive and CEO of Harbinger Technologies, Inc. He has contributed to titles such as *Earth & Beyond*, *Freelancer*, *Kingpin*, and the *Ultima Online* series. Thor is also a contributor to the books *AI Game Programming Wisdom* and *Game Programming Gems 3*, and the editor of the *Massively Multiplayer Game Development* book series.

Gideon Amir—Majorem

gidibarvaz@yahoo.com

Gideon Amir is a mathematician and algorithm developer. He took his first (long) dip into the world of algorithm development serving in the Israeli military intelligence, and continued his venture into the computer industry working at RichFX, Inc. He later moved to Majorem studios where he developed the game engine. He is currently pursuing his Ph.D. in mathematics at the Weizmann Institute of Science, specializing in random processes.

He wishes to thank Yuval Mendelson and Assaf Mendelson for their help and fruitful remarks.

Shannon Appelcline—Skotos

shannona@skotos.net

Shannon Appelcline has a long history of involvement in tabletop gaming industries and has been working in online design since 1999. At Skotos, his design, development, and programming credits include work on *Castle Marrach*, *Galactic Emperor: Hegemony*, *Lovecraft Country: Arkham by Night*, and *Monsters! Monsters! Grendel's Revenge*. Shannon has also been the editor for the *Skotos Article Archive* for the last four years. He has edited over a dozen different gaming columns by many industry luminaries and has personally penned approximately half-a-million words on the topic of game design.

Ramon Axelrod—AiSeek, Inc.

mushroomramon@yahoo.com

Ramon Axelrod served for six years at the Israeli Defense Force R&D in operations research and mathematical decision-making, researching in the fields of large-scale simulations and artificial intelligence. He later was chief software architect of an MMORTS platform at Majorem Studios. Currently, Ramon is the CTO of AiSeek Inc., a startup company developing hardware for accelerating and facilitating development of artificial intelligence in next-generation games.

He wishes to thank Yuval Mendelson and Assaf Mendelson for their help and fruitful remarks.

Richard A. Bartle—University of Essex

richard@mud.co.uk

Dr. Richard Bartle co-wrote the first virtual world, MUD ("Multi-User Dungeon") in 1978, and has thus been at the forefront of the online games industry from its very inception. A former university lecturer in artificial intelligence and current visiting professor in computer game design (both at the University of Essex, UK), he is an influential writer on all aspects of virtual world design, development, and management. As an independent consultant, he has worked with most of the major online game companies in the UK and the United States over the past 20 years. Dr. Bartle's 2003 book, *Designing Virtual Worlds*, has already established itself as a foundation text for researchers and developers of virtual worlds alike.

John Donham—Sony Online Entertainment

jdonham@soe.sony.com

As vice president of product development for Sony Online Entertainment's San Diego studio, John Donham manages the teams producing *EverQuest*, *EverQuest II*, *EverQuest Online Adventures*, *PlanetSide*, two products under development, and SOE's publishing projects including *Champions of Norrath: Return to Arms*.

John started in the online game industry over 12 years ago as a programmer and designer for commercial text-based MUD companies Novalink (*Legends*) and Simutronics (*GemStone III*, *DragonRealms*). Beginning in 1995, John worked as a producer and designer at Simutronics for several MMP products: *DragonRealms*, *ArchMage*, *Hercules and Xena*, and *CyberStrike 2*. During this time, John also helped manage Simutronics' transition from a dependency on online services (such as AOL and CompuServe) to a service-independent Internet game company, helping create the infrastructure needed to run an online game service (Web site, billing system, customer service tools, 24/7 monitoring of the game products). In 1998 and 1999, he managed all product development and live products at Simutronics. In 1999, John moved on to Outrage Entertainment, where he helped the company grow from one development team to two, and he produced the early stages of the single-player console products *Munukuru* and *Alter Echo*. In 2000, John joined Sony Online Entertainment as a senior producer, shipped *Star Wars Galaxies* in 2003, and managed the *Galaxies* live team for the first several months after launch. John then moved on to be the director of development for the San Diego studio, and helped ship *EQ: Gates of Discord*, *EQ: Omens of War*, and *EverQuest II*. John has led SOE's San Diego studio development since October 2004. John would like to thank Fannie Gunton and John Gonzalez for their assistance with his article.

Adi Gaash—Exci-TV

adi.gaash@thrill-factor.com

Adi Gaash is currently the executive producer at Exci-TV, a firm that develops original game content and is a transformer of online and MMP games into the new age of digital TV. Previously, he was the founder and CEO of Majorem LTD, the developer of *Ballerium*, the first real MMP real-time strategy game. Adi has 10 years of experience in multimedia, entertainment, and communication projects.

Tom Gordon—AlienPants

cro@alienpants.com

Tom has been involved in online gaming in the UK since joining the team at BarrysWorld in early 1999, taking over responsibility for community management, the BarrysWorld Web site, dealing with customer Web site hosting issues, and day-to-day support. Since leaving BarrysWorld and forming AlienPants, he has been heavily involved in online and mobile gaming, including creating a live television program that integrated mobile texting with PC and console games cheats, and launching several SMS-based products and services aimed at the PC and console games mass market.

Tom is also involved in the day-to-day running of the world's largest IRC network, QuakeNet, for the past two years. QuakeNet is home to more than 450,000 of Europe's hardcore online games players, with more than 200,000 people online every night, and is rapidly becoming the home of online gaming in Europe.

Brian Green—Near Death Studios, Inc.

brian.green@neardeathstudios.com

Brian Green, often known online as "Psychochild," is an experienced online game designer and programmer. He was an active text MUD developer in college, and started his professional career in 1998 working on the classic PvP online RPG *Meridian 59*. His company, Near Death Studios, Inc., was founded in 2001 and purchased the rights to *Meridian 59* in late 2001. In 2002, the team at Near Death Studios, Inc. commercially relaunched *Meridian 59*. More information about *Meridian 59* can be found at *www.meridian59.com/*.

Jim Hicke—Xtreme Strategy Games

jhicke@xtremestrategy.com

Jim Hicke is a software industry veteran with over 25 years of management and software development experience. Prior to joining the gaming industry, Jim was part of multiple successful high-technology startups. During that period, he served as a director of research and development and a board of directors member for ENFIN Software Corporation, and as a vice president of research and development at MicroTac Software, a publicly traded company. Jim entered the game development industry by founding Chantemar Creations Inc. and shipping his first product, *Steel Reign*, under Sony's SCEA label. Recognizing the potential of the new MMP game genre, Jim joined a team of developers who went on to found Verant Interactive. During his tenure at Verant, which later become Sony Online Entertainment, Jim was solving technical problems unique to the new MMO RTS genre and using his expertise to help the *EverQuest II* team. Jim is now a partner in Xtreme Strategy Games, where he is using his entrepreneurial skills and technical expertise in bringing to market the next generation of games and gaming technologies.

David Kennerly—Fine Game Design

david@finegamedesign.com

David Kennerly directed five MMP games in the United States and Korea. He localized Korea's first world, *The Kingdom of the Winds*, and designed the social system of *Dark Ages: Online Roleplaying*. Before joining Nexon in 1997, he designed *The X-Files Trivia Game* for 20th Century Fox, and troubleshot U.S. Army networks in Korea. David encourages creativity among developers and players. He helped organize MUD-Dev Conferences, and founded an online library of fan fiction. David has authored on game design for ITT Tech, Westwood College, Gamasutra.com, and the IGDA white paper *Persistent State Worlds*.

Joe Ludwig—Flying Lab Software

joe@flyinglab.com

Joe Ludwig is a lead programmer at Seattle-based Flying Lab Software. He designed the core architecture behind Flying Lab's upcoming MMP game *Pirates of the Burning*

Sea. Prior to his official entry into the game industry on Sierra's ill-fated *Middle-Earth Online*, Joe worked on network printserver firmware at Hewlett-Packard. When he isn't programming online games, Joe can often be found in his workshop building fighting robots. Joe wishes to thank his infinitely patient wife Nissa who puts up with his tendency to take on too many projects without the slightest complaint. He is also grateful for all the help the crew at Flying Lab Software provided honing his articles and providing design assistance. Arr!

Craig McDonald—Origin Systems (R.I.P.)

macnugetz@earthlink.net

Craig McDonald is relatively new to the industry, starting at Origin as a game master for *Ultima Online* in 1999. Working at Origin until it closed in the spring of 2004, Craig worked in some capacity in almost all facets of the organization, including customer service, community, and marketing, ending up in quality assurance as the lead for *Ultima Online*. Upon leaving Origin, Craig had a brief stint at Inevitable Entertainment as associate producer on the first-person-shooter, *Area 51*.

He is currently taking a break from the games business, and is working normal hours in the online brokerage industry as a product development manager at Cyber-Trader: A Charles Schwab Company®. Craig also continues his academic pursuits working to graduate with an MBA in May 2005 from the McCombs School of Business at the University of Texas at Austin.

Larry Mellon—Electronic Arts

larry@maggotranch.com

A former university bum, Larry Mellon funded a decade-long school habit as an itinerant programmer across various campus R&D groups. Larry began using automated test and metrics systems in 1989 as a tool to cope with the complexity of optimizing simulations running in parallel across distributed and shared memory supercomputers. Extensions on such tools proved quite valuable in shipping EA's flagship MMP title, *The Sims Online*. Larry went on to build a second-generation test&measure system for other Maxis games, including *The Sims 2.0*. Larry now works for himself, applying automation to all aspects of developing and operating MMP games. His papers on automation and scalable virtual world infrastructure can be found online at *www.maggotranch.com/MMP*.

Larry's overall background with infrastructure for large-scale distributed systems covers 15 years of commercial software development and applied research into synchronization and scaling techniques for MMP military training simulations. As a lead architect in DARPA's Advanced Distributed Simulation, Synthetic Theatre of War, and Advanced Simulation Technology Thrust programs, Larry was a key contributor to the DoD's High Level Architecture/Run-Time Infrastructure 2.0 (now IEEE 1516). He has been in the gaming industry for over four years.

John M. Olsen—Infix Games

infix@xmission.com

John M. Olsen started working on graphics software of various sorts long before graduating from the University of Utah in 1989. He has worked as a game programmer on PlayStation, PC, and Xbox titles for Infogrames and Microsoft over the past several years doing special effects, artificial intelligence, networking, real-time loop design, instrumentation, user interfaces, and whatever else has been thrown his way. He's contributed to the *Game Programming Gems* series and has spoken at the Game Developers Conference. Having escaped the full-time game industry for the moment, he still keeps involved by working on designs and code for both game and nongame side projects with industry friends.

Cory Ondrejka—Linden Lab

cory@secondlife.com

As vice president of product development, Cory Ondrejka manages the team developing *Second Life*, Linden Lab's award-winning user-created digital world. His team has created the revolutionary technologies required to enable collaborative, atomistic creation, including distributed physical simulation, 3D streaming, completely customizable avatars, and real-time in-world editors. He also spearheaded the decision to allow users to retain the IP rights to their creations and helped craft Linden's virtual real estate policy.

Prior to joining Linden Lab in November 2000, Ondrejka served as project leader and lead programmer for Pacific Coast Power and Light. At PCP&L, he brought the *Road Rash* franchise to the Nintendo for the first time with *Road Rash 64* and built the core technology teams that completed multiple products for Nintendo and Sony consoles. Previous experience includes lead programmer for Acclaim Coin-Operated Entertainment's first internal coin-op title and work on Department of Defense electronic warfare software projects for Lockheed Sanders. While an officer in the U.S. Navy, he worked at the National Security Agency and graduated from the Navy Nuclear Power School. Ondrejka is a graduate of the United States Naval Academy, where he was a Presidential "Thousand Points of Light" recipient and became the first person to earn bachelor of science degrees in two technical majors: Weapons and Systems Engineering, and Computer Science.

Jon Parise—Electronic Arts

jon@indelible.org

Jon Parise currently works as a software engineer at Electronic Arts where he has worked on the MMP titles *The Sims Online* and *Ultima Online*. Prior to that, as a graduate student a Carnegie-Mellon University's Entertainment Technology Center, Jon was involved in a variety of research projects ranging from interactive real-time motion capture to a virtual character puppeteering system to interactive animatronics (entertainment robotics). He also holds a bachelors of science degree in information technology from the Rochester Institute of Technology.

Jon is a long-time contributor to the open-source community. He is a core developer in the PEAR and Horde projects, and has been involved with the PHP project for over five years, during which he co-authored *Beginning Databases with PostgreSQL* and *Professional PHP4*. He has also spoken at multiple international PHP conferences.

Jon would like to acknowledge the contributions of Andrew L. Tepper of eGenesis and the support of the *Ultima Online* and *The Sims Online* development teams in the development of his article.

Katie Postma—Ubisoft

guinevere4719@hotmail.com

Katie Postma has been a *Myst* fan since the inception of the series. Through good fortune and hard work, Katie has become the hardworking and much-loved community manager of the Ubisoft Mystworlds community. Katie works and lives in London, Ontario with her husband Rick and her two adorable children Ben and Amanda. Katie would like to thank the Mystworlds Community and Ubisoft for their support, Cyan for their phenomenal games, and Graham for writing this biography because she couldn't find the 25th hour in the day. Katie would also like to thank Ron Meiners, without whom all the work at Mystworlds simply couldn't have happened.

Marty Poulin—Sony Computer Entertainment America

mpoulin@scea.com

After many years of programming real-time embedded systems, Marty became involved with game development in 1999 as part of the startup Playnet/Cornered Rat Software (CRS). With the company's sights set on creating *WWII Online* (an ambitiously scoped MMOG simulation of ground, air, and sea forces of WWII), Marty became the primary architect and implementer of CRS's distributed game server infrastructure and supporting network engine.

During his five years at CRS, Marty explored most facets of game engine design and development, eventually taking on the role of chief of technology development. Marty is now with SCEA working on client/server solutions for developers on various PlayStation platforms.

Justin Quimby—Turbine Entertainment Software

justin@turbinegames.com

Justin Quimby is a lead engineer at Turbine Entertainment Software. Over the past six years, he has worked on *Asheron's Call*, *Asheron's Call: Dark Majesty*, *Asheron's Call 2*, and *Middle-Earth Online*. Currently, he is realizing his childhood dreams working as lead engineer on *Dungeons & Dragons Online*.

John W. Ratcliff—Ageia Technologies, Inc.

jratcliff@infiniplex.net

John W. Ratcliff is a long-time game industry veteran who started with Electronic Arts in the 1980s. John's games include *688 Attack Sub*, *SSN-21 Seawolf*, *Scarab*, *Cyberstrike 2*, and *Planetside*. John is an active member of the development community, contributing code and technology as often as possible. Currently, he works for Ageia Technologies, Inc., a startup technology company in St. Louis, Missouri dedicated to advancing the acceptance of physics integration in next-generation games.

Artie Rogers—NCSoft

artie.rogers@gmail.com

Artie Rogers has been working on design and support for commercial MMP, PC, and console games since 1995. He has been involved with support and content creation for *Ultima Online*, and design and development on *Ultima Online 2*. Artie is currently working as a designer for NCSoft on *Tabula Rasa*, an online game that will be published by NCSoft.

Michael Saladino—Electronic Arts

MSaladino@ea.com

Michael Saladino started making computer games over a decade ago as a low-level graphics engineer in the days of DOS. From there he moved to general systems engineering and then to lead engineering positions. At one time or another, he has programmed most game systems including graphics, physics, sound, AI, world management, game mechanics, tools, and so forth. Extending outside of engineering, he has also worked as a producer and a publishing engineering manager. His company history includes Parallax/Volition, Presto Studios, Microsoft, and now Electronic Arts. His current position has him working as a development director on *Golden Eye: Rogue Agent*.

Michael would like to thank talented mentors throughout his career including Max Elliott, David Norris, and Scott Taylor who have taught him much. Michael would also like to thank his beautiful fiancée Kristen for understanding his passion for this insane endeavor.

Max Skibinsky—HiveMind, Inc.

max@h-mind.com

Max Skibinsky is currently the founding CEO of HiveMind, a Silicon Valley startup dedicated to creating a new genre of social-intensive casual MMP games. Max worked in the fields of enterprise software architecture and development for more than 15 years. He lead the development of 10 highly successful commercial applications, which shipped tens of millions of copies worldwide for diverse clients such as Electronic Arts, THQ, Enroute Imaging, Netscape, and Celera Genomics. Max holds a master's degree in theoretical physics, yet like so many physicists, the beginning of the computing era proved to be too much of a lure.

Skibinsky's work in this book has been influenced by many thought-stimulating brainstorming sessions and online discussions, starting with the *Dictator* engine design in 1995. The author would like to thank Hamilton Hitchings, Sergey Belistov, Sergey Guzeev, Paul Tchistopolskii, Dmitry Devishev, Jorden Woods, Luke Jones and many others who helped author to formulate and crystallize his vision.

Roger Smith—Modelbenders, LLC

mmpg@modelbenders.com

Roger Smith is a chief engineer with Sparta Inc. and the president of Modelbenders LLC. He develops simulation systems for the military, creates commercial courses on simulation and virtual world technologies, and writes a constant stream of technical papers for books, encyclopedias, journals, and conferences. He has presented several full-day tutorials at the Game Developers Conference and teaches simulation courses at a number of universities.

Sean Stalzer—The Syndicate

dragons@LLTS.org

Sean "Dragons" Stalzer has spent the better part of a decade running the legendary online gaming guild The Syndicate (*www.LLTS.org*). As guildmaster of a guild of more than 500 members, across numerous MMP games, he has learned much of what it takes to run a successful guild and what an MMP game needs to offer to attract and retain guilds. As part of a number of player panels and working in direct consultation with developers, that knowledge has been applied to games to achieve a better guild environment for all players. Sean continues to push the envelope of what a guild can achieve in gaming through new partnerships with developers, corporate sponsorships of guilds, and even service marking the guild entity that has become so well known over the years.

Sean would like to thank Wil "Grif" Widmeyer, Dargus and Dwana "Veakari" Hughes of The Syndicate for assisting in the editing of his articles. Sean would also like to thank The Syndicate for their participation in the generation of content for the articles, and Mark Gere, a lead MMP game developer for Microsoft, for his edits and revisions from a developer's perspective.

Don Stoner—DCSI

mmpg@modelbenders.com

Don Stoner is a senior software engineer for DCSI in Germany. He develops military simulation systems for visualizing simulation events, networking multiplayer systems, communicating with real vehicles, and enabling two-way voice interfaces for virtual worlds. He is a former member of Army Intelligence and Special Forces with experience in combat operations, signals interception, reconnaissance, and surveillance.

Shea Street—Tantrum Games

shea.street@tantrumgames.com

Shea Street got his start in multiplayer programming by developing online games for early dial-up service providers before the Internet became what it is today. He has been programming for games for well over 15 years and is entirely self taught, but holds a computer science degree from *Full Sail* in game design and development. Over the years, he has had a hand in creating countless games and providing private consulting to a number of companies for many of their project needs. Shea is currently the lead programmer and co-founder of Tantrum Games.

Shea would like to thank everyone at Tantrum Games for all their hard work and dedication and for being very understanding and patient with him while he was writing for this book. He would also like to thank everyone in all the forums who took part in his discussions and lectures, and anyone who shared a late-night cup of coffee with him. Last but not least, Shea would like to give thanks to all of his friends and family who helped support him through life, especially his father. If it weren't for his father who helped him buy his first computer and got him interested in programming, none of this would have been possible.

Mike Wallis—Turbine Entertainment

mwallis@turbinegames.com

Mike is a seasoned game developer with 16 years of experience. He is currently the senior producer on *Middle Earth Online*, a fantasy-based MMOG being developed by Turbine Entertainment. Prior to joining Turbine, Mike was a key member in the development and release of the sci-fi MMP game *EVE Online*, acquiring the product from the publishing side while at the same time directly managing the game's day-to-day production from the development end. He has managed the production of close to 20 titles for both PC and console platforms, including such high-profile projects as *Sonic the Hedgehog* and projects based on the NBA and *Star Trek* license.

Mike would like to thank Valerie Massey and Erlendur Steinn Gudnason for their contributions to his article.

Graham Williams—UbiSoft

grahamw@rogers.com

Graham Williams is a community management volunteer for UbiSoft and Mystworlds. He writes a technical review column in local distribution. Graham balances his work online while completing his education at the University of Waterloo in Ontario, Canada.

Graham thanks UbiSoft and Cyan for their support during the short tenure of *Uru: Live*, and friends and family for their support.

About the Web Site

Continue the conversation of *Massively Multiplayer Game Development 2* online with our Web site at *http://hardcodedgames.com/mmpgamedev/*.

This site will be updated frequently with development news and commentary from the biggest names in online game development.

MASSIVELY MULTIPLAYER DESIGN TECHNIQUES

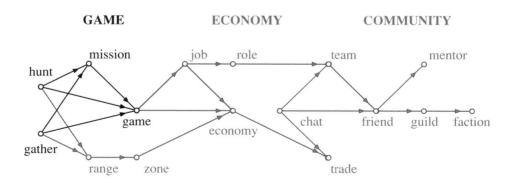

1.1

Virtual Worlds: Why People Play

Richard A. Bartle — University of Essex

richard@mud.co.uk

Ask people why they play virtual worlds, and their response is likely to be some variant of "to have fun." This is pretty well the bottom line for players, but it's not detailed enough to be of much use to designers. *What* do they find fun? *Why* do they find it fun? How does their idea of what's fun *change* over time? What can designers do to make them have *more* fun? And what happens when they *stop* having fun?

Introduction

The hypothesis outlined here asserts that virtual worlds are about the *celebration of identity*. It stems from the observation that different players find different kinds of things "fun," and that their idea of what constitutes "fun" changes along predictable lines as they play. The hypothesis also suggests that there is an age-old precedent for this.

Player Types

The original player types model [Bartle96] divides players into four categories, using two axes that express a player's degree of preference for acting on or interacting with the virtual world itself or its (other) players. Figure 1.1.1 illustrates this as a graph.

Figure 1.1.1 presents four broad types of players:

Achievers: Enjoy acting on the world, and are typically gamers, playing to "win."

Explorers: Enjoy interacting with the world, and delight in discovery.

Socializers: Enjoy interacting with other players, and spend a lot of their time chatting.

Killers: Enjoy acting on other players to dominate them, either through bullying or politicking.

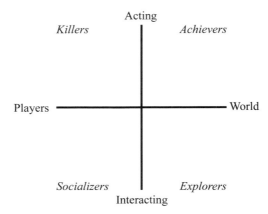

FIGURE 1.1.1   *The original player types graph.*

Flaws in the Model

Although this model has been widely accepted as a useful tool among designers [Price04], it nevertheless has flaws. Two are of particular importance. First, it suggests that players change type over time, but it doesn't suggest how or why they might do so [UnSub04]. Second, all of the types to some degree, but especially the one for acting on players (that is, *Killers*), seem to have subtypes that the model doesn't predict.

A New Player Types Model

The issues were resolved [Bartle03] by adding a third dimension, *implicit/explicit*. The distinction boils down to "thinking before doing." Implicit action is that which is done automatically without the intervention of the conscious mind; explicit action is that which is considered or planned for, generally as a means to achieve some desired goal or effect.

A Third Dimension

This new dimension creates a 3D graph, with eight player types instead of four, as shown in Figure 1.1.2.

Each of the original player types now comes in two flavors.

Opportunists are implicit *Achievers*:

• If they see a chance, they take it.
• They look around for things to do, but they don't know what these are until they find them.
• If there's an obstacle, they do something else instead.
• They flit about from idea to idea like a butterfly.

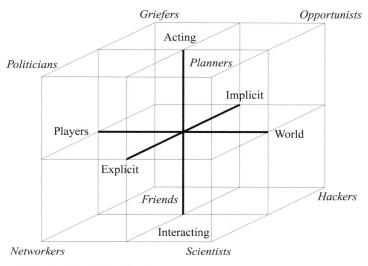

FIGURE 1.1.2 *The 3D player types graph.*

Planners are explicit *Achievers*:

- They set a goal and aim to achieve it.
- They perform actions as part of some larger scheme.
- If there's an obstacle, they work around it.
- They pursue the same idea doggedly.

Hackers are implicit *Explorers*:

- They experiment to reveal meaning.
- They have an intuitive understanding of the virtual world, with no need to test their ideas.
- They go where fancy takes them.
- They seek to discover new phenomena.

Scientists are explicit *Explorers*:

- They experiment to form theories.
- They use these theories predictively to test them.
- They are methodical in their acquisition of knowledge.
- They seek to explain phenomena.

Friends are implicit *Socializers*:

- They interact mainly with people they already know well.
- They have a deep/intimate understanding of them.
- They enjoy their company.
- They accept their little foibles.

Networkers are explicit *Socializers*:

- They find people with whom to interact.
- They make an effort to get to know their fellow players.
- They learn who and what these people know.
- They assess who's worth hanging out with.

Griefers are implicit *Killers*:

- Attack attack attack!
- They're very "in-your-face."
- They are unable to explain why they act as they do, although they may offer rationalizations they'd like you (or themselves) to believe.
- Their vague aim is to get a big, bad reputation.

Politicians are explicit *Killers*:

- They act with forethought and foresight.
- They manipulate people subtly.
- They explain themselves in terms of their contribution to the virtual world community.
- Their aim is to get a big, good reputation.

This new model formalizes the subtypes apparent in the original model, and thus provides designers with a more precise tool for targeting content. However, it's not immediately obvious how this model accounts for the fact that players change types over the course of time. If it could furnish such a development sequence, it would enable designers to create content they might otherwise neglect, and place it where it should be of most use.

Development Sequences

When *MUD1* was in its prime, some five to ten years before the concept of player types was formulated, groups of visitors to the Computer Science department at Essex University would often (as a treat) be allowed to play it. Because these novices were usually seated at separate terminals in the same room, it was possible for the player supervising them to observe how they approached the concept of a virtual world for the first time. It was soon noticed that most people adopted the same initial strategies, but changed their behavior over the course of an hour or so. By following how established players continued their careers after this stage, it was ascertained that this *drift* often (but by no means always) followed a pattern:

1. Newbies began by killing one another.
2. Having tired of fighting, they began to explore the virtual world.
3. Once their knowledge was sufficient, they moved to trying to "win" the "game."
4. Having won, they settled down and socialized.

In traditional player type terms, this would be *Killer* to *Explorer* to *Achiever* to *Socializer*, as illustrated in Figure 1.1.3.

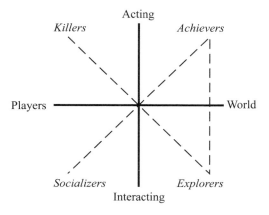

FIGURE 1.1.3   *The Main Sequence.*

Because it's the most popular progression, this is called the *Main Sequence*. It's not the only sequence, however; some players have been observed seeming to oscillate *Achiever* to *Explorer*, for example, and others oscillate *Killer* to *Socializer*.

The 3D version of the player types model helps here. The Main Sequence, using this newer model, would be *Griefer* to *Scientist* to *Planner* to *Friend*, as shown in Figure 1.1.4.

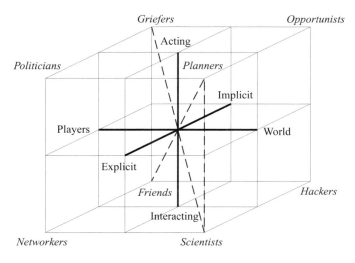

FIGURE 1.1.4   *The Main Sequence in 3D.*

The main sequence is visible in the 2D graph, but there are three other common sequences invisible there. These do, however, show up on the 3D graph, and are shown in Figures 1.1.5, 1.1.6, and 1.1.7.

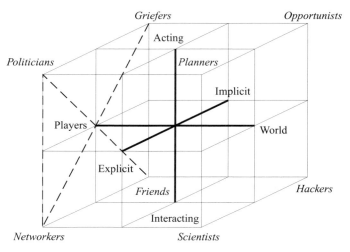

FIGURE 1.1.5   *The Main Socializer Sequence is* Griefer *to* Networker *to* Politician *to* Friend.

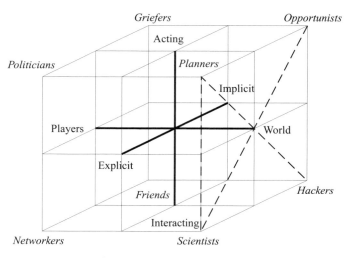

FIGURE 1.1.6   *The Main Explorer Sequence is* Opportunist *to* Scientist *to* Planner *to* Hacker.

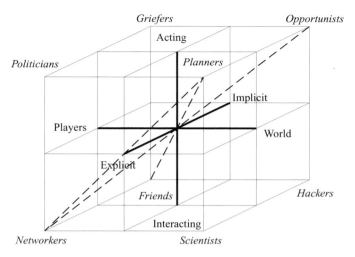

FIGURE 1.1.7 *The Minor Sequence is* Opportunist *to* Networker *to* Planner *to* Friend.

These four progressions are almost comprehensive, but not entirely so because circumstances can make players jump between paths at various points. A player on the Minor Sequence could, for example, feel from his experiences networking that the virtual world itself was less interesting than the people who played it. He might therefore switch to the Main Socializer Sequence instead (although most would stay with the Minor Sequence).

Development Tracks

If we take all the sequences from the 3D diagram and write them out in combination with each other, we get the *player development tracks* of Figure 1.1.8.

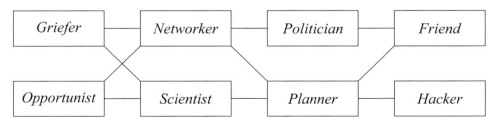

FIGURE 1.1.8 *Player development tracks.*

The sequences all start implicit, then go to explicit, and then return to being implicit. There's an oddness in that although *Networkers* can choose to become *Politicians* or *Planners*, *Scientists* never become *Politicians*; this may be an actual phenomenon, or it may be that it does happen but is yet to be observed.

From these tracks, we can now see a more general sequence:

1. Players start by determining the boundaries of their actions, acting on instinct and their experiences elsewhere in similar situations. They do this either by trying everything that looks reasonable (*Opportunist*), or by pushing to their extremes (*Griefer*).

2. Having determined the basic actions available to them, they begin stringing together meaningful sequences of actions—learning what works in combination with what else. They'll do this either by experimenting (*Scientist*) or by asking someone who already knows (*Networker*).

3. Having acquired the necessary knowledge to operate effectively, they apply it to achieve what they regard as success. Success is measured either by the virtual world (for *Achievers*) or by other players (for *Politicians*).

4. The players finally master their skills to the extent that these become second nature to them. They now understand the virtual world (*Hackers*) or their comrades (*Friends*) implicitly, without having to think about what effects any actions may have on them—they "just know."

This "locate to discover to apply to internalize" path is how learning works in general. Babies will thrash around until they discover that doing *this* makes *this* happen to their foot. They will then combine various sequences of such actions and find that if they do *this* then *this* then *this*, they can kick—moving their legs as a coherent action. They then apply this knowledge in the furtherance of other goals (I want the biscuit, the biscuit is over there—hey, I can toddle over and get it!). Finally, they toddle so much that they don't have to think about it any more—they can simply walk [Adolph03].

So now, we have an explanation of drift in terms of player types. Unfortunately, we still don't know what drives this drift, or why players consider it fun. It's clear that players are learning *something*, but what?

Immersion

A clue as to what the players are learning comes from an understanding of the concept of *immersion*.

What Is Immersion?

Immersion is the sense that a player has of being *in* a virtual world.

It is related to the concept of *presence*—the illusion that a (computer-)mediated experience is not mediated [Lombard97]. Indeed, immersion is seen in presence theory as one of the several forms that presence can take. In virtual world terms, however, although presence is an aid to immersion (because the fewer barriers there are between player and virtual world, the better), it isn't sufficient to cause immersion.

Immersion is also related to the psychological concept of *flow*—a deep involvement that transcends distractions and sense of time [Csikszentmihalyi90]. The two are not, however, the same thing: people can experience flow without reference to their state of immersion. In other words, you can be immersed whether or not you're engrossed, and be engrossed whether or not you're immersed.

For virtual worlds, immersion takes longer to develop than most players suppose. Here's how they tend to see it:

1. If they are playing and feel as if they're in the virtual world, they are immersed.
2. If, while immersed, they are interrupted, this makes them no longer immersed.
3. If, having been interrupted they return and pick up where they left off, they're immersed again.

This view is indeed correct, but what many players fail to recognize is that there are *levels* of immersion—it's not a simple binary concept.

Levels of Immersion

A 2002 survey by Nick Yee [Yee02] identified three of the original player types as being key motivational factors for players (the fourth, *Explorers*, gave way to "leadership"). The desire to become immersed was revealed as a fifth such factor. Immersion is not, however, the same kind of object as a player type. For example, although you can simultaneously be both immersed and a *Socializer*, you can't be both an *Achiever* and a *Socializer*.

So what is immersion, if it's not a type? It's a progression.

There are four main levels of immersion, through which players pass in the order: *unimmersed*, *avatar*, *character*, and *persona*.

The human beings sitting at the computer, interacting with the virtual world, are players. Players control an object with which they are associated within the virtual world, and the way they regard this object indicates how immersed they are. If they regard it simply as an object (as they might, say, a hyperlink), they are unimmersed. If they identify with it enough to consider it their *representative* in the virtual world (a puppet that acts on their behalf), then it is an avatar. If they project their personality onto and through it to the extent that it becomes their *representation* in the virtual world, then it is a character. If they consider it them, in the virtual world, then it is a persona.

To be unimmersed is to use a tool. To be immersed is to invest some (or all) of the self in that tool. An avatar is a doll, a character is a simulacrum, a persona is a person—a player, *in* the virtual world.

Role-Playing

Immersion isn't itself the ultimate aim of virtual world play, but it does help deliver what is: affirmation of identity.

When an actor acts, he takes on the role of a character. In playing the character, the actor comes to understand that character, and through this understanding gains insight into his own situation. An actor can change as a result of playing a character; the character, however, does not substantially change. This is *hard role-playing*, in that the character played remains firmly fixed in its identity. There are virtual worlds specifically set up for this kind of role-playing [Goetz95].

With hard role-playing, you can only learn as you approach a character. When you reach it, you can learn no more from it. This leads to a paradox: as a role-player, you try to become your character, but if you succeed, you're no longer role-playing.

Most virtual worlds, however, use *soft role-playing*. Here, not only does the player change to fit the character, the character changes to fit the player. The very aim of soft role-playing is to align character and player—to find a "you" that you like to be. Perturbations in the character that are received positively or negatively are fed back into the player's self-image; it's as if virtual worlds provide, through characters, a mirror for players to reflect upon themselves. Because you can see yourself, you can't lie to yourself. Therefore, if you don't like what you see, you must change until you do.

Again, the fact that players and characters change to fit one another was noted in the early days of virtual worlds, where it was known as *drift*—the same term that was applied to changes in player type. Although this was a coincidence, we shall see shortly that the two are not unrelated.

Immersion and Identity

As players become more aligned with their characters, they become more deeply immersed in them (and in the virtual world). At the same time that they are experiencing this increase in immersion, they are also progressing along the development tracks as described earlier.

Ideally, players should reach the ends of both at the same time. However, if the virtual world has too much of a treadmill, they could reach full immersion before they finish. This will lead to feelings of frustration—they feel they've won, but the finishing line is still distant. Similarly, if the virtual world allows content to be consumed too quickly, players could finish before they reach full immersion. This will lead to feelings of dissatisfaction—they've crossed the finishing line but don't feel they've completed the course. The job of the virtual world designer is to ensure that most players become their characters at roughly the same time that their playing skills become internalized.

At this point in the theory, we know that players develop along predictable lines (development tracks). We know that they become increasingly immersed as they play. We know that the two progressions should coincide in their completion. What we don't yet know is what drives the process and links the two together.

Myth

The force that propels player development and immersion, gluing them together, comes from what (at first glance) may seem a nonobvious source.

The Hero's Journey

In his 1949 masterpiece, *The Hero with a Thousand Faces* [Campbell49], Joseph Campbell traces a common thread that runs throughout the myths of all cultures. Ancient tales from across the world all follow the same, basic formula—the *monomyth*, or *hero's journey*. Campbell speculated that this was because myth has its roots in the human psyche: a universal need to explain the same social, worldly, and other-worldly concepts that trouble each and every one of us. He drew on myths from Nigeria, North America, Australia, Phrygia, China, Iceland, Bali, Persia, Mexico, Finland, Cambodia, Peru, . . . ; he referenced the epic tales of Gilgamesh, Arthur, Vishnu, Osiris, Moses, Cuchulainn, Buddha, Jason, . . . ; he explored narratives such as Homer's *Odyssey*, Dante's *Inferno*, *The Sleeping Beauty*, *Anna Karenina*, *Faust*, *The Frog King*, ...

The hero's journey is alive and well today as a narrative theory. It has been applied before the event to create stories (as with the movie *Star Wars*), and after the event to explain them (as with *Harry Potter and the Philosopher's Stone*). Some virtual worlds (e.g., *Shadowbane*) deliberately use the hero's journey formula to guide quests for players.

Here, we also apply the hero's journey formula to virtual worlds, only not in quite the same fashion.

The Quest for the Self

The way the hero's journey works is that an individual passes through a prescribed set of stages leading from self-ignorance to self-mastery. The individual travels from the mundane world to be reborn into an "other world" of danger and the unknown, where normal rules do not apply and in which the bulk of their adventure takes place. Having succeeded there, they then return to the mundane world armed with new knowledge and experience (a renewed sense of *self*), to address whatever issue drove them to the world of myth in the first place.

Now in myths, epics, books, movies—and indeed in all forms of fiction but one—it is the protagonist of the myth, epic, book, movie, or whatever who undertakes the hero's journey. Readers identify with this character, and therefore gain an insight into their own situation, but they don't undertake their *own* hero's journey. How could they? Any world of myth must by definition be apart from reality, so how could anyone ever hope to visit one? *You* don't get to be a hero from watching *Star Wars*—Luke Skywalker does.

The single exception is virtual worlds. With virtual worlds, the player *can* and *does* embark upon a hero's journey—not as a *character*, but as *the hero*. The virtual world is the "other world" you visit from the real (mundane) world, and *you* are granted hero status—if you complete the journey.

A Hero's Journey to a Virtual World

There are three phases to the hero's journey:

1. **Departure** takes place in the mundane world (i.e., reality).
2. **Initiation** takes place in the world of myth (i.e., the virtual world).
3. **Return** brings the hero back to the mundane world.

Each of these phases is split into a number of steps, some of which (in the first and third phases) can occasionally be skipped or reordered.

The easiest way to show the hero's journey as it applies to virtual worlds is simply to list the general formula, step by step, as it maps onto the experience of a player of virtual worlds.

Departure

Departure comprises five steps, usually undertaken in the following order:

1. **The call to adventure.**   You see an advertisement, a shelf unit, or a cover disk, or you read an article about the virtual world. Where previously you were unaware of the virtual world's existence, the seed has now been sown.
2. **Refusal of the call.**   There are many reasons not to play—time, expense, fear of looking foolish, to mention a few. For some people, this is as far as it goes; for you, your desire to play overcomes your self-created objections.
3. **Supernatural aid.**   A friend who already plays offers to help you out, or you find a Web site with a welcoming forum; perhaps you peruse a strategy guide. Whatever the source, you feel that you will have support in your endeavor from someone who knows the score. Thoughts of possible failure diminish.
4. **The crossing of the first threshold.**   You install the client software and connect to the virtual world.
5. **The belly of the whale.**   You create a character—a new *you*—and are ready for your adventure. It's a formal *rebirth*.

Initiation

Initiation comprises six steps, almost always undertaken in the following order:

1. **The road of trials.**   Here, a number of obstacles present themselves. In overcoming, evading, or avoiding them, you start to find your feet in the virtual world. This is the *Opportunist/Griefer* stage from the player development tracks.
2. **The meeting with the goddess.**   The "goddess" here is a metaphor for the totality of knowledge. Having determined the extent of your limitations, you become aware of how these stack up against what you will have to know to succeed. For some players, the task looks hopeless and they drop out; for you, it is a call to acquire knowledge you will need if you are to

progress further. This is the *Scientist/Networker* stage from the player development tracks. In terms of developing your sense of identity, the suggestion is that by learning about the virtual world and/or its players, you are learning more about yourself.

3. **Woman as the temptress.** Here, "woman" is symbolic of your old-world origins, and this step marks the turning point between learning and doing. Having acquired the knowledge necessary to continue, are you content to leave it at that, believing you could apply it if you wanted to (but you don't)? Or are you in for the long haul, having faith that what will happen if you continue is better than what will happen if you don't? In player development track terms, this is the boundary between *Scientist/Networker* and *Planner/Politician*—an affirmation of commitment that separates the two "explicit" quarters of the track and the midpoint (in terms of progression, if not time) of the journey.

4. **Atonement with the father.** This is the key step of the hero's journey, and the one in which players tend to invest the most effort. It's what, when you started, you felt the virtual world was "about." It maps to the *Planner/Politician* stage, where you strive to "win"—to be recognized by the virtual world *in its own terms* as being a success. The "father" here is the person who has the supreme power over the player in the virtual world—the designer, in other words, as manifested through the virtual world's design. When the virtual world ultimately acknowledges that you have "won," you gain the closure you need to be able to move on to a different order of "play" entirely.

5. **Apotheosis.** Players wind up here as *Hackers/Friends*. You understand the virtual world, its people, and yourself; you are at peace with all. Challenges from the virtual world, when they arise, are no longer important. It is a period of rest.

6. **The ultimate boon.** This is where the match between hero's journey and the virtual world experience goes a little astray. In myth, heroes typically acquire a token of their achievement (the "boon") that has meaning in the real world; often, obtaining this will be the formal reason why they visited the "other world" in the first place (Jason specifically voyaged in the Argo to obtain the Golden Fleece, for example). Virtual worlds suffer from the same problem as other fictional worlds here, however: the only things in virtual worlds that have a material existence beyond that world are its players. Thus, whatever prize a player may be awarded in the virtual world, it can't be removed to the real world except in facsimile. That said, there *is* one possible candidate object for the boon: the new, wiser you. Although in myth this may well be what the boon is meant symbolically to denote, in virtual worlds the symbolism has to move aside for purely practical/implementational reasons. As we shall see, this has mildly irritating consequences for some later steps in the journey.

Return

Return comprises six steps, usually undertaken in the following order:

1. **Refusal of the return.**   In the virtual world, you have power, respect, friends, and peace. Why would you want to return to the real world?

2. **The magic flight.**   In myth, the hero's return from the "other world" is precipitated by his possession of the boon. The previous owner wants it back; the hero can't therefore stay *and* have the boon, so must escape back with it to the world of the mundane—usually with the previous owner in hot pursuit. For virtual worlds, the identity of the "previous owner" of the boon (i.e., of you) is not apparent. In theory, it should be the developers: they own the boon as manifest in their virtual world (i.e., your character). Unfortunately, developers are content for this boon merely to exist in their virtual world, and the very last thing they want to do is to hound you out. The magic flight is thus robbed of its trigger: you don't want to leave, the developers don't want you to leave, so what might provoke you into leaving? The next step may provide the answer.

3. **Rescue from without.**   The hero's return to the mundane world is often aided by a denizen of that world; in our case, this probably means a family member, a friend, or a work colleague. All they have to do is what they've always done: raise real-world issues. You, however, now begin to listen. Suddenly, for example, "Why do you spend so much time on that computer?" doesn't have such a clear-cut answer as it once did. In myth, the rescue usually occurs in an exciting, upfront, action kind of way; in the boon-as-self of virtual worlds, the issue is not so much that you need *help* to leave as that you need an *excuse* to leave. Once someone in the real world gives you that excuse, *then* you'll be subject to the full array of temptations thrown down by the developers to try to prevent you from going. For virtual worlds, therefore, it seems that although the *magic flight* and *rescue from without* steps exist, their order of appearance is reversed. As mentioned earlier, such a transposition of steps in this third phase of the hero's journey is not unusual.

4. **The crossing of the return threshold.**   Arrival back in the mundane world is something of a shock; you must reconcile your new self with the legacy of your old self. The world has carried on without you, and you must address its outstanding challenges. Although these once seemed formidable, however, they can now be overcome with relative ease (perhaps using the boon). Note that this isn't a complete break with the virtual world, just a parting from it as the most important place in your life: although you could decide to cancel your account, this would only ever be for practical reasons (e.g., expense) rather than symbolic ones. It's not that you *stop* playing, it's that you stop *needing* to play.

5. **Master of the two worlds.** Here, you finally accept your destiny. You have a sense of balance and proportion: your real and virtual selves are the same. You can return to the virtual world at will, but it has lost its mythical significance to you: it's just a place, now, like any other.

6. **Freedom to live.** You can finally be yourself.

Analysis

It seems clear from the preceding mapping that players of virtual worlds follow a hero's journey. However, the match is not quite exact. It's not just the problem with the boon; there are other places where the practice doesn't quite ring true with the theory. Although we can't go into those much here (see [Bartle03] for further analysis), it is worth noting that the critical *atonement with the father* step is not properly satisfied by most commercial virtual worlds. Players feel they have "won" the "game," but they don't get confirmation of this from the virtual world itself; they are therefore doomed to a state of perpetual frustration. They leave without wanting to leave, seeking validation in other virtual worlds that can at best offer but an echo of the acceptance they crave (and, indeed, that they deserve).

Things don't have to be this way, though! If players are *accepted* by the virtual world as having "won" it, they are released from the treadmill to a state of blissful repose. They may stop playing the virtual world *as a game*, but (as master of the two worlds) they won't stop paying to access it. It would therefore seem that the best way for developers to retain their players indefinitely is if they *allow them to leave*. The fact that so many virtual worlds don't do this may help account for their unimpressive retention rates.

Virtual world design theory does have its uses.

Conclusion

There's more to the hypothesis than is given here, but these other points would take several more articles' worth of text to convey. What happens to players who become derailed from the development tracks? Does the development of community have a main sequence of its own? Can the hypothesis explain players from cultures where people identify themselves with the group rather than as individuals? None of these questions is answered, nor are any of the others that you want to ask right now.

Some of these issues are addressed in [Bartle03], but some aren't. All are peripheral to the central thrust of the hypothesis, however, which is this:

- Playing virtual worlds is a kind of hill-climbing activity through identity space.
- The hero's journey is a good algorithm for finding a local maximum, if not a global one.
- Immersion is an emergent consequence of following the hero's journey.
- Players follow predictable development tracks as they play, exhibiting particular playing styles as they do so.

- The player development tracks correspond to the steps of the middle phase of the hero's journey. The other two phases take place in the real world, rather than the virtual world.
- Whatever a player needs to do right now to progress through the hero's journey is what he currently regards as "fun."
- The result of playing a virtual world is that players understand themselves more.

Virtual worlds are a quest for identity. By being someone virtual, you find out who you are in reality. It's this that makes virtual worlds fun, it's this that makes them compelling, and it's this that designers must understand.

References

[Adolph03] Adolph, Karen E.; Vereijken, Beatrix; Shrout, Patrick E., "What Changes in Infant Walking and Why," *Child Development vol. 74 (2),* available online at *www.psych.nyu.edu/adolph/Footprints%20.pdf,* September 1, 2004.

[Bartle96] Bartle, Richard, "Hearts, Clubs, Diamonds, Spades: Players Who Suit MUDs," *Journal of MUD Research vol. 1 (1),* available online at *http://mud.co.uk/richard/hcds.htm,* September 1, 2004.

[Bartle03] Bartle, Richard, *Designing Virtual Worlds,* New Riders, 2003.

[Campbell49] Campbell, Joseph, *The Hero with a Thousand Faces,* Princeton University Press, 1949.

[Csikszentmihalyi90] Csikszentmihalyi , Mihaly, Flow: *The Psychology of Optimal Experience,* Harper & Row, 1990.

[Goetz95] Goetz, Phil, "Literary Role-Play in Cyberspace," *Interactive Fantasy 4,* available online at *www.mud.co.uk/richard/ifan295.htm,* September 1, 2004.

[Lombard97] Lombard, Matthew; Ditton, Theresa, "At the Heart of it All: The Concept of Presence," *Journal of Computer-Mediated Communication vol. 3 (2),* available online at *www.ascusc.org/jcmc/vol3/issue2/lombard.html,* July 5, 2004.

[Price04] Price, Nick, "When Good Things Happen to Bad People," available online at *www.snoozeboy.net/downloads/final_completedoc_frontchanged.pdf,* September 1, 2004.

[UnSub04] UnSub, "'This SuXX0rz; I quit!!!!!': An Examination of Player Exit Motivations in Massively Multiplayer Online Games (MMOGs)," available online at *www.thebeholder.org/research/mmogexit.htm,* September 4, 2004.

[Yee02] Yee, Nick, "Codename Blue: An Ongoing Study of MMORPG Players," available online at *www.nickyee.com/codeblue/home.html,* July 5, 2004.

1.2

The Three Thirties of MMP Game Design

Artie Rogers—NCSoft

artie.rogers@gmail.com

No challenge that Massively Multiplayer Online Games (MMOG) developers face is more important to solve than the problem of how to get players to keep their accounts active and play the game longer than Thirty Days. A majority of games outside the genre have play-through times that fall far short of the 30-day mark, so most gamers new to the MMOG genre aren't used to dedicating that much time to a single game. It is important for developers to recognize this challenge and to develop with it in mind. This article breaks down the player's first Thirty Days into distinct developmental strata that designers should keep in mind when first creating their MMOG.

For the purposes of this discussion, the article outlines and defines three major gameplay strata in terms of time period, goals, and some design possibilities to achieve those goals. The first stratum discussed is the First Thirty Minutes of gameplay. In this stratum, the player will encounter the interface and Heads-Up-Display (HUD), and become introduced to the game fiction and immediate calls to action. The second gameplay stratum is defined by the player's First Thirty Hours of gameplay. In this stratum, the player will have begun to make more tangible goals in terms of advancement and object acquisition. The players have started to define their own direction and achievement priorities individually and among possible adventuring groups. The final stratum is the First Thirty Days of gameplay. It is in this time period that players begin to establish their own personal online community, if they choose to take part in one, or their role in an existing community. This is where the players will want to see progress made along a long-term advancement path for their character, their community, and other personal projects. Each gameplay stratum offers unique design challenges and differences as the player progresses through them. They each have a unique set of goals to achieve to better guarantee that a player will keep playing the game long term.

The First Thirty Minutes

The First Thirty Minutes of gameplay is often considered the most important. It is the first exposure the player will have to the game, its controls, systems, and fictional fabric. This is often the first serious challenge to the player's attention and interest. If the player cannot easily enter in the game world and feel compelled to action by way of fictional setting or promise through interesting advancement, it is unlikely that he will play far into the next stratum. Therefore, while this is the shortest stratum, it can be the most important, as it builds a foundation of action and gameplay that bridges to the other parts of the game.

A few of the primary goals for the First Thirty Minutes of gameplay are providing a smooth introduction into the game, establishing a connection between the player and his avatar, and giving the player an imperative to action. These goals, among others, can be achieved by focusing on Control Tutorial, Character Creation, and Fictional Context.

Control Tutorial

Learning the basic controls of the game will be the first real exposure the player will have to the game because they are the primary conduit the player uses to interact with the world. When building a control scheme it is advisable to keep a few things in mind:

- Keep the controls simple.
- Keep the controls customizable.
- Examine the genre and adopt any control characteristics that seem to be emerging standards.
- Reveal controls during the tutorial on a "need-to-know basis."
- Unfold complex control actions through simplicity.
- Keep the control education experience private.

Allowing complexity to unfold through simplicity is a useful design guideline for all things including controls. With regard to control tutorials, this means revealing control details only when needed, unfolding more involved functionality only when the player needs it through a set of simple controls. This design tenet is also true when educating the player to the different HUD elements in the game. There should be a brief task associated with each new control concept or HUD element to ease the player into the full complement of controls and HUD. Maintaining a tight, focused core of controls that can unfold to offer more variety of actions is important in maintaining a simple control scheme. For example, in a first- or third-person game, many developers design around a W-A-S-D movement control scheme with the mouse look. With that in mind, it is advisable to consider the keys that neighbor the movement keys, and use mouse buttons in combination to allow for a more extensive movement set carefully controlling the expansion of the number of unique keys involved in the control scheme. Simply expanding the control scheme to incorporate a wide variety of individual keys to do very specific things adds an overly complex key component to achieve the variety of control possibilities desired. Most console game control schemes represent a good model for working within a very limited set of core controls, yet using those in combination to result in great versatility through that simple set.

When designing a control scheme it can be helpful to examine the contemporary members of the genre to see if any control elements are emerging as a control standard. Always remember that the main objective with control design is to allow players to navigate and play the game easily, effectively, and quickly. This can sometimes be achieved by adopting aspects of an established control scheme because the player is then already familiar with the controls and doesn't have to learn anything new. Related to this point is to allow players to customize their controls in whatever way they see fit. Again, this contributes to making the control scheme familiar for the player, which reduces the time it takes the player to master the basic controls.

Another point to remember is to allow players to learn and experiment with the base control set in private, away from other players. This allows the players the freedom to make mistakes and experiment without fear of social embarrassment or admonishment.

Following a design principle illustrated in different parts of this article, controls are best revealed slowly and simply. In this case, we will begin with basic navigation, leading the player through Character Creation, and then add and activate different control and HUD elements on a need basis only, as they become introduced to the different core gameplay systems, giving the player plenty of time to get comfortable with each new control or HUD element.

Character Creation

Character Creation is one of the most important roles of this stratum in that it sets the stage for establishing the first connection the player has with his avatar. The avatar is important for a number of reasons:

- It is the social window onto the game world.
- It is the primary object of gameplay and reward.
- It is the primary object of achievement.
- It represents the aspired persona for the player.

These points underline the importance of facilitating the player's connection to the avatar as soon as possible. A well-designed and thought-out creation process must be entertaining, provide a series of advancement choices to the player throughout his introductory experience, and give the player the information he needs to make choices that best fit his gameplay styles.

Character Creation will involve three major decision points for the player:

- Character Path of Advancement
- Character Appearance in terms of body size and shape, and beginning clothing
- Character Identification in terms of names, titles, etc.

Character Path

Typically, the first portion of Character Creation is related to the player's choice determining the general advancement path he wants to take. This can manifest itself by asking the player to choose a race or class for his character that might have some base characteristics reflected in starting attributes and skills. This base attribute and skill configuration normally provides a general advancement direction to give the player some development course to follow. Some MMOGs offer the option to regress or to change advancement paths once in the game so the player can experiment with other advancement paths and adjust his character to fit his in-game interests without having to recreate the character. It is a good idea to grant the player that flexibility, all the while keeping in mind that it is important to give significance to the player's first advancement choice. Giving this first choice lasting importance and having the choice indicate an advancement direction provides the player the opportunity to aspire to some longer term character goals. Therefore, while having the option to change characters after being in game is good, it is best to make that process take significant time and resources, so the players still must carefully consider their choices even if they aren't locked into them forever.

It is important to try to keep the first class or race choices limited. Another goal of the skill or class choice in Character Creation other than giving the players an advancement path to follow is to provide an environment for the player to connect and define his avatar. How to construct these choices becomes a problem of balance between avoiding having the players make uninformed choices about their advancement path, and making the choice significant enough that it provides a clear indication of an advancement path along which the players can aspire. If the players find themselves locked into an advancement path, they will weigh the value of quitting the game versus the task of recreating a character to make up for a mistake made at Character Creation. One option to avoid that problem, in addition to allowing class and skill regression, is to establish advancement tiers that unfold in complexity as the character advances. The player would move from general choices of advancement tendencies, which are significant and establish an advancement path, into more complicated and specific choices as he advances through this gameplay stratum.

Related to the concern of requiring players to occasionally work through character creation, developers want to make this experience entertaining. In the event that the player does have to experience Character Creation again, then it isn't seen as a chore. A good example of this is the ethical questionnaire that was central to the Character Creation process of the *Ultima* series. The player was presented with a series of ethical questions, and his character was built by the answers he gave. The questions were numerous, varied, and interesting enough that going through the process again was entertaining. This was a powerful and entertaining way to personalize the avatar, and was fun for the player beyond its Character Creation purpose.

Character Appearance

Once the player selects the advancement path on which he would like to start moving, he can move on to the next step of Character Creation, which is modifying appearance, which may not be as complex as choosing the advancement direction of the character, but is every bit as important.

The player's appearance should be as customizable as is feasible for the game. It is an important process for the player to further the connection with his avatar by having it match the imagined image of his character. It is also important that the player feel as individual as possible in the social community by looking different even if the character, in skill and ability, is very similar. These customization options should at least include body shape and size, hair style and color, and clothing style and color. The selection process should be easy and intuitive, and the player should be able to rotate and move his character to follow the creation process in action.

Character Identification

The final leg of the Character Creation journey is picking a name or other identifier. The player should be allowed to name his character anything as long as it fits within certain profanity limits. There is a need for unique identifiers for characters from a customer support perspective, at the very least, but there are different ways to positively identify a player without resorting to unique single names. Assigning a surname to a character is one way to allow the players to be called whatever they choose. The important issue here is allowing players to maintain a constant game persona and maintain character fantasy. This solution doesn't compromise the rationale for unique identifiers, and gives the player the naming freedom that is advantageous.

Carefully constructing the process by which a player is first introduced to and bonded with his avatar is a very important step in smoothly transitioning him into normal gameplay. The player will be making important decisions and adjustments to the avatar to meet his fantasy aspirations, so it's important that Character Creation enables him to do this. The player will want the character to match his imagined combination of attributes, look, and personal identification.

Fictional Context

Providing the player with clear direction early in the game is another problem of this introductory period. These fictional imperatives to take action will serve to establish the player's place within the context of the game. During the Character Creation experience and first scenes of gameplay, developers have a captive audience to which they can deliver the global fictional context. It is by creating, introducing, and encouraging the embrace of this fictional role that the player can be more easily directed through the early portion of the game.

Establishing the Fictional Context can be achieved through a series of small quests, none of which last more than five or ten minutes, but all of which contribute to a short story arc that sets the fictional stage of the game and provides the player with the motivation to move forward. The idea is to extend Character Creation and Control Introduction into the first experiences of normal gameplay while not extending them beyond the confines of this first gameplay stratum. While unfolding aspects of Character Creation and Controls, the player is being introduced to the fictional context of his game.

As the game progresses, administration-created fictional plots become less important to the players losing in favor to either the difficulties that revolve around character advancement or the social plots that are generated by their local game community. These plots could be anything from organizing an adventuring group, to discovering the best tactic to gain specific character skills, to becoming the mayor of a player city. Those plots will supersede most other fictional plot lines because they rarely involve the player's specific character or community. However, it is at this time that fiction is most important, when the character is new and those social bonds have yet to manifest themselves, a compelling fictional context can propel the player deep into his game world.

Creating and effectively delivering a compelling fictional context can provide the players with a number of valuable experiences as the developer seeks to move them into the next gameplay stratum.

The First Thirty Hours

While the First Thirty Minutes convinces the players to give the game a chance by way of an interesting Character Creation process, an intuitive Control Scheme, and an exciting entry into the adventure of and their role in the Fictional Context, the First Thirty Hours are the most important in terms of transitioning players to thinking more long term and beginning to establish their own online communities.

As players enter this segment, they'll have working knowledge of the core systems that surround the game and how to get within the environment. Players understand their initial role in the fictional world and have had some gameplay success under their belt as they progressed through the introductory phase of the game. It's at this point that players begin to consider and define their place in the game's community in terms of fiction and group play, more fully explore the game world, and plot some longer term character goals.

Character Advancement

While in the first stratum the player has been introduced into the game world, playing in the second gameplay stratum is the time to get the player introduced to the core aspects of long-term gameplay. The goal is to present the process of questing or engaging in the main mode of gameplay for advancement rewards and the long-term advancement benefits. For the purpose of this article, these two processes are linked as quest presentation is the important gating action to advancement rewards, so aspects of both will be addressed.

A compelling fictional element and logical quest-flow are important when transitioning the player from the constructed game style of the First Thirty Minutes with shorter paths to achievement and fewer decision points with regard to quest selection and advancement choices into a more group-friendly game with more quest options and longer term goals for both the individual and group. Fictional emphasis must be maintained until the point that either the attachment to character or the attachment to group or community becomes so important that they outweigh fictional concerns. When the players first enter the main game world, they should be connected to an NPC or Hub character that will provide the impetus to quest completion.

It's important to lead the player, logically, from one quest to another in a way that feels natural. Other than being compelled to action by an NPC, inspiring the player could also be achieved by some environmental changes that reflect progress through a plot line. For example, an enemy invasion gives rise to certain ambient activities and spawns behaviors on the surface, which, in turn, might give fictional justification to keep a city abandoned. As the player progresses through a series of tasks fashioned to thwart the invasion, the ambient destruction and spawning behavior change such that it is apparent that the player's actions are having an effect. Eventually, as the player continues to complete those tasks, the city could gradually return to a functioning state. This can be achieved in a large-scale MMO with the tracking of player achievements in the region. In this way, the players can be led into action and see immediate consequence and benefit of their actions.

There should be a goal of providing at least 40% of the 30 hours in the form of new quest gameplay. The rest will be taken up by social interactions, nonadventurous character maintenance, and exploration. With the understanding that quests in this stratum should last around 30 to 45 minutes, one needs to construct a series of close to 24 plot-related quests. These quests should further the main plot and continue the education of game systems.

The player will be getting into the meat of the advancement system at this stage, and it's important to keep the pace of achievements and exposure to new content rather brisk during the First Thirty Hours of gameplay. The time between the release of new content, quest time, and character achievement will lengthen as the player progresses through this stratum. By the nature of this gradual spacing of advancement and achievement, the player will begin to formulate longer term goals. The desired result is to lead the players into a situation where they are interested in establishing long-term goals. Advancement system choices are very complex, and can't be fully explored here, but we can touch on a few options. During this stage of advancement, it is important to better define the player's advancement path. People can normally manage and plan decisions between three to four steps ahead given three to eight choices at each step. The fewer decisions at each step, the longer the decision path can be. Therefore, for the purposes of drawing out and lengthening the player's advancement plans, it is advantageous to gradually limit his options as he progresses through this gameplay stratum. Whether one decides to use a standard system of levels and experience pools, or if the system is more about object collection and management, the previous assertion still remains valuable. Frequent reward and access to new systems can generate lasting enthusiasm, but as the player reaches the end of this stratum, the branching character choices should be few, and the time to achievement should be long.

This phase of quests and advancement is important as it propels the player further to character specialization while continuing the player imperative as driven by the game fiction. The introduction of new content will be denser during this stretch of gameplay than later in the game, as the goal is to solidify the bonds between player and character and to set the stage for long-term character development goals.

Exploration

While one task is to try to keep the player occupied with quest completion and pure character advancement, it's also good to remember that one of the most efficient uses of world-building space is through exploration and discoveries of hidden rewards.

There are several goals when considering the Exploration aspect of gameplay:

- The locomotive act itself should be entertaining.
- Provide rewards for exploration.
- Create the space in such a way to maximize the appearance of spaciousness.

When designing travel for an MMOG, developers should try to make the basic act of moving around entertaining and fun. There needs to be a way for the players to vary their movements as they travel from point A to point B. For example, in a typical platform game such as *Mario Sunshine*, the player can perform a multitude of moves, while running, that make running entertaining, such as jumping, sliding, jumping off walls, doing combo jumps, and so forth. While it is understandable that the way in which this locomotion variation occurs will be predicated by the setting of the game, the general tenet that travel needs to be entertaining is still valid. A second point to consider is to create an advancement ladder related to making travel more efficient and entertaining, if possible. *City of Heroes* did this with great success. They built the lowest rung of travel and made it entertaining, and then built in a ladder of travel advancement. In this way, they made travel a fun portion of their game. The fundamental goal to remember with regard to travel is that if you're going to ask the player to spend any significant chunk of time doing anything, then do everything possible to make sure it's entertaining.

Another technique to making travel and movement from place to place more interesting is to link some reward to it. Simple curiosity to explore surroundings is a strong motivator at this stage of the game, as players are still getting used to the game environment. Beyond the natural exploration of their surroundings, players will invest more time exploring a map if they feel these are some rewards behind it. Rewarding exploration inspires players to invest more time in a given map looking for reward. There are many examples of how this can be achieved in an MMO:

- Place hidden portals to small spaces with great reward.
- Reward players for discovering a named geographical location.
- Hide a character who will give a reward for being found.
- If there is a need for raw resources, then a way to encourage exploration is to have a resource spawn remotely.

Exploration rewards are a great way to reduce the laborious feel of pure travel and can inspire players to invest more time in a map area than they might have otherwise.

Smart design is also important in maximizing the entertainment value of exploration. This isn't about pure size, or square footage. This is about smart use of space. Consider theme parks, such as Disney World and Six Flags, and how they can maximize the use of their space. Theme park designers create a space that feels much larger than it really is. Two of the ways in which this is achieved is by dense use of ambient space and by creating several decision points for customers while they walk from point A to point B.

Creating several decision points for the player along a common travel route can create the illusion of a larger space. This can be accomplished with road branching or with events. With regard to road branching, one can see that effect in older cities whose roads do not fit on the grid and there is not a single logical route from point A to point B. The basic design idea one can take from that effect is to build the world in such a way as to provide the user multiple path combinations to the same destination. If a player is going from point A to point B and each has four entrances and exits, each directly connected, then the player can make the same trip in four different ways. However, if you introduce another, smaller connection space between points A and B, which has three entrances and exits, then there are many more path combinations from point A to point B. In this way, the player travels to the same place but can do it in a multitude of different ways, which serves to make the area feel more complex and larger than it actually is. This is because while the players might travel from A to B several times, chances are they won't take the same route each time.

Another way to make traveling more interesting is by using dense ambient spaces to help create the illusion of a larger space. The effective use of ambient space consists of providing those dynamic elements in terms of art and audio that make the space feel fuller of activity than if they were absent. Two great examples of this are the movie *Blade Runner* and the game *Call of Duty*. The street areas of *Blade Runner* are the perfect example of effective use of ambient space. The rain, wide variety of lighted street signs, various persons walking the street, and interesting zeppelins that filled the sky all contributed to the bustling feel of the city and left no space empty and lacking. However, the actual street space that the viewer explored in the movie was small. Another good example of effective use of ambient space comes from the demo level from *Call of Duty*. Having a space with distant fires burning, various anti-aircraft flak, and crashing planes taken in consideration with the sounds of explosions, screams, and gunfire helps to create a full and exciting environment. One of the challenges to the developer is filling in that space, but the end benefit is that travel then becomes less tedious if the player travels through an area that is fundamentally entertaining.

Ego Development

The ability to define oneself in terms of individual achievement and place in a community is by far the most important aspect of this gameplay stratum. These are the two most perilous goals undertaken for this stratum, and, if either fails, it can seriously jeopardize the life of the account and its survival through the First Thirty

Hours. It is imperative that the player is provided with objects of aspiration, opportunities for individual achievement, and chances to find a place and acceptance among the game community.

The most important part of the development of the character's ego is defining its role within a group. It is an MMOG truism that players who find and establish these ties within this second gameplay stratum are far more likely to be long-term players than those who don't. If one considers the nature of social groups, then it becomes self-evident that the larger the social group to which an individual is a member, the less impact the departure of a single member of that group has on the other members, thereby increasing the fundamental stability of each account within a community. For example, if a player is only connected to six other players, and one of the six leaves, it can have significant impact on the remaining players. However, if that social group was increased in size to a 30-member guild, then, generally, any one player who leaves that group has significantly less impact on the other members. Encouraging players to form relatively large adventuring groups becomes a practical matter of increasing the stability of the account base. The developer can approach encouraging group creation in two ways: encourage the player to become an active member within a group, and encourage established groups to recruit new players.

Addressing the first part of the solution, one wants to present the individual player with proper opportunity and incentive to establish ties with an adventuring group on his own. The important thing to remember is to approach this incentive in an additive way and to reward joining a group, as opposed to couching it as the player is worse off playing alone. This article touches on three ways to encourage the player to find a group:

- Make grouping the faster, safer, and more efficient way to level.
- Provide systems that a group can use to gain group-wide attribute or skill benefits.
- Provide some fundamental skill enhancements by being in a group.

The first method to encourage a player to join a group is to provide a situation in which being in a group allows the player to attain his goals in a faster, easier, and safer way. In many cases, MMOG developers want to retain a balance between risk, reward, and time investment, and will adjust experience rewards in a distributed way across a group, thereby reducing the experience reward per party member. This actually can be counterproductive to the end goal of encouraging the player to find an adventuring group. To encourage grouping, one should consider removing all party adjustments to experience. For example, if a player gets X experience completing a quest both solo or in a party, then he will be more likely to want to complete it in a party since the risk is lower. Another incentive is to provide the group with some blanket benefit that the player will inherit if he is a member. If the group can provide individual benefits in the form of increased character abilities or access to new character skills, the player will view the group as another character advancement method, which can remove some of the social pressures related to approaching a group. For instance, if a guild acquires a certain quest object, which when placed in the guild hall as a trophy provides all the members of the guild a skill increase, a character with an interest in that skill has incentive to join that guild. Another benefit would be to link some individual skills or skill-boosts to group play. For example, if a player performs a certain action, such as casting a spell, while playing solo, then it will have a certain effect. If the same player performs the same action while within a certain distance of grouped allies, then the spell could borrow power from the allies and increase the strength of its effect. Or, if a player has a skill that serves only to boost the abilities of allies, then that player will have some inherent incentive to group so that he can get the most out of his character. It is important that the player is aware of these benefits and knows how to build a group. It is then that the player is put into a situation to aspire to become a group member, and the ability to realize that desired position.

At the same time, one wants to provide a very aggressive incentive for existing adventuring groups to recruit the newer members. This system will emerge in the next gameplay stratum.

The First Thirty Days

When players have reached this gameplay stratum, which assumes some of the previous development efforts were successful, one can also assume some of the characteristics of that player and his character. It is more than likely that the player is involved in some adventuring group at this point, whether that's an organized and officially recognized guild or just a loosely associated adventuring group with characters of friends made both on- and offline. It is also likely that the player has formed some longer term goals for both character and group achievement. When the player enters this segment, his goals have begun to elongate in terms of time invested. This is also a time when the individual's attention turns from centered on base character goals to thinking more about group- or guild-specific goals; for example, building a city or decorating a guild house. The player certainly continues to care about his own gain, but the group's benefit is now a major consideration as well. The main areas of design to reflect on for this gameplay stratum would be projects with which the player expends time, energy, and resources; group projects where the player will share group-related aspirations and will expend time and resources to achieve.

Individual Projects

As the player moves through the game, the rate of goal achievement gradually slows down, so that the time between goals is much longer now than when the game began. One challenge is to create a set of activities that a player can work toward on his own that do not have an established end but must regularly build upon itself either in a lengthy advancement ladder or in a regenerative cycle, while providing regular and relatively rapid progress feedback. Here are a few guiding characteristics for these projects, none of which is required:

- Require investment of time, effort, and/or resources.
- Do not fundamentally affect the character's score attributes or abilities.
- Provide regular feedback to report progress.

An Item Collection and a Housing system are two such veteran gaming systems that have proved very popular and very effective in achieving the goals of a long-term individual project.

One common method that achieves these goals is providing a defined Item Collection, which may or may not have character implications, toward which a player may concentrate his efforts. This practice is very effective, as the player will put more time into a centerpiece project with some visible signs of progress. The player can measure progress through either stated or implied collection completion. These collections could come in the form of skill granting or enhancing objects that might increase in power as the collection nears completion. For example, *Diablo 2* employs the power of such an Item Collection through unique sets of equipment and their crystal enhancements. Associated with the difficulty of completing any given collection along with the time required to complete any single collection is the perceived value of the account, which will increase with the perceived difficulty and time invested. The Item Collection may also be objects related to quests or tasks, which might require groups of people to acquire. By requiring a larger organization of players and a large block of time invested in the task, the developers are naturally delaying the completion of these collections. The Item Collection could simply convey a level of quest or exploration achievement in the form of totems or trophies related to different landmarks, or a collection of mission tiles that can be found when missions are completed. In these ways, the developer can present some variety and a distinctive quality to the individual experience of the later game.

Another Individual Project that a developer might provide is a Housing system. The Housing system can involve multiple stages of significant time and resource investment, from a process granting the ability to have a house, to the process of building the house, and finally to the process of maintaining and improving the house. Additionally, House construction can logically sustain a hard time limit that the players can understand and accept. An example of how a Housing system could be played out begins with the player being required to complete a multistaged quest to be granted a plot of land to gain permission to build a house.

The player could submit his petition for housing to the system and get an answer a real day or two later. The player would need to collect enough gold to buy a housing blueprint. Once the player uses the deed on his plot of land, a receiving object will appear to represent the house construction in progress. This object would also act as a container for the resources required for the building's construction. The player would need to collect the amount of wood, steel, and stone that the blueprint requires and deposit them into the house construction object. If possible, the system could grant additional decorative characteristics according to the quality of resources used to construct the house. Once the house has received all the needed resources, construction of the house will begin. After a few days, the house will be fully constructed. One option that could allow for some reliance on group and community is to give the player the ability to allow other players to contribute resources or to interface with the house construction object, which would then lessen the construction time by a certain amount. Once the house is completed, the player could choose to begin work on gaining permission to build a larger house, by going through a modified process similar to the one described. Once completed, the house will require some maintenance to act as a constant wealth and resource sink on the player. Houses become a public representation of achievement in which the player can take pride. It is something that should take a great amount of time and resources, which shouldn't be something that directly impacts the adventuring capabilities of the character. A developer would want to permanently attach the house to the account so that as the house increases in time and resources invested, the more permanent the account becomes. In this way, a Housing system with a ladder of advancement tied to the house can provide for and achieve many of the main goals for this gameplay stratum.

The Item Collection and Housing systems are both largely popular and extremely effective in providing some long-term goals for the individual player. Some other possible systems could include a pet system, whereby the player can collect, crossbreed, raise, and train his pets. A gardening system also can achieve the goals of the individual projects. Again, one could include aspects of collection, crossbreeding, and raising into a garden project the same as elements in the pet system.

Providing a player with some longer term projects to which he can dedicate time, effort, and in-game resources is vital in the attempt to keep his attention for long periods of time. The Collections, Housing, Pets, and Gardens systems are all examples of systems that can fulfill the goals of the Individual project, helping players reach and surpass the third gameplay stratum.

Group Projects

Another challenge for this stratum is to provide long-terms goals and projects for time, resource, and effort investment for groups as well as individuals. Groups, by nature, are more secure sets of players because of the friendship and social ties that develop between one another. However, to help those ties grow stronger and to expand their influence to other players, it is important to give these groups long-term goals and objects of achievement to focus their efforts. Here are three general classes of projects for consideration:

- Win prestige for a guild by marking its achievement in relation to other guilds.
- Institute a City advancement system, where the group would invest time, resources, and effort to advance a city object.
- Have guilds compete against each other directly for objects of prestige or benefit, through contests for individual objects or competition for sections of game space.

While these suggestions just scratch the surface in terms of group object possibilities, they can act as examples to illustrate some of the goals for group objects and how to achieve them.

The simplest form of group motivation is intergroup comparison through some in-game metric with public acknowledgment. One example would be a leader board that tracks which group is the best at doing a particular activity, such as which guild has the most money, or which guild has completed this epic quest the most times or in the shortest amount of time. One way to provide incentive to being the best other than simple bragging rights is by rewarding the group that is best in a given area. For example, track which guild collects the most of a given resource. The winner would gain a base skill increase that lasts until they lose the top position. It is important that people see these rankings in and out of game, such as on the Web page and perhaps an in-game representation associated with a guild center or even posted in the main gaming centers. Linking guilds to some larger community object is a good technique for widening the appeal of inter-guild interactions, as members of this larger community would have vested interest in the success of their associated guild if they stood to benefit. These kinds of contests give a renewable and attractive goal for a group to aspire to for the long term.

Another system for group achievement is a City system that provides a central object on which the group can expend energy and time on, and yields a visible reward and feedback to efforts put into it. For example, a City system could begin when a guild forms, and its formation would manifest itself in a small village. The village would consist of mud huts for each guild member and then a small contingent of NPCs. For the members of the guild to improve their city, they must contribute resources to its town center, and they must increase the NPC satisfaction rating for the town by doing tasks or quests for the NPCs. These tasks could take the form of a specific series of quests or a generic task of removing an enemy or bringing a certain amount of resources. Once they have achieved the needed resources and satisfaction level, the city will increase in size and in number of NPCs. Each group member will then have the option to upgrade his house using resources from the city resource pool, or pass the upgrade, meaning the group would have more resources ready when working for the next level. The new NPCs might bring with them some benefits such as NPC vendors or someone to repair items. The system could continue in this way of having group members improve NPC satisfaction and collect raw resources, and it would then provide a host of different benefits from stores, banks, training centers, and portals to new adventuring zones. This is just an example of a system that could provide long-term goals, incentive for the group to work together and group-wide benefits as a result of group effort.

Another interesting technique to generate group effort and to create some intrigue among groups is to employ some form of Player Versus Player competition. For example, one possible system would involve one guild issuing a challenge to the other over the possession of a Trophy, which would be a decorative object for the guild house and an object that conveys some benefit to all members. Once a challenging guild clicks on the desired Trophy, which is publicly displayed outside the champion guild's guild center or house, they would have the option to challenge the possessing guild for the trophy. It would be wise to institute a couple of limits to discourage frivolous challenges, such as limiting challenges to one per month, and having the challenge cost a certain amount of currency or resource based on the trophy's value to discourage nonserious challenges. Once the challenge is accepted, a notification goes out to both guilds describing the details of the contest. Once the contest is finished and the winner is decided, the trophy is automatically transferred to the winner's guild house or guild center. After the trophy has transferred ownership, there will be a grace period during which the trophy cannot be challenged. This contest of trophies will provide a unifying incentive for the guild to have the resources to challenge for another guild's trophy.

Regional Conquest is another group project system; in this case, guilds seek to conquer game world regions through traditional PvP and to reap the rewards of holding these sections of game land. This system could function similarly to the Trophy competition, except that this competition would be for the rights to adventure in certain sections of land. In this example, the game map would be separated into sections of land. Each section of land is only accessible to the guild that governs the land and their allies. Guilds will challenge and take land from an NPC guild at first. When a guild wants to challenge for the rights to a section of land, then that guild can access a global map, click on the desired zone, and select to challenge for it. They can get metrics on that land before they challenge it, such as creature spawn, special locations, resources spawned, and so forth. The guild must pay a certain "energy" cost to challenge for the land section that is based on a system determined value for that particular section of land, and they must own a neighboring segment of land. This "energy" will be calculated by the contributed items, resources, character energy, or character currency that is added to it. A receptacle exists at the center of the guild's capital city, and players can add money, items, or perform actions on this receptacle to help build "energy" to enable the guild to challenge for a section of land. Once the guild has enough "energy" to challenge for the rights to a section of land, it can issue the challenge to the occupying guild and will have to compete for the section of land in a PvP contest. This contest will happen on the same day and at the same time for each contest so that the guild members can plan around the contest. It also provides a natural hard time limit to help space contests. Contests would be conducted in a controlled setting. The guild will choose which players will enter the competition, by way of a vote or appointment by guild leader. The PvP rule set and map layout will be different for each section to give a variety of gameplay possibilities for each land challenge, from death match to capture the flag to domination. When the time for the contest arrives, the chosen challengers will be transported into the contest map and they will war with the other guild for rights over the land section. Other guild members can choose to watch the contest through the eyes of their guild mates. Once the contest is completed, the losing guild no longer has access to that section of land. They can remain, but if they leave or log out, they cannot return. With a system of conquest such as this, it is important to guard against monopolies. One way to do this is to have each section of land require a maintenance cost that would stack as the guild's empire grew, thereby functionally limiting the size of any single empire. The conquest system provides an avenue for characters of all levels to contribute to the success of the guild. It also provides an incentive to be involved and follow the success of the guild to which the player is associated. It provides long-term goals of land conquest, and regular time invested in getting more land and keeping the land already possessed.

Conclusion

MMOs are far different from single-player games in many ways, and none is more significant than the fundamental design problem related to longevity. Smoothly transitioning the player from a typical single-player experience to a game where content release and character advancement become more rigidly controlled and where social inclusion and achievement play a significant role is difficult. Identifying these phases of gameplay and the design role each plays in the player transition to long term is an important step in achieving the smooth transition. Often, developers will not smooth that transition, or will neglect one of the strata of gameplay, which can result in turning away potential long-term players. This article identified three main gameplay strata that differentiate themselves from each other by what one can expect the player to need in order to move into the deeper and longer elder gameplay. By designing to each stratum, developers can better transition the players to a longer term mindset, and in that way work to stabilize their account base and give the game a longer life.

1.3

Balancing Gameplay for Thousands of Your Harshest Critics

Brian "Psychochild" Green— Near Death Studios, Inc.

brian.green@neardeathstudios.com

Gameplay balance is a difficult thing in computer games, and doubly so in multi-player online games. Balance is about maintaining the fun for the player by providing a game that is neither too hard nor too easy for them. The rapid feedback from online game players and ease of change often mean that there's intense pressure to quickly fix imbalances. It is important for a good designer to know how to balance and maintain balance as a game grows.

This article focuses on best practices for balancing the gameplay during a game's entire life cycle from design to launch to years of maintenance. It also looks at rules for attempting balance for Player vs. Player (PvP) games that are notoriously difficult to balance. Finally, the article looks at times when you *shouldn't* balance a game and benefits of controlled imbalances in the game.

Why Balance? Definition of Balance and Goals of Balanced Gameplay

The best thing about online games is that you can patch the game to fix problems. The worst thing about online games is that you can patch the game and introduce more problems. These two sentences describe why balance in online games is so difficult to achieve in general. The dynamic nature of these games means that balance is a constantly moving target. Because players are interacting with each other, balance issues become much more vital to the designer when compared to traditional single-player games.

What Is Covered?

The concept of balance is huge, so this article by necessity only examines a focused part of the topic. The focus will be on gameplay balance, particularly as it relates to combat. However, designers should be able to apply the general information in this article to other areas such as crafting, economy, and other important aspects of an online game, and learn from specific examples.

Of course, each game is unique, and the solutions to your problems are usually as unique as your game. Therefore, this article focuses on "best practices" in balancing gameplay instead of offering concrete solutions to every problem. Specific examples from existing games are used when appropriate to the topic for illustrative purposes only. Also keep in mind that what works for one game might not be the proper solution for another game, even if the feature was wildly successful in the first game. Be prepared to do your own investigation and consideration when it comes to balancing gameplay in your own game as you learn about what worked in other games.

This article also focuses on game design instead of technical issues. For example, design is concerned with imbalance, whereas cheats are of interest to the technical developers of a game. The designer's job is made more difficult because both imbalances and cheats are referred to as "bugs" and can be hard to tell apart. Although cheating detection and prevention is outside the scope of this article, this is not to downplay their importance; a game cannot be balanced if it is plagued with cheats!

Finally, it is important to keep in mind that multiplayer online game development is a never-ending task, especially when it comes to balance. There is no magic formula that will make imbalances and problems go away forever. Players will discover imbalances long after you launch, and new content will always bring with it the possibility of new problems. You must continuously watch for imbalances as the game grows and develops.

What Is Balance?

First, it is important to define what is meant by "balance" before we get into detailed discussion. It is often hard to define because it is more of an art than a science. Designers will almost always have to work without perfect information since these games are often very large, mind-bogglingly complex, and the player base is too unpredictable to ever gain perfect information. This means that there just isn't a magic equation that you can use to make sure your game is balanced. Moreover, most large online games have multiple interacting components that can complicate the issue; even if the combat system is self-balanced and the crafting system is self-balanced, the interaction between these two internally balanced systems can be completely imbalanced overall.

In practical terms, balance is about fairness to the player. A player should feel that the game is reasonably fair and that his input is meaningful to the outcome of in-game activities. Balance also means that no group of players has an overwhelming advantage over or feels completely inferior to another group of players because of the game mechanics. Balance means that a player can feel a bit of pride about his ability to play the game.

Unfortunately, these aren't objective measurements of the game. Because of the subjective nature of balance, it is vital to realize that player perception truly is reality as far as the game is concerned. If a player thinks something is imbalanced, he will complain about it. This can be very frustrating for designers who see their careful design torn to shreds by someone who thinks there is an imbalance.

It is also important to keep player motivation in mind when considering gameplay balance. Players are usually looking out for themselves, and frame balance issues in personal terms. A player will rarely claim that his character class or template is too powerful; if a player does claim this, you probably have a severe imbalance. Most players will claim that their character is either balanced or too weak compared to other classes or templates. Likewise, other classes and templates will rarely be called too weak. Most of the time, a player will refer to other classes and templates as too powerful, often because of some special power or ability that the player envies. From a player perspective, anything that hurts the player is an imbalance, but anything that helps him is a "strategy." Remember these points of view as you are balancing your game, especially when you are relying on player feedback.

Overall, balance is about maintaining the fun in the game for all the players in your game. Balance means that every player has a fun character that isn't too hard and isn't too easy to play; either extreme will ruin the game. Balance also allows the players to have characters they enjoy and can invest in emotionally and participate fully in the game world. After all, is that not what we want from the players? The more fun they have in our game means the more they emotionally invest in their characters, the more enjoyment they can derive with our game.

What Is Not Balance?

Now that we know that balance has at least something to do with fun and player perception, we should focus on what is *not* balance. There are many common fallacies that designers sometimes believe that can cause problems in balance.

First and most importantly, balance is not necessarily what an individual player truly wants. As mentioned before, players are self-motivated in their view of the game. This often means that a player wants a bit more power than the other players in the game. Unfortunately, while that may be the most fun for the player in the short term, we want to maximize the fun for all the players in the game. This can also lead to players becoming upset with not having enough "fun" in the game, because they will never get exactly what they want; establishing player expectations, which we discuss later, can help counter this. Therefore, giving the players what *they* consider "balanced" is not always balance.

Balance also rarely has anything to do with the amount of time a player has spent in the game. Designers often think that a long, arduous advancement path balances out a very powerful ability in the game, such as the balance curve for wizards in traditional fantasy RPG game systems. This is not balanced primarily because players will always achieve goals faster than you expect; good game players are able to easily optimize games, and will often share this information with other players. It also doesn't matter how long it took to get the power if the player can abuse the power repeatedly right now. This is especially true in games with PvP combat, where the player or players with the powerful ability can use it to stop other players from achieving that ability.

Balance is not purely mathematical. It is understandable for designers to want to try to find some magical equations that ensure balance, but unfortunately, they do not exist. Something as simple as adding +1 to offense while adding +1 to defense may seem balanced on the surface, but can often be completely imbalanced. For example, perhaps the internal game mechanics specify that each point of defense only counteracts .75 points of offense. This can happen if the game mechanics use a weighted ratio between offense and defense. Alternatively, gameplay realities could make this imbalanced even if the mechanics seem balanced upon casual observation. "The best defense is a good offense" is a typical strategy in many online games, so offensive power is seen as more desirable than defensive power. Therefore, the players benefiting from increased offense will probably get more actual power out of the change than the players benefiting from the increased defense.

Designers must also resist the urge to balance gameplay by using complex equations. For example, a designer might want to create a specification based on equations developed by taking the derivative of an equation describing the relation between two elements in the game. The designer may feel that this is balanced because it's complex, but that is not always the case. There might also be problems with implementation, especially in a system that has technological restrictions. In this case, a simple equation might be more correct and easier to implement correctly.

Developers should also try to avoid aesthetic purity in design simply for the sake of such purity. This is when the designer creates a "pattern" in the organization that seems symmetrical; this type of "balance" is often imbalanced from a gameplay point of view. Creating such patterns can be very hard to resist, since it can be very intellectually appealing to have symmetry in the design. An example of this focus on aesthetic purity can be found in *Meridian 59*'s spell school, Kraanan, designed as both pro-combat and anti-magic. These two aspects make a nice symmetry, but this setup made the spell school too powerful. It helped fighter types defend against magic while aiding their native abilities, giving all-around offense and defensive bonuses. It became an overwhelming advantage in the game and very few players choose not to take it. However, due to the player expectations it is hard to change this spell school to be more balanced. The symmetry appeared balanced but caused notable imbalances in practice.

Finally, avoid static balance, which is another case of a focus on the aesthetic purity in the design. The best example of this is providing identical gameplay experiences in different skins. While this may be balanced in theory, it can be extremely boring for most players. One of the attractions of online games is that they are dynamic, so trying to create and enforce a static part of the game goes against the strengths you should be exploiting.

In the end, great game balance is never perfect. Although we might strive for perfection, it is important to remember that an ever-changing online game is rarely going to achieve it due to the ever-changing nature of the game. Designers need to do their best to balance the game, but be mindful of the limitations they are under.

Now that we know what balance is, let's look at practical applications of this knowledge.

Balanced Play: Overview of What Works (and What Doesn't) in Balancing Gameplay

Although this article is about design, it is important that all areas of development work together to balance the game. Do not forget to include areas like Customer Service (CS) and Events Managers in discussions on balance because they will often have a dramatic effect on the balance of the game. For example, a carefully balanced economy can be disrupted if an Event Manager gives out lavish prizes to participants in events. Likewise, the CS representatives can give you feedback from player complaints. Player opinions of the game, the development team, and the balance of the game in general will be influenced by all areas of development. Make sure that everyone works together to achieve this goal; otherwise, you might end up working at cross-purposes [Bartle03].

Time is the one resource that is always in short supply in game development, and online games are no exception. Designers for multiplayer online games also feel additional pressures from the tight feedback loop between developer and player. You can experience the clamor of players demanding a change in real time. Since patches are an expected and even demanded feature in online games, it is not surprising that change is one of the few constants in online game. This puts pressure on the designer to make changes rapidly.

Consider Changes Carefully

All these reasons are why the most important rule in balancing a design is to make all changes only after very careful consideration. Again, every game is unique and has different solutions. It's important to consider the effect that a change will have on your game as a whole. You must also make your changes appropriate to the expectations of your players. Your design solutions must meet multiple design criteria, and careful planning is required to ensure that balance is established and maintained.

It is common to want to make a quick fix to a problem in the game given the often-intense pressures most designers experience from all directions; however, hasty decisions can create more problems than they solve or might even ignore the problem completely. For example, a proposed fix could focus on fixing symptoms but not the actual problem.

It's important to fix the problem and not merely respond to the symptoms. Keep in mind that the symptoms are the most obvious sources of problems upon initial inspection. For example, let's say that you find that the majority of players are killing monsters too fast compared to what you expected. The obvious solution is to change the mechanics so that monsters are harder so combat takes longer. However, if you looked a bit further you might find that the majority of players killing monsters too fast have a particular imbalanced ability that gives them a large advantage when fighting monsters. Addressing this source imbalance is better for the game overall; if you had simply made monsters harder to kill, it would have driven more people to use the imbalanced ability and created an even greater imbalance that the players would come to rely on. Such an entrenched imbalance becomes harder to fix later due to player expectations. It is important to use all the tools available to you in order to make informed decisions.

Data Collection Is Valuable

Data collection can be one of the greatest allies a game designer has when dealing with imbalances. In a live game, you should already be collecting a wide variety of data for customer service purposes; accusations of cheating and technical bugs need to be tracked and verified. Adding a way for designers to access this data will give them tools to improve game design [Kennerly03]. Data shows you what players actually do compared to what they say. Experienced game developers know that what players say and what they do is often very different, and data collection can give you the information necessary to make more informed decisions.

You can use data analysis and trends to help you uncover current or possible future imbalances. For example, a sudden change in player behavior could indicate that an imbalance has been discovered by the players. As the players shift their behaviors to take advantage of this new imbalance, you can take steps early in the cycle to fix problems before they become widespread and more entrenched.

However, it is important to keep in mind that you should not overreact and make hasty changes based solely on collected data. Observed shifts could be the result of a previous imbalance correcting itself automatically through the actions of the players. It is important to evaluate the data collected to see if it is sufficiently balanced. A sufficiently balanced game may not be balanced exactly as you expect.

An example of rather detailed data collection can be found in Raph Koster's discussion of the economy in *Star Wars Galaxies*. Raph shows some of the data collected and some conclusions drawn from the data in an official posting. In his discussion, Raph talks about his observations of the in-game economy from looking at stats. Of particular interest is how the development team discovered the existence of a dupe bug through evaluating the economic balance in the game and noticing that more money was leaving the economy than was entering it through player actions. It is also interesting to read how something that normally hurts an economy, the currency deficit, is actually a healthy response by the economy to balance out the dupe bug that was found. You can find the full discussion at the *Star Wars Galaxies* Web site [Koster04].

Use Player Feedback Wisely

Collecting data can be useful, but remember that balance was defined as being "about maintaining the fun in the game for the players" previously. Therefore, while objective data can be useful, it can't really tell you if the players are having fun, a very subjective point of view. For that, you must get feedback from the players.

It would be nice if it were really as easy as asking players what they thought. As noted before, what they say and what they do can be completely different. You must keep in mind that your players are incredibly interconnected even if they are only able to communicate within your game, so groupthink is an incredibly powerful force that helps players form opinions about if a game is balanced or not. Therefore, most player feedback needs to be properly interpreted. The best overall strategy is to listen to your players but not have your actions dictated by player feedback.

Why listen to players in the first place? Again, we need their feedback to make sure they are having fun. If they are not having fun, they will not be happy and will not remain our players for long! In addition, players are often more knowledgeable about the practical aspects of your game. Thousands of players are going to be more thorough in evaluating your game than any number of designers would be. Players experience your game on a day-to-day basis, whereas designers are mostly concerned with issues on higher levels. Players know the practical side of things, whereas designers usually deal with the theoretical. Given the gulf between theory and practice, players can be a valuable source of information for the realities of gameplay that might escape the attention of even the best designer.

Despite the invaluable nature of player input, it is important to remember that this information is not pure and unbiased. As mentioned before, players are motivated by their own interests. Players who report that their own class is weak and that other classes are too powerful are usually championing their own desires. Much of the feedback you receive from players is similarly biased toward helping the player. This is why it is important for a game designer to evaluate the feedback and try to separate the personal biases from useful data.

Even beyond personal biases, players are quick to complain when things are bad, but are very slow to report when things are going well. This is to be expected, since players are expecting to be entertained; anything that contributes to this is expected, anything that disrupts the entertainment is to be removed. However, this pattern of feedback can be very depressing for a designer who is not prepared for this; you will hear many more complaints than compliments, if you even hear any praise! This can lead to feelings that the game is plagued with problems and that very few good aspects exist. This can also be a tremendous public relations problem if these complaints are made in public forums. It is important to remember that there are good things in the game even if the distribution of reports seems overwhelmingly negative. And, again, it is important to manage player expectations about the game as will be discussed later. Encouraging positive feedback will let you know what strengths your online game has upon which you can expand.

So, how do you collect useful user feedback? One of the worst ways is to collect it from open forums for your game. Almost every game has these forums, and they are almost universally useless for getting good feedback. The biggest problem is that the open forums only attract a small number of players. You will usually only see 10–20%

of your users active on the forums. These will tend to be the hardest of the hard-core players of your game, representing a very narrow and specific point of view. In addition, groupthink and bandwagons can sidetrack discussions. Dominant posters can use the forums to sway people to their side to advocate their narrow point of view. People with complaints will also dominate the forums, since people with complaints are more likely to give feedback than people who are content with the game.

However, *Dark Age of Camelot* set up a very effective program called the "Team Leads" program. They asked respected and active players to become "team leads" and speak to the developers directly about the concerns of a specific class in the game. The selected players would be given access to a restricted forum that the developers would read on a regular basis. These representatives would then collect the feedback from the hundreds of thousands of players and summarize the concerns for the developer.

This was a great program because it was useful for getting feedback from players. The team leads were able to filter out the tremendous amount of feedback from the players. They presented the developers with a focused amount of feedback in a coherent form. The program also took advantage of the fact that players are going to naturally ask for improvements to their own classes first; it even encouraged this behavior! The program was useful to the developers and took advantage of the players' natural tendencies.

Planning Ahead Is Valuable

Even if you are a master at getting useful feedback from players, it will be worthless unless you know what to do with it. It is important to plan for changes to the game.

The first rule is to maintain as much flexibility as possible in your designs. It is hard to determine where imbalances will appear, and restricting yourself in any way will reduce your ability to react quickly and effectively to imbalances as they become known. Unfortunately, there will always be restrictions and limitations, so it is important to know your weaknesses and how to work around them. Plan ahead for things you expect will probably need to be rebalanced. For example, instead of creating static variables to balance an aspect of the game, allow for flexible values that can be changed on a live game server. This will allow you to change balance on the fly without a major patch, allowing you to react to imbalances faster.

The next rule is to plan ahead on how to deal with the eventual imbalances that come to light. Imbalances will happen, so how will you deal with them? Having a plan established beforehand will help you deal with the imbalances more gracefully and easily. The use of flexible values in game systems is a great first step, but there are other ways to deal with the results of imbalances as well.

Let us take an imbalanced economy as an example. Through some flaw in the system, some players have a very large amount of money. How do you fix this problem? One way is to use the tracking system and remove unfairly earned money. Of course, this presents a problem because the original players who took advantage of the exploit might have passed the ill-gotten money to other players already. Do you take away the money the players think they earned fairly through trade with another player?

An alternative to such heavy-handed administrative behaviors is to design in-game contingency plans. A common method to do this is to encourage conspicuous consumption of expensive goods. Usually, this conspicuous consumption comes in the form of rare and desirable clothing, usually black in color, with very high prices. If these clothes have no gameplay effect, then players have spent their money on in-game items that give no discernible gameplay advantage. The economy has had the excess money drained off and can hopefully revert to a balanced state. Of course, part of this design is ensuring that players see these types of objects as desirable through establishing their expectations.

Another design idea can be found in *Yohoho! Puzzle Pirates* and its marketplace. Players can place bids for basic items supplied by the game system for trade skills. Players with the highest bids have their orders fulfilled first and fastest. As the average bid price increases, overall speed increases, draining more money from the economy. This means that an influx of cash will not disrupt the economy overall, just provide more basic crafting items for players. As the money is drained from the economy, the balance will be restored to expected levels.

Determining When Everything Is Balanced

You have made your decisions carefully and thoughtfully. You have received useful and appropriate player feedback. You even have plans for maintaining balance through a design intended to counteract imbalances. Now comes the hard part: determining when you've done your job correctly. When is the game properly balanced?

The most common response from an inexperienced online game developer is to say, "When the players stop complaining." As mentioned before, however, players do not necessarily want true balance. If the game is truly balanced, players will still generally want a bit of additional power for their characters. Most of them will still complain about a lack of balance. A more accurate, although perhaps a little cynical, statement is that the game is balanced when all the players complain equally about the balance between all the different elements.

A better way of evaluating balance is to analyze the data you collect from your game. As mentioned before, you can evaluate the data to see if the game has a reasonable balance, which may not be balanced exactly the way you anticipated. Player behavior in the game is the best measurement to see if a game is truly balanced.

Pre-Balancing: Fundamental Design and Establishing Player Expectations

So, you have decided to develop an online game. Congratulations! You sit down in front of a blank screen and start typing your masterpiece design. What issues are important to consider before the first player ever logs on to your game?

Establishing Player Expectation Is Vital

Without a doubt, the most important job is to establish player expectations about the game. As mentioned before, all areas of development should work together to ensure and maintain balance. The task of establishing player expectations requires support from not only designers, but from all other areas of the development team, especially customer service (CS) and quality assurance (QA). It is important to present a consistent message to the players to develop their expectations in beneficial ways.

What does it really mean to establish player expectations? It means that you give the players a definite impression of what the game will be like so that they know what is standard operation and what is an exploit. It also lets them know what kind of game to expect. For example, if your game is highly focused on PvP combat, you need to establish this fact so that players wanting a noncombat environment are not upset. Players of such a game should realize that direct conflict with other players is part of the game, and not a problem to be dealt with by CS representatives!

On the CS side, you need to establish policies of evaluating and punishing exploiters and cheaters. The same data collection tools that designers can use to evaluate balance can also be used for CS representatives to discover cheats and isolate cheaters. Any amount of balancing is useless if players can cheat and otherwise exploit the system. Finding and punishing exploiters early will establish player expectations that the game may be tough, but it is at least fair. This is especially important in games with a focus on PvP combat.

In general, you should establish expectations about the game as early as possible. Your initial designs should include what the player expectations should be. Defining these expectations will give a clear goal and consistent message to all areas of development. The longer the game exists, the more likely people will be to form their own expectations of the game, which can be difficult for the developers to achieve. If you do a proper job of establishing player expectations, much of the rest of your work should be easier.

Game Types: Class/Level vs. Skill Based

Once we have player expectations established, we should look at some more specific ways of implementing balance in a design before launch. As an example, we will focus on two dominant types of games: class/level-based systems and skill-based systems. This is not to say that these are the only two types of games possible; in fact, we are ignoring many different types of interesting systems that aren't centered on a cumulative-character design. However, these two game types are very familiar to most designers and are good examples to discuss some of the finer points of balance in design.

Class/level-based games focus on the class and level of the character. In general, each character picks a class at character creation and starts at level 1. As the character experiences the game, he advances in level at certain intervals. Occasionally, additional classes are available to the character at later levels. The class and level tend to define what abilities and items the character can use and what the character's overall power level is. These games tend to encourage players to form groups with other characters that complement their characters' powers and abilities.

Class/level-based games are usually balanced, unsurprisingly, with classes and levels in mind. Each class should have a specific and unique purpose in a group. This purpose should be comparable to the purpose of other characters without being dominant or inferior to another. For example, warriors might be able to take hits well and guard the rest of the group from damage, while the cleric can heal the group most effectively. As long as both of these tasks are important to a group, the classes are reasonably balanced against each other. Imbalances usually occur when the abilities of one class are less useful, or if one class has the abilities of another. For example, if clerics can heal fast enough that anyone can take hits as well as a warrior, then the warrior is generally considered underpowered. If warriors can heal as effectively as clerics while protecting other group members from damage, this is generally considered imbalanced. Some games allow some classes to have multiple abilities that are not as efficient as the abilities of a "pure" class. Therefore, a paladin class might be able to protect the group from damage (but not as well as a warrior can) and heal damage (but not as well as a cleric can). Balancing these powers so that each class feels useful to a group and capable in the game is a key to balancing the game overall.

In addition, levels must also be balanced. Level disparity is an important topic in class/level-based games. How do players of greatly different levels interact? On the one hand, if they cannot interact, you run the risk of alienating friends from each other as their levels become more diverse over time. On the other hand, a lack of level disparity can take away the feeling of "power" that players expect from an experienced high-level character. This issue becomes even more important in PvP games. If a high-level character can slaughter a low-level character without much effort, the low-level character will feel the situation is imbalanced. Levels are most balanced when levels have a meaningful but not overwhelming affect on gameplay.

Alternatively, there are skill-based systems. A purely skill-based system is one that has a variety of abilities ("skills") from which the player can choose a limited number to customize his character. This type of system breaks away from the rigid class-based systems mentioned previously, since a player could take a variety of powers that defy easy classification. These types of games also tend to lack a central "level" measurement of overall power; rather, the character's power is the cumulative power from all his various skills. These skills are often accumulated during gameplay, and individual skills' powers can be increased as the player uses the skills.

Design goals for balancing skill-based games are quite different from class/level-based games. Players can define their character's roles and choose their own unique purpose that fits the character. An imbalance usually does not create power disparity between characters because everyone is usually able to gain the imbalanced ability. Therefore, no one feels "left out" unless he chooses not to take the power. However, this also leads to the negative situation where a limited number of "templates" or specific organizations of skills will be seen as the best possible character to have. For example, in *Meridian 59*, players can master between two to four schools of abilities;

conventional wisdom mastering three schools was the best template for many years. When players follow templates, characters start to look similar as the conventional wisdom of which abilities are "more imbalanced" is shared between players. Worse, this conventional wisdom can stubbornly remain a "fact" in the game and result in the players resisting or even failing to adjust for changes made to specific abilities. Because of this, balance usually focuses on allowing for a wider variety of viable player types based on the skills selected for the character.

Another important balance consideration for skill-based games is accumulating and removing skills from the character. The speed at which a character can accumulate skills is important to balance. If a character gains skills too fast, he can become much more powerful in a short period of time, which can overwhelm inexperienced players. However, if a character gains skills too slowly, the character can seem more boring or stagnant. It is also important to consider the result of a player removing skills from the character. Most games offer a "respec" system, allowing players to give up skills in order to gain other skills to replace them. This is useful for players who want to change their skills as the character develops, but it can also indirectly encourage people to redefine their character based on the "super template" that current conventional wisdom encourages.

In general, class/level-based systems are considered easier to balance than skill-based ones. The reason is that there are fewer variables to balance between classes as compared to skills. You also do not have to worry about a single player using a combination of two different skills to gain an overwhelming imbalanced advantage. In a class-based system, such an advantage will usually require at least two different characters to work together, increasing the complexity of abusing the imbalance.

Finally, it is important to realize that these game types are not an either/or situation. Hybrid systems can use aspects of both systems, which present their own unique balance challenges. In *Meridian 59*, the system is primarily skill-based, but the skills are grouped into different "schools" that are roughly equivalent to classes. Therefore, players can choose which skills they want, but higher level skills in one school require the player to master lower level skills first. Players are generally able to select skills from two to four of the seven schools. *Meridian 59*'s system has many of the balance challenges of both class/level-based systems and skill-based systems, such as greater interaction between a single character's skills. However, the game also enjoys some of the positive balance consequences, such as players having defined roles in groups.

Game Mechanics: Transparent vs. Opaque

Now, let's look at design for our game mechanics. We will look at transparent and opaque game mechanics. These terms describe how much information is available to the player about the game mechanics, which can be measured on a sliding scale between the two extremes.

Opaque mechanics mean that as little information is shared with the player as possible. In extreme cases, stats might not even be shared with the player at all. Most times, players will get basic information such as vital statistics and major character attributes, but will not be told derived statistics directly. For example, a player might know that he has "Might 30" and that the Might stat affects carrying capacity and damage, but not specifically know how much carrying capacity or bonus damage that provides.

Opaque mechanics are often desirable because it adds an additional layer of gameplay. The players get to figure out what their stats mean, and what stats are optimal for their style of play. In addition, imbalance can often remain partially hidden from the players since it is not immediately obvious when an opaque mechanic is imbalanced. However, there can also be some serious drawbacks. First, game mechanics are usually documented by a dedicated group of players if there is any gameplay advantage to be had. However, most players are not statisticians, so they will often gather statistically invalid information and make improper conclusions. In addition, you often see players using gathered information as an advantage or even see players spreading false information to confuse rivals, especially in PvP-focused games where misleading a rival can be a significant advantage. Players without accurate information will often complain about perceived imbalances; remember, player perception is reality in online games.

Transparent mechanics, however, give the players complete information about how the game works. Often, games with transparent mechanics will provide numerical information such as raw damage or speed on weapons, armor protection for pieces of armor, and so forth. Although this makes imbalances easier to see, it also means that everyone is on equal footing when it comes to finding imbalances. Developers can also handle complaints easier if all the mechanics are easy to see.

No single online game is wholly opaque or completely transparent. Most games share at least a little information or hide some aspect of the game for the players to discover. Because of this, each game has its own combination of balance issues to deal with based on how much information a player has.

Perfect Balance Is Impossible Before Launch

A designer's goal is to balance the game as much as possible before launch. However, the unfortunate reality is that you will never have enough time or information to achieve perfect balance before launch. It is important to keep this fact in mind as you are designing for balance.

The best thing a designer can do when facing the reality of balancing is to be prepared to scale back some features that will not be balanced before launch. This can be the result of a lack of time to implement, to test, or even to properly design the system. If this happens, prepare to launch without the system. Due to the nature of online games, a system that has a flaw in the core of the design can create problems in the game for many years afterwards. Having to work around this flaw will create much more work in the long run, and completely replacing the system with the flaw can hurt player expectations. However, it is often hard to do overall balance if you are not sure which systems will be done in time and which will not. It is also often hard to make the decision not to launch with a particular feature; veteran online game developer Gordon Walton often accurately describes this as "knifing your babies."

Even if you are certain that a system is balanced, some problems just aren't revealed until after launch. In some cases, it has taken years to discover some imbalances. When players discover a new tactic, or even use an existing option to its full extent, new imbalances can be revealed that were not apparent before. In addition, sometimes players will discover imbalances during testing, but keep the information secret in order to use the knowledge "when it counts" after launch. Therefore, it is very difficult to get enough information before launch in order to achieve perfect balance.

Of course, the dynamic nature of online games means that even if you did manage to balance the game perfectly before launch, it will not remain that way. Unless the game is stagnant, new content will be added to the game. This new content will bring with it the possibilities of new imbalances being added.

So, what is the point of trying to balance a game before launch if it is essentially impossible? First, players will judge your game based on the balance at launch. This means that the more balanced the game is, the more likely players will have a positive opinion of your game. In addition, fundamental design problems can be very difficult or even impossible to correct after launch. Therefore, you must do your best to design a balanced game.

Post-Balancing: How to Rebalance Existing Gameplay

What if you have already launched your game? By now you have found out that the launch isn't really the end of development; rather, it is just a new beginning! Rebalancing the game after launch is a completely different issue.

Player Expectations Change

As mentioned before, it is all but impossible to get perfect balance before launch, so a good designer should be ready to rebalance gameplay. A greater number of players will find imbalances that were not previously obvious, and devious players that found unreported balances in beta will now begin to exploit them. The nature of the game has changed with the launch, and the designer's job continues to be demanding.

Most importantly, player expectations change after launch. After launch, it is much more difficult to manage player expectations. Once your game becomes a service they must pay for, the players become much more demanding. Changes that were acceptable during beta testing become highly resisted after launch. Designers should instead be prepared to adjust to gameplay realities as players will expect the game to change to suit their play style. Overall, players become much less tolerant to change, especially changes that affect them negatively. A designer's job focuses much more on maintenance instead of pure creation after launch. In the long term, however, players will still expect added content to keep the game fresh and interesting.

Balance Changes Over Time

The game's balance will change over time as the game changes. New players will come, new content will be added, new tactics will be discovered, and new challenges will be found. Online games are dynamic by nature, and balance cannot be a static thing.

The most obvious form of change in balance comes as the player distribution changes. Near launch, the game is dominated by newbies as everyone logs on to the game and starts playing. New items are overvalued due to their relative rarity in the game. Low-level areas will be crowded as every player in the game tries to play in them. The world will feel restricted and crowded even though a large majority of it is devoid of any player activity. Just after launch, balance requires that players can work together easily and that enough items enter the economy to be useful to players.

As the game becomes established, the shift in focus goes from newbies to veteran players. Items, particularly common items, are undervalued due to their common and often hand-me-down nature. Veteran players will give newer characters their items as they obtain better objects, changing the item economy. Advanced areas are now overcrowded, since a majority of players is in these areas. Balance requires that players of different power levels be able to interact meaningfully and that newer players have a role in the game.

Finally, balance can change as new developers are brought onto the team to maintain the game. New ideas and attitudes can shift the focus of the game and gameplay, requiring adjustments to balance. New developers can also look at old problems in new ways and find solutions to balance problems.

Making Balance Changes After Launch

So, how do developers make necessary changes to the game when players are resistant to change and the balance of the game is constantly changing?

First, you need to follow the rules of basic project management. List and rate all the known imbalances. Once this list is established and prioritized, it is important to know how fast a fix should be made. Major problems such as money exploits and dupe bugs *must be fixed immediately*; if they are not, they can cause long-lasting imbalances in the game. Important problems such as an ability that gives an overwhelming advantage to a player without an effective countermeasure should be fixed as soon as possible, possibly in an emergency patch. Less important issues like abilities that give a slight unfair advantage to a player can be fixed with normal patching. Knowing which problems fit into which categories can be helpful in keeping the development team's workload to a manageable and uniform level.

When it is time to make changes to the game in order to establish or maintain balance, the type of change made is just as important as what part of the game is changed. In general, positive changes to the game (boosting abilities) are perceived as better than negative changes ("nerfs"). If possible, abilities should be enhanced instead of diminished in order to maintain balance. Players prefer to feel stronger because of change instead of getting weaker. In fact, a weakening of a character could cause players to become frustrated as they feel the investment in their character is "wasted" and that future investment will be similarly worthless. However, negative changes are often easier and more effective in promoting balance; when you absolutely have to "nerf" something, the best policy is often to implement the negative change and steel yourself for the inevitable complaints.

In addition to positive changes, smaller changes are preferable to large changes. A smaller change is less disruptive to the game, and less upsetting to players. A large change also runs the risk of being an overreaction to an existing balance issue, and such an overreaction will require further rebalancing, often in a pendulum-like series of changes that miss the balance point. Smaller changes, however, are often simpler in nature. Changing many things at once can compound the effects of a change. Two different changes intended to promote balance may have too much of a cumulative effect due to their interactions, leading to a new imbalance to replace the previous imbalance. Complex changes are also harder for players to follow, leading them to accuse the developers of trying to sneak in negative changes often called "stealth nerfs" by the players.

If needed, large changes should be made carefully. Ideally, a large change should be done over a period of time to lessen the overall impact. Under this plan, small changes are made every patch, moving closer to the ultimate goal. A good designer should then evaluate the change after every update to see if it has solved the imbalance. Balance is often achieved earlier than expected, requiring a less drastic change than originally expected and avoiding the pendulum-like series of changes.

Balanced Murder: How the Rules Change for PvP Games

Computer games are hard to balance. Online games are generally even harder to balance. However, of all online games, games that focus on PvP combat are probably the hardest to balance. The rules change drastically because players are on both sides of the combat, and a good designer needs to keep this truth in mind.

Player Targets Act Different from Monster Targets

When one player is fighting another, the rules change because the target's behavior changes. When a player uses an imbalance against a monster, it will not complain. You will not see angry posts by orcs in your discussion areas about unfair player tactics. Other players might complain when it seems that the player is using an imbalance against a monster, but usually as a method of getting an enhancement for their own characters. However, when it appears that a player uses an imbalance against another player, you will get a complaint almost every time. The victim will usually demand a change to the game to make it fair. If you do not hear a complaint, it usually means the victim has left the game in disgust, which is not good for the long-term health of the game!

In addition, player targets are harder to attack and kill than AI-controlled monster targets. This is a major selling point for PvP combat, but it also means that the challenge of the game increases. Because player behavior is not predictable, it is harder to balance encounters between different players. For example, players are generally not restricted to specific locations like AI-controlled monsters are. Consequently, players will attack each other anywhere and everywhere they are able to. This means you have to plan for this by perhaps giving players, especially newbies, a bit of extra protection in areas they expect not be attacked.

Because of the nature of PvP combat, balance is a much more sensitive issue overall. Since players are often harder to kill, players are more eager to get any advantage they can find. This means that they will happily exploit any imbalance. Players will be extremely creative in finding and exploiting even the smallest imbalance to gain an advantage.

In addition, as mentioned before, player perception determines reality in these games; anything that helps a player is a strategy, but anything that hurts the player is an imbalance. Unfortunately, in PvP every tactic falls under both definitions since it helps one player and hurts another. This means that it is very hard to tell real strategies from imbalances in the game. Players will often complain about a perceived imbalance unless it is fixed. Once you fix it, however, other players will complain because it was fixed and took away a valuable tactic. Since players only complain when they feel there is a problem, you will not hear from the second group of people before the change. Because of this, advance planning and experience with balancing online games is vital in order to make the most effective changes possible without upsetting too many people.

A Designer's Job Is Harder with PvP

A designer's job is much harder to accomplish when it comes to dealing with PvP. As mentioned before, players are more upset about imbalance in PvP. It is a good idea to look at the reasons why players are more upset about imbalances in these types of games.

The most important thing to realize about PvP is that there is a very real element of ego involved when a player loses to a human opponent. If an AI-controlled monster defeats a player, the player can place the blame elsewhere; when the victor is another player, the result usually comes from the fact that the victor was a better player. No one likes to feel that he isn't a good player. Player victors also taunt their victims and anger them with very specific verbal attacks that carry more truth and thus more weight than anything a monster could spit out. Finally, an opponent with an apparent "I win" power is extremely frustrating to players because the opponent will continue to use (or abuse) the perceived imbalance as often as possible, as opposed to an AI-controlled monster that is not quite so intelligent in using its overwhelming powers, often by design.

Even beyond the attitudes of players, a designer's job is harder because reliable information is harder to get from player feedback. A classic PvP joke asks, "According to other players, who is cheating and/or taking advantage of imbalances in the game?" The answer according to the players is, "Whoever is currently winning the fight!" Players who are sore losers will often give incorrect information about the behaviors of their opponents. Slight imbalances will be blown completely out of proportion. However, players that are taking advantage of imbalances are usually motivated by self-interest and want to keep their advantages. In addition, some players see "complaining to the administrator" as a valid strategy in the game instead of using gameplay methods to counter powers they do not like or feel powerless against.

A good designer must also realize that knowledge is power in a PvP game, especially a game with opaque mechanics. Information hiding and misinformation tactics are advantages that players will use against other players. A player might intentionally withhold information from other players in order to maintain an advantage over other players. Players might make false claims about abilities in order to make them seem weaker and less desirable, again maintaining an advantage over other people who shun the supposedly weak ability. Moreover, players might spread disinformation to make another ability seem too powerful in comparison, often as a way to weaken counters against their abilities, or as a way to divert attention from their own imbalances and advantages.

Finally, a designer's job is more difficult because a PvP game usually cannot ignore the traditional Player vs. Monster (PvM) gameplay in the game. One system affects the other to a large degree. PvM is usually the way to gather supplies used in PvP combat. However, PvP can be used to prevent another player from engaging in PvM activities. It is also much harder for players to fight smaller or easier PvP encounters in order to rebuild from losses, whereas players can easily do the same for PvM encounters. Both PvP and PvM interact in a variety of ways that make balance even more challenging. A designer generally cannot ignore either PvP or PvM aspects in a PvP game; otherwise, the whole game will suffer.

What can a designer do to balance PvP? First, remember that each ability will be used against another player. Each ability should have counters, but nothing that completely eliminates the ability. The counters should have abilities that counter them as well, and not necessarily the original ability. For example, a fire damage spell might be countered by an enchantment that reduces fire damage. The counter to this enchantment might be a spell that eliminates enchantments from a target. This cycle of abilities and counters gives more options to the players and allows them to have meaningful input into a battle against another player, which makes the combat feel fairer and thus balanced.

Perfect Imbalance: Why Not Everything Needs to Be Balanced

After a whole article about why balance is so important and how to achieve it, a section on good imbalances seems contradictory. However, there are times when a limited amount of imbalance is good for the game. These are not so much true imbalances but rather areas where balance is not so heavily emphasized. There's still a balance to these types of imbalances that must be maintained to make them useful in your game.

Imbalance as Gameplay

Many players enjoy challenges. As mentioned before, players are incredibly creative; this creativity allows them to solve problems that are seemingly impossible. It is often useful to provide an "impossible" goal for players and allow them to tackle it as the ultimate sign of mastery over the game. It provides a bragging point to other players, demonstrating their ability at playing the game. This ultimate challenge can be a goal that players set for themselves as they enter the game.

It is important to make this goal optional for the players; the reward for conquering this goal should be significant, but not overwhelmingly powerful. For example, a special piece of equipment that has average stats but a unique appearance is appropriate. If players feel penalized by being unable to do the "impossible" scenario, particularly because they cannot gain a powerful reward, they will feel cheated by it and complain that it is imbalanced. However, it is important not to punish a player for solving the puzzle "too easily!" This can easily lead to frustration on the player's part.

As balance changes, so can the once "impossible" challenge. What was difficult becomes commonplace as the overall power curve increases and players become more experienced with the game. It is important to renew the old challenges with new challenges, not only to provide a real challenge to the players, but to give the people who completed the previous "impossible" challenge a new task to complete.

It should go without saying that these types of imbalances work better in a PvM environment than in a PvP environment. Players will abuse any imbalance to get an unfair advantage over other players, and purposefully coding in a seemingly "impossible" imbalance is asking for abuse. Players will get easily frustrated trying to beat this "impossible" situation against an opponent that can alter his strategies to easily respond to any counters. PvP usually has enough intentional imbalances as it is.

Imbalance for Focus

Another important use for intentional imbalances is to put extra focus on particular areas of the game. Players will naturally seek out and exploit imbalances, so an area of the game with a slight imbalance will draw the attention of the players.

One way to use this is to provide bonuses for more casual players. Putting a slight imbalance into the game can provide a focus for players to center on. An area that rewards players with slightly better experience can draw a bigger crowd, allowing for easier formation of social bonds between players. This can allow more casual players to keep up with the hard-core players by allowing them easier access to the social network. However, a good designer needs to design a way for the hard-core players to not exploit the same benefit to further their own advancement. One way to do this would be to put goals that the hard-core players value, such as challenge and items that provide bragging rights, in other areas away from the area for the casual players.

Imbalances can also be used as information between players. A small but commonly accepted imbalance can be part of the conventional wisdom passed from more experienced players to the newer players. A bit of "secret" information passed along to the new players can make them feel like part of the game, giving them a bit of mastery even at the early levels of gameplay.

Finally, imbalances can give a special aspect of the game more focus. This gives the special aspect more impact and attention than it might otherwise receive. For example, in *Meridian 59*, there is a tree that serves as an in-game memorial to a player who passed away in the offline world. If a player drops a rose near the tree in the game, his character will receive a small temporary increase to an attribute in a game with relatively fixed attributes. This activity is highly profitable compared to other ways of gaining attributes and is slightly imbalanced. However, because of the gameplay advantage, people pay more attention to the tree than they might otherwise; the imbalance provides a focus on the memorial for a fallen friend.

Imbalance as Reality

In the end, a perfectly balanced game is a stagnant and boring game. Changes bring new imbalances that must be dealt with, and a designer's work is never done. A perfectly balanced game also leaves very little room for interesting variation and surprises within the game. Players often want novel experiences; providing only safe and boring, yet perfectly balanced, experiences just isn't much fun.

It's a good thing that imbalances make the game more interesting—perfect balance is impossible to achieve, anyway!

Conclusion

Balance in online games is hard. Balance is about maintaining the fairness and fun of the game with other players. A designer needs to carefully consider any changes made to the game to attempt to establish or maintain balance, regardless of the usually immense external pressures. Data collection and player feedback are the best tools to use for collecting information to evaluate the balance of a game and to make future changes to promote balance. However, players are often motivated by self-interest and competition, leading to feedback that must be carefully interpreted.

Before launch, it is important to establish player expectations. Different designs require different tactics for balancing the game. Different game mechanics within the design require different tactics as well. Achieving balance before launch is impossible. After launch, a designer's job continues. Player expectations change after launch, and it is harder to establish the expectations of new players. Balance changes over time as the player base and the game changes, and a designer must adapt to these changes. Positive and small changes are better than negative or large changes, in general.

Balancing a PvP game is much harder because the target changes. Players act very different than monsters do in both gameplay and their feedback to the designers.

Players get much more upset about imbalance in a PvP game because it affects their characters negatively. PvP games must still have balanced PvM since both systems affect each other. Providing counters to all abilities increases options and fairness in the game.

Finally, imbalances are often useful. They can give focus to areas that might otherwise be neglected. Examples are useful areas for certain players or special aspects of the game such as memorials for fallen players. Perfect balance is impossible, anyway!

In the end, a sense for balanced gameplay comes from experience. This article hopefully gave you some of the basic tools to develop that sense for yourself.

References

[Bartle03] Bartle, Richard, *Designing Virtual Worlds*, New Riders, 2003.

[Kennerly03] Kennerly, David, "Better Game Design through Data Mining," available online at *www.gamasutra.com/features/20030815/kennerly_01.shtml*, August 15, 2003.

[Koster04] Koster, Raph, "Astromech Stats: Economy Stats," available online at *www.starwarsgalaxies.com/content.jsp?page=Astromech%20Stats%20Economy*, April 30, 2004.

1.4

Power by the People: User-Creation in Online Games

Cory Ondrejka—Linden Lab

cory@secondlife.com

As technology moves relentlessly forward, content creation has become the primary factor in development costs for games in general and massively multiplayer, online role-playing games (MMORPG) in particular. For MMORPGs, content requirements are increased both by the need to keep customers engaged for long periods of time and player-to-player sales of game currencies and items. Game developers and publishers have responded to these concerns by engaging in an arm's race with their customers. End User Licensing Agreements (EULA) restrict player-to-player transactions while large content teams release patches and expansion packs in an effort to keep content fresh and interesting. While today these strategies are common within the industry, historically they have not been nor are they the only available options. Players have repeatedly proven that they have both the desire and the need to create content within games. Players create both for their own enjoyment and for the potential real-world economic gain from their effort. A notable example of this desire is that user creation exists within worlds that don't allow user-created content and even in those that explicitly ban economic gains. The pervasive nature of user-created content and free markets, while often at odds with the desires of online game developers, demonstrates the often-missed opportunity to solve the problems of skyrocketing content creation costs and commoditization. User creation should not be added to a world in an ad hoc manner. Rather, effective user creation requires a broad set of requirements and decisions. These decisions have far-reaching implications on game design, interaction with the real world, and the digital world's internal economic structure.

Introduction

It is difficult to create a profitable massively multiplayer online game (MMOG), role playing or otherwise. Beyond the technical challenges of networking, graphics, and security, MMOGs have a smaller addressable market than single-player video games do. Their costs depend heavily on content development. An approach for increasing the addressable market and reducing content development costs is to allow players to create content. User-created content has a long history in online games. First considered a solution to content generation problems in MMOGs [Morningstar90], user creation has been discussed in general terms for several years [Mulligan02b]. The first modern MMOG to be completely reliant on user-created content is *Second Life*, which was released in 2003 [Linden03]. During its first year of operation and growth, *Second Life* built on many of the concepts developed in these older games by making economic and property decisions that maximize quality and quantity of user creation.

A Brief History of Digital Worlds

In 1981, Vernor Vinge changed the course of all digital worlds to follow. Vinge's "True Names" [Vinge81] not only anticipated significant identity- and security-related aspects of the modern Internet, but extrapolated from the already popular multiplayer, text-based games of the time [Koster02] to introduce readers to an immersive, online space that used the real world as a metaphor. Vinge's "Other Plane" transformed online games into places. He also understood that people would want to live there because it would be so much fun to live in a world as malleable as the human imagination [Vinge81].

His imagination transformed text dungeons into digital worlds and proved inspirational to both fellow authors [Gibson84] and programmers.

In 1986, Lucasfilm Games released the multiuser, avatar environment *Habitat* for the Commodore 64 home computer system. Created by Chip Morningstar and Randy Farmer, *Habitat* was a graphical environment of 20,000 interconnected regions that allowed multiple users to travel as avatars, to communicate with each other via text chat, and to buy and sell goods and services. Driven by the complex behavior of its users, *Habitat* grew rapidly despite limited graphics, bandwidth, and processing power. More importantly, it introduced the concept of a shared, virtual space with far fewer game and role-playing aspects than the *MUD1* and MMORPG communities.

Just after *Habitat*'s launch, John Walker, the founder of AutoDesk, wrote the influential white paper "Through the Looking Glass" [Walker88]. Walker demonstrated the importance of three-dimensional, digital worlds that allowed users to create and interact. Neal Stephenson synthesized and extended on all of these ideas in *Snow Crash* [Stephenson92]. Stephenson's "Metaverse" expanded Vinge's "Other Place" by moving it from a playground for the hacker elite to a mainstream, online environment that used the real world as a metaphor for entertainment, socializing, and conducting business.

In Stephenson's vision, the world's wealthiest and most connected people spend their time in the Metaverse [Stephenson92]. With the creations of Walker, Jaron Lanier, and others [Barlow90], plus the early success of *Habitat*, building the Metaverse seemed possible.

Unfortunately, creating an appealing Metaverse proved much harder than expected. Multiple graphical chat environments and virtual reality companies came and went during the 1990s [Koster02], but none of them achieved anything close to the complexity and realism portrayed in *Snow Crash*.

In 1990, Morningstar and Farmer wrote a postmortem of *Habitat* called "The Lessons of Lucasfilm's Habitat." Much like Jessica Mulligan's writings about MMORPGs a decade later, they attempted to encapsulate the critical lessons learned through the creation and operation of *Habitat*. They specifically identified content as a critical problem, both the cost of creating sufficient content to keep *Habitat*'s users engaged and the inefficiencies of central planning with such a large world. They focused on user-created content as a badly needed solution to the problem [Morningstar90]. Their predictions were remarkably prescient, and the many companies that attempted to copy *Habitat*, such as WorldsAway, Worlds, Inc. and Communities.com, did not learn from them [Morningstar04]. These worlds were not commercially successful and their developers are generally defunct, even though some of the worlds are still operating thanks to users taking over the costs of running servers [Palace04]. As Morningstar would say, "You can't tell people *anything!*" [Morningstar04].

So, instead of avatar-driven online communities growing, the 1990s saw another type of online space establish itself as the dominant form: the MMORPG. By late 2004, several million MMORPG subscriptions existed in the United States alone [Woodcock04], although some players subscribe to multiple online games or have multiple accounts [Yee03b]. But where did MMORPGs come from?

MMORPGs and the Status Quo

Others have written extensively on the history of MMORPGs [Koster02], so there is no need to cover that ground again. Suffice it to understand that a very clear family tree extends from Roy Trubshaw and Richard Bartle's *MUD1* through to the current MMORPGs [Bartle04b, Mulligan02a]. They all use character leveling as the primary method of controlling user progress and access to content. Unfortunately, this approach can be bypassed by commoditization and player-to-player exchanges, so MMORPGs rely on their EULAs and intellectual property law.

The status quo in MMORPGs is that their EULAs include language that, to varying degrees, grants rights to a user's creations to service operators. While there has been some user unhappiness related to these terms, most current online games offer such limited opportunities for creation that it has not become a pressing issue. By owning all of the content, world operators can use their EULAs to block buying and selling of digital goods [Sandoval00] and other economic activities.

Enforcing these blockades is at best costly and at worst impossible, so why do digital world developers and operators add these provisions to their EULAs? The developers themselves often don't decide what goes into their games' EULAs, nor do they necessarily fully understand the impact of these decisions. To understand the flaws with current EULAs, the pervasive nature of user creation must be examined.

The Need to Create

The Sims was the first mass-market game to heavily utilize player-created content. *The Sims* allows the player to control the lives of a number of virtual Sims who go about their day attempting to find happiness. Part of their happiness comes from the possessions their homes are filled with, so purchasing items like better chairs and stereo equipment is a focal point of the game. Will Wright and Electronic Arts understood that users would be able to supply more content to each other than the developers could create, so they released the tools to create content before the product was shipped, and now claim that over 80% of the content in use was created by the players [Becker01]. Beyond customization, players have also built stories around screen shots captured in *The Sims*. Over 95,000 of these albums are posted and traded actively among players. The most popular album has been downloaded over 300,000 times [EA04].

This desire by players to make worlds their own extends into games that do not support the type of customization allowed by *The Sims*. In *Ultima Online,* users who wanted to decorate their homes devised elaborate strategies for combining in-world objects to create images that look like real-world items. For example, there are several different techniques for making pianos that involve dozens of different objects, ranging from wooden crates and chessboards to fish steaks and fancy shirts [Stratics04].

User creation does not end at the borders of the game. Machinima is the creation of movies within synthetic realities [Wikipedia04], and very often, the synthetic reality of choice is an existing game engine. It is a relatively new phenomenon, but it is spreading and achieving mainstream success, including the popular *Red Versus Blue* [Delaney04]. *Quake* and *Unreal*, both popular first-person shooters (FPS), are widely used by machinima creators. Film types include simple linear narratives, parody, and abstract exploration of the genre. These films demonstrate the quality and variety that an inspired creator can produce when given the right tools.

Another form of user-created content that extends beyond the game is mods. Mods rely on the fact that many FPSs, and some other games, allow users to modify the game's artwork and gameplay. The more flexible the engine, and again *Quake* and *Unreal* are standouts, the more variety in the mods, turning the original FPS into everything from driving games to architectural walkthroughs. Web sites devoted to mods [PlanetQuake04] provide reviews and an audience. The mod community also acts as a training ground for artists and developers who want to enter the game industry.

Get Over Yourself

User-created content is not guaranteed to be of sufficient quality, however. Many have applied Sturgeon's Law to user-created content [Goodwin02] to argue that user-created content is doomed. Some game developers, artists, writers, and musicians fear user-created content. They say that it takes a professional to provide content that is superior enough for users to engage with and to cause them to return. Raph Koster addressed this concern at GDC 2002 when he told film directors, writers, poets, painters, and so forth to get over themselves because the rest of the world is coming [Mulligan02b].

While it is clear that not everyone can create great content, some certainly can. *Counter-Strike* is a mod for the FPS *Half-Life*. In 1999, two avid FPS players working outside of the game development world created a game with a perfect blend of online teamwork, realism, and tuning. It resonated with players and *Counter-Strike* spread virally through mod sites. It was so popular that Valve Software, the creator of *Half-Life*, decided to commercially distribute *Counter-Strike*. Five years later, *Counter-Strike* is by far the most played online FPS, with tens of thousands of users typically playing at any time [GameSpy04b].

People express themselves through creation and customization. Examples abound, from the popularity of karaoke, cell phone faceplates and ring tones, to the 1.4 million active weblogs [Henning03]. Individuals want to be perceived as creative by customizing their surroundings and to have their moments on the stage. In many cases, it seems that users are waiting for access to the right tools. Fortunately, game developers can leverage this resource, because content development costs are continuing to increase.

The Cost of Content

Increasing graphical capability is driving up the cost of development and is a primary business challenge. This is particularly apparent with MMORPGs, as Sony Online Entertainment's Gordon Walton has stated, because the costs for quality art are rising faster than the market is expanding, and MMOGs require more art than standalone games [RPGVault03].

MMORPGs require a tremendous amount of content. They have to entertain hundreds of thousands of players for hundreds or thousands of hours. Player-to-player interactions, both social and commercial, help keep players engaged, but a large amount of the experience is designed and built by the game developers. Large teams and lengthy development cycles, often 50 or more developers working for two years or more, are the norm. Continued improvements to graphics and CPU technologies will force teams to be even larger.

Crafting vs. Creation

Although virtually synonymous in casual usage, crafting and creation have very different meanings in online games. Crafting also allows users to "make" things, like shirts or swords. However, the act of making is simply to gather the necessary items and then to choose the "make shirt" option. This is the process of MMORPG crafting. Players combine items in specific ways to create other items. Everything was designed and implemented by the developers. The players are simply following a recipe. Recall the *Ultima Online* piano. Players combine objects to make a piano-shaped pile, but these piles do not do anything. You cannot play them. Developers would have to decide to add a piano to *Ultima Online* through changes to the core game and a patch.

Many crafting systems involve the gathering of raw materials, and newer MMORPGs are adding more complicated schemes. It might appear that crafting adds value in the same way as real-world creation. This is not the case. Developers use crafting based on raw materials to slow the rate of production, to limit the crafting of the best items, and to extend the life of content by obscuring which items are the best. Production is slowed because users must take the time to acquire the correct combination of raw materials. Crafting of the best items is limited through artificial scarcity of raw materials. By presenting the users with a larger design space to search through, these items take more time to discover and spread through the community. However, the users are still merely choosing from the set of objects the developers built into the game, and competitive pressures combined with communication between users will force rapid convergence onto the best items. The value of some items will increase due to scarcity, but this is fundamentally different from the value added in real-world creation. Users cannot truly innovate because they are still simply choosing from the items supplied by the developers.

Crafting, even with raw materials, provides no defense from the impact of commoditization because it merely provides a broader set of pre-built content for the residents.

Nor is crafting creation. In the real world, creation requires the application of time and skill to raw materials to produce items significantly more valuable than the sum of their parts. Innovation can lead to entirely new creations, concepts, and ideas. True creation puts the power into the residents' hands. Unlike crafting, commoditization and market forces act as incentives, encouraging innovation and competition between creators [Ondrejka04].

Implementing true creation in digital worlds is a difficult undertaking. Atomistic construction, the scheme developed for *Second Life*, provides an approach for enabling user-created content.

Enabling User Creation

User creation in online games is not new [Koster02], but the shift from text to 3D, physical worlds requires a new approach. Raph Koster mentioned the idea at the 2002 Game Developer's Conference when he suggested giving users the building blocks like LEGO® did to provide an exciting new level of authorship.

This is easier said than done. Atomistic construction is not widely used because it is difficult to implement. It must exhibit both predictable and emergent behavior and requires that components assembled in arbitrary ways function correctly.

Requirements

Predictable behavior allows users insight to explore the design space they are offered. People are better able to approach problems when provided a modicum of structure. Predictable behaviors such as "objects fall under the effect of gravity" or "objects collide with each other" provide these constraints.

Emergent behavior occurs when a set of rules interact in unexpected ways allowing experimenters and innovators to invent truly new creations. For example, users working with the predictable rules of gravity and collision could have a contest to see who could build the longest and most complicated chain of dominoes across the landscape. While simplified online examples exist [Sodaplay04], *Second Life* is the first digital world to provide a real-time, interactive, fully three-dimensional, physically simulated implementation that allows multiple users to create collaboratively in a shared space [Ondrejka03].

Second Life's Atoms

Second Life provides its residents with basic building blocks, called *primitives*. These basic geometric objects—boxes, cylinders, spheres and torii—provide the basis for all construction in *Second Life*. These simple shapes can be cut, sheared, hollowed, and twisted to make more complex shapes and can also be linked together to form compound objects. The users apply textures to these shapes, choose material, and set visual properties. They add scripted behaviors, audio cues, and text displays until they have something with the right look and behavior. Residents upload audio samples and texture maps into the system, allowing tremendous freedom to design. Homes built using this system contain thousands of primitives, hundred of materials, and dozens of scripts and audio cues.

Avatars are similarly customizable through over 200 individual adjustments. Further customization is available via user-uploaded animations and attachments. Attachments are 3D objects created within *Second Life,* adding everything from sunglasses to robotic exo-skeletons to an avatar's persona.

All of this creation happens within the digital world and in real time. Rather than using an offline tool to build a house or to customize an avatar, residents create within the environment and are able to share the creative process with others.

An Example

Building a parachute in *Second Life* demonstrates the power of atomistic construction. It is important to understand that nowhere in the *Second Life* software is there a specific parachute object. Instead, the physical simulation supports moving objects and motor forces. Users rapidly began exploring different types of vehicles and developed realistic and functional parachutes for skydiving and base-jumping.

A parachute in *Second Life* is a combination of geometric shapes with textures providing color and detail. The geometry is constructed within the online world, so other users can collaborate and provide feedback. Real-world textures are uploaded into the system and consist of everything from basic colors to details of cloth and lines. The textures are positioned and aligned in world, providing further opportunity for collaboration. The user can upload audio samples to be played when the parachute opens, as well as appropriate character animations while falling and landing. Residents are then able to purchase a user-created parachute to base jump off tall apartment buildings.

Second Life is running a full physics simulation at all times. Fundamental behaviors like falling and bouncing are as simple as dropping an object. However, the computational power required to fully simulate a parachute down to the tension in its risers and the computational fluid dynamics of its wings is beyond current server hardware. To generate higher level behaviors and effects, and subsequent character animations, a scripting language is used. A script is a small piece of source code that is attached to objects in the virtual world dictating behaviors upon execution. For a parachute, the script handles the user's control inputs, triggers animations, plays sounds, opens the chute, and generates the forces to simulate a smooth decent. The result is a parachute that looks, sounds, and behaves something like a parachute in the real world. In addition, the flexibility of atomistic construction means that the user could modify a basic parachute to add on blinking lights and a trail of ghostly, flaming skulls.

Creation as Communication

Dynamic and accessible creation tools reinforce the fact that creation and self-expression are powerful forms of communication. In the real world, these forms of communication are limited to artists and those with sufficient disposable income. The relatively high average wealth of digital worlds leads to more freedom to communicate through your appearance and your possessions than in the real world.

A collaborative environment allows users to specialize. The parachute created in the previous example exists within a digital world of opportunity. The creator may form a club to teach others how to skydive, hire artists to make beautiful canopies, commission builders to create airplanes for skydivers to leap from, and make movies of her adventures. Parachute lessons excite other residents and lead to competitions for the most stylish drop, best animation, or most accurate landing. Their store sells parachutes, outfits, and private lessons. The creator can build an identity and a community around skydiving, leveraging the talents of other residents.

Collaborative creation has the additional benefit of allowing residents to learn about each other personally. Building with other people is a powerful experience. In digital worlds with atomistic construction, numerous opportunities exist to create with fellow residents as part of the everyday experience, building tighter social bonds within the world.

Smooth Scaling

Another advantage of atomistic construction is that it smoothly scales with processor speed. Currently, commodity server machines simulate around 15,000 objects that range in scale from a millimeter to tens of meters, with many of those objects engaging in behaviors and physical interactions. The real world operates at a much smaller scale, from 10 times smaller for even simple mechanical systems to 10,000 times smaller for chemical and biological processes. While computing a real-time simulation of complex mechanical or chemical processes is years away, every doubling of computer performance moves atomistic creation closer, opening up new creative opportunities. By the end of decade, it will be possible to simulate a parachute, including aerodynamic forces acting on flexible cloth, in real time.

People Powered

True creation empowers users in two important ways. The first is their ability to create what they need, without additional load on the development team. The open-source Web server Apache allows skilled users to make substantial modifications to achieve the desired results. Research has indicated that while the majority of Apache users are initially dissatisfied with the product, their ability to change it to suit their needs results in an extremely satisfied customer base [Franke02].

Second, when a base of users becomes proficient at modifying the product to suit their own needs, they become skilled at teaching other users how to use the product. They are willing to invest their own time and effort to educate others [VonHippel01], because this furthers their own understanding of the system. This is very similar to the behavior seen within *Second Life*, where residents have been willing to teach each other.

Additional Technological Requirements

The ability to generate content at a fantastic rate does incur some additional technical challenges, including storage, management, delivery, and display. These requirements must be understood if user-creation is going to be incorporated into a digital world. The specifics of *Second Life*'s technical solutions have been discussed elsewhere [Rosedale03], but the general issues apply much more broadly.

Storage is an issue, obviously, because of the amazing rate at which users can create content. Unlike a conventional game, where all the content is built beforehand and storage is merely instance management, atomistic construction allows a practically infinite supply of new game objects to be created. The cost of storage is decreasing, but resident creation will outpace any trivial storage solution.

Depending on the implementation, these game objects may need to be available anywhere in the world after a minimum delay. Asking a single, large database to serve all of these game objects is a very expensive and potentially futile approach, so proper thought needs to be put into distributed asset delivery and correct game design choices to support the management scheme that is chosen.

Once the correct assets are found, they need to reach the client. User-creation and atomistic construction ensure that every visit to the digital world will encounter a large quantity of new geometry, textures, audio, and animation, so whether streaming or zone-based, the delivery of large quantities of data must be included in the design. In addition, when building business plans, the bandwidth cost of asset delivery must be considered.

Finally, rendering the user-created content can be a challenge. Development teams work within clearly defined texture and polygon limits and have incentives to create the most efficient content possible. A digital world that supports user-creation must share resources between users and is susceptible to a "tragedy of the commons" [Hardin68]. Play mechanics and the in-world economy can both be used to control what users build, but display engines must be constructed under the assumption that users will create suboptimal content.

A Classic Blunder

It is not possible to partially embrace atomistic construction. User-created content may seem risky to a developer's IP and sensibilities. The temptation is to add an approval process for users' creations. This is a classic blunder. Approval processes do not scale, nor do they automate. Even if they did, it is not possible to vet atomistic construction without destroying its many advantages. Approval processes reduce the quality and quantity of created content by introducing delays and inefficiencies into the development process. Without the powerful forces of free markets and trade acting on content, user-creation will not generate content of sufficient quality to substitute for content generated by the development staff.

Real-World Intellectual Property

Recall that the status quo is for EULAs to grant all rights to the digital world operator and to restrict real-world trade and exchanges of digital currency and goods. Given the problem of ever-increasing content costs, the logical solution is user-creation. However, to fully leverage user creation, economic and legal factors must be considered. Content that users generate must be of sufficient quality to entertain not just the creator, but other residents as well. Real-world economic history provides a wealth of information on what incentives creators require. Intellectual property will be examined first.

Digital Property

While there is still some academic debate around the questions of digital goods and property, there is very little question that items generated using atomistic construction techniques are property in the utilitarian, Lockean, and Hegalian definitions. Utilitarian, because new creation has value to the creator but took time to create, so protections are required; Lockean, because innovation and work add value to the basic building blocks; and Hegalian, because the creator invests himself in his creations [Lastowka03].

However, even if it is property, who should own it? Much like the property question, the answer seems clear when dealing with the results of atomistic construction. Many have invoked the *Monopoly* example to emphasize the contradictions around players claiming to own what are effectively game pieces [Bartle04a], but this is a false example when true creation is involved. A far better example would be to ask whether Adobe owns all of the artwork created with Photoshop® using their .PSD file format, which can only be manipulated and displayed within Photoshop. Obviously, the answer in this case is that Adobe doesn't own the artwork—the creator does!

Moreover, it turns out that allowing ownership has far-reaching economic implications that have only recently begun to be understood.

Property Rights

Hernando de Soto's work in developmental economics, "The Mystery of Capital," provides insight into the critical importance of ownership. De Soto explains that lack of ownership prevents property from being fungible. The vast majority of the developing world's population, despite having potentially valuable assets like homes, land, and businesses, cannot leverage them because they lack ownership, with far-reaching consequences. From unavailable telephone service because their home isn't at a legal address, to a lack of business insurance because there is no license on record, lack of ownership is a tremendous handicap. More importantly for entrepreneurs, untitled property cannot be used to secure loans or to set up a legal business [DeSoto00].

As user creation grows, individuals and businesses will create objects of significant value, and many will be handsomely rewarded for it. However, for some of these creators, the short-term gains will not be their ultimate goal. Instead, these entrepreneurs will see the chance to leverage their wealth to create the next opportunity. In the United States, the primary source of capital for entrepreneurs is the home mortgage [DeSoto00]. For virtual pioneers, the ability to use virtual property as collateral will be a critical step toward building virtual businesses. They will have a hard time convincing the bank to give them the loan, but the process is not even possible if they do not own their property.

William Bernstein argues that property rights are a requirement for sustained innovation and economic growth. While justifiably cautious in his analysis of historical quality of life and economic activity, he makes a strong case that the Industrial Revolution, and the accompanying social and legal changes, was driven by four critical factors: property rights, scientific rationalism, capital markets, and cheap communication and transportation. Without all four of these factors, sustained innovation is not possible, and without sustained innovation, long-term economic growth will not occur [Bernstein04].

Digital worlds have the opportunity to strengthen their own internal economies by choosing policies that reinforce the four factors. In fact, from an economic perspective, property rights and communication are both driven by a factor that world designers have nearly complete control over: the cost of information.

The Cost of Information

Information is a critical component in any economic activity. Lack of it leads to distrust, increased costs, and, ultimately, less innovation. Large payoffs can force institutions to work through high information costs, as the speed of economic change is tied to how fast learning takes place [North94].

Others have recognized the critical nature of information costs. Thomas W. Malone has noted that the decrease in communication, travel, and information costs is a driving force in the move from centralized to decentralized governmental forms, from bands to monarchies to democracies, with corresponding increases in efficiency and economic strength. He then takes the idea a step further by arguing that businesses are following a similar path and are exploring increasingly decentralized approaches to solving problems. Democratic and market-based solutions are beginning to appear in large corporations with tremendous potential gains in efficiency and productivity [Malone04].

If user-created content is going to replace developer-created content, users will need to be innovative and competitive. By allowing creators to retain their real-world intellectual property rights to their creations, they have the potential to make money off their creations. However, before delving into the required economic connections to the real world, an important issue needs to be discussed.

If lower information costs were critical to innovation, wouldn't some form of commons—shared ownership of property within the digital world—be the best choice? This is exactly the question raised by Yale Law School's Yochai Benkler.

Commons, Creative and Otherwise

At the State of Play conference in 2003, *Second Life* changed its EULA so residents would retain intellectual property rights to their creations. During the ensuing discussion, Benkler raised the important point that by limiting creativity in a world intended for people to be creative in, you essentially put up new hurdles to creativity [Grimmelmann03].

Digital worlds thrive on great content. Atomistic construction puts the potential for great content in the hands of the residents and allows the world to leverage their skills and interests. Intellectual property law allows in-world creations to compete on a level playing field with the real world and to evolve within a competitive landscape. The connected nature of the space and zero marginal costs of reproduction mean that the only resources are time, creativity, and innovation. However, for user-created digital worlds to grow beyond early adopters, they must generate content that draws in new and casual users, either as residents or by reaching them through other channels. Great content, content that drives world growth, is critical to achieving this.

What's My Motivation?

While not every creator wants to make money, in a world where residents can do anything, business provides an important global context. These links also provide quantitative measurements of the strength and stability of the in-world economy. This potential for economic links forces a return to Benkler's question. Intellectual property law creates limited monopolies to provide creators the opportunity to sell their creations for more than the marginal cost [Lemley04, Netanel96]. These protections are just as important for *Second Life* creators as they are for creators in the real world.

User-creation requires real-world intellectual property intrusion if residents are allowed to upload content. In *Second Life*, residents upload textures, audio samples, and animations, so structuring a EULA to create an intellectual property commons is not a good solution because it would severely limit what content could be imported into the world.

A commons has additional problems. It limits the creator's choice about whether to commercialize their creations, derivative works extracted back to the real world are devalued, creators can't create trademarks or brands in world, real-world organizations and corporations avoid the world for fear of devaluing their brands, and creations cannot be leveraged because they lack legal standing [Ondrejka04]. Clearly, not all user-creation is hurt by these limitations, but some certainly would be.

Experience within *Second Life* indicates that large groups working toward common goals are required to create great content and experiences. Large groups have overhead and turnover and therefore require additional effort to maintain. Some creations will be built via incremental improvements from a dynamic group, but others will require organized groups and long-term commitments from the participants. Some project leaders will find economic motivations extremely useful.

Time Constraints

A final limitation to overcome is that of time. Creation in digital worlds, even with the best development tools and collaboration, is a time-consuming endeavor. MMORPGs have proven that some people are willing to spend large portions of their lives in digital worlds, but both the perception and reality of online games as a time sink act to limit the number of people who will play online.

Players are busy people, especially the young adults who make up the core of the MMORPG market [Yee03a]. While evidence is mounting that gamers are abandoning television in favor of games [Loftus04], the 20 or more hours per week [Yee04] that most online games demand must be stolen from other activities. Starbucks™ pioneered the idea of a "third space," namely somewhere between work and home where you would spend time. Digital worlds also target that idea, and unlike Starbucks, property rights and economic ties to the real world mean that residents might actually earn money there rather than just spending it.

In the real world, lack of ownership is a fatal flaw in attempts to establish successful free markets. It would be a mistake to think that virtual worlds will be any different. Free markets are required to help distributed, atomistic creation create high-quality content. In fact, one of the few missteps in *Snow Crash* is the fact that its main character has significant virtual wealth but not real-world wealth. For user-creation to be successful, virtual wealth must be convertible to real wealth.

Real-World Trade

Trade with the real world opens up entirely new opportunities and incentives for residents of digital worlds. When combined with atomistic construction, ownership, and markets, trade becomes the economic force driving the evolution of user-created content. This pressure to innovate is critical to generating great user-created content. However, despite the positives, some worry about the impact of trade between the real and digital worlds.

Attempting to Stop Trade

In 2001, Indiana University's Edward Castronova wrote an economic analysis of *EverQuest* and legitimized the academic study of digital worlds [Thompson04] and the interesting human activity within them [Castronova02, Castronova03, Lastowka03]. He has since focused on the "right to play," the idea that real-world economic connections are antithetical to a fun, immersive world [Castronova03]. Castronova asserts that the buying or selling of digital goods damages the game, both because it detracts from the game concept [Bartle04b] and because it begins the slippery slope of real-world laws and regulations intruding into digital worlds. Yale Law School's Jack Balkin focused on the same issues from the direction of First Amendment rights of the game developers to create the game they want to [Balkin05]. All three of these authors use commoditization, the legitimate buying and selling of digital goods for real-world currency, as a litmus test for whether or not digital worlds will be able to maintain their magic circles. The first question is whether this is an appropriate test.

In 2001, Sony banned the sale of *EverQuest* items on eBay [Sandoval00], and in 2004, Turbine followed suit by banning *Asheron's Call* sales [Castronova04]. The generally cited reason for the bans was the right to play, which assumes that digital world developers have a choice about commoditization. The evidence suggests that this is not true.

The removal of *EverQuest* items from eBay did nothing to reduce the black market as other sites such as PlayerAuctions and IGE took up the slack. While use of these sites technically violated game EULAs, infractions were rarely enforced, and the success of these sites indicated a strong demand among the players for player-to-player exchanges of goods and services. In fact, recent announcements from Sony [Colker04] indicate that they are interested in capturing some of this market.

Commoditization may not even be a choice for developers. Modifying the game to prevent real-world transfers requires that all player-to-player exchanges within the game be blocked. Additionally, the transfer of accounts between players must be prevented as well. Stopping all in-world exchanges is required because there is no way to accurately determine if the exchange is the result of a real-world monetary transaction. Certain patterns may suggest real-world involvement, but detecting and proving player intent is difficult and prone to false positives. Developers are left blocking all player-to-player transactions, which eliminates much of MMORPG gameplay. Proving that an account has changed hands, much like proving intent, is practically impossible.

Comparing Harms

The EULA clearly makes a poor litmus test for whether a digital world should be protected from real-world laws and regulation. It is time to return to the question of whether the magic circle is even desirable.

A market exists for digital goods because it takes a significant time commitment on the part of players to reach interesting content. As a result, players with proportionally more money than time have an incentive to shortcut parts of the experience. While this does have the negative effect of having some inexperienced players experimenting with more power and wealth than they would normally have, this negative is not fundamentally different from the effects of "twinking," when higher level players work to allow the rapid progression of new or lower level players, and no policies exist attempting to ban twinking. In fact, twinking has become a well-regarded component of newer MMORPGs [GameSpy04].

The negative must also be compared to the effects of forcing economic behavior into black and gray markets. Companies like IGE [Thompson04], which operate "virtual sweatshops," exist at the whim of digital world developers and have yet to establish strong consumer protections [Cringely04]. Tighter integration with the real world offers residents better economic opportunities, as well as better protections as the services supplying these opportunities are legitimized. The four most popular MMORPGs in the United States—*Final Fantasy XI, EverQuest, Ultima Online*, and *Star Wars: Galaxies*—all combine role-playing components and themed environments with strong secondary markets. Players are voting with their subscriptions and the evidence is they are choosing worlds that balance play and commoditization. More broadly, the real world provides evidence that ownership, trade, and play can coexist and the law has ample precedent for respecting the rules of the game [Balkin05, Lastowka04].

Open Source

Many have used the example of the open-source development of Linux as an example of the benefits of reduced information costs [Malone04, Benkler02]. Projects that share the characteristics of modular development, incremental improvement, and contributors who have a personal stake in the improvements often benefit from open-source development approaches. However, it is important to realize that not all projects meet these criteria. As the dearth of open-source games can attest, open-source development methodologies are less appropriate for some types of projects. Specifically, those that require long time commitments to make useful changes, that aren't modular enough to allow independent additions, or that require strong vision may require benefit for more traditional centralized management.

Developers can still take advantage of reduced communication costs. Asynchronous and remote development approaches can still be used to create great content, but economic gains, whether salary or equity, are a useful tool for working around open-source limitations.

Slaying the Commoditization Dragon

Commoditization of virtual goods is happening and developers have not been able to stop it. Neither buying nor selling is an isolated behavior, with players using eBay and specialized auction and purchase sites, especially for worlds that explicitly ban it. PlayerAuctions, a site that grew as a result of eBay's ban on *EverQuest* items, boasts over 150,000 members [PlayerAuctions04]. It is easy to see why worlds that merely enable crafting are afraid of commoditization.

However, as has been shown, in digital worlds that embrace intellectual property and economic ties to the real world and have true user-creation and innovation, commoditization isn't something to fear. Instead, it is part of the market forces that have historically driven innovation and economic growth. All of the world's residents will experience greater and more varied content, while some will profit from their creativity and ideas. Rather than attempting to block this behavior, digital worlds can benefit from embracing it.

Power by the People

What are residents able to accomplish once they are offered the right tools for user-creation in an environment designed to support creation? What do people do when offered a world where the only constraints are their creativity and time? In *Second Life*, the answers have been very exciting to watch. In the sections that follow, data is drawn from customer usage for 30 days in June and July 2004, when *Second Life* had approximately 10,000 customers.

Robust Internal Economy

Second Life's users have been able to create an astonishing amount of content. At the end of June 2004, after one year of operation, users had created more than four million objects, with a million of those objects currently active in the world. Of those, over 300,000 have scripted behaviors. More than three million pieces of clothing have been made. Over 99% of the assets in *Second Life* are user-created. Users run hundreds of classes and events to ensure that new residents understand how to create and customize within *Second Life*. Derivative works improve and innovate as they build upon the works of each other. Figure 1.4.1 shows the world of *Second Life* in June 2004. Five thousand acres are simulated using a grid of 300 machines.

In *Second Life*, an internal market allows residents to be creators, consumers, or both. Over 10,000 different people used *Second Life* in June 2004. Those people engaged in one million player-to-player transactions and spent over L$130 million. L$, or "Linden Dollars," are *Second Life*'s in-world currency. At the end of June, the total value of the *Second Life* economy was more than L$72 million. The average transaction price was L$91 and there were 34,000 objects for sale in-world, more than double the number of virtual game goods for sale on eBay from all other online games combined.

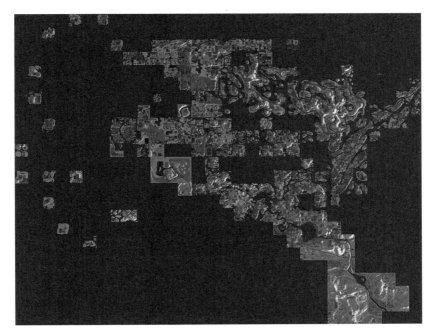

FIGURE 1.4.1 Second Life *in June 2004.*

The collaborative nature of *Second Life* has also led to a strong community, with users linked by group memberships, chatting, and internal instant message (IM) buddy lists. Chat provides a local method of communicating, such as saying "hi" to an avatar standing near you, while IM provides a private method of communicating over any distance. Again using June 2004 data, users sent over 25 million lines of IM. Nearly 70% used IM and communicated with an average of 15 different friends, while the top 10% of connectors communicated with over 150 different people! Almost 70% of users belong to at least one affinity group, and there are 10 groups with more than 100 members. While it has been argued that conflict is required to build strong social bonds, this is obviously not the case in *Second Life*.

Robust Trade with the Real World

In addition to its potent internal economy, *Second Life* also has numerous connections to the real world. Residents upload textures, audio clips, and character animations into the world. Continuing with the June 2004 numbers, residents made over 100,000 uploads. These uploads, whether for personal or commercial use, are effectively a raw material input into *Second Life*. Combined with time and ingenuity, these assets are becoming important components of the internal economy.

Linden Dollars provide the second connection to the real world via third-party exchange and auction sites. Currently dominated by Gaming Open Market and IGE, L$ are actively traded and provide a method for converting L$ into real-world currency. To put the transactional volume into perspective, at current trading rates, the L$130 million would be worth approximately US$600,000. More importantly, over L$16 million with a value of US$77,000 was traded for US$ during June. Many residents are able to cover their costs of playing *Second Life* and some are making a significant profit.

Allowing residents to generate income violates the EULA of nearly every other video game and digital world, much like a world without strong property rights. Publishers argue that restrictive EULAs protect them from the financial risks and lawsuits. For example, Black Snow Interactive sued Mythic Entertainment when Mythic shut down their virtual sweatshop [Dibbell03], although that case never went to court.

However, EULAs that restrict ownership are not the only recourse. Web hosts, collocation services, and bandwidth providers all provide ample evidence that liability can be reduced while still allowing customers to retain their intellectual property rights and ownership. World operators can protect themselves financially and provide their residents security in their creations and commerce. Both are critical components to the long-term success of user-created content.

The Metaverse and Beyond

This article began with a brief historical review. For many who are or who have been working on digital worlds, the Metaverse of Stephenson and his vision of the Street are an inspiration and a goal. Other than his fictional interface technology, are the tools in place to realize his vision? Many products and companies that claimed to have created the Metaverse are now smoking craters. Rather than looking at specific products, an examination of current technologies and strategies is in order.

Building the Street

Stephenson talks about a contiguous, Earth-like world. It is heavily populated, covers a very large area, and is filled with content. The proliferation of various grid and cluster computing solutions provide the computing power to simulate the world. Advances in last-mile bandwidth and streaming technology allow the world's content to be delivered to the users. The limiting factor is content.

As previously discussed, MMORPGs are already limited by content creation. However, no matter how large a game world might become, it shrinks when compared to the Metaverse as described by Stephenson. Currently, the most ambitious MMORPGs are targeting tens of thousands of simultaneous players in a shared space, but a broadly appealing real online world might need to handle tens of millions. A monolithic team cannot create content to entertain that many people on an ongoing basis. Centralized planning simply fails at this scale.

Leveraging the residents themselves to create in a distributed way is the only solution. A proper balance of tools, ownership, and economic incentives allows a small percentage of the total population to create an unprecedented amount of content. For example, *Second Life*'s June 2004 scale, with 20% of the residents' time spent creating content on a regular basis and about 10,000 user-hours per day, generates 2000 user-hours or 1 user-year of content creation per day. That is a content development team of 365 people. After accounting for Sturgeon's Law, this 365-person team is as large as many MMORPG content staffs. Scaled up to millions of user-hours per day, even with only a tiny fraction of time spent creating content, the Metaverse will use a content team larger than the entire game industry. This approach will build the Metaverse.

Ongoing Challenges

The scale, dynamic nature, and economic motivations of user-created digital worlds present challenges that have not yet been fully addressed. Navigation, local versus global tensions, and dispute resolution all need better solutions as these worlds continue to grow.

Navigation is difficult because, on top of the usual real-world challenges, user-creation is incredibly dynamic. Landmarks vanish, people move to new locations, and stores change inventory with much greater frequency than the real world. Easy-to-use tools result in many ephemeral builds that would be worth visiting if there were a way to find them. Parties, protests, and other gatherings happen on a whim as people's paths cross. As the worlds grow, this problem will only get worse. Currently covering 5,000 acres, *Second Life* has already expanded to the extent that no single person can keep track of every new or interesting location, item, or event. Despite extensive search functionality, tracking of aggregate movement statistics, and the ability of users to indicate their own personal points of interest, the world is simply too vast to be individually monitored. Of course, this opens up economic opportunities for reviewers, tour guides, atlases, and the like.

User-creation also creates many opportunities for collisions between local and global desires. One *Second Life* user made a futuristic blimp that flew around dispensing advertising [Farmer04]. What happens when that blimp flies over a medieval village? The more flexibility is built into the world, the more residents will expose tensions between the individual, the group, and the world. Zoning and other rules can resolve some of these problems, but must be balanced against the damage they do to creativity and innovation.

With millions of player-to-player transactions per month, digital worlds are beginning to face some of the same issues as eBay. Working with eBay, SquareTrade has pioneered online dispute resolution and is exploring many of the issues of trust and identity [Abernathy03], which will become increasingly important to digital worlds. Although current online dispute resolution is focused on transactions, it has the potential to help other types of disputes, including zoning and fair use.

As previously covered, reduced information costs maximize innovation but economic motivations are critical to the creation of great content. Copyright and patents exist to provide limited monopolies to inventors in exchange for lowered information costs. Unfortunately, the collision of online technologies and the current era of "strong" copyright does a poor job of maintaining that balance [Lessig04]. Critical components of innovation—namely fair use and the freedom to tinker [Economist02]—are generally limited or blocked in the digital world. Suddenly, only the technologically elite have their fair use rights. Clearly, digital worlds offer an opportunity to explore a better balance, and perhaps will be a source of insight for those looking to improve the real world.

Constitutional Issues?

John Perry Barlow [Barlow96] wrote, "A Declaration of the Independence of Cyberspace" in 1996, focusing ideas from the various online communities of the time.

Barlow's utopian "Declaration" anticipated many ideas that would later be applied to digital worlds. Motivated by free speech issues, it argued that the real world did not "create the wealth of our marketplaces" nor "know our culture, our ethics" and that "[y]our legal concepts of property" do not apply.

As has been shown, for all of its grandeur, the "Declaration" is wrong to ask for separation between the real and digital worlds. Intellectual property and economic ties are critical. However, these connections do raise legal issues that have yet to be resolved, including two very important questions related to the Freedom of Speech.

Balkin asks if the First Amendment should protect the act of creating digital worlds, or will the government have a say in what the game is [Balkin05]? He proposes commercial connections to the real world as a litmus test, although later comments indicate that he recognizes the problems with that approach [Balkin04].

In a similar vein, Peter Jenkins recently wrote an article comparing digital worlds to company towns [Jenkins04]. Building on Balkin and others [Lastowka03], he raises fascinating questions about whether digital world residents have free speech rights. Generally speaking, the First Amendment only protects free speech from being abridged by the government. Jenkins argues that, much like a company town, digital worlds may perform "public functions" that will need to respect free speech rights due to state action doctrine.

Currently, world operators rely on the EULA to provide protections from these questions, but as digital worlds become larger and more profitable, it is inevitable that governments will start asking these questions. The eventual result is unclear, as is whether EULAs will provide protections to the companies relying on them. Perhaps more importantly, understanding of the underlying legal issues can help world creators to understand why freedom of speech may actually be beneficial to their worlds in the long run.

New Opportunities

Digital worlds are just beginning to explore the vast array of uses beyond role-playing. There are still major opportunities to further expand the connections between the real world and the digital in order to improve content creation. As Bernstein suggested, capital markets are an important aspect of sustained economic growth, yet digital worlds have yet to implement true banking, with the currency virtualization and liquidity that banks provide. Much like the navigation question, banking in worlds with property rights and high degrees of innovation is a very real entrepreneurial opportunity that allows residents to improve their world without the development team having to stray from core competencies.

In the real world, Creative Commons [CC04] is attempting to provide a better balance between the cost of information and property rights by offering a wide range of licensing options for creators who do not want a normal copyright. Some of these licenses are a natural fit for digital worlds, yet Creative Commons licenses have yet to be integrated into one.

Digital worlds should be home to social activism [Vertu04] of all kinds. The first major attempt to raise virtual currency for social causes within *Second Life* generated over US$1700 worth of donations within one month. Allowing this type of behavior relates to the questions Jenkins raises about freedom of speech in digital worlds. Are not the communities more committed to the digital world because they are allowed to engage in activism?

By granting residents ownership of their creations, games creators, businesses, and academic researchers are able to freely move into digital worlds. Rather than having to negotiate with the world operator, an entrepreneur can simply decide to test his idea by trying it. With access to a fluid economy, an addressable market and superb communication and creation tools, he may find it significantly more cost effective to explore his idea with the digital world rather than the real one. To Castronova's point, does this behavior destroy the game for the other participants? Obviously, it comes down to how the world is built, but the real world proves that play and work can coexist, and by allowing residents who play to also be entrepreneurs, they will spend more time in the world and work even harder to draw in other residents.

Academic and business research improves the quality of the world in similar ways. By exposing digital worlds to a broader set of users, developers are exposed to applicable real-world knowledge that wouldn't otherwise be available to them. Many areas of research in the real world, from dispute resolution and e-democracy to currency trading and business strategy, can benefit digital worlds if the right connections are established. It is always difficult to spend precious development time and resources reaching out to other businesses and academia, but in the digital world space, the benefits can be enormous.

A Better Place

Digital worlds are best understood as places rather than as games. People spend time there, often want to live there [Castronova02], and engage in the full range of human activities that are found in other places. More importantly, digital worlds have advantages over the real world and offer their residents some amazing opportunities.

For people who have never considered themselves creative or have never had the opportunity to try, exposure to easy-to-use creation tools can be a life-altering event. The productivity of *Second Life*'s diverse users reinforces that people crave creative outlets and find them more enjoyable when they can share the experience. Collaborative creation, combined with the educational and entrepreneurial opportunities that a community supplies, provides an escapism that is a powerful complement to games.

Finally, combining innovation and entrepreneurial activity leads to a long-term shift in trade between the real and digital worlds. Currently, digital worlds are net consumers of real-world content. Users upload textures, audio, and animations, and various real-world IP is thought to be valuable in the digital world [Book04]. However, the creative energy within digital worlds will ultimately become a resource to the real world. The first tantalizing glimpses of this are in fashion, where the same reasons for "cool hunting" [PBS01] in big cities are being applied to a digital world [STD04].

Digital worlds plus atomistic construction provide a space unlike any other, a place where the only limitations are human ingenuity and time. Fashion is only the first industry to take advantage of this, but others are sure to follow. In time, through connections to the real world rather than isolation, Barlow's vision may be realized through the creation of a civilization of the mind in Cyberspace [Barlow96].

Conclusion

This article covered a lot of territory, so a brief recap is essential. The ever-increasing cost of content development is already a problem for MMOG developers and will continue to become more of one as Moore's law continues its relentless drive forward. Allowing users to create content is a powerful way to increase users' connections to the digital world and reduce development cost. However, user-creation is not something to add to a digital world in a casual manner.

The history of digital worlds and MMORPGs was briefly reviewed in order to understand the roots of user-created content and the current reliance on crafting. The differences between crafting and true creation were also covered, including the reasons why crafting fails to protect digital worlds from commoditization pressures. An approach to allow real user-creation, atomistic construction, which has been used successfully in *Second Life*, was introduced. Atomistic construction allows users to create new content in real time by making incremental changes to physically simulated, geometric primitives; has proven easy to use and flexible; and has enabled incredible productivity on the part of *Second Life*'s residents.

The history of these spaces is also an important tie to users' desire to create. Many games demonstrate that users want—need—to customize and create, even if the game does not explicitly support user-creation. However, merely enabling user-creation is not enough to truly offset content costs because undirected user-creation does not result in innovation and continuous improvement. Economic forces are required to achieve those goals. To enable a strong and sustained market, correct legal, economic, and design choices must be made.

Creators need to own their creations. Without strong property rights, history has shown that sustained innovation does not occur. Support for real-world intellectual property enables content to move between the digital and real worlds. This allows creators to choose economic motivations for their creative endeavors, and provides a legal framework for choosing less restrictive IP regimes, such as Creative Commons. Low information cost, a tremendous advantage of digital worlds and a driver of innovation, must be preserved through smart decisions about IP and ownership.

Ownership enables economic motivations, but MMORPGs are attempting to block trade with the real world. Not only are those attempts failing, it is critical to understand that user-created content needs those connections in order to take full advantage of market and economic forces. User-creation can only be maximally effective within a competitive and free market.

By placing user-creation into that situation, many new opportunities appear. Suddenly, the digital world is more like a world and less like a game. Some residents will earn real income within the world rather than just focusing on leveling. Innovation will add features to the world that the developers never imagined. Residents will compete with the digital world provider by creating their own experiences within the world or by offering services that are not provided as part of the game. New legal issues and legislation may apply to the digital world in unexpected ways. New business opportunities outside of the developer's core competencies will present themselves.

All of these can be looked at as opportunities or hindrances, depending on the product and the developer. User-creation is a powerful tool, but like all tools, it must be applied to the correct problems. It is only by thoroughly understanding the implications of user-creation that it will be used effectively to make both games and digital worlds more fun, vibrant, and exciting for everyone.

Further Reading

For more information on user-creation and digital worlds, the references provide a wealth of information. In addition, the following Web sites and mailing lists are excellent sources of data and debate.

- *http://terranova.blogs.com/terra_nova/:* Terra Nova is home to many of the great thinkers and writers at the intersection of research and digital. It also maintains a great set of links to useful digital world Web sites. This article would not have been possible without the insights and arguments from fellow Terra Nova authors.
- *www.kanga.nu/lists/listinfo/mud-dev/:* MUD-Dev, the granddaddy of them all. Everything you ever wanted to know about digital worlds, although historical discussions are often hard to find.

- *http://ssrn.com/:* The Social Science Research Network is home to many papers about digital worlds, their residents, and their economies.
- To learn about legal issues related to digital worlds, Jack Balkin's Balkinization (*http://balkin.blogspot.com/*), Yale's LawMeme (*http://research.yale.edu/lawmeme/*), Ernest Miller's page (*www.corante.com/importance/*), and Susan Crawford's blog (*http://scrawford.blogware.com/blog*) are good places to start, although relevant posts generally end up on Terra Nova as well.

References

[Abernathy03] Abernathy, Steve, "Building Large-Scale Online Dispute Resolution and Trustmark Systems," available online at *www.odr.info/unece2003/pdf/Abernethy.pdf,* July 30, 2003.

[Balkin04] Balkin, Jack, Comments posted to the thread "Jack Balkin on Virtual Liberty," available online at *http://terranova.blogs.com/terra_nova/2004/04/jack_balkin_on_.html,* May 4, 2004.

[Balkin05] Balkin, Jack, "Virtual Liberty: Freedom to Design and Freedom to Play in Virtual Worlds," available online at *http://ssrn.com/abstract=555683,* Virginia Law Review, 2005.

[Barlow90] Barlow, John Perry, "Being in Nothingness Virtual Reality and the Pioneers of Cyberspace," available online at *www.eff.org/Misc/Publications/John_Perry_Barlow/HTML/being_in_nothingness.html,* February 12, 1990.

[Barlow96] Barlow, John Perry, "A Declaration of the Independence of Cyberspace," available online at *www.eff.org/Misc/Publications/John_Perry_Barlow/barlow_0296.declaration,* February 9, 1996.

[Bartle04a] Bartle, Richard, "The Pitfalls of Virtual Property," available online at *www.themis-group.com/uploads/Pitfalls%20of%20Virtual%20Property.pdf,* April 2004.

[Bartle04b] Bartle, Richard, "Paradigm Propagation," available online at *http://terranova.blogs.com/terra_nova/2004/07/paradigm_propag.html,* July 15, 2004.

[Becker01] Becker, David, "The Secret Behind the Sims," available online at *http://news.com.com/2008-1082-254218.html,* March 16, 2001.

[Benkler02] Benkler, Yochai, "Coase's Penguin, or Linux and the Nature of the Firm," available online at *www.benkler.org/CoasesPenguin.html,* December 2002.

[Bernstein04] Bernstein, William, *The Birth of Plenty,* McGraw-Hill, 2004.

[Book04] Book, Betsy, "These Bodies Are FREE, So Get One NOW!: Advertising and Branding in Social Virtual Worlds," available online at *http://papers.ssrn.com/sol3/papers.cfm?abstract_id=536422,* April 30, 2004.

[Castronova02] Castronova, Edward, "Virtual Worlds: A First-Hand Account of Market and Society on the Cyberian Frontier," available online at *http://papers.ssrn.com/sol3/papers.cfm?abstract_id=294828,* January 14, 2002.

[Castronova03] Castronova, Edward, "The Right to Play," available online at *www.nyls.edu/docs/castronova.pdf*, October 1, 2003.

[Castronova04] Castronova, Edward, "Veteran Virtual World Bans eBay," available online at *http://terranova.blogs.com/terra_nova/2004/05/veteran_virtual.html*, July 27, 2004.

[CC04] "Creative Commons," available online at *http://creativecommons.org*, July 27, 2004.

[Colker04] Colker, David, "Game Makers to Try Pay-as-You-Go Model," available online at *www.latimes.com/technology/la-fi-game14may14,1,7538891.story?coll= la-headlines-technology*, May 14, 2004.

[Cringely04] Cringely, Robert, "PayAcquantance—When It Comes to Selling Virtual Property, PayPal Isn't Always Your Pal," available online at *www.pbs.org/cringely/ pulpit/pulpit20040506.html*, May 6, 2004.

[Delaney04] Delaney, Kevin, "When Art Imitates Videogames," available online at *http://nikon.bungie.org/pressscans/wsj.040904/red_vs_blue_wsj.pdf*, April 9, 2004.

[DeSoto00] De Soto, Hernando, *The Mystery of Capital*, Basic Books, 2000.

[Dibbell03] Dibbell, Julian, "Serfing the Web," available online at *www.juliandibbell. com/texts/blacksnow.html*, January 2003.

[EA04] "The Sims," available online at *http://thesims.ea.com/us/index.html?menu= exchange&content=exchange/index.html*, July 27, 2004.

[Economist02] "Tinkerers' Champion," available online at *www.economist.com/ science/tq/displayStory.cfm?story_id=1176171*, June 20, 2002.

[Farmer04] Farmer, Randy, "The Business of Social Avatar Virtual Worlds," available online at *www.fudco.com/habitat/*, July 15, 2004.

[Franke02] Franke, Nikolaus and Eric Von Hippel, "Satisfying Heterogeneous User Needs via Innovation Toolkits: The Case of Apache Security Software," available online at *http://papers.ssrn.com/sol3/papers.cfm?abstract_id=299419*, May 31, 2002.

[GameSpy02] Kosak, Dave, "*City of Heroes Roundtable*," available online at *http://archive.gamespy.com/interviews/february04/cityofheroes/index.shtml*, February 26, 2002.

[GameSpy04] "GameSpy Live Stats," available online at *www.gamespy.com/*, July 30, 2004.

[Gibson84] Gibson, William, *Neuromancer*, Ace, 1984.

[Goodwin02] Goodwin, Jon, "GDC Day 5, Developers on the Future of Online Worlds," available online at *www.kanga.nu/archives/MUD-Dev-L/2002Q1/ msg00758.php*, March 28, 2002.

[Grimmelmann03] Grimmelmann, James, "The State of Play: Free as in Gaming?" available online at *http://research.yale.edu/lawmeme/modules.php?name=News& file=article&sid=1290*, December 4, 2003.

[Hardin68] Hardin, Garrett, "The Tragedy of the Commons," available online at *http://dieoff.org/page95.htm*, 1968.

[Henning03] Henning, Jeffrey, "The Blogging Iceberg: Of 4.12 Million Weblogs, Most Little Seen and Quickly Abandoned," available online at *www.perseusdevelopment.com/corporate/news_shell.php?record=51*, October 4, 2003.

[IGE04] "IGE," available online at *www.ige.com/powerleveling.asp*, July 28, 2004.

[Jenkins04] Jenkins, Peter, "The Virtual World as a Company Town—Freedom of Speech in Massively Multiple Online Role Playing Games," available online at *http://papers.ssrn.com/sol3/papers.cfm?abstract_id= 565181*, July 1, 2004.

[Koster02] Koster, Raph, "Online Worlds Timeline," available online at *www.legendmud.org/raph/gaming/*, February 20, 2002.

[Lastowka03] Lastowka, F. Gregory, and Dan Hunter, "The Laws of Virtual Worlds," available online at *http://papers.ssrn.com/sol3/papers.cfm?abstract_id=402860*, July 19, 2004.

[Lastowka04] Lastowka, F. Gregory, and Dan Hunter, "Virtual Crime," available online at *http://papers.ssrn.com/sol3/papers.cfm?abstract_id=564801*, July 19, 2004.

[Lemley04] Lemley, Mark, "Ex Ante Versus Ex Post Justifications for Intellectual Property," available online at *http://papers.ssrn.com/sol3/papers.cfm?abstract_id= 494424*, February 16, 2004.

[Lessig04] Lessig, Lawrence, *Free Culture*, The Penguin Press, 2004.

[Linden03] "Your Second Life Begins Today," available online at *http://lindenlab.com/press_story_8.php*, June 23, 2003.

[Loftus04] Loftus, Tom, "TV Execs Try to Lure Gamers Back—Golf Players Watch Golf, But Will Video Game Players Watch Games?" available online at *http://msnbc.msn.com/id/4778773/*, April 30, 2004.

[Malone04] Malone, Thomas, *The Future of Work*, Harvard Business School Press, 2004.

[Morningstar90] Morningstar, Chip, and F. Randall Farmer, "The Lessons of Lucasfilm's Habitat," available online at *www.fudco.com/chip/lessons.html*, 1990.

[Morningstar04] Morningstar, Chip, and F. Randall Farmer, "MDC 2004: Habitat Redux," available online at *www.fudco.com/habitat/HabitatRedux.ppt*, 2004.

[Mulligan02a] Mulligan, Jessica, "Talkin' 'bout My . . . Generation," available online at *www.skotos.net/articles/BTH_17.shtml*, January 22, 2002.

[Mulligan02b] Mulligan, Jessica, "Much Water Under the Bridge, Much Beer Over the Dam . . . ," available online at *www.skotos.net/articles/BTH_33.shtml*, September 3, 2002.

[Netanel96] Netanel, Neil, "Copyright and a Democratic Civil Society," available online at *www.utexas.edu/law/faculty/nnetanel/yljarticle.htm*, 1996.

[North94] North, Douglass, "Economic Performance Through Time," available online at *http://members.shaw.ca/compilerpress1/Anno%20North%20Econ%20Perform%20thru%20Time.htm*, June 1994.

[Ondrejka03] Ondrejka, Cory, "Escaping the Gilded Cage: User Created Content and Building the Metaverse," available online at *http://papers.ssrn.com/sol3/papers.cfm?abstract_id=538362*, November 2003.

[Ondrejka04] Ondrejka, Cory, "Living on the Edge: Digital Worlds Which Embrace the Real World," available online at *http://papers.ssrn.com/sol3/papers. cfm?abstract_id=555661*, June 8, 2004.

[Palace04] "About the Palace.com," available online at *www.thepalace.com/ assets/about.html*, July 28, 2004.

[PBS01] "Cool Hunting—What's It Like Hunting for Cool?" available online at *www.pbs.org/wgbh/pages/frontline/shows/cool/etc/hunting.html*, 2001.

[PlanetQuake04] "PlanetQuake Mods," available online at *www.planetquake.com/ quake3/hosted/mods.shtml*, July 28, 2004.

[PlayerAuctions04] "Player Auctions," available online at *http://playerauctions.com/*, July 28, 2004.

[Rosedale03] Rosedale, Philip, and Cory Ondrejka, "Enabling Player-Created Online Worlds with Grid Computing and Streaming," available online at *www.gamasutra.com/resource_guide/20030916/rosedale_pfv.htm*, September 2003.

[RPGVault03] "Online Worlds Roundtable #8, Part 1," available online at *http:// rpgvault.ign.com/articles/455/455832p2.html*, October 22, 2003.

[Sandoval00] Sandoval, Greg, "Sony to Ban Sale of Online Characters from Its Popular Gaming Sites," available online at *http://news.com.com/2100-1017-239052. html?legacy=cnet*, April 10, 2000.

[Sodaplay04] "Sodaconstructor," available online at *http://sodaplay.com/constructor/ index.htm*, July 28, 2004.

[STD04] "Future Fashion 04," available online at *http://spacethinkdream.com/files/ FF04.pdf*, July 28, 2004.

[Stephenson92] Stephenson, Neal, *Snow Crash*, Bantam Books, 1992.

[Stratics04] "How to Make the Piano," available online at *http://uo.stratics.com/homes/ betterhomes/essay_piano.shtml*, July 28, 2004.

[Thompson04] Thompson, Clive, "Game Theories," available online at *www. walrusmagazine.com/print.pl?sid=04/05/06/1929205*, May 6, 2004.

[Vertu04] "VERTU," available online at *http://vertuous.org/*, July 28, 2004.

[Vinge81] Vinge, Vernor, "True Names," *Binary Star #5,* Dell Publishing Company, 1981.

[VonHippel01] Von Hippel, Eric, and Karim Lakhani, "How Open Source Software Works: 'Free' User-to-User Assistance?" available online at *http://papers.ssrn. com/sol3/papers.cfm?abstract_id=290305*, November 19, 2001.

[Walker88] Walker, John, "Through the Looking Glass," available online at *www.fourmilab.ch/autofile/www/chapter2_69.html*, September 1, 1988.

[Wikipedia04] "Machinima," available online at *http://en.wikipedia.org/wiki/ Machinima*, July 28, 2004.

[Woodcock04] Woodcock, Bruce Sterling, "An Analysis of MMOG Subscription Growth—Version 8.0," available online at *http://pw1.netcom.com/~sirbruce/ Subscriptions.html*, March 2004.

[Yee03a] Yee, Nick, "Gender and Age Distribution," available online at *www.nickyee.com/daedalus/archives/000343.php,* January 1, 2003.

[Yee03b] Yee, Nick, "Number of Accounts," available online at *www.nickyee.com/daedalus/archives/000343.php,* February 11, 2003.

[Yee04] Yee, Nick, "Hours of Play per Week," available online at *www.nickyee.com/daedalus/archives/000343.php,* February 21, 2004.

1.5

Games Within Games: Graph Theory for Designers—Part 1

David Kennerly—Fine Game Design

david@finegamedesign.com

One of the hallmarks of a discipline is a precise vocabulary, which signifies a specialized intellectual toolset. Programmers have a toolbox of theories to construct from, such as propositional calculus and data structures. Artists, too, have a palette of principles, such as composition and color theory. The theories contain precise terms whose implications suggest solutions to problems germane to that trade.

For massively multiplayer (MMP) game design, graph theory is an intellectual toolset. With graph theory, a designer can analyze and theorize about structures inherent in MMP games. Within a limited scope of game structures, the designer can trade an ambiguous term for a precise definition, replace a fudge factor with a principle, and evolve lore into science.

A World Without Words

Although the term *graph theory* sounds obscure, you have been using graphs most of your life, such as every time you look at a city map or draw a diagram. A *graph* is a mathematically correct diagram that depicts relationships between *vertices,* which are points or dots. If the graph is labeled, then a vertex may be referred to by its label, such as vertex *a* in Figure 1.5.1. A line, called an *edge*, may connect two vertices. This represents a two-way relationship between the *adjacent* vertices. In Figure 1.5.1, the edge adjacent to vertex *a* and vertex *b* is referred to as {a, b}.

A *digraph* is the abbreviation of the term *directed graph*. Do not be intimidated by the name. All flowcharts and activity diagrams are digraphs. A digraph is like a city map with only one-way streets. In a digraph, an edge is called an *arc*, depicted as a line with an arrow near its *head*, to indicate a one-way relationship between the two vertices to which the arc is adjacent. In Figure 1.5.1, the arc from vertex *e* to vertex *f* is referred to as (e, f). Because an arc has a direction, the tail vertex is adjacent to the head vertex, but the head vertex is not adjacent to the tail unless there is a symmetric

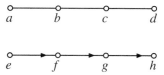

FIGURE 1.5.1   *Graphs and digraphs, labeled and unlabeled.*

arc in the opposite direction. In Figure 1.5.1, the arc (f, g) exists but the arc (g, f) does not. Since all digraphs are kinds of graphs, many digraphs are referred to simply as *graphs*.

A *path* is a sequence of adjacent vertices. In Figure 1.5.1, the graph induced by $\{a, b, c, d\}$ is referred to as a 4-path, P_4, because it contains four vertices. Likewise, (e, f, g, h) belongs to DP_4, since it is a directed (D) path (P) of (4) vertices. Now that we have become acquainted with the primitives, let us apply our knowledge to MMP design.

Hunters and Gatherers

The common activities of many MMPs may be broadly classified as an analogue of hunting and gathering. Often, there are foes to defeat and raw materials to collect, both of which are periodically repopulated. This includes mobile objects (*mobs* for short) such as monsters (in a fantasy setting), villains (in a heroic setting), and hostile aliens (in a sci-fi setting), as well as static objects such as minerals, crops, magical components, and any items provided by the mobile objects, which players call *loot*. By abstracting the collection of resources from a mobile object as *hunting*, and from a static object as *gathering*, we are able to analyze the process systematically, in a way applicable to an MMP in any setting.

A digraph can represent hunting, as shown in Figure 1.5.2(a). A hunter performs the following activities: (s) search or camp for a mob, (g) fight the mob, (l) lose the fight or (w) win the fight, and then start over at (s). To keep the analysis simple, other alternatives are ignored.

A *subgraph* is a graph with a valid subset of vertices and edges. An *induced subgraph* includes every edge adjacent to the subset of vertices. One induced subgraph of a hunt is $\{g, l, w\}$, which represents the fight (g); where the player wins (w) or loses (l), as shown in Figure 1.5.2(b). Using a metaphor to biology and genealogy, a graph theorist calls this digraph a *tree* [Rosen03]. Mathematicians abbreviate such a tree as DT_3, because it is a directed (D) tree (T) with three vertices. DT_3 has a root (g), and two leaves $\{l, w\}$. By omitting preceding vertices, the root of a tree serves as a reference point. Every vertex adjacent to the root is its child. A leaf of a tree means the vertex has no children. Since the arcs are directed outward from the root, the tree in Figure 1.5.2(b) is called an *out-tree*.

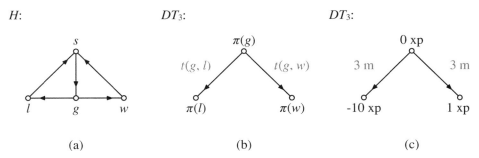

FIGURE 1.5.2 *A hunting (a) game graph, (b) game tree, and (c) its payoffs.*

Game theorists can model any finite and turn-based game as an out-tree [Binmore92]. At each vertex, one of the players chooses an arc. To account for randomness, game theorists invoke a virtual player named Chance, who chooses a random arc. Each leaf is assigned a payoff value, using the Greek letter (π), pronounced "pi." For now, a *payoff* is the value of the points gained or lost at a game vertex, such as $\pi(w) = 1$ xp.

Experience points (xp) are the primary form of payoff in many MMPs. As an example, consider a fight with a gnoll in *EverQuest*. Since most games penalize losing a fight much worse than winning, let us assign simplified values to each leaf: $\pi(l) = -10$ xp and $\pi(w) = 1$ xp, as shown in Figure 1.5.2(c). A game cannot be played at infinite speed, so game theorists assign a time value to each arc. In our example, let us expect two minutes of camping until the gnoll spawns, $t(c, h) = 2$ m, and three minutes of combat, win or lose, so $t(g, l) = 3$ m and $t(g, w) = 3$ m. In an example of an *EverQuest* player versus a gnoll, assume the player is sufficiently fit to freely choose to win (g, l) or lose (g, w).

For an MMP, it is especially important to analyze *extremal cases*, which is the least or greatest member of an ordered set of cases. As the number of players approaches infinity, the probability of every case occurring approaches certainty. For a single player the probability may be negligible, but for all players the probability becomes assured. By analyzing extreme cases, a designer guarantees that all other possible cases occur between the extremes. Let us look at the rate of payoff from a single hunt, shown in Figure 1.5.2(c), where times for camping are ignored. In the *best case of a single hunt*, this hunter wins 1/3 xp/m, or 20 xp/h (experience points per hour). In the *worst case of a single hunt*, this hunter loses at a rate of $-10/3$ xp/m, or -200 xp/h.

However, a usual MMP is not a single game; it is an infinite game. So, let us generalize a game tree into a *game graph*, in which each vertex has a payoff value (π) and each arc a time value (t). By assigning example values, we can depict a *hunt graph*, as shown in Figure 1.5.3(a). For convenience, payoffs of zero are not displayed. A graph theorist generally calls any edge value the *weight* of an edge, and calls such a graph a *weighted graph*.

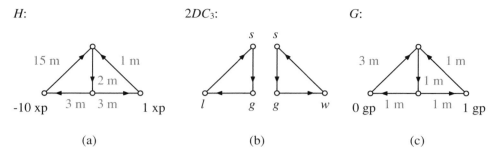

FIGURE 1.5.3   *(a) Hunting and (c) gathering are comprised of (b) payoff cycles.*

A single hunt may be modeled as a directed path in the digraph shown in Figure 1.5.3(a), starting at vertex *s*. In Figure 1.5.3(a), the digraph contains two directed paths that begin and end at vertex *s*, as shown in Figure 1.5.3(b). A graph theorist calls such a path a *cycle*. A cycle with three vertices is called a 3-cycle, or mathematically C_3. The prefix *D* reminds us that this is a directed graph, so both cycles in Figure 1.5.3(b) belong to DC_3. By converting minutes to hours and substituting values from the hunt graph, *H*, we can compute the payoff rate for each cycle, $\pi'(DC_{3l}) = -30$ xp/h and $\pi'(DC_{3w}) = 10$ xp/h.

A gatherer performs the following activities: (*s*) search or camp for a resource, (*g*) gather or refine the resource, either (*l*) unsuccessfully or (*w*) successfully, and then start over at (*s*). In Figure 1.5.3(c), a gather graph displays example payoff in gold pieces (gp) gained or lost. For examples, a gatherer may be an herbalist in *Dark Ages*, gathering flowers and mixing them into potions, or a miner in *Eve Online*, gathering ore from asteroids. With the simple values of *G*, we can compute the payoff rates for each cycle, $\pi'(DC_{3l}) = 0$ gp/h and $\pi'(DC_{3w}) = 20$ gp/h. These payoff rates may be of any kind and may be combined, such as xp and gp.

The hunt graph, *H*, and gather graph, *G*, contain the same number of vertices and have edges that connect these vertices in the same manner. A graph theorist calls any such exact correspondence of vertices and edges isomorphism. The word comes from the Greek *iso-* (equal) and *–morphe* (form). Thus, *H* is isomorphic to *G*. Even if the vertices are moved around or relabeled, isomorphism remains. As an example, look again at the rightmost digraph in Figure 1.5.1. This digraph looks different, but it, too, is isomorphic to *H* and *G* in Figure 1.5.3. These are not the only form a hunt graph or gather graph may have. Moreover, with a game graph, any game system may be modeled.

Flow: The Topology of Optimal Experience

So far, we have discovered the minimum and maximum payoff rates for two infinite games, *H* and *G*, with a single player. However, we are studying infinite, massively multiplayer (MMP) games. A naïve analysis might multiply these rates by the maximum number of players per server, n: such as $n \max\{\pi'(H)\}$ or $n \min\{\pi'(G)\}$. Yet, an MMP further limits the extremal cases, by the maximum spawn rate for the mob or resource.

Usually the game server fixes the maximum spawn rate, and usually player preferences determine the hunt rate or gather rate. The difficulty of the hunting or gathering and the players' preferences determine the kill rate (successful hunting) or harvest rate (successful gathering). In the hunt graph, H, let us extract from the search vertex, s, a consumption vertex, t, as shown in Figure 1.5.4(b). This new vertex, t, represents the fact that the mob or resource is no longer publicly available, because the player, in the economic sense of the word, consumes the mob or resource.

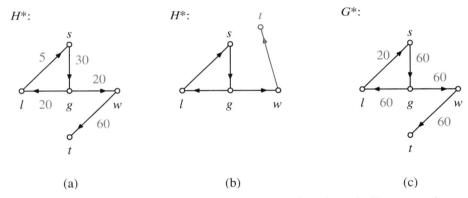

FIGURE 1.5.4   *(a) Hunting and (c) gathering resources flow through (b) a network.*

Figures 1.5.4(a) and 1.5.4(c) depict a special kind of graph, known as a network [Wallis00]. Imagine each edge as a pipe and the flow as liquid moving through the pipes. We can speak of a mob or resource flowing from a *source* (*s*) to a *sink* (*t*). The *value of a flow* is the amount reaching the sink from the source. Imagine a stream of gnolls (H^*) or flowers (G^*) flowing through pipes that player behavior selects.

Figure 1.5.4(a) represents a mob (*s*) being spawned, (*g*) fought, (*w*) killed; and thus, (*t*) consumed. By dividing the number of minutes in an hour by the time for each arc in Figure 1.5.3(a), we obtain the *capacity* of each arc in terms of mobs hunted per hour (*H*/h), shown in the *hunt network*, H^*, in Figure 1.5.4(a). For simplicity, if the hunter loses, assume (*s*, *g*) also equals a portion of return travel time. Likewise, operations from Figure 1.5.3(c), define a *gather network*, G^*, in terms of resources gathered per hour (*G*/h) in Figure 1.5.4(c).

Cannon Fodder

We now want to speak about the common properties of hunt networks and gather networks, so let us group them as a type of *fodder network*, from an old term for nondescript food. A fodder network enables a game designer to measure the rates at which players consume mobs and resources.

Flow through a network cannot exceed the maximum capacity at any edge. No set of players can hunt faster than the server spawns, or consume fodder faster than the minimum time required to kill or harvest it. If minimum capacities are defined, then flow cannot be less than this, either. By default, we assume a minimum capacity of zero, in case a negative value would be absurd. As an example, it usually makes no sense to un-kill a mob, even if it is undead.

Thus, the range of possible values of flow is constrained at either extreme. Minimal flow occurs when no players consume fodder during the given period. Maximal flow occurs when players consume fodder as fast as it is instantiated. In most MMPs, there is a diversity of fodder from which to select. The optimal player strategy is to select the fodder that yields a maximum expected payoff rate. When not all fodder is equally rewarding, the value of a fodder's flow correlates to its reward.

Apples to Apples

It is overly simplistic to compare the raw rates of consumption between all availabilities of fodder. Rare fodder, that is fodder with a lower rate of instantiation, all other things being equal, approaches nearer to its maximal flow than common fodder does. Two reasons support this. Statistically, rarity implies depletion before indifference. A monster that spawns once per day is more likely to be slain than all 1,000 monsters that could be spawned if each were slain at a maximum rate. Socially, rarity increases the prestige of possession. Even a useless but rare item fetches a higher price than a useful but common item. Therefore, it is wise to partition analysis of fodder into categories of rarity, as applicable to the MMP in question. Additional modifiers include intended difficulty; a boss is intended to be more difficult, so a lesser value of flow is desirable.

The Carrot or the Stick

A designer may prune extremal flow of each category of rarity and difficulty. The fodder with the least flow may be said to be the least desirable, attainable, or popular. To increase flow, a designer may increase the fodder's reward, accessibility, or publicity (RAP). The *reward*, in most MMPs, is a combination of advancement, fashion, currency, and advantage. In *Dungeons & Dragons* terms: experience points, exclusive garments, gold, and magical items. There are other rewards, such as prestige and sensorial gratuity, yet for this introductory article, we restrict ourselves to quantifiable rewards. *Accessibility* includes the ease of reaching the location of the fodder, the amount of fodder produced, and the ease of consuming the fodder. *Publicity* includes

NPC gossip, PC gossip, news, guides, FAQs, and other sources of information about the fodder.

If a designer included the item in a crafting recipe for a valued item, then the utility of the item has increased and, if the crafting in question is not already saturated, its flow is expected to increase. The opposite also applies. Decreasing reward, accessibility, and/or publicity correlates to a decrease in flow. However, player-generated publicity cannot be decreased by ethical means. Even if the exploit were made less accessible, once the cat is out of the bag, the publicity of an exploit only increases.

The graph theoretical concepts of fodder can be extended to include missions or quests. As examples, dynamically generated missions in *Phantasy Star Online, Anarchy Online*, and the original *Dark Sun Online* already meet the criteria of fodder. These missions are periodically generated for player consumption. A few additional graph concepts enable us to design missions that are more dynamic.

Story Arc

In one *Final Fantasy XI* quest, "Truth, Justice, and the Onion Way," a new player begins by (*e*) trying to join a kids' club, the Onion Brigade. Its leader, Kohlo-Lakolo, (*f*) sends the player to find a rarab tail (a rarab is a caricatured rabbit). So, the player hunts (strangely not rarabs) or otherwise obtains (*g*) a rarab tail. Upon return with this tail, (*h*) the player is awarded, as initiation, a Justice Badge. Omitting low-level dialogue trees and hidden logic, a directed path, DP_4, may model the player decisions in this quest. In fact, this quest is isomorphic to the directed path in Figure 1.5.1 (*e, f, g, h*). Since a mission graph is a type of game graph, payoff analysis and flow analysis can be applied to this or any mission.

A linear mission (DP_n) has a problem in a persistent game; it lacks replayability. A linear mission is fine as an initiation ritual and many other rituals, but in an MMP, the optimal player strategy is to solve the mission, once and for all. A new player's optimal strategy is to copy the solution, such as by reviewing a quest FAQ on a fan site. Imagine an exam in school that is given every semester. If the exam is identical each time, then new students inherit the solution from previous students. Indeed, this is the optimal study strategy. Oh, did you already know that?

Completing Narratives

Nonlinear missions have been proposed, such as the modular mission [Sheldon04]. In this narrative structure, the mission may be played in any order. This provides a wealth of permutations; a modular mission provides *n*-factorial (*n*!) paths to complete the mission. Such a narrative structure can be depicted as a *complete graph*, denoted as K_n. Figure 1.5.5 represents such a mission with one, two, three, four, or five vertices, denoted as K_1, K_2, K_3, K_4, or K_5, respectively. This graph is undirected, since a player may traverse the mission in either direction.

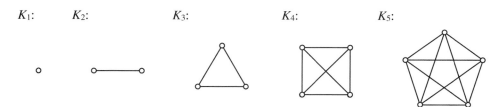

FIGURE 1.5.5   *A complete graph models a modular mission.*

However, writing, designing, and testing completely modular missions are a challenge because there is no guarantee that all $n!$ orders make narrative sense and simultaneously increase the risks and rewards. A game writer may create narrative transitions that glue the narrative modules together, but as the graph reveals, there are $n(n-1)$ transitions that must be written and tested (one for each direction).

Furthermore, unless designed carefully, there is always a unique *minimum spanning path*, which is a path that is adjacent to each vertex and has the least edge weight. A rational player, by definition, avoids non-minimum spanning paths. Therefore, like ants to honey, eventually alternate paths are ignored in favor of the shortest. This can be avoided by balance, but balancing $n!$ paths is hard. A complete narrative is not a poor structure, but it is expensive. However, it empowers a player to permute the narrative.

Composing Narratives

There are several structures between the linear narrative and the complete narrative. Let us consider one: the composite narrative. Most missions are linear, because a directed path (DP_n) contains the least design and testing overhead. However, what if we could multiply replayability while only adding to total development overhead? A little graph theory may go a long way.

Graph theorists have defined binary operations to generate new graphs from old ones. These are analogous to set operations, so use the same symbols, such as $DC_3 \cup DT_3$ or $K_4 - e$. One of the more confusing operations is graph composition [HageHarary91]. In essence, a *composite* creates a copy of a first graph for every vertex in a second graph and then adjoins the vertices wherever the vertex in the first graph had been adjacent. As an example, the composite of a directed 4-path (DP_4) and four unconnected vertices (K'_4) creates the composite path, shown in Figure 1.5.6, with alternating gray vertices for clarity.

As it turns out, a composite path has little overhead, so in mission design, a composite narrative may be accomplished with slightly more design and testing than a linear narrative. Each stage of the mission, as shown in Figure 1.5.6, is guaranteed a consistent relationship with the preceding and subsequent stage, so custom transitions do not need to be written for each arc. Although the mission is still linear, the path varies.

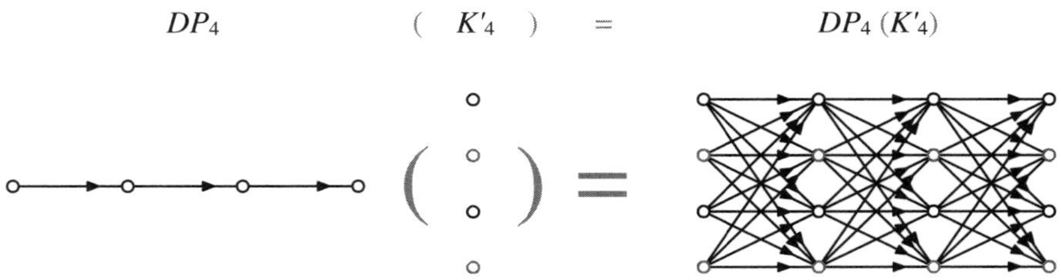

$$DP_4 \qquad\qquad (\quad K'_4 \quad) \quad = \qquad\qquad DP_4\,(K'_4)$$

FIGURE 1.5.6   *Composite graph created from two simple graphs in* Dark Ages.

The example shown in Figure 1.5.6 is from "The Letter" in *Dark Ages*. In this dating quest, a woman and a man unravel a mystery from letters in a romantic dialogue between a missing soldier and his lover. At the first stage (the leftmost column of vertices), the man is given a clue to find the next stage, which is randomly selected from one of the four NPCs of the second stage (second column). The man communicates this to the woman, who initiates the next stage, and so on, back and forth through four stages.

Graph theory elegantly describes the structure of "The Letter" as the composition $DP_4(K'_4)$. The notation, K'_4, represents the complement of a 4-complete graph, which is an *empty graph* of four disconnected vertices. Although technically n^k vertices exist (4 stages and 4 variations produce 16 vertices), each is a variation (K'_4) of a common template (DP_4). While this does not provide a unique style of play each time, it does provide 256 combinations, which entertains players longer at a fraction of the cost.

To verify, we may employ big-theta notation, $\Theta(g)$, which can be summarized as "approaching the growth of the given function, g." Even if a sophisticated player does not wish to repeat an essentially similar mission, the player community's solution requires $\Theta(n^k)$ effort, instead of $\Theta(n)$ for a linear mission. And a composite narrative only costs $\Theta(n + k)$ development time. Thus, replayability has been multiplied while only incrementing development time.

Designing Dependency

A player ingeniously subverts a narrative that lacks activity dependency by performing it out of order. *Anarchy Online* provides an example for analyzing activity dependency in a mission. Figure 1.5.7(a) illustrates the "Assault Pack Quest." The player is (*b*) asked by Mr. Blake to (*e*) deliver a radio transceiver to Echholt, and then (*w*) offer the receiving lieutenant a whiskey to (*a*) receive an assault pack [RPGExpert04a]. As shown in Figure 1.5.7(a), suppose this takes 10 minutes to travel from Blake to Echholt (*b*, *e*) and then 8 minutes to travel from Echholt to whiskey (*e*, *w*) and 8 minutes to return to Echholt to receive the assault pack (*w*, *a*). The writer's intended order (*b*, *e*, *w*, *a*), Figure 1.5.7(b), costs the player 26 minutes.

Yet the optimal order (b, w, e, a) only costs 14 minutes, shown in Figure 1.5.7(c). An activity digraph illustrates why. In Figure 1.5.7(d), an arc, indicating one activity must be completed before another, joins each activity vertex.

One technique to restore narrative structure is a composite narrative. In Figure 1.5.7(e) a composite narrative reveals nine possible missions, by randomly proposing three destination NPCs $\{e, f, g\}$. If the NPC randomly selects an item $\{w, x, y\}$, and these items are expensive or distant from each other, then the optimal player order equals the writer's intended order (b, $\{e, f, g\}$, $\{w, x, y\}$, a).

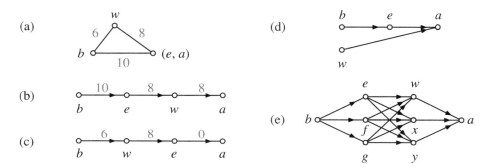

FIGURE 1.5.7   *Activity analysis of an* Anarchy Online *mission.*

Alert readers have noted that the structure of this mission resembles "Truth, Justice, and the Onion Way." Likewise, in "Truth, Justice, and the Onion Way," an activity digraph isomorphic to Figure 1.5.7(d) reveals that the rarab tail is not necessarily obtained in that order. In fact, the optimal order is to get the rarab tail before Kohlo-Lakolo asks for it.

Loopholes

Besides mission design, graph theory provides conceptual tools for debugging a mission. A mission is a cursed blessing for a game designer. As a blessing, it provides an opportunity for the designer to script an entertaining experience. As a curse, the nuances of the scripting language as well as the complexity of the mission logic provide opportunities for unintended exploits. Missing a single validation permits a player, who completed the mission, to get its reward ad infinitum.

Recall that a *cycle* is a path that starts and ends at the same vertex, so a cycle is literally a loop in a graph. In a mission, a cycle represents a state that may be returned to, which may be desirable, such as a validation dialog, or undesirable, such as an infinite increment-gold loop. Inspecting a detailed mission graph for cycles can prevent such an exploit.

Take a Walk, and I'll Pay Your Feet

To a graph theorist, a *walk* means any sequence of adjacent vertices, including backtracking or cycling through the same vertices. A walk in a game graph, therefore, traverses edges, which requires time (t) and provides a payoff (π). The limiting factor of how far a player may walk is the time available. Analyzing such a walk can expose an exploit.

Figure 1.5.8 illustrates how. In *City of Heroes*, two popular modes of gaining experience points (xp) are hunting (h) and missions (m). Let us contract a mission until only three stages are distinguished: mission entrance (m_1), nearly finished (m_2), and finished (m_3). If a player becomes disconnected during a mission, the mission is reset (r). This forms a reduced game graph G^*, which is composed of four payoff cycles. These correspond to the four plays: hunting (DC_1), missions (DC_4), aborting missions (DC_{3h}), and resetting missions (DC_{3r}).

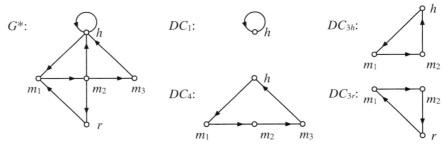

FIGURE 1.5.8   *This* City of Heroes *game graph contains four payoff cycles.*

In 2004, a mission exploit existed in *City of Heroes* that permitted higher xp/h (experience points per hour) [RPGExpert04b]. Mission villains offer a more rewarding rate of experience than hunting, and finishing a mission offers an even higher rate. Finishing a mission is clearly the designer's intent, so where is the exploit? Let us model an exploit scenario by assigning a payoff (xp) to each vertex and a time (minutes) to each arc in the reduced game graph, G^*. Simplified values for each payoff arc are listed in Table 1.5.1.

Table 1.5.1   Payoff Arcs in a *City of Heroes* Game Graph

Vertex	π(xp)	Arc	t (min)	Arc	t (min)
H	5	(h, h)	5	(m_2, m_3)	5
m_1	0	(h, m_1)	15	(m_3, h)	10
m_2	60	(m_1, m_2)	30	(m_2, r)	1
m_3	20	(m_2, h)	10	(r, m_1)	1
r	0				

Let us discover the exploit. Suppose a player has 180 minutes to play during a single session and wants to maximize xp/h. The payoff cycles in Table 1.5.2 comprise four attractive walks in Table 1.5.3. The player may hunt for three hours. Since each hunt cycle (DC_1) takes five minutes, the payoff equals $36DC_1$, which yields 60 xp/h. Alternatively, the player could attempt missions for three hours. Each completed mission cycle (DC_4) takes 60 minutes, so there is time for three missions ($3DC_4$), which yields 85 xp/h.

Table 1.5.2   Payoff Cycles in an Infinite Game

Cycle	Path	π(xp)	t (min)	π' (xp/h)
DC_1	(h, h)	5	5	60
DC_4	(h, m_1, m_2, m_3, h)	85	60	85
DC_3h	(h, m_1, m_2, h)	65	55	71
DC_3r	(m_1, m_2, r, m_1)	60	32	113

Table 1.5.3   Some Payoff Walks in a Three-Hour Game

Walk	π(xp)	t (min)	π' (xp/h)
$36\ DC_1$	36(5)	36(5)	60
$3\ DC_4$	3(85)	3(60)	85
$3DC_3h \cup 3\ DC_1$	3(65) + 3(5)	3(55) + 3(5)	70
(h, m_1) $\cup 5DC_3r \cup$ (m_2, m_3)	0 + 5(60) + 20	15 + 5(32) + 5	107

Two less obvious options exist. One is aborting the mission (DC_3h), which takes 50 minutes, so there is time for three aborted missions and three hunt cycles ($3DC_3h \cup 3DC_1$). This yields 75 xp/h, which is less than finishing each mission. Clearly, it pays to finish a mission; or does it? The last cycle is resetting the mission just before finishing by logging out and returning to begin anew. This cycle (DC_3r) takes 32 minutes, so there is time for five resets and one complete mission: (h, m_1) $\cup 5DC_3r \cup$ (m_2, m_3). The reset exploit yields 107 xp/h per hour, which is about 25% better than finishing missions.

Although this is not a serious problem for *City of Heroes,* suppose it were. Then, how do we solve it? One solution reduces experience gained per mob in the mission, so that the payoff of the nearly finished mission vertex yields $\pi(m_2{}^*) = 20$ xp. The difference, 40 xp, is added to the finishing vertex, $\pi(m_3{}^*) = 50$ xp. Because we balanced the payoff for finishing, the complete mission cycle (DC_4) remains the same. In this scenario, the reset exploit equals ($\pi(m_1) + 5\pi(DC_3r^*) + \pi(m_3{}^*)$) / t, which yields $(0 + 5(20) + 50) / 3 = 50$ xp/h. Since this is about 17% less than hunting, the exploit has been eliminated.

Conclusion

Graph theory offers a consistent vocabulary to analyze and design the structure of a game, and it offers solutions to MMP game designer problems. We hope you will consider its inclusion in future design and analysis.

Part 1 of this article demonstrated graph theory's benefit to the analysis and design of micro-game systems, such as hunting, gathering, and missions. Part 2 explains how graphs may model macro-game systems, which compose an economy and community. Figure 1.5.9 provides, in black, an activity digraph of the MMP graphs we covered here. Because Part 1 discussed the fundamentals of game graphs, networks, flow analysis, and payoff analysis, Part 2 may introduce several advanced applications.

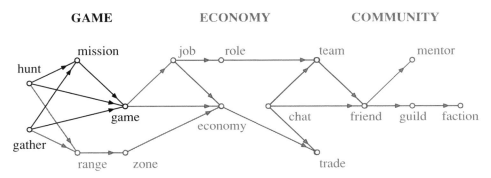

FIGURE 1.5.9   *The MMP, from micro-game systems to macro-game systems.*

References

[Binmore92] Binmore, Ken, *Fun and Games: A Text on Game Theory,* D.C. Heath, 1992.

[HageHarary91] Hage, Per, and Frank Harary, *Exchange in Oceania: A Graph Theoretical Analysis,* Oxford University Press, 1991.

[Rosen03] Rosen, Kenneth, *Discrete Mathematics and Its Applications,* Fifth Edition, McGraw-Hill, 2003.

[RPGExpert04a] "*Anarchy Online*—Assault Pack Quest," available online at *www.rpgexpert.com/1590.html,* March 11, 2004.

[RPGExpert04b] "Supreme *City of Heroes* Guide," available online at *www.rpgexpert.com/1985.html,* March 3, 2004.

[Sheldon04] Sheldon, Lee, *Character Development and Storytelling for Games,* Premier Press, 2004.

[Wallis00] Wallis, W. D., *A Beginner's Guide to Graph Theory,* Birkhäuser, 2000.

1.6

Worlds Within Worlds: Graph Theory for Designers—Part 2

David Kennerly—Fine Game Design

david@finegamedesign.com

What sets a massively multiplayer (MMP) game apart from a standalone game? At the micro level of gameplay, an MMP shares a lot in common with a single player or multiplayer game. Only at the macro level can we observe structures impossible in a standalone game.

Using concepts from Article 1.5, such as a payoff cycle and a network, we can construct a simple model of macro-game systems. Loosely speaking, macro-game systems form the skeleton of the MMP economy and community. The similarity of the concept to macroeconomics is inevitable, since we are going to investigate an economy. After our investigation, we can then identify a web of player interaction, which comprises the community.

However, before we can begin to model an entire economy or community, we must understand how to connect its micro-game subsystems. Our new toolbox from Article 1.5 contains sufficient techniques to connect the fundamental structures: the hunt graph, gather graph, and mission graph. Recall that each of these is an instance of a game graph, for we are about to construct a new game graph that contains them all.

Making the Connection

Uniting a mission graph, hunt graph, and gather graph is a straightforward operation and illustrates the interaction of each game system. A mission often includes *fodder*, which is anything to hunt or gather. A mission may also include a submission, a game within a game. Therefore, we appear to possess a backbone to which to attach micro-games. What is missing is a model of space to interconnect each micro-game.

In most MMPs, the player participates in a two-dimensional or three-dimensional space. The simplest representation of space is a grid, which graph theorists have studied. In Figure 1.6.1, a *grid graph* represents a tiny two-dimensional ($G_{3,3}$) and three-dimensional ($G_{3,3,3}$) space. This representation is not exact, except in an orthogonal tile-based game, such as *The Kingdom of the Winds*, in which the player can only move in the cardinal directions. Still, the grid graph is a good place to start. From a grid graph, a level designer can construct any spatial graph, by adding or deleting vertices or edges.

$G_{3,3}$: $G_{3,3,3}$:

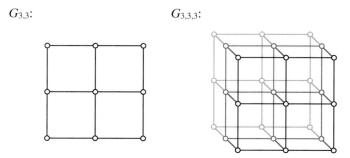

FIGURE 1.6.1   *A grid graph simplifies 2D and 3D space.*

However, to model even a modest MMP requires a grid graph with millions of vertices. To reduce the size of the grid while retaining design information, we need a design-dependent method to cluster vertices together. Let a *range* be a set of positions whose occupants may see and target any other occupant of the set. In a classic MUD (multiuser dungeon), this is usually a room, because each mob in the room can usually target each other mob.

In an MMP that emulates continuous space, there is no simple method to cluster the boundaries of a static range. Yet for most MMPs, there are two criteria: proximity and visibility. Two objects that are close are proximate and in range, except when an obstacle blocks visibility. For example, boxes and walls block targeting villains in *City of Heroes*, returning the message "target blocked," and targeting a villain that is not proximate returns the message "out of range." The target does not have to be a mobile object; any object suffices. As an example, in several *City of Heroes* missions a player targets a crate. Using proximity and visibility to simplify, let a *range graph* represent spatial relationships between each range.

A range combines multiple positions; therefore, many objects may exist within the same range vertex. A single range vertex may contain multiple mobs, resources, or missions. To avoid confusion, rather than placing an object in a range vertex, *connect* the object to a range graph. Draw an edge from a vertex in the range graph to the initial vertex of the mission graph, hunt graph, or gather graph.

Figure 1.6.2(a) gives an example from *EverQuest*. A gnoll hunt graph (*H*) is connected to a range graph (*R*) in Highpass Hold. This represents the fact that a player vertex adjacent to a range vertex may target, and therefore interact with, any fodder or mission adjacent to the same vertex. Graph theorists call the set of vertices adjacent to a given vertex its *neighborhood*. Therefore, any two objects with an intersecting neighborhood are in range of each other.

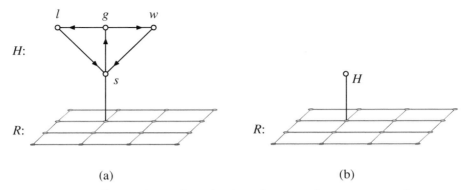

FIGURE 1.6.2 *Connecting and condensing a hunt graph to a range graph.*

A player, too, can be connected to a range graph, which represents that the player is in range. This enables the graph to represent player-to-player interaction, such as trade, crafting, or player-versus-player (PvP) combat.

In the Zone

Sometimes a designer needs an overview of the game server. A territory of range vertices can be condensed to a single vertex. A graph can represent any collection of territories, where an edge represents territories that share a common border. A convenient territory on the global-scale is the *zone*, which is a territory that requires loading. A *zone graph* represents each zone as a vertex and each portal between zones as an edge. For example, *Asheron's Call* dramatically depicts transfer through a portal as a magical tunnel in space-time, whereas *City of Heroes* dresses its portals as subway stations. Although a seamless world does not contain zones, this terminology applies to a contiguous area supported by a single server.

The designer may analyze a range or zone graph for optimal strategies. Figure 1.6.3 represents a zone subgraph (*Z*) of Windhurst Woods 2-neighborhood in *Final Fantasy XI*, plus a hunt graph (*H*), player (*P*), and mission graph (*M*). In the example from Article 1.5, "Truth, Justice, and the Onion Way," the optimal order is (a) hunt for a rarab tail, (b) travel, and then (c) speak to Kohlo-Lakolo, as shown in Figure 1.6.3. Because this walk has no redundant edges, it is superior to the default walk.

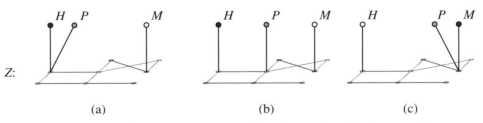

FIGURE 1.6.3 *In* Final Fantasy XI, *a zone subgraph reveals optimal quest order.*

Getting to the Point

Homeomorphism is simpler than it sounds. It is like taking an airline flight with or without layovers. In either case, you traveled from the same origin to the same destination. The word comes from Greek *homeo-* (similar) and *—morphe* (form). A graph that is homeomorphic is not necessarily isomorphic, but the concepts are related.

One method of simplifying both the presentation of a game graph and gaining insight into the graph is through the operation of homeomorphic *contraction*. It is like an airline itinerary without a layover, or a macro for a game command. For a player, two games that possess homeomorphic game graphs are strategically identical.

The *degree* of a vertex equals the number of adjacent edges. To simplify an undirected graph, contract each vertex that has a degree of exactly two. To simplify a directed graph, contract each vertex that has an in-degree of exactly one and an out-degree of exactly one. To retain time information (t) in a game graph, sum the two edges that have been combined. To retain payoff information (π), sum the contracted vertex with its child.

Homeomorphism provides insight into the decisions being made by the player. For example, Figure 1.6.4(a) shows a player's map of Highpass Hold [EQAtlas99]. From this a simplified range graph, Figure 1.6.4(b) is drawn. Contracting the intermediate vertices of Highpass Hold from R yields R^*, as shown in Figure 1.6.4(c). Once spawn locations and other interactive locations are connected to R^*, interactivity can be analyzed.

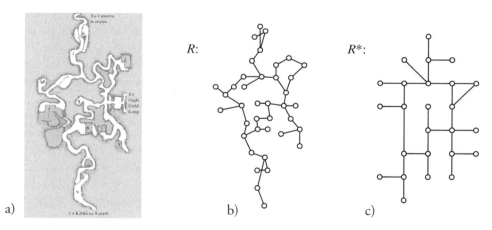

FIGURE 1.6.4   *Highpass Hold homeomorphism in* EverQuest.

Career Path or Caste System?

Players are engaging in long-term strategies when they choose which class or job to play and how to advance. Because increments of advancement vary, job levels between

MMPs are incomparable, yet the fundamental structures of job decisions are comparable. Just like a mission or a maze, a job system is homeomorphic to a sequence of decisions. A *job graph* reveals the structure of these decisions. Each vertex represents a job, and level, from which a decision begins or ends, and each arc represents an alternative.

A few examples illustrate job decisions open to a player. *EverQuest* employs a strict class system. A long directed path, DP_{65}, characterizes *EverQuest* class advancement after character creation (prior to *Omens of War* expansion). Given 15 classes and 65 levels, an out-tree (DT_{16}), shown in Figure 1.6.5(a), depicts that there is a single decision vertex, the root. *The Kingdom of the Winds* offers specialization at a higher level, called a *subpath*, so its job tree is homeomorphic to $(DT_5 \cup 4DT_4)$ shown in Figure 1.6.5(b). The union of an out-tree and a bipartite graph $(DP_7 \cup K_{6,9})$ represents *Final Fantasy XI* job graph, shown in Figure 1.6.5(c). In addition to the major decisions shown, each of these games has further options for job advancement, such as a secondary job in *Final Fantasy XI*.

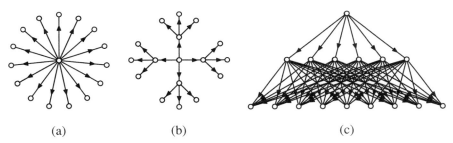

      (a)   (b)   (c)

FIGURE 1.6.5   *Job graphs of (a)* EverQuest, *(b)* The Kingdom of the Winds, *and (c)* Final Fantasy XI.

Roleplaying

Almost all MMPs are cooperative, and almost all cooperative games emphasize player specialization. An RPG often commits a player to a specific role. In most MMORPGs, players have defined the tactical roles as tank, healer, nuke, buff, and debuff, which are summarized in Table 1.6.1.

Table 1.6.1   Common MMORPG Tactical Roles

Role	Description
Tank	Absorb incoming damage.
Healer	Heal damage.
Nuke	Deliver damage.
Buff/Debuff	Augment damage delivery and degrade incoming damage.

In most MMORPGs, the job designates a role, yet there are many ways to divide the pie. A job may have multiple roles, and multiple jobs may share the same role, or subdivisions of that role. Therefore, a job is not a role. One job may be part buff and healer for example. However, if the game prevents a single player from being efficient at all roles, then an optimal team is comprised of specialists. Some examples from games are shown in Table 1.6.2.

Table 1.6.2   Example Role Correspondences

Tactical Role	City of Heroes	Final Fantasy XI	The Kingdom of the Winds
Tank	Tank/Scrapper	Warrior/Monk	Warrior
Healer	Defender	White Mage	Poet
Nuke	Blaster	Black Mage/Thief	Mage/Rogue
Buff/Debuff	Controller	Red Mage	Poet/Mage

A *tactical role graph* presents these staple roles as a signed graph, shown in Figure 1.6.6. A *signed graph* represents positive and negative edges between vertices. Conventionally, the negative relation in a signed graph is depicted as a dashed line. A dashed black arc from (*n*) nuke and (*e*) enemy indicates damage delivery role, and a solid black arc from (*h*) healer indicates healing. A dashed gray arc from (*b*) buff/debuff indicates degrading damage delivery, and a solid gray arc from (*b*) buff/debuff indicates augmenting damage delivery. Even without knowing the details of the game mechanics, the graph gives an appreciation of which jobs make better soloists and which do not, such as buff/debuff and healer, since they have no damage arcs of their own. Yet their multiple healing and buff arcs, respectively, give an intuitive appreciation of their efficiency in a team.

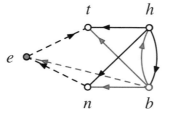

FIGURE 1.6.6   *A tactical role graph depicts the influence of each role.*

A role graph does not have to be based on the *Dungeons & Dragons* tactical model. Various designs lend themselves to role graph analysis, such as farming flax in *A Tale in the Desert*. One efficient team strategy is to divide the labor of farming between three players in the form of three roles: planter, weeder, and harvester. An activity digraph reveals the necessary order for each of these activities, which is the stated order. The team coordinates its behavior in series. Therefore, instead of felling a foe, the team farms flax.

When analyzed together, a role graph and job graph give insight into the distribution of desirable jobs on a team. In *Dark Ages*, there are five classes, and an advanced player may choose a secondary class. Therefore, the *Dark Ages* job graph ($DP_6 \cup K_{5,5}$) has some similarity to *Final Fantasy XI*, shown in Figure 1.6.5(c). However, a class imbalance, or rather an imbalance of roles within the tuples of classes, occurred [DAHelp04].

A *tuple* is an ordered set, in this case the order being the original class and the transfer class. A player with the class tuple (monk, warrior) efficiently performs the role of tank and nuke ($t \cup n$). Additionally, the class tuple (wizard, priest) performs the role of nuke, buff/debuff, and healer ($n \cup b \cup h$). Therefore, optimal team selection consists of a small subset of the 25 class tuples. To balance, a designer may augment the ability of a pure class (e.g., warrior, warrior), so each job retains a niche in the role graph.

Trading Bits

A key trait of an MMP is an economy. In-game trade is a significant activity that is only possible in an MMP, since the game is persistent and contains a market of other players.

A network may model an economy; indeed, graph theorists have applied networks to solving several economic transportation problems. This is more complex than the fodder network examined in Article 1.5, because there are many alternate paths. In an *economic network*, let a vertex represent an abstract container of an item. A player, in this context, may be a container, just as an area, mobile or static object, or a nonplayer character may be. An arc in an economic network represents a transfer of an item from one container to another.

To be a network, the graph must have two sets of distinguished vertices: sources and sinks. Let the source be any container where an item is created, and a sink be any container where an item is destroyed. In general, sources and sinks are synonymous with faucets and drains [Simpson99]. Common sources include fodder, rewards, crafters, and developer sales. Common sinks include NPC merchants, item usage, and decay.

A condensation graph is a graph in which several vertices have been contracted together. By contracting all elements that belong to the same category, such as all players of a shared economic function, an economy graph may be condensed to its essential system.

A Tale in the Desert has no combat, so all decision-making occurs in gathering, the economy, and the community. This MMP offers a rich tapestry of decisions to make in several of its crafting activities. As shown in Figure 1.6.7, even the simplest homeo-morphism of the chime graph for experimentation in the acoustics laboratory retains 52 of the original 100 vertices [AWID04].

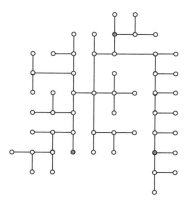

FIGURE 1.6.7   *A* Tale in the Desert *chime graph.*

In the *Final Fantasy XI* quest, "Truth, Justice, and the Onion Way," there are two items in flow. A rarab tail is created and destroyed, and a Justice Badge is created. On a diagram, the source of the rarab tail is a creature. Although a player may gain the rarab tail from another player, that player must obtain, through a path of transactions, the tail from the source. The rarab tail has a sink, which is at the completion of the quest. Subsequent to this sink is the source of the second item, the Justice Badge, which Kohlo-Lakolo gives to the player.

Lubricating the Economy

A designer may *troubleshoot* the economic network. In electronic communications, this term means to isolate a defective component and fix or replace it. First, identify desirable flow. The desirable flow for an item is a range that varies with the population size, style of gameplay, and utility of the item. Once this range has been defined, two methods exist—theoretical and empirical—for troubleshooting. Theoretical methods require deducing the expected flow of an item through each vertex. Empirical methods require measuring the actual flow of the item through each vertex.

Once this has been accomplished by either means, the expected or observed flow may be compared to the desirable flow. A vertex with low net flow is indicated by the sum of incoming arcs being greater than the sum of outgoing arcs, as shown in Figure 1.6.8. Thus, graph theory models *hoarding*. A designer may directly or indirectly modify the values of some of the arcs adjacent to the hoarding vertex. On the outgo-ing arcs, the designer may increase the rewards, accessibility, or publicity (RAP).

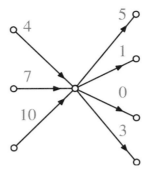

FIGURE 1.6.8 *Hoarding in an economic network.*

As a general example, *Ultima Online* increases the accessibility of many items by providing offline vendors. Instead of requiring both players to be online simultaneously, *Ultima Online* vendors only require one player to be online; therefore, the item in trade is more accessible for a buyer. These vendors are effectively personal consignment stores, which sell items. As another example, *Final Fantasy XI* auction and vendor system also increases accessibility. Alternatively, a new outgoing arc may decrease hoarding. For example, a new quest may be created that is a sink for an item, such as a rarab tail. This creates a new arc and rewards a player for depositing the item into that sink.

Keeping Your Options Open

One economic exploit from *Ultima Online* is the famous bandage bug [Dibbell03]. For brevity, this example is dramatically simplified. Suppose there are two NPC merchants. Each may be modeled as a tree connected to a zone graph, shown in Figure 1.6.9(a). Suppose a player can purchase 50,000 gold worth of cloth from the first merchant (V_1), and make bandages to sell to the second merchant (V_2) at 54,000 gold, all in 20 seconds. The optimal path may be extracted, as shown in Figure 1.6.9(b). A profit of 4,000 gold occurs each 40-second roundtrip, or 360,000 gold per hour. Julian Dibbell speculated that 20 machines running 10 automated sessions of *Ultima Online* each could generate up to $20,000 per day [Dibbell03].

From reviewing the graph, several solutions appear. Out of these, raising the cost of cloth is not desirable, since it hurts all other players. Alternate solutions include increasing the distance or difficulty of the optimal path between the set of merchants, to lower the rate of profit. *Ultima Online* chose to apply a classic economic theory: a diminishing margin of return. As more bandages are sold in a short period, the value of each additional bandage diminishes.

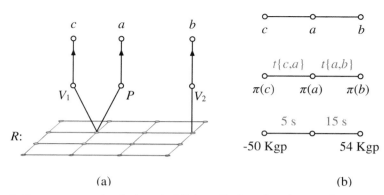

(a)   (b)

FIGURE 1.6.9   *Analyzing the* Ultima Online *bandage exploit.*

Originally, *Ultima Online* attempted to connect the sink to the source and thus create a closed economy [Simpson99]. Such design appears elegant, but a closed model is missing something: the rest of the world. A designer should hope that the economy is not a closed system, because a new customer's subscription acts as a source of new wealth. If the economy is a closed and balanced network, then each new subscription (at the source) must be balanced by a cancellation (at the sink). Therefore, an unbalanced source and sink MMP economy is not only convenient, it is relevant to a commercial service.

Community Building Is the Web

Universities, when considering where to construct permanent walkways between buildings first let the students trample on the grass until the foot travel has worn paths of natural usage. In an MMP, community discovery is the first step to community building; that is, learning what communities already exist.

At the micro-level of community, a single signal is transmitted from one player to another. The most common instance of a signal is chat, so a *chat graph* represents each player as a vertex and an edge as two-way communication within a given timeframe, such as an hour, a day, or a week. Chat is the atomic activity that constructs an MMP community. Therefore, a designer may detect communities in a chat graph. For example, a frequency-weighted chat graph of *TinyMUD* correlates to social involvement of its users [Cherney99].

In a well-designed MMP, community and game systems are as interwoven as a tapestry. Community interweaves with economy through patterns of trade. At the lowest economic level of detail, a *trade graph* represents an arc when one player has traded a significant set of goods to another player. Just as anthropologists have analyzed trade graphs in Micronesia, so may designers analyze trade in MMPs. For example, a vertex with a high degree indicates a potential for wealth [HageHarary91].

The job system also meshes with the community. Artifacts of this may be discovered in a *team graph*, which depicts an edge between players who have formed a team within a given time period. Social assertions, such as the popularity of a job and the cliques of cooperation, are directly observable in the team graph. In analyzing a graph, a *clique* designates a set of vertices that are completely connected. In any community graph, a clique corresponds to a social unit. For example, all members of a team, by definition, form a clique in a team graph.

Chatting, trading, and team formation each occur within a single session. The atom of a multiple session relationship may be detected in a *friend graph*, which depicts an edge between a pair of players that list each other on their respective friend lists. A one-way arc is less meaningful, because a one-way friendship is a weak bond. From a friend subgraph, an isomorphism to another subgraph, such as a chat subgraph or a trade subgraph, correlates to a social bond.

As the population grows, a friendship becomes as invisible as a drop in an ocean. Therefore, a *guild graph* displays a guild vertex with an arc from each player who belongs to that guild. Since each member has the same neighborhood, as depicted in Figure 1.6.10(e), the members are said to be *N-equivalent*, or neighborhood-equivalent. Oftentimes, a guild is a socio-economic unit, so chat graph, trade graph, and friend graph cliques are expected within a guild neighborhood, which represents communal activities. Figure 1.6.10 shows all these subgraphs.

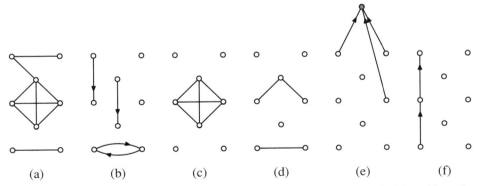

(a) (b) (c) (d) (e) (f)

FIGURE 1.6.10 *Subgraphs of (a) chat, (b) trade, (c) team, (d) friend, (e) guild, and (f) mentor.*

Ritual and ceremony are fundamental social activities. One of the most basic of these is observable in the *mentor graph*, which depicts an arc between a novice and a mentor. As an example, *Asheron's Call* gained popularity for its allegiance system, which was a new mentor/guild design based on the old pyramid scheme. In 2004, after discovering that a linear path (DP_n) was the optimal mentor graph, Turbine redesigned the rewards to eliminate this exploit [Beckers04].

Community graphs can influence design, as there are many forms of communication models, from channels, to teams, guilds, and structures in between. As an example, *Final Fantasy XI* employs a linkshell, which has some properties of a friend list and a guild. As another example, *Puzzle Pirates* employs both temporary jobbing on a pirate ship or permanent membership in a pirate crew. Graph theory reveals that many undiscovered designs exist.

Axis and Allies

In addition to a graph of only one kind of relationship, graph theorists have specified methods to model nonequivalent relationships. The simplest of these is a diametric opposed relationship, such as alliance and enmity. A *faction graph* is an undirected, signed graph representing positive and negative mutual relationships between sets of players or nonplayers, known as *factions*. For convenience, the reflexive arc (an arc from a vertex to itself) is implied and not drawn.

Faction graphs apply to several MMPs. As an example, in 2004, *World of Warcraft* planned to have two opposing factions, the Alliance and the Horde. This may be modeled as K_2, as shown in Figure 1.6.11(a) with a relationship of enmity (a dashed edge). *Dark Age of Camelot* (Mythic) embeds into its logo three opposing realms: Albion, Midgard, and Hibernia. Each relationship, which is mutual enmity, can be modeled by a signed graph, K_3, as shown in Figure 1.6.11(b). This has significant interaction consequences, as only enemy realms may attack each other.

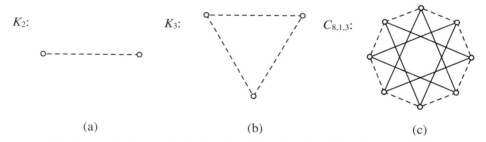

FIGURE 1.6.11   *Faction graph of (a)* World of Warcraft, *(b) realms in* Dark Age of Camelot, *and (c) religions in* Dark Ages.

As another example, there are eight gods in *Dark Ages* (Nexon). In Figure 1.6.11(c), each of these gods has two allies (solid edges) and two enemies (dashed edges). This *Dark Ages* religion graph is a *circulant graph*, which is a generalization of a cycle. In this case ($C_{8,1,3}$), there are eight vertices, and the first and third proximate vertices are adjacent. This author designed several game consequences for these relationships, such as consecrating an item (an economic source), mass worship (a player ceremony), desecrating an item (an economic sink), and group prayer (a player ritual). Thus, the factions, economy, and ceremonies are interwoven.

Conclusion

Any MMP game system, micro or macro, can be modeled as a graph, so graph theory is a rich field with solutions to MMP game designer problems. Figure 1.6.12 illustrates an activity digraph of the graphs this pair of articles has introduced. For a glossary of the graphs and terms covered, plus up-to-date links to new information, you may visit the author's Web site [Kennerly04]. From the point of view of the *web graph*, an entire game server is only a single vertex, so an MMP is a world within a world.

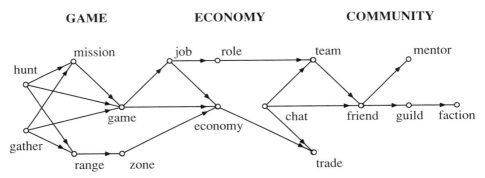

FIGURE 1.6.12   *The MMP, from micro systems to macro systems.*

We hope you will consider graph theory in the design of a future MMP or analysis of an existing one. A precise vocabulary, a robust intellectual toolset, and imagination can design a wondrous world. Just as a pioneer mathematician Arthur Cayley applied graph theory to predict undiscovered molecules, a pioneer designer can apply graph theory to invent new game structures.

References

[AWID04] "Acoustics Lab," *A Wiki in the Desert*, available online at *http://atitd. centauri.org/wiki/Acoustics_Lab*, July 13, 2004.

[Beckers04] Beckers, Alex, "Allegiance Experience," available online at *http://ac. turbinegames.com/index.php?page_id=157*, January 12, 2004.

[Cherney99] Cherney, Lynn, *Conversation and Community: Chat in a Virtual World*, CLSI Publications, 1999.

[DAHelp04] *Dark Ages Help*, available online at *www.dahelp.com*, July 31, 2004.

[Dibbell03] Dibbell, Julian, "Corrections, Corrections," available online at *www. juliandibbell.com/playmoney/2003_06_01_playmoney_archive.html*, June 6, 2003.

[EQAtlas99] EQAtlas, "Highpass Hold—Map," available online at *www.eqatlas. com/highpassholdmap.html*, 1999.

[HageHarary91] Hage, Per and Frank Harary, *Exchange in Oceania: A Graph Theoretical Analysis,* Oxford University Press, 1991.

[Kennerly04] Kennerly, David, "Webs Within Webs: Graph Theory for Designers—Appendix," available online at *http://finegamedesign.com/graph*, August 29, 2004.

[Simpson99] Simpson, Zachary Booth, "The In-game Economics of Ultima Online," available online at *www.mine-control.com/zack/uoecon/uoecon.html*, April 7, 1999.

1.7

Guild Management Tools for a Successful MMP Game

Sean "Dragons" Stalzer— The Syndicate

dragons@LLTS.org

Guilds play a vital role in the online gaming world. A complete set of guild management tools is required to both allow guilds to flourish and to help retain them as customers. Since MMORPGs have existed for many years, a set of expectations exists in players' minds that defines the minimum set of tools needed to manage a successful in-game guild. As guilds continue to grow in size and longevity, players will require additional features that will make running a guild or participating in a guild more rewarding. This article presents MMORPG features that should be implemented to support a successful, vibrant guild community. Features are categorized as either required or optional but nice to have. Guild functionality helps separate one game from another.

Why Is It Important to Have a Good Suite of Guild Management Tools?

As the MMORPG genre evolves, there is an increased focus on group- and guild-level content, which is often referred to as "raid" content. A raid could be defined as gathering large groups of players together to accomplish a goal that could not be accomplished alone or in small groups. The evolution to raid-level content was driven by the trend among players to form guilds. The creation of raid-level content and defining it as the "end game" has further pushed players to join guilds. Raid content has caused guilds to grow larger in order to have the forces available to overcome those challenges. Since guild membership is high among the player base, a good set of guild management tools is necessary for Guildmasters to successfully manage their entities and for players to get the most out of being in a guild. In addition, one criterion used by large well-known gaming guilds, like *The Syndicate* (*www.LLTS.org*), to choose which MMORPGs to participate in is the completeness of the Guild Management tool suite. Thus having a more complete set of guild management tools will aid in attracting and retaining guilds and players.

Mandatory Guild Management Features

There are a number of features that most players would agree that a game must have in order to meet the basic needs of a guild. The list of mandatory features does evolve over time. As players get used to also having optional features, those features become mandatory. Games that only include the bare minimum set of mandatory features will be less attractive to gamers. As such, it is wise to consider the following mandatory feature list and the optional list. The basic features that a game needs to have include:

- In-game detailed guild roster
- Guild ranks with customizable levels of authority
- A guild chat channel
- The ability to add and remove members anywhere in the gaming world
- The ability to remove members while offline
- A customizable guild message of the day
- Display guild name over a character's head

In-Game Detailed Guild Roster

Every successful MMORPG to date has had some form of in-game roster available to at least the Guildmaster of the guild. Some of the more successful MMORPGs, like *EverQuest*, have elaborate rosters, and players have now come to require a roster and to expect to have advanced features incorporated into the roster. At a minimum, the in-game roster should list the Name, Critical Statistics (e.g., level, race, and class), Guild Rank, Public/Private Notes about the character, and the Last Date Online for that character. The list should be able to be sorted by all of those categories. Finally, the list should have an option to export it, from the game, into a text file that guilds could then use to manage their rosters outside the game.

Guild Ranks with Customizable Levels of Authority

Most guilds will have some level of hierarchy within the guild. It could be a very simple one of Guildmaster and Members, but most will have a more complex system involving officers, newer members, veteran members, raid leaders, and other such classifications. There are also many functions within the game relating to guild management, and there may be different ranks within the guild that will perform those functions. Each guild should have the option to assign the power to perform those tasks to various ranks and then to assign those ranks to members. The ideal scenario is one that allows the guild to create their own ranks and name them what they wish and assign the powers to them independently of each other. For example, a rank could have the add member permission but that wouldn't inherently give that rank the remove member permission.

Some of the common powers that should be in an MMORPG include:

- Add/Remove Members
- Promote/Demote Members
- Set the Message of the Day
- Add/View Public and Officer Notes
- View/Speak in Guildsay
- View/Speak in Officer Chat
- Grant/Remove Access to Guild Property
- Declare War/Peace

A Guild Chat Channel

Being able to communicate between guildmates is a cornerstone of any guild. Part of the reason why guilds exist is for the social aspects of gaming with friends or with people who share similar goals. Thus, the ability to communicate with guildmates, in private, is a key feature of any MMORPG. All games should include at least one method of chatting with guildmates in private, such that nonmembers could not read the text. That chat channel should display text in a color different from other game-related text so it is easy to distinguish guild chatter from other game information. The most common color used for guild chat is a bright green. Members should be able to customize chat channel colors to suit personal preferences, but by default, the guild chat color should differ from other chat colors. If the game uses a method of logging in to and out of channels, then the guild chat channel should be automatically opened every time a character logs in to the game.

The Ability to Add and Remove Members Anywhere in the Gaming World

Global, server-wide commands are another cornerstone feature of guild management. This class of command is most prevalent when it comes to adding and removing characters. One of the key player complaints in early *EverQuest* days, for example, was the inability to get a guild together to add the members due to players being low level and monsters being far too difficult to move everyone to a common spot. Thus, later games began to add the ability to add and remove players from anywhere within the game. Any member who has been granted the permission to add or remove a member should be able to issue the command from anywhere in the gaming world to anywhere else in the gaming world.

The Ability to Remove Guild Members While They Are Offline

Guild rosters can grow very large over time as players make secondary characters, or as players quit guilds or retire from the game they are playing. This can lead to many characters still in a guild roster that should not be there. It is possible those characters could be used to spy on the guild of which they used to be members. It is possible that accounts are closed and those characters could never again log in to remove themselves or to be removed. Thus the ability to remove any character from the roster, even if that character is not online at the time, is important in a successful guild management tool suite. An optional feature, in the same vein as the remove option, that would be a "player pleaser" is to add the ability to extend invitations to join a guild to players who are offline. Next time those players log in, a pop-up box could appear indicating the guild and the person who extended an invitation to them, and they could select to accept or decline it.

A Customizable Guild Message of the Day

Messages of the Day serve as a valuable guild communications tool and should be included in all MMORPG designs. The commonly accepted definition of a Guild Message of the Day (MotD) is a series of text that appears when a player logs in to the game, the contents of which is customizable by the Guildmaster or empowered officers. Some of the purposes they serve include alerting players to bugs or issues, reminding players of upcoming raids, and passing along critical or time-sensitive guild information. The MotD should be in the form of a pop-up box that comes up every time a character logs in to the game and not simply the first time the character logs in for that day. The MotD should also be retrievable via a menu option or hotkey command. The MotD should be of sufficient length to allow several sentences of description to be included. Setting the MotD should be a configurable guild permission that can be granted to various guild ranks by the Guildmaster. Anyone with that permission should be able to set the MotD or edit the existing one. Finally, whenever the MotD is set or changed, it should automatically display to all members who are currently online.

Display Guild Name Over the Character's Head

The showing of a guild's name, floating alongside the player's name, over the character's head has become a standard in online gaming. Some games have chosen to include a toggle to turn off that display, but most have not. The ability to indicate a player's membership within an organization is a source of pride to many players and one of the ways guilds can project power and influence in the gaming world, attract new recruits, and be held accountable for actions their members take.

Optional/Nice to Have Guild Management Features

The MMORPG business is very competitive and the inclusion of extra features for guilds can make or break a player's decision to participate in a particular game. In addition, as more of the "nice to have" features get included in more games, they will become mandatory because players' expectations will change. The following list includes some of the optional guild management features that a development team should consider adding to an MMORPG:

- The ability to Alt-Tab out of the game
- Customizable guildhalls
- Customizable titles that can be granted to members
- Optional guild structures
- Guild Bank/Storage with levels of access control
- In-game "'post-it" note board for members
- Customized text colors by guild rank
- Optional game-managed dues system
- Ability to set up an in-game guild application system
- Ability to manage the guild via Web pages
- Guild flagged/owned equipment
- Officer placed waypoints and camp spots
- Guild crests on items
- Guildmaster incentives
- In-game Guild Calendar

The Ability to Alt-Tab Out of the Game

A common pet peeve among players is being forced to remain inside the game world for the duration of their gaming session. Those feelings develop because a significant amount of the guild experience takes place outside the game engine itself. Many guilds use chatzones/posting forums to communicate. For additional real-time, more secure and flexible communications, guilds often use Internet Relay Chat (IRC) servers. E-mail is a commonly used communications tool by guilds. Fan sites receive millions of hits a month from players because they contain strategies, guides, and their own forums in which players and guilds participate. Thus, locking players within the game itself for the duration of their play session either forces them to log out from the game to look things up and make use of those communications tools, or causes them to be less connected to their guilds. Strong guilds with strong connections among members can continue to add value and fun for a player long after the game itself has ceased to be fun. For example, *The Syndicate* polled its members and found that more than half of the polled *Ultima Online* (UO) players would not be playing UO if they were not members of the guild. Thus, allowing players to alt-tab out of the game, or to play the game in a window, allows players to make use of those guild tools, thus strengthening the guild's value to them and causing them to participate in the game for longer.

Customizable Guildhalls

Players like to own virtual property. Part of the reason to play online games is to amass a collection of virtual "stuff" that is larger than that of other players. By extension, guilds like to own guildhalls. They are a symbol of power and serve as a focal point for in-game activities. One common issue that developers face, some months after a game goes live, is that of having gold sinks to keep the virtual economy in line. The developer's need for gold sinks and the desire by guilds to have guildhalls complement each other. Guildhalls can be made to be expensive. They can be customizable so new features could be added for a price. To prevent guildhalls from cluttering the landscape or add lag to the server, they could exist in instanced areas outside the normal play area.

Some examples of customizable features that guilds could "sink" gold into include:

Guild Storage Space: Access to storage could be controlled by the customized guild ranks and the amount of storage could be increased for a fee.

Class/Race/Skill Trainers: The ability to hire NPCs to take up shop in the guildhall and train members.

Banker: Accessing a player's bank is a very common occurrence. The ability to hire a banker to work out of a guildhall would be added value for guilds.

Post-It Note Board: A space that could be added to the guildhall where players can leave short notes to other members.

Guild-Owned Vendors: The ability to hire an NPC to take items the guild places on him and resell them to nonmembers.

Guild Arena: A private PvP area where members can duel, practice PvP skills, or have private guild contests.

Teleportation Gates: The ability to buy portals to key game locations or major towns. If members were to base themselves from the guildhall, they could more easily get to major locations.

Increased Guildhall Size: Size matters. Many guilds like to have the biggest and best of everything. Allowing players to upgrade the size of a guildhall addresses that desire. In the case of using instanced areas for guildhalls, this could manifest itself both in the "portals" that members of that guild enter to reach their guildhall, and inside the guildhall, there would be more rooms or more space to add on other features.

Internal Member Housing: Players also like to own personal houses. Members of guilds often want to live near each other if possible. Therefore, adding the ability for members to "rent" rooms to live in with additional personal storage space and perhaps the ability to upgrade them would marry the guildhall and player housing issues together.

Furniture: Furniture and other room decorations (tapestries, fireplaces, etc.) are basically eye candy. However, as the *Ultima Online* model demonstrates, furniture is a very popular form of eye candy. Three of the seven, 7th Anniversary Gifts players could choose from in UO are in the form of eye candy for player houses and guildhalls.

Customizable Member Titles

Besides having customizable ranks, adding customizable titles that also display over a player's head or that were listed in the guild roster is an attractive feature to players. Being able to label a character "the Best Bunny Slayer" or "Guild Quartermaster" is something players enjoy. If the length of custom titles were limited and filters added to prevent obscene and indecent words, titles can add value without creating more issues. *Ultima Online* is an example of a success story that uses customizable titles grantable by the Guildmaster.

Optional Guild Structures

As a general rule of thumb, players dislike being forced to do things. One example where this sometimes comes up is when players are forced to pick from a list of developer-defined guild structures. While some guilds fit well into those structures, many do not. For the guilds that do fit into them, they can offer added value. Therefore, when a guild is created, an option could exist to pick from a predefined guild structure or instead choose a "player managed" structure that would have no game imposed structure to it other than having an assigned Guildmaster.

Some examples of predefined guild structures that could be made available, as options, to players include:

The Democracy: If players chose that option, the Guildmaster would be the person with the highest vote count. A new vote would automatically take place at some interval, and when a character logged in during the voting period, a pop-up box would appear and the player could vote for any member.

The Council: Some guilds are based around a small group of players managing things. In those cases, each council member is, more or less, equal. Therefore, in this optional guild type, a certain number of people could be specially invited by the character who founded the guild, and they would become council members with equivalent power to the founder.

The Dictatorship: Most guilds fit into this category, and thus it is handled by the "'player managed" category described previously. One person is in charge and cannot be removed by the members of the guild, but the members are free to quit and form their own guild if they do not like how the Guildmaster runs things.

Player choice, with the option to have a predefined structure or not, is the key to this optional guild management feature. Allowing the base templates to be customizable and allowing the guild to change templates later are also important. Choosing no template at all is the option many guilds will take, but offering some predefined ones will help set one game apart from another.

Guild Bank Account

Even if guildhalls are not added to an MMORPG, the addition of guild storage space is a feature that players would widely support. The *Wish* MMORPG is an example of where this was implemented. The Guildmaster, and any rank within the guild that has been granted permission to do so, gets two options when speaking to the banker: an option for their personal bank box, and one for the guild bank box. The size of that box could be customizable, perhaps based on guild size or on buying upgrades to it. Access to the bank box should be configurable via the customizable guild ranks and could have the levels of No Access, View Bank Contents, Add Items to Bank, Remove Items from Bank, Add Currency to Bank, and Remove Currency from Bank. Optional logging of what is added and removed and by whom that could be toggled on by the Guildmaster would be an added-value feature as well.

In-Game Members-Only "Post-It" Board

Even if guildhalls are not added to an MMORPG, the addition of a guild post-it note board or an in-game e-mail system will be of added value to players. *World of Warcraft* went the route of the in-game e-mail system (that also allows sending and receiving of items), which addresses this need, in part. The other aspect of this feature is the ability to leave notes that more than one person or the entire guild could read. The guild-level feature could also be controlled by powers granted to the different guild ranks. The powers could include No Access, View Post-It Notes, Add Post-It Note, and Remove Post-It Notes. All notes could expire within some duration, except perhaps those that were left by the Guildmaster or certain empowered officers who can make persistent/sticky notes.

Customized Text Colors by Guild Rank

As guilds get larger, the guild chat channel gets more cluttered with conversations. Too much "green spam" will subconsciously make the readers begin to tune it out. One option is to limit what guildsay can be used for, by having guild rules that are enforced. Another useful feature would be to have an option to differentiate the text color of a member based on rank. Perhaps if guildsay was bright green, then the Guildmaster's text might be green but underlined or bolded, whereas the officers may have their name show up in blue while the text following it is green. An optional method to allow text to stand out for key members of the guild would be of added value, especially to larger guilds.

Optional Game-Managed Dues System

Not all guilds will collect dues, but some do to support guild expenses. If "gold sink" options like customizable guildhalls are added to a game, then guild dues will become an attractive option to many groups. The addition of a system whereby empowered officers could set the amount and the frequency of dues and have the game automatically collect them would be of great value to guilds that have a dues system. At the specified frequency, when the character logs in to the game, the amount of the dues is deducted from that character's bank account and deposited into the guild's bank account. If the character doesn't have the amount in his bank, his name could be highlighted in a different color in the guild roster, and the next time that amount is added, it would be withdrawn. Allowing the Guildmaster and empowered officers to tag characters to not have dues taken from them would allow a system to be targeted at only "main" characters and not affect secondary characters or inactive yet still guilded characters. Finally, a message should be displayed to each character who had dues withdrawn alerting him that his guild dues of a certain amount were paid and that the next dues payment will be withdrawn on whatever the next due date is.

In-Game Guild Application System

Most established guilds have a Web site and an application form or e-mail address that players can use to apply to join. However, not all players want to go through those processes to join a guild, but would prefer instead to handle the process within the game itself. Thus, the addition of an optional application system that a guild could choose to use would solve that player's need. The system could allow players to access information about a guild in game. Such a customizable requirements page where the guild could list its process and requirements to join would offer value to many guilds. That could optionally lead to a customizable form that players could fill out. That form could be viewable online by empowered members, and a copy could be sent to the Guildmaster via e-mail.

At the very least, including a customizable form that allows a guild to broadcast its requirements to join, its core values, and a list of what it feels it offers to gamers is a positive step for all players as they seek a guild to call home.

Web-Based Guild Management Tools

Guildmasters would be very pleased if given a set of guild management tools that could be accessed via the Internet. Allowing Guildmasters to log in to a secure Web site and then manage certain aspects of the guild system is definitely an added-value feature. Whether from work or school, or simply if the Guildmaster is unable to log in at that moment, being able to perform basic guild management functions offline can help resolve issues and strengthen guilds. Some of the features that could easily be handled via that secure Web page include:

- Removing a Member
- Promoting/Demoting a Member
- Setting the Message of the Day
- Managing the Powers Granted to Each Rank
- Adjusting Guild Dues Amount and Frequency
- Accessing the Guild Roster

Guild Flagged and Owned Equipment

Fighting over loot and the tension that develops when loot leaves a guild due to members quitting is a common and large source of issues for many guilds. One possible solution to the problem would be to add an option to flag pieces of loot as being owned by the guild. By way of example, if the über boss Vorpal Bunny was killed by a raid and dropped a rare sword, the leader of the raid could look inside the corpse, get the item's description, and have a checkbox on the item that flags it as "guild equipment." If this flag were to be checked, the guild that the raid leader belonged to would now own that item. What that means, in practical terms, is that whoever ends up looting the item is essentially borrowing it for an indefinite period of time. Should that person ever quit the guild or get kicked out, that item would be placed in the guild's bank box and could be given out to another member. If the item were deemed to be such that it should never be traded to anyone else, then upon quitting or being removed from the guild, the item would simply be removed from the game.

Guild Waypoints and Camp Markers

One of the drawbacks to online games is the inability to quickly and unambiguously define what a person means when he says "Go There!" A system of guild-placed waypoints and camp markers would help resolve that issue. A picture is said to be worth a thousand words, and a route marker and a camp spot marker could certainly save many words and headaches for guilds.

Empowered officers in the guild could be given the ability to create waypoints and/or camp spot markers that are visible to members of the guild in the main game window and on the member's map. Those markers could automatically expire after a period of time. The course to get from point A to point B could be plotted and the eventual raid/camp spot could be clearly marked. This would be of added value to all guilds that raid or to guilds and players that PvP regularly.

Guild Crests on Items

Another form of both player pride and guild pride (and is another "gold sink") would be the ability to create a guild crest, in game, and place that crest on items. *World of Warcraft*, for example, allows the Guildmaster to create a tabard in the guild's chosen colors and choose from a variety of emblems to place on it. All members can buy one and wear it. This system could be expanded to allow the guild's crest to be placed on shields, armor, cloaks, backpacks, and other items. If the ability to dye those items in the color of the guild were also added, it would give guilds an even greater ability to differentiate themselves from other groups and show guild pride while serving as a gold sink to help take currency out of the economy.

Rewarding Guildmasters

Asheron's Call attempted a model to reward Guildmasters for creating a successful guild. That model turned into a giant pyramid scheme, but the thought behind it was valid. Developing a strategy to reward a Guildmaster for creating and maintaining a stable guild is a valuable tool that developers should not overlook. Stable guilds result in longer term players. Having longer term players means more revenue for the developer. Guildmasters who have an additional "carrot" to work toward will be willing to invest more time in creating a stable guild, thus directly benefiting the game and the players. It would behoove a development team to put some thought into creative ways to reward Guildmasters without creating massive pyramid schemes within their gaming world. Caps on the max reward and rewards that are tied to longevity versus short-term results might solve that issue.

In-Game Guild Calendar

Adding the ability for guilds to add entries to a calendar that is displayed in game to members would be a great and very useful feature. Whether it is a hunt sponsored by a member, a guild raid, a wedding, or just someone's birthday, many guilds have events going on very frequently. A way to see those events in some sort of calendar format would be a useful tool. Externalizing that data to the Web and allowing the Guildmaster to add and remove entries via the Web-based guild tools (discussed previously) or perhaps link it to their Web site would be an even greater asset to guilds.

Conclusion

MMORPGs have been in existence for a number of years. Over that time, players have developed expectations on what a game needs to offer them from a guild management perspective. With an ever-increasing number of MMORPGs entering the market, often faster than old ones are retired, the competition for the pool of gamers is intense. One way to attract customers to a game is to provide a robust guild system that includes all of the features players require and innovative features that separate one game from another.

This article explored a number of mandatory features that players simply expect every game to have. Games that do not provide at least this basic set of features position themselves at a disadvantage to other games before the first subscription fee is ever taken.

This article also outlined a number of optional features that, if implemented, would add value to the gaming experience for players and guilds and help separate a MMORPG from other games on the market. These features are the ones players would like to have, but are currently offered by few, if any, games.

The idea behind all of the features discussed in this article is to make the guild entity more valuable to the player and thus promote guild stability. Guild stability means longer term player retention, which means more revenue for the developer. In addition, a wider and more comprehensive list of guild features is one factor guilds use when making the decision to choose one MMORPG over another.

1.8

A Stock Exchange-Inspired Commerce System

John M. Olsen—Infix Games

infix@xmission.com

One of the best resources for game ideas is the real world. There are examples everywhere of things that could make games better, if only we can figure out how to avoid the uninteresting bits. MMP games almost always have within them the concept of commerce between players, or a way for the players to buy and sell things within the game. In the simplest case, the game includes merchants who usually buy things for a fixed fraction of the normal sale price, and have infinite supplies of everything they sell.

This article deals with a much more interesting system where players can easily trade items among themselves, with only a small portion of the economy based on trading with computer-controlled market members. This is done using time-proven techniques gleaned from limit order techniques of stock and commodities markets of the real world, where players place items up for sale at a specific price, and can also place orders for items at a specific price, allowing the commerce software to match up the buyers and sellers as needed whether the players are online or not.

Applying these techniques to a game requires a handful of features. First, an inventory system that allows ownership of items is needed. In addition, you need a way to generate a unique identifier for any given object within the game, such that two items that are identical in all respects to the players will always produce the same tag. In the database world, this would be a key field in the table of allowed inventory items.

A final requirement is some sort of base currency used to conduct business. A fully barter-based system is possible, but is completely outside the scope of this article. Typically, games have a coinage system, either a single coin type that is used to measure all pricing, or a set of coins with different values such as copper, silver, and gold. Any coinage system works as long as the values of the coins are constant relative to each other.

Database

It is assumed that any full-scale MMP game will have some database engine to handle game and user data. This could range from the large-scale commercial databases to the free MySQL database system. The most efficient choice is to implement your commerce system using whatever database is already in use by the other facets of the game.

A small number of database tables will be needed for the commerce system to work. You will need a table of objects, a table of participants, and a table of orders listing things being bought and sold.

The first of these is the table of objects within the game, and it is likely to already exist in some form within the game design to keep track of the types of things players may own. One complication to this table is if your game uses compound objects, where multiple objects may be attached together temporarily or permanently to create a new object. As long as you also generate repeatable identifiers for your compound objects through direct lookup from those objects or by creating a virtual database entry for each compound object, everything will work out the same.

You may need to limit items allowed within the market system to those either owned by the player or already for sale by someone else to prevent players from "fishing" for item names in the game equipment database. The database will still contain all the possible items, but they will not be accessible until some player has that item and puts it into the commerce system.

The table of participants within the market system includes all players within the game, and borrows again from a table that is likely to already exist within the game design in a form that is very close to what you need. The only thing likely to be missing from your player list is a way to include nonplayer merchants within that list so you can have a single uniform interface for commerce between players, and between a player and a computer-controlled merchant.

Depending on your design, it may work better to have two separate tables of participants so you can segregate the player participants from the nonplayer merchants. You would then access the data through a view that joined the two into a single logical table.

The last table you need is a table of orders. This table holds all buy and sell orders of all the players and nonplayer merchants within the game.

Transactions

Commerce transactions can include four main actions: buying, selling, querying price, and canceling orders. Buy and sell actions may result in instantaneous transactions if objects with matching prices exist in the market, and otherwise result in long-term database entries until a matching action is found. Price queries instantly access these database entries to report quantities for sale, quantities desired, and price. Cancellations provide a way to remove buy and sell actions from the market.

With both buy and sell transactions, you can easily force a First In First Out (FIFO) transaction order by controlling the traversal of your transaction table when searching for matches. That way, if two buy orders for an item have the same price, the one that has waited the longest would be filled.

Buy

To greatly simplify things, buy orders may be either a market order where the buyer simply pays the lowest currently listed sale price, or a limit order where the buyer specifies his desired price. All buy orders should look for items only in the current list of objects being sold through the transaction table.

Due to the inherent risk associated with market orders, you should not include them as an option because of the support issues it could generate. If two identical items are for sale, one for a single coin and one for thousands, it would cause a great deal of stress to have the cheap one be sold right before a player placed a market buy order for that item and got stuck with paying thousands of times more than he had planned. By eliminating market orders, you simply tell the second player that the item was no longer available at his requested price.

The recommended way to allow players to buy items is using a limit order, where the players specify a limit on how much they are willing to pay for the item. It could very well be that they end up paying less for the item, but they will never pay more than their limit.

Buy orders will always go through immediately if the item is for sale with sufficient quantities below or equal to the player's specified price. When buying items, the application searches the outstanding sell orders, counts up the purchased quantity starting at the cheapest, and stops when the limit price is less than the offered sale price or when the desired quantity is reached. This is shown in the pseudo-code later in this section.

Once the desired quantity is reached, or the desired price is exceeded, or the player can buy no more of the item, the current transaction will be completed. If the player did not receive the quantity he wanted, the order is saved in the transaction table for later purchase with an appropriately reduced quantity.

It may be that you want to add an "all or nothing" option, where an order is never partially filled. The order would be saved in the transaction table until the entire amount could be purchased. The added complexity would need to be weighed against the extra functionality. This feature is not included in the following pseudocode.

As a matter of convenience, you can populate your order form limit price with the current lowest price for the object being ordered by the player. In most cases, this will be what the player wants to do, so the added convenience will make the transaction easier for the player.

```
Quantity_wanted = order size
Limit = player's maximum allowed cost per item
For each matching item in the Sell Order list,
```

```
      sorted cheapest first
            Quantity_available = count in the sell order
            Quantity_allowed = (int) (available_funds /
                                      Sell Order price per unit)
            If(Quantity_allowed > Quantity_wanted)
                  Quantity_allowed = Quantity_wanted
            Price_each = unit price for this Sell Order
            If(Quantity_allowed < 1)
                  //Player can't afford any more.
                  //Done processing this order.
                  Break
            If Limit < Sell Order price per unit
                  //Remaining items cost more than limit.
                  //Done processing this order.
                  Break
            If quantity_available > Quantity_allowed
                  //Player will buy part of the sell order
                  Quantity_this_Seller = Quantity_allowed
                  Value = Quantity_this_Seller * price_each
                  Charge buyer for Value
                  Credit Sell Order owner with Value
                  Sell Order quantity -= Quantity_allowed
            Else
                  //Player will buy the entire Sell Order
                  Quantity_this_Seller = Entire Sell Order
                  Value = Quantity_this_Seller * price_each
                  Charge buyer for Value
                  Credit Sell Order owner with Value
                  Delete Sell Order since it is now empty
            Quantity_wanted -= Quantity_this_Seller
      If Quantity_wanted > 0
            //Player wanted more than they got
            Create a Buy Order for Quantity_wanted at Limit
```

Sell

When entered, sell orders only look for items in the list of unfilled buy orders to see how much can be sold immediately. The highest priced buy orders are searched first for matches. The actual sale price can easily exceed the seller's specified limit because the price paid is that listed by the buyer. For example, if someone will pay 500 for something, and you offer one for 400, you will get the offered price rather than your limit price. No sales will occur for buyers offering less than the seller's limit price.

To sell items when the sell order is first entered, count the quantity to sell starting at the most expensive unfilled buy order, and stop when the limit price is greater than the offered purchase price or when the desired quantity is reached. As with buy orders, any remaining quantity will be stored as an outstanding sell order that will be looked at each time someone wants to buy that type of item.

```
      Quantity_to_sell = order size
      Limit = player's maximum allowed cost per item
      For each matching item in the Buy Order list,
      sorted most expensive first
```

```
Order_Quantity_wanted = count in the buy order
Price_each = unit price for this Buy Order
If Quantity_to_sell < 1
        //Player sold them all
        //Done processing this order.
        Break
If Limit > Buy Order price per unit
        //Remaining items offer too little.
        //Done processing this order.
        Break
If Order_quantity_wanted > Quantity_to_sell
        //Player will sell all they have.
        Quantity_this_Buyer = Quantity_to_sell
        Value = Quantity_this_Buyer * price_each
        // Reduce the quantity that buyer wants.
        Order_quantity_wanted -= Quantity_this_Buyer
        Charge Buy Order owner for Value
        Credit seller for Value
Else
        //Player will sell some and fill order
        Quantity_this_Buyer = Order_quantity_wanted
        Value = Quantity_this_Buyer * price_each
        Charge Buy Order owner for Value
        Credit seller for Value
        Delete Buy Order since it is now empty
Quantity_to_sell -= Quantity_this_Buyer
If Quantity_to_sell > 0
        //leftover un-sold quantity
        Create a Sell Order for Quantity_to_sell at Limit
```

Price Query

Any in-game commerce system needs a way to query for current prices and quantities available for sale, as well as the prices and quantities for outstanding unfilled buy orders. Price queries will happen with high frequency, so it is a good thing that it simply reads from the database, as that is much faster than transactions that require writing to the database.

As in the real world, there is no such thing as a guaranteed price quote. It could be that you checked the price just before someone bought the item that was offered at that price, making it no longer available at that price. The best you can know is the current price at the time of inquiry.

It is possible to allow locks to be placed on items to temporarily guarantee prices, but that additional complexity is not likely to be needed. The economy will probably be paced slowly enough that players will usually get the prices they see in a quote when they buy an item a short time later.

Cancel

Players should be able to cancel an order at any time, but need to be aware that a transaction could occur before they do. It would be particularly convenient to offer users a way to cancel all outstanding orders, rather than making them go through one by one.

Canceling either a buy or sell order consists of just removing the specific order from the orders database table.

Other Transactions

There is a host of other possible transactions that mirror things you can do with a real brokerage, but for a game, most of them are overkill that can be safely ignored. This includes such things as options, futures, and investment funds. Adding those to a game doesn't sound particularly appealing, as they can be a lot of work on the programming side, and confusing on the customer side.

Processing Trades

One great advantage to this system is that there is no need for players to be connected to the game for trades to occur, and when connected they do not necessarily need to be in a particular area of the game dedicated to trading.

Players may set up a series of trades at the end of their gaming session, and then disconnect from the game. Upon returning to the game later, they can check the status of their trades to see how things are going.

From a software perspective, trades can only occur when a new buy or sell order is placed. The system does not need to continually check for matches between buyers and sellers. This is because the only way for a price to suddenly come into the range of a player's order is for someone to have placed that order. This simplifies the coding of the system so the more expensive checks and database modifications only happen when an order is actually placed. This reliance on user input helps to distribute the load over time automatically due to the random nature of players connecting and disconnecting over time.

Should you have a way to directly modify the buy and sell orders of computer-controlled merchants, you will want to implement those as canceling and re-entering the order so the system traverses the database properly looking for new trades that can occur at the new price. Directly modifying the table of active orders can cause problems where items that could be traded are not.

One absolute requirement for this commerce system to work properly in processing trades is that the buy and sell orders must be done serially with a single process rather than distributed across a network or run in parallel. This requirement protects the system from item duplication schemes where multiple players attempt to buy an item at the same time. Unfortunately, it also limits the trading volume to what a single dedicated commerce server can do, but a single database access point is likely able to handle many transactions per second with a database designed with well-chosen keys. It would also be possible to warn players if the transaction backlog begins to grow, and either cancel the transaction or let the player know that it could be a little while before his transaction is completed.

World of Warcraft has a commerce system that has several similarities in the way it processes trades, and bears investigation as a system that includes many of the key features mentioned here.

Reports

The game creator is responsible for tracking the in-game economy, and identifying areas of potential trouble within the game. A consistent and well-designed set of reports and graphs can aid greatly in keeping track of the economy. They can be used to track prices of the commonly traded game items to better understand how the full economy is faring.

Charts and graphs are also very useful to players, so you should consider allowing players to access the data, such as graphs of an item's value over time. Giving this information to the players can aid in making the economy more self-balancing, because players will be able to see areas where there is an imbalance in prices due to new supplies of materials, or when supplies are reduced. This will, however, increase the burden on the game administrators and designers to notice and quickly fix pricing mistakes, and cases of pricing and commerce abuse.

A report that finds rapid price swings or sudden quantity spikes or drops can alert you to players taking advantage of corner cases you might not otherwise find. This could be the result of a new addition to the game that dramatically alters the value of other items because of ways in which multiple items can interact. You could also have a computer-controlled vendor configured incorrectly that overpays or undercharges for an item. A good report system can catch all of these cases to help keep things flowing smoothly.

Another thing that can prove very useful is a set of reports listing the top owners, buyers, and sellers for any given item. This can help you track down game loopholes as soon as players start to take advantage of them by highlighting the sudden increase in volume on an item, or when a particular player starts buying or selling a lot of an item that was previously rare or rarely traded.

Game Balance

Some issues will always need attention due to griefers who will try to damage the game in any way they can. Hoarding of items could lead to them being very scarce, allowing players to demand huge amounts for a normally common item. These issues are best solved with computer-controlled vendors that can be configured to put clamps on the minimum and maximum prices for any given item by placing both a buy and sell order for that item.

For example, a computer vendor may offer an item for sale at a price of 100 and buy it at a price of 50. That would force all players to list the item for less than 100 in order to sell it, and a buy order for less than 50 would probably never get filled because players will sell to the vendor first.

Computer-controlled vendors with price clamps can also be used to slow or prevent price inflation and deflation since they can hold the price for a particular item to a reasonable range, no matter what else happens to the game economy. These computer vendors can also prevent hoarding of basic commodities by always offering them for sale at a standardized price.

It is also very important to control how rare objects enter the game, making it difficult for a particular player or group to corner the market and dictate the price for an item. Certain market-upsetting behaviors such as cornering the market and hoarding can also be discouraged by not allowing a player to simultaneously have both buy orders and sell orders for the same item. Allowing such practices could essentially force all players to buy the item at an inflated sale price if you are not careful to randomize the buy and sell orders at a given price when determining who is matched up for a transaction.

If your economy has too many cash sources and not enough cash sinks (places to spend money where there is no permanent item obtained), you can charge a transaction fee for each order placed to pull money back out of the economy. Since you don't want to artificially increase the price of cheap items excessively, a percentage could be worked into the transactions to slightly inflate the cost of items that a buyer must pay, while maintaining the current amount given to the seller.

One game balance issue you will need to address is the choice of when players are allowed to buy and sell items, and when they are allowed to pick up things they purchased. One easy way to keep players from selling their high-end loot while camped at the bottom of the dungeon in which they found it is to force players to be in a trading area to pick up bought items, and require them to be there when they place buy and sell orders. Items being sold must be removed from the players' active game inventory, so they can't carry around something they are selling.

Conclusion

While not suited to all types of MMP games, many game designs would benefit from a trade system based on current stock markets. The stock exchanges of the world are part of a system that has been proven through long-standing use, although some care must be taken to prevent a market crash just as in the real world.

It also pays to know where to simplify your economy and where to leave complexity in for the players. As a general rule, leave out the boring, tedious, time-consuming or difficult parts of reality. Few players will want to spend time micromanaging their account when they could be playing with friends.

As you implement your economy, you can gain a great deal of loyalty from your player base. You give them a real stake in the behavior of the game economy while still keeping things within reasonable bounds with both your automated price limits and your reports and graphs to identify and quickly correct abuses and unintended pricing problems within your economy.

1.9

Alternatives to the Character Grind

Artie Rogers—NCSoft

artie.rogers@gmail.com

One of the unique design challenges facing an MMOG developer is how to provide compelling gameplay in such a way that customers want to spend months and even years playing the game. Attempting to do this often becomes a balancing act between providing enough rewards for time investment rapidly enough to encourage the player to continue investing time, and controlling the rate at which rewards are granted to avoid adversely impacting the perceived value of the reward by getting it too quickly and preventing the player from exhausting the current supply of rewards. Primarily, the rewards in an MMOG come in the form of some content, whether that content comes in the form of new hunting or questing areas, or simply exposure or access to new character or game systems. This act of careful content management with an eye toward rewarding time invested is key to the success of building a strong connection between the player and the game. The core problem is that players will consume content as quickly as they are allowed. One way to solve this problem is to simply control the speed at which that content is released or becomes available to the player. A common tactic used to achieve this is to use the customer's character as the key to content, meaning as the character increases in level, the player gains access to more of the game. Developers then attempt to control the speed at which the player advances through the character levels, thereby limiting the amount of content the customer can consume over a given time period. This technique of tying content release to character advancement is commonly referred to as controlling content through a Character Grind.

In a general sense, a Grind refers to the situation whereby the player performs a group of related actions that are viewed by the player as primarily a means to an end, and whose main design functions are as a method of controlling the release of content or as an object for time investment. One can see the inherent value of Grind elements in an online game just by its definition. Time investment is often related to perceived value in an object, a psychological effect that the Grind seeks to exploit. In addition, the time required to execute this Grind helps to control the release of content. As in the case of the Character Grind, the character becomes the single key to content. This is the case as characters below a certain level are functionally excluded from particular areas of the game until they achieve the target level. The Character Grind is typically modeled after the *Dungeons & Dragons* system of advancement with some actions contributing to an experience pool; when the players hit a certain threshold of experience, their base abilities and/or skills are added to or improved. This article outlines the purpose behind the Character Grind, highlights some of the inherent weaknesses with that design focus, and offers a host of alternatives to the Character Grind that will serve to vary gameplay experiences for the customer.

Goals of the Character Grind

The Character Grind achieves several goals for the designer:

- It becomes the key to content management.
- It provides incremental content rewards related to the character's advancement.
- It gives a central object for time investment.
- With the first and second goals, it provides incentive to the player to Grind in the game.

Commonly, the player's primary game goal is increasing the character's access to game content, which is meted out in carefully measured amounts through advancing the character's base skill set. This rewards the players just enough for them to continue to Grind on the character, thereby gaining access to more game content and so on. The Character Grind is useful as being the key to managing content, and to give regular content-based rewards, and also gives the player an object for time investment. As the time invested in a character increases, so does the perceived value of that character. This increased perceived value helps to strengthen the connection between the player and the game. The Character Grind is a very useful and appealing design technique simply because it allows the designer to provide a solution to a number of MMOG problems in a single system.

Problems with the Character Grind

However, there are also a number of problems inherent in most Character Grind systems. These problems are not always evident in all the manifestations of the Character Grind, but they commonly occur in mainstream MMOGs:

- Level Separation
- Grind-related activities viewed as only a means to an end
- Placing responsibility of content management in the players' hands
- If relied upon too heavily, gameplay variety becomes diminished
- Time investment burden required to slow content consumption

The first major problem with the Character Grind is that if the content's availability is linked to character ability or advancement, and this advancement is controlled by the time spent in the game, there's the real possibility that social groups will fracture, as some players will have access to content that others do not because some members have more time to invest. This phenomenon is commonly referred to as *Level Separation.*

The next problem with the Character Grind is that it commonly means that the activities related to character advancement or world interaction lose their entertainment value by the very nature of being a Grind. If the activities are designed to be a means to an end, the players will perceive them as such, and attention to the activity itself is lost as the player only looks to the end reward.

Another common problem with the Character Grind is that it puts the responsibility of content management in the hands of the player. This becomes a problem because the game design must slow content release to fit the advancement speed of the players who spend the most time in the game so that they won't consume all of the available content too quickly, while at the same time trying to provide enough content to the casual players to keep them satisfied.

The final problem with the Character Grind to be touched on here is the time requirement that many MMOGs ask of their players in order to advance their characters. This time investment requirement can be prohibitive since it is gauged to the hardcore audience, which is needed for the Character Grind to fulfill its purpose of content management. These problems commonly found with the Character Grind prompts one to want to explore other methods of providing effective content management.

Alternatives to the Character Grind

Remembering what the Character Grind provides and its problems is important in exploring options to it. There are many advantages to seeking alternative ways to achieve the goals of the Character Grind:

- It can eliminate the problem of Level Separation.
- It allows the designer to provide more avenues for content releasing gameplay.
- It allows the designer to explore other mechanisms to manage content, thereby alleviating some of the time burden from the player.
- It allows the designer to provide a wider variety of gameplay, which is valuable in itself, resulting in a more diverse and interesting gameplay experience for the player.

A number of different alternatives to the Character Grind achieve many and sometimes all of the same goals. This article explores Character Grind alternatives such as:

- Using Collections as both a key to content management and character advancement.
- Using the passage of real time as a method of content management.
- Providing for a variety of online projects, which may or may not relate to exposure to new content, for both groups and individuals.

All can be used as effective alternatives to the Character Grind without inheriting the common problems associated with it.

Collections

Collections are very common throughout the history of games and hobbies, and there are several current examples of their popularity in games, both computer and table-top. Collections can be used as a form of character advancement and expression, in terms of new actions or enhancements, or can simply be a tool of social expression. One could argue that the most powerful collection isn't one that impacts the character's abilities, but is simply sought because of the interest in the item in and of itself. There are many examples of how Character, Social, and Item Collections could be realized in a game, and how they can achieve the same goals as the Character Grind while avoiding many of the associated problems.

Character Collections

Character Collections are related to the advancement or improvement of base character skills and abilities. They can be used to replace conventional Character Advancement with a Base Skill Collection, or they could be the primary method of skill enhancement for the player with Skill Augmentation Collections. Both methods can alleviate many of the traditional Character Grind problems.

With Base Skill Collections, the player collects in-game items to gain access to new character skills. This can replace a traditional RPG advancement system in part or completely. The players could either be completely dependent on these new skill items to advance their abilities, or the design could employ a combination of moving through a traditional advancement system and finding these skill items. This example will explore a system that completely departs from the traditional advancement system. This system most resembles the card collection games. For example, the players will collect skill cards or objects. Each object corresponds to a specific character ability. While the total number of collectibles is large, players are limited in terms of how many cards they can have active on their character at any one time. Player will have a bank to draw from to compile their "active" deck. In this way, the character's skill becomes bounded in that all players have the same number of active skills. The abilities can therefore be balanced in terms of inherent strength across the board. The veteran gamer advantage comes through their flexibility, which is gained by having a larger bank of cards at their disposal. This collection method is powerful in a number of different ways:

- Level Separation is diminished because each player can only have a certain set of cards active at any one time.
- Working to a full collection is a time-consuming task, as each card will have a different method governing its availability from base rarity to some time restriction on availability.
- Designers can augment the available card pool once the game is live.
- Designers can control the rarity of any single card or card group.
- Players invest time into the skill object bank, thus enhancing their character value yet not fundamentally increasing the character's power.

Many of the currently popular card collection games work off this design to great success, as they have a wide audience of players who spend time collecting cards, while trying to perfect the cards in their "active" deck.

With a Skill Augmentation Collection, the player collects objects that are only related to skill enhancements. This doesn't address the problem of Level Separation, as it only deals with the enhancement of existing character skills. However, it can provide an avenue for time investment that, if designed properly, will not adversely affect the balance of character power within a certain skill range. Collections of this kind can be a very powerful tool as an incentive to enhance the skill increases the character experiences through level advancement. *Diablo*, *EverQuest*, and other popular RPG-style games use these skill-enhancing collections to great, positive result either through collecting parts that require assembly to activate or in the form of rare objects that bring the augmentation with their use. They could manifest as a combination of those ideas, such as a rare usable object that is part of a set of objects that can provide an additional benefit once all the objects of a set are found and used. Here are a few examples of augmentation object effects when used or equipped:

- Enhance a given skill, such as increase damage or increase rate of attack.
- Enhance a given attribute, such as increasing endurance, so players can take more damage or run further.
- Enhance a given skill or attribute for all the players in the group who fit a certain criteria.
- Provide protection against a certain class of attacks, such as immunity to fire.
- Provide some visible effect such as invisibility.

As you can see, these objects don't have to be limited to adjusting attributes or skills. They could be used for group augmentation or for altering the appearance of the player for gameplay or social reasons. Skill Augmentation Collections are a powerful incentive to exploration and achievement as players seek to improve their abilities while working on advancing in level.

Item Collections

Item Collections are classified as such because they do not fundamentally alter the abilities of the character in terms of granting new skills or augmenting existing skills. Instead, these items center more on social activities. Prestigious Item Collection and Entertainment Item Collection are two examples of such social-centric collections.

Prestigious Item Collections are simply collections of a pool of items that represent some in-game achievement. These items could also be thought of as Trophies. These items give an alternative form of reward to the player who seeks to gain fame within his local game community by collecting them. There are several examples of these kinds of items. Some of the "rares" from *EverQuest* are items of prestige that also affect character abilities. They fill a dual function as items that increase character abilities and as items that communicate the character's achievements to the community. The prestige aspect is a huge draw for many players above and beyond the skill increase they enjoy. The acquisition of these items could be linked to the defeat of some unique enemy, or could be linked to the completion of some mission campaign. These items could also be linked to exploration, in the form of an item that is only found in some remote or difficult to find location. It's also possible to distribute these items through some in-game competition, such as a skill competition against the computer or another player. The Prestige items are important because they enhance the social aspect of the game. They universally communicate achievement to other members of the community, giving the player pride in the community and increased perceived value in his character, and providing a goal to which other players can aspire.

Another type of item collection that can lead to great benefit is the Entertainment Item Collection. These items consist of objects that provide some unique entertainment value, such as objects that provide in-game lights, particles, or music when used. Their effect in terms of appeal and complexity could stack as a player found more pieces of the collection. *Animal Crossing* does this to great effect with the musical plants. Another example could be an assortment of in-game orb objects the player collects. Orbs of this collection would produce a musical note and a light effect when used. There would be a collection board into which the player could insert the orbs. When the player uses the board, the series of notes would play in order. When placed in a special order, the notes would be played and dynamic lights displayed to represent a song of the player's creation. In this way, the player would be motivated to expand his collection to better entertain members of his community. This kind of collection helps to enhance the social ties by providing an interesting outlet for entertainment, and as with every collection, the time invested relates to the perceived value of the ollection.

Entertainment Item Collections and Prestigious Item Collections are two Collection types that stress the social potential of the collection on an individual level.

Social Collections

MMOGs are, by nature, very social games, whether or not people actively choose to interact with that society. With that in mind, one should remember that collections don't always have to involve physical objects that the player collects. Therefore, while the Item Collections refer to items that might have some social role, these collections refer to a collection of Social Connections or Social Approvals. These Social Collections could be based on an individual or on a group level. Plenty of incentive can be provided in either case.

The most obvious Social Collection that one could include in an MMOG design is Social Connection Collection. This collection could manifest itself in several different ways, from collecting fealty from a group of followers, to amassing a complex social network, to lobbying the local game community to vote for you in an online game election.

One example of a Social Connection Collection can be seen in the *Asheron's Call* fealty system. It demonstrates the power of campaigning for peer fealty in the game. Players swore fealty, which created a pyramid structure of shared experience with benefits rising exponentially as the fealty network grew in size. In this case, the benefits were directly related to character growth through an experience-based system, and it worked well for what it was. A criticism might be that the system would have been more effective if the group, as a whole, would have gained some guaranteed benefit by size as well, instead of having all the system granted benefits move upward. However, it is a good example of a Social Connection Collection that gives strong incentive to create a social group.

The Sims demonstrated the interesting appeal of working for social acceptance as a barrier of advancement and a content management tool. Granted, this was in a single-player environment, but the same principles for the collection of Social Connections could apply to an online game. Borrowing from that example, Social Connections could be one barrier for advancement down a particular path. For example, a player could be working up the ladder at a magician's guild. To advance down that path, the player would have to collect a certain number of social connections within the guild as part of the requirement for advancement. One could leverage this tactic in a different manner by allowing the players to build social networks in the way in which online networking services function by connecting friends together through their relations to other people. In this example, an individual player's power and value to a community would increase with the size of his social network. A community's abilities would be influenced by its collective connections. In this case, that individual's value to the community is based on his social network. This value gives incentive to the player to grow his own collection of connections, and drive the community to strengthen and expand its own social network by courting those players with the larger social networks.

Voting is an easy incentive to expand one's collection of Social Approval. For example, a player could join a local game community by being accepted into a player-established city, and then to gain standing within the community, the player must acquire votes from a certain number of citizens of that city. The player is encouraged to establish a wide variety of social ties within the community to garner the necessary votes. The elected position is attractive since it is used to gain access to new content that could be in the form of new system functionality, such as various governmental controls, or government buildings whose access is limited to social status within that community determined by a certain number of votes.

These Social Connection or Approval Collections easily translate into a guild activity. The collection could be encouraged by having guild membership size as a prerequisite for gaining a guild house, or perhaps guild size could be a requirement for some larger activity. It could also be seen in a community's attempt to increase its city size to gain access to other content in terms of systems, group-wide benefits, and other incentives. These benefits could manifest themselves in the form of self-governing tools, or the city itself, once it reached a certain size, could allow players to open portals to different game spaces not otherwise accessible to the game community. If the players within that guild or community want to gain access to that content, they will have to meet predetermined levels of Social Connections.

Collections can be a powerful and flexible tool when designing systems that require time investment and control the release of content. They serve as a possible alternative to the typical Grind.

Real-World Time Control to Advancement

Another very powerful tool to use in content management and controlling character advancement is simply using a Real-Time Element. The passage of time is a system with which players are familiar and will accept if the rule is established from the onset. Introducing time as a hard rule to any system gives the designers exacting control over the advancement of the game population in a certain skill and the consumption rate of content. These two areas are not left to the ingenuity of the player base to shortcut the system, which they would be if they were governed by a Grind-based system. Time passage is a strict phenomenon that cannot be circumvented even by the most resourceful player. Time passage can be used to reasonably control the release of certain content, and can also be used to govern the rate of character advancement. Using the passage of real time grants the developers several advantages in that it provides tight control over any system and understandable and predictable controls to the player.

Seasonal/Environmental

One method of using time to manage content release is by linking events to certain time periods of the day, week, month, or year. This can be in terms of an object's availability or of a system's activation. There are several examples of how this system can function in a game under different time periods.

One could limit access to certain flora or fauna to particular months or seasons of the year. This allows a developer to logically control the release of content over the year. Players are familiar with that behavior because it mimics real-world interactions; it is this familiarity that makes the system easier to accept. Certain flora and certain fauna are only available during certain seasons of the year. Some plants will only bear fruit during certain seasons of the year, and some animals might spawn in different regions according to season. *Animal Crossing* uses this technique very effectively. Many of the creatures that a player collects in *Animal Crossing* are only available at certain time periods during the year, and simply don't exist in the game world outside of that time period.

It can also be useful to control content access on a smaller time scale than seasonally or monthly. One could also control access to certain game spaces simply by time of day. This is also a system that *Animal Crossing* used, and more interestingly, it harkens back to some of the older *Ultima* games. In these games, access to some objects or game systems is limited by time of day inside the game, which is translated to some real-time passage. The stores are also only open for business during certain times of each day. Another example from the *Ultima* series is that some content was limited due to the phases of a pair of fictional moons. Each moon would cycle through phases according to a real-time schedule, and certain locations were only available when each moon was in certain phase. In that way, content access was limited and its consumption was controlled.

Introducing seasonally sensitive events and tying access to some content to real-time passage is a very controlled and understandable system of content release at the developer's disposal.

Character Advancement

Time can also be useful when controlling the advancement rate of a character. If the developer wants to rely on character level being the primary key to releasing content, time can be a very powerful tool in making the consumption of that content predictable. It can also be very useful when appealing to those players with limited time available to play the game, because they aren't as penalized for not having time to play. There are a few general ways in which time can be introduced in acceptable ways.

A well-known method of controlling character advancement in MMOGs is using what is referred to as the "Full Brain" advancement control, which is the advancement restriction that allows a character to advance a set amount over a certain time period. This type of control can be hard or soft, meaning its limits can be hard or disincentives may activate after a certain amount of advancement has been achieved. There are several examples of the soft "Full Brain" system being experimented with in the MMOGs, such as *Ultima Online*'s "Power Hour" and more recently with *World of Warcraft*'s resting recommendations. Both systems offer the introduction of real-time controls of advancement and have experienced differing degrees of success.

Another way to introduce a time element into character advancement is to link advancement through in-game occurrences or to the completion of an in-game event. For example, a training school exists in the game that is only accessible during specific seasons, and the training requires several days to complete before the player has access to the new level skills, in which case a game day translates to a certain time period in real time. This same effect could be achieved by creating an "absorption" time where the player acquires the new skill, but it only becomes fully useful after a real-time period has passed. These rigid time controls on advancement help tremendously when planning a release schedule for content.

The introduction of a real-time element into character advancement gives the designer exacting control over the advancement rate of the player base. In this way, the designer can better manage the release and consumption of content and can limit the effects of level separation as time invested has less of an impact.

Online Projects

The act of Grinding can be a powerful tool in building game loyalty and increasing the customer's perception of the grind object's value, whether that object is the character, a pet, or an in-game house. It is beneficial to consider placing Grinding activities into areas of the game other than character advancement to avoid the problems associated with Character grinding. Two general groups of online projects would be those designed for the individual and those designed for groups or the community at large.

Individual Projects

The Individual Online project is an important class of gameplay of which the Character Grind is a member. The two key attributes to an Individual Project are that it should require regular time investment, and should provide the player with regular feedback communicating progress, both of which will increase the perceived value of the final product. One can refer to real-world hobbies for inspiration when creating effective Individual Project; hobbies such as crafts, pets, and gardening can prove to be useful guides. There are several different ways an Individual Project can manifest itself in an MMOG.

A Pet system is a useful and proven way to provide renewable gameplay that requires a certain time investment and provides regular feedback to the player as he commits to the training or rearing of a pet. The player would teach the pet various actions or series of actions, some of which might affect gameplay and others that would be purely social. The player would be required to care for the pet, expending time and resources on its upbringing and training. The value of the pet would grow with the cost and time invested in its upkeep and training. The strength of the connection between player and pet is demonstrated regularly in and out of computer games. Introducing a Pet system achieves many of the goals that the Character Grind seeks to solve.

A different Individual Project similar to the Pet system would be a Gardening system. In this example, the player would need to have a home location where he can interact with a defined segment of land, planting and growing various appropriate plants. The player could choose to plant any sampled flora in the land area he governs. Each plant would require a different resource to grow. The plants would require regular interaction, and progress could be tracked by regular appearance changes, such as browning of the leaves for abusive upkeep, and vibrant greens and blooming flowers for exceptional care. The plants would yield some useful adventuring items or social items, such as healing berries or glowing fruit.

Another example of an effective system of Individual Projects is a Crafting system. The Crafting system supplies an activity that requires some time investment. It gives the players results from their labors, in which many players take pride. Invariably, with any Crafting system or trade heavy system, a social environment emerges from the players who are interested in that aspect of the game. The presence of a Crafting community and society can provide another barrier to exit in addition to the perceived value of the character and the crafted objects that can come from the time invested in their creation.

Individual Projects provide important tools to keep the player interested and invested in the game. They provide activities that can be done without group coordination, and a central object for time investment. They can also inspire community creation. Individual Projects solve many of the problems that face the Grind design of MMOs.

Community Projects

Community Projects can be just as effective as Individual Projects in creating a place for time investment, regularly communicating progress, and providing an effective

Grind location. However, the unique strength of the Community Project is that it can appeal to many players at the same time. Providing a centralized goal and purpose to a group can help serve to solidify the social bonds between the members of the community. A number of different example projects can provide all the benefits of the Character Grind and more.

Advancing a Guild House is a Community Project on which players can Grind, as a group, and see the fruits of their labors. The Guild House would require a certain level of resources, crafters of a certain skill level, and a guild of a certain size before it could be constructed. Beyond its initial construction, upgrading the Guild House could follow the same creation process, and upgrades could affect size and bonus functionality. For example, a Guild House that has increased in level might have an altar room where guild members can receive a daily buff. The Guild House would become the key to content and elder game systems, as a Guild House could grant access to portals to new areas of gameplay or be the starting point of some conquest-styled elder gameplay. The advancement of the Guild House would be affected by any level of resource contribution, thereby empowering members of all skill levels to contribute to the project's success. Advancing a Guild House gives a centralized community project that will act as a time sink, provide visual and functional feedback to progress, and serve to strengthen the bonds between guild members as they each contribute to the achievement of a common goal.

Regional warfare is another unifying project that could involve the entire community or guild. For example, the game map is divided into discrete zones that each community could possess at any one time. To invade a given zone, the community would first need to amass a certain amount of energy, which is measured by contributed resources such as money, items, or raw resources. To invade a zone, the community would have to pay the cost to invade in energy. Each zone has an associated cost relative to its value, which would be calculated by creature difficulty, the rarity of resources, the presences of portals inside the zone, and any group benefits that come with possession of a zone. For example, a zone could be costly, relative to other zones, if it held a wide spread of creature difficulty, an access portal to an underground mine with rare resources, and an enchanted area that grants benefits to the crafters of the community and grants a bonus to those who craft within the enchanted area. Once the community decides to invade, the members of both (if the zone is already occupied) communities are notified, and within a set time period, a contest will be held to determine who will control the region. The contest is a player-versus-player (PvP) contest on an isolated map with defined conditions of victory. Once the winner is determined, that region becomes accessible only to members of the winning guild. The time invested impacts the perceived value of the guild empire and the recently taken region. As in the last example, the reliance on the community will strengthen bonds as members work toward a common goal. Any character of any level or any skill distribution can contribute to the success of the community.

Another idea that achieves the same goals as the conquest is one where the community works to advance a City. For example, the City begins as a tiny collection of huts with a single NPC. The players can interact with that NPC to run various tasks or quests. The results affect the NPC's satisfaction with the city, which increases with each quest completed. Once the NPC is of a certain satisfaction rating, another NPC will join the city showing it has increased in level. This NPC will take up residence in the city and bring with it some inherent benefit to the community, such as being a Tinker or Trader, which gives characters local access to a vendor. The players would then work on increasing the satisfaction rating of the new NPC. Once both NPCs reach a certain satisfaction rating, another NPC will join the city, and thus the city will grow in level, size, and function. The City becomes a gateway to new systems and content. For example, a new NPC might come into town and establish a training center that opens access to a new Skill pool for the players. Another NPC could enter town and be responsible for the construction of a portal that gives access to a new gaming region to the community. If the city required tasks to be completed and resources to be committed to it, it would provide a unity of purpose and bonding cause for all the members. Developers could use this City as the key to content, and it would fulfill the time investment and social enhancing roles of a Community Project.

Guild House, Conquest, and City Development are just a few ideas that fit within the goals of a Community Project.

Examples of Using Those Ideas in Combination

All of these ideas were presented as basic building blocks, but they can come together as a combination of different ideas and restrictions. Here are some additional suggestions about how to combine the previous ideas into workable Grind alternatives:

- Using the collection of skill objects to control character advancement could benefit from a real-time element. The developers could create a Skill Object release schedule to carefully control the game community's access to certain skills.
- Acquiring achievement badges could benefit from a real-time component. Players can gather these badges at a measured pace. These badges indicate the completion of an in-game event or series of events, or they could represent the position within a system-run organization or guild.
- A time element would logically fit into the idea of the Community Project of Conquest or City Advancement. Developers could create time limits on the number of regions that could be invaded in a given time period. With regard to City Advancement, it's possible to have NPCs construct their own dwellings and have that process take a certain amount of real time. In the latter case, it might be useful to give the players some limited control over how long that process will take by having them burn resources in an effort to expedite the process.
- The idea of collections would be useful in the idea of City Advancement. Developers could create dual-use objects, ones that have a use in City Advancement and some use in a mini-game. These objects would take on some community interest while retaining the importance of the mini-game competitions, if players had to wager a game piece.

Conclusion

Many useful design theories came together to create the current form of the Character Grind. Influences from old role-playing games, to psychological theories of value and attachment, to second- and third-generation MMOs who try to make the Grind better all have contributed to the current assortment of issues related to employing the Character Grind. The negatives it can bring to an online game many times outweigh the benefits seeing as the benefits can be achieved in a variety of ways. Many developers suffer under the negatives operating with the erroneous assumption that the Character Grind must be part of their design. There's no reason why these theories and design beliefs can't be realized in a variety of different ways within an online game. Providing different Grind objects and Grind alternatives allows developers to avoid the problems that are a by-product of the Character Grind.

1.10

Telling Stories in Online Games

Shannon Appelcline—Skotos

shannona@skotos.net

Artwork initially attracts players to our games, and *gameplay* keeps them there day after day, month after month. However, a third element gives us the most opportunity to expand our games beyond the narrow niches they currently inhabit, an element that's largely ignored in many games—storytelling.

Storytelling

Storytelling can truly enthuse our players, leading them to encourage friends to play, and can make our games something that will be remembered not just next week or next year, but for decades to come.

The most successful storytelling games of decades past make this clear. Most designers of our generation remember the *Ultima* games well: the interactions with Lord British, the virtues of the avatar, and the many people and places met during the quests required by the game. Likewise, other games with solid bases in storytelling stand out, among them *King's Quest*, with its plots heavily based on fairy tales and folk lore; *Adventure: The Colossal Cave*, with its volcanoes, bears, rusty wands, and golden eggs; and *Zork*, with its underground empire and hidden caves. We'll remember these games long after the latest FPS about beating up prostitutes and running down civilians has disappeared from the shelves, and that's because they had stories. They *told* stories.

By telling stories in our own online games, we can create this same opportunity to make our games bigger than they otherwise might be.

The Storyteller's Craft

There are many storytelling mediums, including plays, radio programs, novels, short stories, movies, and television shows. Each of these mediums approaches storytelling in a different way; each focuses on different aspects of storytelling to take advantage of the strengths of the individual mediums. In radio, well-described settings are irrelevant, because the stories live entirely in the minds of the listeners, while action is usually represented by sound effects. In movies, storytelling is compact and lean, because there are a mere two hours to tell a plot through from beginning to end. In long-running television series, there's plenty of time to stretch events out, over months or years of storytelling, but at the same time, individual plots are confined to an hour, with exciting punctuations every 10 to 15 minutes, as required by commercial necessity.

Although each of these mediums approaches storytelling differently, each still depends on the same five building blocks of story telling: *setting*, where the story takes place; *character*, whom the story happens to; *backstory*, what happened before the story; *plot*, what happened during the story; and *theme* (along with its cousin, *symbolism*), what the story really means (see Figure 1.10.1).

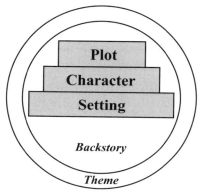

FIGURE 1.10.1   *The building blocks of storytelling.*

Although online games—which are interactive, ongoing, and peopled with tens of thousands of participants—are a very different medium from those that have come before, these five building blocks can still be used to introduce true storytelling into online games. The methods may not be quite the same, but the lessons learned from thousands of years of telling stories can inform and improve the storytelling in our online games.

Setting

Setting is the most basic of the storytelling building blocks. It forms the foundation of a story, the basis upon which everything else is built. As already noted, it's "where the story takes place," but there's a lot of opportunity (and need) for expansion of that basic precept.

At its most basic level, setting describes the *geographic* basis for a story. Where does it happen? In a city? In a village? In the wilderness? Is it set in a snow-bound castle nestled on the top of an ancient mountain? Does it take place around a singular oasis, deep in the Moroccan desert, near a long-buried temple? In New York City? In the outskirts of London?

Setting can also describe the *political* basis of a story. Is it set in a repressive fascist regime where everyone is killed at the age of 21? An open society where everyone watches everyone else through an infinitely large network of cameras and monitoring software? A communist society where everyone really does try to help everyone else, *from each according to his ability, to each according to his need*?

Past this political core, setting can also encompass *societal* rules of all sorts. How does the society feel about marriage? Work? Fidelity? Loyalty? Love? Hate? One of the wonders of creating a setting is that you can toss up all the rules that we tend to take for granted in our world, and see how things might be in a very different place.

Although these three cores—geography, politics, and society—define the most basic ideas needed to outline a setting, they're only a start. You only have to look outside your window to see the infinite complexity possible in any setting. Any setting is made up of sub-settings and sub-sub-settings. You could describe a city, then a specific precinct in that city, then a block within that precinct, then a specific house. It's like fractal geometry, with each change of scale and location revealing more things that must be described. Therefore, when describing a setting, as when describing everything, you gloss: you decide what's important and you pay attention to that. Geography, politics, and society are good places to begin.

Writer's Rules: "Show, Don't Tell"

Most of the lessons we've learned about how to tell stories over the centuries have come from writers, as they've been the ones who most often actually talk about their craft— and more important, write about it, filling libraries with books that describe how to write. Writers also tend to be fairly clever people, so many of their "rules" about writing come packaged in handy little aphorisms, easy to digest and easy to remember.

Throughout this article, we'll meet some of the most famous and most common aphorisms about writing by writers. They're nuggets of wisdom that have been refined down to their diamond core, and thus are some of the suggestions that, as game designers, we're most likely to find guidance from.

"Show, Don't Tell" is probably the core precept of all writing. It's a lesson that a beginning writer will hear the first time he talks with a professional (and probably will hear again and again, as his writing is rejected until he has this rule down flat). This rule means that it's neither very inspirational nor evocative to simply tell your viewers what's going on. Instead, you need to show it, or if you prefer *dramatize it*, to bring action and excitement to a potentially boring explanation.

Think back to *Star Wars* and you'll probably remember a few of the more dramatic scenes: Luke returning home to find his uncle and aunt dead, their house burned out; Luke swinging across that big chasm in the Death Star; and Luke scream-ing out as Ben is struck down by Darth Vader. How much less dramatic would these have been if they'd been described rather than dramatized? How much less touching would Luke's grief have been if we hadn't seen his anguished yell as his mentor fell, but instead only heard him tell Han "I was devastated when Ben died"? George Lucas showed rather than told.

(And, to offer a counter-example, in *Babylon 5*, creator JMS often fell back on the "infodump," a quick way to tell a lot of information without showing it. Several times throughout the first season, one character told another, "This is the fifth of the Baby-lon stations. The first three were sabotaged before completion, while the fourth disap-peared within 24 hours of going active." Imagine how much more dramatic it would have been, instead, if we'd seen the fate of the first four stations as a lead-in to the first episode. In fact, consider how much more dramatic it *was* when we finally saw the fate of Babylon 4 in the first season episode, "Babylon Squared," rather than just hear-ing about it as part of yet another infodump.)

The precept of "Show Don't Tell" really applies to every aspect of storytelling. It's listed here, because it'll apply to everything else we'll discuss. However, it also does have particular application to setting. Once you've defined your setting, you'll have pages and pages of notes about it: its weather, its laws, its political structure, and much more. Whenever you can, *show* those ideas about your society, rather than telling them. If it's illegal to throw out paper in your near-future dystopia, arrest a player for doing so rather than just handing him a cold list of rules; if everyone in the society can become ruler for a day, pick a player, or at least let a player see someone get picked for the honor. In each case, the setting will immediately become that much more real for the players, because they see it in action rather than just reading about it.

Describing Settings Generally

The basic definition of setting as geography, politics, and society does a pretty good job of outlining how to describe it (see Table 1.10.1). You figure out the basic ele-ments of setting, and you write them down. The most important rule for describing setting, however, is, *mind the details*. Setting isn't just about the big things ("it's a jun-gle world"), but also the small things ("what is the only place in the galaxy where the rare starshine flower grows, which blossoms once a year, on the summer solstice"). The preponderance of small details—used when appropriate—is what will prove to your readers (or viewers or players) that you actually understand a setting and know what makes it tick.

Of course, these details have to be a compromise; as already mentioned you need to know when to gloss as well. The art of describing a set is in some ways Zen-like: you must describe next to nothing while implying you're describing almost everything.

Table 1.10.1   Settings Checklist

√Geography
√Politics
√Society
√Details

Describing Settings in Online Games

When considering online games, setting is probably the most important building block of storytelling, because it, like backstory, best matches our understanding of how a game works. When we offer a game to players we're providing a sort of blank slate—a canvas for players to take their actions upon—and the foundation of that canvas is the setting.

As such, the simplest use of setting in an online game is *as a game background*. This means that you show it on the map that's printed in your instruction manual and you depict it graphically as the background through which characters can run, walk, and fight. It's primarily the geographical setting that shines here: your background's climate, what it looks like, how its houses are built, what its people wear, and so forth.

Similarly, you can use your setting as a *cut story*. When you introduce your game at the start through full animation, or when you cut between important scenes (something less important for online games than for the older single-player RPGs), these are more opportunities to really show off your setting. It'll all be pretty superficial, just as that use as game background was, but still it's a chance to make sure your setting is consistent, and to give your players the smallest hints at the background underlying the game.

The most important use of setting in an online game, however, is as a *game driver*. Your setting should affect just about everything that happens in your game (or, to go back to our recently learned cliché, you should be showing your setting, not telling). When a player takes an action within a city, the responses should be based on the setting: has he broken a taboo? Has he made a gesture that the citizens find bold and generous? Has he broken a ridiculous law? Has he inadvertently made a commitment that he didn't intend?

The details will drive your game.

If you've done a good job describing your setting, and this may be a job that takes a developer months or years, it should be a unique place, probably quite different from whatever society we consider our own. In this case, everything that is done in that setting should be considered by its own rules, and that should have marked effects on every other aspect of your game.

Character

Characters are the people who inhabit your setting (and thus your creative work). They bring life to your setting, and inevitably form the basis of plot. Like settings, characters can be defined in a number of different ways.

The most obvious description of a character is through his *physicality*. What does he look like? Is he tall or short? Lean or muscular? For that matter, is the character a male or a female (or something else)? Does he wear glasses? How about sideburns? How about clothes? Physicality can also describe more than just the obvious visual aspects. Is his voice a quavering alto or a sturdy baritone? Does it sound scratched and cracking due to decades of nicotine use, or calm and soothing? Further, what does the character smell like? (Or, if necessary for your type of game, what do they feel and/or taste like?) By definition, a character's physicality is the most superficial way to describe that character, but it's what we humans, as visual beings, are apt to notice first. It can be very frustrating to have a movie or TV show ruined because two characters looked too much alike, and you could never figure out what was going on. The same issue of mistaken identity should be dutifully avoided in any creative endeavor (except, perhaps, Shakespeare's plays and situational comedies, where mistaken identity is an intentional and humorous part of the story).

You can also describe characters through their *personality*. This is the outward face that they present to the world. It's the way that they act and react: the potentially unfathomable actions that they take and the emotions that we can only guess may underlie them.

Finally, we can describe characters through *psychology*, which is what actually makes them tick. Does a character have a deep sense of loyalty? How about an Oedipal complex? Is he bipolar? Does he hate snakes? These underlying psychological quirks can (and should) explain the personality that we see.

(*History* is a fourth way to define characters that we'll ignore for now. It describes what a character has done, and how that's changed him. However, history is really encapsulated in another building block of storytelling, backstory, which we'll come to shortly.)

Writer's Rules: "We Like What's Like Us"

Characters are very important elements in most fictional works, and thus every writer has a rule or two about them. This one is, perhaps, one of the most crucial. Generally, characters in stories *must* be sympathetic. They must be someone we care about, because that makes us care about the entire story. Without that personal connection, stories at best are unemotional, and at worst are plain boring [Card88].

And, whom do we care about most? People who are like us. People who share our trials and tribulations, who are just working to try and make it from one day to the next—people who we could be.

Marvel Comics stumbled upon this rule in 1961 with the release of *Fantastic Four #1*, then again in 1962 with the release of *Amazing Fantasy #15*, the first appearance of Spider-Man. Before then, most comic characters had been untroubled upholders of the peace, but with the introduction of the Marvel Age of comics, we now had heroes with problems [Wright01]. Ben Grimm had become a monster, a Thing. He'd often be awash in self-pity; sometimes he even fought with younger teammate Johnny Storm. Peter Parker, meanwhile, was always running short of money, was picked on at school, had an ailing aunt, and when he was Spider-Man, no one understood him. In other words, Ben and Pete were people like us.

Writer's Rules: "No One's a Villain in Their Own Mind"

Perhaps the flip side of the coin is this: villains are people like us, too. No one says, "I'm going to be evil," or "I'm going to be a bad person." Rather, people make decisions that affect other people in a negative way because *they think it's the right thing to do*. They have a belief system of some sort that makes their incomprehensible actions comprehensible and perhaps even necessary—to them. Understanding this creates the basis for truly understanding one category of characters that may inhabit your works.

Comic books, science-fiction TV shows, and action movies are all pretty bad at presenting one-dimensional villains with little underlying purpose to their evil actions. However, *Buffy the Vampire Slayer* has managed to do a bit better, particularly through the evolution of vampiric bad boy Spike. Here was a villainous vampire who originally came onto the show simply to make some trouble. However, as the character evolves we learn that he's always been a "fool for love" and that his evil actions were almost always the result of an unfulfilled desire for acceptance.

Writer's Rules: "Characters Must Change"

In traditional mediums, the most important rule for characters is this: "Character must change . . . and that change must come from within." [Kaufman02] In other words, stories are usually about a journey, one in which the main characters are different people when they get to the end than when they started. These changes may be physical or societal, but they tend to come from a character's deeper understanding of their own selves.

We can see these changes in many of the exemplar stories we've already discussed. Luke Skywalker and Buffy the Vampire Slayer, in particular, walk very similar paths (a path called *the Hero's Journey*, as it happens, which is discussed elsewhere in this book). Both begin their story with little understanding of what they'll be called on to do; through their journey, they find deep reserves of strength within themselves, and by the end of the story, they've proven themselves to be leaders, ready to face whatever challenges the world places in their way.

The idea of changing characters is, perhaps, one of the most uncomfortable ones for the medium of online games, and that comes out of central questions about how characters can (and should) be used in online games.

Describing Characters Generally

The first step in describing a character in an online game (or in any medium) is to truly understand that character (see Table 1.10.2). For minor characters, you won't need to understand much, but for major characters you want to have a handle on every aspect of the character previously mentioned—physicality, personality, and psychology. It might be useful to fully describe how the character looks and dresses (or draw him or her, if you're so talented). Afterward, it might be useful to write up some questionnaires, and then answer them for your character. How does he feel about marriage? About death? What's his favorite dessert? His favorite song? What climate does he like and why? How does he feel about politics? (Questionnaires available at online dating services might give you an excellent set of Q&A for your most important characters.)

Table 1.10.2   Character Checklist

√Physicality
√Personality
√Psychology
√Details

Once you have a good understanding of your character, your next job is then *not to infodump that to your players*. To make a memorable character you just need to include one or two details: a physical element (his loud ties, the shuffle to his step); a quirk (his love for cats, his nervous tic of tapping his fingers); or a goal (to dethrone the president, to save the environment). Everything else should be background, the basis for how he acts and how other people react to him. If you try to dump everything on the players at once, they won't be able to tell what's important, and their eyes may just glaze over, because you've told rather than shown.

Describing Characters in Online Games

A much more difficult question is how characters truly fit into online games. To a certain extent, it's not an entirely comfortable combination, because in online games you actually have two different types of characters: gamemaster characters and players.

Gamemaster characters are, out of necessity, background. They shouldn't be the stars of the show, and thus you shouldn't place too much emphasis on them. However, players, who are the stars, are largely independent. You can't move them around like chess pieces, as you could with characters in a novel.

Nonetheless, you can still use lessons learned for characters in many useful ways in online games.

For *gamemaster characters*, you can do your best to make sure that they're fully fleshed out, so that they're realistic human beings (or whatever race of beings happens to inhabit your game). You should understand everything about them (if they're important enough), you should make them sympathetic, and you should make sure that even your villains have reasons for doing the things they do.

For *player characters*, you can only offer tools. Make sure that your players have the ability to flesh out the physicality, the personality, and the psychology of their characters as much as they wish. Prompt them with questions that will make them think about who their characters are without requiring that they answer those questions. Beyond that, you should give your players' characters the opportunities to change without making that a requirement either. Have your game face them with hard questions that will test their beliefs and their morals. Some players will simply go on the set way they decided on at character creation, but others will see the opportunity for change and seize it. These will be the players who create characters that will be remembered and written about long after they've retired.

Plot

If character forms the heart of *who* is in your setting, plot forms the heart of *what* happens there. It forms the basis of all action and all change in your story, and is the important backbone that keeps your entire story together.

In its simplest form, plot is described as "a beginning, a middle, and an end," or, if you prefer, as "introduction, rising action, climax, falling action, and denouement." In general, this means: first, we introduce the situation, including the characters, the setting, and the problems that the characters will face. Second, because of those problems, actions start to occur, perhaps because of the characters, perhaps in spite of them. Third, we reach a confrontation where the characters come face to face with their problems and either conquer them, or don't. Fourth, the action slowly dies out in the wake of the climax; and fifth, loose ends are tied up and the story is ended.

Writer's Rule: "If There's a Gun . . ."

This entire rule goes something like this: "If there's a gun over the fireplace at the beginning of Act I, it must go off by the end of Act III; and, conversely, if a gun goes off by the end of Act III, then it must be seen over a fireplace during Act I." This particular rule has even made it into popular culture, where singer Aimee Mann says, "I won't find it fantastic or think it absurd / When the gun in the first act goes off in the third" in her song "Frankenstein" [Mann95].

The rule correctly describes two different aspects of plot:

- First, everything that's part of a story (and thus part of the plot) must be significant. You don't want to throw elements in that have no plot (or thematic) significance. In other words, if we, as viewers, see that gun, then we understand, because of the covenant we have with the storyteller, that it's going to be significant.
- Second, the rule states that if something is going to be important for the resolution of a story, then we'll know about it well before the resolution. (The opposite tact to this is called introducing a *deus ex machina*, or literally, a "machine from the gods." It means that when we reach the climax of a story, when everything

seems lost, suddenly something comes out of left field to resolve the plot in a way that most readers would consider "unfair.")

Mystery novels and films are perhaps the form of literature that either most carefully adhere to this rule or else most bitterly regret not doing so. In a good mystery story, we see all the clues clearly beforehand—all the guns over the fireplace as it were—and thus the ending is clearly broadcast, but only to the most astute viewer. Conversely in a bad mystery story we learn in the last 10 pages that the victim actually had a lost twin brother, and that he is the true assailant, not the seven other people that we'd been led to suspect throughout the story.

Finally, and without giving anything away, M. Night Shyamalan tends to be a master of this rule in his movies, including *The Sixth Sense*, *Unbreakable*, and *Signs*. All of his twist endings are well telegraphed to the vigilant viewer.

How well or how poorly a story telegraphs itself through careful attention to all plot elements can be a strong basis for whether a story fails or succeeds.

Describing Plots Generally

Every storyteller has his or her own method for describing plot.

The simplest descriptions of plot generally summarize it in a sentence or two. Creators who believe in this sort of description of plot usually claim that there are only a limited number of plots under the sun.

Leo Tolstoy is often credited with saying, "There are only two stories in all of literature: a man goes on a journey, a stranger comes to town." Jack Hodgins meanwhile lists three types of plot: plots of character, plots of fortune, and plots of thought [Hodgins01]. Other authors list out other types of plots in numbers that increase up to dizzying heights—until you look at an outline of 71 different possible plots and wonder what use it is.

Perhaps more usefully, plots can be described structurally. Most can be described as three-act plays, as mentioned earlier, with a beginning, a middle, and an end, but that's not the only method to describe plots. Other plot structures include *episodic plots*, where barriers are gradually overcome, with no increase in tension; *mountain plots*, where those same barriers cause increased tension as they mount; and *"W" plots*, which are used in Hollywood to describe a clean set of two low-points and two high-points over the duration of a story [Appelcline00] (see Figure 1.10.2).

Movies overall provide one of the most specific and most reliable structures for plot of any medium. The general movie "W" plot is laid out like this:

1. Act I (20–30 minutes)
   a. The establishment of characters and setting—We learn who the story is about.
   b. An inciting incident—Something happens to shake up the characters' world.
   c. A turning point—Characters make a decision to move out of their comfortable world.

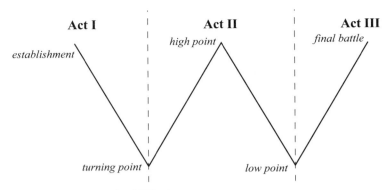

FIGURE 1.10.2 *The "W" plot structure.*

2. Act II (60 minutes)
   a. The beginning of a journey—This may be metaphorical, but whether metaphorical, emotional, or physical, the characters leave their life behind.
   b. A series of challenges.
   c. A high point where all appears well.
   d. A sudden turnaround, followed by a point of no return—A character makes a decision or takes an action from which there is no coming back.
   e. Another series of challenges.
   f. A low point where all seems to have failed.

3. Act III (20–30 minutes)
   a. A moment of truth, understanding, or realization.
   b. Another series of challenges—Characters slowly crawl up from their low point.
   c. A final battle—All is won (or lost).

Once you've studied this structure, it's hard to watch a movie without seeing the plot points drop one by one: an inciting incident occurs within the first 10 minutes, and the characters go on a journey within the first 30; around the 60-minute mark everything is going great, but then there's a sudden turnaround and things get worse and worse, until the 90-minute mark where things hit a nadir, then start to improve, until the climatic confrontation at the end of the movie [Siler01].

Turning once more back to *Star Wars*, we can see that it fits this structure like clockwork. In Act I, Leia is captured and her droids are sent to Tatooine (inciting incident), which eventually leads to the Lars homestead being destroyed (turning point). In Act II, Luke leaves home (beginning of journey), meets friends and foes before heading off in the Millennium Falcon (challenges), and finally closes in on Alderaan (high point). But then, in the second half of Act II, things turn bad: Alderaan is found destroyed (turnaround), and the Millennium Falcon is caught in a tractor beam (point of no return), forcing them to face more challenges in the Death Star (challenges), before Ben is finally cut down (low point). Then in Act III, Luke finally connects with the Force as he starts shooting down Tie Fighters (moment of realization), and this leads to his assault on the Death Star itself (final battle).

When you're describing your own plots, perhaps you won't want to go into that level of detail, but somewhere between the one-line description and the careful three-act outline you'll find the level of description appropriate for your own story.

Describing Plots in Online Games

Like character, plot is a slightly uncomfortable fit for online games, once more because your viewers are actually interactive participants. Generally, if you try to force a plot on players you'll be accused of "railroading" them, meaning that you're shunting them down a set avenue (your plot) without giving them any chance for personal decision.

This still leaves us with the least meaningful method of displaying plot: *cut stories.* As with setting, you can tell the core story of your game through introductory and intergame animations. It's just not particularly deep, however, and may be skipped by many players.

However, there's already a well-established method for railroading players in many online games: *quests.* They tend to have set starting places (being told to get the Gizmo from faraway Garbaz), set middles (getting to Garbaz), set climaxes (getting the Gizmo), and even set denouements (returning the Gizmo to the QuestMaster). More carefully adopting plot structures to these quests by carefully outlining and then defining the middle section of the quest as a series of obstacles—of setbacks and points of no return—will likely make your quests more evocative, more meaningful, and more memorable.

(*City of Heroes* is a recent game that has made very good use of quests, through missions that are given out by contacts. The most important missions actually chain together, creating a larger story than would have been possible with any individual quest.)

Plot can also serve as excellent *metastory*, and this may actually be where you have the most opportunity to impress your players. By constantly advancing the overarching plot of your entire game world—and particularly by basing those advancements on player actions—you can tell a story at the global level. At the same time, this global story *has* been impacted upon by players, and *will* definitely impact your players as you change your setting and characters to adapt to the plot itself. If your game is slowly being overrun by dark forces from the north; or if there is a new rise of magic in your lands; or if the ruins of an ancient race are being uncovered on the rim of the galaxy, then you have the opportunity to slowly advance this metastory, and you can do that best by making sure a well-structured plot underlies your decisions.

(*Asheron's Call* was one of the first online games to really push the idea of metastory through changing events, and thus new quests, items, and movies that appear on a monthly basis.)

Finally, you should consider *player plots* in online games. These are stories told by your players themselves, with or without the support of your game administrators. Supporting them can be very time consuming, but they allow your players to become very important creative forces in your world, rather than you having to assign that task to administrators. Typically, only the smaller games have managed to succeed at this type of plotting, and mainly by giving players extraordinary creative control over a game. (At Skotos, we've been very successful in this regard with our premier game, *Castle Marrach*; privileged players run most of the plots within the castle using fairly powerful creative tools while they in turn enable less-privileged players to engage in plots of their own.)

Although regular, closed plots can sometimes be hard to develop in online games, there are a number of potential methods to create open-ended plots, which have a beginning but no well-defined middle or end.

The simplest method to create open-ended plots is the *plot seed*, where a problem is introduced into a game without any well-defined method for solving it. The players are thus able to come up with the answer that best suits them—but without the meaningful results that could have come about from a more structured plot.

Likewise, many online games simply substitute *conflict* for plot, usually player versus player (PvP) conflict. Although conflict is indeed at the heart of plot, the converse isn't true. The result will probably satisfy your players in the short term, but presumably, if you're considering storytelling building blocks, you're looking for something deeper than that.

Backstory

Setting, character, and plot are without a doubt the three most important building blocks of storytelling (see Table 1.10.3). Two others are still notable, but less important: backstory and theme. Backstory is, simply, what came before in your story. Call it history if you like (or legend or myth or even yesterday). It can apply to any element of storytelling mentioned so far: setting (what things used to be like), character (what people used to be like), and plot (what previously happened).

Table 1.10.3   Backstory Uses

√Setting
√Character
√Plot

Writer's Rule: "The Past Is Prologue"

The writer's rule for backstory simply means this: what's gone before is only important as it affects what's happening right now.

So, your main character had a dog that was hit by a car when he was 15. Is that important? Only if there's going to be some pivotal event involving dogs, cars, or 15-year-olds in your story. Otherwise, it's really cool that you know this fact about your character's past, and you should use it to modify your understanding of who your character is, but you don't actually need to tell your viewers about it.

Think of how long a prologue is, compared to the length of an average book. That's probably about as much explicit backstory as you need to give.

Describing Backstory Generally

There seem to be two main schools as to how backstory should be described. Some creators meticulously describe it, writing out tedious histories and myths and language structures, which they then use to form the basis of their creative work. J.R.R. Tolkien is perhaps one of the most renowned to have described his backstory in such a manner, as is shown in the 100+ pages of appendixes in his *Lord of the Rings*.

If this tact is taken, it's important to understand that these notes are generally meant to be *your* background, not background you're going to hand to your viewers. (As ever, show, don't tell.)

The opposite tact is, simply, to fudge it: to never worry quite how the backstory works, but rather to define it as you go along. This has the possibility of saving you a lot of work, and of creating a backstory that's more generally relevant to the story that you actually end up telling, but it also has the potential to blow up in your face if you're not careful. *The X-Files* has always seemed like a good, modern example of on-the-fly backstory that never seemed to gel right. The TV show's "mythology" episodes, laying the foundation for an alien invasion with government oversight, never seemed to really work out, and as killer bees, black oozes, and Gigerian aliens were added to the mix, things started to make less and less sense.

The best answer to the question of describing backstory is probably a compromise: do some of it ahead of time, so that you understand the general strokes of your world's history before you try to lay out your plot, characters, and setting. In addition, when you later do add details on the fly, make sure that you incorporate them into your original backstory, so that later additions won't contradict them.

Describing Backstory in Online Games

In online games, you have one advantage over more traditional mediums: there's a general understanding among players that backstory may be presented outside of the game itself, through printed manuals and through Web sites (although whether players bother to peruse these backstories is an entirely different question). There's no harm in all at using these methods to describe your backstory, as long as reading it isn't a requirement for playing your game. However, the best method for including backstory in the game is the same as that of most other storytelling building blocks: you need to show it. Much as with your setting, you should make sure that your backstory is a living, breathing part of the world you created, not just a cold list of what came before.

Theme

Of all the building blocks of storytelling, theme is probably the most poorly understood and the most disrespected. Theme is *what a story is really about*, meaning the deeper messages that a story is trying to convey. To put it another way, theme is "the story behind the story."

Thus, you could say that *Star Wars* is a story about growing up, while *E.T. the Extra-Terrestrial* is about growing up and acceptance and friendship, and *Rocky* is about perseverance against all odds. Theme isn't magic and doesn't have to be particularly deep; it's just an abstraction of a story's plot.

Unfortunately, theme was destroyed for many of us by high-school English teachers. Some turned theme into rote (such as man vs. man, man vs. nature, and man vs. himself, which are actually really *plot* listings, no matter how they're usually presented in American Literature classes). Others found absolutely ridiculous themes in books, pop songs, or other creative works—or else turned theme into some magical thing that you could only see if you were smart enough.

The Taming of the Shrew is a good example of a school-taught play where teachers tend to find ridiculous themes, causing students to hate or misunderstand the idea of themes. It's clearly a story of the importance of gender roles and of conformity. However, it's often taught as being a diatribe against misogyny or an ode to feminism, which is very apt for the politics of today, but not for the story that Shakespeare wrote, where Kate eventually accepts her gendered role, and thus her place in society.

English teachers also seem particularly apt at taking pop culture creativity, be it the songs of the Beatles or modern Rap artists, and trying to explain what they *really* mean—and getting it totally wrong.

Theme isn't magic, and it isn't even particularly hard: it's just the underlying and overarching meaning of a story.

Very closely related to theme is *symbolism*, which is simply the idea that an element in a story actually represents something different. Perhaps light means love and safety, darkness fear and danger. Symbolism is only particularly important as it relates to the theme of a story, and beyond that, it's a bit of intellectual tomfoolery.

Writer's Rules: Theme Happens

Many English classes teach this one wrong, too. Theme isn't something that you have to carefully introduce from the first moment of conception of a story. Rather, it's something that happens naturally.

Upon completing the first draft of a story (or the outline for your in-game plot), you'll often note that a particular theme seems to be recurring. You keep returning to the idea of safety compromised or paradise lost or whatever. Only then, in your second draft, do you try to reinforce this theme, perhaps by making the core message in your central story clearer, perhaps by introducing additional subplots that either reinforce the core message or offer a counterpoint to it.

TV dramas often take this tact, but they often overdo it as well. *Dawson's Creek*, in the middle of its run, built almost every episode around a central theme. Like most TV shows, *Dawson's Creek* tended to have three plots in each episode: a core "A" plot, which was the backbone of the episode; a secondary "B" plot, which got a fair amount of time; and a tertiary "C" plot, which filled up the last 5 or 10 minutes left.

Dawson's Creek's themes tended to be fairly simple. You'd have an episode about truth in relationships or the difficulty of change, or whatever. The "A" plot would then offer a point for that theme ("Dawson tells Joey the truth about how he still had a girlfriend when they slept together"), then the "B" plot would offer a counterpoint ("Pacey doesn't tell Audrey about his sexual indiscretions"), and then the "C" plot would offer another point, often somewhat removed from the first two ("Grams admits to her granddaughter that she's seeing a new man, now that her husband is five years gone"). It was highly formulaic, and probably overdone; perhaps the problem was that they weren't allowed to develop naturally, as theme should—but they still do offer examples of how theme can be expanded from its initial germination.

Symbolism, again, works much the same. When you've finished your first draft of a story and realize that it's full of fire or ice or smoke or whatever, you have to start thinking about what that element really means, and then start using it correctly within your story.

Describing Theme Generally

There's little more to be said about how theme is described generally: the writer's rule of letting it appear naturally and then nurturing it is a pretty good outline of how to use theme. The most important thing to understand beyond that is that you don't actually state or describe theme. Rather, you imply it.

Describing Theme in Online Games

For a game, you should generally think about what you want your game to say: what is its core message? *EverQuest* doesn't seem to have a core theme: it's a game about hacking and slashing without a lot of deeper meaning. Meanwhile, it's possible that *Ultima Online* has managed to inherit at least some of the themes of its single-player ancestors, which were about fellowship, friendship, and maintaining a hard line of morality even through difficult circumstances.

Your game doesn't have to have themes, but as with all the building blocks of storytelling, it'll probably be more meaningful if it does.

Storytelling in the Twenty-First Century

The building blocks of storytelling are thousands of years' old, dating back to the first time a caveman told a story about his hunt around a low-burning fire, hoping to hold back the terrors of the night. However, as we enter the twenty-first century, and as we consider the possibilities of our new online medium, it's becoming obvious that the path is open for dramatically new types of storytelling.

First, we have the opportunity to tell stories in bright new *genres*. Fantasy, and to a lesser extent science-fiction, have been the watchwords of computer games since their inception, and even more so for the world of online games, whose only hits (*EverQuest*, *Dark Age of Camelot*, perhaps *Asheron's Call*, *Star Wars: Galaxies*, and *Ultima Online*) fit into this category. There's a lot of room beyond these narrow genres for telling different types of stories—built around mystery, romance, thriller, and many other categories— we just haven't figured out how to yet. Likewise, historical and modern-day recreations through online games seem prime categories for development.

Closely related, *setting* has a lot of room for change in online games. Settings in online games don't have to be connected together in intuitive physical ways; they could instead be connected through common themes, common ideas, or even chronological connections. Likewise, we don't have to keep telling stories at the same scale. Why not make online games where characters represent entire empires rather than individual entities, or where they instead represent entities part of a larger whole, like cells in a body? We've thus far been confined by our understanding about how the real world works, but there's no reason this needs to be the case in virtual worlds. Our *backstories* will change as our settings do.

As already discussed, we have plenty of room to learn more about how to use *character* and *plot* in online games. We need to learn better how to involve real human beings and still allow them meaningful character development and access to important plots.

Finally, that leads us to *theme*, a storytelling element that will change in the twenty-first century by its mere inclusion in online games.

Conclusion

Storytelling, along with artwork and game design, is one of three creative forces upon which modern online games are built, but it's also the one that is most frequently ignored. By paying more attention to the basic building blocks of storytelling, we can create online games that are more memorable and perhaps more meaningful.

These building blocks include:

Setting: The underlying geography, politics, and society upon which a game is built.

Character: The physical, personal, and psychological description of the people who inhabit your game.

Plot: A combination of introduction, rising action, climax, falling action, and denouement, which together describe the actions of your game.

Backstory: The description of what came before for your setting, characters, and plot.

Theme: The description of the underlying messages of your game, which may include use of symbolism as well.

These building blocks must be changed and adapted for use in online games, but thousands of years of writer's rules and lessons learned can help us get a head start on telling *good* stories in our online games.

References

[Appelcline00] Appelcline, Kimberly, *Plot Strategies*, available at *www.skotos.net/articles/ PlotStrategies.html*, Skotos Tech Inc., 2000.

[Card88] Card, Orson Scott, *Characters & Viewpoint*, Writer's Digest Books, 1988.

[Hodgins01] Hodgins, Jack, *A Passion for Narrative*, McClelland & Stewart, 2001.

[Kaufman02] Kaufman, Charlie and Donald Kaufman, *Adaptation*, Columbia Pictures, 2002.

[Mann95] Mann, Aimee, *I'm with Stupid*, Geffen Records, Inc., 1995.

[Siler01] Siler, Megan, *Fundamentals of Screenwriting*, Lectures, UC Berkeley, 2001.

[Wright01]Wright, Bradford W., *Comic Book Nation*, The John Hopkins University Press, 2001.

Additional Credits

This article could not have been written if not for four years spent talking about writing and game design on a regular basis in the column *Trials, Triumphs & Trivialities* for Skotos Tech. Articles that were particularly crucial in the development of this piece include:

"This Blessed Plot: Seeds, Conflicts & Other Non-Plots" (12/2002), available at *www.skotos.net/articles/TTnT_99.shtml*.

"The Elements of Good Scarytelling, Part One: Haunting Themes" (10/2002), available at *www.skotos.net/articles/TTnT_94.shtml*.

"Future Memes, Part One: Overview and Genres" (1/2002), available at *www. skotos.net/articles/TTnT_55.shtml*.

"Future Memes, Part Three: Settings and Physics" (1/2002), available at *www.skotos. net/articles/TTnT_57.shtml*.

"Movies, a Structure for Plot, Part One" (2/2001), available at *www.skotos.net/ articles/TTnT_22.html*.

1.11

Great in Theory: Examining the Gap Between System Design Theory and Reality

Justin Quimby—
Turbine Entertainment Software

justin@turbinegames.com

One of the largest problems facing the game industry is the formalization and advancement of game design. As players become more sophisticated, they expect more "fun" from games and lower barriers to entry. In the same way that pen-and-paper games evolved from complex battlefield simulations, to rules-heavy role-playing games, and recently to games focused less on numbers and more on storytelling, so too are game designs evolving. Another critical factor is that development budgets continue to increase. Because of budget-pressure and customer expectations, developers need to innovate in a low-risk manner.

The problem is exacerbated in the subscription-based massively multiplayer (MMP) games. Compared to single-player games, where fewer data points exist, evaluating the validity of a particular MMP game design theory has a greater margin for error. Although MMP developers eagerly study single-player games, the differences in game scope, lifespan, and player behavior limit the application of some of the ideas. For example, in a game where hundreds of thousands of people play for years, no single player can have the power to destroy the world. Therefore, developers rely on instinct, lessons from radically different genres, and other experimental methods to design their games [Lawrence04] [Rickey04]. This article analyzes the theories behind the design, the implementation, and the ultimate fate of the spell economy.

Spell Economy Mechanics

At the time of its release in 1999, *Asheron's Call* was full of revolutionary ideas, from a seamless landscape without zones to a storyline that advanced through monthly content updates to a global spell economy. The spell economy is a deceptively simple concept: the power of a spell is inversely related to the frequency of its use. Therefore, the more frequently a spell is cast, the less powerful it becomes. One player alone during the course of regular play cannot significantly degrade a spell. Only through large numbers of players casting a spell can its power decrease. Conversely, spells that are rarely used gain power, so undiscovered and under-used spells increase in effectiveness (see Figure 1.11.1).

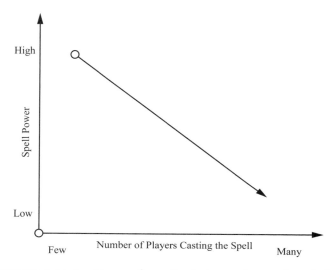

FIGURE 1.11.1   *Power of a spell relative to the number of players casting it.*

Turbine had several goals in designing the spell economy. By making the knowledge of a spell's formula valuable, the spell economy should create an information economy where players trade spells for currency and favor. In *Asheron's Call*, the only way to learn most spells is through experimentation. Players cannot simply buy a scroll to learn how to cast Flame Bolt. The game does not give players the ability to cast every spell; they need to discover the spell formula themselves or persuade other players to tell them the formula. As a result, players may experiment to find new or under-used spells, which is an interesting alternative gameplay dynamic to combat. Furthermore, the spell economy deepens spell casting, rather than the rigid gameplay that governs most fantasy magic rule sets. However, the most audacious goal was that of using the spell economy to create interesting social dynamics. Players may form cabals to perform research and then guard their results from outsiders. Turbine hoped that groups would attempt to cajole or bribe information out of tight-lipped wizards.

From this very simple concept, many interesting game dynamics come into play. In theory, players have an incentive to hoard their spells. Knowledge of how to cast the Force Bolt spell translates into a more effective character. This game mechanic has the potential to appeal to a variety of playing styles.

Learning Spells

An analysis of the spell economy requires an understanding of how players learn spells in *Asheron's Call*. A player learns spells through experimentation with spell components to discover the spell formula. If the player selects the correct components and casts the spell on an appropriate target, the spell is added to the player's spell book. Each spell has a unique spell formula, comprised of five to seven spell components. There are 72 spell components and seven slots, meaning there are over 100 trillion combinations of components, so a player has an enormous possibility space to search through to find spells. Several factors limit the spell search space, to reduce player frustration. First, the order of the spell components is consistent, with one slot for target type, another for the school of magic, and so forth. Furthermore, each spell component has a consistent meaning from spell to spell. For example, the component Birch Talisman means "other-targeted" in a Flame Bolt spell and "other-targeted" in a Force Bolt spell (see Table 1.11.1).

Table 1.11.1 Spell Formula for Flame Bolt 1

Component Type	Specific Component
Power	Lead Scarab
Action	Hawthorn
Concept 1	Powdered Onyx
Concept 2	Turpeth
Target	Birch Talisman

For higher-level spells, two components, called *tapers*, are customized to the casting player. The tapers are determined by running the player's unique ID and the spell ID through a formula. This customization means that even if one player gives the formula for a spell to another player, that player still must determine his customized formula.

Implementation Details

At the heart of the spell economy is a simple object, which is loaded by the master server upon startup. Every time a spell is cast, the server-side representation of the player queries the spell economy for the current power of the spell. Once the spell economy determines the updated power of the spell, the casting player is informed and spell casting continues. In the multiserver environment of the Turbine Engine, communication with the spell economy requires sending a message across the server network to the machine where the spell economy resides. Once the spell economy completes its calculations, a response snakes back to the machine controlling the character.

The global spell economy performs a simple computation to determine the new power of a spell. The power of a spell is a float multiplier. The spell economy contains a hash table whose key equals the ID of the spell. Each time a spell is cast, a constant value is removed from the power level of that spell. The spell economy periodically increases the power level of each spell by a constant amount. The casting of a spell deducts a fraction of the spell power and then returns that new value to the caster.

```cpp
class GlobalSpellEconomy
{
public:
    // called when a player casts a spell
    float CastSpell( SpellID sid );
private:
    // called by a regularly by a heartbeat function
    void RechargeSpells( void );
    // modifies the power of a spell and returns the
    // new current power level
    float ModifySpellPower( SpellID sid, float mod);
    // hash of all spells and their power
    hash_table< SpellID, float > m_SpellPower;
    // amount to deduct from a spell's power when cast
    float m_CastMod;
    // amount to recharge a spell's power
    float m_RechargeMod;
};
float
GlobalSpellEconomy::CastSpell( SpellID sid )
{
    // reduce the power of the spell by the constant
    float curr_power = ModifySpellPower( sid,
                                         m_CastMod );
    return curr_power;
}
void
GlobalSpellEconomy::RechargeSpells( void )
{
    // loop through every spell and recharge them by
    // the preset amount
    for (SpellID sid = 1; sid <= MAX_SPELL; sid++ )
    {
        float curr_power = ModifySpellPower( sid,
                                             m_RechargeMod );
    }
}
float
GlobalSpellEconomy::ModifySpellPower( SpellID sid,
                                      float mod )
{
    // modify the power of the spell
    float curr_power = m_SpellPower[sid];
    curr_power += mod;
    // bounds check the power of the spell
    BoundsCheckSpellPower( curr_power );
    // update the stored spell power
    m_SpellPower[sid] = curr_power;
    return curr_power;
}
```

This system of a persistent unique for the global spell economy operates well under light load conditions or in a single-server environment. When the system undergoes heavy load, the master server becomes a major bottleneck, as tens of thousands of spell casts route through it. As a result, the global spell economy became a distributed system, with each server having a local copy of the current global spell economy's power table. Each server gathers spell-cast information while dispensing the cached spell's power level. Every half-hour or so, the individual servers upload their spell cast histories to the master server, which then calculates the new spell power ratings and broadcasts these ratings to the rest of the server farm. This distributes the load for spell cast requests among the game servers, thus removing the bottleneck.

Player Feedback Mechanisms

Players do not care about the engineering design of a system, but instead focus on how they can interact with that system. For the spell economy, a player receives feedback on the current power of a spell through three mechanisms. The first is through combat feedback. A player can check the numeric value of the damage caused by Flame Bolt as reported in the chat window and note that it is more effective than Force Bolt. Second, a text message indicates the strength of the global spell economy. The text could range from, "The magic flows through you," to, "The magic blazes within you!" or, "The magic rushes powerfully through you!" Finally, each player's spell book displays the "charge" of a given spell for that particular player.

Difficulties of the Spell Economy

The ultimate test of a game mechanic is how players receive it. The spell economy enjoyed a tremendous amount of community excitement before the game's launch. After the game shipped, players began to note some issues with the spell economy. One problem with its implementation is how spell power affects spell damage. After rolling the raw damage for a spell, the damage is then multiplied by the power of the spell. Damage is rounded to the nearest whole number. In *Asheron's Call*, spells such as Flame Bolt 1 do a base damage of 8 to 15. As a result, it doesn't matter whether the power level is 0.95 or 1.05. If the random number rolled for damage is 8, then the spell does 8 points of damage. The range of damage done by spells does not provide enough of a spectrum for the spell economy to subtly influence spell damage amounts.

For players to embrace a game mechanic, they must be able to understand and regularly predict the results of that game mechanic. The feedback that players received was not sufficient to easily explain the arcane nature of the spell economy system. The feedback mechanism of a vague text message regarding the strength of a spell was not sufficient to allow players to judge the effectiveness of their spells [Live02].

At its core, the spell economy allows other players to affect the potency of a player's spells. This takes control away from the player without sufficient explanation. Players want dependable damage outputs. This left some players angry at the spell economy because it caused apparent random fluctuations in the effectiveness of their character. For a large swath of the player base, spells and swords are equivalent. Since the damage done by a sword does not vary based on how many players use swords, spells should not vary either. Every player is concerned with the abilities of their character first and then the rest of the world. The spell economy took some of that control away for spell casters.

The spell economy depends on players keeping a spell's formula secret and infrequently used. This means that the "value" to a player to keep a spell formula secret is greater than the benefit he derives from giving it away. That theory does not take the nature of social interaction on the Internet into account. A discoverer gains more recognition and respect from publicizing a discovery than by secreting information away. Gaming sites thrive on new information and lists of content. Ultimately, players want to be able to read overviews of quests and instructions on how to cast the newest spell. Players created automated bots for the game client that ran through spell component combinations to automate the spell discovery process. Within months of the game's launch, a large percentage of all spell formulas were available on the Web.

The Fate of the Spell Economy

Asheron's Call succeeded. The spell economy, despite its promise as a social mechanism and variation on traditional magic systems, did not achieve its goals. In June 2002, the Live Team removed the spell economy from *Asheron's Call*. Some of the crucial hypotheses behind the design of the spell economy did not pan out after the game shipped. People enjoy bragging about sports victories, personal achievements, and real-world scientific discoveries, so why should game discoveries be any different? Ultimately, there was not enough value to players to keep a spell formula secret.

Conclusion

Turbine learned a tremendous amount from the development of *Asheron's Call*, and we continue to learn from the live team that keeps the game vibrant and active. The lessons learned from the spell economy are incorporated into every system that Turbine now designs. It is a testament to the quality of *Asheron's Call* that more than five years after its release, it continues to draw new players without the spell economy.

References

[Lawrence04] Lawrence, J. C., "Discussion of MUD System Design, Development, and Implementation," available online at *www.kanga.nu/lists/listinfo/mud-dev/*, 2004.

[Live02] AC Live Team, "Letter to the Players," available online at *http://classic.zone.msn.com/asheronscall/news/ASHEletter0602.asp*, June 4, 2002.

[Rickey04] Rickey, David, "Engines of Creation" columns, available online at *www.skotos.net/articles/engines.shtml*, 2004.

MMP ENGINEERING TECHNIQUES

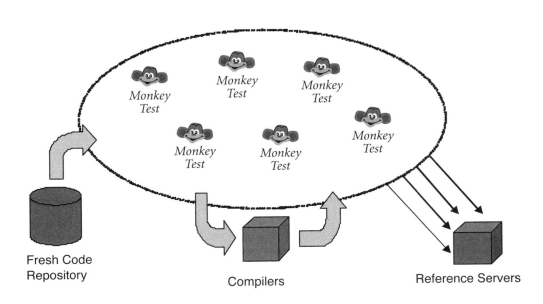

Fresh Code
Repository

Compilers

Reference Servers

2.1

Automated Testing for Online Games

Larry Mellon—Electronic Arts

larry@maggotranch.com

Online gaming requires a strong commitment to testing. The Quality of Service bar is quite high in a subscription-oriented business, while a continual flow of new content in turn generates continual, costly regression testing over years of operation.

The testing of massively multiplayer (MMP) games is much more difficult than the testing of a single-player game. Single-player games lack the nondeterministic execution problem that hinders the reproduction of errors while debugging large-scale distributed systems. Similarly, generating the input of a single player is easier and cheaper than simulating the activities of hundreds to thousands of online players: a required ability to examine server behavior under peak load conditions.

Automated testing can greatly reduce the QA cost of MMP game regression, providing an excellent return on investment over the years of operating and extending your game. However, its real value lies within the development team. *Automation provides push-button access to accurate, repeatable, measurable tests.* This new ability can be used during your game's implementation phase to load test server software, to improve stability of the code base while under development, or to measure completeness against milestones.

Automated testing supplies hard data when making key business and development decisions. Measurable tests applied very early in the development cycle expose the true state of completion and risks, focusing the development team on the key roadblocks in enough time to successfully react to the data.

What Exactly Is "Automated Testing?"

Automated testing is simply using software and hardware to increase the accuracy of, accelerate, or scale portions of the testing process. The most common strategies are systems to generate repeatable inputs against your game, tools to evaluate pass or fail for a particular test session, some form of "test session executive" for controlling the processes and output of a distributed system, and tools to manage large volumes of tests and their results across both manual and automated testing.

173

There are several automated testing tools on the market you can evaluate. Odds are you'll have to custom build at least some of the tools for your particular development approach and make some changes to your game's implementation to simplify automated testing. You'll also have to invest in hardware to run the tests, staff to craft, analyze, and maintain the tests, and maintain the testing system itself.

Automated testing can be difficult to correctly integrate into your shop, but the potential payoffs in higher quality, shorter development schedules, and lower operational costs are too high to ignore. *The lowest-risk and most cost-effective approach is to begin your project from day one with automated testing.* It is much easier to design in hooks for automated testing that to retrofit hooks in existing software. You also get more use out of your investment if the testing system is available to developers from the beginning (see Figure 2.1.1).

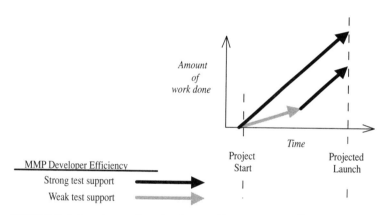

FIGURE 2.1.1 *Increasing developer efficiency pays off, and the earlier the better.*

Automation Architecture

Figure 2.1.2 provides a high-level view of the major automated test components, their relationships and primary functions, and how they connect to the game. This architecture is an extension of one successfully used in an automated testing system built for *The Sims Online* (described further at *www.gdconf.com/archives/2003/*).

Test Session Executive

This component must support developers and test servers in the building, starting, and monitoring of one to many clients connected to a specified server instance.

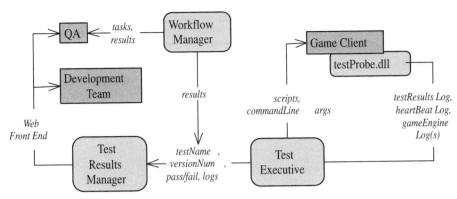

FIGURE 2.1.2 *Major components of an automated testing system.*

Support for parallel execution of test sessions will radically increase the overall output of test servers. Another useful feature is the ability to override specified server-side components with local developer instances. The executive is also responsible for the gathering of raw data, initial evaluation of test results, live monitoring of log files, and posting the results to the Test Results DB. A GUI is highly recommended to simplify the process of configuring and running hundreds to thousands of tests per day across test servers and individual developers, and serves to make the tests more accessible to nonengineers. *The easier it is to add, configure and run tests, the better off you are.*

A Test Session Executive must also have some mechanism to evaluate if any given test session has passed or failed. You'll need a flexible mechanism that permits many forms of testing, and ideally some way for developers to easily trace which inputs caused which specific failure. For regression testing, simply compare a specialized "test validation log" from a known good test run against the current test results. You'll end up looking at the raw logs a lot: use formatted text to speed the evaluation process, sample validation logs may be found in Tables 2.1.1 and 2.1.2. Restricting validation log output to the minimal data related to the current test greatly simplifies failure analysis. Note that simple text differences, insignificant numerical variance, or irrelevant data will cause a diff () to fail. *Monitor and improve your validation logs to minimize false fails: a test that repeatedly and incorrectly cries wolf wastes everybody's time.* Finally, load testing requires a different type of pass/fail from regression testing. Load testing simply needs to know if any given *transaction* (a requested operation on the remote server) passed or failed, and the response time for each transaction.

Table 2.1.1   Example Script and Validation Log for Core Functionality Testing of Inventory

Scripted Command	Validation Log File Entry
emptyInventory	emptyInventory: SUCCESS
addToInventory Knife	addToInventory [Knife]: SUCCESS
log currentInventory	Inventory Contents: Knife
addToInventory Balrog	addToInventory [Balrog]: SUCCESS

log currentInventory	Inventory Contents:
	    Knife
	    Balrog

deleteFromInventory Balrog	DeleteFromInventory [Balrog]: SUCCESS
log currentInventory	Inventory Contents: Knife

Table 2.1.2   Example Script and Validation Log for Core Functionality Testing of a Toilet Object

Scripted Command	Validation Log File Entry
buyObject Toilet	buyObject [Toilet]: SUCCESS
waitUntil Toilet EXISTS	waitUntil [Toilet Exists]: SUCCESS
logMsg Testing Toilet Core Functionality	# Testing Toilet Core Functionality
logMsg Only 'Use' & 'Clean' should be available	# Only 'Use' & 'Clean' should be available

logCurrentInteractions Toilet	Toilet: Currently Available Interactions
	    Use
	    Clean

log Msg Make sure Motives work	# Make sure Motives work
setData currentAvatar.Motive.Bladder 20	setData currentAvatar.Motive.Bladder [20]: SUCCESS
useObject Toilet 'Use' currentAvatar	useObject [Toilet :: Use] currentAvatar: SUCCESS
waitUntil currentAvatar.Motive.Bladder > 40	waitUntil [Bladder > 40]: SUCCESS
logMsg Motive Test passed!	# Motive Test passed!
logMsg 'Flush' should be a new interaction	# 'Flush' should be a new interaction

logCurrentInteractions Toilet	Toilet: Currently Available Interactions
	    Use
	    Clean
	    Flush

Test Results Manager

Testing a system as large and complex as an MMP game generates a lot of data. Your team will need assistance in sifting through it. The ability to filter out noise and look for patterns across tests will make using your system much easier. *The faster you can get the clear, summarized results of a test to the people who need it, the more useful is your entire testing system.* Further, game development tends to have many "rush" stages. Data that arrives too late to factor into critical, hour-to-hour decisions about the current build and the current worries is simply not useful to the development team. Plan for a flexible series of Report Generators that provide high-level summaries of a single test or of a series of related tests. Drill-down access to specific test results, failure conditions, historical results, and searches/comparisons across individual process logs is essential to getting your investment in automated testing ingrained in the day-to-day development of your game.

Workflow Manager

MMP games can have a very broad feature set, which in turn entails a broad set of test suites and many testers. Workflow tools can dramatically accelerate the dissemination of testing tasks, the coordination of automated and manual testing, and the collection and aggregation of all results. A number of QA workflow and reporting tools are commercially available. Make sure that whatever you buy or build supports fast, easy changes to test specifications: they will vary as much—or more—than your game design. Bonus points if the workflow tool is capable of integration to your local automated testing system, coordination of testing tasks split across manual and automated testing, or controlling the manual triage process for failed automated tests. *Highly accurate reports with built-in summaries of full or partial regressions should be made available—in real time—to the entire team.*

testProbe

testProbe is the only testing component that directly attaches to a testClient. Best done as an optionally loaded library to minimize intrusion, the testProbe module is responsible for generating input events against the testClient (via script or algorithm), hooks to test or set internal game variables, and heartbeat logic to signal hung client states to the Test Session Executive. Note that the Executive is *not* required to run a test. Developers may easily run and rerun a test inside a debugger by using the same path as the Test Executive: scripts and command line arguments. *TSO*'s cheat system provided an excellent starting point for our testProbe module.

Implementation Options

The architecture described in the previous section supports several implementation options. The following sections discuss in more detail specific implementations and their relative merits in MMP testing.

Generating and Synchronizing Test Inputs

Correctly matching your input mechanism with how you plan to use it is critical to success. The most flexible approach is to emulate the observed or predicted actions of players via *scripted play sessions*. This supports most forms of testing and can be made highly similar to actual fielded conditions. Generating mouse and keyboard events can be done without modifying the game code, but generally require higher maintenance and can be prohibitively expensive as a load testing rig. Other forms of generating input include algorithmic event generation, event recorders, a packet snooping/replication approach, and class-level unit testing. All are useful techniques, but each supports a limited number of testing types. *Given the cost of building and maintaining an automated testing system, use a single, configurable test client that can support many types of testing.* Other major input requirements include the ability to synchronize the actions of single or multiple clients, and the ability to repeat the synchronized inputs against a single build (while debugging) or across builds (while regressing). *In general, the more repeatable a test is, the more useful the test becomes.* Strong repeatability is defined as (1) running the same test against the same build 100 times should produce the same result 100 times *and* (2) running the same test across differing builds will also produce the same result (game defects and design shifts excepted). When randomized inputs are necessary, seeding the game's random number generator from a script will often be enough to support repeatability.

There are several approaches for creating test clients and several, sometimes conflicting requirements. Keeping synthetic clients up to date while the game code is still under construction burns precious development time and increases the chances of being wrong. Your best bet for a testing client is the shipping client itself.

A nullView Test Client

During the development of an automated testing system for *The Sims Online*, we simply refactored the game code itself to improve testability. As shown in Figure 2.1.3, a Presentation Layer shim was inserted between the GUI of the client and the client-side game logic. We then attached a scripting system to the same entry points as the GUI (via the Command pattern) and moved the graphics system into an optionally loadable library. *Changing your game's architecture to include a Presentation Layer and an optional viewing system provides a lightweight test client, controllable via script, which by definition is indistinguishable from a shipping client.* Maintenance becomes trivial. As game features and network protocols evolve in the shipping client, they are automatically available and up to date in the test client!

Some of the issues to watch out for when using a nullView client include:

Error feedback and UI/logic entanglement: When we removed the GUI from *TSO*'s shipping client, we found that the remaining game code had very little error detection logic in it. Visual anomalies were the usual way to detect problems in transporting data to the client. We ended up having to retrofit error handling into the game logic. We also found that the code to control the UI's dialog boxes and screens was heavily intertwined with the underlying game logic that fetched and manipulated data from the servers. This was solved with refactoring: when the Presentation Layer shim for a given feature was inserted, UI logic was pushed above the layer, and data manipulation logic was pushed

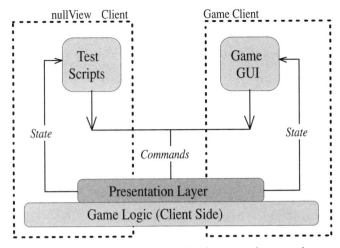

FIGURE 2.1.3   *Use a subset of the shipping client as the test client.*

below the layer. *Including a Presentation Layer in the initial feature design is* much *cheaper than refactoring after the code is built.*

Execution cost: Your nullView client must be lightweight enough to run tens to hundreds of testClients per CPU for large-scale load tests. Process startup costs and memory footprint were the driving factors for the performance of *TSO*'s nullView client.

Internal event timing: There was one serious bug with *TSO*'s nullView client. A few types of client→server events were tied to timers affected by the inclusion or exclusion of the CPU-intense graphics system. This resulted in heavier load by a nullView client than a shipping client. You should maintain a set of calibration tests that compare idle packet rates of nullView and View clients.

Maintenance: Due to time constraints, the separation of view and nullView clients was not as clean as one would like. This created a recurring situation where a change was made to the shipping client that would break part of the nullView client. We solved this by simply adding the use of the nullView client to the project's Sniff Test (described later in this article, Sniff Test is a short regression test of critical path code, run by engineers prior to a checkin). Two interacting clients, one client being nullView and the other a shipping client, resulted in faster and better tests for developers and less work for the testing team. *Strong abstraction in the Presentation Layer increases maintainability, as does minimizing/avoiding #ifdefs when removing the graphics.*

Hanging code: When a client hangs and there is no view to observe what happened, did the hang actually occur? Well, sadly, the answer is yes. We found adding state-driven timeout handlers with a script-controlled timeout value to be highly useful when debugging such problems. Timeout handlers should report what conditions they were waiting for, what the values were when the timeout fired, and what the values should have been.

Ordering Events for Single and Multiple Client Test Sessions

MMP games often need to have multiple inputs into a single test session, coming from multiple processes. To make such tests accurate and repeatable, there must be some way to order the input events across processes. The more common case is the requirement to order events within a test. *Sequential ordering and time-based ordering are insufficient for most testing applications.* User actions are often dependent on a game state change from the previous action, such as using a skill-building object until a threshold is reached, or external actions, such as the arrival of a new avatar in a room. Sample synchronization primitives include:

WaitUntil `<localState> <operator> <X>` is an easy, flexible mechanism to accomplish synchronization and/or validation. WaitUntil simply blocks the execution of a test script until the "<operator> <X>" returns TRUE. For example, "waitUntil avatarCount greaterThan 3" blocks testClientA's script until two or more additional test clients become visible to testClientA. Due to the large set of potential <localState>, a data-driven approach to defining new state probes is recommended.

Rendezvous `<mark>` is useful if there are multiple scripts executing in parallel with occasional synchronization points.

WaitFor `<time>` is useful to simulate time delays. Timing variants across builds and hardware preclude waitFor from being a reliable synchronization mechanism.

RemoteCommand `<remoteClientName> <remoteCommandString>` simply passes the command string to the specified client. The command string is then executed by the remote client's scripting system. Command strings may be individual commands, such as "route localAvatar nextRoom," or more complex such as "run scriptName.txt" or "setData localAvatar.happiness LOW."

Tables 2.1.1 and 2.1.2 shown earlier provide example tests using the preceding primitives. Atomic operators are assumed to improve readability. In the Inventory test, note the use of indirect inspection of the result of commands. *When testing, never trust a primitive's return code in evaluating the success of an operation.* A useful metaphor is your teenage son. If you ask him if he has cleaned his room, he may reply "yes." But if you want to know if the room has actually been cleaned—to your standards—you'll independently inspect the result of the operation. Dumping the contents of the inventory to the log via an independent operation provides much stronger validation: Was the operation successful from the viewpoint of someone using the Inventory? Does querying the Inventory find the new item? Did adding the new item overwrite an old item? Did deleting one item trash a different Inventory item?

This test is written to the *core functionality* specification level; in other words, does the most common use case succeed? More advanced testing might include edge cases, such as adding maxSize+1 items to the inventory, deleting the same item twice, or deleting a nonexistent object.

The combination of waitUntil and remoteCommand provides the strongest mimicry of actual user behavior and supports the broadest set of test conditions. The most common form of multiclient scripting for *TSO* used one master client to perform most testing actions, with remoteCommand calls to one or many puppet clients created in and dedicated to that test run. Another possibility is to execute the script from the server, pushing out remoteCommands to one or many puppet clients. The downside of this approach is lack of visibility into the state of remote clients, one of the very things under test.

Event Recorders

Developers seem drawn to Event Recorders like moths to a flame. Recording all game/mouse/network/whatever events while playing the game and playing them back is a bad idea. The problem is that you have an entire team modifying your game's logic and the meaning or structure of internal events on a day-to-day basis. For *The Sims Online* and other projects, we found that you could only reliably replay an event recording on the same build on which it was recorded. However, the keystone requirement for a testing system is regression: the ability to run the same test across differing builds. *Internal Event Recorders just don't cut it as a general-purpose testing system.* UI Event Recorders share a similar problem: when the GUI of the game shifts, the recording instantly becomes invalid.

However, the notion of a Recorder is very valuable in that it allows you to essentially play the game to craft a new test. For *TSO*, after discarding two event recorders, we shifted to a Recorder in the Presentation Layer. This *Semantic Recorder* captured the abstracted game operation performed by a player via his local GUI and wrote out the script step(s) required to emulate said operation. This was tremendously useful in recording tests portable across builds, but scripters still needed to add control and validation logic to the captured events. The most effective use of the Semantic Recorder was in saving the steps to build complex house structures. Note that Recorders can, under some conditions, also capture defects from a live environment. However, the distributed nature of an MMP game limits the usefulness of this approach. Defects are often the result of interleaving logic threads across N processes, whereas a Recorder only captures local events.

Algorithmic Testing

A powerful form of testing is to dynamically generate events from an algorithm, not a script. A surprising amount of content testing is possible by writing a few algorithms and exploiting gameplay mechanics. An excellent example is *TestAllObjects*, a *TSO* primitive that queried the game to dynamically build a list of all possible interactions an avatar could have with all possible objects within reach, and then sequentially pushed those interactions onto a test avatar. By invoking *TestAllObjects* on preconfigured levels (aka houses) with strategically placed objects, we could easily create a single, short test that routed an avatar completely through a level while triggering all possible interactions in that level. This technique was successfully applied to the initial version of *TSO*, but was only usable in testing content, not client/server operations. A later version of *TestAllObjects* was much more useful in the single-player game *The Sims 2.0*. The following combination of three algorithms could exercise a majority of the game content:

1. for each <avatarType>: CreateNewAvatar
   2. for each <objectCategory>
      3. BuyAndPlaceAllObjects <currentCategoryName>
      4. TestAllObjects <currentAvatar>

A broad test is thus cheaply accomplished, albeit with limited correctness verification. *Combining algorithmic testing with automated Error Managers (discussed later in this article) is extremely effective, if an algorithm can be found to match the characteristics of your game.*

Implementation Options: Test Control Executive

A mechanism to control and observe your test clients is required. Adding control hooks into the game is your best option, but the hooks need to be as unobtrusive as possible. The approach shown in Figure 2.1.4 uses the following:

Process Executive: Capable of configuring, starting, and stopping N test clients and ancillary server-side processes. The Process Executive uses a heartbeatMonitor to repeatedly snoop on a heartbeat log occasionally updated by the test client. Checking for "no recent log entries" or "no forward advancement of client time" accurately detects crashes and most forms of client hangs.

Data Manager: Provides real-time monitoring of the outputs of controlled processes and archives test results to the central test server. Supporting developers with local analysis functions such as searching game logs for asserts and error messages is very valuable in reducing the triage time for a failure, as is configurable e-mail notification at various stages of a test run.

Test Session Manager: Responsible for running structured series of tests (sequentially or in parallel) against specific client/server combinations and aggregating the test results (e.g., "20 of 25 login stability tests failed").

Pass/Fail Evaluator: Flags "same" or "different," when comparing the logs of the current test run against the logs of a successful run. Note that this is *not* a complete pass/fail decision. Automation merely summons a human to examine the difference and assess if it is irrelevant, due to a valid game design change, a bug in the test, or a defect in the game itself. See Tables 2.1.1 and 2.1.2 shown earlier for examples of feature-specific validation logs.

Test Trigger Manager: Continuously monitors outside world events that would trigger the need to run a new test. Possible triggers include the time of day, new Builds being available for test, reported failures from other tests, or new code has been checked into the central repository.

Plan for flexibility in your Control Harness. You'll need to adjust how it works to best fit it into your development practices, and something new will always crop up. In *TSO*, we started with a collection of Perl and Shell scripts as the Control Harness; this let us get up and running quickly, but proved to be limited as we continually extended functionality. Switching to Python was a big win. It must also be very easy to add new tests: a drag&drop file/folder metaphor is useful to organize and add tests. Adding a new test can be done simply by creating a new folder and test script in a directory tree of test categories. The new test is then instantly available from the UI. This also supports easy reconfiguration of the testing hierarchy as needs and knowledge advance.

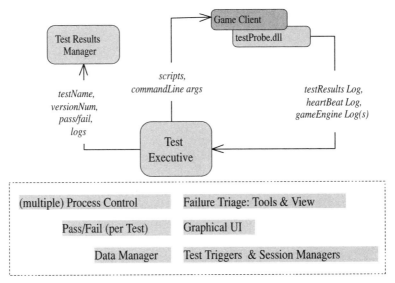

FIGURE 2.1.4 *Major requirements for a Test Executive.*

Information Management

Information management is critical to the success of your automated testing system. A large-scale test run involving tens to hundreds of processes can generate a massive amount of raw data, but usually only a small fraction of that data is relevant to tracking down any particular problem. Further, finding patterns across series of tests is difficult as the number of test results per build increase. Figure 2.1.5 describes an approach that revolves around a central Web site—a *Console*—that your entire team can use to find out what currently works and what does not.

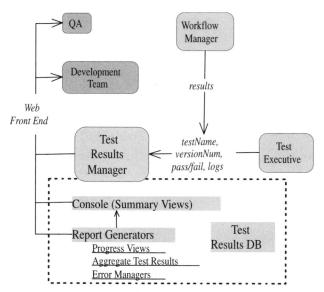

FIGURE 2.1.5   *Internal components of a Test Results Manager.*

Automatic *Report Generators* can summarize detailed test reports to "good," "bad," and "differences from the last build" for the Console. They can also constantly scan for *critical events* and immediately flag them for human attention. *The Console presents progress charts, alerts, and errors to help focus the efforts of your development team.* Drill-down access from the Console to individual test results and log files assists your team in quickly triaging specific failures. You'll also need some way to filter out known failures that will take a while to fix—this keeps the noise level down and helps ID new problems, not just constantly flagging existing problems.

Similarly, you will need some mechanism to deal with transient failures. *MMP games are nondeterministic systems.* It is quite possible for a test to pass 80 out of 100 runs, and crash or hang the remaining 20. For *TSO*, we ran *calibration tests* on a regular basis, repeating the same test hundreds of times to assess how deterministic the result was. The initial results were very scary. Of game functions considered "critical path" (the collection of features or code paths that, if broken, prevents a majority of the development team from progressing on their daily tasks, and/or prevents the bulk of the automated tests from succeeding), no feature would consistently pass. *TSO*'s critical path consisted of six primitives: Login(), createAvatar(), buyLot(), enterLot(), buyObject(), and useObject(). Failure rates on the critical path ranged from 70% to

30% per element during the initial fielding of our testing system. One critical path feature, EnterLot, over 30 repetitions, could function correctly, or it could fail due to crashes and hangs, or work, but evict the owner and transfer all possessions to another avatar just entering the lot! We eventually ran all important tests several times in each test session and defined any feature that passed more than 85% of the time as "good enough" for initial development purposes. We slowly raised the bar to 95% as the features stabilized. *Calibration tests measure the accuracy of data used to make key business decisions and clearly expose nondeterministic failures.*

Historical analysis is also very important; the result of a test in the past and what checkin caused the test to stop passing are vital clues in tracking down problems. Further, an interesting psychological phenomenon exists with most developers. Failures reported by automated testing are often considered the test's fault, not the still-wet code that was just checked in. And of course, that is a possibility. The game's correct behavior might have shifted, the test might have been relying on invalid game behavior to work correctly, or there might be a bug in the test itself that is only just now rearing its ugly head. *The law of large numbers is a testing group's best friend.* If a test has passed 50 times a day for the past two weeks, yes, it could still be broken. However, the onus is now on the developer to show why a specific code checkin caused a previously working test to stop working, and your team as a whole has an excellent starting point to begin tracking down the cause of any problems.

Crash Managers: Many odd crashes occur "in the wild," where the flow of networked events is unpredictable and real user actions and real user data produce unexpected effects. *A Crash Manager is a type of Error Manager: a Report Generator that analyzes game engine errors instead of test results.* Client and server crash logs (generated from manual testing, automated testing, and Beta user's gameplay) are pulled from the Test Results DB and aggregated into daily high-level reports. Your Crash Manager should also support some way to filter out crashes in areas of the game known to be currently incomplete, such as shutdown failures. Table 2.1.3 shows a sample view of these high-level results, with drill-down access to the raw data, accessible to the entire team from the Web-based Console.

Table 2.1.3   Sorted Lists of Crashes and Log Files Help Prioritize and Fix Serious Errors

File	Line #	Frequency	Game Version	Raw Logs
graphics.cpp	12,000	45	1.44.5	Click to view
simulator.cpp	812	4	1.44.5	Click to view
fnord.cpp	42	1	Beta	Click to view

Asset Tracking: Large-scale games require thousands of asset files such as sound, textures, and animations to support their broad feature set. Similar to the Crash Manager, a specialized Error Manager (Table 2.1.4) can collect reports of missing asset errors, as reported from clients. An interesting variant is the inverse of missing asset errors: reporting all assets that were found and used in a broad game regression. Compare the list of used assets versus assets on your shipping manifest; any assets on disk that are not used are good candidates for removal when you're pinched for space on your final disk images. Table 2.1.4 also gives insight into overused asset files, such as a sound that is repeated too often in live gameplay. For an easy implementation of some types of Error Managers, simply create an automated metric that counts and reports to a central Web site, as shown in Article 2.6 in this book.

Table 2.1.4   Finding and Grouping Errors via Automation Speeds Bug Fixing

Missing Assets (Sound Files)	Count	Context	Game Version
Squeak	33	stepEvent	1.44.5
Groan	22	deathEvent	1.44.5
Shriek	1	mockEvent	1.44.4

Get your Report Generators in place early, and constantly improve them to meet on the ground, current conditions. A good rule of thumb: if you have to spend time each build boiling down the results of a test run to a meaningful result, you need another Report Generator.

Applications of Automated Testing

A myriad of applications exist for automation in the development of MMP games. The value of each application will vary across projects; a little "back of the envelope" math will help you prioritize and plan testing applications.

When crafting new testing applications, note that the strength of automated testing lies with its ability to repeat massive numbers of simple, easily measurable tasks. Automation breaks down as individual test complexity increases. Douglas Adams, speaking at the 1997 SCO Forum, summed up the problem nicely when he said that the basic difference between computers and us is that they are blindingly stupid, and capable of being stupid many, many millions of times a second. Repeating simple tests hundreds of times and combining the results is far easier to maintain and analyze than using long, complex tests.

Measuring simple tasks is surprisingly useful. It provides clarity into what needs doing next, replacing opinion with fact. It is also much easier to establish and agree on simple tests, and they are relevant much earlier in the development cycle than complex tests are. As shown in Figure 2.1.6, the exact specification of the game varies considerably in the early stages of development as designers experiment with differing gameplay and presentation options. Further, game implementation generally follows an incremental development approach: the initial implementation of a feature is usu-

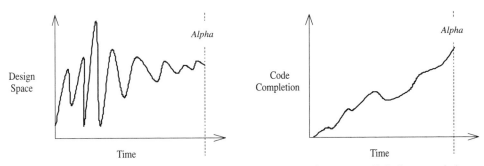

FIGURE 2.1.6 *Applying detailed testing while the game design is still shifting and the code is still incomplete introduces noise and the need to keep rewriting tests.*

ally restricted to *core functionality*; in other words, the minimum subset required to support basic gameplay. Applying a test with shipping-quality level of detail before Alpha is pointless. Keeping such detailed tests up to date with design shifts is expensive, and running them is irrelevant; you'll only find bugs that won't be addressed until post-Alpha anyway. Core functionality tests are immediately applicable and retain their usefulness over time. *In the early development phase of MMP games, the value of automated testing is in measuring, stabilizing, and scaling core functionality, not testing for shipping quality.*

Automation applications fall into four broad categories:

Stability: Constant testing of core functionality greatly increases the stability of the code base and of the servers. This increases developer efficiency by reducing broken builds and dead servers that impede their day-to-day tasks. *Automated testing keeps developers moving forward, not stalled due to codependent components, broken builds, or having to continuously triage and repair once-working code.*

Scale: Testing the behavior of servers at peak load cannot be done without automation. Finding and diagnosing scaling issues is much easier with a repeatable test than with live users.

Content: Verifying that thousands of assets are correctly hooked up and functioning correctly across all types of avatars and all conditions with all tuning factors being correctly balanced is a formidable task. The cost of content testing can be tremendously reduced via automation.

Semi-Automated Tests: Automation may be used to generate raw data for live testers to evaluate. Something as simple as entering all in-game locations and generating screenshots of graphical effects works very well. *Using automation to provide cheap, broad coverage of the game and live testers to evaluate the results combines the strengths of both forms of testing.*

Automated test results may be applied during game development in three basic ways:

Focusing development: Focusing on true, measured problems, not perceived or potential problems, saves on time, effort and team stress levels.

Tracking progress toward launch: The more complex the feature set and the larger the number of connected clients, the more difficult it is to accurately measure the progression of the game's development. Further, team size and code codependences constantly interfere with and muddy the view of forward progress. *Automated testing allows very precise measurements—each and every day—of how close the game is to launch.* Load testing clearly shows how many clients at what level latency a given server instance can support, where automated unit tests running against each build show which features are currently working and to what level of completion, per feature. Again, core functionality testing is the best bet here. Full feature completeness is too difficult to define before the features have been play tested, and would not pass until after Alpha anyway.

Flagging problem areas: Flag problem areas of a build for in-depth manual testing. Remember, computers are stupid. Always have manual testers triage automated testing failures to gather additional data and add human judgment to the pass/fail process.

Many of the applications listed in the following section were very successful in accelerating the implementation of *The Sims Online*, a client/server game with shards ("Cities") consisting of hundreds of server-side processes, thousands of simultaneously connected clients, and a persistent database for tens of thousands of avatars ("Sims"), their houses, and their possessions. The applications are largely independent from each other, so pick what seems most appropriate for your project's needs. Sniff Tests, Monkey Tests, and Load Tests are the best starting points.

Stability During Development

Automated testing from the very beginning of development greatly stabilizes your game's infrastructure and feature set. *Once a piece of shipping code is working, why let it stop working?*

Build Regression: Running a series of tests against each new build with consideration of what worked in the last build immediately shows when a defect has been introduced into your code line. Your Build Acceptance Tests should be light-weight; quick feedback is essential to the test's value, and shorter tests are easier to interpret and maintain. You can then fail the build, pass it with an immediate bug report, or update the test itself, should the changed test result turn out to simply be a valid change in the game's behavior.

Sniff Test: A fast pre-checkin regression test run by developers before checking in new code. A *Sniff Test* is very lightweight, exercising only the critical path of game code that, if broken, prevents other developers from working (see Figure 2.1.7). QA Smoke Tests cover much more functionality and take much longer to run—20 to 80 minutes versus 2 to 10 minutes for a Sniff Test. Incompatible client/server/DB changes, crashing login servers, and broken builds seriously impede developer efficiency across the team; therefore, a small time investment per checkin can pay big dividends across all developers. Sniff Test was very

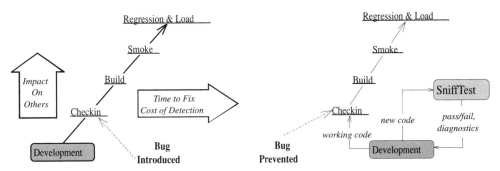

FIGURE 2.1.7 *A fast pre-checkin test of critical path code keeps the development team working instead of fighting fires.*

useful on *TSO*. It provided a baseline of what was known to work across a complex set of codependent components, a common benchmark runnable from any machine. As a pre-checkin gate, SniffTest helped save developers from breaking something important that was related to their code change in some mysterious but definitely catastrophic fashion. *Sniff Test is your best barrier to introducing bugs that slow your team's forward progress.* Keep in mind you're adding a recurring cost to every checkin, so don't try to cover everything! Running a Sniff Test should consist of no more than pushing a button and then reading some e-mail or getting some coffee while it works.

Monkey Tests: Programmers love monkeys; thus our choice of a monkey metaphor was perhaps inevitable. Monkeys also turned out to be useful in making the automation system more understandable to *TSO*'s production staff. A monkey avatar (thanks to Bob King) gave a nice anthropomorphic feel to the tests and helped drive home the message that an automated test was just a repeatable series of any avatar actions. Figure 2.1.8 shows how Monkey Testing was used to continually measure the stability of the Mainline code repository. Every hour of every day, a series of Stability Monkeys would grab the latest code checkins and compile a new test client. Each Monkey would then repeat a single test several times against that day's Reference Server and report aggregate results for that hour. For *TSO*, each Hourly Monkey Test corresponded to one core functionality unit test against each element on *TSO*'s critical path. This gave us three extremely important results:

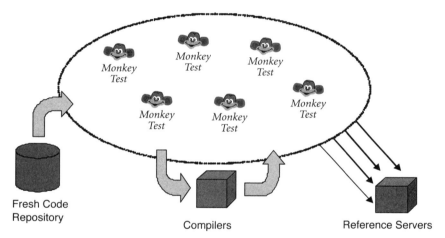

FIGURE 2.1.8   *Monkeys continually compile and test client features against reference servers.*

- A constant health indicator for both the game's code base and the Reference Servers (under nonstop use by the entire development team) that instantly and clearly flagged show-stopper problems.
- The Reference Servers, although not heavily loaded, were constantly in motion. This exposed race conditions not seen when single tests were run sequentially by developers.
- The Reference Servers also began to slowly age and data sizes slowly increased. This exposed corrupted buffers, memory leaks, and data scalability issues very early in the production cycle.

Repeating each test several times and aggregating the results is extremely important in an MMP game. Nondeterministic failures can cripple the forward progress of your team and are very difficult to track down. *Monkey Testing provided clarity in under-*

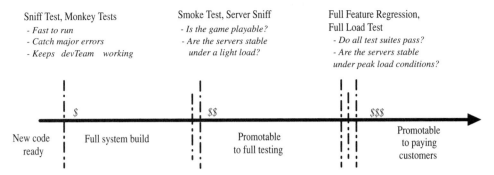

FIGURE 2.1.9 *Hierarchical Comb Filters catch completely fried builds with very cheap tests, very early in the pipeline. Expensive tests are only run on builds known to pass earlier filters.*

standing where we were, a reliable measure of forward progress, and a trip wire when new problems were introduced.

Hierarchy of Tests: Figure 2.1.9 shows a staged series of *comb filters*, each increasing the level of test coverage as a build candidate progresses down the promotion pipeline. Pre-checkin Sniff Tests and Monkey Tests are lightweight but catch common and/or mission-critical defects. Post-build smoke and stability tests answer the question, "is this reproducible build worth spending detailed testing effort on?" Finally, detailed, expensive QA regression testing and load testing are only done on builds known to be functionally correct.

Unit Tests (class level):   Development strategies such as Extreme Programming rely heavily on automated unit testing, with tools such as cppUnit, jUnit, and nUnit being easily available. While unit testing is quite useful in some testing applications, several limitations exist. First, finding class-level "units" in game code that can be extracted and executed outside of the game as a whole simply may not be possible (another argument for building code with automated testing as a design requirement). Second, meaningful unit tests at the class level are difficult to come up with. The tests are written by a programmer, usually with little testing experience. Once you've passed in some good and some bad arguments to your method calls, where do you go from there? Next, the unit tests are not directly tied to the user experience, and thus are not likely to reflect true fielded conditions, nor will producers and managers be able to properly understand and prioritize fixings problems found by class-level unit testing. Finally, class-level unit tests do not support system-level tests against features or scale, or component integration tests. *Class-level unit testing is restricted to a small spectrum of the overall testing requirements for MMP development. It is best done in addition to system and subsystem testing, not instead of.*

Unit Tests (feature level):   Feature-level unit testing meets most of the desirable unit test characteristics, with far fewer limitations. They are also easier to do with legacy code and are more tied to the user experience; thus, test results are more understandable to Development Directors and Producers who are removed from the code. Feature-level unit tests also map nicely to use-case analysis, an excellent mechanism to establish realistic test cases. One essentially creates a series of storyboards describing how a user would interact with each feature, and what observable effect his action should have. *Scripting use cases at the core functionality level is the best starting point for a new feature.* The downside of feature-level tests is that your load penalty is high: the entire game client comes in for each test. Using a nullView client largely mitigates this effect. There is also a greater risk of side effects from other features disturbing the feature under test.

Scaling the Servers

MMP systems break down under heavy load. There are so many moving parts and so much more data flying around, something that works just fine when the developer checks it in goes "spang!" when 2,000 clients are churning out data. *Testing for stability at scale is one of the most important things you can do with automation. Get the bugs out before the paying customers show up!*

Load testing should be done very early in the development cycle. It provides clear, *measurable* views of what does and does not work at scale. *TSO* used a technique we called Scale&Break to focus development on the key roadblocks. Scale&Break is simply taking the Alpha-grade server code and running a load test. Slowly increase the number of connected test clients until something crashes. Fix whatever crashed and repeat the test to verify the fix. Then, increase the number of test clients and start over, repeating until you reach your target load. *Scale&Break replaces opinions on what will prevent scaling with facts, and in enough time to address the inevitable issues.* Note again the importance of repeatable tests. They will yield more than enough problems to fix, and give you a way to verify that they've been fixed. Randomized inputs should be saved until your servers are working reliably at scale. Similarly, begin testing with common use cases. Testing for extreme edge conditions before the average case reliably passes is wasted (and noisy) effort.

The following is a list of the metrics obtainable from an automated testing harness (see Figure 2.1.10) and their importance:

Average client latency: Player lag at peak server load is an extremely important measure that directly impacts the player experience.

Number of supportable clients: Allows you to establish how many servers and how much bandwidth will be required to support your projected market, while meeting minimum end-user performance requirements.

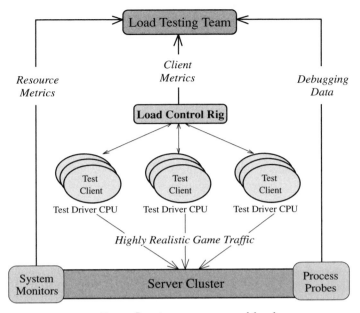

FIGURE 2.1.10 *Data flow in an automated load test.*

Meantime between failure (Client and Server): On average, how long can a server cluster stay operational at peak load? Similarly, how long will the client last without crashing or locking up?

Resource utilization: CPU, memory, network traffic, and page faults are essential metrics when optimizing servers.

Process metrics: What activities inside each server-side process are driving the resource issues identified previously?

Content Testing

MMP games contain a great deal of content, content that is continually being extended and modified over years of operations. Testing such content is expensive, but is also invaluable. *New content can significantly disrupt the playability of existing features, throwing your economy or tuning levels out of balance.* Closely monitoring your content keeps users happy and designers sane. Examples of content testing include:

Comprehensive coverage testing, stress testing, and randomized input testing:
When combined with the two Error Managers (described previously), exhaustive coverage testing is extremely useful in tracking pre-launch feature completeness. Simply have test clients perform all possible operations in all possible combinations, and fix all the problems your Error Managers collect for

you. Of course, open-ended gameplay prevents truly exhaustive testing from being a viable option. A reasonable approximation is to use a combination of broad, shallow coverage across the full feature set and focused stress testing against selected components with known risks. Randomized inputs complete your test coverage by jumping through unexpected combinations (just like real users), but should not be used until the game has shown stability under repeatable inputs. Excellent results have been achieved with *algorithmic testing*, as defined earlier in *Implementation Options*.

Testing Graphics: Computers are traditionally weak at testing visual effects. Simple bitmap comparisons tend to be quite brittle; minor variances will frequently trigger false failures whereas a human tester can apply judgments such as "close enough" or "minor change, not a bug." Algorithmic comparisons that find edges or do fuzzy comparisons of shapes and colors are possible but expensive and can be unreliable. Your best bet here is to combine the strengths of automated and manual testing: use automation to place the game in many repeatable situations (in-game locations or artificial reference tests), and then save snapshots of the screen for later evaluation by manual testers. Snapshots can either be screenshots, reflecting an instant of time, or small video recordings, reflecting a span of time. This technique was used very effectively in *The Sims 2.0*. The automated tests provided very broad coverage, tens to hundreds of snapshots per build. Manual testers and/or artists would then quickly flip through the snapshots, looking for visual anomalies and drilling further into any identified problem areas. Make sure you have an easy way to tie a found problem back to the (repeatable) test that generated the error, that it is easy to compare related tests (such as the same reference test against DX 7/8/9 hardware), and to see what was the last "known good" snapshot for any given test.

Tuning Tests: Another form of comprehensive testing possible via automation is that of checking tuning values for key gameplay values. For example, create an artificial test environment that contains all damageable objects, then run a series of tests where an avatar wields all possible types of weapons and hits all damageable objects, and then use a Report Generator to chart the results similar to those in Figure 2.1.11. You could also have avatars endlessly perform all forms of skill-building tasks and measure the time it takes to transition each level. Testing AI balance is also possible via artificial test environments: place the AI in a simple situation of N possible choices for a long period of time, and then measure if the right choices were made the right percentage of the time.

Test Suites: Many games will have a series of formal "test suites," extracted from game design docs to establish content correctness via a series of very specific command and validation steps: "do <this action> and make sure the game responds with <a specific state change>." Test suites are excellent candidates for automation, but be very careful. . . . First, do *not* try to use these tests during the

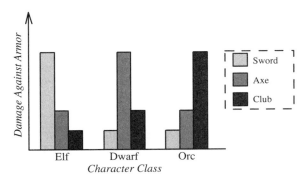

FIGURE 2.1.11 *Automation allows exhaustive testing of all types of characters against all types of objects, skill gain rates for every class for every skill, and any other key gameplay variables.*

early stages of game development. By definition, the game is not done yet, ergo these test suites will generate a huge number of errors, errors that nobody really cares about until the game is closer to done. Further, running detailed tests against a system that doesn't quite work yet produces even more noise; trying to track back a specific failure to one of many potential causes is a difficult proposition. Finally, any detailed tests you write early in the development cycle will inevitably have to be rewritten as the game design evolves. *Save your detailed tests until Core Functionality tests are passing and the content has stabilized.*

Applying Automation to Your Project

The easiest and cheapest way to do automated testing is one very simple rule: When you check in new code, you also check in the automated test that exercises the new code.

If an existing test does not exercise the new code, then the developer provides a new test or extends an existing one. The best approach is to first write the test for a feature during the design phase and then implement the feature, only checking in the new code when the automated test passes. Tailor the test to "first checkin," core functionality quality; in other words, expect the new feature to work in the most-commonly used code path but not handle all edge cases or necessarily meet performance requirements. More detailed tests can be written as development continues on the feature.

Kent Beck's writings on test driven development provide considerable data on the value of writing the test before the code. Issues with interfaces are quickly and cheaply exposed, developers can continually refer to the fast, repeatable test case while cutting new code, and a tangible, *measurable* artifact exists to document a feature and keep it running over years of extensions.

Other techniques to add automated testing have been successfully used, but are more expensive. One option is to add an additional developer to the team with the sole responsibility of adding automated testing hooks to other people's code. This works, but is very inefficient. Adding testing hooks as a design requirement is far easier than reverse-engineering existing code to add hooks. Another option is to add testing engineers to the QA side of the shop, at a cost of increased labor and generally lower testability if they can't modify the game itself to increase its testability.

You'll need to spend a fair amount of time integrating automated testing into your development cycle, but there is a huge payoff. Be flexible. A good integration effort will morph the tools, development process, and game code until a simple, seamless process exists. *Integration of automation is critical and difficult; a senior engineer with support from both development and QA is required for success.*

Be prepared for things to go wrong; automated testing is tricky and few game developers have experience with it. That means that legacy code and development practices will have to be modified to effectively use automated testing. Your best bet is continual analysis of how effective your testing system is, and continual improvement to make it faster and easier to use on a day-to-day, hour-to-hour basis.

Some useful rules of thumb when integrating automation into your game's development cycle include:

Keep tests short and simple.   Get in, test one thing, and get out. The longer a test, the more it costs to maintain and triage when it fails, and the more likely some side-effect thing gets in the way of what you are actually trying to test.

Your tools must be easier to use than not to use.   For each type of test report your system spits out, sit down with the developers who are supposed to use it, and walk through the process of fixing a problem found by the automated testing system, and how they would know if and when the problem was reported as fixed by the testing system. If they can't instantly find everything they need, change your UI to make it so.

Keep your Sniff Test short and push-button runnable.   Everybody runs it. Do feature-specific testing via other tests, with the exact same push-button.

Rapid triage support.   IDing the cause of a test failure is critical, but that's hard in MMP development. The cause of failures may involve complex interactions across processes on distributed machines. By dropping all logs in the TestResults DB, a series of Event Reporter 'bots can look for and report critical event failures and ID patterns across logs. Use real-time reporting of failure results to a central site. *Keep improving your triage system until your development team can instantly ID the basic problem uncovered by an automated test.* Rapid triage is a must-have during development to streamline troubleshooting and repair and it will pay dividends for years to come.

Run thousands of tests.   Buy some hardware and have it cranking 24x7. Repeat tests tens to hundreds of times to build statistical certainty into your results. You'll be amazed at the variance, especially as you scale.

Summarize everything.   Most people don't need or want the details. Use automation to scan the detailed test results and produce high-level views of good versus bad, passed versus failed, this build versus last build, and so forth, with drill-down access to the raw data from each report.

One of your biggest problems will be inserting this technology into your development team. There is a high payoff for doing so, but changing how people work is always difficult. Start using automated testing from day one in your development cycle before people are under the gun and set in their ways. It is more cost effective and lower risk. You will also get more use out of your investment.

More data on how and why to apply automation in MMP development can be found at the author's Web site: *www.maggotranch.com/MMP.html.*

Conclusion

Automated testing can help you produce a higher quality game in less development time, providing accurate measures of progress as you go.   Further, basing development decisions on hard data, not opinion, saves time and reduces stress. Such tools have a great return on investment for games with years of operation, but supporting automated testing in an MMP game is not a trivial task. Automated testing affects many aspects of your code design and development practices. Starting a project with automated testing is much easier than adding it late in the development cycle, and is more effective.

Automation augments manual testing, it does not replace it.   Use automation for repetitive, simple tasks with clear pass/fail criteria, or use automation to generate test data for humans to evaluate pass/fail. Use humans for creative testing, use automation for tasks involving scale; broad exhaustive testing for accurate analysis of key game tuning values and content completion; or testing tasks requiring a high degree of repeatable accuracy. Enjoy!

Acknowledgments

Much of the knowledge in this article was painfully gleaned from implementing *TSO's* automated testing system, which would not have existed without the vision and executive support of Luc Barthelet, Gordon Walton, and in particular, Chris Yates. Many of the successful design constructs were the result of discussions with the executive team, Greg Kearney, Steve Keller, Chris Kosmakos, Jeff Marshall, and Darrin West. Sniff Test's success was dependent on strong leadership from the executive team, *TSO's* director of development (Dominique Phillipine), and *TSO's* engineering leads.

2.2

Massively Multiplayer Scripting Systems

Jon Parise—Electronic Arts

jon@indelible.org

Back when I was a graduate student at Carnegie Mellon's Entertainment Technology Center, a group of five of us developed a real-time interactive show for the Carnegie Museum of Natural History's Earth Theater, a 210-degree panoramic theater composed of five side-by-side projection screens. A small network of computers served the five digital projectors to create a single unified image. The theater generally presented "traditional" pre-rendered shows that were specially mastered for this unique display system, but our goal was real-time interactivity. The generous folks at LithTech had made their 3D engine available to us for use in our in-house projects, and we set about adapting their system to this new challenge.

We were immediately presented with a challenge near and (maybe not so) dear to every multiplayer game developer's heart: how do you design an interactive content delivery system for a networked environment? Furthermore, how do you make the system accessible to the nonengineers who will be responsible for developing the content itself?

My ultimate solution involved embedding a Python interpreter and exposing the core LithTech interfaces to the Python scripting environment. One of the five computer hosts was designated the "master" and ran the authoritative version of the script. The other hosts were kept in sync using a simple network stream of positional updates.

The Python system provided us with an unanticipated amount of flexibility. It allowed us to make core changes to the rendering and networking systems without affecting the show content. It also enabled the content producers (i.e., the scripters) to work in parallel to the rest of the engineering efforts. This early success made me a tremendous proponent of scripting systems for interactive content, and when I later became an engineer on *The Sims Online* and *Ultima Online* development teams, a solid scripting system proved to be the only viable option for supporting the dynamic content of a massively multiplayer (MMP) title.

Design Questions

Let's begin by discussing some important design questions:

Does your game need a scripting system?   While one of the goals of this article is to extol the virtues of scripting systems, not all games require them. For example, if the game's design doesn't call for large amounts of interactive content and employs relatively simple rule sets, there is little to be gained by introducing the added complexity of a scripting environment (although it could be argued that such a simple game could be written *completely* in script).

How much of your system should be exposed to the scripting environment? This is obviously a matter of tradeoffs. On the one hand, exposing the majority of the game systems to the scripting environment yields the greatest return on "scripting system investment," with the measurable benefits generally being in the area of development flexibility. Unfortunately, this comes at the maintenance and development cost of the scripting infrastructure itself.

On the other hand, building your features using your implementation language primarily (e.g., C++) reduces code duplication, but to the detriment of your scripting system's ability to fully interact with your core game systems.

When do you trade execution speed for development speed?   In general, your scripting system's interpreted code is going to execute slower than your compiled code. This is why most developers wouldn't dream of writing their core graphics or physics components in an interpreted language. However, compiled code pays a price for its speed advantage in that it is essentially static once it's been linked and executed. Interpreted code, however, can be removed, reloaded, and rebound inside of a live process, three features that are incredibly important to a rapid development environment.

For whom is the scripting system intended?   Lastly, when designing your scripting environment, it's important to establish your target audience (or "customer"). Are you developing your system so that your team's engineering staff can quickly iterate on core game code? Is your goal to enable your designers to prototype (and perhaps ultimately implement) their game systems? Are you planning on making your scripting environment available to your customer service team or the players themselves?

You likely find each of these customers important, albeit to different degrees, and each brings its own set of unique requirements.

Architecture

If you have the luxury of starting your game's system architecture from scratch, you have numerous organizational choices. One of the most important choices with regard to your scripting system is whether you will embed your interpreter inside of your game (i.e., you treat it as another system component) or whether you plan to run your entire game from within the interpreter. While hybrid architectures are possible, nearly all implementations adhere to one of these two models.

Games such as *The Sims Online* and *Ultima Online* follow the first model. The interpreter is "ticked" at some fixed interval from the main game loop once other system tasks, such as networking or graphics updates, have been handled. The interpreter does its share of work, which often results in modified game state, and then the loop iterates again. Most would consider this a traditional execution model.

The alternate approach, employed by *Disney's Toontown*, loads all of the game components into the interpreter. The main game loop might even be written in script itself! This interpreter-centric approach relies on your scripting environment's ability to access and manipulate your nonscripted game components (using some kind of foreign function interface; *Toontown* uses Python extension API), but the end result can be a very flexible and satisfying organization.

Synchronicity

MMP games are inherently client-server based, and synchronizing game state between the clients and servers is a core design challenge. While the larger problem of synchronization is out of scope here, the impact it will have on the design of your scripting environment is entirely relevant.

One possible implementation mimics the traditional Web technology model: all of the primary scripting (i.e., the scripting that controls the game's "business logic") occurs on the server. These scripts affect some change in game state, which the server broadcasts to the clients. The (thin) clients are therefore completely ignorant of the scripting environment's existence. This is the approach adopted with great success by *Ultima Online*.

A variation on this model adds nonsynchronous client-side scripting support. To make another Web technology comparison, this is akin to the client-side JavaScript support. The server-side scripts can focus entirely on shared world logic, while the client-side scripts can perform local, latency-sensitive functions (such as graphics-related tasks). It's debatable whether this simplifies or complicates the game's code, however. On the one hand, it means that server- or client-side scripts become more succinct; on the other hand, the two scripting environments need to work in concert to achieve a unified experience. Either way, the result is clearly complex and necessitates careful planning to implement correctly.

A third model involves a true parallel simulation: identical scripts execute in lockstep on both the client and the server. In other words, both the client and the server maintain a completely up-to-date representation of the world, and the same scripts execute using the same data on both ends of the network connection. This offers the low-latency advantages of a non-networked game while introducing the notion of a shared world. Unfortunately, it also introduces all of the problems inherent to parallel systems (namely, handling synchronization and drift).

The Sims Online adopted this last execution model due to the simulation-centric nature of the gameplay. The game's interaction-based interface also lent itself to discrete events and state changes that could be easily broadcast between client and server. It did introduce the problem of whether one end of the simulation could be completely trusted, however, so the attitude that only the server contained the authoritative representation of the world was adopted. To this end, each client-initiated interaction had to be authorized by the server before it was applied to the shared simulation, and the game's scripting environment was molded to support this organization.

The Scripting Language

The scripting language is the centerpiece of your scripting environment, and it would be unwise to select a scripting language until all of your system's requirements have been defined. Understanding the requirements upfront will also provide a basis for narrowing down the wide array of available scripting language solutions to just the ones that fit you game's needs.

Using an Existing Language

Many developers choose to adopt an existing general-purpose scripting language, such as Python, Lua, or LISP. Implementations are generally freely available and redistributable given appropriate crediting, and most are developed under an open-source model that encourages contributions, rapid release cycles, and wide-scale testing and adoption. In summary, most of these languages can be considered mature and community-supported.

However, the fact that these are general-purpose languages needs to be emphasized. They might offer functionality that you simply don't need (or even desire), resulting in a "heavier," and possibly less manageable and secure scripting system. For example, Python might be your language of choice, but does your scripting system require threading, socket, and file IO support? Granted, you could restrict or disable those modules, but that may introduce additional maintainability overhead, depending on the interpreter's design.

Moreover, adopting a third-party scripting system introduces a strong dependency on an externally developed product. In addition to the obvious technical concerns, this may also generate business complications. For example, open-source solutions hardly ever come with support contracts or guarantees, and there are cases where the licensing terms might prove a hindrance.

Still, the advantages of using an existing scripting language often outweigh these concerns. You can virtually eliminate the development cost of designing and implementing a language interpreter, and you reap the benefits of externally maintained documentation, code libraries, and support resources. These latter benefits are especially important when you are faced with the task of training new team members on your game's scripting system.

Should you decide to adopt a third-party system, be sure to budget time and resources to study its internals and make any necessary modifications that might be needed to fit your requirements. A significant portion of your game will be based on this technology, and you will need to support it to the same extent as any internal development components. For example, you will need to make a substantial investment in the "glue" code that integrates your game with your scripting system, so it will behoove you to develop an understanding of the work involved in designing, using, and maintaining this component of your game system early in your development process.

Rolling Your Own Scripting Language

There are many cases where using a third-party scripting system is not desirable. For some, the game's requirements might dictate an application-specific, nongeneral scripting solution. Your requirements may call for strict or constant-time execution and rigorous memory management, or you may be concerned with deploying third-party code with your final product (perhaps due to licensing restrictions). Your development studio may also have an existing internally developed scripting environment that may be easily adapted to suit your needs. All of these are valid reasons for not adopting a third-party scripting system.

For others, however, the engineering staff might be uncomfortable introducing externally maintained code into the project (perhaps invoking the dreaded "Not Invited Here" mantra), or they might relish the challenge of developing the system themselves (which could be a recipe for disaster!). Or, perhaps there are legal requirements that prevent you from using a third-party solution in your product. In these cases, it might make sense to develop a custom, proprietary scripting system for your game.

Building a scripting language is no simple task, however. An effective system is more than just an interpreter; you'll also need at least a basic compiler, debugger, and profiler. Unless your engineering staff has experience in these areas, you could be introducing a significant development risk.

With that being said, a number of large, successful MMP games are built upon custom scripting solutions. *Ultima Online* runs on a C-like text-based scripting system called Wombat, and the objects in *The Sims Online* are all developed using Edith, the object-centric, tree-based development environment that implements the SymAntics system. Each of these systems had unique needs (*Ultima Online* was originally developed over seven years ago before most modern third-party solutions were mature or even available; *The Sims Online* was built on top of the original *The Sims* code base), which justified the development of a proprietary scripting system.

Scripting Language Integration

Once your scripting language has been selected, it will need to be integrated with the rest of your game. As mentioned earlier, your scripting engine can either be embedded inside of your larger application, or your game (a la *Ultima Online*) can be implemented in terms of your scripting engine (*Toontown*).

Regardless of which organization you choose, you will need to consider how you will expose the rest of you game's functionality to your scripting environment, and vice versa. This "glue" code is generally implemented as a set of wrapper functions that simply invoke native code functions from script (after performing any relevant argument and result conversions). Unfortunately, this often results in large amounts of support code; once the native routine is written, the wrapper function needs to be written that will expose the function to script. A generic function call layer could be implemented, but at the loss of performance and tight-coupling. A preferable solution to the maintenance problem is something like *Toontown*'s internally developed "interrogation" system, which scans the native C++ code's resulting object files and generates Python bindings for all of the specially decorated routines. This yields performance-friendly native code bindings without the maintenance cost of handcrafted wrapper functions (at the expense of the potential bloat often associated with automatically generated code).

Objects

MMP online games are inherently object-based. While this doesn't necessarily call for an object-oriented programming environment, the scripting system must at least be object-aware, and, in nearly all scripting implementations, the "object" is the basic operand of nearly all common operations. In fact, most game scripting systems consider "object" a standard data primitive (just like "integer," "float," and "string" values).

In the scripting environment, an object is generally represented by some kind of unique handle (e.g., an object ID) that maps back to a concrete game object instance. It is the "lowest common denominator" for game system interactions and may polymorphically represent everything from player objects to static world objects to effects objects.

Some more object-oriented scripting environments support the notion of object-based namespaces. This allows script-accessible data to be stored on an object. The better implementations will use some kind of introspection or reflection mechanism to make accessing data even more magical and convenient. It may also mean that script routines may run in the context of a specific object (as member functions).

Most scripting environments allow you to extend a game object, implemented in native code (such as C++), using the scripting language. For example, your native game code could define a base NPC object from which your scripting environment could derive multiple specific types of NPCs: merchants, thieves, guards, and so forth. This adds to the flexibility and general maintainability of your game logic, and promotes rapid development, prototyping, and deployment.

All of this results in an object-centric scripting environment, so take care in how your object-management routines are designed and implemented, as most of your game's functionality will depend on them. Seemingly simple decisions regarding object access or scoping rules may result in future difficulties, such as *Ultima Online*'s inability to access objects that are being served outside of the current process.

Persistence and Game State

Persistence is a common problem in developing MMP games, and it will likely have an impact on your scripting environment as well. Your scripts won't be concerned with how the data is persisted, but you will always want to ensure that they're acting on the most recent, authoritative data, regardless of the state of the world. Persistence also comes into play when you consider how scripts will operate when players and objects cross server boundaries.

This introduces a side discussion concerning the general expectations that scripted code can place on the state of the world. For the most part, you will want to ensure that your scripts will always execute in a consistent, stable environment. For example, you probably don't want to worry about your script code being preempted by another execution thread, especially if your scripting engine isn't aware of such concepts, so you may want to treat your script callouts as critical sections (conceptually, at least).

Development and Maintainability

Once your scripting system is up and running, your development team will have to actually start using it to build game features. It's in these day-to-day operations that the quality of your early design choices will quickly become apparent.

Editing

Most, but not all, scripting languages are text-based. Creating and editing a script doesn't require anything more than a basic text editor. If it offers advanced search and syntax highlighting features, it's even better. However, will your scripter developers be able to edit scripts on their local machines, or will they need to work directly on the servers? Will they have to transfer their scripts to the server using an FTP-like mechanism after each edit, or will the script distribution system be part of the game client itself? What needs to happen in order for the game processes to reload the changes? How will your development team review changes to script code?

The answers to these questions are just as tied to the requirements to the rest of the system as they are relevant to the scripting system itself, so they can't be answered, or even discussed in detail, here. However, they are important questions to ask because they will all affect your team's ability to rapidly develop scripted content. Because scripting lends itself to rapid iteration, each additional step that needs to be performed in order for the developer to see the result of his changes increases overall turnaround time and reduces developer efficiency. Optimizing your scripting system (and your game as a whole) for rapid iteration will definitely pay off in the long run.

Your scripting environment may require a custom editor, as is the case with binary resources. If this is the case, as it is in *The Sims Online*, your development team will become responsible for maintaining the editor application as a key element of the development suite (on an equal level of importance with your compile and build tools).

Concurrent Development

Only the smallest development teams can get away with not planning for concurrent development, and MMP online games are seldom developed by small teams. A good portion of your in-game content will probably be written in script, and your developers will be rapidly iterating on your script files, so your scripts will be an area of high contention throughout the life of your project's development. Given that, it makes sense to plan for concurrent script development.

If your scripting language is text-based, you can take comfort in the fact that most modern source control systems, such as Perforce, offer excellent three-way merging capabilities. However, you still need to take care with files that simply cannot be merged automatically, such as a list of enumerated values. Most development teams are comfortable with this.

If your scripting language is based on binary files, merging is probably out of the question, and you'll need to treat each binary file as an "exclusive" resource (meaning only one developer can make changes to it at a time). This was the case on *The Sims Online*, where each world object's script data is stored in a single file, preventing multiple developers from working concurrently on the same object. Our solution was to "explode" each binary file into a collection of smaller resources (many of which could be converted to merge-able text files), thus increasing the granularity of our "exclusive" resources.

A third approach is an appealing hybrid solution: maintain the script code in a text format and deploy a compiled binary version. This combines the benefits of both approaches: the source code can be easily edited, reviewed, and merged, and the runtime performance can be optimized. Such a system is currently being tested for *Ultima Online*, and the initial results look quite promising.

Script Code Library

Once your scripting environment is up and running, you'll find yourself inclined to write large amounts of your game code in script. This will naturally lead to the establishment of a collection of supporting game routines written in your scripting language. Be sure to budget resources for the development and maintenance of this library of script code. Developers often neglect this part of their code base because of the tendency to view script code as subservient to native, compiled code. The result is a sloppily organized, often unconnected, library of script functions.

You will want to apply the same software engineering principles to your script code that you would afford your native code. Script code should be organized into discrete modules, and scripts should only import the modules they require. In the compiled code world, not following this practice results in lengthy build times. In the interpreted script world, similar delays may be realized every time a script is loaded at runtime, depending on how the scripting engine handles just-in-time compilation and caching.

You may also want to apply the same kinds of code documentation standards to your script code that you mandate for your native code. For example, you could decorate your script code with Javadoc- or Doxygen-style markup, which can be used to generate code API references. Your scripters, especially those joining the project in the later stages of development, will surely find such a reference invaluable.

Lastly, you should enforce the same kind of code review standards for your script code that you apply to your native code. This is doubly true of source code changes that span both your native and script code bases.

Debugging and Profiling

Any modern development environment—compiled, scripted, or otherwise—requires a debugging system in some form or another. At the very least, developers are accustomed to being able to fall back to so-called *printf()*-style debugging, but most demand a more robust, feature-rich debugger that allows them to step through live code and observe data changes.

Your script debugger will also play an important role once your game is deployed. Should your scripts experience errors in a live, production environment, you can automatically invoke the debugger and have it report its back trace to the development team for triage.

Code profilers tend to be used less often than debuggers, but they're still incredibly important development tools. Script code profilers are especially useful in load-test environments, as they will help your development team focus on performance "hot spots" before the responsible code goes live.

If you've chosen to use a third-party scripting environment, there's a good chance that a debugger and profiler already exist. They may not be the optimal solutions for your client-server environment, but they should provide enough functionality to make your developers productive, and you can always extend them or write your own. If you're using an internally developed scripting system, you will also be writing your own debugger and profiler.

Deployment

Once your script code is authored, debugged, tested, and profiled, it can be deployed into a live server environment. How this is accomplished is largely tied to the design of the rest of your game systems. However, it will directly affect the level of service you are able to provide to your players. For example, the *A Tale in the Desert* team prides itself on its ability to transparently deploy script changes to their production environment; the script is recompiled on the fly, and players don't experience any downtime.

Conclusion

With the ever-increasing costs involved in developing MMP online games, scripting systems are one of the few investments that always seem to pay off in the long run. At this point, if you haven't already adopted a scripting system for your MMP online game, we hope you're now reconsidering your development plans. And if you are already using a scripting system, we hope this article has provided you with some new ideas and perspectives that you can use to improve the usefulness and efficiency of your scripting environment.

Happy scripting!

2.3

Real-World MMO Object Sharing

Joe Ludwig—Flying Lab Software

joe@flyinglab.com

One of the major focus areas for massively multiplayer (MMP) games is keeping object state in synch between hosts and communicating state changes and events about those objects. Not only do the client representations of objects need to be kept up to date with servers, but servers often need updated views of objects from other servers. The system you have in place to share objects between entities is one you want to just work so that you can focus less on technology and more on the game itself. This article discusses the object sharing and notification mechanism that "just works" for *Pirates of the Burning Sea*.

The system described in this article is very similar to the Observer/Observable Design Pattern [Otaegui03] approach. There are also several commercial middleware solutions available. You can find out more about them in the middleware section toward the end of the article.

Basic Architecture

The core components in the shared object system are objects and listeners. Objects are the actual game entities containing data that needs to be kept in synch between servers and client, stored persistently, and loaded as static data for the world. All shared objects are derived from a base class that defines various accessor functions and knows how to serialize shared objects. Listeners are objects derived from a pure virtual base class that are notified when various object events occur. Together, these two classes allow objects to be shared across the network, come in to and go out of view, and be kept up to date.

All of the examples will use the following object classes. This is a simple sample class. Our project has around 120 such classes of varying levels of complexity, and that number is growing. The `CPackedData` class is one we use to pack and unpack network messages; you probably have a similar class you can drop into that role. The `flsSharedObject` class is the base class for all shared objects:

```
class flsSharedObject
{
public:
    // accessors
    int getLocalId() const { return _localId;}
    int64 getId() const;
    flsSharedObject *getObjectFromId(
        int64 iFullId);
    flsSharedObject *getObjectFromId(
        int iDbid, int iLocalId);
    flsSharedObject *getParent();
    flsSharedObject *setParent(
        flsSharedObject *pNewParent);

    // listener methods
    static void addClassListener(
        int iDbid, flsListener *pListener);
    void addListener(flsListener *pListener);
    void removeListener(flsListener *pListener);

    // object methods
    void addToDatabase();
    void removeFromDatabase();
    void writeToDatabase(bool bWriteDirtyOnly);
    virtual void markDirty();
    virtual void makeClean();
    void sendEvent( int iEvent );
    void createAllListeners();

protected:
    // virtuals
    virtual void postCreate();
    virtual void postUpdate();
    virtual void preRelease();
    virtual void preAddToDatabase() {}
    virtual void preWriteToDatabase(
        bool bWriteDirtyOnly) {}
    virtual void postWriteToDatabase(
        bool bWriteDirtyOnly) {}
    virtual void postRemoveFromDatabase() {}
    virtual void preDestroyPacket(
        flsListener *listen){}

    virtual void preBuildPacket(
        CPackedData *packet,
        bool bUpdate, flsObjectListener *listen) {}
    virtual igBool preParsePacket(
        CPackedData *packet, bool bUpdate)
        { return true; };

private:
    // data
    int _localId;
    flsSharedObject *_parent;
    bool _dirty;
}
```

The virtual methods in this class are called at various points in the object life cycle as detailed in the next section. We arrived at this set of methods through some painful trial and error as the shared object system has evolved. Each shared object has a 64-bit unique ID in two parts; the high 32 bits are the class database ID (DBID), and the bottom 32 bits are the object's local ID within that class. On a server, any object can be read from the database with that ID. On the client, the set of objects published by the server is maintained, and any object in that set can be retrieved from its ID. Example shared object classes follow:

```
class flsShipMotionData : flsSharedObject
{
        float _pos[2];
        float _vel[2];
}

class flsShip : flsSharedObject
{
    string _name;
    int _shipType;
    int _shipHealth;
    flsShipMotionData *_motionData;
}
```

For these classes to be used effectively on the client, listeners must be implemented to watch for object creation, updates, and destruction. All listeners derive from the flsListener base class:

```
class flsListener
{
    virtual void create(flsSharedObject *obj){}
    virtual void update(flsSharedObject *obj){}
    virtual void event(flsSharedObject *obj,
        igInt event ){}
    virtual void destroy(flsSharedObject *obj){}
    virtual void preDestroy(flsSharedObject* obj){}
    virtual void sendPacket(flsSharedObject *obj,
        CPackedData *packet){}
}
```

The virtual functions on flsListener are called as part of the object life cycle that is detailed in the next section. Here is an example of two listeners used for the creation and updating of client-side ship models:

```
class flsShipModel : flsListener
{
    virtual send(flsSharedObject *obj)
    {
        // perform initialization
    }
```

```
        virtual void update(flsSharedObject *obj);
        virtual void event(flsSharedObject *obj,
            igInt event);

        virtual void destroy(flsSharedObject *obj)
        {
            // perform cleanup
        }
    }

    class flsShipManagerListener : flsListener
    {
        virtual void create(flsSharedObject *obj)
        {
            flsShipModel *pNewModel = new flsShipModel;
            obj->addListener(pNewModel);
        }

        virtual void preDestroy(flsSharedObject *obj)
        {
            flsShipModel *pModel =
                findModelFromObject(obj);
            obj->removeListener(pModel);
        }
    }

    // somewhere at startup
    flsShipManagerLister *pShipListener =
        new flsShipManagerListener;
    flsSharedObject::registerClassListener(
        flsShip::getShipDbid(),
        pShipListener);
```

Game Objects

One of the core classes in the system is the flsSharedObject class. It is responsible for packing and unpacking objects for sending across the network. In the system used by Flying Lab, this is accomplished by way of reflectance; the pack method iterates through the fields on an object's class packing the data in each field, then iterates again while unpacking on the other side.

We are fortunate to have access to a data definition language (DDL) that came with our graphics engine and provides us with reflectance. The reflectance methods give us runtime access to the fields of each class so we can walk the list of fields to add each of them to a packet. This allows us to add fields to the shared object system automatically by adding them to the class.

If you do not have a similar system in place, you may have to implement pack/unpack methods for your classes. Pack and unpack methods are notoriously difficult to maintain, so whatever you can do here to automate this process will save you tons of time by the end of the project. Your DDL will need to allow you to specify which fields are shared (and which should be ignored by the system), which are to be sent across the network, and which need to be sent again on updates.

Object Messages

Object messages in the shared object system come in one of four forms: create, update, event, and destroy. These same four messages are used to call listener methods on the server and client. Together they allow a listener on the server to transmit data to the required clients, and listeners on the client to update the 3D scene or UI to reflect the current state. More details on listeners are available later in this article; for now it is enough to know that object listeners are registered to one object, and class listeners are registered to listen to all objects of a class.

All of the methods for these object messages take the object as an argument. This is because a single listener can be added to multiple classes or objects and may, as detailed later, receive updates for objects that are children of the object they are actually listening to directly.

Object listeners receive create messages when they are added with the `addListener()` method. Class listeners on the client receive create messages when a new object of that class is loaded from the database (on the server) or sent down from the server (on the client.) This message is the listener's chance to initialize itself or to create the client-side representation of the object. In the example code, `flsShipManagerListener::create()` creates an `flsShipModel` object and adds it as an object listener on the ship. This sort of thing is typical in a class listener. The object listener can perform whatever initialization it needs to perform in the create method.

Class and object listeners receive update messages when an object they are listening to is cleaned with the `makeClean()` method. Any code changing a field should call `markDirty()`, and then at regular intervals `makeClean()` should be called in order to distribute the changed data. This will mark the object as clean and communicate the changes to all listeners. We call `markDirty()` in accessor functions and `makeClean()` at the end of object pulse methods and command handlers to keep the objects up to date. Our `markDirty()` method also marks the object dirty for writing to the database, a flag that is not unset when `makeClean()` is called.

When `sendEvent()` is called on an object, an event message is sent to all that object's listeners. We use events to indicate major state changes in addition to sending an update message with new data because listeners often only care about the high-level "ShipHasSunk" event instead of having to check every so often for the lower level "Water in holds has exceeded twice cargo capacity."

Initially, we didn't have events in our shared object system, but once we added them, we started using them in many places to replace large blocks of state tracking code. We currently use them for posting user notification messages ("Your ship has sprung a leak"), driving UI updates ("Your ship has sunk out from under you"), and state notification for ships other than your own ("This ship is now in a boarding action"). It's amazing how much effort goes into breaking ships in an age of sail game.

Destroy messages are much like create messages. The `preDestroy()` method is called on class listeners when objects are unloaded from memory on the server or client. For object listeners, `destroy()` is called when the listener is removed. This message is an opportunity for object listeners to clean up the 3D scene or UI to account for the object that is disappearing.

Object Message Sizes

By default, each field in a shared object is sent to the client when that object is created and in updates. This can result in a lot of redundant data being sent very frequently and will quickly bloat the amount of data sent by the server beyond reasonable limits. To prevent redundancy and to hide data that the client may not need, we have two flags per object field: `sendOnUpdate` and `storeInPackets`.

If `storeInPackets` is not set, the field is never sent to the client in any form. It is only kept in server memory for server use. Use this for fields that the client doesn't have a use for, like the internal timestamp when the ship was created, or for fields that you don't want the client to know, like the amount of ammunition an enemy has remaining.

If `storeInPackets` is set, but `sendOnUpdate` is not, the field is sent in the initial packet for an object, but not in any subsequent update packets. The value of this field is valid on both the client and server. Use this field for information that the client needs to know, but that doesn't change like the name of a ship or its ship type.

For fields that are sent in update packets, they are sent in every update packet, even if they have not changed. It is a good idea to keep the setup fields sent on update as small as possible for this reason. You can also keep the update size down by breaking frequently updated data into its own object or implementing the per-field dirty flag described in "Areas for Expansion."

Object Lifecycle

Creating and manipulating objects in the shared object system requires that the game code follow some specific patterns. These guarantee that every object has an ID when it needs one, clients learn about objects in the right order, and the send-update-destroy progression goes as expected. Everything in the lifecycle on the server depends on reference-counting the objects and unloading the object when its last reference is released.

On the server, the lifecycle for object creation looks like this:

1. Object is created by game code.
2. Game code performs initialization of the object.
3. Game code calls `addToDatabase()` on the object.
4. Object is sent to any class listeners for objects of its type.
5. Game code modifies the object and calls `markDirty()`.
6. Game code calls `makeClean()` causing `update()` to be called on all listeners.
7. Game code saves the object with `writeToDatabase()`.

```
flsShip *pShip = new flsShip; // step 1
pShip->_name = "SomeName";    // step 2
pShip->_shipType = 123;
pShip->_shipHealth = 100;
pShip->addToDatabase();       // step 3
// step 4 happens automatically in addToDatabase()
pShip->_shipHealth = 90;      // step 5
pShip->markDirty();
pShip->makeClean();           // step 6
pShip->writeToDatabase();     // step 7
```

Object use after creation is similar:

1. Game code retrieves object with `flsSharedObject::getObjectFromId()`.
2. Game code modifies the object and calls `markDirty()`.
3. Game code calls `makeClean()` causing update() to be called on all listeners.
4. Game code saves the object with `writeToDatabase()`.

```
pShip =(flsShip *)            // step 1
    flsSharedObject::getObjectFromId(shipId);
pShip->_shipHealth = 50;      // step 2
pShip->markDirty();
pShip->makeClean();           // step 3
pShip->writeToDatabase();     // step 4
```

Object destruction is just a matter of calling `removeFromDatabase()`:

1. Game code retrieves object with `flsSharedObject::getObjectFromId()`.
2. Game code calls `removeFromDatabase()`.

```
pShip =(flsShip *)            // step 1
    flsSharedObject::getObjectFromId(shipId);
pShip->removeFromDatabase();  // step 2
```

On the client, object lifecycle is controlled entirely by messages from the server. The client is sent object creation messages, object update messages, and object destruction messages for each object:

1. Shared objects system receives creation packet.
2. Object is created and `create()` is called on all class listeners of that type.
3. Shared objects system receives an update packet.
4. Object is modified in memory and `update()` is called on all class and object listeners for the object.
5. Shared objects system receives a destroy packet.
6. `preDestroy()` is called on all class and object listeners.
7. Game code removes all references to the object.
8. Object has its ref-count reduced to 0 and is released. During this process, `destroy()` is called on all listeners.

Calls to destroy() happen so late in the process on the client that they are rarely useful. Subobjects of the object may have already been destroyed when this happens. Clients implement preDestroy() instead, which is called before the object is actually freed. This is done so the client does not attempt to use data in the object that may have already been deallocated.

Object Hierarchy

The previous example code had one object referring to another in a parent-child relationship. These arrangements are very common in games, where a character may have an inventory object, which, in turn, is a list of equipment. It is also useful to move information that updates frequently (such as ship position) into its own object so that the frequent updates are made to objects that are as small as possible. This sort of hierarchical relationship between objects is well supported by the shared object system.

The first piece of this puzzle is the _parent field. The parent field is a pointer to the parent object of the object in question. When addToDatabase() is called on an object, the parent pointers of all children are set to the object, and then addToDatabase() is recursively called on the children. All object messages (create, update, event, and destroy) are passed up the parent chain, first calling the object listener, and then calling the class listeners. Therefore, if a child object of class A has a parent object of class B and is made clean, first object listeners on the child are called, then class listeners on A, then object listeners on the parent, and finally class listeners on class B.

When a new child object is created, first its parent pointer is set, and then addToDatabase() is called. This results in createAllListeners() being called, which calls create() on each listener. If the object has already been added to the database, the game code will need to call setParent() and then call createAllListeners() directly.

Network Listeners

Client connections use network listeners to transmit object state to the client. They are responsible for packing up object creation, update, and destruction messages and transmitting them. They derive from the same flsListener class as other listeners, but instead of updating state, they pack up the object and send it to the client. Network listeners can even register with other listeners and get called when those meta-listeners get a object message call.

Because a single object can be referred to by multiple other objects, or appear as a result of multiple listeners, network listeners maintain a reference-count per object to keep track of what objects they have already told the client about. They will get one destroy() call for every create(), but they may get four creates and four destroys, so this ref-count is to prevent the server from sending the same object to the client three extra times, and then requesting that it be destroyed three extra times.

If the network listener receives a create() call for an object it has not sent to the client, it sends a create packet for the object and sets the reference-count to 1. If a create() call is made for an object that has a positive reference-count, the count is incremented. A destroy() call for an object with a reference-count greater than 1 causes the reference-count to be decremented, while a destroy() call for an object with a reference count of 1 results in the destruction of the object. The network listener should display an error message or assert when destroy(), update(), or event() are called for an object without a reference.

Unreliable Updates

Often, the situation calls for sending updates to the client that are unreliable. If you are going to send an object update again in a fraction of a second, losing one update isn't going to matter much to your client. We accomplished unreliable updates by adding some fields to classes that require them:

```
bool _reliableDirty;
int _lastTimestamp;
```

Each time markDirty() is called, both _reliableDirty and _dirty are set. When makeClean() is called, it branches based on what sort of dirty state the object is in:

```
if(obj->_dirty)
{
    // send unreliable update here
    obj->sendUnreliableUpdate();

    obj->_dirty = false;
}
else if(obj->_reliableDirty)
{
    // send reliable update here
    obj->sendReliableUpdate();

    obj->_reliableDirty = false;
}
```

This means that if your object reaches a steady state, a reliable update will be sent with the final state in it so the client will be up to date even if the last unreliable update was lost. The functions sendReliableUpdate() and sendUnreliableUpdate() don't actually exist in our system; we use a global flag to indicate to all network listeners that the update it is about to receive should be unreliable and set the flag in makeClean(). For these reliable updates to be sent, makeClean() must be called frequently. Our pulse timers clean objects such as these every 0.3 to 1.0 seconds depending on the object.

The timestamp field allows the shared object system to ignore update messages that are older than the most recently processed update. Making this work requires that the server and client have their clocks in synch, so you will have to send periodic time updates from the server to all clients. When an object update packet goes out, the timestamp is included at the front. If the timestamp is older than the last timestamp stored in the object on the client, the update is ignored.

Additional `flsSharedObject` Methods

There are a number of methods defined in the example code that have not been discussed. These are all virtual methods to allow classes to override the generic behavior with their own specific behavior. Most classes don't need them, but they often come in handy.

The `postCreate()` and `postUpdate()` methods are called on the client after a create or update method has been processed but before it has been announced to listeners. These are useful for fixing up nonshared fields to point to static resources; for example, fixing a cannon object to point to the cannon type object the client loaded from disk. Class listeners can't be used for these functions because the order in which class listeners are called is not guaranteed.

Before any work is done in `addToDatabase()`, `preAddToDatabase()` is called. This allows the class to perform any work it wants to perform on a brand new object before it is written the first time. The `preWriteToDatabase()` method serves the same function for writing already created objects. These are also both good places to put object verification debug code.

Our list class uses `postWriteToDatabase()` to write its contents; there are a variable number of them, so they can't be fields, and the normal recursion doesn't apply. `postRemoveFromDatabase()` is used by shared object lists for the same reason. This class also uses the `preDestroyPacket()` method to call destroy on all of its contents so that the contained objects are guaranteed to be destroyed before the parent. We don't use these methods outside of the list class.

The `preBuildPacket()` and `preParsePacket()` methods are used by classes to expand on or replace their automatic packet generation. We implemented a subclass of shared object, `flsTimestampSharedObject`, that supports unreliable updates and update timestamps using these methods. If you remove all fields from shared objects for a class, you can use these methods to entirely do your own packet generation.

Storing Objects in a Database

We use the shared object system to do all of our object persistence. In addition to per-field network flags, each field has a flag to determine whether it is stored in the database. By default, all of them but pointers to nonshared object classes are stored. Exactly how we perform this storage and retrieval is beyond the scope of this article, but the short version is that we build one table per class with the fields as columns and use class reflectance and the DDL to build SQL queries to read and write the objects.

Challenges with Shared Objects

The shared object system we use at Flying Lab is reasonably efficient and very functional. Using it is not without challenges, though. There are strict requirements placed on the game code for object lifecycle, and breaking those requirements creates bugs that can't automatically be detected. Unreliable updates can arrive out of order, and any that do must be ignored, or they will cause problems. The system also has some execution and bandwidth overhead.

Because unreliable updates via UDP often arrive ahead of the create/destroy stream that travels via TCP, it is possible to get them out of order. The two forms this takes are: 1) receiving updates for objects the client has not yet heard about, and 2) receiving updates that refer to objects the client has not yet heard about. The first problem is easy to detect, and simply ignoring these updates works; another update will be along at any moment anyway, assuming you are calling `makeClean()` frequently. The second problem can also be resolved by ignoring the messages, but it is more annoying because detecting that the seventh field in a message refers to an object that isn't available involves processing the first six fields. We deal with this by only displaying "I haven't heard of this object" error messages for reliable updates.

Efficiency is a tougher nut to crack. Some bandwidth efficiency approaches are discussed in the next section. In addition to bandwidth, however, building packets on the fly based on runtime reflection information on the class involves a lot of branching and looping and isn't as optimized as hand-generated code would be. The trade-offs in development have been worth it so far, but we may end up needing to write custom pack/unpack routines for some high-volume classes to overcome this problem.

Areas for Expansion

A number of features could be added to this system to increase its utility. Right now, listeners can only be registered per-object or per-class; they could be registered globally. An object view listener can be devised that keeps two server objects in synch with each other for presenting summary information to the client. Support for viewer-specific field filtering would be nice for hiding partial information about objects. Tracking object dirtiness per-field can also reduce bandwidth use.

Global listeners probably aren't much use for game systems themselves, but they can be used to track performance and usage metrics for the shared object system. Each `create()` and `destroy()` could be measured per-ID to watch for object thrashing; that is, objects that are being repeatedly loaded from the DB only to be thrown away again. If this is done with a global listener, the instrumentation can be turned off by simply not registering that listener.

An object view listener allows one object to update its state based on changes to another object. Clients can then listen to the view object and receive multiple updates in one message. Depending on how advanced your field information is at runtime, these updates may be able to be applied to the view object automatically.

Another enhancement that we have considered is allowing each field to be assigned a view level. Listeners would register with a view level when they were added to an object, and would only receive fields at their requested view level or below. We have not added this yet because of the complexity it adds to the system and the opportunity for bugs it represents, but if your game requires it, a per-field view level may be a useful enhancement. It would allow you, for example, to announce what flag a ship flies to players who are within 1000m and the name of the captain to players who are within 100m. Each view level would include all of the information from all the previous levels, plus whatever fields are added at that level.

Finally, the bandwidth requirements for updates could be greatly reduced for many classes if the dirty flag were per-object-field instead of per-object. Update packets can have field flags added to the start of the packet that contain a bitfield indexed by a field ID that determines which fields are present in the packet. For packets that are frequently updated but don't always update the entire object, this may be useful. Another option is to break some of those objects into multiple objects so that they can be updated independently.

Middleware

We wrote our own shared object system at Flying Lab, but that is not the only way to do it. At least two commercial middleware packages exist, and should be evaluated before starting on your own system. Quazal [Quazal04] and ReplicaNet [Replica04] both have evaluation versions available and have been reviewed [Jones03] online.

We don't have very much familiarity with either product. Quazal seems to have quite reasonable prices for their small-scale multiplayer product and absolutely absurd prices for their MMO package (US $69,000 plus 4–6% royalties, or $495,000 royalty-free as of this writing). Most middleware companies are happy to negotiate on price, so you may be able to drop that price considerably. ReplicaNet's prices are more reasonable (US $5000 royalty-free); they deserve an evaluation if you are in a position to license such a library.

Conclusion

The flexible shared object system we use at Flying Lab has saved us months of development time. We don't worry about object packing or how updates work when we are writing game code. Building such a system for your game will save you similar amounts of time.

The system outlined in this article is not perfect. It has some peculiarities that need to be overcome by training your engineers, and has plenty of room for improvement. It is, however, good enough. We use the system for all game object state, sending potentially hundreds of object updates each second. And when you have an entire MMO to develop in addition to your object communication layer, "good enough" is just right.

References

[Jones03] Jones, Kevin, "Network Middleware Comparison," available online at *www.gamedev.net/features/reviews/productreview.asp?productid=240*.

[Otaegui03] Otaegui, Javier F., "Observer/Observable Design Patterns for MMP Game Architectures," *Massively Multiplayer Game Development*, Charles River Media, 2003.

[Quazal04] Quazal.com, "Quazal: Multiplayer Connectivity," available online at *www.quazal.com*.

[Replica04] ReplicaNet, available online at *www.replicanet.com/*.

2.4

MMP Server Cluster Architecture

Joe Ludwig—Flying Lab Software

joe@flyinglab.com

As server speed increases every year, so does game complexity. For the foreseeable future, massively multiplayer (MMP) games will continue to demand more than all but the most powerful and expensive hardware that can be delivered in a single box. This article is about why it is often a good idea to split each world instance across multiple server machines, and how you might go about it once you decide it is necessary. The approach outlined here describes how to have the features hosted on one machine fail over to another machine if the first one should fail, how to launch processes on multiple machines, and how to reduce the impact of fatal server bugs.

Definitions

Throughout this article, the term *cluster* is used. This refers to the set of physical machines that make up a single world instance. Each machine could host a variety of different game features by running a server process of one of the types detailed here. Exactly what features are hosted on any given machine will depend on the needs of the cluster when the process for that feature is launched. Each machine in the cluster is likely to be hosting multiple processes.

Goals

The cluster architecture described in this article is designed around three goals: availability, scalability, and ease of implementation. Each of these goals competes against the others for attention, and a balance must be struck between them; they are listed in the order of priority used to develop the multiserver approach.

Availability refers directly to the uptime of the service. A service that never goes down outside of scheduled downtime has high availability, and a service that goes down constantly has low availability. Loss of part of the service for ten minutes is bad; loss of the entire service for even one minute is worse. Losing player data is terrible; corrupting player data beyond recovery is catastrophic.

The cluster architecture is scalable when it does not place undue limitations on the number of players supported in the game world. To a lesser extent, it should not place undue limitations on the number of players supported in an area within the world. There is always an upper limit for technical reasons, but it should be high enough that the limits desired by operations, art production, and game design are lower, allowing those three parties to fight over it and leave us out of it.

The cluster architecture should allow us to write code in support of the first two goals without getting in the way of coding a fun game. Systems should be flexible and extensible wherever possible. The architecture must make debugging as easy as possible. A programmer who is required to stop seven processes by hand, recompile, and then start seven processes again before testing a one-line fix is a) wasting a lot of time with processes instead of coding interesting gameplay, and b) soon going to need a nice white jacket that fastens in the back.

The Golden Rule

Avoid single points of failure at all costs.

A single point of a failure is a piece of hardware or software that, if it crashes, brings down a cluster or the entire service. Having machines with two power supplies and mirrored drives means that you don't have to shut down unexpectedly when a power supply shorts and the resulting power surge fries a hard drive. If you have a system with at least one single point of failure, Murphy's Law states that that's the one that will fail.

The real benefit of avoiding single points of failure is statistical. If it only takes one component failing to bring down your service and that component takes one hour to repair every time it fails, a nine-hour mean time between failures means you have 10% downtime; this isn't good because many of your users will spend that tenth hour searching for the "cancel subscription" button. If your system is designed in such a way that *two* such components must fail at the same time for the service to come down, your chances of losing component B in the hour that component A spends being serviced is 10%. Multiply the two together and you end up with 1% downtime, or 99% uptime.

Your uptime per component is hopefully much higher. Ninety-nine percent uptime per component and requiring two components to fail at once means that you have 99.99% uptime for the service. Ninety-nine percent uptime means that you will be down for one hour about every four days; 99.99% uptime means that you will be down for one hour about every 13 months. That's certainly a respectable number for your non-life-threatening game services.

Multiprocess Architecture

If your entire service runs in one process (multithreaded or otherwise), that process is a single point of failure. A deadlock or errant pointer access can easily throw an exception that takes out the service and probably does so frequently. Fixing the bugs is good, but that only lasts until the next crashing bug is coded. A better solution is to distribute your service onto multiple processes.

Having multiple processes on the same machine is better from an availability point of view than a single process, but you still have a single point of failure for the cluster: if that machine fails, so does the service. Splitting your cluster across multiple machines and putting multiple processes on each is the answer. It also increases the amount of RAM and CPU time available to your cluster as a whole, which improves scalability.

Server Directory

The key to the multiprocess system is the server directory database. All processes in the cluster update their status in the database every five seconds. This enables any process in the cluster to query the database for servers to connect to and to detect when a process has died or stopped updating. The server directory database has two tables in it: the cluster table and the process table. Any database server can be used as a server directory database; you probably already have one that you are using for many other things in the game. If you have not selected a SQL server, MySQL [MYSQL01] is free and is what Flying Lab Software uses.

Using a database for this process tracking accomplishes one of the goals: it allows a single process per cluster to see the current status of the cluster and restart failed processes automatically, and increases availability. This process is called "big brother," and is described in greater detail in the next section. Storing the information in the database allows a new big brother server to take over without the need for additional data transmission if the primary big brother process fails, removing a single point of failure.

The cluster table is a list of all the clusters that have ever registered with the database. It also maps a cluster name to an ID to speed up the process table. The cluster table has the following columns:

`id` (**int**):   The ID column is populated when the cluster registers with the database the first time. The value is used in the process table to tie each process to a cluster. This column should use whatever modifier allows you to select IDs automatically (which is autoincrement in MySQL).

`name` (**character string**):   The name column is the name of the cluster. This can be a key into your string table or the name itself, but it should be meaningful. This name must be a unique key to prevent accidental duplicates.

`up` (**bool**):   The up column is used by the operations client to tell the cluster when it is time to shut down gracefully. This column defaults to false.

`primary` (**int**):   This column contains the instance ID of the big brother process that controls the cluster.

`version` (**int**):   The version of the game running on this cluster. If your version numbers don't fit in a single column, this may actually be multiple columns. This is used to restrict the list of clusters offered to the client and to prevent version mismatch problems between processes.

The process table is a list of every process running in every cluster. It is filled by the processes themselves and updated continuously. The process table has the following fields:

cluster (int):   The cluster ID of the cluster of which this process is a part.

processType (int):   The type of the process. This is one of a set of public constants that are known to the process code and the operations client. One of these values should indicate big brother.

instanceId (int):   The ID of the process within the type and cluster. This may be significant, or it may just be the next available ID. Together, instanceId, processType, and cluster must define a unique key. The table should have a key to allow the database to enforce this restriction.

address (unsigned int):   The IP address of the machine on which this process is running.

tcpport (int):   The TCP port number that this process is listening on, or 0 if it is not listening for TCP connections.

udpport (int):   The UDP port number that this process is listening on, or 0 if it is not receiving UDP traffic.

status (int):   The number of players active on this process. If this number is negative, the process is not active yet. A well-defined set of negative values can show specific process status to the operations client. Server processes should update their row frequently during startup and shutdown to aid in debugging.

lastupdate (time):   The time when this process was last updated. If this time is more than 10 seconds in the past, the process is probably down because each process updates its row in the process table every 5 seconds.

Together, these two tables provide an accurate picture of the state of the cluster. From them, the operations client can tell which clusters are up and down, what versions the clusters are running, and the state of each server in the cluster. The operations client can also start up and shut down servers.

Big Brother

Big brother is a process type that runs on each machine in the cluster. The purpose of this process is to keep the other processes up and running. Each big brother process is in one of two modes: primary or secondary. The mode of the process determines what work it has to do.

A big brother in secondary mode is waiting in the wings to take over the cluster if the primary becomes unresponsive. Every five seconds, each server in the cluster updates its status in the process table. Secondary big brothers also monitor the last update time of the primary. If the primary's lastupdate time is ever more than 10 seconds in the past when a secondary big brother checks on it, the secondary declares itself primary in the database, but doesn't actually restart any servers. If the process is still marked as primary five seconds later when it polls the database again, it has successfully taken over the cluster.

The primary big brother is responsible for starting servers. At launch, it builds a list of servers that should be up at all times. Every five seconds, the primary queries the process table for processes in the cluster that have not posted an update in at least 10 seconds and attempts to start new processes to take over for each of them. If the up flag is not set for the process, this does not occur.

First, the primary picks a machine to host the new process by finding the least-loaded big brother in the list (which may be the primary itself). Then, it records the time, sends a Start Server Process message to the big brother process for the target machine, and marks that a request was sent. When this message is received, big brother immediately sends a Start Server Process Acknowledged message back to the primary, and then launches the process. When the acknowledgment message is received, the primary big brother marks it. The primary big brother will not attempt to start a process that it has sent a request for within the past 10 seconds, or one that it has received an acknowledgment for in the past 30 seconds.

In addition to monitoring the process table, the primary big brother process is also responsible for cleaning up the old rows in that table. Every five minutes, the primary deletes any process table row with a last update time that is at least five minutes in the past (see Figure 2.4.1).

Setting Up Big Brother

Setting up a machine to participate in a cluster is relatively simple. First, you need to figure out how to launch the process itself. Then, you have to provide necessary configuration. Once you have done these two things, big brother will take care of itself.

Big brother itself reports into the process table, but the primary is not able to start another big brother process, so this must be done another way. On a server running Microsoft® Windows®, the process should run as a Windows service [MSDN01]. On a Unix server, big brother can be started by a server boot, which is a shell script that spins endlessly spawning the process again whenever it exits. Whatever the method, big brother must start automatically after each reboot and restart after each crash.

Big brother needs to know some things to do its job, but not very many. It needs the address and database name for the server directory database. It needs the name of the cluster of which it is a member. It also needs a list of servers to spawn to keep the service running. Other than that, all of the configuration is on the processes themselves and is defined by the list of machines that register in the database.

On startup, big brother connects to the server directory database and looks up the cluster ID. If the cluster isn't listed, the process adds it, remembering that ID. If the attempt to add the cluster failed, it is probably because another big brother got there first, and the ID can now be looked up. Once it knows the cluster ID, the process can start pulsing every five seconds for its normal operation.

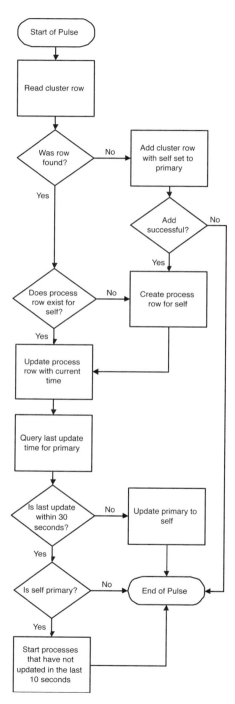

FIGURE 2.4.1   *Main pulse for big brother.*

Starting Up or Shutting Down a Cluster

Shutdown is much more interesting than startup, so we will talk about shutdown first. Every process in the cluster should monitor the up field for its cluster table row. If this is ever false, big brother processes should revert to secondary mode and all other types of processes should exit. By setting this flag, the operations client can start up or shut down the server.

Starting up a cluster is just a matter of setting the up field to true. The big brother processes have already elected one of themselves to be primary, and when this field becomes true, the primary automatically starts launching other server processes.

Process Types

Big brother is only one of several process types that the cluster needs to function. The second most important type is the connection server. There are also processes to handle login, chat, and zone services. The exact set of process types depends heavily on the game's design. See Figure 2.4.2 for a typical set of process types.

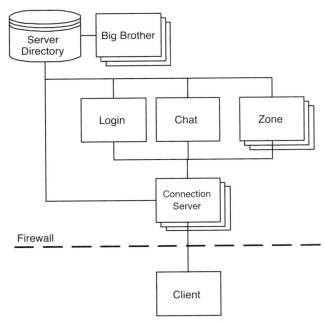

FIGURE 2.4.2 *Connections between the processes in a cluster.*

This architecture description uses the word *zone* to mean a section of the world that is self-contained. The links shown in Figure 2.4.2 show no ability to act across zone boundaries. If your game has a continuous world, this can be accomplished by having the zone servers connect to each other and share game state across those connections.

Connection Server

The connection server process forms the front-line connection between the client and the rest of the servers. Although these servers don't do much on their own, they are the workhorses of the cluster. They constantly shuttle messages back and forth between the various other processes and the client. They are also responsible for all the TCP retransmit work due to lost packets on the Internet. There are many connection server processes running at any given time to greatly increase the number of players supported by a single cluster.

The connection server is also responsible for the zoning procedure. It maintains the connection state for a client and controls the saving and loading of the client's character through the zone transition. If a zone server goes down, the connection server can keep a connection active for reloading once that zone comes back up.

The primary responsibility of the connection server is message pass-through. The same system is used for messages from the client and messages from another cluster process. When a message needs to be sent to another process for a specific client, an envelope message is sent first. The envelope contains identification information for the client so that the internal process can tell what player the command is from. When an internal process, such as a zone server process, needs to send a message to the server, it sends an envelope message to the connection server to indicate which client the message is intended for, and then sends the message itself.

Client Connection States

Connections from a client to the connection server begin in the Accepted state, and from there move into one of the other states listed here. The current state of the connection controls what messages the connection server will process from the client, and what messages the connection server expects from other processes.

Accepted: The connection has been established from TCP's point of view, but nothing else has gone on. Depending on your game's communication needs, the state may immediately change to Login.

Login: In this state, the client can send SendLogin messages that are passed through to the login server. A successful one results in the login server sending SetCharacterSelection to the connection server, which sends a summary of available characters to the client and moves the connection to CharacterSelection.

CharacterSelection: The client is logged in and is selecting a character. A successful SelectCharacter message results in a CharacterLogin message to the chat server and a ZoneLoadCharacter call to the zone process occupied by that character. The state is then switched to Zoning.

Zoning: A zone process is loading the character. If a zone server reports ZoneLoadCharacterComplete, the state changes to Ready and the client is sent ConnectionReady. If the zone process disappears, the state changes to ZoneDown.

ZoneDown: The character is in a zone that isn't currently up. The character stays in this state until the zone comes back up (at which point, ZoneLoadCharacter is sent and the state changes to Zoning) or they disconnect.

Ready: The character is connected and playing. If it switches zones, its zone server sends ChangeZones, which changes the state back to Zoning.

Dead: The connection is dead to us. No more data from the connection may be processed, and after five minutes in this state, it will be disconnected. This state is used for any case where a player is booted automatically by the game but needs notification of why (banning, duplicate login, etc.). The connection persists long enough to let the client read the reason, at which point the client is disconnected. The five-minute timeout handles hung or hacked clients.

Ongoing Interprocess Connections

Many cluster processes need to connect to other processes to do their work. The list of processes to connect to depends on the game design and the needs of the connecting process. The mechanism used to make the connections is always the same.

Every five seconds, the process queries the process table for the list of active processes. The results of this query are compared to the list of processes to which connections are required. If a process of the right type exists but there is no active connection, one is initiated. If the process' IP address and port number have changed, but there is already a connection to a different process, that connection is broken and a new connection is initiated to the current process. This system of retrieving process lists out of the server directory database relieves big brother of the burden of telling processes where to connect.

Login and Chat Processes

The login and chat process types are examples of processes of which each cluster only needs one. Like all the other processes, big brother starts these. Each connection server connects to these processes via TCP, and passes login or chat requests from the client to the appropriate server.

The login process is responsible for verifying user passwords and logging out old connections with the same account. SendLogin messages from the client are passed through to the login server. If the username and password are correct, the Login server will send LoginSuccess to the client and SetCharacterSelection to the connection manager. At this point, the login is added to the list of logged-in characters. If the login was already present, ForceLogout is sent to the connection server that holds the old login so that the old client can be disconnected. If the username is unknown or the password is incorrect, LoginFailure is sent to the client.

The chat server is responsible for distant communication between players. Nearby chat is handled by the zones since they know where the characters are in the world. The chat process handles direct chat, group chat, and guild chat. The chat server may also be responsible for character name service (e.g., telling the client the character ID associated with the name "Roland Weathersby").

Depending on the design of your game, there could be many other cluster-wide processes. If the game supports in-game e-mail, then e-mail deserves its own process. If message boards are supported, they should be on their own process. Depending on the complexity of the system, guilds could share the chat process with other services or have their own process.

List the systems in your game and divide them up between processes in a reasonable way. One tip is that your high-volume processes are going to be your least-stable processes; whenever possible, high-volume services should not share a process with a mission-critical process. In addition, the game should be able to function without a process, or that process becomes a single point of failure.

Zone Servers

Each cluster has a zone server for each region of the game map. Games that support instanced areas for missions may have additional zone servers to support those instanced areas, or some zone servers may do double duty. The zone server is responsible for enforcing all game rules related to movement, combat, inventory, world object interaction, and anything else that your game's design requires.

All of the zone processes are not necessarily running the same code. In the case of our game, *Pirates of the Burning Sea*, we have some zones that are entirely sailing ship based and some that are entirely avatar based. These two parts of the game have very different movement requirements, and so run different bodies of code. In our case, they actually run the same executable and half the code is never executed for each type of zone.

The zone server is the process that holds the majority of the vital player data. This server should save player data as frequently as possible. If your game involves frequent movement between zones, this is a natural save point, but you should consider saving more frequently than that either based on time passed or when a major event (leveling up, buying a new ship, etc.) happens to the player.

Additional Processes Outside the Cluster

There may be some processes that are running outside the cluster to provide services that are shared between clusters. There may be a metrics server process to which all the cluster servers connect that gathers metrics from each server and stores them in a database. There could be a bug or user petition tracking process that manages these tickets across servers so GMs don't have to be logged in to a particular server to help users there. What form these take depends on what your operations and customer service teams need.

One obvious addition would be a server directory process that communicates the list of available clusters and their status to the client. It would read the server directory database and package up the relevant bits to send to the client. This process would load balance client connections between the connection servers by sending each client to the least-loaded server. Moreover, because this process only needs to read from the database, there could be any number of them running at a time to provide redundancy and extra capacity.

Debugging in the Multiserver Architecture

When you have a single monolithic server, it is easy to debug your server. You just launch the server from the debugger, connect a client, and away you go. When your cluster is made up of dozens (or hundreds) of processes, debugging is not as easy. You cannot simply launch every process each time you need a server. In addition, big brother is designed to start replacements whenever a process stops responding, which would certainly happen if you set a breakpoint on a zone server.

The solution is relatively simple: include a way in the big brother configuration to tell it not to launch servers of a particular type. If you are debugging a zone server, tell big brother not to launch zone servers. All of the other servers in the cluster will come up automatically, and when you launch your debug zone server by hand, it will add itself to the server directory database and the connection server(s) will automatically connect to it. In fact, if your client is still up, it will automatically zone back into the world when its zone server returns.

Of course, this ability to hot-swap servers flies out the window if you change the protocol used by your game and then relaunch the zone server. It could be unable to interpret anything it receives from other cluster processes or the client. In situations like this, you will have to bring down the entire cluster and restart with the new code.

If you are trying to track down a problem but aren't expecting to change code, you could also attach a debugger to an already running server and debug that way. If you attach a debugger, you will need to set your big brother configuration to allow very long timeouts for cluster processes or it will replace your process while you're scratching your head at some bizarre call-stack.

Weaknesses in the System

As you may have noticed, the server directory database is actually a single point of failure. Sure, the processes on a cluster can keep running while the database is down, but they are unable to report status, spawn the additional processes needed for instanced zones, or spawn new processes when old ones go down. Many database servers have solutions for this problem, usually having to do with automatic fail-over to back up servers. At a minimum, your processes should automatically reconnect to the database if it fails.

Another potential issue with the system is the overhead. Processes are much heavier than threads, and each additional process has an extra copy of much of the code. The very things that add redundancy to the system reduce its efficiency. Use of DLLs or other shared libraries can reduce the extra code space used to some extent. Duplicate static data is a tougher one to solve. If all the processes need to know the list of all weapons available in the game, that list will be in memory many times on every machine in the cluster. This is a price you pay for redundancy, because one process going haywire and overwriting half of the weapon list and then crashing is going to have no effect whatsoever on another process.

This system also has no means by which big brother can move a heavily loaded process from one machine to another. If 50% of your players decide to go to the same location at the same time and your chat server happens to be running on the same machine as the zone server for that location, then chat service suffers for all players. This is a difficult problem to solve, as the chat service would be disrupted by such a move, and the zone server holds a large amount of data that would be time consuming to move. The risk of overloading servers can be reduced if servers shut themselves down when no players are actively using them. This is not possible for servers that are used continuously, like the chat server, but other server types can probably restart without impacting any players. If a connection server stops accepting new connections, eventually it will run out of players and be able to shut down. A zone server hosting a part of the world that does not hold any active players can shut down until a player moves into that region of the world.

Conclusion

This article presented one vision of how to split your service into multiple processes running on a cluster of machines. It emphasizes availability and scalability and makes some trade-offs in ease of development to achieve those goals. Although the nitty-gritty details of passing messages, spawning processes, and connecting to databases were not covered, most of the key procedures were presented, so you should not have any problem implementing this system on top of your existing network layer. Although it is not perfect, this approach solves the most important issues that we need solved for our clusters.

Adapting this architecture to your game design is not a trivial process. You will need to identify what shared processes your game needs, and what tasks the zone servers should perform. There are decisions to be made here that have lasting impact on the game's design, so the earlier they are resolved, the better. This article should serve as a baseline to adapt to your game and let you avoid some pitfalls along the way.

References

[MSDN01] Microsoft.com, "Using Services," available online at *http://msdn.microsoft.com/library/default.asp?url=/library/en-us/dllproc/base/using_services.asp*.

[MYSQL01] MySQL.com, "MySQL," available online at *www.mysql.com*.

Massively Multiplayer Games Using a Distributed Services Approach

Shea Street—Tantrum Games

shea.street@tantrumgames.com

With our need and desire to attain the ever-limitless world that massively multiplayer (MMP) games are expected to be, we find ourselves limited by content, story, hardware, and software. Fortunately for us, the latter two can be more easily thwarted than the prior. In the past, enterprise servers and software have been the bulging band-aid for the industry. However, taking a step back and remembering that less is truly more, the need for the expensive hardware and a team of rocket scientists to create the server backend is no more. No longer is the idea of throwing money and power at the problem a solution. With a distributed services approach, a developer can now use consumer off-the-shelf hardware to take any number of players limitlessly through any world they create.

Overview

As it stands now, there are only a few client/server models in which to set up an online game. The most basic of these is the straight client/server approach (see Figure 2.5.1). In this approach, a client connects directly to the game server. When any critical events associated with the game server happen, all players are disconnected. This model limits the number of players based on a single piece of hardware, the server. An adaptation of this model segments the world to be run on separate servers. When the player needs to travel from one part of the world to another, he must be disconnected and reconnected to the appropriate area server. This now virtually removes the limit of total number of players in the world, but still limits the number of players in one area with critical events localized to that affected area server.

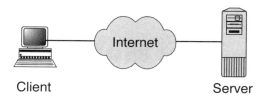

FIGURE 2.5.1   *Basic client/server model.*

A further modification of this model adds in a proxy that the players connect to in order to access separate parts of the world (see Figure 2.5.2). These parts of the world are handled by separate servers that the player is passed along to by the session server. This removes the need to disconnect the player totally from the game while passing the player from one area to another, by keeping the player connected to a session server. Adding more players to your world is now bound to the number of session servers, but still limits the number of players in one area.

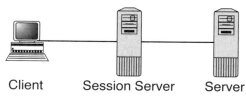

FIGURE 2.5.2   *Client/server model with a session server.*

Until now, these models and mutations thereof were the industry's de-facto online game setup. With the limitations on the number of players, game-hindering system crashes, player connection transfers, and multiple copies of the world simulation on all area servers, one would have to ask, "Is there a better way?" The answer is the distributed services approach.

The Distributed Services Approach

Like the aforementioned models in the previous section, the distributed services approach still requires the player to make connection to a session server that we refer to as a *frontend service*. After the connection is made, the frontend service captures all player data and then communicates to the appropriate service servers through the unified network (see Figure 2.5.3).

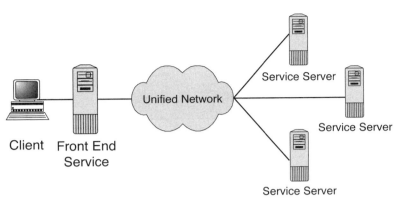

FIGURE 2.5.3 *Distributed services approach.*

What Is a Service?

Unlike the area server mentioned earlier, the service is a single task-oriented part of the world simulation. These services grouped together form the entire world simulation. A service's task can be a collection of similar game functionality. By breaking the game's functionality down into separate services we gain a more flexible and scalable world. The service can now handle all of the player's task-specific actions. Since individual servers handle a smaller part of the simulation, they are more optimized for the task they serve. This also allows the hardware they run on to be scaled more cost effectively as the game's players grow or decrease in number. An example of the services setup can be seen in Figure 2.5.4.

Service Class

The *Service* class is the most basic building block of the distributed services approach and forms the base for all of the services with which a unified simulation would deal (see Figure 2.5.5). At the most basic level, the Service base class is totally devoid of any specific logic and only supplies a simple framework on which to be built. A Service is assigned its own name and ID that designates it as a unique service so it can be located and communicated with at any point. Communications with and between services are all done through the unified network by a message dispatching system of callbacks [Randall02].

Unified Network

The unified network is the name given to the total server backend as well as the *UnifiedNetwork* utility class (see Figure 2.5.6). The UnifiedNetwork is the glue that binds all the services together to form a single unified network of operations. It is a singleton class that is a wrapper for the communications and management of the networking

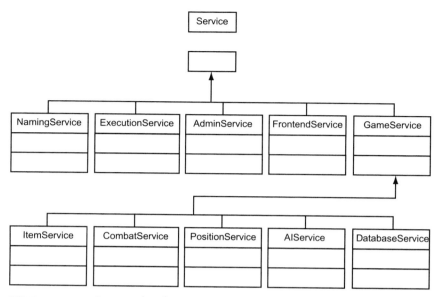

FIGURE 2.5.4   *Service class hierarchy.*

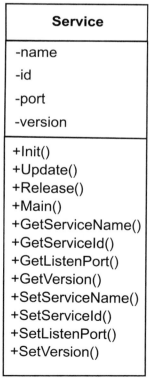

FIGURE 2.5.5   *Service class diagram.*

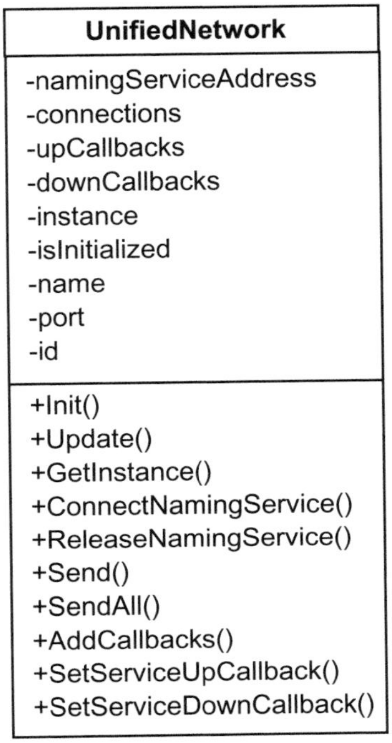

```
┌─────────────────────────────────┐
│         UnifiedNetwork          │
├─────────────────────────────────┤
│ -namingServiceAddress           │
│ -connections                    │
│ -upCallbacks                    │
│ -downCallbacks                  │
│ -instance                       │
│ -isInitialized                  │
│ -name                           │
│ -port                           │
│ -id                             │
├─────────────────────────────────┤
│ +Init()                         │
│ +Update()                       │
│ +GetInstance()                  │
│ +ConnectNamingService()         │
│ +ReleaseNamingService()         │
│ +Send()                         │
│ +SendAll()                      │
│ +AddCallbacks()                 │
│ +SetServiceUpCallback()         │
│ +SetServiceDownCallback()       │
└─────────────────────────────────┘
```

FIGURE 2.5.6   *UnifiedNetwork utility class diagram.*

layer. This class is the "magic" of all inter-service communications. In the simplest of definitions, it handles all the micromanagement of network messages for each individual service, the establishing of connections, and regaining of lost ones. A service starts up its UnifiedNetwork by initializing it with its service name. In turn, the UnifiedNetwork then connects to the naming service and registers the service by name and acquires an assigned port address and ID number. At this point, all other services can now communicate with this service, but it does not have the capability to listen yet. To do this, the service needs to register its callbacks with the UnifiedNetwork. The UnifiedNetwork becomes a catch-all of all incoming messages for this service. It then routes these messages to the appropriate handling functions in the callback list. In addition, the service can register up and down callback lists as well. These callback lists are handling functions for when the service relies on other services' state of being active or inactive. With this in place, communication with other services is as easy as calling it by name through the UnifiedNetwork and sending it a packaged message. Since multiple services can have the same name, there is the choice of broadcasting the message to all those services by their shared name or by sending to an individual service using its unique ID.

Required Services

Now that we have a base framework of the Service and UnifiedNetwork classes, we need to establish a list of all required services to bind the distributed services system together.

Naming Service

The *NamingService* is no more than a glorified DNS server. It keeps a database of all registered services along with their unique IDs and port addresses (see Figure 2.5.7)

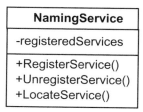

FIGURE 2.5.7   *NamingService class diagram.*

Execution and Administration Services

The *ExecutionService* launches on the service server startup to tell the *AdminService* that there is a server available to execute whatever service is needed at the moment. It also acts as a remote terminal service for the AdminService client allowing it to accept commands to administrate the server on which it is running. The AdminService controls all these services and servers. It keeps a running knowledge of what services are currently active and inactive, and then dictates to the ExecutionServices what services to start up on its servers. The AdminService operates autonomously and also works as a trusted shell client to the ExecutionServices for user inputted commands (see Figure 2.5.8).

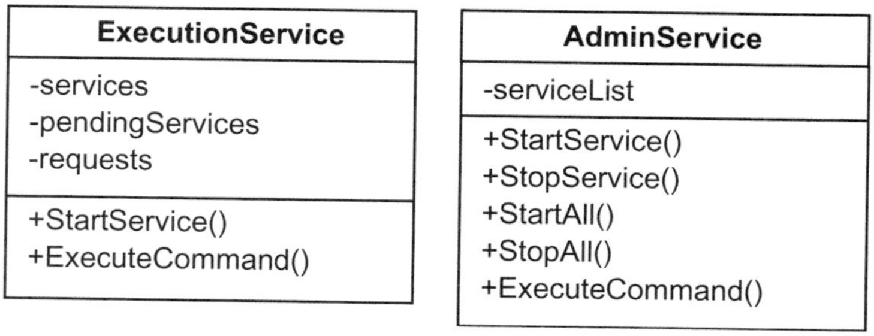

ExecutionService	AdminService
-services -pendingServices -requests	-serviceList
+StartService() +ExecuteCommand()	+StartService() +StopService() +StartAll() +StopAll() +ExecuteCommand()

FIGURE 2.5.8   *ExecutionService/AdminService class diagrams.*

Frontend Service

The *FrontendService* is the client entry point for any game that uses the distributed services approach. It is game specific; there is no set structure to its implementation. The only function it needs is to allow clients to interact with the game world and vice versa. As stated earlier, the max concurrent player population of the game world is based solely on this service; therefore, the optimization of this service is critical for game execution.

Guidelines for Constructing Game Services

Game services, like the FrontendService, are game specific and have no set structure in their implementation. However, there is a framework of mind that one must keep in creating such services.

Smaller Is Better

When segmenting the game into services, it's best to segment these services so as to have little or no dependencies on other services. Even though all services need to communicate with each other to create the entire world, it's the FrontendService that depends mainly on the other services so as to compile the data into a representation of that world for the player. These game services communicate only with other services to retrieve the small amount of data they need to perform their task-specific operation, only to push their processed data to another service for direct usage. The benefit of keeping the task for each service small is to allow the service to maximize the number of player operations in the game world on a single server. The flipside to this is that a service can be too small. It's best to keep in mind that some game functionality is better packaged together to form a single service.

Talk Less, Say More

The ideology in this is that when a service has a specific operation to perform and requires external data to achieve its goal, the service asks another service for the data in one request. That service then bundles all the data, returning it to the service in a ready-to-use format. This eliminates flooding the network with many smaller requests. In an example of a combat service inquiring about a player's active weapon, the combat service would request from the item service that data. In return, the item service would return the active weapon and all other pertinent information such as statistics on that weapon, even though the combat service only requested the name of the active weapon.

Server Mates

As alluded to earlier, some services are better off running together on the same server. An example of server mates, in the case of all instances, is the ExecutionService running on every service server. When you have broken up your tasks into what services you want to run, it's sometimes best, and required, to have two dependant services running on the same service server. Knowing what services are best run together on the same server can be dependant on game mechanics.

Game Service Construction Example

Let's look at the construction of a simple ItemService. First, we need to identify the objectives that the ItemService is to accomplish, what other services are going to be using it, and how much.

Objectives

- Persist game items to and from the database.
- Add and remove items from player inventories and the world.
- Update item statistics.
- Permanent removal of destroyable or consumable items.

Service Usage—Who and How Much?

This simple ItemService needs to communicate with the combat service, the position service, the FrontendService, and the DatabaseService. When communicating with the CombatService, it is the ItemService's job to return the active item being used by a player and its stats. In regard to the PositionService, the ItemService tells the PositionService whether to add or a remove an item from the world. The ItemService relies on the FrontendService for information in regard to a player's involvement with items. The DatabaseService is the bank for the ItemService to deposit and withdraw items in the world.

ItemService Class

Now that we have defined what the ItemService needs to accomplish its task, we now can move on to implementing the *ItemService*. Like any other service, it is implemented and inherited on top of the Service base class. Creating this class is as easy as defining its functionality and binding to its callbacks (see Figure 2.5.9).

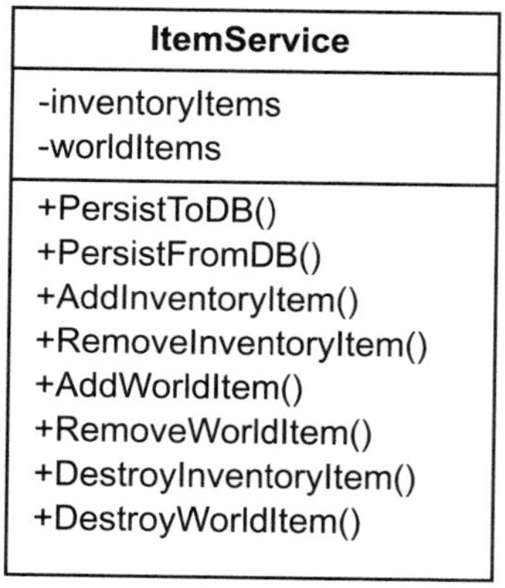

ItemService
-inventoryItems
-worldItems
+PersistToDB()
+PersistFromDB()
+AddInventoryItem()
+RemoveInventoryItem()
+AddWorldItem()
+RemoveWorldItem()
+DestroyInventoryItem()
+DestroyWorldItem()

FIGURE 2.5.9   *ItemService class diagram.*

Where Do We Go From Here?

Now that the distributed services system is in place, what more can be done? Things like service version control, crash protection and recovery, hot swappable services, shadow and watchdog services, and live updates are only a few of the features that give this system its robust capabilities. To read more about these features and other aspects of the distributed services system, refer to [Street04].

Conclusion

As mentioned at the beginning of this article, the need and desire for a limitless world is great. With the distributed services approach, the grief of worrying about the hardware and software is gone. No matter the target number of players or the size of the world, the backend of this system will scale accordingly. Whether the total number of players rises or falls, the distributed services system can be scaled by hardware upgrades or the number of service servers running. The developer now has more time to focus on the content and story, rather than worry if the software and hardware will support such.

Even though we have provided the tools, creating an MMP online game can be one of the greatest and hardest endeavors a developer could ever embark on. The complexity of the task and the scale of the work are just as equally massive, and if not, extensive at best. Therefore it takes a lot of forethought and creativity to come out with a successful and balanced online game in the end. Even if a developer does not want to believe or admit to such, the players run the show once an online game goes live. All a developer can do is to guide, nurture, and help further build up the game from that point on. Good luck.

References

[Randall02] Randall, Justin, "Scaling Multiplayer Servers," *Game Programming Gems 3,* Charles River Media, Inc., 2002.

[Street04] Street, Shea, "Keeping a Massively Multiplayer Online Game Massive, Online, and Persistent," *Game Programming Gems 5,* Charles River Media, Inc., 2004.

2.6

Metrics Collection
and Analysis

Larry Mellon—Electronic Arts

larry@maggotranch.com

"When you can measure what you are speaking about and when you can express it in numbers you know something about it, but when you cannot measure it, when you cannot express it in numbers, your knowledge is of a meagre and unsatisfactory kind."

Lord Kelvin, speaking to the Institution of Civil Engineers, 1883.

Metrics for the Massives

Everyone has some variant on the old saw, "if you can measure it, you can improve it." And we need them all, for there are a lot of things to track and improve in a massively multiplayer (MMP) game. The performance of the infrastructure is a prime use of metrics to engineers, while in-game economic measures and player activity numbers are more favored by game designers, community reps, and marketing. There is also the need to find players who are associated with higher numbers of service calls and player complaints, and to monitor the live systems for anomaly events that signal trouble.

Note the volume of data to sift through. A server cluster with tens to hundreds of interacting server-side processes, hundreds to thousands of connected players per cluster, and potentially millions of registered users can easily generate gigabytes of metrics data per day. *Automating the collection and summarization of metrics is critical in the day-to-day operations of your game.*

There also exists the intriguing possibility of data mining on the user base to find ways of increasing the game's profit margin over time. Casinos are an interesting sister gaming industry that has done extremely well with this business practice. We have an unprecedented ability to observe and measure our players' predilections and preferences and tune our games accordingly over years of operations. However, we also have to trade that off against potential privacy issues: walking that fine line without alienating customers requires a careful approach.

The Business Case for Metrics

Metrics systems cost a significant amount of money. However, they don't directly put pixels on the screen for your customers, which generally lowers their priority when tasking game team engineers. This is a strategic mistake. *Metrics replace opinion with fact, providing clear views into the inner workings of complex, large-scale systems.* Be it the expensive interactions of server-side processes or the unpredictable actions and interactions of your player community, metrics augment the talents of your entire team by focusing their efforts on key, measured issues and visualizing the results of their changes.

Over the years of developing and operating your game, it pays off to measure and continually enhance your service to reduce your recurring costs and make your subscribers happy. You can continually measure and tweak the balance of key tuning values in your game, closely monitor content usage and resource utilization, and plan long-term extensions based on observing what features are currently and historically the most popular with your customers.

Metrics are even more useful in the development phase of an MMP game. The complexity of tens to thousands of interacting processes with highly variable user inputs and network connections produces odd peaks and valleys in performance and stability that cannot be predicted in the design phase. You need to see actual numbers on packet rates, error rates, response times, and CPU/memory consumption at scale from both controlled field tests and live operations to optimize and stabilize your game. The sheer scale of an MMP game makes more things go wrong than in smaller games, and the distributed nature of the problem makes it harder to quickly track down problems. *Development goes faster if your team can clearly measure problems and quickly observe the effects of their changes.*

Further, players never do quite what you expect. You'll need to closely monitor things like the economy to keep fair gameplay; cheating and unbalanced inflationary income costs you in developer fire-fighting time and generates unhappy subscribers. Similarly, you need to track other gameplay factors such as character class balance, weapon effectiveness, and skill level increase rates. No matter how careful you are during design, players will find a seam and ruthlessly exploit it. Even a perceived imbalance affects gameplay; players will avoid a class they've heard is too weak. *Unbalanced gameplay costs you in both the player experience and underutilized content.*

Most importantly, you can measure your customers. Player metrics allow you to analyze what your customers like to do in your game, what they spend their hard-earned money and time on—a glimpse into who your audience is. And if you know your audience, you can improve your product and expand your market.

Harrah's Casinos—a multibillion-dollar corporation with casinos spanning the globe—has found this concept extremely useful. Total Rewards—essentially a frequent gambler plan—provides Harrah's with bet-to-bet activity of registered players, who in turn get rewarded with perks and privileges for participating. Harrah's ended up with what amounts to a detailed, long-term study of their repeat customers, providing their entire management hierarchy with direct analysis of profits and costs and actions per player and per game feature, today, and over time. A TeraData warehouse collects the raw information, which is then used to continually tune the operations of the casinos to make their repeat customers happier, and help establish the most effective use of operational dollars.

Total Rewards is widely considered one of the best computer-based customer loyalty programs ever devised, winning Harrah's a Technology ROI award in 2004. Harrah's executives and customers alike love the program. John Boushy, CIO of Harrah's, in a speech at the DCI CRM Conference in Chicago in February 2000, said that they were achieving over 50% annual return-on-investment in their data warehousing and patron database activities. He thought that this was one of the best investments they had ever made as a corporation and that it would prove to forge key new business strategies and opportunities in the future.

Metrics augment your team's creative and technical talent in their drive to stabilize, scale, and tune your game during development, and intelligently react to measured reality over years of operations. You should have a functional metrics collection and analysis system in place by the time the first client is talking to the first server.

Classes and Applications of Metrics in MMP Systems

There are three basic classes of metrics in MMP games:

Players: Tracking in-game actions and events, such as time spent in various activities, most frequented areas of the game, or blow-by-blow views of battles; extracting player patterns from persistent data, such as the most/least popular possessions and character classes; customer service metrics, such as involvement rate in service calls and complaints; and social networking data, such as average number of friends per player or the key players in the community.

Game engine: CPU, memory, and bandwidth consumption per server component; average frame rate or latency across clients; and failure rates and types per server component are all common examples.

Economy: Tracking the daily levels of inflationary income from all sources; identifying player spending patterns; and tracking the daily results from all types of money sinks.

Applying the preceding metrics allows iterative improvement over the years of developing and operating your game. Find something that isn't going fast enough, or your players aren't using enough, or breaks too often, or costs too much to operate, and find a way to measure it. Your team can now take action and see if each given action had the desired effect of making the measure go up, or go down. *Whatever you measure, it needs to be quantifiable, reliable, and easily accessible to be useful.*

While individual metrics are clearly specific to a particular game, their application will tend to fall in one of the following categories. For each category, a sample chart is provided, drawn either from metrics used in the fielding and operations of *The Sims Online*, or from the author's active imagination.

Day-to-day operations benefit from historical tracking of metrics and the ability to see abnormal patterns the moment they develop. A giant spike in one source of inflationary income may indicate an exploit. Similarly, abnormal spikes in certain types of network packets may indicate a hacker attack, or simply be used to track down the root cause of mysterious server crashes. Customer service reps and community managers will benefit from the ability to see what players are doing, make a change, and then directly observe the results of their change. Time-view charts of server resource metrics such as CPU or memory usage, key server events such as crashes or DB slowdowns, and aggregated player inputs are very enlightening to your operations team. Examples of such automated, daily reports are given in Figures 2.6.1 through 2.6.3.

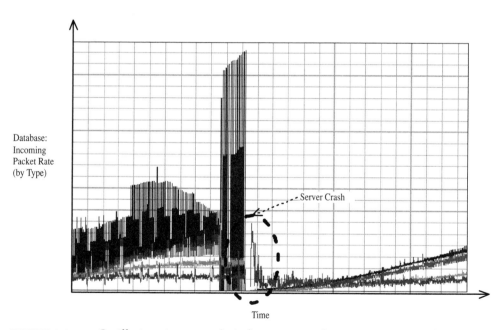

FIGURE 2.6.1   *Oscillations in one packet's data rate is a clear starting point when tracking down the server crash.*

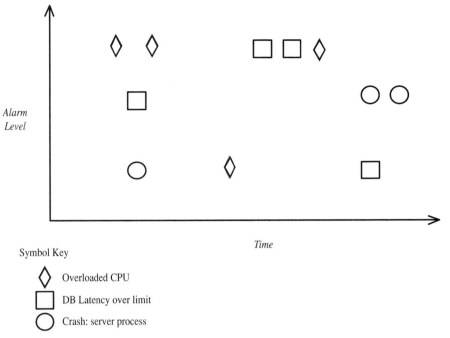

FIGURE 2.6.2 *Time-driven views of key events further help track down related system failures.*

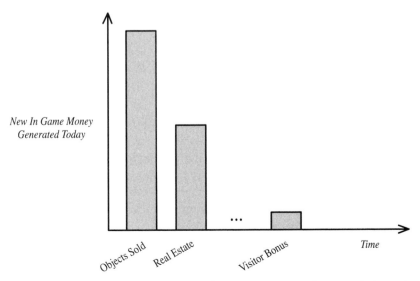

FIGURE 2.6.3 *Abnormal spikes in the economy can indicate unbalanced gameplay and/or exploits.*

Highly realistic load testing is possible by accurately measuring the server inputs from live Beta users and producing an input profile of an average user. Figure 2.6.4 visualizes the process of capturing the Beta user data and iteratively tuning the load testing rig until the input generated by N scripted test clients matches the actual input from N live players. Controlled load tests may then be done against candidate server clusters, using hundreds to thousands of copies of this representative user. Accurate, large-scale load testing allows capacity planning and server stability analysis well in advance of launch. For further information on load testing, see Article 2.1, "Automated Testing of Online Games."

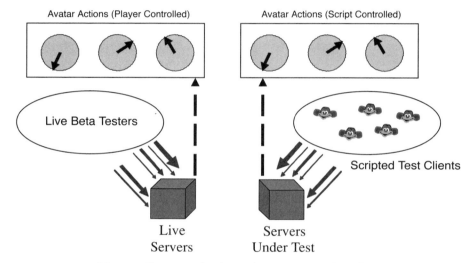

FIGURE 2.6.4   *Metrics allow your load test clients to precisely reflect measured user behavior.*

Content completion may be also measured. Thousands of sound, texture, and animation assets can easily exist in an MMP game; tracking what is where becomes difficult at that scale, and things continually keep breaking as new content is released. Metrics can provide your team with accurate information of what happens in a controlled test session, allowing content bugs to be easily found and fixed before being released to paying customers. A more detailed examination of this approach is presented in Article 2.1.

Long-term extensions to your game will benefit from high-level analysis of player behavior. Marketing can use metrics as fodder for press releases and viewing the effectiveness of in-game events. Tuning values may be changed to balance character classes and weapon damage levels based on how they are being used by players, or to increase socialization opportunities (see Michael Steele's excellent talk on social networks at *www.gameconference.com/2004_archive* for applications and visualizations of such data). Players may be guided toward underutilized content, and new content may be developed with direct, observed knowledge of what your player community likes to do. Similarly, infrastructure metrics allow your engineering team to optimize recurring costs, such as resource hogs or constant system failures that aggravate your customers and consume precious response team hours. Examining the behavior of differing classes of players and/or differing slices of time is another extremely useful application of metrics. Charting all activities of new players over their first 30 minutes within your game is an intriguing example. Looking at why some new players become long-term players and others do not could allow your design team to increase the conversion rate from samplers to subscribers. Examples of such automated, daily reports are given in Figures 2.6.5 through 2.6.8.

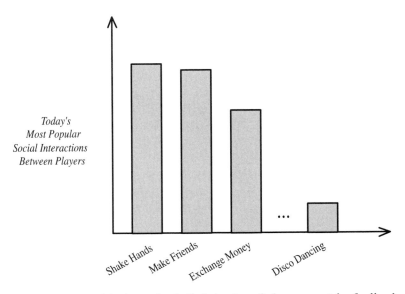

FIGURE 2.6.5   *Tracking the daily behavior of players provides feedback into the game tuning and community management processes.*

Customer level profit/cost analysis is an intriguing use of using metrics to establish which customers generate the most profit, and which customers cost the most to support. If griefers are costing your studio more money in service calls and unhappy subscribers than you make from them, get rid of them. However, of even more value is identifying *types* of players and their impact as a class on your profit margin and the areas of your game that they favor. Once identified, tuning your game to attract more high-profit players seems like a legal way to print money.

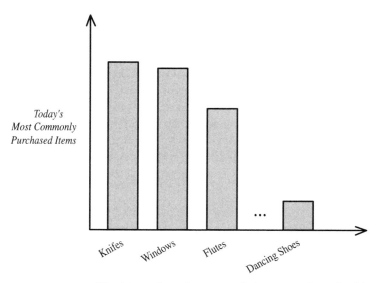

FIGURE 2.6.6   *Tracking what objects people buy provides valuable glimpses into your audience's desires.*

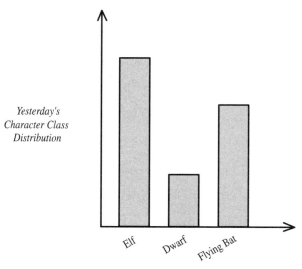

FIGURE 2.6.7   *Imbalances in the chosen character classes are easily identified.*

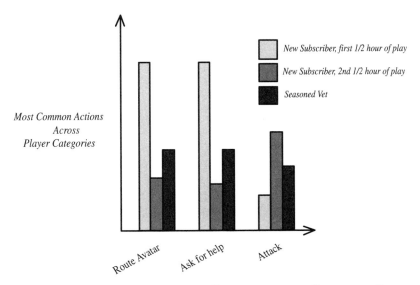

FIGURE 2.6.8 *Breaking down overall metrics into smaller groups of players shows interesting patterns.*

You could also expose some metrics to guild leaders as a perk—free to you and valuable to them. Some guild leaders already track things like member effectiveness in battle and participation or contribution levels. Making guild leaders' lives easier attracts them to your game and strengthens your community.

Architectural Components of an MMP Metrics System

Your metrics collection system is responsible for two major tasks: collecting raw data and providing fast access to summarized data views. Ease of use for all functionality is critical—allow users to easily add new probes, customize new data views, aggregate multiple tests into single reports, set alarms to look for dangerous data patterns, and drill down to specific test results. Metrics should be available as either time-view charts or summarized charts representing a block of time (such as all player actions over a day), and historical (such as today's numbers versus yesterday's numbers). A similar architecture to the one in Figures 2.6.9 through 2.6.11 was used to collect data for *The Sims Online* and was found to be both powerful in use and cost effective to build.

See *www.gdconf.com/archives/2004/* for further data on *TSO*'s metrics system.

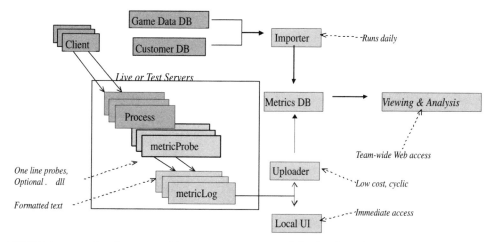

FIGURE 2.6.9   *A reference architecture to capture and display key player and server metrics.*

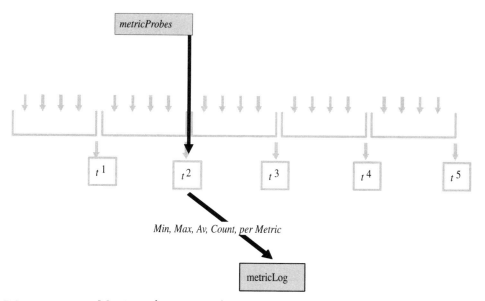

FIGURE 2.6.10   *Metric probes capture data at an event level, recording each time window's data in a memory buffer. At the end of each time window, summarized results for that window are written out to disk and the counters are reset.*

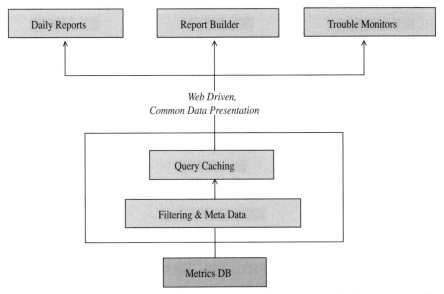

FIGURE 2.6.11 *A common viewing system with easily extended reports provides fast, easy access to metrics across the entire development team.*

Implementation Options

There are many possible solutions to collecting metrics. The best solution will depend on the needs and implementation characteristics of your specific MMP game, but in general, your solution will lean in one of two directions:

Full collection: Every event, every action, every atom, for all players and processes, all the time.

Partial collection: Only collect selected events, and/or collect aggregated behavior, not individual events.

The obvious problem with full collection is managing the raw data. Some quick back-of-the-envelope math tells us that a 10-shard game with 5,000 play sessions a day per shard, each averaging two hours, is collecting event data from 100,000 player hours. Assume for the sake of argument one user event per minute and you get 6,000,000 player events per day to store. But wait, there's more! Don't forget your infrastructure data: millions of additional events per day.

Transporting and storing the raw data with minimal impact on server performance is certainly achievable. The more subtle problem with collecting that much data is simply trying to understand it. Manually surfing hundreds of megabytes of raw data to find certain specific problems or repeating patterns is not a viable solution.

You need tool support to automatically produce high-level, aggregated views of data that show you what you need to know, not drown you in meaningless noise.

Given that most applications of metrics will deal with aggregated data, partial collection options are a very appealing choice—much lower in cost with a "good enough" level of service. The downside is that you'll need to identify very clearly what high-level reports will be needed and provide sufficient flexibility to allow additional reports down the road. A strong possibility is to collect only aggregated behavior metrics for server-side processes and collect event-level behavior metrics on your players.

There are three basic collection points for metrics:

Client-side collection: Highly accurate views of player activity are marred by privacy concerns and a weakness to data spoofing by the end users. Some metrics such as FPS and accurate latency data can only come from the client-side. Gathering such data from internal play testers and Beta testers should not be an issue, but tread carefully before pulling data from a paying customer's machine.

Server-side collection: Highly accurate views of internal server events and of player activity that directly impacts server performance are easily provided with considerably fewer privacy issues.

Data mining: Fascinating data about your players may be extracted from both the Persistence database of your game (where client possessions and character descriptions are stored) and the customer service database (where billing records and service histories per player are stored). From this data you can easily build tables showing things like the distribution of character classes across your customer base, or the top 10% of user accounts involved in customer service incidents this quarter.

Common Risks

A lot can go wrong in both the application and development of your metrics systems. When we started the metrics system for *TSO*—less than four months before launch—we found the dusty skeletons of several other metrics systems, either failed, obsolete or extremely limited in application. *The best way to keep a metrics system working is to have it constantly in use. Support as many applications as you can with a single, data-driven metrics system.* You end up with less code to build and maintain, a common UI, and the ability to easily compare server metrics against the player activity metrics that drive server performance.

Metrics systems of this scope are also hard to build. You will need a strong tools team with senior engineers working hand in hand with the development team to make success possible. Further, bear in mind that metrics are in part a development tool. *The deadline for a functional metrics system is* not *launch day; your team needs access to metrics long before the game hits Alpha.*

Once you've built successfully a metrics system, your next biggest risk is drowning in the sea of data it will produce. Automatically producing high-level data views, alarm 'bots to constantly scan for patterns of "risky" data, and flexible tools to surf the data waves and filter out irrelevant noise helps keep your head above water.

People hate to get probed; just ask any alien ship. If you collect the wrong data, or allow even the perception that you're snooping where you shouldn't be, severe customer backlash can result. Don't be sneaky, be very open about what you are collecting, and how. Collecting metrics strictly server-side largely derails the privacy issue. You could also follow the model of the electronic Neilson TV monitors or Harrah's Total Rewards program: have participation in a detailed, client-side metrics program provide desirable perks and privileges to volunteer players.

You also have the Schrödinger's Cat dilemma: the very act of observing your system can change its behavior. Dumping out gigs of data per hour will drive your ops team up the wall, so be very aware of your probe's impact on server performance, and have metrics to automatically measure the load of collecting metrics.

Finally, a metrics system involves software, and that means bugs. Business decisions are constantly being made based on the data from your metrics software. Be very aware of the possibility of defects and correlate key measures across differing sources.

Conclusion

A strong commitment to metrics will have a significant impact on the development and day-to-day operations of your MMP game. However, collecting metrics at the scale and complexity of an MMP game is nontrivial. Use a strong tools team and work day to day to improve the usability and effectiveness of your tools.

Finally, remember that knowledge is power. *Fielding a metrics system early in the development cycle of your game allows your entire team to make decisions based on fact, not opinion.* Development goes faster, and a stronger game results. Enjoy!

Acknowledgments

The success of *TSO*'s metrics collection system was heavily dependent on the design and implementation skills of Jeff Marshall and Moe Hendawi.

2.7

Delta-Compression for Heterogeneous Data Transfer

Jim Hicke—Xtreme Strategy Games, LLC

jhicke@xtremestrategy.com

Massively multiplayer online games often have various game systems that require presenting statistical and historical data to the gamer. This data could be anything from a quest history list, or a guild management system, to the statistics on the selected NPC. Not all classes of data need to be seen at once, and most of this data changes over time.

While efficient hand-optimized techniques are used to transmit player and NPC locations, it is possible to use polymorphic techniques to transmit other data structures. This article discusses a generic way to send game system data structures and keep them up-to-date with a small amount of bandwidth.

There are several problems that need to be solved related to this data. The data is often dynamic and changes need to be optimally transmitted. The number of objects for which data is available can be vast, and the data needs to be delivered on a need-to-know basis. Game systems are in a state of flux during development, and the technique used to encode data must be flexible and easy to change. The system presented in this article addresses all of those issues and creates a framework for easily dealing with heterogeneous data in an online game.

Basic Considerations

It must be decided when to use a generic technique verses customized techniques to send data between the client and server. Certain classes of data demand an optimized approach, such as player and NPC locations. These locations and associated statistics, such as health, should use a technique similar to an FPS such as *Quake 3* [Hook04]. The basic optimizations that can be achieved in such techniques rely on having a known state data structure and sending optimized deltas of it using a custom bit-field. Larger and more complex data structures, such as those composed of variable-length constituents, lend themselves to the generic approach.

No matter which approach, generic or custom, is used to compress the data, it must be sent over the network. UDP is the protocol of choice for online games, as it minimizes lag and imposes a low overhead for sending data. The "unreliable" in UDP is a misnomer; the odds of a low-level data packet being dropped are the same for UDP and TCP/IP. The TCP/IP protocol handles the retry and out-of-order issues. Unfortunately, it also tries to affect systemic bandwidth issues that might be causing packet loss by reducing the packet send rate, sometimes dramatically. This might be good for Web sites, but it is unacceptable for games. The protocol must be fault tolerant, predictable, and have low latency. Game developers don't like other protocols between their server and their game. The motto "Better never than late" drives the underlying philosophy of gaming network protocols [Simp01]. For this reason, most games use UDP to send data packets and they manage the dropped and out-of-order packets themselves.

To have a polymorphic system to deal with network data, there needs to be a unified way to specify object instances. The approach used by this system is a unique identifier called the ObjectID. The ObjectID can be used to get a reference to the instance data of an object, and uniquely defines this instance within a game simulation server cluster. Pointers cannot be used, since the data needs to be streamed between processes. It is assumed that the object lookup, using the ObjectID, is extremely fast and returns a pointer to a base type that has the polymorphic characteristics in which we are interested.

```
CObject* pObject = gObjectManager.Lookup(uObjectID);
```

Within this system, any reference to an object within an object is assumed to be by ObjectID.

The other requirement is for each object to have a way to stream itself to and from a data buffer. The generic solution deals with all data as a stream of bytes with no knowledge of the internal structure of the object. Each new gaming system has only to supply the streaming methods to become part of the solution. The streaming required for this system is not necessarily the same as the streaming required for persistent storage. It is likely that only a subset of the server data needs to be transmitted to the client. This implies that there is another client-specific class associated with each server class. The server class can supply a method to stream out to the client-specific class format, or it can create the client-specific object and use its streaming method. The first technique is faster; the second is easier to maintain.

Constructing the System

The first step to constructing the system is to add the ability to track which ObjectIDs the client is interested in. In effect, the client is interested in a copy of the object and change events related to the object. In this regard, the system is an implementation of the publish/subscribe protocol, where the game server acts as the event broker and the client acts as the event consumer [Zhen01]. Once the server cluster knows which objects the client is interested in, it can start tracking them for delta compression.

An interesting issue regarding the client subscribing to the game cluster is how it gains knowledge of which ObjectIDs to request. There needs to be a bootstrapping of information to the client. The client will need to know its own ObjectID and those of the visible NPCs. From there, it should be possible to discover other ObjectIDs of interest by looking at the data returned from subscribed objects. One approach is to give the client an organized set of relevant ObjectIDs in a default data object that is published to the client on initial connection. For example, this object can contain the ObjectID of the Quest History Object, the Guild Object, the Housing Object, and so forth. Another approach is to create game system-specific messages that subscribe to specific objects that are related to the player, such as "this player's quest history." When the gamer opens a user-interface window to show the information, the client subscribes to the appropriate ObjectID (see Figure 2.7.1).

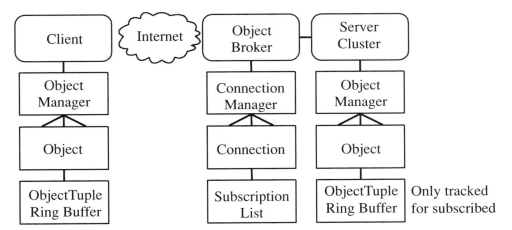

FIGURE 2.7.1   *Delta compression system.*

Object Manager

Since the data is being synchronized with a delta compression technique, there needs to be a way to refer to versions of an object instance. The simulation frame sequence number of the server, which owns the object, is an obvious choice. This will be called the FrameID. The tuple (ObjectID, FrameID) uniquely defines an object instance at a point in time. This will be called the ObjectTuple. It is usually sufficient to use the lower 8 bits of the FrameID as an unsigned integer to determine the relative "age" of an object, as this will save on bandwidth.

The Object Manager will need to keep a history of ObjectTuples for a certain number of frames in order to have the required baseline data to construct an object using delta compression. The ideal data structure is a ring-buffer of the required data held in a cache for ObjectIDs to which a client has subscribed. There is no need to keep history information for unsubscribed objects. This ring buffer is used on the client to obtain the baseline data buffer used to decompress the data as indicated by the delta compression packet. It is used on the server to construct the delta compression packet based on its knowledge of the most recent baseline available to the client.

There are two ways to keep the last known FrameID up to date on the server. The explicit approach is to have the client send a periodic message to the server with the highest FrameID successfully decompressed. This has the advantage of being accurate but imposes an upstream bandwidth cost. The implicit approach is to assume a certain rate of lag and use that metric to decide how old a FrameID to use as the base data. In this approach, the client sends a message back to the server if the indicated base FrameID is not available in its cache. This message includes the client's highest known FrameID. The server responds by increasing the assumed lag on that connection and resending based on an older FrameID. This approach requires no upstream bandwidth once the lag rate estimate is refined for the connection, but is subject to more overhead on the server.

The Object Manager supplies the following methods:

```
class CObjectManager
{
public:
CObject* LookUp(unsigned int ObjectID);
void Add(CObject* pObject);
void Delete(unsigned int ObjectID);
bool RingBufferGet(
unsigned int ObjectID,
unsigned int FrameID,
char* pBuffer,
int size);
bool RingBufferAdd(
unsigned int ObjectID,
unsigned int FrameID,
char* pBuffer,
int size);
};
```

Required Polymorphic Behavior

The base class of the object returned by the object manager supplies the following methods:

```
class CObject
{
public:
virtual bool ReadStream(
    const char* pStream,  // IN - Stream buffer
    int nSize);           // IN - Size of buffer
virtual int StreamSize(); // Returns size required to
  // stream out the data
```

```
virtual bool WriteStream(
    char* pStream,          // OUT- Stream buffer
    int nAlloc,             // IN - Allocated size
    int& nSize);            // OUT- Generated size
unsigned int CObject::GetFrameID();
virtual bool IsExpired();
bool IsInitialized();
};
```

These streaming methods are a minimalist implementation, as most games create some sort of streaming object that handles the bookkeeping. The `GetFrameID()` method returns the FrameID for the object. This is used to determine how old the data is by comparing it to the currently known simulation FrameID. The `IsExpired()` method is used to determine if the object hasn't been updated in a reasonable amount of time, where reasonable is defined by the class. The `IsInitialized()` method is used to determine if the object has been updated at least once by the server since the subscription request.

Delta Compression

The basic premise behind delta compression is that the changes to a large data structure are small during each simulation frame and, therefore, only the changes must be transmitted. The generic solution to this problem is a function that takes the baseline buffer and the current buffer and produces a delta buffer that describes how to modify the baseline into the current buffer. Another function takes the base line buffer and the delta buffer and creates the current buffer. This is the underlying technique for source control systems and program patchers. The following functions are used to perform this processing:

```
bool CreateDelta(
    char* sourcePtr,        // IN - baseline
    int sourceLen,          // IN - number of bytes
    char* targetPtr,        // IN - current data
    int targetLen,          // IN - number of bytes
    char* deltaPtr,         // OUT- delta buffer
    int deltaSize,          // IN - allocated size
    int& deltaLen);         // OUT- bytes generated
int ApplyDelta(
    char* sourcePtr,        // IN - baseline
    int sourceLen,          // IN - number of bytes
    char* deltaPtr,         // IN - delta buffer
    int deltaLen,           // IN - number of bytes
    char* targetPtr,        // OUT- current data
    int targetSize,         // IN - allocated size
    int& targetLen);        // OUT- bytes generated
```

The delta buffer contains a sequence of codes and data. The codes execute on the base data, combined with the delta buffer data, to create the new data. The new data is used as the streaming source for the object to update itself. This set of codes supports data that increases and decreases in size, so it is appropriate for use with variable-length strings and arrays. Table 2.7.1 describes a basic delta compression code system.

Table 2.7.1   Delta Compression Codes

Code	Parameters	Description
COPY	length	Copy <length> bytes from the source buffer and increment the current source buffer location.
REPLACE	length data[length]	Copy <length> bytes from the delta buffer data and skip past <length> bytes in the source buffer.
INSERT	length data[length]	Insert <length> bytes from the delta buffer data. Keep the source buffer location the same.
DELETE	length	Skip past <length> bytes in the source buffer.
REPLICATE	length offset	Copy <length> bytes from the source buffer, starting at <offset>.Do not change the source buffer location.
REPLACE_RLE	count data	Replicate <count> bytes of <data>.

It is possible to get creative with the codes and the algorithm to create them. Keep in mind that encoding is slower than decoding in most algorithms. It is also possible to squeeze the buffer size further by using bit fields instead of byte codes. For example, the code DELTA_COPY16 could be implemented so that it contains the length field in the lower 4 bits of its byte code. This assumes, of course, that there are no more than 16 total compression codes so that each code fits in a nibble, leaving a nibble for a parameter.

Messages

Tables 2.7.2 and 2.7.3 describe the messages used by the system to manage the subscribed data.

Table 2.7.2   Messages Sent by the Client

Message	Description
MSG_OBJECT_SUBSCRIBE	Start a subscription to an ObjectID.
MSG_OBJECT_FRAMEID	Send the highest FrameID for an ObjectID. This is used when the server sends a baseline FrameID that the client doesn't have. It can also be sent periodically by the client to give better data to the server at the expense of upstream bandwidth.
MSG_OBJECT_UNSUBSCRIBE	End a subscription to an ObjectID.
MSG_OBJECT_RESET_ALL	Tell the server to reset all state information about this connection and resend all data. This is useful for debugging.

Table 2.7.3 Messages Sent by the Server

Message	Description
MSG_OBJECT_COMPLETE	A delta packet based on the default constructor of the object.
MSG_OBJECT_DELTA	A delta packet with a specified base FrameID.
MSG_OBJECT_DESTROY	Inform the client that the particular ObjectID, to which the client is subscribed, has been destroyed.

Fault Tolerance

Fault tolerance is built into the system by the use of the ObjectTuple, the history ring buffer, and acknowledgment messages. The client easily discards out-of-order packets because it compares the FrameID of the currently known ObjectTuple with the incoming delta packet and drops any that are not newer. Delta packets that are dropped by the network, within the limits of the ring buffer, are a nonissue because the client keeps a history list in its ring buffer and a new delta packet arrives shortly. If the client receives a delta packet with a baseline that it doesn't have yet, it informs the server of its most recent ObjectTuple and the server bases the next delta packet on that version. If the server no longer has that version, it sends a complete new copy of the data.

Client Algorithm

During each frame:

```
FOR each subscribed ObjectID
IF !pObject->IsInitialized() AND time since last request is greater
than x milliseconds
            SEND MSG_OBJECT_SUBSCRIBE
     ELSE IF pObject->IsExpired()
            // We haven't seen an update in a while
            // remind the server we're still interested
     SEND MSG_OBJECT_FRAMEID
```

In response to messages:

```
ON MSG_OBJECT_COMPLETE:
     CREATE pObject
     pObject->ReadStream(buffer)
     INSERT pObject into ObjectManager
     INSERT buffer into Ring Buffer under FrameID
ON MSG_OBJECT_DELTA:
     IF the FrameID is not in the Ring Buffer
            // Send highest FrameID we have
            SEND MSG_OBJECT_FRAMEID
     ELSE
Get the buffer for the FrameID
            Apply the delta to create the new buffer
     pObject->ReadStream(buffer)
     Insert the buffer in the Ring Buffer
```

Server Algorithm

During each frame:

```
FOR each connection
FOR each subscribed ObjectID
IF first update
SEND_MSG_OBJECT_COMPLETE
ELSE IF (object changed AND minimum update time passed) OR maximum
update time passed
        IF last known FrameID is not available
                SEND MSG_OBJECT_COMPLETE
        ELSE
Create Delta from last known FrameID
SEND MSG_OBJECT_DELTA
```

In response to messages:

```
ON MSG_OBJECT_SUBSCRIBE:
        Add ObjectID to list of subscribed objects
ON MSG_OBJECT_UNSUBSCRIBE:
        Remove ObjectID from list of subscribed objects
ON MSG_OBJECTID_FRAMEID:
        Update last known FrameID for this object
```

Unsubscribing

It is important to maintain as small a subscription list as possible to reduce bandwidth and server processing time. The way to deal with dropping a subscription to an ObjectID is to use time-to-live values on the subscription. The client can also send an unsubscribe message when it determines that all systems on the client are finished with the ObjectID, but it should still use the time-to-live concept for greater reliability. Any "dangling" subscribed objects will clog the system. The client tracks the time from the last subscribe message and reissues the subscribe message within the time-to-live interval for all active ObjectIDs. For example, a UI window that subscribes to an object would have to call a method in the Object Manager to indicate that it is still interested in the ObjectID. The Object Manager would then check the time-to-live value and reissue the subscribe message as needed. When the ObjectID is no longer requested by any system on the client, it will fade from memory when the time-to-live is exceeded.

Dealing with Dropped Packets

The system automatically compensates for dropped packets by the nature of the base FrameID concept. There are, however, some techniques that can be used to deal with connections that are prone to dropped packets. Assuming that the situation is detected, the server can send duplicate messages since the system is tolerant of that situation. This, of course, increases the bandwidth use and can make the situation worse. This technique is reserved for connections that are prone to dropping packets due to line noise or ISP issues, as opposed to connections that are flooded with data.

Dealing with Lag

The main effect of lag on this system is in the coordination of known FrameIDs. This has a ripple effect on the amount of data sent over the connection, which can exasperate the situation. The larger the difference between the base FrameID and the current FrameID, the larger the delta pack required. Since there is a finite limit to the bandwidth, and it is often small on massively multiplayer (MMP) games, the best solution is to slow the update frequency. This can be done across all of the objects, or some heuristic can be used based on knowledge of the data types.

Pitfalls

As usual, performance is the bottleneck of many gaming systems, and this one is no exception. The problem with buffer-based delta compression is that it has to touch a lot of memory to generate the delta packet. This can lead to performance issues. In addition, the algorithm for generating the delta packet needs to be as fast as possible.

The algorithm for generating the delta packet needs to be a greedy algorithm that operates in linear time. While this won't generate the smallest delta packet in all cases, it will perform well in the average case [Burns97].

Extending the System

Any system can be made better, and this one is no exception. While this technique will automate the delta-compression of network data, it does nothing for the tedious task of writing streaming methods. Although it is trivial to write the streaming methods for each new class, why not automate them?

A simple C++ parser can be written to read through the header files. The section of members that needs to be streamed can be marked with special comments, recognized by the parser. The parser can generate C++ code to implement the streaming methods. This code can then be compiled into the system. The two-pass process can be automated with makefiles. Once this system is in place, the data can be reorganized without worrying about the streaming methods.

Conclusion

MMORGs evolve over time by adding new game systems that may have complex data structures associated with them. The best games evolve over time so the ability to quickly implement new features on a stable platform is highly desirable. Polymorphic solutions to heterogeneous data transfer can speed development and reduce bandwidth. The techniques described in this article allow one to concentrate on developing new game mechanics without having to worry about network traffic.

References

[Burns97] Burns, Randal C., and Darrell D. E. Long, "A Linear Time, Constant Space Differencing Algorithm," in Proceedings of the 1997 International Performance, Computing and Communications Conference (IPCCC), IEEE, 1997.

[Hook04] Hook, Brian, "The Quake3 Networking Model," available online at *www.bookofhook.com/Article/GameDevelopment/TheQuake3NetworkingModel.html*.

[Simp01] Simpson, Jake, "Networking for Games 101," available online at *www.gamedev.net/reference/articles/article1138.asp*.

[Zhen01] Zhenhui, Shen, and Srikanta Tirthapura, "Self-Stabilizing Routing in Publish-Subscribe Systems," available online at *http://clue.eng.iastate.edu/~snt/research/debs04.pdf*.

2.8

Architecture and Techniques for an MMORTS

Gideon Amir—Majorem

gidibarvaz@yahoo.com

Ramon Axelrod—AiSeek, Inc.

mushroomramon@yahoo.com

In a massive multiplayer online real-time strategy game (MMORTS), thousands of players share the same contiguous virtual space. Each player controls dozens of units (in contrast with MMORPGs) and can battle with/against any number of players simultaneously. The players need to receive information in the immediate surrounding of all their units. As these units can be very far apart and see many other players with thousands of units, the amount of information that must be transferred to the client machines to keep their world state consistent is far greater than those required in the MMORPG genre.

Dealing with this tremendous flow of information poses one of the greatest challenges of the MMORTS game genre [Jaecheol01]. Naïvely, updating all the information (in excess of 50KB/sec) around each of the players' units all the time is impractical in today's low-bandwidth modems. Even if every end user had equipment capable of reaching this kind of throughput, the cost of such communication load will be tremendous to the game provider.

The new game genre also poses new demands in other areas such as content creation and data presentation to the user. For example, a new level of demand on computational resources is needed for Artificial Intelligence (AI), both for players and for the computer adversaries needed to act against these players, as typical virtual worlds might include millions of AI units. Moreover, the large maps needed to house thousands of players are problematic for standard path-finding techniques.

In this article, we describe the algorithmic basis needed for implementing an MMORTS game capable of sustaining hundreds of units for each player, all of which can affect their surrounding. We focus mainly on the task of keeping data *consistency* across all servers and all connected clients with *minimal bandwidth*, while keeping acceptable perceived latency. Stated differently, we need to send only the relevant information for each client and in a way that fits nicely into 1 to 2 KB/sec.

The final sections describe how the algorithm devised can also benefit other parts of the system (clustering, graphics, etc.) and deal briefly with other problems of MMORTS games.

Basic Techniques

We will start with the most naïve approach to the problem of sending all relevant data to each client. The idea is to generalize the algorithms like [TNL01] used in MMOG with a single avatar for sending relevant data, so that it loops through all the units of each player. This can be best understood by the following pseudocode:

```
for (each connected player P) do {
    for (each element E of player P) do {
        for (each element U near E) do
            Create message updating element U's state
    }
    Compress all messages to player P
    Send messages to player P
}
```

The compression algorithm can take into account the fact that many consecutive elements *"U"* near each other have similar characteristics, such as similar unique identifiers (ID), sharing a close position and engaging in the same action (all attacking, all moving, etc.), and achieve a fairly good compression ratio.

The first step for optimizing the algorithm comes from noting that a lot of information is covered by more than one element of the connected player (usually in RTS, players move their units in fairly large groups—and all see more or less the same things). Although it is possible to simply flag each element *"U"* if it has been sent in order to avoid retransmission, we will take a slightly longer route, which will prove more useful at the end.

World Segmentation

We divide the world into small square regions (see Figure 2.8.1), which must be bigger than the highest line-of-sight (LOS) radius, so that a unit in a square can only see up to the adjacent squares. The region should not exceed the LOS by much so that the adjacent squares will not include excess information that cannot be seen. Note that this bears vague similarity to sections of grid solutions (see [Ferguson01]), but for different purposes.

For each region, we keep track of all the elements in the region and of all the players who should receive information about that region or part of it (players *viewing* the region). This makes updating the state of the world relatively trivial as is illustrated by the following pseudocode:

```
for (each region of map R) do {
    for (each connected player P viewing region R) do
        for (each element E in region R)
            Create message updating element E's state
}
for (each connected player P) do {
    Compress all messages to player P
    Send messages to player P
}
```

Keeping track of the elements in each region is pretty straightforward, but keeping track of the list of players who view the region is somewhat trickier, as it depends on their elements in adjacent regions as well. To do so, we assign for each viewing player entry in the region a bitfield, which designates from which adjacent squares (or this one) it is viewed. When the first unit of a player enters a region, all the squares adjacent to it are marked as "viewed" by that player (the player is added if he is not yet present and the proper bit is set). When the last unit of that player leaves the square, all bitfields in adjacent squares are updated, and players who do not see a square are deleted (see Figure 2.8.1).

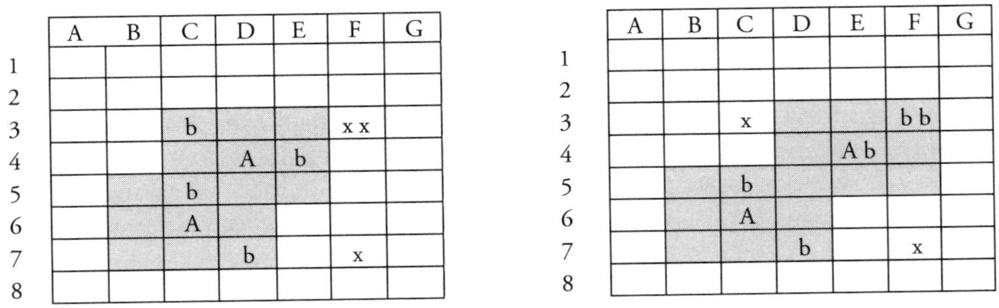

	A	B	C	D	E	F	G
1							
2							
3			b			x x	
4				A	b		
5			b				
6			A				
7				b		x	
8							

	A	B	C	D	E	F	G
1							
2							
3			x			b b	
4					A b		
5			b				
6			A				
7				b		x	
8							

FIGURE 2.8.1   *World segmentation on the server before and after unit A in D4 crosses to E4. The gray areas are regions marked as viewed for the player who owns units A. Units that belong to other players are marked as b (viewed), x (not viewed).*

This solution still falls short of the mark, as can be easily seen even by considering the conservative scenario given in the introduction: a player and four allies attack an enemy base guarded by five players; each of them also has 100 units, totaling 1000 units. This scenario already requires each client to be sent updates of about 1000 units approximately twice per second. Even at 6 bytes/unit after amazing compression (a single second of battle can contain updates to several abilities: HP, mana, xp, carried items etc., and each update must also contain the unit's unique identifier), the updates exceed standard modems and will cost the game provider a fortune. Since MMORTS games contain units that persist over many weeks, it is necessary to provide additional data to support them (more configurable options and abilities), which adds to the amount of data that must be transferred.

Advanced Methods for Bandwidth Reduction

The next step in reducing the communication bandwidth is to note that many of the changes in the state of an element do not necessarily require update messages to be sent, because the updates are predictable. For example, if a moving unit continues moving in the same direction, there is no need to send updates of these movements. Updates will be sent only when the unit changes direction or stops. Many network games use action prediction of the user mainly to cut the response time, not bandwidth. If the user chooses the trivial predicted action, the client will start executing the move at once.

It is possible to make a slightly more elaborate prediction scheme that can also take into account more "active" decisions (assuming one choice is favored over the others). The server runs the prediction algorithm against the actual state, and if the prediction fails for any reason, it sends corrections to the clients about it.

RTS games offer the opportunity for a far more elaborate prediction scheme. Since the units are usually given "complex" commands (build here, attack there, etc.) and the AI is responsible for decomposing it into step-by-step actions, many of the units' actions are entirely predictable by the same algorithm. Therefore, if we send these complex commands at low rate and perform the same low-level-AI routines on the server and all viewing clients, we could achieve very good bandwidth while keeping the state consistent.

The output of such a prediction algorithm might depend on the unit itself and its surroundings. For example, the movement of a unit A following another unit B depends on the whereabouts of unit B, as well as on the obstacles lying in its immediate path; target selection might depend on all of the local enemy units. Typically, the low-level-AI dependencies are restricted to a certain radius around the unit creating a *dependency bubble*. For the output of the algorithms to be consistent between the server and all the clients, they have the same commands, and the relevant information inside the dependency bubble must be identical on all of them.

Developers of MMORTS games should also consider the following issues:

The computation power on the server restricts the possible prediction power.
Naïvely, one could send only very complex actions, such as the user's actions, in large time intervals, and all clients can predict everything from it. However, such actions usually require vast amounts of computation. Using the movement example, the entire path of a unit can be constructed from the true destination. However, even using a fully optimized A* there is no way a server can deal with more than a few thousand units (when millions are needed). Therefore, we should restrict ourselves in practice to actions that are computationally simple. Examples include retaliating to attacks by close creatures, or simple steering (e.g., walking few tiles, following another unit, moving with an offset).

Since the actions of units depend on other units in the dependency bubble, the order of processing is a significant factor.   Suppose that B changes its direction in the preceding example. If A is processed first, it will not be aware of the changing direction and will continue in its previous heading. However, if B is processed first, A will change its heading to match. One way to achieve the same processing order on the server and all clients is to process all units according to their unique identifier in ascending order. To avoid ordering advantage/disadvantages, one has to process in ascending order and descending order interleaved turns.

Another related issue is the consistency of the data in the dependency bubble. For the prediction to be accurate, all data in the dependency bubble must be available and current. On a client machine, for units positioned near the end of the viewable region, part of their dependency bubble falls outside this region, so one cannot use the prediction and still be consistent with the server. As mentioned previously, once the prediction fails, the server must send corrections to the client, resulting in the need for continuous updates of units near the end of the viewable region.

The practical question is how to implement a simple system on the server that will know which unit requires continuous updates and which unit can use prediction. One possible solution is to generalize the segmentation to regions by dividing the regions on the server into two types for each player: the CUR (Continuously Updated Region) and the PUR (Prediction Used Region). The PURs of a certain player are those squares that hold his elements, and the CURs are all the remaining viewed squares. Figure 2.8.2 illustrates a scenario similar to that in Figure 2.8.1.

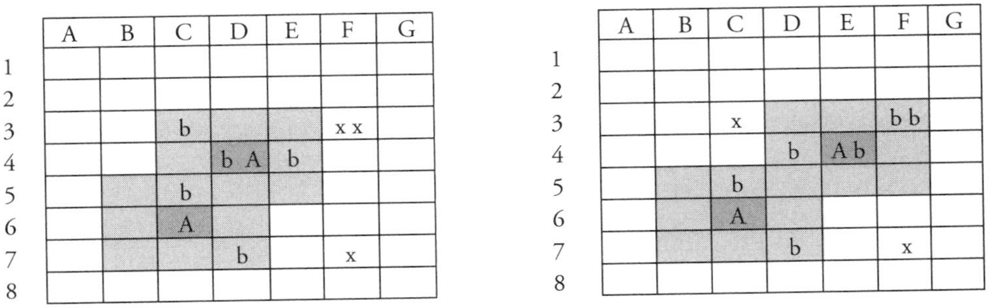

FIGURE 2.8.2   *Advanced world segmentation on the server before and after unit A in D4 crosses to E4. The light gray areas are regions marked as viewed for the player who owns units A. Light gray areas are CU (continuously updated) and dark gray areas are PUR (prediction used). Units of other players are marked as b (viewed), x (not viewed).*

Intuitively, having only those squares that hold the player's elements as his PURs will only provide mild results, as most of the viewed area still needs to be continuously updated. It is also possible to define the eight adjacent squares as PURs, and only the squares around them as CURs, giving better PUR/CUR ratio. However, in practice, the gain from such a choice is small, as the distribution of elements is far from uniform. Units of different players get close to one another only for interaction (allies move together and trade, enemies fight, etc.), which usually drives them to the same square. In fact, careful choice of square size can ensure that the CURs are usually very empty even in very large battles with thousands of units and many players. In addition, increasing the number of PURS and CURS results in a wider area on which the client must be updated, ultimately resulting in larger bandwidth.

To complete the discussion, the data-updating algorithm now looks something like:

```
for (each region of map R) do
    for (each connected player P viewing region R) do
        if (Region is Border for P){
            for (each element E in region R) do
                Create message updating E's state
        }
        else (region is Inner for P){
            for (each element E in region R) do {
                if (Prediction fails due to user change)
                    Create message updating E's state
            }
        }
    for (each connected player P) do {
        Compress all messages to player P
        Send messages to player P
    }
```

It should be noted that the algorithm also provides data that lends itself to compression. As mentioned earlier, even without any proper world segmentation, a compression algorithm is quite effective because many consecutive elements U are near each other, have similar unique identifiers (IDs), and probably engage in the same action. The advanced world segmentation allows a far better compression ratio:

• The world segmentation essentially ensures that consecutive units lay close to each other.
• At the complex action level, more units are engaged in the same action than at a step-by-step update (since in RTS, units move in formations that have the same complex action).
• The game elements are processed in an ascending/descending order so that IDs can be even more tightly packed.

Reusing the World Segmentation for Other Purposes

The world segmentation algorithms suggested in the previous section could also be used on the server and client machines to facilitate/accelerate other common RTS tasks.

Clustering: One of the more compelling ways to divide the workload of maintaining an MMORTS server cluster between individual machines is according to spatial world position: each server deals with all the game elements and players that are in a certain area. The world segmentation algorithm can be extended to have a seamless world map across servers and allow shrinking and growing of server areas in real-time (each server is responsible for a certain region, but a small patch of squares around it is still updated by adjacent servers—still *viewed* by that server. Having data in this patch continuously updated by other servers allows for a fast and easy passage of units across the seam).

3D graphics rendering: It is impractical to keep a mesh of the entire world in MMORTS games. Rather, the mesh is constructed in real-time on a need basis and a cache is kept of recently viewed areas. It is in general very convenient to construct the meshes for areas that match the segmentation, and to keep regions that are marked as viewed by the player longer in the cache (as they are inherently viewed more). With a slight effort, even fog-of-war calculations can take advantage of the viewed/unviewed division.

The data structure can be easily used to answer queries like, "What elements are positioned at a certain location?" and "Which elements are near/around a location?" This greatly accelerates choosing targets for attacking units as well as other actions.

AI: The proper segmentation lends itself easily to creating a tiered approach. First, one builds a scaled-down version of the map needed by defining each square region as a tile on a scaled map. Then, same-player groups of units that are geographically close together are aggregated together on the scaled map. This can be repeated iteratively.

Distributing AI to Clients

Because a great deal of AI is needed in RTS, simply adding a few more computers at the server farm is not sufficient to support the performance requirements. Since the connected users have a lot of CPU power at their disposal, it is logical to try to harness that power by distributing AI processes to the clients.

We will focus on the technical issues of distributing processes, and will not dwell on the legal and semi-legal ones, most of which can be covered by adding one more term to the terms of use paper players accept as part of the installation. Still, it is worth mentioning that when one plays a regular, offline RTS, the client uses part of the CPU for playing "opponent" AI. We suggest that distributed AI in MMORTS games does essentially the same thing.

Returning to technical issues, distributed AI still has to conform to the low bandwidth restriction. This has great impact on the type of distributed algorithms possible:

We provide only guidelines.   Fine-tuning depends greatly on the architecture of the MMORTS and of the AI and the exact algorithms used. More detailed discussion and specific solutions lie outside the scope of this article.

The game should distribute CPU intensive algorithms, which require little input data and short output answers.   Examples include terrain analysis routines (e.g., choke points), optimization algorithms over spaces with many variables (e.g., resource allocation and management), and searching of large data-spaces that are built on the fly.

Favor strategic, long-range planning that needs only minor changes afterward over tactical short-range decisions.   Favor sending strategic, long-range planning that needs only little changes afterward to the client's overall tactical short-range decisions, which change rapidly and require constant updating.

If distributing tactical unit decisions is important, transfer control of entire NPC armies to a client and do not divide them across clients.   There is significant interdependency between units inside an army but little interdependency between units of different armies. Therefore, playing few NPCs of each army on each client will increase the bandwidth tremendously.

All MMOGs share a common problem: content creation.   The need for filling an enormous virtual world is a time-consuming and expensive task for game designers, who in turn seek automated solutions. Since the AI in RTS games includes many routines for "building," it is tempting to apply them also for automatic content creation. The local flavor of these tasks makes them ideal candidates for distribution.

After deciding *what* to distribute, we are faced with the practical question of *how* to build a task-distributing manager. We start by collecting information about the bandwidth available for each client and processing power to decide which clients can deal with additional tasks.

Next, each time there is a need to send a location-based query (e.g., terrain analysis) or transfer control over an NPC army to the AI on a client machine, send it to the most appropriate player(s). The algorithm should try to pick players already viewing the regions relevant to the query in order to reduce traffic. For playing NPC armies, this achieves even better bandwidth reduction because all the squares in which these NPCs reside are turned into PURs of that client. For reasons of security and robustness, send the queries to more than one client and keep only the majority result, which avoids dependency on any one client.

The pseudocode for such a system is shown here:

```
for (each pending distributed job J) do {
    get list L of players viewing regions of J
    sort list L according to size of viewed region of J
    for (each player P in list L) do {
        if (player P hasn't got enough CPU or bandwidth)
            erase P from list L
    }
    if (not enough eligible players remained)
            add players not viewing the region to the list
    send query to top 3 players
}
```

Note that the list of players viewing regions of J can be formed very quickly by using the advanced world segmentation explained previously.

Conclusion

MMORTS provides great challenges to both designers and programmers. This article covered mainly the architecture and the algorithms needed to achieve low bandwidth per client (1–2 KB/sec) for transferring updates on large armies comprised of thousands of units. The basic idea common in many network games—*only send information relevant to the client*—was supplemented by world segmentation and complex actions. The suggested scheme also helps other areas of the MMORTS such as clustering and AI.

References

[Ferguson01] Ferguson Mitch, and Michael Ballbach, "Product Review: Massively Multiplayer Online Game Middleware," January 2003.

[Jaecheol01] Jaecheol, Kim; Eunsil Hong; Yanghee Choi, "Measurement and Analysis of a Massively Multiplayer Online Role Playing Game Traffic," available online at *www.apan.net/2003_busan/34.doc.*

[TNL01] Torque Network Library project documentation, "Torque Network Library Design Fundamentals," available online at sourceforge.net at *http://opentnl.sourceforge.net/doxydocs/fundamentals.html#fundamentals.*

2.9

MMP Engineering Pitfalls

Justin Quimby— Turbine Entertainment Software

justin@turbinegames.com

Engineering for an MMP is a difficult beast. Not only does building a game require an extensive code framework and tool sets, but requirements change not based on new functional specifications, but instead on "what is fun." In the 10+ years of Turbine Entertainment Software's existence, the company has grown from a small garage developer to a professional-grade development company with two studios and multiple projects in development. In that time, Turbine has learned a tremendous amount in all areas of MMP development, from art to design to engineering. This article examines how Turbine addresses some of the MMP engineering pitfalls.

Scheduling

Given the size of the engineering effort that MMPs require, effectively scheduling the engineering team is critical to delivering a good game on time. Developing an MMP is a team affair. Proper direction and planning can ensure that the engineering team works effectively. A full discussion of scheduling philosophies is beyond the scope of this article; however, two points in particular merit discussion.

Crunch Time

Crunch time is a form of mandatory overtime for the team, usually involving 12- to 14-hour days and up to seven days a week. Crunch times vary in length from a week or two all the way to the course of a year or more. Today at Turbine, crunch times are infrequent, limited in duration, focused toward a specific goal, and are never built into the schedule. Before declaring a crunch period, the leads and production team work to clearly define the goals for each engineer. When the engineer completes his tasks, his crunch is over.

Unmanaged engineering crunch for MMPs development is not an effective development strategy. Crunching just to catch up hurts morale and leads to poor quality code as engineers become tired and discouraged. When scheduling engineering tasks, do not use crunch to make the deadlines. Although long hours of crunch periods allow for the rapid completion of engineering tasks, it leads to staff burnout. Losing engineering staff can be devastating to the development schedule. When you lose an employee, the time to recruit, hire, and train a new employee will drop months of time off the engineering schedule.

The engineering effort on MMPs does not stop when the game ships. Engineers should not take two months off after the game ships. The post-ship period is the critical time when hundreds of thousands of players hammer on the game and any crashing bugs must be fixed as soon as possible. If the engineering team is burned out at ship, then server-crashing bugs will take longer to fix. Longer downtimes lead to people leaving the game, which can lead the game's subscription numbers into a downward spiral. Give the engineering staff a chance to be rested post-ship by cutting features rather than relying on extended crunch time.

Slack Time

Flexibility is crucial when building an MMP. Toward that end, it is critical to build designated slack time into the schedule. Numerous events can demand additional engineering effort during the course of development. Important press demonstrations, new features that become apparent once the game is well along in development, and market pressures all demand additional engineering time. Without slack time built into the schedule, two things can occur: engineering crunch time or the loss of features. In some cases, losing features is not an option. If another game adds a feature to the benchmark of basic MMP functionality, then that feature has to be part of your game.

When scheduling engineering, always take the long perspective. Look back over the past several years, noting the cause of all large schedule shifts, and build those into the engineering schedule. Numerous resources exist online describing the development cycles of MMPs [Gamasutra04]. Events that are guaranteed engineering drains are conventions and publisher press affairs. For conventions, the Electronic Entertainment Expo dwarfs all others. Always assume that a demo will show at E3, and build slack time in for last-minute demo features and debugging. When it comes to adding new features, engineering must always weigh new capabilities against the risk to product stability. Many years ago, this author added new game code at the last minute for a companywide demo. In front of the entire company, the game proceeded to repeatedly crash; the solution would have been to use an older and far more stable version.

Communication

As team sizes grow, ensuring good communication becomes increasingly important for the engineering lead. Without good communication, engineers may spend weeks implementing a feature that duplicates the effort of another engineer. Perhaps a content designer stops work while waiting for a bug fix, not knowing that the fix was made the week previous. Beyond the top-down communication of lead to staff engineer, peer-to-peer communication works extremely effectively. One technique that began informally in the engineering department is the sending of "today" messages. Every day, an engineer sends out an e-mail to all the engineers with the subject line "today." The message contains a brief paragraph or bullet list of what the engineer did that day and what he is planning to work on the next day. If the engineer faces a particularly nasty problem or has hit a roadblock, that item gets noted as well. On Fridays, engineers augment their daily summary with a summary of their week. The specific format does not matter, just the content.

Other engineers peruse the today messages of the rest of the engineering team to stay abreast of what folks are working on. Leads can use these today messages to track a specific engineer's progress over the course of weeks and try to address any planning problems. Public today messages also create a forum for public glory and accountability. When Bob's today message reads, "worked on combat formula" for three weeks, other engineers will gently chide Bob about slacking off. In addition, when Chad notes that he has finished the new crafting system, other developers will congratulate him.

Engineers need to know what other engineers are doing, and should know the current tasks of the designers and artists. Today messages provide a great resource for peer-to-peer communication. Every production department at Turbine has adopted today messages as a great communication tool.

Floor Plans

Today messages, team meetings, and design documents are all useful tools, but face-to-face discussions are the most effective form of communication. Without in-person interactions, system design documents and schedules do not convey the whole picture. A team completely isolated without real-life interaction will never achieve the synergy of a team with great communication. Turbine encourages "face time" through discouraging personal offices. The difference between the seating arrangement of the development teams for *Asheron's Call 1* and *Dungeons & Dragons Online* reflects this commitment to communication.

Turbine's layout grew organically during the process of building *Asheron's Call 1*. Each engineering team had a room. Each team sat together in their room, but those rooms were well removed from each other. Walls and twisty corridors separated the game systems, user interface, server, and core technology engineering teams. Cross-team communication was infrequent. The camaraderie and friendships of the engineers allowed them to overcome the communication barriers and ship *Asheron's Call*. For *Dungeons & Dragons Online*, the team operates in a pit model. No one, not even the executive producer, has an office. Dedicated meeting rooms allow for private meetings or extended whiteboard discussions. While this arrangement leads to a louder work environment, it has been critical to the team's rapid iteration development cycle. Team members recognize the importance of taking long or loud conversations to meeting rooms to preserve the general work environment. By having designers, artists, and engineers sitting in close proximity, the time it takes to go from system design to first-pass implementation to first content to first iteration has been cut dramatically. Open floor plans, in Turbine's experience, help the team members bond and develop the sense of community important to excellent software development.

Engineering Process Techniques

Much has been written on the discipline of software engineering in the last 20 years. Regardless of the actual implementation, language, or development environment, there are numerous mechanisms that if adopted will speed up development and aid you when demo deadlines loom.

Revision Control Systems

Numerous software post-mortems discuss the importance of using a revision control system (RCS). Having a central repository of game assets is crucial toward ensuring smooth development. Without a repository that can be backed up offsite and restored, the engineering team is only one lightning strike away from total project disruption. Turbine currently uses Perforce for all of its projects. Regardless of which system the development staff uses, several key features assist the development process. The RCS must be able to handle the scale of the game's data and code set. MMPs have enormous amounts of content and code. An RCS that bogs down at more than 20 users and 2 gigabytes of files will hurt the development team. The ability for a developer to operate with multiple active "change lists" allows engineers to compartmentalize their work and make minor fixes while in the middle of implementing a new system. One tool that Turbine engineers find invaluable allows them to scan their machine for stray files they forgot to add to their "change list." This lessens the chance that an engineer will overlook checking-in a newly created file.

Of all the RCS additions and modifications that Turbine uses, the most useful is the public notation of every check-in. Details of every check-in, along with a file list, are mailed out to a dedicated Outlook public folder. This mechanism ensures that every engineer is accountable for every check-in. There are no "stealth" check-ins. A public archive of all check-ins serves as a convenient way for developers to stay abreast of all the changes going into the game. QA can watch the check-in list to verify that an engineer did in fact check-in code to fix a bug.

A Build a Day Keeps the Producer Away

An important part of Turbine's development culture is having the game functional every day. If the build is broken for long stretches of time, engineers can become lazy about fixing their particular system because other bugs prevent the testing of their code. Daily builds reinforce a culture of responsible engineering. A system is not finished until it is fully functional and integrated into the game. QA also benefits from having a rapid turn-around time to test new systems. A daily build means that a fix checked-in on Tuesday can be tested on Wednesday, rather than the following week. Perhaps most important, daily builds mean that if a last-minute demo is needed, the producer can simply fire up the previous night's build, rather than requiring a build performed on an engineer's machine without any QA verification.

Automated Build System

Building the game data files and executables in a dependable and simple fashion is important in all software development. An unreliable build system leads to engineering heartache. During the development of *Asheron's Call 1*, the build system grew organically. The build system could create all the necessary components, but the system was incredibly arcane. Very little logging existed, so when official builds failed, engineers scrambled to determine the source of the problem. Occasionally, the game was fine but the build system had hiccupped.

Developing an automated build system is a crucial part of Turbine's development environment. Automating as much as possible in the build system reduces the need for human input to create a build, which in turn diminishes the chance for human error to cause a broken build [Irving00]. There are numerous steps involved in turning code and art assets into a game package. Turbine's current build environment automatically obtains the latest versions of all files, compiles client and server executables, compiles preprocessing tools, and runs them over the data tree to build client and server data files. Once all the executables and data files are built, the system builds an installer for the client and creates zip packages for the debug client, release client, and server. These zip packages are then copied to an archive machine, and an e-mail with a full log is posted to a public folder. From start to end, the build system requires no human input.

If there are any problems with the build, full path links are included to the log files, so developers can click on the hyperlink and immediately jump into determining the source of the compile or data problem. The system is written in Perl and maintained by the core technology tools team. The build system is modular and each step can be executed individually. As a result, this system is the same system used by individual developers during their game development cycle. Engineers can compile code, artists can integrate artwork into the game, and designers can build dungeons and tweak stats on their local machine, all under the umbrella of one system.

The Power of Shame

In addition to the nightly build machines, the *Dungeons & Dragons Online* team uses a low-end machine to perform continuous builds. The machine gets the latest source and data, performs a limited executable and data build, mails out the results, and then repeats the cycle. Since this machine is not doing a full clean build, these builds occur several times a day. These frequent builds allows developers to verify that their recent work compiles on a separate machine. It is always better to wait an extra half hour to ensure that no files were missed than to break the overnight build! The machine has come to be referred to by the team as the "Shaminator," since it helps avoid the shame of breaking a build.

Tools, Tools, Tools

People play MMPs not for technology, but for content. Ultimately, the purpose of engineering is to enable the design team to create content. If the engineering team implements systems that content does not know about or does not want, that engineering effort is wasted. Supporting the content creation team is critical to making a good MMP [Ragaini00]. Toward that end, a focus on tool development is critical for engineering. During the course of developing *Asheron's Call 1*, tools development occurred intermittently alongside the development of the core technologies of the game, such as the physics engine and combat gameplay. The world and dungeon creation tool was incrementally built as the project progressed by a variety of engineers.

When Turbine embarked on developing *Asheron's Call 2: Fallen Kings* (AC2), one of the first decisions was to staff up a dedicated tools department. By assigning engineers to tool development, Turbine was able to create a toolset far superior to that employed on AC1. Bugs were fixed and features added in the course of days rather than weeks or months. The improved usability, stability, and performance of the toolset translated directly into improved efficiency for the content team. The success of the tools team during the AC2 development cycle led to the creation of a permanent tools team within Turbine's core technology group [Frost03].

Play the Game

In today's marketplace, players will not pay for a new MMP with partially implemented systems and broken features. The engineering team must deliver a smooth and solid end-user experience. One simple tool to help an engineering team focus on code quality is a team "play-day." A play-day is simply an hour or two in which the entire development staff plays the latest QA-approved build of the game. By forcing the entire team to play the game, the harsh light of truth comes to bear on the game. The team experiences the game as a player sees it. Players do not use admin commands or operate in latency-free environments. Therefore, if the synchronization of avatar animations when buying items from a vendor is flaky or completing a quest crashes the server, then the play-day highlights that problem. Playing the game in its entirety rather than looking just at individual systems stresses the connections between all of the game's systems. These connection points often are the boundary cases for engineering systems that are the source of most bugs.

Regularly scheduled play-days also reinforce the importance to the team of not breaking the build. The shame of being responsible for canceling a play-day drives home the importance of consistently having a functional game build! Play-days are also a chance for engineers to show off their newest system, which motivates engineers to finish systems, rather than tuning and tweaking them for weeks.

Turbine began using play-days when developing *Asheron's Call 1*. Play-days were ad hoc, run by various team members when they wanted to bang on a particular system. However, these play-days were neither regular nor teamwide. As a result, systems would break and not be fixed for weeks. Turbine recognized the value of play-days, and during the course of development on *Asheron's Call 2* instituted regular play-days. They are now standard operating procedure for all games in development at Turbine.

Code Quality

The revenue from subscription-based entertainment comes from the customers who pay every month. If players leave after a month or two, the game will fail. If the game crashes regularly or does not run well on reasonable hardware, customers will not continue to subscribe. Perhaps even worse, people who buy the game only to have it crash will tell all their friends not to buy the game. This negative buzz can kill any title. The importance of maintaining customers for as long as possible translates into two focus areas for engineering: maintainability and stability.

Engineering work on an MMP does not halt when the game ships. Maintainable code is crucial for the live team to address bugs after the game ships. No game will ever ship completely bug-free. Engineers must prepare for the inevitable bugs that players discover, by creating code that is easy to understand and nonfragile.

The first step toward an understandable code base is the application of uniform coding conventions. The existence of naming standards, comment formats, and class layouts is far more important than the specific details of the conventions. Consistent naming conventions are tremendously important when new engineers join the project or an existing engineer needs to trace code flow through unfamiliar territory. Turbine had several different coding styles during the development of *Asheron's Call 1*. Some engineers used Hungarian notation [Maguire93] [Simonyi77], while others eschewed it for verbose variable names. The importance of a unified naming convention was driven home by the time spent supporting *Asheron's Call 1* post-launch. Every engineer who traced a bug through several subsystems, each with its own naming convention, realized the value of standards. Today, Turbine has coding conventions that are shared across all projects.

A crashing game is a failing game. Code must be stable. Attaining stability requires a defensive-based mindset where engineers police themselves. Engineers must constantly ask the questions, "How can I verify the input provided to my system?" "How could my system potentially fail?" Peer reviews of new code allow fresh unbiased eyes to see problems before the code is checked in [Mozilla04]. Institutionally, Turbine embraces code reviews of major systems to catch bugs and as a means of knowledge transfer between engineers. One specific technique that serves Turbine well in achieving stability is the liberal use of asserts. Turbine also uses a dynamic logging system for on-the-fly debugging. Having the capability during a play-day of turning on logging for a specific system that is experiencing problems, such as vendor transactions, is invaluable toward finding problems in the dynamic environment of an MMP.

Conclusion

Modern MMPs require a long and difficult engineering effort. This article reviewed several potential problems in the MMP development effort and how Turbine addresses them. Ten years ago, Turbine was a company of four guys in a basement with a dream. Today, Turbine is a large company with two offices, two shipped MMP games, and multiple games in development. Hopefully, the lessons learned by Turbine's engineers will help your engineering efforts:

- Scheduling crunch time is a bad idea.
- Build slack time into the engineering schedule.
- Today messages work as a peer-to-peer communication mechanism.
- Pit environments engender communication.
- Use a high-quality revision control system.
- Aim for functional builds every day.
- Use an automated build system.
- Provide a system for engineers to verify the build on another machine.
- Recognize that engineering serves content development.
- Build a dedicated tools team.
- Play the game as a team regularly.
- Develop unified coding conventions and enforce them.
- Think about the live team when designing systems.
- Always focus on stability and tools to improve stability.

References

[Frost03] Frost, Paul, "Postmortem: The Tools Development of Turbine's Asheron's Call 2," available online at *www.gamasutra.com/features/20030820/frost_01.shtml*, August 20, 2003.

[Gamasutra04] various, "Postmortem," online at *www.gamasutra.com/php-bin/article_display.php?category=5*, 2004.

[Irving00] Irving, Francis, "Automating the Build Process," available online at *www.gamasutra.com/features/20001208/irving_01.htm*, December 8, 2000.

[Maguire93] Maguire, Steve, *Writing Solid Code,* Microsoft Press, 1993.

[Mozilla04] Mozilla Organization, "Frequently Asked Questions About mozilla.org's Code Review Process," available online at *www.mozilla.org/hacking/code-review-faq.html#1*, August 31, 2004.

[Ragaini00] Ragaini, Toby, "Postmortem: Turbine Entertainment's Asheron's Call," available online at *www.gamasutra.com/features/20000525/ragaini_01.htm*, May 25, 2000.

[Simonyi77] Simonyi, Charles, "Meta-Programming: A Software Production Method," Stanford University, Xerox Palo Alto Research Center, 1977.

2.10

Animated Procedural Skies

John M. Olsen—Infix Games

infix@xmission.com

Nearly every massively multiplayer (MMP) game needs a sky, and there are as many techniques for rendering skies as there are games, with some looking much better than others. A great sky needs to lend a feeling of reality to the game through its subtlety and variety. This article demonstrates a method for building a multilayered animated sky using fully procedural methods. By combining carefully chosen sky-dome geometry, procedurally generated textures, and dynamic layering and movement, you can create a sky that will add greatly to the ambience of your game.

Introduction

Each visual effect can be used very well in some games, while not working well at all in other games. Animated procedural skies will be most useful in games where the player can see the sky from ground level, or from a fairly low altitude if airborne. The visual effect is not as impressive if players end up flying high into the sky because they expect to be able to reach and travel through the clouds. Additionally, sky-rendering code is wasted in isometric-style games where no sky is visible.

Limitations to this technique are fairly straightforward. First, care must be taken when the sky borders terrain that uses range-based fog. When using range-based fog, you must match the fog color and the horizon edge color as closely as possible to minimize the sharp edge that can occur between the fogged terrain and the sky. Second, a full horizon of terrain should be rendered to prevent the player from seeing below the edge of the sky dome.

With this effect, you will gain realistic and dynamic cloud cover. Part of this realism is due to showing wind speed and direction, and the inclusion of haze at the horizon. This haze can be easily seen on a clear day in the real world by comparing the darker color of the overhead sky with the lighter hazed color at the horizon.

Sky Dome Geometry

The actual scale of the sky dome geometry is arbitrary if rendering is done in the correct order. By drawing the sky first, you can choose the most convenient size for modeling the sky dome. Putting all vertices at a distance of one unit from the origin would be a good choice to make the math simpler and more intuitive.

A cone model is the simplest to use, and can have three or more sides. Using three sides and a base would give you a tetrahedron, which is similar to a flattened four-faced Platonic solid as seen in Figure 2.10.1. With a low number of sides, you may get some visually detectable edges as clouds move across those boundaries. A cone should be fairly short relative to its base size. This keeps the clouds at a more uniform scale as they move from one side, across the top and back down the far side, making it appear that the horizon is a long distance away. Having a sky dome with eight sides as shown in Figure 2.10.2 can additionally simplify the math for both the geometry and texture mapping, which will be covered later.

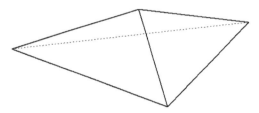

FIGURE 2.10.1   *A minimal pyramid sky dome, a flattened tetrahedron.*

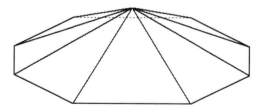

FIGURE 2.10.2   *An eight-sided conical sky dome.*

Other platonic polyhedron models can also work well, but are more complex to create and to map with textures. An icosahedron (20-sided solid) is often used due to the relatively spherical surface, but only part of the full shape is needed in most cases, as shown by the darker lines on the top and middle of the object in Figure 2.10.3. The bottom five triangles in Figure 2.10.3 may be eliminated since the horizon will appear somewhere along the middle band of triangles. When using an icosahedron, the camera location needs to be moved up from the center to be closer to the top so clouds at the horizon will be scaled to look farther away.

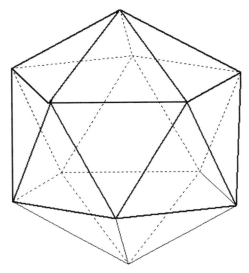

FIGURE 2.10.3   *Using an icosahedron as a sky dome.*

Cube maps should be avoided with this technique since they need to be rendered with built-in stretching to help hide the corners and edges.

The base sky color can be varied for day and night cycles, and previous work has covered this in a wide range of detail. Many of these techniques are listed on the Virtual Terrain Project Web site [VTP04].

As mentioned earlier, rendering order is important. Your scene should be rendered with the sky first, then the world, followed by any user interface elements.

There are some additional requirements for rendering a sky dome when you are building it to an arbitrary scale rather than putting the sky polygons out past your farthest scene geometry at their true apparent distance. You need to draw the sky with no translation whatsoever, so it is always centered at the camera location. You also need to turn off Z writing so your regular scene rendering works properly to overlap the sky. Finally, you need to rotate the sky dome based on the rotation of the camera around a vertical axis. This method of rotation keeps the sky properly oriented with the rest of the world.

Cloud Textures

Cloud textures for this technique need to repeat along both the X and Y axes, so they can be tiled in either direction with no visible seams. These textures can be generated either from bitmaps or procedurally.

If a photograph of real clouds is used, the textures will need to be doctored with a photo editing program to make it tile along both axes. High-end graphics programs usually come with filters and tools that simplify the process of turning a nontiled bitmap into a tiling bitmap.

If an image of pre-rendered clouds from some cloud rendering software is used, you still need to make sure it tiles properly, but some tools take care of that for you by making it automatically tile as it builds the cloud texture bitmap.

If you decide to go with fully procedural textures built right into the application, there are still several options available. Kim Pallister has described a method for generating single-layer procedural clouds using accelerated graphics hardware [GPG01], and Mike Milliger has written about procedural texturing as well [GPG02]. You can also build them by using a simple smoothing algorithm on an array of random points to get your initial cloud density values, or you can use a tiling variation of a Perlin Noise function [Perlin99] to build the data.

In any case, whether using pre-rendered textures or building your textures on the fly, you will want to put the cloud pattern into an alpha channel and make the entire color channel white. The reason for this is that you want each layer of cloud to show through as they are all rendered one on top of the other.

One exception to the rule of making your textures tile on both axes would be the case where you build a single texture that is designed to span the entire sky. Due to the layering techniques that are presented later in this article, this isn't a particularly good choice for this sky rendering technique.

The thickness of the cloud coverage can be varied by subtracting a constant amount from the alpha channel of the texture, and clamping the values so they do not wrap around or go below zero. As seen in Figure 2.10.4, you can vary from heavy cloud cover to just a wisp or two by varying the amount subtracted from the alpha channel.

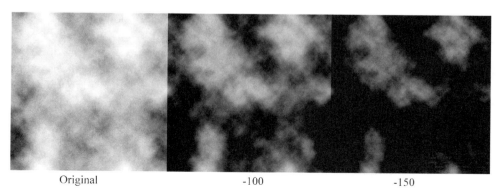

Original   -100   -150

FIGURE 2.10.4   *Varying levels of cloud cover by subtracting values from each index.*

There are ways of making the cloud pattern even more dynamic. As a first step, you can vary the amount of cloud cover over time. This requires a periodic update to the cloud texture as you rebuild it from your base texture over time.

Another possibility for dynamic textures is to rebuild the base texture with a varying pattern over time. If using Perlin Noise, you can make your texture be a two-dimensional slice out of a three-dimensional noise space. For example, you can use your X and Y indices into the noise as your pixel coordinates, and change your noise function Z index over time to create an animated two-dimensional texture. When you do that, you get an interesting effect of clouds forming and dissipating as they move across the sky.

Updates to your sky texture do not need to be done every frame, whether based on simple clamping or rebuilding the base texture. In fact, updating the cloud textures only every few seconds should be sufficient unless you want a surreal time-lapse effect where the clouds seem to boil as you watch them move.

It is always a good idea to double buffer the sky textures if you plan to alter the cloud textures over time. Whether you modify the source texture that is not actually used for rendering, or the final rendering texture, you will be able to avoid stalls in the video card by double buffering. This will keep your game's frame rate much more uniform, rather than having a slow frame every time you update the cloud texture. These stalls occur when the GPU tries to lock and render to a texture when that texture is already locked for modification, or when it is locked for rendering and you attempt to lock it to change it. Only one lock at a time is allowed.

Movement

Static clouds are unrealistic. You don't want the players of your game to look at the sky and know what direction is North because that's the direction of a particularly shaped cloud. This lack of movement can be handled by picking a direction for constant prevailing winds, but that also is somewhat unrealistic.

To add more flavor and interest to your clouds, both the speed and direction of the wind can be modified over time. Once again, we can rely on random noise data to provide our input. In this case, we need single points marching through a two- or three-dimensional array of noise. One random sample indicates the direction, and the other the wind speed.

Some scaling is in order in both cases. If you would like the wind to tend toward a particular direction, you can set a base angle, and scale the directional noise to vary within a given number of degrees of that value. If you want it to blow randomly in any direction at all, this can be done smoothly by choosing an arbitrary base direction, and scaling the random value to some multiple of 360 degrees. If you scale to just 0–360, the wind can never go from 360 degrees directly to zero, so scaling it to at least two times 360 is recommended as shown in Figure 2.10.5.

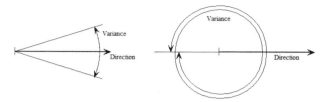

FIGURE 2.10.5   *Prevailing and random wind, with average direction and variance shown.*

Some care must be taken in choosing how fast the wind direction can change. It should be hard for players to notice the changes in direction over time unless they are specifically watching for it. You do not want the changes to be fast enough to be a distraction.

Wind speed is another consideration where you may want to always have some wind blowing to keep your clouds moving. In that case, you set your minimum wind speed, and add to that based on a scaled random value that determines your current wind speed. As you apply noise functions to both wind direction and speed, you will get a graph similar to that shown in Figure 2.10.6 when the speed or direction is graphed over time. The minimum and maximum values are horizontal lines that will always constrain the random line on the chart.

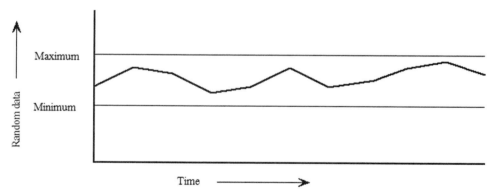

FIGURE 2.10.6   *Speed or direction input data varying over time.*

With a wind speed and direction specified, you need a way to actually animate the cloud pattern across the sky dome. One of the simplest ways to do this is to modify the UV mapping that determines how the texture is applied to the polygons. You will need double buffering on the vertex list the same as already mentioned for the textures to keep from stalling the graphics pipeline, since you will be modifying the UV information in that vertex list every frame.

There are some tricks that can make the UV mapping much easier to deal with. First, note in Figure 2.10.7 how the vertex coordinates for an eight-sided sky cone all lie in an XY plane when viewed from above. You can take the conveniently scaled XY coordinates in Figure 2.10.7 and map them to cover the UV range as many times you would like the pattern to repeat across the sky. Copying the values straight across as shown will cause the pattern to repeat twice in each direction.

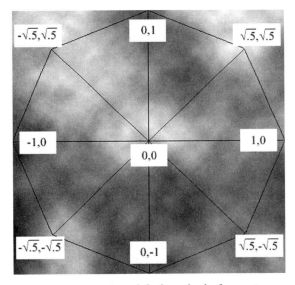

FIGURE 2.10.7 *Simplified method of mapping XY coordinates into UV on a sky dome.*

To get the cloud pattern to properly repeat, you must make sure that the texture mode is set to wrap rather than to clamp, which would simply repeat the last texture pixel to the edge of the polygon.

Once this layout has been created, translation of the sky texture becomes an issue of simply adding a constant delta to every UV each frame, and swapping in the newly modified vertex buffer for use on the next frame.

Care should be taken with this technique to not allow really large UV values, since some graphics cards will generate jittery and jumpy textures due to round-off error when the UV values get too large. To avoid this, every time a UV's distance from the origin is over a certain threshold, translate all the UV values uniformly back toward the origin.

To prevent large UV values and the associated jitters, a simple distance check can be made that will use very little CPU time. Find the minimum and maximum U and V coordinates independently as you go through the vertex list. If the maximum values are too large (say, over 100) or the minimums are too small (below –100), you can subtract that minimum or maximum U or V value from each vertex. There is no need to compare actual distances, or try to always do both U and V translations at once.

On modern graphics hardware, this UV translation technique could be replaced with a texture translation matrix. In that case, you still need to be careful of large translation values causing texture jitter. Rather than adjusting the UV values, you would just subtract an integer amount from the X or Y component of the translation matrix.

There is another method of animating clouds that does not require direct manipulation of the UV data. If you are using a fully enclosed sky sphere such as a full icosahedron instead of a half-sphere dome, you can rotate the sky geometry. This method is not recommended because of the difficulty associated with texturing the sphere. You would need to guarantee that the entire sky sphere's textures look good, and this takes special care and effort. It also requires texture techniques that are much more complex than building a wrapping 2D texture.

Layers

A properly formed sky will need several layers ranging from the base sky color to the clouds, and finally to a haze layer. The combination of the base layer, multiple cloud layers, and the haze layer will give you the visual complexity that will lead to more realistic skies in your game.

The base sky color does not need any geometry since you can clear the frame buffer to the background sky color, or just draw a two-dimensional box to fill the scene with the desired color if you do not want to fill the entire screen.

The haze layer is needed because skies are usually lighter toward the horizon due to the additional scattering of the light traversing a larger volume of air. The haze texture itself ramps from fully opaque at the edges to fully transparent through most of the middle area. If this haze texture is created using white as its base color, you can use vertex coloring to add interesting lighting effects for different times of day and night.

The sky color can be controlled dynamically by making this haze texture white, and using vertex coloring to alter the sky color as needed in synchronization with drawing an appropriate background color. The color used for the haze layer should be the same as the fog color used for range-based fog on the terrain to minimize the harsh transitions between fogged terrain and the sky.

Haze layers, unlike clouds, are not dynamically translated. Rendering order is also important in getting the effects to look right. Haze must be drawn after all the clouds have been drawn. That way, the clouds fade to the haze color along with the rest of the sky, obscuring the clouds as they reach the horizon. Figure 2.10.8 shows how all the various sky layers can stack together to make a complete sky.

FIGURE 2.10.8   *Base color, three cloud layers, and haze combined.*

Multiple cloud layers at different scale values and translation speeds lend an interesting parallax scrolling that gives the sky a much greater apparent depth. Two layers of clouds are needed to get the parallax effect, and more than three tends to not be all that noticeable. Varying between one and three layers can be built into the game as a function of the weather or the location to lend some variety to your skies.

Adding too many cloud layers may slow your rendering, since each pass is filling the entire screen with alpha-blended polygons. Go with the least number of layers that gives you the effect you are after. One way to improve performance on modern graphics hardware is to combine as many cloud texture layers as possible into a single draw command. Many graphics cards will allow as many as four simultaneous textures.

The translation speed of the clouds should be scaled relative to the size of the clouds. If your second cloud layer is scaled to half the size of the first layer, the second layer of clouds should move at half the speed of the first layer.

The actual scale value between layers can have a strong impact on how well the effect works. If you scale by powers of two, that means that at some point your textures could line up in odd ways all across the sky, making it more obvious that it is tiled. For this reason, it works better to select scale values that do not line up well with each other.

Prime numbers work very well as scale values since they are not subject to being multiples of each other. Three scale factors that tend to work fairly well are 3, 7, and 11, because they are reasonably close to doubling the scale each time, but still do not line up their seams exactly. Depending on the size of your base cloud texture you will need to scale these three numbers (or whatever other numbers you choose) by some value to get your cloud density to look right.

Conclusion

Dynamic skies can be done effectively by animating their movement in multiple layers, and can be done cheaply by creating the textures on the fly rather than relying on the time and skill required to build tiling textures by hand. Although excessive layers can put a burden on the video card, the effect can be done with few enough layers that it will not be a large burden on your real-time budget.

Parallax scrolling has been used successfully to convey depth for decades in a range of computer games and cartoons, so it is a well-proven and understood concept. This is simply a new application of old technology to an area that isn't always done as well as it could be.

Even after you have completed everything as described, there are several areas left for exploration and experimentation. Vertex coloring of the haze layer and background color can be done to add sunset effects, and lens flares and the sun can be rendered within the sky and clouds by adding them in as an appropriately layered rendering effect.

References

[DeLoura01] DeLoura, Mark, *Game Programming Gems 2* (Generating Procedural Clouds Using 3D Hardware, by Kim Pallister), Charles River Media, 2001.

[Perlin99] Ken Perlin's GDC Hardcore presentation on noise is available online at *www.noisemachine.com/talk1/index.html*, December 9, 1999.

[Treglia02] Treglia, Dante, *Game Programming Gems 3* (Procedural Texturing, by Mike Milliger), Charles River Media, 2002.

[VTP04] Virtual Terrain Project sky effect links are available online at *www.vterrain.org/Atmosphere/*, July 14, 2004.

Time and Event Synchronization Across an MMP Server Farm

Roger Smith, Modelbenders, LLC and Don Stoner, DCSI

mmpg@modelbenders.com

The server farms that support massively multiplayer (MMP) games contain hundreds of computers, many of which represent geographic areas that are so close or intertwined that the operations on these machines need to be tightly synchronized. As the richness of game content and cross-server interactions increases, the need for synchronization grows as well.

In this article, we describe algorithms that have been developed for parallel and distributed simulation systems to provide guaranteed synchronization of event execution and time advance across any number of networked computers. Modifications have emerged that customize the original algorithms to make them more efficient for interactive virtual worlds.

The goal of this article is to describe the algorithms in terms that can be understood by an experienced programmer, provide the necessary computer code to begin implementing the techniques, and explain the costs and benefits of using these techniques.

Introduction

Synchronization of event execution and time progression across parallel and distributed computers has been an issue in high-performance computing circles for decades. The programmers who created massive models of nuclear blast effects found that their simulations were too big to be handled by a single processor of any size. Therefore, they turned to parallel computing to give them the horsepower to run these in a reasonable amount of time. However, that immediately created a new problem of synchronizing the events that were occurring on these multiple independent processors.

Since then, distributed computing has spread to a number of other application domains. Interactive training for the military and computer gaming are two of the most popular. Massively multiplayer games (MMPGs) are the most extreme form of distributed computer game and demand event synchronization just as the nuclear models and training simulations do.

Impacts on the Massively Multiplayer Experience

MMPGs like *Asheron's Call* find that event and time synchronization across machines in their server farm is a major issue. Jeff Johnson of Turbine Entertainment says that, "the biggest problem that Turbine has in managing its seamless worlds' server-side is in dealing with asynchronicity and serializing server game state at arbitrary points of execution" [Johnson04]. Generally, MMPG server systems follow one of two major architectures: 1) the zone-based model where objects are represented on a single machine that is responsible for a specific geographic area of the virtual world, and 2) the distributed (or seamless) model in which objects are represented on multiple servers and their state values and event lists must be constantly synchronized [Beardsley03]. Although the second model desperately requires a reliable synchronization mechanism, even the zone-based model contains game events, boundary conditions, and system management operations that require synchronization.

Poor or nonexistent synchronization across servers impacts both the players' experience with the game and the ability to manage and control operations within the game engine. In some cases, inconsistent event execution can result in different outcomes of event sequences on the servers and potentially expose this inconsistency to the player client machines [Smith00].

Synchronization is a difficult thing to achieve and does impose performance costs and operational limitations. However, the increasing complexity of MMPGs and the growing horsepower and bandwidth that drives them is going to justify the resources for synchronization, just as these resources have opened the door for better AI and physics in the past.

Available Solutions

There are a number of different solutions to the event and time synchronization problem. Each provides slightly different capabilities at different performance costs. The first, most common, and least-expensive is the *best effort* method. This calls for each message receiving process to buffer messages, order them according to their timestamp, and execute them in the hope that all of the sent events for the buffered period have been received. When a late message is received, the event managing software must make a decision to either execute the event late or delete it. This decision is usually very specific to the game and the type of the event. It is essential that this decision is made deterministically and applied identically on every machine. However, even a deterministic algorithm cannot deliver uniform results on multiple machines. Message delivery delay varies from one machine to the next, and the buffering of events does not result in the same events being included in the buffers on every machine. For example, consider an event E1 sent to computers M1 and M2. On computer M1, event E1 may have been received, ordered, and properly executed. However, on computer M2, event E1 may have arrived late and been subject to either late execution or deletion. This uncertainty of results is a major motivation for the creation of more predictable synchronization algorithms.

A second popular method of synchronization is using a *central timeserver*. One process is anointed as the master of all time progression. Its job is to set the pace of execution for all game processes in the server farm and to determine when conditions warrant moving forward, slowing down, or stopping. This method improves on *best effort* in that all of the processes are slaved to one master and thus remain much more closely aligned in time. However, it does not provide any mechanism to guarantee that messages are executed in the same order on multiple machines. Moreover, as the "master of time," this process can ignore the performance issues of heavily loaded slave processes, allow them to fall behind, and create opportunities for causal event violations. Many of the message passing algorithms that have been created to address this problem are actually ad hoc or partial implementations of synchronization algorithms we are about to prescribe.

The leading method for reliable event and time synchronization is the *Chandy/Misra/Bryant* (CMB) algorithm and several useful modifications of this algorithm. CMB requires exchanging messages between servers that define which event timestamps have been executed and determine the readiness to move forward to the next time increment [Fujimoto90]. In this article, we describe CMB and some modifications that are particularly useful to MMPGs.

Another synchronization method that is very popular within academia and some analytical communities is *time warp*. This is a very exotic method that is difficult to understand, implement, and modify for an MMPG. Readers interested in this technique should dig into the references provided at the end of the article [Fujimoto00 and Smith00].

Time in the Virtual World

Before explaining CMB event and time synchronization in greater detail, it is important to establish some basic properties of time management in simulations and games. Some of these characteristics are required to create a simulation that is causally consistent, and others are necessary to enable CMB to work.

Virtual time is real: When discussing the subject of time in a virtual world, the significant value is the time that is created and managed by the software, not the "real time" experienced by flesh-and-blood players. When we manage time advance in a game, we are often attempting to align virtual time with real time, but all events and the entire digital world are referenced to virtual time, not real time.

Discrete step size: In a game, time moves forward in discrete increments. In many systems, these steps are so small that it appears to the player that time is moving continuously. However, that is an illusion, just as a movie appears to present a continuous moving image even though it actually has a step size of 24 frames per second (fps). Effectively, the step size defines an increment that is small enough that all events scheduled in that period can be treated as if they occurred simultaneously.

Monotonically increasing: Game time is always monotonically increasing. This means that event timestamps always increase or stay the same. They do not ever go backward. This is an important property because it means that if a process generates an event with a timestamp of 100 on it, it will never again generate an event with a stamp of 99, 98, or any other value less than 100.

Event timestamps: All events in a simulation are timestamped. There are no orders, commands, inquiries, or reports that are created without a stamp indicating the time at which they should be executed. It is not so important to stamp them with the time that they are created, although there is some value in that as well; the essential time is that at which the event must be executed by the game.

Network message lag: The delivery of messages across a computer network always takes time and induces lag. Therefore, messages on the receiving end are "old" in that they represent the state of the sender some delta milliseconds in the past. Additionally, there is no guarantee that messages sent will be received in the order in which they were sent, or even received at all.

Limited remote information: The receiver of messages always has a limited amount of information about the state of the sender of the messages. This limitation has a direct impact on the content of messages and the reasoning that must be performed on the receiving computer.

Managed Synchronization

It is possible to provide much more reliable synchronization than the best effort described above. Following are several of the leading solutions for event and time synchronization.

Chandy/Misra/Bryant Algorithm

CMB is known as a "distributed k-reduction algorithm." It can be used to synchronize any number of independent processes running on different processors or on the same processor. Using event timestamps from all of the participating processes, the CMB algorithm calculates the "Global Virtual Time" (GVT) for the entire group. GVT is the minimum timestamp on all exchanged messages. Virtual worlds generate and transmit events that are scheduled to be executed at some time in the future. GVT identifies the latest timestamp on events that can safely be processed without creating a causal error. All events up to and including those at GVT can be processed without worry that a synchronized process will create another event in the past of GVT.

When implementing CMB, the infrastructure that receives the event messages maintains one queue for each of the other remote participants in the synchronization.

As events arrive from the remote processes, they are logged in the appropriate queue (Figure 2.11.1). The GVT mechanism evaluates the timestamps in each queue and identifies the lowest value in the queues. That timestamp becomes the next GVT value, and all events with that timestamp are released to the modeling software for execution. Events with higher timestamps remain in the queue awaiting future release. As events are released, it is possible for one or more of the queues to become empty. When this occurs, the mechanism cannot advance the value of GVT because it cannot determine what the lowest timestamp for the associated process will be. Therefore, when this occurs, GVT must remain at its current value until an event arrives to fill the empty queue. This algorithm is illustrated in the following code sample [Perumalla04]:

```
/* basicGVT illustrates the original Chandy/Misra/Bryant algorithm —
   without mods */
void basicGVT( void )
{
/* integer used for iterating through the list of processes */
int processIndex = 0;

/* integer used for iterating through the event queue of each process*/
int queueIndex = 0;

/* Initialize stop */
        bool stop = NULL;

/* Next Global Virtual Time "nextGVT" initialized to some large
   number */
nextGVT = setNextGVT (99999);

/* This while loop iterates through each of the processes and their
   queues, and checks for the lowest timestamp.*/
while ( ((processIndex < numberOfProcesses) && (stop == NULL)) ;
processIndex++)
{
        /* If event queue is not ordered, check every event. If or-
           dered, just check the first event. This for loop iterates
           until the queue is empty */
for (queueIndex = 0; e[processIndex][queueIndex]; queueIndex++)
{
/* Checks the timestamp to see if it is the new minimum and sets
   nextGVT if it is. */
nextGVT = min(nextGVT, e[processIndex][queueIndex]->timestamp);
        } /* end for */

/* If the current "processIndex" queue was empty. */
        if (queueIndex ==0)
{
/* stop calc*/
                stop = 1;

/* Sends a NULL message.  Null messages are required to keep the
   process from entering a deadlock state. */
                sendNullMessage ( );
```

```
            } /* end if */

    } /* end while */

    if (stop == NULL)
    {
            GVT = nextGVT;
    } /* end if stop */

    } /* end basicGVT */
```

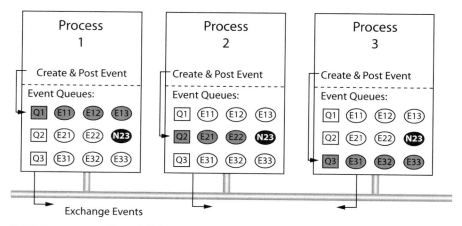

FIGURE 2.11.1   *Chandy/Misra/Bryant event queues to calculate GVT.*

Empty queues can result in a deadlock in which process P1 is awaiting an event from process P2, while P2 is waiting for an event from P3, and P3 is awaiting an event from P1. To break this deadlock, CMB implements "Null Messages" (the black messages in Figure 2.11.1). These are not true executable events; they are messages that simply carry the timestamp for the next event that a process intends to generate. Null Messages are usually generated at a scheduled rate that is driven by the largest acceptable deadlock time. The original CMB algorithm generated a Null Message after each real executable event. This essentially reduced deadlock time to zero, but at the cost of doubling the number of messages being sent between computers. The newer timed-release mechanism is much more bandwidth economical, but at the expense of a short deadlock period.

The computation of GVT is so simple that the CPU expense is almost insignificant. The real impact is that it regulates the pace of all processes to match that of the slowest process in the synchronization. This is one of the features that later modifications have improved upon.

Advance Request/Grant Modification

CMB was designed for analytical simulations such as nuclear blast studies or models of national air traffic patterns. When this algorithm migrated into the military training domain, specific modifications were made to improve its performance. In a military training simulation, there can be thousands of objects sending event messages to dozens of different computers. Evaluating the timestamp on all of these messages proved redundant and unnecessary. During a given time step, thousands of objects generate event messages with the same timestamp. Under these conditions, the GVT algorithm found itself comparing thousands messages with the same timestamp.

To reduce these comparisons, an "Advance Request" and "Advance Grant" message pair was created. Advance Request was a request by the process to move to a specific time in the future (Figure 2.11.2). In most cases, this corresponded to the timestamps on the thousands of event messages. However, it reduced the number of timestamps to be compared for GVT from a number on the order of the number of objects in the virtual world (n*10,000s), to a number on the order of the number of processes running (n*10s). In the case of large object databases, this can represent an improvement of three orders of magnitude. When the GVT algorithm determines the next safe timestamp to advance to, it provides an Advance Grant message to those processes that are allowed to move to their requested time. Processes that had requested a time further in the future do not receive a response and are expected to wait until they receive a grant—usually after a slower machine has caught up to that time.

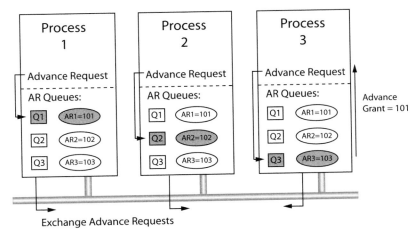

Exchange Advance Requests

(Distributed events are not shown in these queues. They are handled separately.)

FIGURE 2.11.2 *Advance Request Messages reduce cost of GVT calculation.*

The changes to the original method shown previously are limited to the while loop. In this snippet of sample code, it is clear that the number of events being evaluated has been significantly decreased through the elimination of the entire inner for loop:

```
/* This while loop iterates through all of the processes, and looks
   for the advanceRequest message with the lowest time. It then sets
   the nextGVT to that time.  Note that this algorithm only checks
   each process once for an advance request rather than iterate
   through each processes entire queue.  */
while ( ((processIndex < numberOfProcesses) && (stop == NULL)) ;
processIndex ++)
{
/* Checks the process for an advance request */
      if (e[processIndex]->advanceRequest)
{
/* sets the nextGVT to the advance request time if it is less than
   the current minimum*/
                      nextGVT = min(nextGVT,
e[processIndex]->advanceRequest);
}
/* Sends a null message if the queue is empty */
else
{
/* stop calc*/
stop = 1;

/* Sends a NULL message.  Null messages are required to keep the
   process from entering a deadlock state. */
sendNullMessage ( );

      } /* end if */

} /* end while */

if (stop == NULL)
{
/* Sets the Global Virtual Time "GVT" to the new time obtained from
   the advance request */
      GVT = nextGVT;

/* Publish Advance Grant message.  Once this is published processes
   are allowed to move to the requested time and execute events for
   those times.*/
sendAdvanceGrant(GVT);

} /* end if */
```

This modification significantly improved the performance of calculating GVT. However, it did not improve the situation in which the slowest process was regulating the entire family of processes involved in CMB.

Lower Bound Timestamp and Lookahead

The next major modification to CMB is often referred to as the Lower Bound Time Stamp (LBTS) method [Mattern93]. This takes advantage of the fact that most simulations and games have a defined, discrete time step size. Under the traditional GVT method, when one process is operating on events at time 100, other remote processes are allowed to process all events up to and including those with stamp 100. However, using LBTS, remote processes recognize that a simulation operating at 100 right now will generate future event messages with timestamps of 100 plus one time step. Therefore, if a process' step size is 4, a remote simulation can be given permission to execute all events up to and including those with stamps of 104, knowing that the first process will not generate a message at 101 because it is not capable of doing so. Under the exact same conditions, LBTS is more aggressive than GVT and allows faster processes to move ahead of slower ones by some fraction of one step size. This can be extremely useful when different processes use different step sizes. In some cases, there are simulations with a step size of 1 working together with others using a step size of 2 or 3. (These are conceptual numbers that illustrate the ratio of size. An actual simulation process would use a step size such as 100 milliseconds, 200 milliseconds, or 1 second—which have ratios 1:2:10 and can be exploited by LBTS.) When this happens, the simulation using a step size of 1 will find useful work to do with stamps, or 103, when the simulation with step size of 2 would otherwise have regulated it back to 102 under GVT (see Figure 2.11.3).

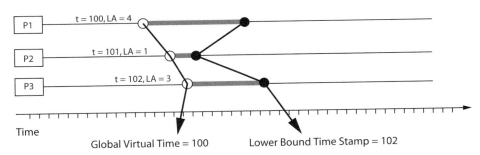

FIGURE 2.11.3   *Comparison of GTV and LBTS.*

This slight modification can maintain causal consistency across the family of servers while also reducing the drag caused by the slower machines. The changes necessary to implement this are entirely limited to the `if` statement on `advanceRequest`. GVT is no longer equal to the lowest advance request value, but to the lowest of the sum of each process' advance request and its look-ahead value.

```
    if (e[processIndex]->advanceRequest)
        {
    nextGVT = min(nextGVT,
  (e[processIndex]->advanceRequest + e[processIndex]->lookAhead));
        }
```

Deconflicting Simultaneous Timestamps

The previous discussion provides the general solution to the synchronization problem. However, several unique issues must be dealt with to allow this mechanism to work. In a multiserver game, it is desirable to have all events processed in the same order on each server. This goes beyond time ordering them. It includes processing those with the same timestamps in the same order on multiple machines. Several interesting mechanisms have been created to support this [Fujimoto00].

Assume that the game time-step size is 100 milliseconds. Then, a timestamp value would have 100 milliseconds as its smallest digit. A timestamp value of 12345 would represent 1,234 seconds and 500 milliseconds into the game. To support absolute ordering of events, this number must be augmented with more information. Some researchers point out that this is almost equivalent to stamping events with a unit smaller than the game's native step size. However, other techniques are a little more complex than that.

The first option is to add an ID number to the timestamp that is an incrementing counter that resets to zero each time the game ticks to the next step. This means that every event is tagged with a time, such as 12345, but also receives a counter. Therefore, its time and ID number might be 12345.002, followed by an event stamped 12345.003, 12345.004, and so on. This inclusion of an ID number works very well for indicating the order in which events are created. It also allows a receiving process to use this information to identify any event messages that are missing. In this article, we use "." to delimit the information, which is a useful method for explaining the concepts. However, in practice these values may fit into different digit positions within a single large integer or may be stored in different variables.

However, the order in which messages are created is not necessarily the order in which they should be executed. This has led to the practice of creating an "age" and a "priority" for messages. The "age" identifier is like a generational indicator. Events that are stored in the initial starting data set have an age of 0. When one of those events causes another event to be created, the created event has an age of 1. When that one causes an event, it will have an age of 2. If an event of age 3 triggers the creation of two new events, then both of them have an age of 4. This insures that whenever an event is caused by another event, the causal order between the two is maintained. When age is combined with the unique ID described earlier, it insures that an ordering algorithm always places two sibling events in the order in which they were created. Adding age as part of the timestamp can be done in many ways, but we will illustrate it as "timestamp.age.ID" or "12345.002.004" in which 12345 is the actual timestamp, 002 is the age, and 004 is the unique ID.

Priority indicates specific events that should be processed ahead of others. These are usually events that have a need to be executed very quickly after being sent. For example, in an FPS game, any explosion events should have a higher priority than player-to-player chat messages. The use of a priority stamp can replace the use of age or be combined with it. Retaining all of these pieces of data may result in a timestamp that includes "timestamp.priority.age.ID."

The age and ID modifications were created to improve synchronization within a time step. Priority allows the sender to specify which events should be addressed first.

Conclusion

This article described algorithms that are designed to synchronize event execution and time advance in distributed simulations and virtual worlds. These techniques have been in use for many years in the high-performance computing community. As MMPGs become increasingly complex and comprehensive, they develop a similar need for strict synchronization between some or all of the servers within the server farm. The Chandy/Misra/Bryant algorithm and the modifications shown here are the most applicable event and time synchronization algorithms that can be applied in this environment. At one time, the speed of computers and networks limited the use of these algorithms to simulations with timestep sizes on the order of one minute. However, as hardware performance has improved, it has been possible to bring these algorithms into simulations operating with 1-second or 100-millisecond timesteps. Continually improving hardware performance, algorithm optimization, and the complexity of distributed virtual worlds will make these methods accessible to simulations with even smaller time steps in the future.

Like all new additions to game software, the computational costs and impacts of the new algorithm must be balanced against the benefits provided. Many games and even military simulations operate sufficiently well without strict synchronization. The purpose of MMPGs is to provide a believable immersive experience. The demands for accuracy are not as high as those for modeling nuclear blasts or chemical reactions. Algorithms such as CMB will earn their way into MMPGs as they become better understood, the costs for implementing them are known, specific MMPG optimizations emerge, and the complexity of MMPG worlds increases.

References

[Beardsley03] Beardsley, Jason, "Seamless Servers: The Case For and Against," *Massively Multiplayer Game Development*, Charles River Media, 2003.

[Fujimoto90] Fujimoto, Richard, "Parallel Discrete Event Simulation," *Communications of the ACM*, Association of Computing Machinery, 1990.

[Fujimoto00] Fujimoto, Richard, *Parallel and Distributed Simulation Systems*, Wiley-Interscience, 2000.

[Johnson04] Johnson, Jeff, "Massively-Multiplayer Engineering," *Proceedings of the Game Developers Conference*, available online at *www.gdconf.com/*, 2004.

[Mattern93] Mattern, Friedeman, "Efficient Algorithms for Distributed Snapshots and Global Virtual Time Approximation," *Journal of Parallel and Distributed Computing*, Vol. 18, No. 4, 1993.

[Perumalla04] Perumalla, Kalyan, "libSynk: Source Code for Time Synchronization," available online at *www.cc.gatech.edu/computing/pads/kalyan/libsynk.htm*, July 2004.

[Smith00] Smith, Roger, "Synchronizing Distributed Virtual Worlds," available online at *www.modelbenders.com/Bookshop/techpapers.html*, December 2000.

2.12

Anti-Cheat Mechanisms for Massively Multiplayer Games

Marty Poulin—
Sony Computer Entertainment America

mpoulin@scea.com

So, you have this shiny new MMP game and it has lots of horsepower and a paint job that belongs in an art gallery. You only have one problem: your neighborhood is pretty tough. You have the hacker and cheater gangs trolling the streets just looking for that next joyride. How are you going to keep from being the next victim?

Introduction

Creating an MMP game is a demanding task. To be successful requires a very diverse skill set, creativity, and management of resources. Taming all of the challenges to produce an MMP game that attracts a large player base will likely take years and millions of dollars for development.

With All That Time and Investment, Wouldn't It Be a Shame If Something Were to Happen to It?

If you received that last statement in an e-mail, you would immediately start asking questions to see if the threat was real and if your game is really secure. The problem is although the threat is real no one is sending you a note to let you in on it. Your game will be under attack from the day it launches until the day you pull the plug.

This threat has several names, including *hacker*, *cheater*, and *griefer*. These names are familiar because they have become an ever-present threat in online games. Each is a different facet of what can destroy your customer's experience. Let them run rampant and no matter how stunning your graphics, realistic the physics, or completely intuitive and addictive the gameplay, you could still end up signing papers at the unemployment office.

While any game is susceptible to cheaters, an MMP game that is dependant on a subscription-based revenue model has potentially much more to lose. If a hacker can crash your servers at will, a cheater finds a way to become invincible, or a griefer finds a way to kill every new player that spawns, the game will hemorrhage players. Luckily, there are steps you can take to keep these threats at bay and your customers happy.

Know Thy Enemy

In our competitive society, cleverness is valued over strength, and deception is rationalized against insurmountable foes. We idolize the underdog who tricks the oppressive system. Games are a reflection of society and a way to have fun exploring its constructs. It is no wonder that deception and trickery are basic ingredients in some games.

Although the term *cheater* vilifies these individuals, they rarely see themselves as evil. To them they are simply playing the game within the game. The real challenge is not to play by the rules, but to see how they can bend or break them without having to pay the price.

At the same time, the rewards for cheating are hard to resist. In online games, competition and bragging rights are an aspect of the design that players crave. Gaining status at the expense of others is part of the game design for some games; the means of gaining that status by cheating is of little consequence to the cheaters as long as they are not caught.

Of course, status is even sweeter if the cheater can gain it by exposing the real triumph, the cheat itself. Cheaters crave recognition for outwitting the system even more than winning in the game. It is this need for recognition that pushes cheaters to share their exploits and techniques.

This sharing of cheats and hacks becomes a self-perpetuating cycle. As each cheater exposes his exploits and receives praise, even more cheaters want to be like that cheater, or prove that they are even better. Eventually, there is a game outside the game that is being played between the cheaters in their own community.

As if status alone was not reason enough, we may also have to combat another of the oldest reasons to cheat—greed. Entrepreneurial players have figured out that other players are willing to pay real money for virtual loot. This by itself is not necessarily bad. In fact, some games are actually trying to get a piece of the action by selling the loot directly. The problem is that where there is money to be made, someone will always figure out how to exploit the system to make more money.

The Cheat Lifecycle

Two groups of cheaters are important. The first is the hacker who creates the hacks and exploits. The other is the user of the exploit. Each of these has a specific role that is important to recognize.

In reality, a hacker by himself is usually not a problem. One person cheating has a limited influence on the overall perception of the game. If a player is duped once or twice by some "133t" cheater, he may chalk it up to bad luck. In addition, we can usually eventually track down a lone cheater and find a way to eliminate him from the game.

The real problem is that hackers feed off the accolades of the people they can get to use their exploit. This distribution to cheat users amplifies the hackers' effect on the game world and on the perception of your player base. If players are cheated every time they play, the game will be perceived as unfair and the players will lose any interest in playing it.

In attacking this problem, it helps to understand that there is a lifecycle to a cheat. A hacker spends a certain amount of time discovering or designing and then testing the exploit before he distributes it. The time it then takes for an exploit to become rampant can vary from hours to weeks depending on the game community.

One of the reasons why adoption can take longer is the amount of risk the cheater perceives in using the exploit. The perceived value of an exploit is a measure of the potential reward if it is used vs. the potential for loss by being caught. There will always be some users who will be willing to take a chance on an exploit, but many others will wait to see if the first group is caught.

The better we are at detecting and punishing cheaters, the less people will want to cheat, and the smaller the audience and impact of the would-be hacker. This is, of course, easier said than done. It takes time to detect and design a fix for an exploit. In some cases, we won't even be able to pinpoint who is cheating until we add mechanisms to detect the cheat. The longer it takes us to do this, the more we lose.

In addition, as we are working on the next detection and fix, the hacker is merrily engineering his next exploit. The faster he is able to develop his exploits, the more exploits we have to combat. If the cheater can create exploits faster than we can detect and counter them, we will have lost the fight.

To make sure we have a fighting chance, we have to make it as hard as we can for the hacker to develop his exploits so that we have time to counter them. If a hacker has to work for several weeks to develop an exploit that lasts for couple days, in which time he will most likely get caught and exposed, chances are the cheater will move on to greener pastures. In the end, the harder and riskier we make it for the cheaters, the fewer cheaters we have to deal with.

The Threats

Knowing why a cheater cheats is a start, but we must understand the nature of the exploits the cheater wields in order to develop ways to counter them. In an attempt to categorize these threats, we've broken them down into the following taxonomy:

Altered client executable: By modifying the client executable, the cheater can manipulate the client completely.

Altered client data: By modifying the client's data files, memory, or messages, the cheater can manipulate the client sometimes more easily and effectively than altering the client executable itself.

Eavesdropping: By examining client data or messages, a cheater can gain superior knowledge of his enemy's location and capabilities, giving the cheater the equivalent of radar or extrasensory perception.

Compromised execution environment: By wrapping or replacing shared libraries, the cheater can eavesdrop on or modify any information that the client executable attempts to pass or retrieve from the operating environment.

Player automation and augmentation: Since the input systems on computers are outside the control of the program, it is relatively simple to inject control from an external program instead of the user and enhance or replace player actions.

Insufficient authentication: By stealing the identity of other players, it is possible for the cheater to gain their loot and perpetrate acts that may be blamed on his victim.

Denial-of-service attacks: There are several ways in which a cheater can block, disconnect, or lag his opponents. In addition, the cheater may choose to attack the server, and block, lag, or deny access to all users.

Bugs and design flaws: No system is perfect, and in even the best implementations there are likely to be issues regarding out-of-order execution, race conditions, and validation of data and rules that can allow the cheater an advantage if discovered.

Abuse of rules or functionality: Even if the game systems are operating as designed, it is possible for a cheater to take advantage of loopholes in the rules or activities outside the ability of the rules to enforce.

Insecure servers: Even assuming all the game systems are secure, an experienced hacker may be able to gain access to the internal network, systems, and data.

Abuse of power, trust, or position: In any game, there are positions from game managers to the developers themselves that are entrusted to keep the game running and secure. Unfortunately, the people in these positions do not always do the right thing.

The breadth of the problems this list illustrates can be quite daunting. Anti-cheat truly does impact every part of the game design and development process, and we do not expect that this list is complete, or that the solutions covered here will provide the best solutions for every game.

Anatomy of a Cheat (Hacking 101)

As mentioned earlier, cheaters who create cheats like to refer to themselves as *hackers*. Regardless of the skill level of the hacker, for most basic cheats the tools and procedures used to hack a game are pretty much the same.

Memory finder: Takes snapshots of a game's memory and displays the difference between snapshots within a range of values specified by the cheater.

Trainer: A program that modifies the program and/or data memory of the game during runtime in response to input from the cheater.

Trainer maker: A program that automates the creation of trainer programs.

Disassembler: A program that will convert a game executable into human-readable assembly instructions.

Debugger: A program that is used to stop a game's execution when specified memory locations are accessed, and display instructions and memory contents.

Patcher: A program that creates a patch that can be used to create modified game executables with the cheaters hacks applied.

Where does one start to hack a game? By finding the memory that controls the behavior the cheater is looking to modify. For example, if a cheater wants to find where his ammo count is kept, he can use a memory finder program to first take a snapshot of the game's memory at 25 rounds, and then take another at 24 rounds. The cheater then instructs the memory finder to display all the values that started at 25 and then ended up at 24. Repeat this procedure a few times and the cheater has a pretty good idea where the ammo level is being stored.

If the memory that the cheater is looking for is in a static location, then each time the program is run, that value will be stored in the same relative location. All the cheater needs to do then is use a trainer maker to construct a trainer program that can respond to an input and set the ammo level to whatever value the cheater desires.

If the memory is dynamically allocated, the cheater will instead have to use a debugger to stop the program whenever the value is accessed. From here, the hacker can locate the static pointer to that value. With the static pointer, the cheater can once again create a trainer that can find and modify the values he is interested in or modify the game code itself to keep it from changing the value.

With a working cheat in hand, the cheater can decide to either distribute the trainer, or modify the code in the program itself and distribute a patch instead.

Advanced Hacking

While the most basic hacker or "script kiddie" can perform the previous hack, this is only the tip of the iceberg. Like most learned techniques, there is a great variation between the skill levels of each hacker.

The most advanced hackers know how to program perhaps as well as the developers of the game, and have also developed more specific skills that enable them to take your game apart piece by piece. An advanced hacker is likely to know assembly language, and how it relates to API calls and advanced data structures. This hacker will even be able to identify the language you created the game in and may be able to effectively rewrite your game line for line.

Trusted Clients (The Myth)

The first fact that we have to accept is that the client cannot be trusted. The client executes on the cheater's box, and he has all the tools he needs to reverse engineer any part of the systems you have so diligently constructed. A skilled hacker can bypass every check your team creates in probably less time than it took you to implement it.

While we may be able to make the process described previously more difficult, there is no one magic bullet. Attempting to ensure that the client is trustworthy can be a rabbit hole, and the tit-for-tat game with hackers can easily escalate until your programmers are spending more time on anti-cheat than on new features.

To get ahead on this game, you have to start before the hackers and attempt to keep one step ahead of them. Don't wait for each hack; instead, be proactive and design your code to be more hack resistant. Identify perceived threats early in the development cycle so that you can implement a combination of different countermeasures and detection systems as soon as possible.

In addition, you will have to remain vigilant, identifying new threats on a continuing basis. If a new cheat is postulated on a message board or detected in another game, assume that your game is next. By immunizing your game at the first sign of a threat, you can keep from being the next victim.

One way to get ahead of the hackers is to follow the rules discussed next for client side anti-cheat.

Rule #1: Clean the Code (Picking Up the Bread Crumbs)

One way to make a hacker's job easier is to leave symbols in the code. Whether these are debug symbols or string literals, they can give the hacker a good idea where to start looking for a particular function. If that were not enough, since the hacker can easily set a break point in his debugger and look at raw memory, runtime strings are almost as vulnerable.

In the case of string literals and runtime strings, you should make an effort to ensure that either is at least obfuscated whenever possible. Running your source code through an obfuscation processor that lightly encrypts your string literals and dependant data files can make it that much harder for a would-be hacker to see what you are doing.

Rule #2: Always Encrypt Important Values

If the value a hacker is looking for is encrypted, the cheater is left with just the changed memory and little indication of which location he is interested in. Encrypting need not be expensive or hard to accomplish. The following code uses XOR to lightly encrypt values for most integral types.

```
// simple encryption class for integral types
template <typename T, int key>
class SimpleCryptMem
{
        T       _value;
public:

        void setValue(T value)
        {
            _value = value ^ (T) key;
        }
```

```
T getValue()
{
        return( _value ^ (T) key );
}
};
```

In our classic ammo-level hack, if the memory had been encrypted where the hackers would have simply looked for the values they were interested in, they now have apparently random values. Unfortunately, while this obfuscation may thwart some cheaters, many will only be slowed down. The cheater can still locate all the changed locations, and by keeping any one of them at a previous value determine which ones they are looking for and eventually a way to control them.

Rule #3: Never Store Important Values in Static Memory Locations

Finding a value in memory to modify is typically an iterative process that usually involves restarting the client. If the value the cheater is trying to locate moves each time the game is restarted, the job of locating and modifying values becomes that much harder.

By allocating a small amount of random padding at program startup, subsequent allocations appear random as well. This combined with ensuring that important values are located in dynamic memory means that these values will be stored at a different relative location each time the game is run.

There are already some memory finders that compensate for this technique. An additional random padding added to some allocations can (at the cost of a few extra bytes per allocation) further obfuscate a value's location. This functionality can be implemented overriding new() in the base class of some objects, but remember to turn this feature off for debugging.

One way to significantly raise the bar is to combine dynamic allocation with encryption, and move memory around *as* it is used.

```
// Simple scatter memory encryption class for integral types
// Relies on a custom allocator to retain efficiency and
// inhibit memory fragmentation.
template <typename T, int key>
class ScatterCryptMem
{
        T*      _pValue;
public:

        ScatterCryptMem() : _pValue( myNew(T) ) {}
        ~ScatterCryptMem() { myDelete(_pValue); }

        void setValue(T value)
        {
                myDelete(_pValue);
                _pValue = myNew(T);
            *(_pValue) = value ^ (T) key;
        }
```

```
T getValue()
{
        return( *(_pValue) ^ (T) key );
}

};
```

In this example, each call to setValue() allocates a new destination for the value being written. Since where the value is kept moves each time it is written, a memory finder will have a much harder time identifying which memory has changed. In this case, the only stationary location that is changing is the pointer to the value.

This technique will probably not deter an experienced hacker who understands the underlying code, but it may be enough to deter most script kiddies.

Rule #4: Anti-Cheat Systems Should Be Autonomous

While for most code, it is a good idea to completely separate concerns and share common components, this can be the wrong approach for anti-cheat systems. The more dependent your anti-cheat systems are on common code and interfaces, the easier it will become for a hacker to find a common place to disable all of the detection systems.

If all of your detection systems depend on a single variable or call to ReportCheat(), it becomes a simple matter of finding that one call to disable every detection system on the client. Optimally, there will be no common code between your detection systems. Robustness and layering should be attained by overlapping responsibility without interaction or common code.

One way to support code reuse while maintaining autonomy is to inline selected anti-cheat code. Since the code is replicated instead of called, it then becomes more difficult for a hacker to intercept and disable it. Of course, this can lead to code bloat, so some care must be taken.

In the previous code examples, each accessor should be prefixed by a FORCE_INLINE macro directive. Although C++ will normally inline member functions that are defined within the class declaration, it is not guaranteed. Creating a FORCE_INLINE macro that is defined as __forceinline for MSVC++ helps ensure that the compiler inlines the code.

Rule #5: Detection Is a Dish Best Served Cold

An effective way to throw away any advantage that obfuscation might bring is to alert the hacker that he has been detected. The difficulty of locating and overcoming a problem is usually directly proportional to how reliably it can be replicated and how soon after the problem the symptoms manifest.

By alerting the hacker with some direct consequence of his actions, we are giving him feedback that he can use to find the anti-cheat system he has tripped. For an experienced hacker, it does not matter if the game pops up a dialog box, a detection message to the server, or the game suffers an apparent random crash, that action can be traced back directly to the detection system that activated it.

Of course, allowing the cheater to continue playing has its own set of problems. The first and foremost of these is the effect that the cheater has on other customers. To minimize this, the level of interaction a cheater is allowed should be limited. If a cheater cannot permanently gain resources or harm another player, you have effectively created a sandbox for the cheater.

The amount of time that you allow a cheater to remain connected should depend on several factors.

- The amount of confidence you have in your ability to limit the cheater's effect on the system. (How good is your sandbox?)
- The threat perceived from the cheat detected. (The perceived threat from a player manipulating the ammo count may be significantly less than some unknown client checksum error.)
- The amount of time that is needed to effectively obfuscate your detection system.

In the end, it is never a good idea to allow a cheater to play for an extended time. Regardless of what level of threat you perceive from the cheater, he should be disconnected at some random time within several minutes of detection.

Rule #6: Be Consistent to Remain Obscure

You have probably heard tales about someone stealing expensive assemblies by smuggling them out one piece at a time. The key to this scenario is to not act suspicious. If the employee walks in every day with a lunch box and leaves every day with the same lunch box, there isn't much to suspect. However, an employee walking out pushing a large box might raise some eyebrows.

To remain obscure, we should embed detection notification in many of the messages (perhaps all) that are already being sent. The server can then disconnect the cheater at a random time, or ban the cheater and alert a Game Manager to review the incident. The learning curve becomes pretty steep when the cheater's first indication that he has been detected is finding his account deleted.

Rule #7: Do Not Allow the Game to Run Offline

When a client is playable offline, hackers can run their tools without notifications being sent to the server. If we ensure that the client is connected to the game server whenever it is being run, we help increase the likelihood that a hacker is detected before he can complete his hack.

Note: A nice side benefit is that debugging/hacking a connected application is difficult since the connection frequently drops during breakpoints. Of course, this can also annoy developers who are attempting to develop the game as well. Be sure you are able to compile out some anti-cheat features that can slow development. As already noted, never disable anti-cheat at a single common point, since it breaks autonomy.

Rule #8: Don't Feed the Cheaters

While there may always be some people who will cause mischief for mischief's sake, we are always going to be better off if we can find ways to take away the rewards for cheating. If we eliminate the temptations, the people seeking them may find greener pastures.

One of the simpler things we can do to take away the carrot is to stop feeding the cheater's ego. By publicizing a fix for a cheat, we acknowledge that the cheater caused enough of a problem to get a reaction. For the hacker, this is the game: he finds a cheat, you react, and then he finds another. If the cheater is playing a game with you, opt out of the game. A developer never wins by engaging the cheater.

Rule #9: Overlap Anti-Cheat Functionality

When properly designed, each detection scheme can bolster the other rather than rely on it. If the cheater gets by one detection system, the next is ready to trip him up. With enough layers, it is possible to make the job of creating a hack so difficult that it just isn't worth the cheater's time to do it.

Of course, this can also be a challenge that is hard to resist. To hack the unhackable would be quite a feather in some cheater's cap if he were to pull it off. This reminds us to never feed hackers by proclaiming what a good job we do. The only accolades a well-protected game should expect are the lack of negative reviews about cheaters.

Rule #10: Limit the Way Cheaters Can Interact with the System

Another way to keep the carrot away from the cheaters is to limit the ways he can interact with the world. To an extent, griefing and other antisocial behavior can be functions of incomplete game design. All developers should be involved in thinking through the many ways that the elements of a game can be abused, not just the game designers. This is definitely an area where more eyes and perspectives can make a significant difference to how your game plays out.

Antisocial behavior often has indirect rewards. As an example, if people are camping at spawn points, it is possible to turn off the kills awarded to the camper. Unfortunately, the camper might want to control the odds in a battle by reducing opposing forces at the source, or he may just enjoy inflicting grief on other players. While it can cause other problems, turning death off entirely around a spawn point can totally eliminate camping.

There are features in a game that may be deemed worth the trade-offs of antisocial behavior. Simply recognizing that the feature will cause some antisocial behavior is not enough. A concrete plan to counteract this influence should be developed, or the feature may end up being more trouble than it is worth.

Client Validation

While validating the program and its data will not ensure that the client is trustworthy, it can certainly add another obstacle for the cheater. By performing a simple cryptographically secure hash function on the executable and key data files at startup, we can catch some of the more obvious and redistributable attempts at hacking the game.

In general, the more secure and exacting the hashing algorithm, the more processing it will take to accomplish. On modern processors, the 50% performance penalty of MD5 over CRC32 is scarcely noticed if accomplished in a background thread used to load the files from disk. Managing impact on frame rate may be more of a question of properly scheduling or distributing file loading rather than the performance of one hashing algorithm over another.

Of course, there will still be times as we attempt to push the client's machines to the melting point that the extra processing required to generate any digest or sum may be too much to bear. In those cases, if you must still load files it is a good idea to randomly check a subset of the files you are loading, especially ones considered key.

Since the cheater can use trainers to modify your program's memory on the fly, it is also important to look up and verify key segments of code and static data in memory during runtime. Spread these checks out over apparently random times and locations to obfuscate the calls and manage system overhead.

Distributed Data Validation

In addition to obscuring dynamic memory, we can also validate it. This next step is to mirror separately encrypted copies of important data. These copies can be separately encrypted and used to validate that memory hasn't been altered. To hack a value, the cheater now has to find every location where you scattered the mirrors and attempt to compensate for each encryption scheme.

```
// Mirrored memory validation and encryption class for integral
types.
//      Relies on custom allocators to inhibit memory fragmentation.
template <typename T, int mirrorSize, int key>
class MirroredCryptMem
{
        T      *_pValue[mirrorSize];
public:

        MirroredCryptMem () { memset(_pValue,0, sizeof(_pValue)); }
        ~ MirroredCryptMem ()
        { for(int i = 0; i < mirrorSize; i++) myDelete(_pValue[i]); }

        void setValue(T value)
        {
                for(int i = 0; i < mirrorSize; i++)
```

```
                    {
                            myDelete(_pValue[i]);
                            _pValue[i] = myNew(T);
                            *(_pValue[i]) = value ^ (T) (key ^ i);
                    }
            }

            T       getValue()
            {
                    if (!_pValue[0])
                            return T();

    T value = ( *(_pValue[0]) ^ (T) (key ^ 0));

                    for(int i = 0; i < mirrorSize; i++)
                    {
                            if ( value != (*(_pValue[i]) ^ (T) (key ^ i)) )
                                    setHacked(this);
                    }

                    return value;
            }

    };
```

This is, of course, memory and processing intensive and should be used only on highly vulnerable values or ones that change infrequently. One of the subtleties of this implementation is that while it always catches an altered value, it only returns that altered value if it is referenced by _pValue[0]. This maintains the illusion that there is only one value rather than multiple values.

False Positives

One word of caution; Just because your validation indicates the program or data is invalid doesn't mean that the player is cheating. One source of bad sums can be bad memory, CPU, and so forth on the player's system. In practice, you may find that the number of players with shaky hardware (especially over clocked systems) may be a small but significant part of your customer base.

One way to deal with this inconsistency is to provide the players with a tool that checks the integrity of the system and alerts them of problems when they install the game. If your tool indicates to the players that the system is unstable, point them to resources to help make it stable before they are allowed to complete the install. Doing so will help ensure you get less false detections, and the customer and customer support will be much happier.

That said, you will still get false positives. The way we deal with this is to gauge the amount of trust you have in a detected cheat. While a seemingly random check-sum error may be suspect, one that matches a known cheat may be much more decisive. Regardless, you should never rely solely on any one trigger as proof that the player is cheating. Instead, use the detection to temporarily ban the player (limiting the potential threat) and alert staff to take a closer look. Only after a system has become very mature and has a stellar record with no false positives can its indications be truly believable.

Compromised Execution Environments

If the cheaters can alter the program and data both on disk and in memory, it should be no surprise that they can also modify system libraries and intercept calls to the operating system itself. Because of the complexity of the systems that the game relies on, it is unrealistic to consider categorizing and validating all of the resources on which the game may depend.

One way to limit this task is to *not* use shared libraries where possible. Creating your own shared libraries can be tempting to manage complexity and updates. Unfortunately, this only makes it simpler for the cheater to intercept calls and transparently compromise those calls without being detected.

Instead of attempting to validate every possible underlying system, it is more realistic to identify the ways in which the execution environment has typically been hacked in the past. Two examples of execution environment exploits are the infamous *wallhack* and *speedhack*.

Speedhacks (Time Travelers)

By changing the perceived rate of the clock on the client, a cheater can accelerate his interactions with the world. By making time move faster, what is perceived by the hacked client as a walk can appear supersonic to the rest of the game world. If a cheater can move faster than the other clients can interpolate, the cheater may appear to teleport.

Each client clock has a certain amount of drift. In implementing a global game time service (GTS), you may already be implementing a system akin to NTP where the game compensates for this drift by adding a few microseconds to the client's clock each game loop to keep the client in sync with the other players.

When the cheater accelerates the client clock, the client starts to drift (many times dramatically) from the global game time base. If you include timestamps in every packet, the majority of cheaters can be detected by simply checking for timestamps against the server's GTS. If the client is drifting beyond what is acceptable, he is cheating.

If the cheater does manage to bypass all of the client detection checks and manipulate the client's GTS such that it appears accurate, then other server-side validation systems must be relied on. As with all data, nothing from the client is trusted. A simple check of the velocity of the player can indicate a cheat regardless of whether the player is manipulating time or just poking new positions into the client.

Wallhacks

A simple wallhack works by intercepting render calls and altering them so that walls are transparent or fog is turned off, allowing you to see your enemy. Other tricks involve using the same calls to intercept the rendering of specific targets and either rendering them in front of all other objects, or changing their color to stand out, making them simpler for you or an aim-bot to shoot.

One way to detect this hack is to use the same trick that aim-bots use. Since the game is sending the objects to the card, it should have a good idea what is on the screen at any time. By sampling the rendered image at controlled instances (perhaps with test objects rendered in the back buffer), it is possible to detect if some objects are not rendered correctly. Of course, since a bug in either the graphics card or driver could cause an object to render incorrectly, it is quite possible to get a false positive.

Foiling the Eavesdroppers

Pay no attention to that man behind the curtain . . . So, where is everyone's attention? It's behind the curtain of course. In our case, the curtain is the nice shiny picture we paint for our players on their screen. There are many ways for them to pull back this curtain, ranging from the wallhacks mentioned earlier to memory debuggers that will let you count and examine in-memory objects.

Wouldn't it be great if they pulled back the curtain and no one was there? This is the goal of content occlusion. The client can't see what we do not send them, and the graphics engine can't expose what isn't rendered.

The holy grail of occlusion is to run the simulation entirely on the server and not send any object that cannot be seen to the client. Unfortunately, we don't have the processing power to do this, and even if we did, server-to-client latency would cause serious inconsistencies for the client.

To keep inconsistencies to a minimum, we have to establish the effective interaction volume or frustum for a client. This frustum is determined by a number of factors, including the types of interactions and how fast the client can move, and turn in relation to how fast you can update the client about new objects and events.

This effective frustum will always contain more objects than the actual real list of objects with which a client could interact. Therefore, the client will need to pay particular attention to what objects it renders and what ones it does not. A cheater can make his walls transparent, but why would he if there isn't anything rendered behind it?

Since there will always be more objects in memory than are rendered, it will always be possible for a cheater to find that memory and find a way to act on it. However, the more we can limit this list of extra objects, the less advantage a client can gain by cheating, and the less motivation the cheater has to cheat. We know a hacker can eventually go through the trouble of finding and acting on any information that is on the client; the goal is to make it as hard to do and of as little value as possible.

Encryption

Obfuscation is not security, and then again, neither is encryption. While encryption can be quite secure between two secure endpoints, we do not operate in that world. In games, the client is always insecure and can always decode the messages. By hacking around inside the client, the cheater can even discover the keys using an external app to decrypt transmissions or files.

If the client has hard-coded encryption and decryption keys, the cheater can use them until the next patch of the game, and then spend a few minutes to find them again. To make this process harder, we can exchange keys when we start a new connection. The typical scheme would be to use public/private key encryption with some derivation on the Diffie-Hellman key agreement protocol.

While this is much better than using a hard-coded key, it still has some problems. The classic compromise is a man-in-the-middle exploit. In this cheat, a proxy is placed between the client and the server that intercepts and decodes communication going in both directions. Since the proxy did the actual exchange of keys with each endpoint, it knows how to encrypt and decrypt all the transmissions.

The usefulness of a man-in-the-middle or proxy exploit is that the proxy can protect or augment the client by manipulating and inserting packets. If someone shoots at the cheater, the proxy can throw away the hit message. The proxy can decode the positions of other players and display them, or if in range, the proxy or aim-bot can automatically send a hit message with the target coordinates for the cheater.

Encryption and Obfuscation Synergy

Of course, we can add an extra hard-coded or third-party certificate, such as the Station-to-Station (STS) protocol does, but that only gets us back to step one since this value can also be discovered by the cheater.

A more devious solution is to obfuscate the key exchange in such a way that it makes it difficult for the proxy to determine when the key changes or where to look for the new key. By encoding key changes into our different update packets or keying encryption off world state and time, we can make it very difficult for a man-in-the-middle to be clever enough to keep up. To be useful, the proxy would have to approach the complexity of the game itself, just the effect we are looking for.

As illustrated, the actual encryption scheme that is used is less important than the method of keeping the keys secure. The selection of a particular encryption scheme should depend on the requirements of the system in which you operate. If the client is changing keys every minute, would it really matter that someone were able to crack the encryption in an hour's time? That answer depends on the lifetime of the data being encrypted.

Another factor in encryption scheme selection is speed. It is quite likely that this is not an issue for the client, considering the small amount of data passed between it and the server. The server, however, must encrypt and decrypt messages from every client. The extra overhead can quickly reduce the number of clients that a server can maintain.

Whether you use RSA, DES, AES, or some other encryption scheme, you need to examine the lifetime of the data and the performance impact [WeiDai04] on the server to ensure that your selection works for the game you design.

Note: The export restrictions on cryptography were significantly reduced starting in 2000, and as of this writing allow for the export of products containing some levels of cryptography. It is important that you keep up to date with the current regulations and laws regarding cryptography [Export if you intend to use it in your product.

Leaky Pipes

With encryption secure, the proxy exploit is less useful, but can still cause mischief. One incident that illustrates this was when a not-so-ingenious cheater noticed that specific packets were of a certain size. By dropping those packets, such things as the hit messages or the cheater's position in the world wouldn't be fed to the server, effectively rendering the cheater impervious or invisible.

Since hit messages are accumulated on the server as well as the client and sent via a reliable protocol, dropping hit messages only prolongs the inevitable. For positional and other updates, it is possible to aggregate or randomize packet sizes to obscure which packets are key. Unfortunately, the proxy can still do the equivalent of pulling the plug by dropping all outgoing packets. Since dropped packets are common on the Internet, differentiating between a cheater and someone who simply has a bad connection is difficult.

One way to combat this exploit is to reduce the mobility and interactions of the client depending on the quality of the connection. If the client stops receiving notifications that its updates are arriving, it can slow the simulation significantly. The server would also limit the amount of movement between the last good packet and the most recent.

Tying the motion of the client can be quite effective, especially in first person shooters, but can be problematic in, for example, an air combat-sim. An aircraft hanging in mid air tends to quickly break the immersion of the simulation. Then again, an aircraft's guns or control surfaces jamming can be used to keep the immersion going. The only trade-off is that a player with a bad connection will be at a disadvantage (sitting duck) if the connection acts up during combat.

Broken Pipes

Another exploit that is masked by the inherent unreliability of the Internet is the broken pipe or disco cheat. By pulling the plug on the game at certain times, the cheater may be able to gain an advantage if some transactions do not complete.

One example of this is that when a cheater is about to die or otherwise be penalized, he quickly disconnects from the server. If the connection dies, the cheater cheats the system or other player of the kill and saves himself another death.

One solution to this is to detect when a player has engaged in a battle and then rule that that player lost if he is disconnected. While there will be players with bad connections that may suffer from this rule from time to time, it may be better than rampant death cheating.

Denial of Service

Denial-of-service (DoS) attacks can take several forms. Perhaps the most publicized is the Distributed DoS (DDoS) where a hacker takes the time to use a number of servers to send enough packets to bury your service. Depending on the method employed, there may be filtering that can be done at your router, or your security admin may suggest that you arrange for bigger pipes and more servers to weather the storm.

The next common attack is directing a DoS attack at another customer. By disconnecting your opponent, you can potentially either keep yourself from being killed, or if scoring systems allow it, being awarded a kill. One simple way to eliminate client-to-client DoS is to use a strict client-server topology. If all messages go though the server instead of between peers, there is no way that the hacker can learn the IP address of his target.

Of course, this is not always practical since there may be traffic that you want to go between peers, such as voice over IP (VoIP). If this is the case, any peer-to-peer advantage that disconnecting an opponent might reap must be eliminated from the game design. This will leave the open countermeasures for the broken-pipe exploit.

One DoS method that can be particularly embarrassing is when the hacker manages to convince your server to be the source of the attack. If you have some transactions that are triggered by an easily spoofable protocol like UDP, take the time and a few extra messages to ensure that the target of the response is actually the requester as well.

Dynamic Systems (How to Be a Moving Target)

Regardless of the encryption, obfuscation, and additional layers of checks and validation, given enough time a determined hacker will find a way to make people's lives miserable. That is why one of the most important things that you should manage is time. By becoming a moving target and changing faster than the cheater, we operate faster than the cheat lifecycle.

As already discussed, changing encryption keys over time makes encryption significantly harder to crack. While this works well against external attacks, the code itself remains static. Like any stationary target, the code, whether it succumbs to skill or simple trial and error, will eventually be compromised.

One way to make the code itself a moving target is to schedule frequent releases. These shouldn't necessarily coincide with any feature release. Instead, create a script that randomizes the link order of your modules, forcing some into different locations. Swap out modules that have the same functionality but work in different ways, like encryption schemes or levels of indirection. If the code is constantly shifting, we frustrate the hacker's attempts to find and exploit vulnerable pieces of code.

Authentication

One of the great advantages of the Internet is that you have a level of anonymity that allows you to explore without worrying about repercussions of that exploration. The downside of this is that some people will take advantage of their anonymity to exploit since there are no consequences.

If your login scheme is totally anonymous, then count on the fact that cheaters will have no qualms about trying to exploit your system. Allowing anonymous login is equivalent to giving hackers an invitation to run amuck.

Verified logins at least require the players to verify that they have a valid e-mail account somewhere on the Internet. While slightly better than an anonymous login, this may not be much of a deterrent since it only takes a few minutes to set up a new e-mail account.

A subscription has several advantages (besides actually paying your salary). The first is that players who pay for a game are much less likely to try to disrupt or exploit the game. Next is the fact that most subscriptions represent secured accounts. In most cases, you can track a subscription down to a single person and lock him out permanently.

So, why doesn't everyone just require a subscription to play? The simple truth is that we want to attract new players, and since a certain segment of the online population will not buy a game until they try it, you are stuck with a compromise.

What compromise is worthwhile? That depends on your circumstances. One intermediate step is to require a credit card, but not charge it until they subscribe. This allows you to secure the account and acts as a good deterrent. You may end up with fewer players, but will also inherit fewer problems.

Identity Theft

Of course, none of this is any more secure than anonymous login if we can't ensure that it is difficult to steal the identity of other players. Encrypting passwords is a good first step, but most passwords are actually compromised by either poor password selection or scams perpetrated on the players.

Both of these can be limited through education and ensuring that the player base knows the threats. In addition, you need to ensure that authentication systems are not vulnerable to brute-force dictionary attacks by limiting login attempts to a reasonable number before deactivating the account and notifying the owner through e-mail.

While it is possible for a cheater to temporarily deny a player access to his account by blowing out the attempt limit on his password, that is much better than the player losing his account to the cheater. One additional countermeasure for this DoS exploit is to ensure that a player's login name is different from his player name, and educate your players to not divulge their login names.

Transaction Validation (Trust No One and Nothing)

A comprehensive data validation system is not as simple as the few lines of code necessary to ensure that a buffer isn't over-run. A typical message system is comprised of a hierarchy of parsers that extract collections of elements or structures that are in turn propagated into other layers of the server.

The sooner invalid data is detected and dealt with, the less it will affect other systems. While it is important for the parsers to validate the lexical constraints and syntax of the data they process, the parser does not have knowledge of the constraints of other layers.

To allow the parser full knowledge of the constraints of all the other layers of the system would break encapsulation and lead to the spaghetti code that encapsulation and layering are designed to limit. Instead, each call should add additional data validations wherever there is a potential mismatch or conflict on the data constraints necessary for proper operation.

For example, a client may report that it has a velocity of 10 kph. This is a perfectly valid value since it falls within the range of velocities of at least some of the avatars in the game. The actual velocity allowed for the avatar modeled for this client may be determined by other layers that take into account the class, type, and health of the avatar along with any additional game rules.

Once bad data is detected, it needs to be logged so that someone can deal with it later. What to do after that becomes contextual. In some cases, it is okay to simply throw an exception and continue on; in others where there are numerous dependencies, it may be necessary to continue executing with a modified data set.

Dynamic Constraints

It is also important to expose any constraints that can influence gameplay. For example, a BFG may produce seven damage points and a plasma rifle only five. During gameplay, the producers discover that for proper balance, the rifle should inflict six damage points.

While you could hard-code this validation, it is likely to change over time for each model in the game. In time, this ends up being more work for the programmer and makes the system brittle.

In the previous example, the person who creates the model for the plasma rifle is the domain expert. Since the expert will tune the data, it may be a good idea to put the constraints for the model in a separate configuration file associated with that model. The easier this information is to edit and test, the more robust the model will become.

By exposing these constraints and others controlling scoring and the validation of actions, the production team (not the programmer) can create an iterative set of tests to explore and tune the game until it is intuitive and fun.

The problem with making your constraints dynamic is that it is all too easy to create new soft constraints that violate the hard constraints of the procedures and objects that use the data. By requiring each layer or API to maintain its own constraints, we ensure that the person who knows the hard constraints of a procedure has ensured that that procedure will always work as designed, and it may also be tested against the full range of input to verify that it does.

Statistical Analysis and Data Mining

Unfortunately, validation and tripwires are not always enough. Players will find a way to manipulate any system to their advantage. Even if the system appears to be acting normally and all the validation is happy, there may still be undetected attempts at manipulating the system.

Detecting more subtle manipulations requires instrumentation of your data. By adding metrics to many of the items that can contribute to the success of a player or group in the game, you can in turn create constraints that validate if players are progressing as expected.

If someone has an extremely high kill-to-death ratio, or is collecting more loot per hour than 10 other people per hour, it is time to look into whether the player is using an aim-bot or some other exploit. Of course, some players really are just that good, so it is important to check for false positives before taking action.

This instrumentation is also useful to detect things like game imbalances. If you introduce a new weapon, it may have implications you did not count on or find in beta. What may have been a small tweak can totally change the game's dynamics. Perhaps that is what was intended. In the end, your game is a dynamic entity that you will tune and change over time, so you must be able to tune your instrumentation over time as well.

Cheat Reporting Systems

Regardless of how diligent you have been in your testing, there will always be people who figure out how to get around your best efforts. Due to this, it is important to monitor the data already being collected, and the actual interactions going on in the production system.

How can we do that? Well, we could employ a host of people to sit and watch different segments of the game world and look for suspicious activity. Unfortunately, the game worlds tend to be large and complicated and it is unlikely that you would be able to afford the number of game managers that it would actually take to do this. In fact, even if you could, it is likely that they would miss some of the exploits even if they are occurring directly under their noses.

Reporting Communities (Neighborhood Watch)

One of the tools that revolutionized law enforcement was the telephone. By installing police phones throughout a city, a police officer could effectively respond to problems from a much larger area. Rather than having to watch every street and hope to see or hear suspicious activity, they could be called out to investigate activity reported by any citizen.

This same idea is employed in modern games. It is not uncommon to employ at least one Community Manager to be online whenever the game is running. The Community Manager responds to messages from the players directing them to problem areas. In addition to pinpointing where an exploit is most likely occurring, it gives the players a perception that their issues are being looked at and handled. Part of the Community Manager's job is to walk the beat looking for anything suspicious, but that is more of a random deterrent rather than an effective means of detection.

Filters and Aggregation (Looked Like a Cheat to Me)

If there are 30,000 players online, it is unlikely that one Game Manager would be able to police all the exploits that are going on at any one time. In addition, it can become a simple task of crying wolf in one part of the world, and while the Community Manager is distracted, perpetrate an exploit in another.

One way of aggregating their presence is to enlist the help of a trusted group of players to act as the Community Manager's eyes and ears. If you have a good pool of trusted volunteers that are educated on what to look for, they can sort out the real issues from someone crying wolf.

Putting in a tool set that allows trusted volunteers to answer the call and help where needed is an excellent community-building tool and amplifies the Community Manager's presence. They can also be a liability, so it is crucial that effort be spent on education and accountability through logging and review of activates. Moreover, since a volunteer is not an employee, never act solely on his input for disciplinary activities.

As a cautionary note, while volunteer groups are an excellent resource, they must also be managed carefully. You must ensure that you do not treat your volunteers in ways that would be misconstrued as employees. Volunteers are used effectively in quite a few games, but mismanagement can cause problems, or worse, law suits.

Reputation- and Trust-Based Systems

Reputation- and trust-based systems are modeled after real-world social systems that allow players to manage cheating and anti-social behavior themselves. The basic definitions employed are:

Trust: A peer's belief in another peer's capabilities, honesty, and reliability based on his own direct experiences [Wang03].

Reputation: A peer's belief in another peer's capabilities, honesty, and reliability based on recommendations received from other peers [Wang03].

In a typical reputation-based system, there may be a trusted third party (the server) that acts as a repository for recommendations. A common example of this is eBay, which acts as a recommendation repository. It is up to you, the consumer, to review the recommendations from other consumers to determine your own trust in a provider.

Since it is possible for individuals to post deceptive recommendations, a reputation system can be easily skewed. It then becomes the responsibility of the consumers to review the recommendations of any recommender to further determine the level of trust they place in each recommender and the recommendations they post.

A trust network or web attempts to formalize this process of determining the level of trust of recommenders by establishing a formula to weigh trust that is propagated by trusted sources. For example, if Bill has 70% trust in Sally, he may decide to place 60% trust in anyone who Sally recommends as being trusted at 100%.

Many variations of trust and reputation systems can be quite complex with what may be unclear advantages and disadvantages. It is possible that a game design that incorporates these systems could provide a mechanism to effectively isolate a cheater. Designing an MMPG with a built-in trust or reputation model that is effective in reducing the influence of cheaters while not interfering with other aspects of a game is a challenge—a challenge that we leave for you to explore.

Terms of Service (and Other Legal Mumbo Jumbo)

This is where we proclaim that we are not lawyers. We have been exposed to these concerns from the developer's side and do have some insight into some of the pitfalls, but you should consult with your own legal council to ascertain the best course of action for your company.

There is an art to crafting a Terms Of Service (TOS) agreement that says what you want, is legally competent, and can be read and understood by a normal player. If you cannot understand your terms of service without your lawyer interpreting it, there is a good chance that none of your players will either.

People can sign all sorts of contracts they don't understand, but if neither party understands what a contract entails, it is very unlikely that either party is going to enforce the contract correctly. The player is also not likely to be happy when he is taken to task for not complying with section 342, part 15, paragraph 2.

The basic goal when creating any legal agreement is that it is clear, concise, and simple. Like most things legal, this involves more don'ts than do's:

- Do not confuse the TOS with other documents. The TOS is *not* a EULA, "Privacy Policy," or a "Code of Conduct."
- Do not narrow your rights by tying responses to specific actions. In essence, as a business providing a service, you have the right to refuse service to anyone for any nondiscriminatory reason you want. Turning this into a laundry list dilutes your rights and confuses the player.
- Do not let anyone play the game without agreeing to the TOS and Privacy Policy every time he plays.
- Do spell out the disposition of virtual and intellectual property.

The TOS informs the player that he can be denied service. The Privacy Policy informs the player that you will be collecting personal data on his activities and what you will use it for. Used together, these contracts provide the rights to find out who is cheating and then take action.

The reason it is important to have the player agree every time he plays is that a player may lend his account to another player. This new player may not have seen the

EULA or the TOS if it is presented only once. In addition, you will most likely have to update these policies over time to take care of new features or correct deficiencies. Ensure that you build in a mechanism to push a new TOS and Privacy Policy to players each time they play the game.

Note that when you use personal data (anything associated with an individual) to impose restrictions or penalties, there are specific recourses that may be outlined in laws pertaining to the collection of personal data. In other words, you may have to implement some sort of appeals process in addition to exposing the data in question.

Data Privacy

In addressing data privacy laws, one of the most important terms to understand is "Personal Information." Personal Information is individually identifiable information about an individual that is collected online, such as full name, home address, e-mail address, telephone number, customer number, cookies, processor serial number, IP address, MAC address, or any other information that would allow someone to identify or contact the individual.

This definition is significantly the same throughout all the privacy laws. The importance of this term is that any data associated with "Personal Information" is considered "Personal Data" and is potentially governed by privacy laws.

Data that does not contain or is not associated with "Personal Information" is considered anonymous and is apparently not affected by most privacy laws. For example, you would be allowed to collect anonymous statistics including what would be considered private information, as long as none of the data could be considered or was associated with "Personal Information."

Unfortunately, anonymous data is not particularly useful when we are trying to track the activities of an individual to see if he is cheating. While it may be possible to collect data on an anonymous account and then boot that account, it would not be possible to bar that individual from re-entering the game. To do this, we need to associate data on cheating with "Personal Information."

Once we start collecting "Personal Data," we run into several laws that affect the collection of data depending on where you are in the world. As an MMPG, it is likely that even if you do not market explicitly to other countries, you may still have customers from those countries. If that is the case, it is important that you adhere to laws in your country, and in others.

Several laws that you may be constrained by include:

- The United States "Children's Online Privacy Protection Act" of 1998 (COPPA), which applies specifically to customers under the age of 13 [COPPA].
- The European Union Privacy Directive [EUPD].
- California Online Privacy Protection Act of 2003 (or AB 68) [AB68].
- California SB 27.

Collecting "Personal Data" will most likely subject you to some aspect of these laws. To comply, you should consult with a lawyer for specific constraints of each law, and ensure that you have a clearly defined Privacy Policy that is posted for players and strictly enforced internally.

One way to comply with privacy laws is to participate in an appropriate "Safe Harbor" program. These were initially enacted in response to COPPA and sanctioned by the U.S. Federal Trade Commission, but have since been expanded by the U.S. Department of Commerce to include compliance with "The European Union Privacy Directive."

System Data and Statistics

While you are collecting data, you may also want to include information related to bugs, crashes, and the environment in which they happen. Tracking down a bug on a player's system can be an impossible task without some means of either replicating it or getting some sort of log. In addition, some bugs are dependent on the hardware and OS on which the program is running.

By including a provision in the TOS to collect data about the game and the player's system, you can start to get a firm grasp of where your production bugs are and how to fix them. One side benefit of this is that you also get statistics on what platforms your customers are using so that you can make judgments on what hardware and software to support.

The law on collecting this type of data isn't clear. If you do not associate this information with personal data, the statistics should not be significant to the player, but without a clear indication that you are collecting this data in the TOS, you can run a risk that players will believe you are spying on them.

To make customer support more effective, you may want to associate system data with a customer. If a specific customer has been having a problem and reports a defect, it can be very useful to know that it started to happen when he installed card X or version 2.4 of the game. This association with personal data would have to be reflected in the TOS and Privacy Policy.

Virtual and Intellectual Property

One other thing that is crucial that you spell out in your TOS is the disposition of virtual property and intellectual property. In general, you should make it clear that virtual property does not in any way belong to the player, and that there is therefore no obligation to compensate him for any real-world loss endured by its loss. Tying virtual property to real-world monetary value can be a Pandora's box that should be treated with extreme care.

Likewise, the ownership of intellectual property (IP) needs to be clearly spelled out for player-created content. To be on the safe side, you may want to steer clear of player-created content, since the ownership of IP may not be determined by either your EULA or TOS:

1. "Minors are generally prohibited by law from signing away their IP. Even if they lie to VW developers and say they aren't minors, the developer doesn't get to enjoy any IP rights signed over to them by such players" [Bartle04].
2. "Many countries give moral rights to authors (i.e., content creators) under article 6bis of the Berne Convention. Some go further; decreeing that these are basic human rights that as such cannot be signed away. In most of the EU, for example, there are rights of integrity (the author can object if distortion of the material prejudices the author's honor/reputation) and rights of attribution (the author can demand their name appear on their work). The first of these could be particularly painful for VW developers to guarantee" [Bartle04].

Why is all of this important to anti-cheat? How you would react if in deleting the account of a hacker you ended up being sued for damages from the loss of virtual or intellectual property tied to it. Dealing with cheaters could become a costly activity indeed.

Integrating Anti-Cheat into Development

If anti-cheat sounds like a lot of work, it's because it is. It is quite easy to either have a major part of your development budget spent on anti-cheat, or not have enough.

Choose Your Platform

Most modern game consoles have anti-cheat built in and support staff who can help you make sure your game is virtually immune to hacking. This won't keep people from exploiting bugs and weaknesses in your game design, but a closed platform where the manufacturer can help ensure that the execution environment hasn't been tampered with is a real advantage.

Buy What You Can

If you are going to use a middleware game engine, part of that evaluation and buying process should be evaluating the level of support provided for anti-cheat. If possible, visit the forums of other MMOGs that are using the engine and perhaps even contact the other developers to figure out how much of a problem cheating is. A good analysis of what problems there are in the code and how well they are addressed over time can tell you if that snazzy new engine is more trouble than it's worth.

Then again, the features of that engine may just be too compelling to abandon based on your security analysis. When you are negotiating to purchase the game engine, make sure security is an issue that is brought up. If you are a small company, you may not be able to influence the game engine provider alone, but perhaps if enough of us do the same, engine providers will start listening.

Third-Party Security (Farm It Out)

Another way to get help is to look into third-party anti-cheat systems. Several have sprung up in the last few years. The advantage here is that you get some of the headache managed for you, and get a dedicated team whose focus is anti-cheat.

Staying one step ahead or even behind the hackers can be a full-time job, especially for a small company with a limited number of developers. We are able to spread that burden around by using middleware vendors who focus on anti-cheat. Alone, it may be a burden to support a staff just to keep the hackers in check; together we can aggregate the cost.

Make IT Part of the Team

While not specifically part of game development, having a secure game network is a crucial concern. Game networks and backend systems are a complicated and at times susceptible infrastructure. Even if you are 100% successful in thwarting cheaters in your code, it will be of little consolation if a hacker manages to break into your server set and access your database or disturb gameplay.

Having someone on your IT staff whose first priority is security helps ensure that the security concerns of the network come first. A good security admin will have first-hand knowledge of the mechanics of a DoS attack or the vulnerabilities of an encryption protocol to packet sniffing, and keep up-to-date with the numerous other types of exploits available. In addition, the security admin should work closely with the system architects to ensure that none of these concerns is inherent in the software design.

Write Secure Code

Regardless of how much you are able to purchase from middleware vendors to mitigate the burden of anti-cheat, there will always be parts of the system that you end up writing and maintaining. In the end, you cannot abdicate your role in creating secure code and combating cheaters.

That said, before you even start coding, you should develop a set of requirements that clearly state the security goals of each portion of an application. If your security requirements and goals are unclear or underspecified, there is little hope of implementing a solution that meets them.

If these goals are the foundation of your security plan, then peer review and security auditing are the hammer and nails that complete the implementation. By using peer reviews and auditing procedures to iteratively apply requirements to each system in design and during implementation, you ensure that each security concern is identified and implemented.

A focus on security from the outset influences the design of the system as a whole. By taking a holistic approach, security is addressed in relation to individual systems and how they work together. A strong encryption routine will not be much good if the real exploit is in the data being fed into it. A secure system is only as secure as its weakest link.

As the complexity for the systems and countermeasures we create evolves, it is all too easy to create dependencies that lead to brittle systems that are difficult to maintain. In addition, the more complex the system, the more bugs it will have, and the harder it will be to find them. This complexity can add up until the developer doesn't completely understand the system and how it could be compromised.

To combat this, we have to make sure there is a clear separation of concerns. By layering anti-cheat measures, we compensate for the weaknesses of individual links with overlapping systems. Each anti-cheat measure becomes a discrete system that can be understood independently of the rest of the code.

Testing

No matter how good your developers are, there will always be things that are missed. To uncover these omissions, you need testing. To have confidence that a system is resistant to cheating, effective testing needs to be integrated at many stages of development.

The first line of defense for any system is the unit test. In unit testing, for each function you want to create, you will first create a unit test that will capture the requirements and design constraints for that function by defining and then exercising its constraint or limits.

The importance of this for secure code is twofold. First, it makes the developer think about the expected functionality, and the failure modes of a function. Just as importantly, by implementing specific tests for the desired result, failure modes, and extreme input limits, we get concrete feedback that our code indeed performs as designed.

While unit testing ensures that each unit performs as advertised, it does not verify that the system as a whole works as expected. To do this, we create a more elaborate test that simulates real users called a "Functional or Regression Test."

For functional tests to be truly effective, we must consciously develop tests that exercise a system as expected, and do the unexpected. One example of this is to ensure that not only do we send messages in sequence, but also out of sequence to test for race conditions and dependencies. By violating many of the assumptions a system is developed against, we can start to get a more realistic picture of some of its weaknesses.

Load testing pushes the interactions with the clients to the limit, and the interactions with subsystems and the hardware on which it's running. Since it's much easier to be anonymous when you are one of thousands, peak load is a good target for cheaters. In addition, since there may be race conditions or other vulnerabilities that only show up under high load, it is another extreme for the cheater to explore and exploit. Of course, if all of this isn't enough to include anti-cheat in the load test regiment, consider what would happen if a cheater managed to compromise or bring down a server during your busiest period.

Fourth is the venerable "Closed Beta Test." The importance of the closed beta test is that it is not dependent on the developers. All of our assumptions and preconceptions are left at the door when we hand the game to the beta testers. It is their task to push the system to the limit and figure out scenarios about which we have yet to think.

To be completely thorough, a beta test should have three components. First is ensuring that the game performs as it should under normal input. This is a type of sanity check that we haven't been fooling ourselves that the game actually works. Next is to encourage the testers to misuse the game. By asking them to find out what happens if they do stupid or malicious things, we find some of the holes we have yet to consider.

Exploitation and Cheating in a Test Environment

The last is what we like to call the "cheat test." The cheat test encourages the testers to methodically try every cheat and hack at their disposal against the system. While the usefulness and necessity of this test is obvious, there are security concerns that it generates as well. For example, what if one of your testers decides to hide the fact that one of the hacks actually does work? In this case, we have not only promoted cheating, but have also given a cheater a proving ground for his wares.

The solution here is to institute blind testing. Just as you don't tell the cheaters in the production game that you have detected them cheating, you don't tell the beta testers either. As long as they check a box on a Web page before they run each exploit detailing what they are doing, we can validate on our side that the hack is detected and handled. If testers neglect to tell you about a hack that they are about to run and you detect it, you exclude them from cheat testing in the future.

In addition, you should enlist some of your production staff to stay current with new hacks and exploits on your game and others and do independent checking in-house. If you really want to pursue this, you need to consider hiring an experienced hacker to do additional testing. However, hiring a hacker may be akin to inviting a tiger to dinner.

Conceptually, one of the side bonuses of engaging hackers in your testing and to a limited extent making them part of the team is that they then have a function that gives them prestige. Instead of working hard to exploit your game, they can instead get accolades for protecting it from the exploiters.

When you have completed your testing, it is important that you fix the weakness in the code, and, where possible, add functional tests that can be run to validate the fix. In time, your functional test will become an extremely effective cheater that is on call whenever you want to test your system.

The Open Beta Litmus

If all of this testing weren't enough, every once in a while you may want to perform an "open beta." While closed beta testing is excellent, you will never reach the level of exploitative activity that you can when you open your gates to the unwashed hordes.

During an open beta, you may want to stress your system as far as it can go. More importantly, since it is a beta and you are looking for how the system can break, you may need players that will bend the rules and aren't afraid to try to exploit the system. This is an excellent time to test how well your game design holds up to exploitations and how well your validation, tripwires, and instrumentation work to detect cheaters.

Of course, with an open beta you have the same inherent problems any time you interact with hackers. By providing too much feedback, you make it easier for them to figure out that you are detecting them, and how to get around detection. Second, if you do not take action on the hackers, the other players in the open beta will assume that your production servers must be full of cheaters as well.

It is possible to walk a fine line with an open beta. Our countermeasures for exploits should prevent harm to the system and other players without letting a cheater know he has been detected. Because of this, the majority of cheats should not affect other players.

To manage the cheats and cheaters that we do not have adequate countermeasures for, we take advantage of the cheat lifecycle. By only running the open beta for short periods of time and allowing only a limited number of players (on a lottery basis) each day, the cheater will not have direct feedback that he has been excluded because he was cheating. In fact, the hacker may develop a false sense of security that will prompt him to become careless if he ever does become a customer.

Building Fences Between the Sheep and the Wolves

While one of the best ways to get to know your opponent is to invite him to dinner, it is likely to be a very tense meal. When the food starts flying, you don't want your customer sitting at the same table if you can help it. The simplest way to keep your customer's experience untarnished is to have these two eat in separate rooms, or in this case game worlds.

It is almost never a good idea to let unsecured accounts onto your for-pay game worlds; this does not mean that you preclude your paying customers from joining in on the beta. The level of play and testing on the beta world will be much better if you have good participation from your for-pay players. At the same time, since it is a separate game world, they will understand the chaos that ensues without tarnishing their for-pay world experience.

Wolves in Sheep's Clothing

One thing to remember when you invite your opponents to dinner is that they are learning as much about you as you are about them. In addition, your angelic paying customer base isn't necessarily above cheating either; they just are not fond of the idea of getting caught. An open beta gives any wayward customers a way to test your defenses without jeopardizing their paying account.

Manage Expectation

Yes, some people will still experience the bad effects of cheating on your open beta, but it should be significantly less than in most open games. Since it is a beta and not production, a large number of these cheats may even be considered bugs in the system that you are trying to fix. Since only you know that your system is stable, you can examine open testers' bug reports for clues to cheats that you may not yet detect.

Isn't even one cry of cheating on your servers enough to tarnish your reputation? Not likely. Sure, if the person crying wolf is a reporter, it could smart for a bit, but if you are doing a good job of keeping cheaters out of your production game, your good reputation will spread.

When Is It Enough?

No matter where you work, there will be a limited set of developer resources that you can use to develop and maintain a product. To ensure that all of your priorities are met, you need to balance these resources against the tasks at hand.

Defining Expectations

To set priorities, you first have to define expectations. Our expectations are a set of requirements that define a successful rather than unsuccessful project. To this end, expectations do not define our wants, desires, or dreams, only the subset of those that will predicate our success as a company.

One valid expectation is that the game be perceived as stable. This is not saying that there aren't any bugs. Even on well-structured projects, plausible estimates of between 5 and 30 errors per 1000 lines of code are common. In light of this reality, what stable does mean is that the majority of users will not experience defects that hamper their ability to enjoy the game.

With some new MMP games weighing in at around two million lines of code, that's between 10,000 and 60,000 potential bugs to find and fix, without even taking into account the bugs in drivers and the operating system. With the complexity of today's MMPG, the quality of the software must be closely managed indeed.

Regardless of how good a job you do or how few bugs exist in your code, someone will always find a way to exploit some aspect of your game. The success of anti-cheat must be measured by the same sort of litmus we use to validate the quality of our code. The majority of the players should not encounter cheating that detracts from their ability to enjoy the game or are perceived to be significantly worse than any other game on the market.

The problem with this last definition is that we also need to take into account the boundary condition of a cheater who manages to pull off a cheat so significant that it tarnishes the ability of the game to attract players. If a cheater manages to repeatedly bring down the system or steal a significant number of accounts so that it disrupts the gameplay for a significant period of time, the game is going to be in big trouble.

Determining Exposure and Threat

To start determining what exposure you have to these boundary conditions, you must first determine the following:

1. What needs to be protected?
   a. Personal and financial data
   b. Game data (e.g., player accounts and possessions)
   c. Stability and access to the game
2. What are the threats and vulnerabilities?
   a. Hackers
   b. Cheaters
   c. Griefers
3. What are the implications and the costs if the threats mature?
   a. Legal liability
   b. Loss of productivity
   c. Reputation
   d. Perceptions of your customers

By identifying these three things, you can start to prioritize the threat to your business as a whole and which threats mean the most to your company's survival. With this knowledge, it becomes simpler to determine the appropriate response to each threat and what measures are needed to protect your game from them.

Conclusion

In architecting an MMP game, it is easy to underestimate the impact of anti-cheat or the priority and place it should have within the development process. Anti-cheat is a big task that has implications for almost every level of planning, development, and production. Just skimming the surface as we did in this article hopefully illustrates the scope of the problems and some of solutions that should be employed.

References

[Bartle04] Bartle, Dr. Richard A., "Pitfalls of Virtual Property," The Themis Group, April 2004. Available online at *www.themis-group.com/uploads/PitfallsofVirtual-Property.pdf*.

[AB68] Information of California's Online Privacy Protection Act of 2003 (or AB 68) and California SB 27 can be found online at *http://practice.findlaw.com/top10-0704.html*.

[COPPA] Information on how to comply with COPPA is available at *www.ftc.gov/bcp/conline/pubs/buspubs/coppa.htm* and *www.ftc.gov/os/1999/10/64fr59888.htm*.

[EUPD] Information on the European Union Privacy Directive can be found online at *www2.echo.lu/legal/en/dataprot/directiv/directiv.html.*

[Export] Current encryption export restrictions are administered by the Bureau of Industry and Security (BIS) part of the U.S. Department of Commerce, and can be found online at *www.bxa.doc.gov/Encryption/default.htm.*

[Wang03] Yao, Wang and Julita Vassileva, "Trust and Reputation Model in Peer-to-Peer Networks," Third International Conference on Peer-to-Peer Computing (P2P'03), IEEE, September 1–3, 2003. Available online at *www.cs.usask.ca/grads/yaw181/publications/120_wang_y.pdf.*

[WeiDai04] A recent comparison of the speed of various encryptions schemes can be found online at *www.eskimo.com/~weidai/benchmarks.html.*

2.13

The Quest for Holy Scale— Part 1: Large-Scale Computing

Max Skibinsky—HiveMind, Inc.

thequest@h-mind.com

Massively multiplayer online persistent state worlds (MMP/PSW) are undoubtedly one of the most exciting and technologically challenging development goals in existence today. True believers will argue at length that MMP games are the one and only future king of the entertainment universe. They believe that in the long run, MMP games will replace traditional static-content cable and TV with fully interactive experiences specially tailored to the interests of individual customers.

However, if we were to ask an outside expert without any gaming industry affiliations to judge our industry achievements to date, he would find some of these claims puzzling. How can these worlds be termed "massive" if they can't handle more than a few thousand simultaneous players per world, for instance? That would be quite surprising for an enterprise Web server administrator, accustomed to millions of visitors on his Web server. A database expert from a financial processing center would be amazed to learn that at most the "persistency" of online worlds is limited to a couple of dozen numeric fields per player, with any other changes to the world erased just after a few minutes ("liveness" of dropped items being one of many examples). In other words, MMPs are still nor massive, nor persistent on the same *scale* as deemed normal in enterprise software.

Yet, why would we care about MMP scalability? After all, it is a fairly technical issue, when the main challenges limiting MMP growth today are not technological. MMP games must break out from the hardcore PC gamer niche into the mass market entertainment, and make a transition from the PC to next-generation online capable platforms like PS3 and Xbox2 and various mobile devices. In reality, however, these challenges are in fact closely related.

Let's suppose you have built a successful MMP for consoles, and are now expecting a hefty 3–5 million user subscription growth per year like a typical console title. That is quite a success story! Or is it really? We know from current titles that it is extremely hard to put more than roughly 50,000 total users on a single world instance (represented by a one-server cluster) using current MMP architectures. When we deal with the PC niche market we can expect 250,000–500,000 players, and splitting the game into 10–20 worlds or servers is acceptable. Now imagine you have to split a 5-million user base of console players into servers. Instead of 20 servers, we may have them up into 100–200 different servers! In other words, you will fill a server with players and launch a new server cluster *every other day* for a year. The chances of two friends joining the game and seeing each other in the same world would be pretty slim. Let's keep in mind that a console player would be quite different from a hardcore PC gamer. They can't be expected to understand the notion of different servers, connection outages, or have enough technical understanding to run *traceroute* to your server in a customer support call. Casual players will expect to insert the disc and start playing in few minutes, and they will take no excuses for not seeing friends or family in the game, especially if they are the ones who introduced them to the game in the first place. Current high costs of a PC MMP launch will look like pocket change compared to costs of launching a successful console MMP world, if we opt to use the same architecture as current PC MMP servers do. If MMPs are ever to penetrate the mass market, it will be an unavoidable requirement for the MMP industry to create new types of technological frameworks needed to handle the correspondingly larger number of subscribers.

Today, the main potential of the MMP genre remains largely locked. There are many hard reasons why progress on scalability and persistence within online worlds has been fairly slow. We can compare progress during the last decade in scalability versus, for example, 3D graphics, taking the original *Meridian 59* and *City of Heroes* as our points of reference. So, why can we easily create million-user Web sites, yet we must break MMPs into tiny bits of a few thousand simultaneous players each? What challenges must be solved to create a single MMP populated by millions of players living in the same world?

In this article and the next, we are going to cover the technological barriers currently stopping us from building truly massive worlds and get an overview of promising technologies that can help us overcome them. We are going to look at characteristics of MMP-type scalability, and what makes the needs of MMP games unique. We're also going to share a couple of interesting discoveries from personal research on building a truly massive and persistent online environment.

Large-Scale Architectures

The challenge to build a massive and persistent computing environment is by no means new to general computing. Over the years, different large-scale architectures come and go in prominence; however, never fully disappearing from sight. At a high level, we can identify four main types of architecture:

- Client/server (C/S)
- Peer-to-peer (P2P)
- Grid
- Distributed systems

Let's review the specifics of each architecture and how they relate to MMP needs.

Client/Server Systems

Tracing their legacy all the way to mainframe systems, the vast majority of enterprise-class networks rely on a client/server (C/S) networking architecture. This architecture can be defined as a set of centralized servers processing all transactions for multiple clients in a real-time environment. Each client is primarily an input and output station for the central servers.

This was the setup of the original mainframe/terminal systems deployed in the 1960s, when terminals were given minimal functionality. In the mainframe design, little thought was given to interactivity between users. Instead, all terminal communication was independent of the other terminals and completely dependent on connectivity with the central server.

For C/S architecture, the bandwidth, storage, and processing are fully centralized and the level of interactivity is generally configured to be real-time. As a result, there is a strong requirement for high performance and responsiveness on the server side.

Here are major C/S architecture strong points:

Time tested: C/S technology is so mature and widespread, there are virtually no unknown factors about using it. It's a technology that is well understood and easy to implement.

Single point of control: Controlling the server allows operators to oversee and monitor all activity performed by clients. Any changes on the server will automatically affect all the clients.

Strong security: With the server safely stored in a datacenter, it becomes very challenging to compromise system functionality from the outside.

Modular scalability: The datacenter can be extended and scaled up by adding more server instances serving client requests.

Without any doubt, just as it was in the 1960s, client-server remains the dominant architecture today. Besides being the architecture behind every Web server and financial datacenter, one may consider even technology bellwether Google to be just a vast mainframe, which is accessible to your terminal in the form of a browser. See [Oren04] for a bit of historical perspective.

Client/Server Scalability for MMP Games

All MMP games deployed today use a client/server architecture. Let's look at the typical scalability of such a C/S system. As shown in Figure 2.13.1, a characteristic sign of C/S systems is a dependence on datacenters with both high bandwidth and high processing capacity. IP packets from all client stations must come to a single location, get processed by the server cluster, and have updates sent back to all clients in real-time. To support an increasing number of clients, we must add more machines to the datacenter and increase both incoming and outgoing bandwidth capacities accordingly without losing system responsiveness. As an interesting side note, Google data shows that the main issue of scaling datacenter processing power is not computer power, but rather dispersing heat of all working CPUs. At the time of writing, the Google datacenter consumes roughly 4 MWatt of power on about 20,000 CPUs. Roughly, 70% of this power is spent on dispersing heat, with 30% power spent on actual computing.

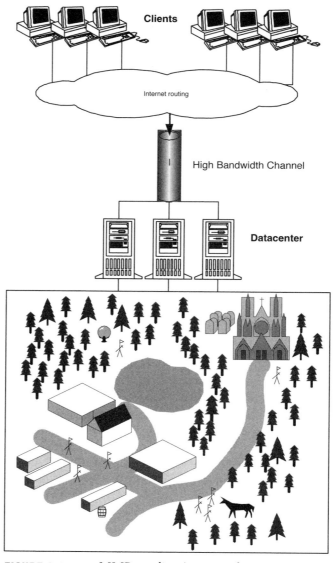

FIGURE 2.13.1   *MMP on client/server architecture.*

One of the fundamental weaknesses of the C/S architecture is its dependency on a single physical channel to the datacenter. This connection represents a single point of failure for the whole service, and a major scalability bottleneck and point of congestion. If for any reason this connection is overloaded, interrupted, or, worse, physically damaged, all users of your datacenter will be adversely affected. In addition, it is worth noting that unless your datacenter is connected directly to one of the Internet backbone servers, any connectivity or scalability issues of the independent ISPs on the way to the backbone will have a high chance of affecting very large numbers of your players, which will be perceived as problems with your MMP server. There is the possibility to geographically distribute datacenters to avoid a single point of failure. However, in such a case, these datacenters will operate independently of each other and should be considered effectively separate servers. Alternatively, if clients of different datacenters must be mutually aware, it will require real-time datacenter synchronization, thus becoming a trivial case of grid architecture, which we review later.

The good news is that given the long history of C/S deployments, the methods of deploying and maintaining 24/7 operational datacenters are well known. However, they all tend to require large capital expenses up-front and significant maintenance costs. A large part of the current high costs of an MMP launch and its maintenance derives directly from the high expense of maintaining a commercial quality datacenter. [Humble04] contains interesting data on an *EverQuest* datacenter.

If the client/server approach is so well known and stable, being further enhanced during the Web revolution of the 1990s, why is this approach not working out for MMP architectures? Unfortunately, there is a principal difference between scalability of Web-based C/S systems and MMPs.

The historical C/S design assumptions revolve around independent, noninteractive terminals. As a result, C/S networks are very effective in cases where each client is carrying out activities independent of the others (such as making Web requests and receiving Web responses). Simple C/S architectures of n nonmutually interactive users scales as $O(n)$, which means as the number of users grows, our support needs for both CPUs and bandwidth will grow as a linear function from n. Modern Web servers actually scale even better as $ln(n)$ due to content caching across similar user requests. However, the assumption of mutually noninteractive users is completely wrong for MMPs. This weakness of C/S architecture becomes apparent when we realize that in general an MMP world on C/S scales as $O(n^2)$.

Let's look at this gameplay situation set in a high fantasy genre. Assume we have a total of four interactive actors at the scene. Let's suppose that one of the actors makes a single action visible to the other actors. The server must get an action request packet, process it according to global and local world rules, and update the observers. Considering that the success or failure of the action is not guaranteed, the original actor should be considered one of the observers as well. Therefore, the single action by one actor in the scene of four produces a total of at least five packets. Every actor in the scene will also act in parallel, giving us in general $n*(n+1)$ traffic packets for a single action, which is the previously cited $O(n^2)$ bandwidth function. The same reasoning can be repeated for server-side processing. Since every action of every actor has the potential of affecting everybody in the scene, the server simply can't determine the outcome by processing each packet linearly as it is received. Instead, all $n*(n+1)$ actions create the current processing context, which can be resolved only as a whole, again making processing times and memory consumption an $O(n^2)$ function. (See Figure 2.13.2.)

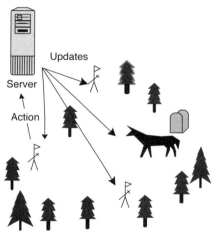

FIGURE 2.13.2   *Single-action C/S processing cycle.*

However, we just looked at a single small scene with four actors. Each $O(n^2)$ would be just a crowd in a small world locality—will it really matter for the whole world? Yes, it will. Many small crowds can be represented as $Sum(i, O(n^2))$. Let's suppose we keep adding more and more users to the world. With more users joining, the world density is going to increase, which means crowds are going to increase as well. That means each n_i member is going to grow linearly with world population, and the $Sum(i, O(n^2))$ will grown as general $O(n^2)$. Another explanation can be given from thermodynamics. With an increased number of particles in a closed system, the number and amplitude of local fluctuations is going to increase. For an MMP world, that means on statistical average we would have more crowds with more participants. Therefore, a world with enforced locality rules still scales as an $O(n^2)$ function.

$O(n^2)$ scalability unfortunately renders the C/S architecture unsuitable for high-performance large-scale MMPs. In practical terms, it means that one can't practically build a reliable C/S MMP system for constantly increasing numbers of users. In such a system, CPU and bandwidth capacity will grow as a square factor from the number of users, and it will always run out of capacity quicker than the linearly growing user subscription revenue paying for the bandwidth and processing power. Various methods can be employed to hide or at least delay the inevitable moment of $O(n^2)$ reckoning on a C/S MMP system. They are very familiar to MMP players: world sharding, splitting world into zones, short visual or action ranges, prevention of large crowd formations, and so forth. Yet overall, they are just different means to keep the potential n^2 value smaller than existing capacity.

Let's do some simple numerical modeling. Suppose we will give each actor three parallel update channels: movement, item use, and actor action. If we optimistically assume each channel will consume two integers (8 bytes), then we will have 24 bytes of data and about the same in supplementary IP data. Using various packet optimization techniques, let's suppose we keep each dataset under 50 bytes. Assuming the server processes update their state every three seconds, with N crowds by n players, and assuming the player controls only a single in-world character (which is really wrong for many games such as an RTS), we will have $N \cdot n \cdot (n+1)\dfrac{50}{3}$ bytes/sec of server bandwidth. How many crowds will there be on a server with T simultaneous players? Let's assume one-third are dedicated solo players who find the very idea of collaborating and playing together with other human beings in an MMP world morally disgusting. We can surmise another third is not part of the large crowds since their current activities don't require it to be so. Therefore, we will assume about a third of players will be crowded. How large will each crowd be? This will obviously depend on the number of population centers, contested structures, or large-scale collaborative or confrontational player gatherings. Let's assume our world will have at least 100 of such crowds forming structures or causes. This number is very high compared to current titles. In *Dark Ages of Camelot* there are hardly more than a dozen castle sieges going on at same time. *Lineage II* offers five castle sieges per world during a two-week cycle. However, let's assume we will have enough content to have so many crowd-forming locations, since for C/S operators it will be beneficial to increase this number. With constant world population of additional crowds, it will decrease the size of each crowd, and reduce the explosive effect of factor.

Therefore, with $N = 100$ and $n = \dfrac{T}{3 \cdot N} = \dfrac{T}{300}$ giving us $100\dfrac{T}{300} \cdot \left(\dfrac{T}{300}+1\right)\dfrac{50}{3} = T \cdot \left(\dfrac{T}{300}+1\right)\dfrac{50}{9}$ bandwidth. Finally, how does T (simultaneous players) relate to the total world population W? Assuming the average players spends four hours a day playing the game, with players distributed equally across different time zones, we will have $T = W\dfrac{4}{24} = \dfrac{W}{6}$ giving us: $\dfrac{W}{6} \cdot \left(\dfrac{W}{6 \cdot 300}+1\right)\dfrac{50}{9} = \dfrac{W^2}{1944} + \dfrac{50 \cdot W}{54} + \dfrac{50}{9}$ bytes/sec $\approx \dfrac{W^2}{243}$ bits/sec. Since we expect our W to be in hundreds of thousands and millions, then for rough analysis we can easily discard nonsquare members of this polynomial. The maximum number of potential MMP players in a single world can be approximated as

$\sqrt{B \cdot 243}$ where B is bandwidth in bits/sec available in a given datacenter. The author has intentionally presented all steps rather than just giving final and trivial formulas so that readers may experiment with models using different assumptions.

Despite being extremely optimistic in our modeling, Table 2.13.1 spells complete doom for the C/S architecture as an acceptable choice for large-scale MMP games. Even a highly expensive OC12 connection won't be enough just to put all of the current players of *EverQuest* into a single world. State of the art in fiber optics OC-192 connections won't be enough to accommodate the player base typical for any console title.

Table 2.13.1 Max Players by Internet Connection Type

Connection	Speed	Max MMP Players
T1	1.5 Mbit/s	19,000
T3	44.7 Mbit/s	104,000
OC3	155.5 Mbit/s	200,000
OC12	622 Mbit/s	390,000
OC192	10 Gb/s	1.5 million

Looking at the historical data and existing research at our disposal, we see that a C/S architecture for MMPs currently can be labeled as a low-technology risk, but with a high operational cost, capable of serving in the low thousands of users in the same world and having scalability limits for future growth. If C/S can't serve MMP needs in the long-term, what are the alternatives?

Peer-to-Peer Networks (P2P)

From a logical perspective, P2P networks are the exact opposite of C/S systems. If C/S systems are based on strict differentiation between noninteractive clients and a centralized server, P2P assumes fully capable and interactive clients, each having an equal role with his peers. One may think of a P2P network as a collections of peers, where each one can assume the role of client and server simultaneously, with a "classical" C/S system being just a degenerated case of P2P network with a single peer assuming the server role.

Historically, P2P is almost as old as traditional C/S. From the birthplace of the Internet as a collection of peer ARPANET hosts, to current decentralized Usenet and DNS systems, we see deployments of P2P architecture. In fact, looking back in history, choices between C/S and P2P seem to be fully determined by cost and availability of a given system. Expensive systems that had to be shared usually started out as C/S. Yet, if the systems for whatever reasons were already widely deployed or in abundant supply, then some form of P2P network between such systems would be established.

As music industry executives are painfully aware of, P2P networks are very low cost to deploy, scale extremely well, and don't have single point of failure issues as C/S systems do. Ironically enough, the first Napster was in fact hybrid C/S and P2P solution, with its C/S component creating the potential of a Napster shutdown on the technical side. KaZaa and Gnutella being true fully decentralized P2P systems don't share such weakness. To date, P2P networks have shown significant technical and economic advantages over traditional C/S solutions. Most P2P networks currently in existence are file-sharing networks in which users interact and help each other by sharing file resources with one another. These networks can effectively scale to tens of millions of users with little cost to all involved (beside the aforementioned music industry executives).

As a matter of fact, even people who never shared music online are among the hundred of millions of users on a strong file-sharing P2P network. That of course is e-mail with its network of P2P mail hosts sharing files with e-mail messages.

Let's sum up the main strengths of P2P networks:

Highly scalable: A P2P-powered network enables all users to operate with good performance.

$O(n^2)$ solution: In a P2P network, each additional player brings in additional load on the system as a client, and own resources as a server as well. Therefore, the system net power and cumulative bandwidth grows automatically with each added player.

Massive processing capabilities: Every node in the network can contribute idle resources for processing. When resources of a given node are fully used, a P2P network will always have an abundant supply of other nodes to take the extra load.

Massive storage capability: By relying on the storage capacity of the clients, large-scale P2P file sharing networks can provide hundreds of terabytes of storage at no additional cost.

Low hardware expenses: The majority of processing and storage takes place within the network; there are typically few if any centralized resources.

Low bandwidth requirements: There is no single datacenter, and connections are formed dynamically between peers as needed. As a result, there is no centralized bandwidth requirement or limit.

Dynamic topology, no single point of failure: The extreme flexibility of P2P networks makes them very resilient to attacks and catastrophic infrastructure failures. The same flexibility allows for various optimization algorithms to be used dynamically to achieve deployment-specific goals. [OpenP2P01] offers thorough classification of various possible P2P topologies.

Improved latency: Average round-trip time in a dynamically formed P2P network is significantly less than round-trip to a fixed C/S datacenter.

As opposed to the client/server model, the bandwidth and storage for P2P networks are nearly completely decentralized (see Figure 2.13.3). As a result, the bandwidth, storage, and processing power are supplied by the user community. There are many more very appealing characteristics of P2P systems. You can refer to [P2P01] for further study of their characteristics.

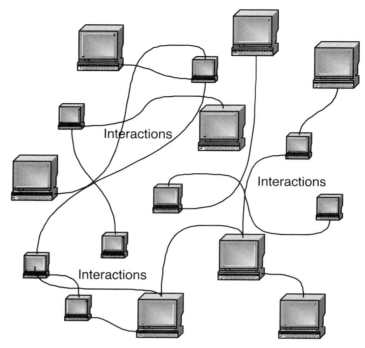

FIGURE 2.13.3   *Autonomous P2P network.*

However, it's impossible to speak about P2P networks without mentioning some of their natural weaknesses. These weaknesses are a direct consequence of their decentralized structure. The very features that make P2P networks so resilient and scalable are making them hard to control, and what's even more critical for MMP needs is that they are even harder to secure. There is virtually nothing in a traditional P2P network that may guarantee that data streams coming from the P2P network are from a legitimate source and have not been tampered with. There is also no reliable way to establish data authenticity. There is no way to control behavior of the P2P network as a whole, besides a few nodes in close proximity (referred as "horizon" in P2P literature).

Grid Computing

The formal definitions of grid computing still remain somewhat fuzzy. Grid computing in its most general form can be thought of as a network of mutually aware servers, serving an even larger network of clients in classical C/S fashion. Since datacenters are now distributed and can form dynamic connections between each other, from a client perspective they become a single very robust virtual datacenter. A grid can be thought of as a C/S architecture taken to the next level with additional degrees of flexibility.

We should differentiate between internal grids (formed by computers within any given enterprise) and open cross-organizational grid environments, which can be globe-spanning, such as Globus Alliance (*www.globus.org/*). Internal grids are basically an optimization of idle computing capacity already existing in an organization, and while it may increase a given organization's productivity, there is little value in internal grids for MMP deployments (beside greatly speeding up your development with Xoreax IncrediBuild® by turning your corporate LAN into compilation grid). However, as long as the resources of an open grid are inexpensive, this architecture can provide tremendous network scalability and performance without incurring the costs that its client/server design would imply. Most open grids today are part of research projects that rely on universities, governments, and large corporations making available supercomputers, mainframes, and large computing structures at little or no cost.

Grid architecture highlights:

Scalable, high-performance network: The grid combines the power of existing datacenters and servers into a single virtual super-server. New dimensions of scalability (by geography or latency) become available.

Massive storage capability: Servers and datacenters in a grid can provide terabytes of storage at no additional cost to the network.

Low bandwidth constraints: The grid servers are generally favorably located near an Internet backbone, so they have an abundant supply of bandwidth to serve clients and to maintain a state of consistency with other grid servers.

Low hardware expenses: The majority of processing and storage takes place within servers contributed to the grid, so little additional resources need to be supplied.

However, typical advantages of a centralized client/server network (visibility, oversight, security, and control) are not transferred to an open grid environment. Since an open grid consists of decentralized servers not necessarily owned by a single entity, there is no possibility of direct management of the grid servers. These servers may be very different machines running a plethora of different operating systems. It is also much harder to monitor in real-time or make changes to the operations or performance of the network. In other words, developing for a grid usually means developing on the lowest common denominator capacity that will be uniform from an ancient mainframe to Linux boxes, which makes a grid architecture a somewhat harsh hosting environment.

Observing practical developments in the last few years, it seems that grids are ideal when there is a large set of uniform, computationally intense tasks (e.g., DNA or math-intensive research), which can be easily distributed across servers, disregarding differences between the specific operational environment of each grid server. (See Figure 2.13.4.)

However, the main shortcoming of the grid architecture for an MMP scenario is the lack of a better than $O(n^2)$ solution. At the end of the day, a grid only provides state synchronization between datacenters and client connection routing to a specific datacenter. After a connection is created, the client interacts with the datacenter in typical C/S fashion. If for whatever geographical or gameplay reasons too many clients need connection to the same datacenter, its processing and bandwidth will immediately grow as $O(n^2)$.

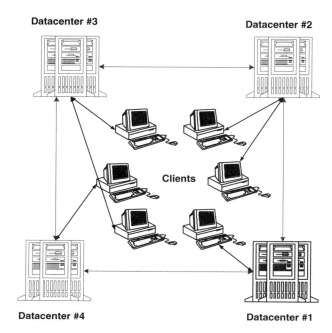

FIGURE 2.13.4   *Grid computing network.*

Undoubtedly, grid systems will offer a compelling alternative when the MMP industry grows beyond the limits of a single datacenter, yet it will be more of a temporary fix rather than a long-term solution.

Distributed Computing

Distributed computing is a close cousin of P2P networks. We can consider distributed computing as a specific case of P2P network, where the primary focus of the network is the computing power of each peer station. Popular file-sharing P2P systems are harnessing bandwidth and storage capacity of each network node and employ real-time communications to form a dynamic distribution topology. Instead, distributed computing is focused on contributing computing power. Real-time connections and network topologies are of little significance, where each station may work on a given computational task for days before making a single connection to the network.

Distributed computing projects have shown great promise for very large-scale computational projects. One of the very impressive achievements for distributed computing is the SETI@Home (*http://setiathome.ssl.berkeley.edu/*) project at Berkley University. The workhorse of the project is a sophisticated custom screensaver utility, which is available for free download to anyone willing to contribute his idle computer time to search for extra-terrestrial intelligence. Screensavers run during idle periods, performing processing by requesting work units from the SETI@Home server, doing math-intensive analysis, and sending calculated results back. At the time of writing, SETI@Home has accumulated over 2 million years of CPU time and performed about 6 billion (that's 6,000,000,000) TeraFLOPs. To put it in perspective, one of the world's fastest supercomputers IBM built for the National Weather Service at a cost of $200 million would have to run for almost for two years nonstop after it reaches its full 100 TeraFLOP/sec potential in 2009 to perform the same number of computations.

Unlike real-time P2P networks, distributed computing offers an interesting solution to the security problem. Given the resource abundance of P2P networks, distributed computing can easily find corrupted data and malfunctioning nodes simply by repeating the same processing a number of times at different nodes. Considering that the majority of nodes will turn out correct results, and it is extremely unlikely that different errors will produce exactly the same erroneous final result, processing defects and data loss become easily noticeable.

Since distributed computing is not a real-time system, it can't be used in the present form for MMP purposes. Yet, this model as showcased by SETI@Home offers many important implications for our needs. For now, let's just note for future use the capacity of distributed computing to harness the vast combined idle resources of user stations and provide good security.

MMP of the Future

Now we know all prevailing large-scale architectures used in enterprise software development today. Using this knowledge, let's put on our MMP developer hats and think what traits our ideal MMP solution should have. We are fully counting that MMPs will break into the mass market, and that our user base will start growing into the millions. What should we prepare for?

1. First, we must achieve acceptable MMP scalability with regard to the $O(n^2)$ problem. Our MMP should accept millions of users and operate normally.
2. Performance should be maintained. Despite a huge number of players sharing the same environment, we must process all data in real-time without losing responsiveness.
3. Security will become an even more critical factor for MMP games, as our user base grows into the millions. Attacks against truly massive MMP worlds can reach the same level of intensity as constant probing for vulnerabilities of popular operating systems. On top of that, we have to admit that item and character auctions have become an integral part of the MMP domain. Traditionally, game security is breached to gain unfair advantage over other players or to ignore rules laid out by the game designers. However, online auctions raise the stakes for MMP worlds even higher. Any security vulnerability automatically becomes a source of commercial gain and an easily repeatable activity that will generate profit to participants. No need to say that the natural human tendency to break rules and explore limits of any system will be magnified one-thousand fold if such activity will

lead to an immediate monetary gain. Therefore, any security vulnerability potentially may become a source of huge exploitation, causing enormous damage to your franchise on all levels.

4. Storing user-created content becomes an interesting challenge in a large-scale MMP world. Let's say you want to give all your players the ability to save a single custom texture of their own face (made with a digital or phone camera) and you are willing to give them 1 MB of memory for this. On a standard C/S solution with a 1-million player base, you will quickly end up needing $10^6 * 10^6$ bytes = 10^{12} = 1000 GB of server-side storage just for that single feature. If you add custom clothing, building, clan war songs, or maybe even player-created lands, your server-storage requirements will simply explode. Here we are getting another $O(n^2)$ function, for slightly different reasons. Each user can contribute a large amount of content initially, and as times goes on he may continue to create and contribute content. Therefore, just like processing and bandwidth, we may want to have our system storage capacity scale with the user base.

5. Controls become an important factor, considering the use of P2P and distributed systems. We must ensure we have access and management rights over each critical part of the system, as well as some means to detect and solve errors. On C/S, we gain that automatically. Less so on a global grid, and there is virtually no direct control in a P2P network.

6. Resilience—the world's ability to withstand catastrophic failures outside of the game world operator's direct control—is key. Overall, resilience is not strictly required (as demonstrated by the *Anarchy Online* and *Shadowbane* launches) for MMP operators, yet highly recommended (as demonstrated by *Anarchy Online* and *Shadowbane* subscription dynamics). Going mass market with MMP games will require quite a different stability of service than what unfortunately came as the historical norm in PC MMP games. It's better to have a system prepared to handle critical failures in parts outside of our direct control, and have the ability to recover from them.

7. Last, although perhaps it should be first, is the cost. How much it will cost us to deploy all the necessary hardware and connectivity resources prior to launch? What will our burn rate be to operate it? Can we operate the service with positive margins?

Let's look at an analysis matrix (Table 2.13.2) to measure all four standard enterprise architectures by these metrics, using the following rough grades:

Poor and high cost: Unacceptable
Average: Acceptable for now, yet there are problems preventing long-term use
Good: Acceptable for long-term use; room for improvement
Excellent and low cost: Best possible approach we can envision at the moment

Table 2.13.2   Analysis of the Four Standard Enterprise Architectures

Architecture	Scalability	Performance	Security	Control	Resilience	Cost
Client/Server	Poor	Poor	Excellent	Excellent	Average	High
P2P	Excellent	Excellent	Poor	Poor	Excellent	Low
Grid	Average	Good	Good	Poor	Average	Low
Distributed Computing	Not real-time	Excellent	Good	Average	Good	Low

As it was easy to predict, C/S and P2P end up almost mirror images of each other, with grid and distributed computing being specific subclasses of their base architectures. However we see there is no clear winner. Each standard architecture has weak points preventing it from long-term use for large-scale MMP needs.

Now it is time to use what we learned and get to the work at hand. Let's design a large-scale MMP architecture that will meet our requirements.

Conclusion

We reviewed all fundamental types of large scale architectures. Client/Server, P2P, Grid and Distributed Computing have their own venerable place in history of computer science, yet all of them fall short of the modern needs of ultimate MMP platform. While we see that different architectures expose various critical features we need, yet no existing architecture provides a complete feature set.

Now its time to use what we learned and get to the work at hand. Lets design a large scale MMP architecture which will meet all our requirements.

References

[Btfl02] The Butterfly Grid, available at *www.butterfly.net*.

[Freenet03] Freenet's Next Generation Routing Protocol, available at *http://freenet. sourceforge.net/index.php?page=ngrouting*.

[Humble04] Humble, Rod, "Inside EverQuest," *Game Developer Magazine*, May 2004.

[Ice04] "The Internet Communications Engine," available at *www.zeroc.com/ice.html*.

[Oaks02] Oaks, Scott; Bernard Traversat; Li Gong, "JXTA in a nutshell," available at *www.jxta.org*.

[OP2P01] Minar, Nelson, "Distributed System Topologies," available at *www. openp2p.com*.

[OP2P02] Gnutella protocol specifications, available at *www.openp2p.com/topics/p2p/ gnutella/*.

[Oren04] Oren, Tim, "Joel on APIs: A Historical Perspective," available online at *http://due-diligence.typepad.com/blog/2004/06/joel_on_apis_a_.html.*

[P2P01] *Peer-To-Peer: Harnessing the Power of Disrupting Technologies,* O'Reilly, 2001.

[Zona02] Zona Inc., Terazona: Zona application framework whitepaper, available at *www.zona.net/whitepaper/Zonawhitepaper.pdf.*

2.14

The Quest for Holy Scale — Part 2: P2P Continuum

Max Skibinsky — HiveMind, Inc.

thequest@h-mind.com

The following is the result of the author's personal research from 1994 to 2002. Some ideas can be traced to very early MUD-inspired experiments. Others are derived from applying lessons from Napster, KaZaa, SETI@Home, and many other incredible innovations that have happened during the last decade in computing.

Before proceeding further, let's make an important disclaimer. The following findings are results of the author's theoretical research, mathematical modeling, and prototyping. However, knowing the track record of the correlation between academic research and practical large-scale deployments makes the author extremely cautious in recommending this as an undisputable guide for practical implementation. Rather, the author would prefer to view this as a basic concept model, a coherent collection of ideas for further brainstorming. If for any reason you see a discrepancy between practical results and assumptions used in this paper, by no means feel constrained by them. The P2P Continuum architecture is deliberately made from fairly independent modules, so you are free to discard the ones that do not meet your criteria, and retain the others.

P2P Continuum is a platform framework that strives to retain the best features of client/server, P2P, grid, and distributed computing in a manner ideal for large-scale MMP deployment. P2P Continuum achieves this by forming a hierarchical and secure P2P network with centralized oversight that distributes the majority of processing, bandwidth, and storage requirements across the devices employed by the interacting users.

If anything is certain, it is that P2P and distributed computing architectures offer such amazing degrees of flexibility and customization that it will come as no surprise that there will be many possible P2P architectures that can be very successful in serving MMP needs.

Continuum Concepts

Before formulating the technical specifications of the P2P Continuum, let's establish some common concepts.

The Holy Trinity

Hopefully, readers have noticed many similarities between existing large-scale architectures. In one form or another, an architecture has just three basic responsibilities:

- Provide connectivity between all system components (clients and servers)
- Process system from current state to the next
- Retrieve data required for processing and store results of processing

From this perspective, it is easy to see that P2P file-sharing networks are merging bandwidth and storage capacity of each station into a single network. SETI@Home, however, is dependent only on stations' processing power.

The P2P Continuum goal is to merge distributed bandwidth, processing, and storage into one seamless and secure computing infrastructure (see Figure 2.14.1).

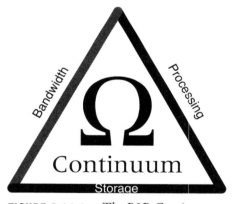

FIGURE 2.14.1   *The P2P Continuum.*

Significant Changes

Let's revisit our dramatic encounter in a high fantasy genre depicted in Figure 2.14.2.

What are the possible outcomes of a given encounter? Obviously, there are roughly three possibilities. Adventurers may win, slay the monster, and cause some sort of persistent data change (monster is gone, its treasure is distributed into the adventurers' inventory, adventurers gain experience, monster lair marked as "abandoned," etc.). Alternatively, the monster may slay the adventurers and cause an opposing set of changes (adventurers' items added to monster lair, adventurers teleported back or

FIGURE 2.14.2   *Fantasy Land.*

marked as "dead," etc.). Finally, there is a possibility that either the adventurers or the monster, after noticing the situation is not proceeding according to plan, will successfully disengage from the encounter, leaving no noticeable data changes short of some health and ammunition expenses.

If we analyze network traffic in the middle of such an encounter, the complexity of the data exchange will give very little indication that the cumulative data changes can be in fact so simple. Adventurers and monsters will move around, use items, cast spells, get harmed and get healed, lose and regenerate mana, and so on. In fact, we can easily model a situation with infinite consumption of bandwidth and processing power with a complete net zero of resulting data changes. Imagine the monster hurting a character for X damage every round, with the character healing himself for X health the following round and regaining the used mana.

Now things are getting pretty interesting. If we transmit all such packets back and forth to the server in typical C/S architecture, this is in fact a complete waste of server resources. The server should be concerned only with data changes it needs to persist in the server database. (There is an obvious security consideration that any data from the client station can't be trusted and must be verified from multiple independent sources. We review this and other security aspects later).

Let's split the traditional C/S data stream into two categories:

Significant changes: Cumulative state changes that have noticeable long-term or worldwide consequences. Significant changes are not a specific action or result; rather, they provide an integrated total of a whole series of actions. If the net result of a given action set is zero, they simply don't generate a significant change. Typical examples of significant changes would involve character inventory, gain of experience, or actions leading to a persistent world state change. Significant changes are rare in the general case, with world actors typically causing just one set of significant changes in a 15- to 30-minute period.

Real-time changes: Required to maintain local state consistency and represent character actions and the immediate environment response to them. That would be common character movements and gameplay actions.

Real-time changes consume orders of magnitude more bandwidth than resulting significant changes do. Obviously, if we somehow unload the RT stream from the server and update the server only with significant changes, we will greatly improve the scalability and performance of our datacenter.

Immediate Action/Reaction Manifold

Attentive readers undoubtedly noticed a certain weakness in the author's reasoning during the discussion of P2P architecture. The author boldly stated that P2P solves the $O(n^2)$ scalability problem, reasoning that in a P2P network each player brings in his own resources as a server as well. Simple numerical modeling will easily show the author's nefarious intent to mislead the naïve. As we know, an n player scene generates $n*(n+1)$ update packets and processing context. Switching to a P2P architecture brings in n servers to the scene, thus making bandwidth/processing scalability a function. Unfortunately, this $O(n)$ function now describes scalability of a *client* station, which unlike a datacenter won't grow as needed. Therefore, as soon as the service load of $n+1$ grows above resources of a given station, even the P2P architecture won't be able to scale.

To address this, let's introduce the concept of an *immediate action/reaction manifold*. In the general case, the majority of actions in MMP games are limited to a certain object set they can affect, and actions taking place closer to a player are likely to play higher importance than actions taking place farther away. Sword swings can affect in real-time only a small radius of nearby actors, while archer fire will have longer reach and a narrow action tunnel (see Figure 2.14.3).

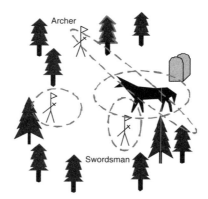

FIGURE 2.14.3   *The players' immediate action areas.*

Realistically, players can react to only so many evolving changes in their immediate surroundings. It will be pointless to give them a real-time data feed for every object included on the visual horizon. For this purpose, let's call the set of objects that the player may affect with his actions in real-time the *player action manifold*, and call all other players and objects that may (in real-time) affect a given player's *reaction manifold*. In our example, the Monster is within the Archer's action manifold, while the Archer is within the Monster's reaction manifold. In other words, these sets of objects are the ones that are likely to require immediate player consideration or reaction. Nearby opponents swinging a sword or faraway archers bending the bow in the player's direction will be part of the given player's manifold. Yet any number of swordsmen 20 feet away and archers not targeting a given player won't be part of his manifold unless they move or change orientation.

This concept offers a way to provide a reliable workaround for high-density crowds in a P2P architecture. If a given crowd grows larger and larger, so $n+1$ updates start to overwhelm player stations, first we will limit real-time update streams only to objects in the player's action and reaction sets. If the crowd will grow even larger, thus increasing its density, we will use prioritization logic on the given manifolds, which will choose the most important updates a player must receive in the real-time channel, while keeping the rest of world changes to the non-real-time cumulative significant updates channel. Practically, this will be the equivalent of splitting a very large crowd into an ever-increasing number of smaller subcrowds. By using a logical set of objects, we can govern this split by game design priorities of individual action/item combinations. Considering that modern player stations can reliably participate/host a multiplayer game with about 32 participants, even if a the crowd will grow to infinity, our architecture will stabilize into an ever-increasing number of overlapping action-manifolds, each consisting of at most 30–50 actors in a given moment in time. Undoubtedly, in such over-crowded conditions, a player won't enjoy a full real-time update of every object in the scene, yet he will still have an acceptable player experience offering him the most critical information about the immediate gameplay situation. Significant non-real-time updates will keep bringing the rest of the player horizon up to speed with a few minutes' delay.

Attentive readers may ask at this point, "but why can't we use this very approach for C/S and dramatically improve our server scalability?" Indeed, this approach can be used to distribute load on a server cluster. However, as we pointed out in the very beginning, one of the C/S bottlenecks is the fat line coming to the datacenter. Even if server/cluster is distributed by action/reaction manifolds, all packets have to arrive from clients to a single router, and update packets have to be sent back from a central location. Bandwidth load on the C/S pipe will be the same $O(n^2)$. What we are really getting from P2P architecture is not the ability to avoid $O(n^2)$ growth, which is unavoidable. Rather, it gives us the ability to uniformly spread out our bandwidth needs through an ever-increasing set of P2P connections in ever-increasing numbers of $O(n^2)$ zones. Action/reaction manifolds help us prioritize most important update packets when $O(n^2)/n$ becomes higher than a given station's bandwidth capacity.

P2P Subserver

By the definition of a P2P network, each station will perform the role of client and server. The client role is easy to understand since it is similar to the traditional C/S client of the MMP world. Clients receive server updates, display corresponding state changes on the game client, receive player input commands, and transmit them to the server. Yet, what would be the role of a server in a P2P environment?

We will define a P2P subserver as a completely isolated component of a client station that behaves and operates autonomously from the view of the client. The player MMP software license agreement will require the contribution of certain storage and processing budget for network tasks by the player station. The P2P subserver will use these storage and processing resources when the software is running, and will perform a number of different roles within the network. For example, the processing role would consist of receiving a set of world objects, processing them, and accepting client connections to the server in the typical C/S manner. We will discuss other sub-server roles later. For now, let's just note one other important role besides processing: routing, controlling, and governing connections of underling P2P subservers.

Taking our cue from SETI@Home, we should also include the P2P subserver packaged as a screensaver that any player may want to run when his computer is idle, giving him informative updates about current world events as content in the screensaver.

Security Considerations

Probably the hardest problem for practical MMP P2P solutions will be establishing full network security. Since P2P subservers will reside on client stations, it opens a possibility of many various security attacks on subserver data, processing, integrating, and transmission.

To establish the strongest possible security, we should approach the problem from two independent directions. The first approach should be *social*, making it meaningless for each member of the MMP world to violate world security. Nonetheless, some people will do so anyway. To address that, let's make it *technologically* impossible to gain anything from such security attacks.

First, let's review *social* techniques we should use:

Players should never process any data related directly to themselves or entities in which they may have interests.   P2P Continuum should use current player location, guild, or kingdom affiliation to insure he is always processing data that has absolutely nothing to do with his current gameplay situation. Considering that the world is much larger than the area of interest of a given player, this is a fairly easy requirement to meet. Malicious players still will have the ability to hamper gameplay of other people, yet this removes their potential to benefit from such activity.

Players should not be able to determine what data his P2P subserver processes or stores. Similar to a distributed computing approach, we can have P2P subservers serve the gameplay situation in a real-time manner, yet do a trailing non-real-time consistency check of dataset processing. If the same dataset from a given P2P subserver shows discrepancies relative to what is shown when the data is processed by different P2P subservers shortly afterwards, we know the original P2P subserver is suspect.

Collect trust. Retaining a peer track record will go a long way to establishing peer trustworthiness. Statistically, hackers and exploiters represent a small percentage of the gaming population, and the challenge consists of detecting them early and not relegating any important tasks to such suspect stations. The combination of repeatable processing, mutual crosschecks, and building a trust ranking will allow us to process data only on reliable P2P subservers as well as not assigning Continuum critical roles to yet unproven nodes.

Dynamic topology. Something can and will go wrong. No matter how hard we try at the design stage, security holes will be found sooner or later. To limit the potential damage from such attacks, P2P subservers should routinely (e.g., every hour) replace datasets for which they are responsible and switch to different peers for mutual crosschecks. Therefore, if an attack is successful, the attacker will gain access to inconsistent and constantly changing data fragments rather than a persistent location he may exploit.

Processing Cluster

As it becomes clear from security considerations, we cannot delegate any particular processing to a single P2P subserver on an ongoing basis. However, a group of subservers may form a fairly consistent processing entity, especially if such groups are formed and reformed dynamically. Let's call such group a Processing Cluster (see Figure 2.14.4).

P2P Clustering gives us many impressive advantages:

Consistency monitoring: Every result will be crosschecked by peer subservers on a continuous basis.

Network resilience: Since each client now receives multiple copies of update streams (which should be equivalent unless the cluster is under security attack), it may simply use the first one received for the game client update. Furthermore, if connectivity problems eliminate half of the existing connections, none of the clients will notice any gameplay interruptions while the Continuum routing governing this cluster will immediately search for replacements.

Improved latency: Since it's possible to optimize processing clusters based on Internet location of clients they are currently serving, it will lead to noticeable reduction in round-trip latency for each client. Instead of having a round trip to a datacenter halfway across the country, Continuum routing should pick up clustering subservers unrelated in gameplay and located in the local Internet vicinity.

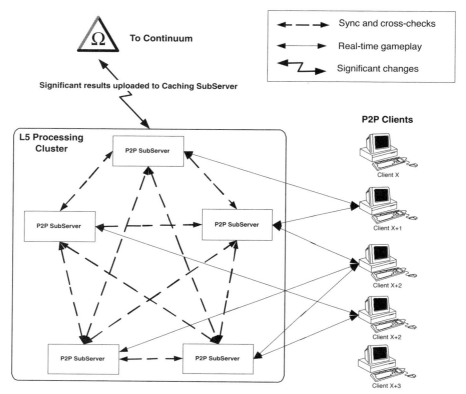

FIGURE 2.14.4 *P2P Processing Cluster.*

P2P Authority

The P2P subserver and cluster will be the workhorse of P2P Continuum, yet what will provide the "big picture" of our network? Unlike file-sharing networks, we do have a well-defined state of the whole world, and each P2P subserver will see only a small part of that whole.

To this purpose, let's introduce P2P Authority. P2P Authority, located in our datacenter, will serve a role similar to the main MMP server in a standard C/S deployment. The difference will be that the P2P Authority will not concern itself with real-time changes, or even immediate significant changes. Rather, it will collect and serve only a small set of system-critical data and maintain database integrity with the Continuum URLs of a full world data. P2P Authority will not try to keep a full copy of the current world state (as we know from user content consideration, it will grow faster than we can add datacenter capacity), yet it will know which P2P subserver is responsible for holding each piece of data or performing a specific duty. Considering each P2P subserver availability as unreliable, the P2P Authority should strive to maintain at least three duplicates of everything, and locally cache data or Continuum duties in case of a resource shortfall. P2P Authority will also become the control center for our network, moving away from a fully decentralized and therefore uncontrollable autonomous P2P network.

Based on each node's Internet topology, trust level, performance, and history, the P2P Authority assigns present P2P subservers into hierarchy in various roles. Each subserver entering the Continuum is assigned to be managed by at least three other subservers with routing authority (see Figure 2.14.5).

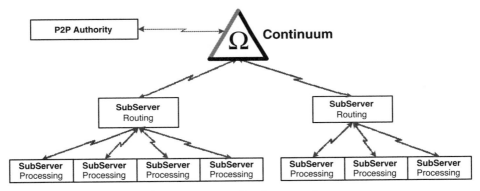

FIGURE 2.14.5   *P2P Authority manages Continuum subservers.*

P2P Continuum Stack

Now, let's turn our attention to more technical details of the P2P Continuum implementation. First, let's establish general layers of the P2P Continuum technology stack. As usual, we will consider each layer of the stack, dependent only on interfaces of underlying layers and exposing clean higher level interfaces to the layer above (see Figure 2.14.6).

Infrastructure

Infrastructure is the low-level plumbing of the P2P Continuum. The infrastructure layer governs how players receive and install the software by downloading a small bootstrapping installer from the P2P Authority datacenter and file sharing a full installation from Storage nodes. The infrastructure layer checks for client updates and then runs the game client and a local instance of P2P subserver. The infrastructure provides access to resources contributed to the Continuum by the local station.

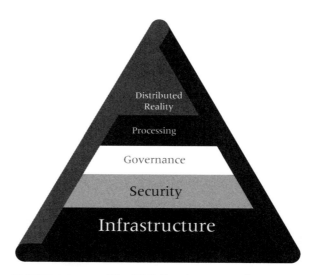

FIGURE 2.14.6   *The P2P Continuum stack.*

Security

Now, let us review the *technical* means of a defense from security attacks. P2P Continuum security must solve the challenge of securing the same holy trinity: bandwidth, processing, and storage.

Thankfully, Public Key Encryption (PKE) will allow us to establish a pretty good security for all three aspects of our network. You can refer to [Schneier95] for a detailed description of PKE, but for our needs, let's just notice the most important practical consequences of PKE:

- Any Continuum station could create two specific strings called a private and public key pair. The private key is never transmitted across the network. The public key is made available to everyone on the network.
- Any set of data can be encrypted (albeit slowly) with either of these keys, when using public domain algorithms,
- The only computationally feasible way to decrypt such data will require possession of the other key.
- Then we can establish two secure operations:
  - Reliable secure data authoring (signing)
  - Reliable secure data transmission and delivery

Let's suppose we have a P2P Authority that is about to place a new client software update onto the network. Other P2P subservers will receive a packet with a request to update their software—yet how can they know that these orders in fact came from the P2P Authority and not from a hacker directing them to a URL with a corrupted version? To solve this, the P2P Authority can encrypt the request and update file with its private key. Since all stations know the P2P Authority public key (and if they don't, they can grab it with a single request from a well-known URL since it's not a secret), they can decrypt the update packet and the file with the update. Hackers have no way to gain possession of the P2P Authority private key short of breaking into the P2P Authority datacenter, in which case, the network will already be fully compromised. A private key is the only way to create encrypted data that can be unlocked with the public key. Practically, the full dataset is not signed; rather, only a small digest of it is signed. Client stations may create their own data digest and compare it with the decrypted digest to determine if this data is indeed authored by the P2P Authority.

The opposite process is used when the client wants to send some data securely; for example, to his managing P2P subserver waiting for significant world updates. In this case, the P2P subserver in charge of updating a higher level node will encrypt a set of significant world changes with the managing node's public key. Since no one else possesses the private key to this data, only the managing node will be able to decrypt world changes transmitted from the client, even if the client had to travel many caching or routing subservers in the network before reaching his destination.

It should be noted that there will be as many private-public key pairs in the system as there are nodes. One node will never transmit its private key to the other node, although each node will expose its public key. Private keys will allow secure delivery to a given node and authentication of results originating from a given node. For example, subserver S1 wants to send data D to subserver S2, yet for whatever reason can't reach it directly and wants to cache data on Caching subserver C until such time S2 becomes available. S1 will sign and encrypt data for S2 with its public key, thereby generating publicKeyS2(D), and then will encrypt it for C, generating publicKeyC(publicKeyS2(D)) in an escrow scheme. Only C can decrypt the outer layer to get publicKeyS2(D) data, and it can authenticate with publicKeyS1 that it was actually authored by S1 node. But C doesn't have privateKeyS2, so the data D itself is inaccessible for C. When S2 gets publicKeyS2(D) from C, it can decrypt it with the private key and verify the S1 signature. This only establishes that the data is authored by the S1 station; it doesn't mean the data itself is trustworthy.

To be completely correct, we must note that PKE is too slow for a real-time communication channel. Standard practice will be to use PKE to securely exchange the symmetric block cipher keys between communication nodes, and then use very fast symmetric encryption. All of the previous scenarios remain true, with the difference that there will be one more additional layer of symmetric encryption. In short, remember that securely storing a secret private key in a node insures it is the only node that can author data signed by this key. By owning public keys of various other nodes, you can create a data packet that can be decrypted only by a destination node.

Now, let's apply PKE to our needs:

Bandwidth security: Any communications happening between the P2P Authority, P2P subservers, and client agents will be encrypted with appropriate PKE and symmetric keys to establish data authenticity and make packet sniffing and man-in-the-middle attacks impossible.

Processing security: Any executable code and execution environment should be signed by the P2P authority, with the Infrastructure layer reporting client executable files and memory space hash sums upon entry into the P2P Continuum. That still doesn't offer 100% security, since correct hash sum values and challenge/response codes could be reverse engineered on the client side, yet it makes it much harder to tamper with system executables.

Storage security: All files and persistent datasets should be digitally signed with the keys of stations authorized to create such data. This allows us to securely store and propagate any amount of files and data across the Continuum. Every client should check for appropriate data signatures before using any files/data received from the Continuum.

Of the three, we only fail to guarantee processing security, since there is no reliable way to prevent client-side code tampering. However, this is exactly the purpose for which we introduced the concept of the P2P Cluster. Each cluster will be configured to perform a trailing comparison of results emitted by other members of the cluster by data packet reflection from clients. If any member of a P2P Cluster is compromised, his results will vary from other uncompromised stations. When other stations detect repeatable inconsistency, they will report the P2P subserver in question to the P2P Authority or delegated routing node, and a new processing cluster will be formed. Compromised stations will be ejected from the Continuum (see Figure 2.14.7).

Governance

After secure communication, processing, and storage are established in a network, we must consider how it should be governed.

Centralized P2P networks, such as the topologies in [OP2P01], can be set up by making a central node (which is the P2P Authority in our case) to manage all peers. However, this solution is not truly scalable since it will require more and more resources from our datacenter with increasing numbers of remote nodes. Instead, let's postulate that the P2P Authority will be the master source of trust and control in the system (provable by possession of the master set of private keys), which will delegate its authority to top-level, most-trusted, and performance-reliable subservers. These subservers in turn will delegate authority and control to underlying subservers, thus creating a trust-based hierarchy of control. Thus, the P2P Continuum will be organized as a trust reliability hierarchy with the P2P Authority at the top. The job of this hierarchy will be to provide a dynamic network topology of subservers and clusters, dynamically route client stations to appropriate processing clusters, and cache and store significant results from gameplay processing of each cluster.

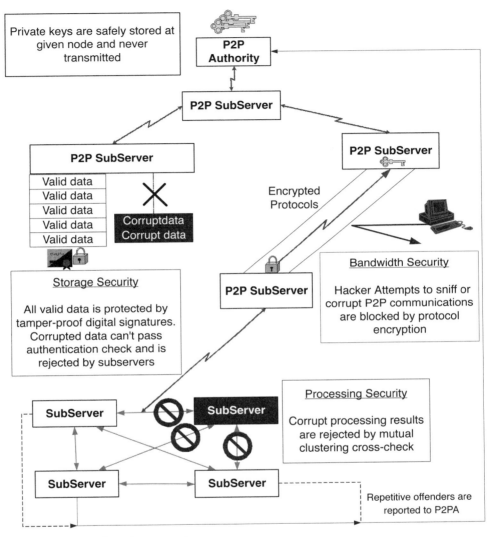

FIGURE 2.14.7   *Security protections.*

For this hierarchy to work, we must now formalize the different roles subservers may perform in this hierarchy. Such roles can be categorized as:

Discovery: Find other subservers with specific roles within the network and maintain a directory of available subservers.

Routing: Form processing clusters from available processing subservers and direct clients to clusters responsible for given world areas.

Processing: Maintain a set of game state objects and process them according to current rules.

Caching: Short-term storage of significant changes for propagation across the P2P Continuum hierarchy.

Storage: Long-term storage and file sharing, such as user-created content or large sets of persistent world object states.

Multicasting: Transmit state changes to large parts of the network.

Authentication: Use security protocols to establish client control rights over given objects and verify trust and intermediary authenticity of given data.

Depending on hardware specifics and idle capacities of a given player station, the hierarchy should assign different roles and duties to given P2P subservers. One may think about subserver roles as seven independent server-side components living under the same P2P subserver process. Obviously, it would be of little sense to turn on a Storage component on a user station with almost no free hard drive space, or make a user station with low memory a processing node. Therefore, each P2P subserver in the hierarchy will perform only a specific subset of services that are most efficient for a given configuration.

One perspective on the P2P Continuum hierarchy is to think of it as extremely real-time sensitive, unreliable and redundant at low level, and non-real-time, cumulative, reliable, and less redundant on higher levels. Each subserver is tracked from its first day in the P2P Continuum for its security and reliability, and the hierarchy will filter upward the most reliable, powerful, and trustworthy nodes. World operators may choose (and probably should) to reward players of such stations with in-game bonuses and reduced membership fees (see Figure 2.14.8).

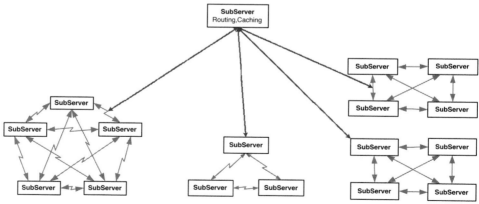

FIGURE 2.14.8   *P2P Continuum hierarchy.*

Governance: Routing Authority

Routing subservers hold a special place among all possible roles of the P2P subservers since their role is critical for the real-time functioning of the P2P continuum. Routing nodes will dynamically form processing clusters from available subservers to deliver optimal processing and networking performance. Subservers and clusters are rotated by authority subservers on a continual basis: first, due to the need of regular reshuffling for security reasons; and second, to optimize each cluster's network latency with regard to clients it is currently serving (see Figure 2.14.9).

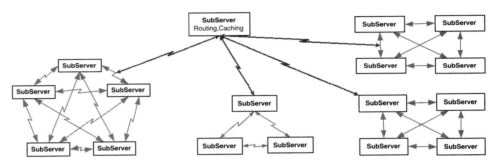

FIGURE 2.14.9   *Routing node controls clusters.*

Processing

In fact, we already covered much of the processing layer, since it will be nothing else than interfaces to form, run, and manage P2P clusters. A typical cluster life cycle may look like the following:

1. Routing subserver determines the need to form a new cluster. For example, players approach a previously unserved part of the world, or due to regular cluster rotation.
2. Routing subserver uses the discovery subserver to locate available processing subservers with given characteristics (processing power and Internet topology location).
3. Routing subserver uses the discovery subserver to locate storage and caching URLs of nodes currently holding required world state.
4. Routing subserver commands select processing subserver to form the cluster and load up world state from given URLs.

5. Cluster forms and compiles stored data and cached significant changes into single world area state. Cluster reports to discovery nodes that it now governs given world area.

6. After cluster reports readiness, subserver sends new cluster URL to client stations of players approaching given world area.

7. Players establish gameplay connection with given cluster.

8. Cluster processes game state, updates client station subscribers of object state changes, and receives player input. Cluster may use discovery and storage nodes to load up additional world information as needed.

9. Cluster reports cumulative significant changes to at least three Caching nodes.

10. Cluster is disbanded if players leave or by routing subserver request.

11. As an optimization parameter in the processing layer, we will have the option to form processing clusters with few or many subservers. Depending on the world area load and population, we may opt to form clusters of different power.

Distributed Reality

In the final layer, we are going to assume that the world size is significantly larger than the sum of all observable area by currently active players. This choice borders on game design decisions, yet so far, it would be true for all existing MMP games. After all, there won't be much interest to play in a constantly overpopulated world.

With such an assumption, we can use an approach rooted in solipsism philosophy that if something is not observable it doesn't currently exist. In our Continuum, if a tree falls in the woods, and nobody is there to hear it, the aforementioned tree would have never been loaded in server memory in the first place, never processed, and therefore never really fell over.

Let's call the superset of all action and reaction object manifolds a reality bubble. For example, all entities participating in a castle siege or large-scale army battle will be part of the same reality bubble. Entities that can't affect in real-time entities belonging to any given bubble by definition will belong to another bubble. In mathematical terms, a reality bubble will be a group acting only onto itself. Therefore, the smallest bubble will be a single actor. When two actors approach each other's action/reaction manifolds, their reality bubbles join.

We will process the reality of our world by tracking reality bubbles based on player activities, and assigning reality bubbles to P2P processing clusters for real-time game play. Depending on the number of players in a given area, complexity of interactions and sensitivity to real-time updates, clusters of different power and subserver count should be formed. For example, town crafting areas and bazaars will obviously be less demanding than massive castle sieges (see Figure 2.14.10).

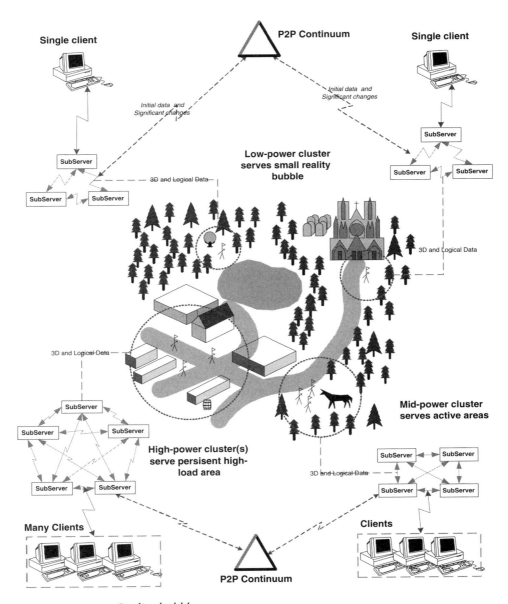

FIGURE 2.14.10   *Reality bubbles.*

Conclusion

The author hopes the reader now has a better grasp on the unique challenges of building a truly scalable P2P platform for large MMP games (see Figure 2.14.11). Unquestionably, this article covers only the high-level topic in very broad strokes, with much detailed work still outstanding. Certain aspects are currently further researched by the author, and some have not yet been touched by analytical thought. Readers should keep in mind that as any high-level analysis, the author used a somewhat cavalier approach to a number of fundamental implementation issues. Even the simple aspect of making subserver-subserver or subserver-client connections will require an additional peer-reflection sublayer if both communicants are located behind firewalls. NAT will also require special handling by the Infrastructure layer. Splitting a CPU budget between client-side middleware (3D, physics) and subserver middleware (AI, logic) will require nontrivial heuristics depending on current gameplay and the Continuum hierarchy configuration.

The P2P Continuum approach shouldn't be considered to live in a self-contained vacuum, related only to MMP or gaming technologies. Just the opposite, the author believes there are already a number of technologies maturing in enterprise space that may find many direct uses in various places of the Continuum stack. JXTA [Oaks02] already offers many important insights on implementation strategy for Discovery, Routing, and Multicasting subserver roles. Certain properties of the Freenet project [Freenet03] could be used by Caching and Discovery nodes for fast location of world data and responsible clusters. Gnutella [OP2P02], FastTrack, and Overnet provide a virtually complete model for a file-sharing-based Storage subserver. Web Services [MS00] are a natural choice to expose subserver services to each other and to implement a loosely coupled framework to allow further expansions of Continuum functionality.

References

[Btfl02] The Butterfly Grid, available at *www.butterfly.net*.

[Freenet03] Freenet's Next Generation Routing Protocol, available at *http://freenet. sourceforge.net/index.php?page=ngrouting*.

[Ice04] "The Internet Communications Engine," available at *www.zeroc.com/ice.html*.

[Lang84] Lang, Serge, "Algebra," 3rd Edition. Springer-Verlag, 2002.

[MS00] Web Services, available at *http://msdn.microsoft.com/webservices/*.

[Oaks02] Oaks, Scott; Bernard Traversat; Li Gong, *JXTA in a nutshell,* O'Reilly, 2002.

[OP2P01] Nelson, Minar, "Distributed System Topologies," available at *www. openp2p.com*.

[OP2P02] Gnutella protocol specifications available at *www.openp2p.com/topics/ p2p/gnutella/*.

[P2P01] Peer-To-Peer: Harnessing the Power of Disrupting Technologies, O'Reilly 2001.

[Schneier95] Schneier, Bruce, *Applied Cryptography: Protocols, Algorithms, and Source Code in C,* Second Edition, John Wiley and Sons, Inc., 1995.

[Zona02] Zona Inc., Terazona: Zona application framework whitepaper, available at *www.zona.net/whitepaper/Zonawhitepaper.pdf*.

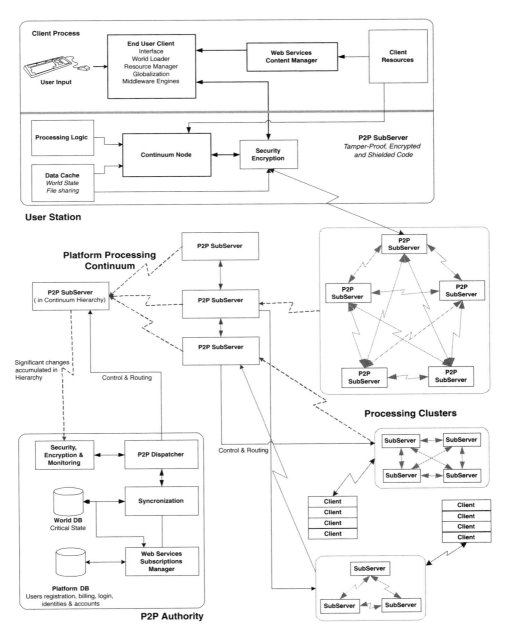

FIGURE 2.14.11 *Vision of P2P Continuum in action.*

2.15

Optimization Techniques for Rendering Massive Quantities of Mesh Deformed Characters in Real-Time

John W. Ratcliff—Ageia Technologies, Inc.

jratcliff@infiniplex.net

Most massively multiplayer online games require the ability to render many on-screen characters simultaneously, whether these are player avatars or nonplayer AI entities. These characters typically are composed of a complex shader, applied to a deformed mesh, and linked to a hierarchical skeleton, which is animated by a collection of artist-generated blended poses. While rendering anywhere from one to ten characters in real-time on modern hardware is fairly straightforward, any attempt to extend this to dozens, if not hundreds, of simultaneous characters will quickly bring any 3D engine to its knees.

This article presents a variety of techniques that allow you to render as many as 100 deformed characters with only a single call to DrawPrimitive. There is no single magic bullet solution; instead, many varied strategies are employed that impact every part of the tools chain and the 3D engine to prevent bottlenecks from occurring.

Mesh LOD (Level of Detail)

Reducing the geometric complexity of your character meshes at a distance is the most obvious optimization technique available. Unfortunately, sometimes people think it's the only method available or required. Mesh LOD is simply the first in a long series of techniques that are required to achieve the ultimate goal of rendering as many as 100 characters with a single draw call.

Mesh LOD is a widely documented technique where triangles are reduced on a character mesh by collapsing edges that are near coplanar. Mesh LOD plug-ins are available with most 3D authoring packages and are a built-in feature of DirectX called "progressive meshes." Many of these implementations are based on the work of Microsoft research fellow, Hugh Hoppes.

When you decide how many LODs your game needs, there are many factors to consider. Is your game primarily first person or third person? How close can the camera get to an object and how far away? How large are your characters? How much of an LOD "pop" are you willing to live with?

There has been a lot of research and development in the industry on the topic of real-time LOD generation. These techniques work fairly well, but, unfortunately, they solve only one problem: they reduce the geometric detail of the object only. What they cannot do is completely remap all of the UV channels to a different texture map or apply an entirely new skeleton to the object. As you will read later, these are key optimization techniques required to reach our goal. For this reason, mesh LODs need to be created manually by your artists. That is not to say the artist cannot use an automatic mesh reduction tool to assist in creating these LODs, but he will need to tweak each by hand afterward.

It may still be viable to use automatic mesh reduction techniques to smooth the transition between levels of detail. Additionally, automatic reduction of skeletons is feasible to some extent by removing leaf nodes (fingers, toes, and facial features) algorithmically.

The number of LODs required for a character in a game would typically be anywhere from three to six models. One of the most critical aspects of LOD is not just how to reduce geometric complexity for things very far away, it is also to eliminate extreme complexity when things are very close to the camera. In massively multiplayer online games, there is a general trend toward customization of your character, including detailed facial expressions and hand gestures. To accomplish this, character models often have many bones and a lot of geometric complexity. This is all great, of course, but you have to ask yourself, "at what distance do I need to see this detail and when I can I throw it away?" It turns out that the distance you can pull the camera back and start dropping subtleties like finger bones is really quite close indeed. Just a couple of meters and you can eliminate a lot of detail that is really only relevant when the camera is zoomed way up close on someone's face. The point here is that you should never have more detail than you need at any particular camera distance.

You will need to provide a very important tool to your artists that lets them tweak the LOD curve on a character-by-character basis, and preview these settings in the engine in real-time. It might be possible to make a first-guess approximation of the distances for each mesh by examining the size of the object in world space, but it is still important to allow the artists and designers to tweak these for finer control.

You should also allow the game engine to be able to lock a character to a specific LOD to make sure there are no artifacts. It can be somewhat amusing to play a game with your character locked at the last and final LOD; a stick figure running around with a rocket launcher is always worth a laugh.

This raises another issue of relative size. If a character is so far off in the distance that he is little more than a couple of pixels tall on the screen, it's doubtful you need to render him in much detail, and chances are you don't need to be rendering the 20 pieces of flair he has attached to his character. The bottom line is, don't process, render, cogitate, or waste any CPU for things you cannot practically see. On more than one occasion, we have seen developers consume enormous amounts of CPU computing the graphics characteristics for objects that were not even on the screen at the time.

Skeleton LOD (or Why Your Artists Are Going to Hate You)

This is the real reason you had your artists create all of those Mesh LODs to begin with. Modern 3D accelerators can handle an enormous amount of polygon density. However, if you want to have hundreds of objects on screen, the power of multiplication kicks in and that "few-hundred triangle LOD" can explode quickly when multiplied times hundreds if not thousands of objects in the scene.

Once you start spending time in a performance monitor, such as Vtune, you are quickly going to find yourself CPU bound just dealing with the thousands of bones all of those skeletal models represent. It is not enough to simply reduce the geometric complexity of an object; you *must* reduce the complexity of the skeleton. If your character has emotes, facial expressions, and hand gestures with articulated fingers, you might easily see as many as 100 bones in your base skeleton. Therefore, even if you reduce the mesh complexity to 50 triangles at the last LOD, you are not going to have much success if you are still animating, blending, and processing 100 bone skeletons for each model.

What this means is that for each mesh LOD your artist created, he must reassign the bone weightings to each, touching fewer and fewer bones each time. In this fashion, after the first or second LOD, most of the bones in the face and fingers should have been removed, and at the final LOD, only a small number of transforms should be touched to make your stick figure walk. Surprisingly, even if this stick figure is only a couple of pixels tall on the screen at distance, that tiny bit of motion goes a long way toward convincing your eye that it is physically correct.

For skeletal objects that are not mesh deformed—for example, vehicles, weapons, or other complex articulated objects—we recommend completely rebuilding entirely new skeletons for individual mesh levels of detail. The weapon in your game with the spinning chambers, rotating gizmos, and other complex machinery may look very cool up close and personal, but you certainly don't want to be processing all those bones when the same weapon is 50 meters off in the distance.

Texture and Shader LOD

Artists love shaders. They are shiny and sparkly and make your eyes happy. The problem is they are also quite expensive. In fact, you can make all of the optimizations already described and it will be for naught if each of your characters uses a different customized shader. Therefore, the lesson to be learned is that you can have all of the custom shaders you want on characters at your highest level of detail, but as soon as things get away from the camera at all, you desperately need to switch to a unified system.

Ultimately, the goal is to render these hypothetical 100 characters in a single draw call. Therefore, by definition, all of these characters must share the same texture assets and the same shader, since either represents a state change requiring a unique draw call. Needless to say, this is not an easy thing to do.

Due to the nature of first-person perspective rendering, the detail level you need for a texture asset drops dramatically at a very rapid pace as it gets further off into the distance. As a sanity check, during testing and preview, you can even store "warning" colors in the mipmap chain of the textures just to prevent artists from over describing their assets. By default, modern graphics processor units (GPUs) will kick in the texture mipmap chain at a ridiculously aggressive rate. This is done to speed up the overall throughput and, in fact, if you change the mipmap bias on any 3D graphics card you can generally see a radical drop in frame rate.

For this reason, you will often find that artists are creating textures that are hardly ever visible at their highest mipmap level. To prevent this from occurring, your meshes need to be re-texture mapped as they go through progressive mesh levels of detail.

Now, if you thought your artists hated you for rebuilding all of the skeletons, they are really going to hate you if you make them reapply UV mapping to every single mesh LOD in the game! Fortunately, this task can be automated as part of the tools chain. Your artists can go ahead and make their awesome high-resolution skins for each of the characters in the game. Then, it is your job to make sure no one ever gets to actually see them unless the camera is two centimeters from the character's face.

As part of your tools pipeline you will need to create a module that will automatically merge skins from multiple character models into single large texture sheets. These unified textures should be organized based on how you predict character models will be grouped on the screen. Therefore, if, for example, there are two creatures that would hardly ever be seen at the same time, you wouldn't group their skins together. However, character models that are frequently seen side by side should share texture assets as they move through successive mesh levels of detail.

Another tool you can make available to your artists is one that automatically generates skins for characters. In the suite of tools available in Granny, provided by Rad Game Tools (*www.radgametools.com*), is a plug-in called "Granny Cast." This plug-in allows artists to assign many unique textures to all parts of a character. Then, as a post-processing step, it will unify all of those textures onto a single large decal and reassign the UV mapping on the mesh at the same time.

The ultimate goal of this is so that when you get to your final LOD, there should be a single massive texture sheet containing tiny little thumbnails for the skin of every character model in the game. While this is a difficult and challenging goal to achieve, it is absolutely necessary to achieve high throughput in your rendering pipeline. If you do not, no matter what other optimization techniques you might implement, every mesh has to be rendered with a separate draw call simply because it uses a different texture asset.

The tool you write to do this will need to load full-resolution texture maps, reduce them in size, and assign them to a location on a series of decal textures. It must then remap the texture-coordinates in the deformed mesh to the offset locations in these new decal textures. Additionally, the material assignment needs to refer to this new texture asset. This can be done as an automated batch process so that it is transparent to how the artists texture their meshes. The artists simply assign UVs to all of their mesh LODs against a single full-resolution skin, and the automated tool will handle texture reduction, UV generation, and material assignment automatically.

Rendering Optimization Techniques

Once your artwork has been prepped using these guidelines, you should now be able to realize the benefits in your rendering pipeline. First, let us consider this example, that way off in the distance, say 50 to 200 meters, is a large group of NPC monsters heading your way. By now, each of those creatures should all be mapped to a single massive decal texture and using just one shader technique, even if assigned to slightly varying levels of mesh detail.

While we will discuss skeletal optimization in a moment, it is important to make sure your pipeline treats all matrices as persistent data. This is a critical optimization and not obvious at first when 3D engines often build matrices on the fly or use stack-based methods. If matrices are considered persistent for a complete frame, you can then reorganize your rendering pipeline so that, as data flows through it, render requests can be accumulated for batch processing in one fell swoop. Moreover, you can also prevent the recalculation of matrices if you know they are persistent or don't need to change. Matrices should not be calculated on the fly, unless absolutely necessary, and should be passed by a pointer that is known to be valid for either the duration of the frame or the lifetime of the object.

Once you have these hypothetical 100 mesh-deformed creatures accumulated in a single batch, replete with persistent matrix palettes and shared material properties, you can now focus on getting them sent to the GPU as fast as possible. Modern-day GPUs detest state changes. Were you to attempt to upload 100 unique matrix palettes and perform a discrete draw call for each creature, even if there were no material changes, you would stall the GPU so much that your throughput would be a tiny fraction of the device's capabilities.

In the current version of DirectX is support for instanced geometry. A technique that allows you to render hundreds or thousands of objects in a single draw call by submitting the transforms as a vertex stream and using the frequency divider to determine how many times to loop over the input mesh data. However, this is useful in only a few limited situations. It tends to work best for massive numbers of very low poly-count objects with one transform apiece. You certainly would want to consider rendering rocks, trees, and small objects that have only a single transform using this technique.

However, for mesh-deformed characters the correct approach is to perform deformation in software, using the CPU, and accumulate the results into a single locked vertex buffer. Once all 100 creatures have been software skinned into a single VB, you can then render them in a single call to Draw Primitive. Since you will have provided the data in exactly the format the GPU desires, one large chunk of vertex data with a very basic and simple vertex shader, the throughput will be astounding.

Of course, you may be legitimately concerned about the amount of CPU you will be consuming by performing mesh deformation in software. There are some tricks to use here as well. Since you are running the skinning process in software, you can be more creative in how you make this code path work. You can reorganize your vertex data to be SIMD friendly and can write your mesh deformation routines to take advantage of the SSE instruction set. Finally, the main optimization you can achieve is by reducing the fidelity and the quality of the deformation itself.

Typically, a deformed mesh is assigned four bone weightings, and the deformation involves four transforms on the vertex position *and* the vertex normal; followed by an average computation. For highest levels of detail, you will probably have tangent space normals as well, which should be removed from the lower mesh levels of detail. While four bone weightings are fine and often needed when watching a character very close up, they are hardly necessary at a distance. In fact, you can begin dropping the number of bone weights that contribute to the final solution at a very aggressive rate. For vertex normals, more than one bone weighting is hardly ever necessary. Moreover, past a certain distance, the mesh is such a crude approximation that you can probably ignore transforming the normal at all. You should experiment with these settings and decide for yourself what loss of fidelity is acceptable. With these optimizations, objects at a distance are performing only a single matrix transform per vertex using the software skinning path. The total throughput you can achieve using this approach is well balanced by the vast increase in GPU utilization you will gain by submitting all of these characters in a single call.

There are two small items of note when thinking about software skinning. Because you are running your deformation in software, it is not necessary to upload the matrix palette to the GPU. You should have a single master matrix palette for each character so that, as your meshes touch fewer and fewer bones, you will automatically touch less memory. You will not have to do any operations to somehow collate a smaller matrix palette; an expensive operation you would have to do were you skinning in hardware. It is also important to note that in addition to accumulating transformed vertices, you will need to accumulate indices as well.

Multiplayer games typically operate in terms of a very large coordinate space. Floating-point numbers have a relatively small amount of precision, and if you try to deform a character at a large integer coordinate, say something like 5,000 meters from the origin, you will experience a number of extremely ugly artifacts, including vertex wobbling and texture swimming. To avoid this, you may find it necessary to move your characters relative to a virtual origin, where (0,0,0) is the current camera position.

Skeletal Optimization Techniques

Once your artists have reassigned bones weightings on each mesh LOD to fewer and fewer bones in the base skeleton, this will create a number of requirements for your engine. When you load a base character skeleton, and its subsequent mesh LODs, you will need to build a mapping table between each deformed mesh and the full-resolution skeleton. First, locate which bones are referenced at each mesh LOD by looking at the bone weightings in the mesh itself. Next, walk the skeletal hierarchy and find every bone that is required for this LOD. At this point, you will have a mapping table, at each LOD, of only the bones that are required to render that mesh.

At runtime, when you rebuild the skeletal hierarchy, you will only need to touch the bones that are active relative to the current LOD. In this way, the application might still be setting bones for the purposes of game logic, and that data will be cached when needed, but only the bones that are active for the current mesh LOD will be rebuilt when rendered.

Another rather obvious optimization is to not rebuild the skeleton for objects that haven't moved. This can be done rather easily by simply having a "dirty" flag that indicates whether the skeleton needs to be rebuilt at all. Remember, it is a key component of this model that all matrices in your entire engine be considered persistent to support frame-to-frame coherence.

Another somewhat questionable optimization technique is to not rebuild the transforms every single frame if an object is very far away. However, this approach causes the displayed character to look very "choppy" and is generally considered unacceptable to the user. However, slow frame rate is generally not considered acceptable either, so you will need to make an aesthetic choice about trading off visual fidelity for overall throughput.

There has been a lot of focus on strategies to minimize the amount of CPU spent recomputing skeletal hierarchies. The reason for this focus is because any time you spread this much matrix manipulation across hundreds, if not thousands, of objects (some composed of as many as 100 bones as their highest LOD), you will quickly consume a significant portion of your overall CPU budget. And, of course, let us not forget the single most important optimization technique of all: *do not rebuild skeletal hierarchies for objects that cannot be seen!* What this means is that you need to be careful to avoid binding gameplay logic to transforms that are primarily used for rendering purposes. Our recommendation is that when you need relative transforms for game logic, you have a separate code path to accomplish just this task, or be satisfied with an approximate transform when a character is off screen. If you write an engine that presumes every single bone in every single skeleton is recomputed every frame at full resolution, the least of your problems is going to be rendering the characters.

One more optimization to keep in mind is deciding when to calculate the current LOD in the first place. The LOD computation is itself a little expensive, since it requires a square root to be performed and a table lookup. When your artists initially set up their LOD curve, they did it based on the default field of view in your game. However, most games today will have situations where the field of view changes; a typical example is using a scope on a sniper rifle. When this happens, you have to multiply the distance of the object from the camera times the current field of view so that when a sniper zooms way up on a character off in the distance, it doesn't render him as a stick figure. Now, the LOD computation is not itself so terribly awful, but anything multiplied times hundreds, if not thousands, of objects is going to add up. A simple optimization is to only recalculate the LOD every so often, since it is generally harmless if it lags a few frames behind (as long as the field of view has not changed).

Animation Optimization Techniques

The techniques used to optimize your animation pipeline are closely tied to the approach you use to LOD the skeleton. The first and most important optimization technique is to form a mapping between the tracks in an animation and *only* the bones that are active at the current LOD. You certainly don't need to be sampling b-spline animation curves for facial expressions on a character 100 meters from the camera.

The next optimization technique is to reduce the amount of simultaneous animation tracks that can be blended onto a single skeletal instance. Animation blending is a key component used in most games to make characters move in a seamless and realistic way. However, as objects recede into the distance, many of the subtleties that arise from blended animation sequences are lost.

As before, it is of the utmost importance that you do not render, animate, or rebuild the skeletal hierarchy for a character that is not visible on screen. One solution is to create an over-described bounding sphere around your character model and only process the character when its sphere intersects the view frustum. With an over-described sphere, the character will be flagged as "visible" when it is near the edge of the view frustum but not yet inside it. This is useful when important graphic effects are associated with the character model that you might want to see before the character itself enters the view, especially since these effects may require the skeletal hierarchy to be current to display properly.

Another opportunity to optimize character animation is to sample the animation data at a lower frequency than the current frame rate. This will result in a stuttering quality to the character animation. However, when you reach a completely saturated situation, with hundreds of animated characters on screen at once, a little bit of stuttering is usually a reasonable trade-off for a better sustained frame rate.

Vehicle and Weapon Optimization Techniques

You might make all of the optimizations already suggested only to find you are stalled rendering the weapons, objects, vehicles, and other small objects that are in the scene. For this reason, it is worthwhile to make sure your mesh deformation pipeline can handle typically nondeformed objects as if they were. Rather than rendering a vehicle as 10 different pieces, each with a unique transform, you might instead treat it as a single deformed mesh. Once you do this, whether it is for your vehicle or other small game objects, all of the optimization techniques outlined for characters will apply to these objects as well. It is also very important to reduce the skeletal complexity for these objects as they move through the LOD chain.

Finally, remember that calling "render" on any object should never actually render it. It should be placed in a queue "to be rendered" so that it can be collated for optimal batch processing when enough data has been accumulated. Since you used persistent matrix transforms, that data is guaranteed to be valid until the end of the frame, without requiring any memory copies to be performed in the process. In short, don't post something "to be rendered" and then delete it shortly thereafter. In cases where you have a large number of low poly density instanced items with a single transformation matrix, taking advantage of the new hardware instancing API will probably be your best choice.

Customized Characters

All of the techniques outlined so far presume you have relatively fixed character models that can be authored in a specific way to take advantage of these optimizations. However, many massively multiplayer games have a strong focus on individuality and customization of an avatar. The idea of having every character model unique does not map well toward our effort to manage mesh, skeleton, and textures as single unified batches.

While you can allow the user to make some basic modifications, like scale on his character or swapping in and out his choice of heads and still realize most of the benefits of these techniques, any excessive amount of individualization is going to take you virtually back to square one. The only real solution to this problem is that if a user is allowed to customize his character extensively, you must incorporate many of the steps previously outlined in the tools and authoring phase directly into your game engine. Your goal would be to, on the fly, produce a unified mesh, texture assets, and reduced skeleton set. This is not an easy task, but there is really no other way to realize the benefits of batch processing of skeleton reduced deformed meshes without reorganizing your data assets to fit.

Certainly, the vast quantity of NPC characters and monsters you may have in your game will benefit since there is usually much less customization applied to these assets.

Conclusion

Hopefully, this collection of combined techniques will ultimately lead to higher throughput when rendering large numbers of mesh-deformed characters in massively multiplayer games. This was certainly the case in *Planetside*, a game engine that used to some degree most of these techniques. Taking advantage of these optimizations will impact every aspect of your content creation pipeline, tools development, 3D engine, and game logic.

MMP PRODUCTION TECHNIQUES

Peak Simultaneous Usage as a Percentage of Total Subscribers

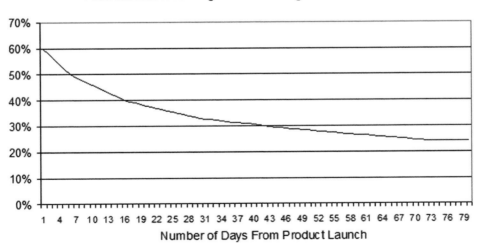

3.1

Large-Scale Project Management

Michael Saladino—Electronic Arts

MSaladino@ea.com

Projects across the industry are becoming more complex, and in few genres is this more evident than in massively multiplayer (MMP) games. Publishers are pushing for a shorter turnaround on their investments, hardware complexity is increasing, and end users are demanding larger and more interactive content. All of this results in ever-growing development teams. At major studios like Electronic Arts, Sony, and Microsoft, teams of over 100 people are becoming the status quo. This article looks at what the new project management looks like in terms of team hierarchy, rigorous scheduling, strong process, and resource handling. This article proposes a collection of guidelines that has been used in directing large-scale projects at Microsoft and Electronic Arts.

Building Your Hierarchy

For decades, computer games were developed by small teams with a few dozen people at the most. This helped promote the idea that a couple of managers could deliver a game in its entirety. One producer, one lead engineer, one art director, and two dozen artists and programmers building the game was how most products were being constructed. However, with larger, modern teams comes the necessity for hierarchy to maintain direction and order. Deciding on your hierarchy or organization chart is the first step in building a stable and productive development team. However, what does hierarchy really mean for a large-scale project?

First, hierarchy is a way of reducing the number of direct reports to a single manager. This is normally done by selecting subleads below the manager. If you have 1 lead engineer and 20 programmers all reporting to him, you need to select subleads to reduce the communication load on the manager. Pick four or five engineers along major functionality lines such as multiplayer, AI, game mechanics, frontend, graphics, and systems. The goal should be for each sublead to have two to four reports, and those four or five subleads all report to the lead engineer. This is the most fundamental purpose of hierarchy: reducing communication requirements by empowering subleads to take ownership.

By reducing the number of direct reports one manager has to deal with, you are clearly reducing his daily and hourly communication needs. Studies in the military, arguably one of the greatest achievements in management structure, find that an individual manager functions best when he's only handling three or four people directly. From this author's experience in game development, someone can effectively produce assets for a game whether art or code and maintain three or four direct reports. Once you hit six to eight, the manager's ability to produce drops extremely low as he spends his days managing almost exclusively. Moreover, if you cross over into double-digit reports, an individual's ability to manage effectively is affected. Therefore, keep direct reports in the single digits. If the manager is also expected to produce assets for the game, keep the number of direct reports below five; otherwise, the manager will be a full-time manager.

While the direct result of hierarchy is improved communication handling, there are other indirect and subtle improvements of which to take note. Workers in small groups tend to feel more individual empowerment. When a person is in a cube farm and is treated just like the other 30 engineers surrounding him, he can begin to lose identity. A feeling like an assembly line worker can take hold, which is usually detrimental to the person's overall production. Creating subleads in control of small groups can keep a person feeling like a major contributor even if it's only in the small group. Most engineers would rather identify as one of three engineers building AI rather than one of thirty engineers building a game. It's simply more personal.

Of course, this benefit also has a drawback: people becoming isolated from the game as a whole. If an artist does nothing but paint household object textures for months on end, it can be easy to lose the forest for the trees. The detail that they're focused on grows in size until it becomes the whole world, which can be good in the short term but is often bad for the long. Remember to always keep people attached to the overall product. Have weekly team meetings where you show off the game as an end user would experience it so every person can look and say, "I did that part." If you think about this issue in a psychological way, people in the game industry were most likely all smart children in their school days. Therefore, take them back to the joy of seeing their work posted on a board with a gold star for everyone to see. Even if the grown-up cynic in them openly scoffs, a part of their childhood will appreciate the attention.

Delivery vs. Functional

Once your team grows to the point where more hierarchy is required, the question becomes how to divide the team? If you imagine a small startup with 6 engineers and 20 artists, most people would split the team up into functional groups. Five of the engineers would report to one lead. The art team would be cut up into modelers, texture painters, musicians, and animators, each with a corresponding lead. This layout would work well, but when your game requires 10 times this many people, does a functionally based organization still make sense?

Do all the administrative assistants at IBM report to a single lead administrative assistant? Do all the engineers at Microsoft report to a single lead engineer? Can you imagine what would happen if they did even with a deep sublead hierarchy like the one described earlier? It would be abject chaos because a functional hierarchy is useful at handling functionally dependant communication but little else. This causes a hierarchy based on functional lines to not scale well. Our true tasks in constructing a game are not functionally pure, but instead require constant cross-functional communication. So, let's try something different: a hierarchy based on delivery instead of department.

A delivery group for a game would be the frontend team. This group would definitely include engineers and Photoshop® artists. It might also include usability experts, 3D modelers, and Flash scripters. We now have many different disciplines all reporting to a single frontend manager with possible functional subleads beneath like a lead frontend engineer. The team is given a single mandate from the team leader: deliver the frontend needed to ship the game. The frontend manager would drive all external information gathering such as the frontend design documents and technical certification requirements from third-party consoles. However, the majority of information needed to build this unit has been isolated within the walls of the frontend team, and only teamwide critical information ever needs to be floated out of the group.

Other delivery groups could include game mechanics, systems, multiplayer, or a standalone server. These are areas that can be sliced from the whole and driven with minimal external communication because a delivery group is cross-functional by nature. Included in the multiplayer group are the levels teams that will construct the multiplayer levels. There are modelers, designers, and texture painters. We include the engineers who will build the client/server architecture and extend the single-player experience to include multiplayer. By making these divisions through the overall team, you can reduce the problem from 160 people making one product to four teams of 40 making four products. In addition, if you draw the lines cleanly and have a strong management team at the top of those four products, you'll be able to keep a rolling integration of these components during development.

Pure Art Directors

However, delivery groups aren't the best solution for all problems. While they keep a smaller team focused on a subset problem, you do wind up with an unfortunate long-term issue with people having managers who aren't of their discipline. For example, imagine an animator being assigned to a group that's going to deliver the melee system for a role-playing game. His manager is handling different disciplines and may not really understand an animation skill set or career. How will this relate to the animator's ability to get promotions? Perhaps the animator is significantly better than how the melee system turns out due to engineering issues. How will the animator's pure talent be seen unless a more senior animator is somehow in the equation to rate his long-term value to the company?

This is why functional leadership is needed. Notice that we did not say management, because these are two very different beasts. To manage as stated previously is to handle information flow. Leadership is to inspire your team and motivate them to become better than they currently are. An art director or even more specifically an animation director for the previous example needs to be in place to help drive quality and identify long-term career growth for the functional team. No one reports to the art director, technical director, or game design director because he is the holder of the pure art. They push the quality limits without having their hands in the schedule or management flow. Therefore, by including these functional leaders in the team you allow managers to drive delivery teams while allowing pure art owners to help inspire individuals with a functional language that they share.

Producer vs. Development Manager

The next line we need to identify comes in the form of the producer. Many small companies have a producer come up with ideas, schedule them, and then push the team to maintain vision and deadlines. What a schizophrenic position. To be expected to both develop brilliant new ideas and have the resolve to cut them when needed. No wonder so many titles scream madly past their delivery dates. It's like allowing an author to edit his own book or giving a director complete control over the final cut. Maybe there are a few true geniuses where this is a good idea, but for the rest of the human race, it's a recipe for disaster. The idea man will always want the final result to be grander in its ultimate pursuit for perfection and you want him thinking that way. You need another person to be the scheduler, manager, and all-around "get it done" man. Enter the development manager.

A development manager is a producer's alter ego. When the producer is blue skying, the development manager is there to attach the anchor of reality. The development manager's job is to maintain the schedule and manage the time of his reports. A successful development manager seldom gives the producer exactly what he wants but instead masters the art of delivering 90% of what the producer wants but at half the cost. Each delivery group should have a development manager at the helm making sure that milestones are being met at the same time as pushing to deliver the best approximation of the producer's vision. It's a checks-and-balance system in its truest form. Why expect these two halves to exist in a single person when you can instead hire two people, each of whom is uniquely suited for the positions? (Plus, the arguments between the two heads are now externalized and are fun to watch.)

Quality Assurance

The last detail in initial team layout we'll discuss is quality assurance (QA), also known simply as test. Test is regularly the most overlooked aspect of game development. However, as projects increase in size, this is another detail that can no longer be ignored. With larger games come larger test requirements. The sheer number of options in online and especially MMP games creates test matrices that can barely be fathomed. This is why attaching testers to a team earlier is better, and also why our industry as a whole must start treating QA as a viable job and long-term career.

The first major step with integrating test is at a company level. Most companies sadly still view testers as 19-year-olds who can barely spell. In addition, unfortunately, if that's whom the company expects in the positions, then that's what the company will pay for and that's what the company will hire. However, major software development companies like IBM and Microsoft have known for decades that software test is a career for mature QA experts. It's a real job with a real skill set often staffed with people from engineering. A strong test group needs strong organizational management, a solid engineering department, and plenty of headcount. Normally, only the last item is supported by companies and only in the form of cheap contract labor. This reality needs to change across our entire industry.

If you can convince your company that you need to integrate test early, hire a few engineer testers. They are engineers that know how to build test cases to stress test bare code systems. They can architect automated testing suites to limit the human equation when dealing with massive test matrices. Sit them with a deliverable team and get them involved in the day-to-day business of the product. A test engineer working with his team should be involved in the architecting process with an eye toward automation and how certain decisions might increase or decrease required hands-on test time. A correct decision early in the engineering process can save hundreds of hours for testers at the end of the project.

Schedule

With a hierarchy layout selected and filled, the next step in proper management is to have a schedule. A schedule is every manager's first line of defense in nearly all situations. Need more headcount? Point to the schedule and show that you need the people. Need to cut a feature? Point to the schedule and show that you don't have time for it. Your schedule is how you effectively explain what you're doing to other people. However, building a meaningful schedule is a rare art in this industry.

Task List

Above all else, understand what a schedule is: management's expression of the producer created game design document (GDD). Hopefully, at this point your producers have delivered a GDD, because without one, your schedule will be fiction no matter what you do. The GDD contains every level, every weapon, every item, every online statistic, and every feature that will go in the game. It describes these features in enough detail so that the workload can be estimated, but not in so much detail that it will prevent real-time experimentation by the team. This is the schedule's starting point.

Take the GDD and break it into tasks, first at a high level, and then reduce each section over and over again until you have a resolution between a month and a week per task. Avoid the temptation to resolve any task finer than a week at this early point, as this will translate into wasted work since you're looking at the project as a whole from the beginning. Games can take thousands of man weeks to build, so don't pretend like you can estimate details that will take a few days a year from now. This exercise will result in a task list of thousands of items across all functional groups. It's always a daunting first look at the game.

Talent vs. Drive

You next need to apply your resource pool (people) to the task list. You should have a rough understanding of what your company is expecting to spend on your headcount and you probably already have names for most of the people if they're coming from other recently completed projects. Therefore, it's time to connect people to tasks. However, before you start attaching people solely on their individual skill set, let's look at a concept for categorizing workers: talent vs. drive.

All workers can be rated along two axes: talent and drive. The talent axis represents their general skills in their respective art form, be it engineering, texture painting, or animating. It's a qualitative measure of how effectively they would solve a problem given a finite amount of time such as eight hours a day. The drive axis represents their desire to succeed and work long hours. They are for lack of a kinder word, *workaholics*. When a person is mapped against these two axes, you get an understanding of what you can expect from him and how to best apply him to the problem of shipping the product.

The first type of person from this matrix has low talent and little drive. This is the easiest person to deal with—fire him. Get him off your team immediately. There is nothing more destructive to a team than low-performing individuals who are warming a seat to collect a paycheck. These people are net losses and therefore should be removed.

The next person you'll find is the highly skilled but nonworkaholic worker. These people have often been in the industry for a long time, which is why they have developed such a strong talent. However, for one reason or another, they have little interest in killing themselves for the team. They want to work their eight hours and go home. Maybe they've been burned too hard in the past. Maybe they have a family. Maybe they just like getting out of work because they have other interests. Whatever the reason, they need to be managed uniquely to who they are. Give them tasks that exploit their skill sets. If a person is a physics engineer, make him integral in architecting your next physics engine. If he's an animator, give him the most challenging animation set you have. However, because of their limited hour set, making sure they track tightly to their schedule is critical. Luckily, their own sense of pride in their abilities is often the best motivation for them getting tasks done on time.

In the other corner of the matrix, you'll find the low skilled but highly motivated individual. This is quite often a rookie straight out of school or someone who has spent a few years in the industry but at a small startup that wasn't teaching him well. They will likely spend most of their time behind on their schedule, but they will be the first to stay late and work all weekend to catch up. That's the nature of being a rookie in our industry.

In the final corner of the matrix, we have the superstar, the person who is so talented and so driven to do his best that he can take on anything. He's done everything his job might ask of him and much more. His work output is miles above everyone else's. The classic phrase that "80% of the work is done by 20% of the people" is referring to him. These are your team leaders, and they should be used to not just produce, but to motivate the team members as a whole to reach beyond themselves and deliver no matter what. These are most likely the kinds of people you'll want in your pure art director positions, whether it's art, engineering, or game design.

Task Assignment

With these three groups of people ready to work (remember, you fired the first group), you need to match them to tasks. Start with the highly talented but lower drive individuals. Put them on tasks that match their talent perfectly. Put them in areas that are the most constant and less subject to wild change. For engineers, game mechanics and frontends are often too chaotic for these people, so put them in core systems like animation or physics. These systems issues are some of your most difficult problems and will need their uniquely strong talent. However, at the same time, keep them out of leadership roles, since you'll want someone willing to do the late nights when necessary. Nothing is more demoralizing to a late night than seeing the team lead go home.

Next, put in your superstars. Since they're so talented and driven, you can put them on almost any task. Moreover, because of their desire to work, putting them in leadership positions will help drive the entire team. They will raise the flag when needed and charge up the hill or even over the cliff if that's what is needed. Your superstars will be your last line of defense from missing milestones, and they're the first people you should trust when something goes wrong.

Finally, we need to attach the rookies with heart to the task list. Due to their inexperience, selecting tasks that are lower risk is always best. Keep them in positions where they can receive mentorship from more talented engineers. Be mindful that their tasks will be the most likely to run long even if the tasks are easy. However, their effort should be phenomenal as they attempt to prove themselves in the industry, so make it clear what is expected from them.

Dependencies and Time Estimates

With people attached to the tasks, your next step is to identify dependencies. Start with true dependencies that exist because one task cannot possibly begin without another being completed. A good example is that texturing a character cannot begin until the model for the character is completed. No matter what clever tricks a manager comes up with, you cannot finish texturing a character unless the model is done. That is a true dependency and it must be called out. The secondary form of dependency is an artificial dependency, which we will get to later in this article.

The next component of the schedule is time. As the manager of the schedule, you should have enough knowledge to make a rough pass and assign time estimates. We recommend including your particular functional "art" director, whether that's a technical director, visual effects director, lead engineer, or whomever in order to get a more balanced guess. Once your initial guesses are on paper, gather your team and get their input on the question of time. Don't share your estimates with them, but instead just give them the list of tasks. Give them a day or two before the meeting to become familiar with the list. Then, in the meeting, call the tasks out one by one and explain the details. Briefly discuss the task as a group, have everyone write their time guess on a piece of paper, and, like judges at the Olympics, raise their opinions. If the estimates are all about the same, you can feel confident that you have a reliable estimate from your best minds. If the estimates are wildly different, then you know that the scope of the task is poorly understood by the group and further discussion is needed. This exercise often turns into a negotiation between the managers and the person who has been assigned the task. If an agreement cannot be made, go with the estimate from the person who has the task, because in the end it's his task and he has to do the work.

Finalizing the Schedule

You now have a list of tasks, basic dependencies labeled, people assigned, and estimates for time. From our experience, many managers in our industry stop here and use this task list to drive a project, and while task lists can be very helpful for short-term development (one or two weeks at a time), they are horribly ineffective for long-term development. A task list does not really show if a given project is going to be done in time for next Christmas because artificial dependencies have not been introduced. Artificial dependencies exist when two tasks cannot be done at the same time, not for any functional reason, but simply because the same person is scheduled to do both tasks. This is where true parallelism can be found in a schedule and where adding people can help finish the game quicker.

With all of this data at hand, hooking it up into a scheduling database is the final step. This is the moment when you'll truly see what the timeline of your project looks like. Start with each person working an effective six hours a day, which is a normal eight-hour day with meetings and such removed. Make sure you mark off vacations and assume that every person will take about one week of PTO every four months. In addition, insert your major milestones into the schedule. Validate that they don't fall on weekends or the aforementioned known vacations.

When you view your data in the schedule for the first time, you'll probably notice that a small percentage of your team is wildly out of proportion from the rest, such as a poor animator who isn't done for three years. This is where workload balancing comes in. Start moving tasks from the overburdened to those who are finishing early. One thing to remember as you move tasks around is that you're moving a task from your ideal worker to someone else. Consider if you need to extend the time estimate because the new person handling the task isn't as skilled or familiar with the task. Moreover, if after this shifting of tasks, you are still over on time, begin inventing "To Be Hired" positions to pull the work into alignment with your milestones. These new hires can be used to overcome artificial dependencies, but remember that they cannot overcome true task dependencies.

You now have a working schedule in your hands. Keep it in a place where everyone on the team can see it, whether that's on the network or printed out and hanging on a wall. Everyone needs to be familiar with his or her place in the schedule. In addition, as the owner of the schedule, it's your job to keep it updated daily. A schedule is a living document that needs to change continuously to reflect new realities. When milestones pass, take a day or two to completely revamp it if needed. Even go as far as once or twice in a project, start over from scratch and compare the new schedule to your old. If they are about the same, you can feel confident in it. If it changes dramatically, your old schedule has probably deviated too far from reality.

Handling Milestones

Your next major step to organize your team is to look at your daily process. These are the steps you take on a daily basis to help verify that your schedule is real and that your target dates are obtainable. Process is a major difference between successful teams and those that flounder in death marches. Is there verifiable movement forward at all times, and if there isn't, what's being done about it?

Begin by setting your milestone schedule. Milestones are a critical aspect of any long-term development process. Much like using hierarchy to divide communication flow, milestones will divide a project temporally into more manageable pieces. Effective milestones should be spaced six to eight weeks apart. We have seen projects work as tightly as four week deadlines, but that's often too rushed except for short-term projects such as expansion packs. Six to eight weeks gives the team enough time to rip out major pieces, sew it back together, and deliver a new and stable version of the game. It also allows for one or two calm weeks where the team has normal business hours after each milestone.

Once you have your delivery deadlines laid out, you need to verify daily that the team has forward momentum. This can be achieved with "dailies," which is a term from the film industry. Basically, it's when the management team and executives look at the bleeding-edge development from the trenches. In the film description of the term, it's simply a collection of takes showing what was done today on the set—and it's essentially the same thing for game development. It's a regular time of the day, say around 6 P.M., where everyone can see what new thing went into a level, check out the new water effect, or see a new NPC dropped into the game. It also helps drive everyone's daily work. Each manager who is going to show something at the dailies knows about it when the day begins, so his effort can be focused on getting these items integrated into the build.

Demo Hell

As any development team knows, the external demo is always a nightmare. Whether it's a third-party publisher or your own chief executives coming down for a visit, a demo can ruin any schedule. The common reason for this is that what is good for building a game often makes a lousy demo for an executive. For example, we could show someone a game that looks and plays no differently between now and three weeks ago, but we know that we ripped out the old collision and physics system and replaced it with a new one that's much faster. In other words, massive amounts of work were completed, but that's not something that goes over well in a demo environment. Instead, teams are often pushed to throw together poorly built pieces as long as they show well. So how can you keep demos from running your team off the schedule?

A demo can be bad because it often takes your team on tangents that have nothing to do with the final game. E3, the industry trade show every May, is traditionally a huge time sink for all projects that is always mismanaged. Therefore, let's start by scheduling the demos we know about. Align your internal milestones with your major demos. No reason to deliver an E3 demo only to follow it awkwardly two weeks later with an internal milestone. Add one week of throwaway work per person per demo on the schedule and be prepared to use it. Check with your publisher for other demos they might be looking for, such as European tradeshows or a yearly game press wine n' dine. You can't allow your team to be surprised by these important deliveries.

However, in the cases when you never saw it coming, there are steps you can take to survive the unexpected demo. Keep in mind that when an executive wants to see your game, it's probably been a while since he last saw it. Therefore, why show him the bleeding edge of your development process? During your regular development schedule, look at your daily build every day and determine whether it's something you would show to an executive or marketing representative. Is it stable? Is the frame rate high? Does it play well? If yes, put it aside as a "showable" build. Make sure you get a good build once every week or two and just collect them. This way, whenever a surprise demo pops up, show them your last good build instead of derailing your current progress by trying to throw together a good build at the last minute. The further away from the daily process a person is, the less likely he'll be able to tell if your demo is truly "up to the minute," which works in your favor.

Slipping Milestones

When measuring your team's progress, you will likely run into the dreaded word *slip*. Slipping is the idea that your team was not able to meet its scheduled delivery on one front, or even worse, all fronts, and a slip can be disastrous for your team's morale and your project's finances. Slips make publishers and executives lose confidence in your project's management, and without this you'll find yourself in danger of receiving wild "course corrections," small marketing budgets or even cancellation. However, it's this very fear that often makes people do the wrong thing when their schedule starts to slip: they lie about it. They tell their boss and their boss' boss that everything is great and right on time. However, in reality, they are only postponing the inevitable when they miss their deadlines.

The most important rule about slipping a schedule is to only do it once. Learn from your mistakes on the first schedule. Honestly look at what happened and figure out what went wrong. Were the initial estimates far too low? Is your team far less skilled than you thought? Maybe you haven't been able to acquire the headcount you requested. Are your producers constantly strong-arming you into adding new features? Whatever the problem, you need to acknowledge it and let the appropriate people know. You need to have hard discussions about a major course correction. Moreover, don't let someone convince you of another milestone if you know it will slip, too. Too often, teams wind up replacing one bad milestone for another, and before they know what has happened they are in a death march with no end in sight. The most common reason for this is that some managers don't want to honestly move milestones to where they should be because they don't like giving bad news. Why tell the team that they're three months behind when you could instead tell them that they're only one behind. What about the other two months? We'll burn that bridge when we come to it. Hit the team once with bad news and then prove to them that it won't happen again.

Resource vs. Features vs. Time

At this point, we have all the pieces needed for success in place: a deliverable hierarchy of management, pure art directors for leadership, a schedule based in reality, and a milestone schedule to take us from the beginning to the end. However, what are the tools that a manager uses to maintain these pieces throughout the project? There are three variables a manager can control to one degree or another: resource, features, and time. These three variables when combined describe your game. Maybe you're a large budget blockbuster that needs to be done in record time. Maybe you're a critical success done by a small startup. As a manager, your balancing of these variables is how you help fit your game into the marketplace your company desires.

Resource

Resource is headcount. It's the number of employees your team is capable of using. The most obvious way to control headcount is through hiring and firing. Firing is mostly useful in our current discussion for freeing up headcount in order to hire someone else. A classic rule of thumb for managers is that you should always churn your bottom 10%. You should stack rank your team every six months, which is the process of ranking the value of everyone on the team against everyone else and placing them into a stack. Once done, removing the lowest performers is an excellent way to keep fresh ideas coming into the group.

Open headcount is the other side of the coin in the form of hiring. Whether your company is growing and creating new open headcounts, or if you've just laid off a percentage of your bottom performers, how you fill that open headcount is critical. The first rule is to take your time. A full-time hire is one of the most expensive things your company can do in benefits, relocation, and training time. Don't rush into hiring someone because you need the help. A bad hire can damage your team just as much as a good one can help. Therefore, spend time every day reviewing résumés and conducting phone interviews. Always have people coming in for in-person interviews, which should take an entire day spread out over a few of your top people. In addition, if your own recruiting isn't moving fast enough, consider external recruiters. While they can be expensive, sometimes the urgency of the hire demands more applicants crossing your path, which an external company can easily do.

Borrowing headcount is another effective solution that's much cheaper than hiring. Quite often in a large company, while one team is crunching another may be in a lull. This is a great time to borrow resources for your project. Since they're already employed by your company, there is no startup cost as with a new hire, your department just has to take over the salary expense. Borrowing can also be more useful for quick resource solutions if you can borrow someone with previous experience with your team members and technologies. The downside of borrowing is the political ramifications that often come with borrowing. When you borrow an employee, his manager just lost a headcount, which even during noncrunch periods is often a difficult thing to allow. The best way to get other managers to accept borrowing is to accept it yourself. Be the first person to offer your own employees when they aren't working at full capacity.

Contracting can also be an effective solution, especially when considering the cyclic nature of our business. Quite often, companies will ramp up full-time hires to get a game out only to have to let them go once the work dries up. Therefore, instead of repeating the cycle endlessly, consider contracting for short-term resource solutions. There are no ramp-up costs other than equipment, and there are no benefits, although most contractors charge at a significant hourly rate to make up for this. You can also consider off-site contracting if the circumstances allow. Off-site usually works best if you're subcontracting many workers from another company with their own management infrastructure in place as opposed to an off-site individual working from home with no oversight.

Features

Your next variable to control is features. This is the list of requests that come from your producers that you used to originally create the schedule. Remember, your producer's job is to create the best game he possibly can, and this often directly translates into the number of features he can include. As a manager, you'll spend most of your time figuring out how to deliver the gameplay the producer wants without necessarily giving him every feature he asks for. Therefore, cutting features is a critical aspect of controlling the development process.

All games should have a simple phrase that describes what the game is, a 50-word or less description as to what the essence is. Asking how a given feature directly relates to this overall concept is often a quick way to get something cut. Another good way is to ask how a given feature is going to increase sales. We often receive large specifications for frontend designs complete with 3D worlds and every feature ever seen in all games. However, how many reviewers write about how cool the frontend of a game is? Or how many times have you heard some kid at the local video game store tell his friend why this game has the coolest matchmaking screen. Relating tasks to the bottom line is a quick way to get the attention of executives when trying to make a cut.

Feature creep, or allowing new features to get into the game after design lockdown, is something that always happens. Despite everyone's best intentions, features will always be thought of late. Your job as a manager is to make sure that any new feature that comes in is worthwhile and doesn't put your deadlines at risk. Probably the most common feature creeps that are allowed into a game at the last minute come from focus testing. This is when dozens of nonindustry game players get a sneak peak at your game and tell you what they like or don't like about it. Well, if the people running the focus tests identify a common thread among the dislikes, those issues are often raised to the level of "must address," which can come in the form of a new feature. In addition, companies often have vice presidents who have ideas about how to improve a game at the last minute, and those also become "must address" issues. When allowing a new feature to enter the schedule, determine if you have the bandwidth. If not, try gaining a headcount to handle the new request. If that's impossible, try cutting another feature that isn't as desired. If that all fails, then we have to call in the third variable—time.

Time

The final variable to control is time. A common joke we tell when a schedule looks hopeless is that the team would stand a better chance of success if they redirected their efforts into creating a time machine. Time is probably the most difficult of the three variables to affect, because it requires moving your ship date. This is perhaps the most wide-reaching variable since it not only affects your team, but also affects marketing, sales, distribution, and studio-wide fiscal earning results. Very little is as hurtful as falling out of your given quarter for shipping. However, not much else can benefit a team as greatly either. Three extra months for a given project can be huge for stabilization, final polish, and continued focus testing. In addition, projects that require and receive an extra year or more can find themselves in a position to correct massive development mistakes like choosing the wrong rendering engine or designing disliked characters. Changing your ship date is the last thing you want to do with your project, but sometimes it can be the only thing that can save it.

Conclusion

Massively multiplayer games are among the largest development efforts in our industry. The work often requires hundreds of people over many years to ship a high-quality MMG, and these realities are changing the way game teams are managed. The basic hierarchy of management is changing. Proper scheduling and the ability to measure progress in a meaningful way every day is taking a heightened importance, as is knowing how to balance the tools in your management toolbox to keep your team moving forward. All of this is critical for the next generation of games, which are only becoming larger in scope and more complex in technology. In addition, at the front of this boom is massively multiplayer with its free-form gameplay and online technology hurdles. It's a place where management goes to truly prove itself.

Effective Quality Assurance—How to Manage Developers

Craig McDonald—
Origin Systems (R.I.P.)

macnugetz@earthlink.net

Individuals who will benefit the most from this article are QA managers who are looking to improve their department's relationship with development, and development leads who are looking for insight into why QA works the way it does. This article presents qualitative advice on how to identify areas that are contributing to adversarial QA/development relationships, and ways to improve these relationships, ultimately leading to more efficient development processes that result in higher quality games.

This article is not a discussion of testing methodologies and practices. Although this topic is of equal importance to successful MMOG development, it goes well beyond the scope of this brief article. In addition, most of the literature discussing software quality assurance possesses this quantitative focus. Unfortunately, the most statistically sound testing methodology is utterly useless in the face of trying to navigate through a development process that fails to take QA seriously. This article focuses on how to increase QA's credibility with development, and nurture a relationship that benefits the entire organization.

Relationships

Successfully building an amicable relationship with the development team is a critical factor in establishing a successful QA organization. The nature of the relationships you build will dictate developers' willingness to adopt and adapt to new QA processes that affect them. This becomes even more important in the context of how QA and development have historically interacted with each other.

In the past it has been the norm for development to work in a vacuum, only to throw code over the wall to QA with little direction as to what changes have been made, and subsequently what needs to be tested. Historically, QA's first exposure to the inner workings of a new game system is through discovery, and trial and error. The inherent problem with this approach is that QA cannot easily differentiate between legitimate bugs and intended design. Testers will report issues that are not bugs, or even worse, ignore bugs under the assumption that they were part of the design. As testers report more illegitimate bugs and miss the real ones, the QA organization loses credibility with the developers. As this credibility is lost, developers find it all too easy to brush off real issues because they simply do not believe what the tester is reporting.

Phrases like, "It works on my standalone," or "You don't have the latest code published" only exacerbate the situation, leaving testers feeling frustrated and angry that the fruits of their labor are not taken seriously. The burden of changing this old way of thinking inevitably falls on the shoulders of QA, and this task can be insurmountable in the face of an adversarial or jaded relationship with the developers.

Start at the Top . . .

To gain maximum development buy-in for QA's interests, you should start with the producer. Ultimately, the producer is the captain of the ship, and is going to be the most effective and influential evangelist on the development team. The proof of this is in practical application.

Ultima Online's most recent producer came onto the scene in 2002 in the middle of development of the expansion pack, *Age of Shadows*. The QA supervisor at the time had had little success in getting the development team to adopt practices that would have ensured more efficient processes and quicker turnaround between development and QA. He seized the opportunity to start a fresh relationship with the new producer, communicating his concerns and suggestions on how they could work together to improve the existing process.

Establishing this relationship early proved invaluable. The supervisor found himself invited to relevant meetings from which he had previously been excluded. Design documentation improved dramatically. Testing time actually became part of the scheduling process instead of an afterthought. For the first time in years, the producer delayed publishes based on QA's input. By starting the relationship on a positive note, the QA supervisor gained an extremely valuable ally.

A Strange Bedfellow . . .

Although the producer is the optimal person to start with for relationship building, you may encounter producers that view QA as an obstacle to be overcome instead of as an equal partner in the development process. When dealing with producers like these, it is essential to acquire other allies in the company; otherwise, you are signing up for frustration and endless crunch.

One such ally, although uncommon, is in marketing. Marketing is affected the most by any changes in the schedule. Retail shelf space, advertising, promotional events, and most other components of the marketing mix must be scheduled and budgeted months in advance. Marketing's ability to successfully build momentum that results in higher sales is contingent upon accurate information regarding the development schedule. If the schedule was made without QA's input on required testing time, that schedule is at risk.

Contrary to the producer's likely response to the scheduling deficiency, throwing QA on crunch is not the best solution. If your concerns are falling on a deaf ear in the producer's office, your next stop should be at the door of the marketing director or product manager. This person will be all too willing to listen to information that will negatively impact his marketing plan.

The Importance of Crashing Meetings . . .

Meetings are arguably the least productive aspect of the development process. They tend to drag on, and meaningful action items arising out of meetings are few and far between, especially if there is anyone attending with even a marginal propensity for being disruptive.

Unfortunately, despite their drawbacks, significant decisions are all too often made in meetings. Even worse, many decisions are made in meetings without QA's input even though they will ultimately affect the nature and content of what needs to be tested for a given development initiative. This inevitably leads to QA working unnecessary crunch because the schedule was not appropriately adjusted for the additional testing time required that resulted from a set of decisions that were made without consulting QA.

As a QA manager, the obvious solution is to go to all of the relevant meetings. The problem is you are probably not getting invited to all of them. For this reason, you should not be the least bit shy about crashing meetings. If you find out a meeting is being conducted that will affect testing time or resources, you should be there, regardless of whether you were officially invited. However, in an effort to nurture the relationship with development, you should first approach the meeting owner and ask for an invite. This is the courteous thing to do, and it allows the meeting owner to correct the oversight on his own. It also allows him to maintain control over his meeting. Reserve crashing as a last resort, but never rule it out as a viable option.

Dates

Dates rule our lives, and have a significant influence on the scope and success of our games. Marketing likes to get in front of certain dates to increase sales. Holiday season represents drastically increased retail spending; however, the market is saturated at this time of year, which increases competition. During the summer there is usually a lull or even a drop in subscribers because all of the college kids have gone home for the summer. Rarely do these sales heuristics coincide with a development schedule, so there is always a great deal of negotiation between development and marketing to arrive at a date that can positively impact sales while at the same time allowing sufficient time to finish a compelling, high-quality game.

As a QA manager, it is imperative that you are involved in these negotiations. Testing is almost always an afterthought in these discussions. Even worse, testing time will be reduced over cutting features nine times out of ten. Ultimately, quality will be sacrificed, crunch will be inevitable, and testers will become burned out and frustrated. To prevent these things from happening, you must take an active role in setting dates with marketing and development.

There Is Never Enough Testing Time . . .

Box products are drastically different from MMOGs in countless ways. From a QA perspective, this holds true with respect to traditional Alpha, Beta, and Final definitions. MMOGs will never be bug free. Their complexity, sheer number of simultaneous users, and frequent updates make this impossible. For these reasons, there can never be enough testing time. However, the direct costs associated with lengthy testing schedules and the opportunity cost of delaying a release will never allow you the time you need. Therefore, when making estimates on testing schedules it is always wise to pad for uncertainty. However, it is extremely important to use discretion and experience when padding; otherwise, you will lose credibility with your estimates.

Your Initial Estimates Should Not Include Crunch . . .

Crunch leads to quick turnover, excessive overhead costs (overtime for hourly employees, and feeding the team), and diminishing returns on productivity. There are a select few personality types that work well in a crunch environment, but these individuals are few and far between. Most people will burn out, and become less and less productive in the face of a death march. It is arguable that the benefits of working 12-hour days and 7-day weeks are outweighed by these negatives.

Granted, some degree of crunch is inevitable. Individuals will give inaccurate time estimates, weather will knock out the power or prevent people from being able to come into work, hardware will fail, and critical members of the team will move on to bigger and better opportunities at other companies. However, crunch should never be included in the schedule. Crunch should only be used to make up for lost time in the face of these unforeseen events.

The Logistics of Beta Testing . . .

Beta testing is inherent to any game development and testing process, especially with MMOGs. As stated earlier, there is never enough time to test given the resources available to you and the complexity of the game you are developing. Beta testing is a great way to have thousands of eager eyes looking for the problems that you are going to miss in-house. However, a productive beta test must be well planned and conducted over a long enough period of time to be able to react to the wealth of feedback it will produce.

All aspects of a beta test require significant time investments that must be accounted for in the schedule. These include, but are not limited to:

- Identifying and recruiting thousands of testers
- Distributing the client either through download or mailing discs
- Setting up the infrastructure to efficiently receive feedback from the testers
- Getting that feedback to development in a timely manner
- Allowing development enough time to react and address the issues that the beta testers have reported

The administrative and logistical requirements for a successful beta test are no small matter. Adequate time and resources must be dedicated to a beta test; otherwise, it is simply not worth doing.

Solid Numbers

In the previous section regarding testing time, we discussed padding estimates to account for uncertainty, and that the propensity to pad too much can result in loss of credibility. This can be prevented by supporting your estimates with solid numbers. Development is notorious for underestimating how long it will take to design and technically implement a system; therefore, it is not surprising that they tend to do the same with the amount of time it takes to test those systems. Empirical evidence is the best way to overcome this bias toward underestimation. Marketing, development, and management are not going to support resource allocation and scheduling estimates based on hunches. You must back everything up with solid numbers.

Metrics Must Be Meaningful and Accurate . . .

Given the right tools and experience, the possibilities for metrics to report are endless. Mean-time to failure, knock-on rate, fix-failure rate, and countless other QA measures are all legitimate metrics that you can report to development, but are they going to be meaningful, and more importantly, useful to the people to whom you are reporting them?

The best way to identify useful metrics is to solicit the development leads. They will know what information is going to be useful and valuable to their respective teams. Once the metrics have been identified, they must be presented in a digestible format. Spreadsheets filled with numbers will most likely end up in the recycle bin. Visual representations are much easier to digest. There are tools such as DevTrack that make this task very easy; however, this is an expensive application that many studios can not afford. An excellent tool that is accessible to anyone with a Windows-based system is Microsoft XL. With a little practice, this application has endless possibilities for reporting testing information in a format that is meaningful and easy to read.

Aside from soliciting the development leads, two metrics are relevant to any MMOG development project. The first is fix-failure rate. This metric quantifies failed fixes development has attempted. It can be meaningful to the development leads and the producer because a high fix-failure rate can indicate a lack of thoroughness with respect to bug fixes. Again, the proof of this can be seen in practical application. The aforementioned QA supervisor for *Ultima Online* started calculating and reporting fix-failure rates for the developers, which was relatively high. As a result, the development leads implemented a policy that required developers to test their own fixes on a published test center (instead of their standalone development box) before setting their bugs to "Awaiting Verification" in the bug-tracking database. The fix-failure rate improved drastically.

The second metric is simple: open versus closed bugs. By representing this metric graphically it is easy to see how close the project is to completion. As the number of open bugs starts to level off, and the number of closed bugs starts to increase at an increasing rate, the graph will show the two starting to converge. Once the two lines get close to each other and eventually cross paths, you can be reasonably confident that the project is almost finished.

Ways to Make Data Collection Easier . . .

Defect tracking is not the only source of useful metrics. Over the life of a project it is extremely important to know how you are tracking against your scheduling estimates. This information is reflected in the time it takes to write and run test suites, regress bug fixes, report bugs, and how downtime beyond your control will impact your schedule. This information can be tracked through XL; however, this method is manual and labor intensive.

An alternative solution is to automate the process. This means you will need dedicated QA engineers, which can be a tough sell to management because they are much more expensive than the average tester. However, the payoff with such an implementation is huge. Manual data tracking is virtually eliminated, and pulling historical data to assist with scheduling estimates on future projects is reduced to the push of a button.

Team Morale

Your team's morale can seriously affect your ability to maintain a positive and productive relationship with development. During long periods of crunch it is inevitable that unforeseen problems will stop work or force tedious work to be redone. It is all too easy to assign blame for these problems to someone outside of your immediate realm of daily contact. QA blames development and vice versa, leading to increased tension between the two groups. For these reasons, it is imperative to keep morale up, especially during crunch and high pressure deadlines.

Ways to Keep Morale High . . .

Recognition and reward are critical factors in maintaining morale. Nothing is worse than hard work going unnoticed, especially if it was done over late nights and weekends. Take every opportunity to recognize the efforts of your reports through e-mail, in person, and publicly in meetings. This sends a clear message to your people that they are important to you and you appreciate their work. Rewards are just as important. Small gestures (gift certificates, lunch on you, a few days off) are just as effective as large ones (promotions, bonuses).

An often-overlooked method of keeping morale up is proactive disclosure. As a manager it is easy to take for granted certain pieces of information that are relevant to your reports' day-to-day experiences. Without an accurate disclosure of news and events surrounding the project, your people will take the bits and pieces of information they are able to obtain through the grapevine and draw their own conclusions. Generally, these conclusions are pessimistic at best, and are based on completely inaccurate data.

Another way to increase morale is to facilitate meaningful involvement and participation. Bring testers to meetings that involve systems on which they have worked. Encourage your reports to spend face-time with developers to resolve issues as opposed to doing it through e-mail. These practices enable your testers to voice their concerns to active audiences, further validating the notion that the development process is a symbiotic relationship between QA and development rather than two functional groups working independently of each other.

Conclusion

By no means is this article meant to be a decisive guide for fixing all of the problems in a development environment. A more appropriate use of this information is as a general guide to facilitating a better working relationship between QA and development. Adversarial relationships can destroy morale, productivity, and most importantly the potential to create lasting value with a high-quality game. Successfully managing your relationship with development can make the difference between a stagnant organization, and one of perpetual process improvement.

The producer and the development leads are your keys to success. These individuals can become evangelists for your cause. However, failure to acquire these allies can be mitigated by having friends in marketing. Marketing directors and product managers become very attentive to anything that can impact the schedule. Allocating appropriate testing time will never be an exact science, but making intelligent estimates based on historical evidence and solid empirical data can greatly increase your credibility. With respect to data, always remember your audience; otherwise, your reports will never be read. Always be aware of your team's morale, and disclose as much information to them as possible regardless of whether it is directly applicable to their daily activities.

Applying these ideas and practices will not ensure your success; however, they will greatly increase your potential to achieve it. No organization is perfect; however, all organizations have one thing in common: they are all made up of people. By focusing on the people, positive relationships can be nurtured to achieve an efficient and productive development process that results in the creation of great games.

3.3

Small Fish in a Big Pond: How Small Developers and Publishers Can Succeed in Promoting Their MMP Game

Mike Wallis—Turbine Entertainment

mwallis@turbinegames.com

Like any other facet of the massively multiplayer (MMP) game industry, there is no shortage of opinions when it comes to strategizing about the best way to promote and generate interest about a game. From print advertising and Web banner placements to interstitials and pop-ups, the debate isn't so much about what to do as when to do it and how often. In our efforts to create a successful position for the existence of *EVE Online* in the hearts and minds of MMP consumers, we used all of the preceding options in addition to community management techniques, newsletters, and specialized promotions—such as the affiliate and buddy programs. The result was a game we were proud of with a supportive throng of followers and impressive sales figures. It was not an accident that this sleeper gem from Iceland became "the little game that could."

State of the MMP Industry, Early 2002

In early 2002, the active MMP playing field was relatively small, but there were over 100 titles in development. The existing "500 lb. gorillas" included *Ultima Online, EverQuest, Asheron's Call,* and the newly released *Dark Age of Camelot.* Other subscription-based MMPs that were surviving included *World War II Online, Motor City Online,* and *Anarchy Online.* Finally, there were a number of major projects on the horizon for release in the next one to two years: *Star Wars Galaxies, Earth & Beyond, The Sims Online, Shadowbane,* and *City of Heroes. EVE Online* was yet another of those MMPs scheduled to release in fall 2002, but how could a small developer (CCP Games) and publisher (Simon & Schuster Interactive) hope to carve out a customer base for itself among all those heavy hitters?

David vs. Goliaths

There were multiple Goliaths we would challenge for a coveted portion of the MMP market, in our case: Electronic Arts, Sony Online, and Microsoft/Turbine Games. We were going up against seasoned veterans with much greater financial backing than we could ever hope to bring to the party. Our goal was not to lure their customers away, for we knew *EVE Online* was a different genre of game than the fantasy sword & sorcery *Ultima Online, EverQuest,* or *Asheron's Call.* Instead, we sought to offer an engrossing alternative to the fantasy genre, although that was something two other games in development—*Star Wars Galaxies* and *Earth & Beyond*—were also hoping to achieve with their space-based/sci-fi themes. We always felt that developers/publishers Sony Online/LucasArts and Westwood/EA, both with vastly superior development budgets and advertising dollars, could squash us when it came to generating awareness through traditional methods: print advertising spends and online media buys. Therefore, we realized early on it was not feasible to tackle the leaders head on by outspending them with advertising dollars. Instead, we "took it to the streets" by using guerilla marketing tactics to generate awareness and publicity for *EVE Online.*

Pre-Release

The objective of the development team during pre-release was to spread the word about the game to raise awareness. Initially, you only want to do this one place and one place only: the game's official Web site. This is where you want your fans, those who will become the hardcore disciples, gathering to exchange ideas and speculate about your upcoming MMOG and how it will advance the genre. As development continues and the project gets closer to its release date, you will need to spread your efforts out to other MMOG fan and news sites, conduct exclusive interviews, IRC real-time chats, and magazine previews.

These early potential customers are looking for a key piece of information: whether your game is what they are searching for in an MMP. We began by making comparisons between *EVE* and other released games (not MMPs) to give the 50,000-foot (extremely high-level) view of our game a solid frame of reference. The two games we compared *EVE* to were the space trading classic *Elite* and the trading/action/story driven *Privateer.* This allowed us to establish what our high-concept was right out of the gate without drawing attention to our competitors.

Within the first 6 to 12 months of development, the information you release must be carefully guarded—not for competitive reasons, but because the game you ultimately release will differ significantly from your early design plans. During the development process, certain features may wind up on the cutting room floor for a myriad of reasons. If you have not shared the details, no one will be the wiser. If you've spoken of them publicly, their absence may come back to haunt you. Ardent fans who are closely following your incubating game are likely to dig up old message board posts from your team, old interviews, past FAQs, and so forth. Having to backpedal can hurt your credibility, and these are the people you will want to believe in you on the inevitable day when you have to announce an unpopular, but necessary, change to their virtual world.

In view of these facts, we tried our best to disseminate information early. We did not have a community manager yet, so we appointed one key member of the development team to act as a designated spokesperson; his responsibilities included making informational posts now and then on the official site. The comments do not have to be specific. Vague or generic statements are generally enough to keep your fledgling community engaged and returning to your site. For *EVE*, we would release stories related to the game fiction as well as information about things that we were certain would remain, such as the ships and player races.

Think carefully before implementing message boards. With the opening of a forum comes much responsibility. It is your way of saying to potential subscribers that you are open for business and ready to hear what they say. Is there someone already in place on the team who could handle the additional responsibility of managing a growing Web community? If not, it may be wise to wait until such a person is in place. Untended forums can become hotbeds of unwanted content festering on your Web site. You may choose to frequent existing forums on fan and news sites for a while to draw attention to your Web site, and then announce the grand opening of your own boards when your community team is in place and ready to oversee them.

The important thing here is not so much to give the future players a voice in how you should proceed in developing your game, but for your team to be visible on your own site. Schedule your updates regularly; perhaps every three weeks in the first stages of development. Do your best to stick to this schedule, as even small deviations can result in rumblings of impending doom from the fan base you are seeking to cultivate.

Approximately one year prior to release, it will become necessary to appoint or hire an official online community manager (CM). It becomes this person's responsibility to serve as the mouthpiece of the development team and to pass along relevant and major parts of game information to the fans. This CM or online community representative, OCR as some companies call them, needs to strategically lay out when it is best to release information, working in conjunction with the dev team to make announcements after a particular internal milestone has been achieved. That way, the CM and the dev team are working on ostensibly the same schedule.

The producer should also post project status updates to the official Web site every four to eight weeks. The update should include a high-level view of the development situation—accomplishments made over the past month and what objectives the dev team aims to complete in the near future. At this stage, a diary or daily blog format is too specific and detailed. Try to keep it at a higher level, one to two pages total. This information will be picked up by portal MMP sites and may get the game mentioned in mainstream gaming news sites as well.

In addition to posting key information during regular updates to the official Web site, we also picked three or four key major *EVE* "fan sites" and MMP portal sites. "Fan sites" are Web pages set up by members of the community on their own initiative, dedicated to specific games that interest them. To those sites, we would grant exclusive interviews with the team or give them the ability to moderate and host a real-time IRC session with several dev team members. Besides the obvious PR benefits, this also serves to drive the enthusiasm of those key sites for maintaining and promoting your game as a viable upcoming MMP option for players. In addition, this rewards the most loyal fans, perhaps giving incentive to others to create more new fan sites. It is that goal you are aiming to achieve—to be talked about among the MMP crowd well before your game is released.

Real-time chat sessions aren't absolutely necessary, but do have the potential to have a good return for a small time investment. While the chats themselves only cater to a very small, extremely hardcore group of players, the logs of the sessions can be invaluable. The transcripts will be posted to various fan sites enabling anyone who was unable to attend the chats the opportunity to read what was discussed. They also allow fans to feel closer to the dev team and will succeed in giving the overall community a stronger sense of cohesiveness. We felt involving two to four dev team members for an hour was certainly worth the goodwill gained. We held IRC sessions approximately once every four to six weeks or soon after special announcements were made, such as release date changes, major press releases, or in response to a major competitor's announcement. Conducting chat sessions after special announcements was done to keep rumors from brewing out of control, to answer questions, and to reinforce faith in the game's development.

Build Trust Among the Community

Over the course of development and management of the community, you will undoubtedly become frustrated with them at times. However, that should never deter you from your responsibility to them of distributing information intelligently and honestly. Be clear and consistent about your message; this will benefit the project in the long run. The fans (who will become future paying customers!) will remember what you've said in the past and call you out if you deviate from those statements or go back on your word. If a major gameplay feature has changed, explain to them why. If a particular feature's nuances are still up in the air or may not make it into the released version, make that clear. Don't be afraid to say that things are still undergoing balancing and tuning, because the reality of MMP games is that those tasks will take place well past the release date. Keeping the community informed in this way helps to establish a much-needed level of loyalty by illustrating to them your commitment to bring them the best game possible.

Use the official Web site and message board to communicate your information. Be sure to have your CM monitor fan and news sites to ensure they are picking up the news. If they aren't, it would behoove you to create an e-mail distribution list, put those sites on it, and blast out the information as it becomes available, ensuring that they all receive the same news at the same time.

As with real-world politics, having information equates to having power. You'll need to be careful about showing favoritism between Web sites. The operators of such sites can go from being your greatest allies to huge thorns in your side if they detect you are favoring a rival site. Make sure you are aware of this. What we did during *EVE*'s development was to rotate our exclusive content among several of the largest fan sites, thereby ensuring that each site had its chance to scoop its competitors at one point or another. This method, when properly managed, serves to stir up friendly competition. It is a more hands-on approach, but when under the responsibility of a quality OCR, can go a long way in promoting awareness about your game.

Trolls and Flamers

Despite your best efforts to please everyone in the community, you will eventually be plagued by message board troublemakers known as *trolls*, who enjoy their online experience by making others unhappy. Insulting others on a forum is referred to as "flaming," and trolls love to start flame wars. What should you do when faced with their (seemingly) endless onslaught of disruptive posts? We found out the best thing to do is to simply ignore them. You should remove posts that are highly offensive or lock threads that serve no purpose to foster the community in a positive way. Monitor their every post, however, and if they violate any of the forum policies and posting guidelines (you do have those, right?), then issue a warning to the troll/flamer privately via e-mail. Public warnings can be appropriate under certain circumstances, but only if done in a calm, professional, and polite manner. It never pays to lower yourself to their level by thrashing them on the forum. Multiple warnings can and should lead to temporary bans (suspensions) from the forums. Multiple temporary bans should become permanent. The bottom line is that you need to follow through with any threats you make, because if you issue empty threats that you don't back up with action, you will lose control of the boards and they will be running you instead of the other way around. Keeping the forums on an even keel will encourage the good contributors to keep posting and your community will flourish.

When responding to community questions on the message boards, know that you don't have to answer each and every question—to do so would require an incredible amount of time that could probably be better spent elsewhere. Pick and choose the questions to respond to carefully. You'll find that some posters will try to goad you into a response by complaining loudly; the squeaky wheel gets the grease, so to speak. Others will try to repeatedly ask the same question in different ways. However, make a conscious effort to answer a few questions every day. This lets the community know you are present and responsive. Ultimately, by building trust with the community, they will often become your champions in the face of trolls and flamers.

Consider choosing your most trusted and obvious message board leaders to become "moderators." Give them the opportunity to help you maintain a professional and positive atmosphere on the forums.

Alpha and Beta Testing

Players will come in droves to sign up to be a beta tester for your game. Most will apply because they want a free game to play, but others are legitimate potential customers with a desire to get a glimpse at the next "revolutionary MMP." The testing community can be very helpful to the quality assurance process. Hundreds and thousands of players are immensely more capable of putting strain and stress on both the hardware and software than a dozen QA employees can. These external testers are creative and resourceful in discovering gameplay holes and exploits that could never have been exposed by a small in-house team.

Such a large number of beta testers presents an interesting logistical problem, however. How can you manage and document each and every bug that is filed into the database by the testers? Filtering out the noise (trivial bugs or those that do not provide enough information) and duplicate bugs from the legitimate ones is a daunting task for any QA group. Early on in the *EVE* beta test phase, we realized we had to employ the community for assistance in this difficult task. Therefore, we asked who among the most active testers on the message boards and in the IRC channel would like to volunteer to be "lead" testers in order to assist in organizing the testing community and sorting through the bug reports. From our group of volunteers, we had 30–40 testers take up the challenge. These testers became part of an elite "bughunter" group on which the dev team relied heavily.

We used two main methods of communication to convey information to the beta test group: online real-time chat, IRC, and a special beta tester-only message board. Due to the sensitive nature of our still-in-development game, we had all beta testers agree to abide by the nondisclosure agreement, or NDA. This kept them from talking about the game outside of the beta IRC channel and the exclusive message board. Perhaps we were lucky, perhaps it was due to the strong cohesiveness of our community—built through the efforts listed previously—that created a level of trust, but we had very few leaks of information prior to release.

The online beta tester chat channel would be password protected and moderated by members of *EVE*'s volunteer program, as well as one or two members of the developer's QA team. The QA team would pass along information to the testers in the IRC beta channel. IRC would be used for the real-time problems and critical things we needed testing results for immediately. Higher level or more general bugs/balancing issues would be posted to the login/password protected beta message board by either the QA team or our community manager. We'd also have a designer or producer post to the beta forum to answer questions or to give updates. Similar to staying in touch with the main community, it is necessary to post semi-frequently to the beta forums to let the players know the team is available and responsive to questions and concerns—although in this communication outlet, you can discuss things in greater detail since the beta testers are all under NDA and already have knowledge of the game's play mechanics.

Finally, you will certainly have your share of doom and gloom predictors among the beta community. For the most part, ignore them, because responding to their taunts only provokes them further. Let your beta community defend the game. It is productive to have players who offer some criticism in order to provide a reality check. However, if they end up becoming more of a headache than they're worth, issue warnings (cite the policies and procedures), and finally ban them from the beta test all together. Don't be afraid to do this—making an example out of one or two troublemakers goes a long way—others will remain in line. When you ban people, make sure you ban them from the beta test, both the beta and main forums, and the beta IRC channel—cover all your bases. Finally, send an e-mail to the offending player(s) and reiterate that they are still bound by the NDA and may not discuss the game. Chances are that they will, although they will no longer have access to your site, so they will take their story to other sites. This is when your good relationship with the fan and news site operators can work to your advantage. You will be amazed by how swiftly they will come to your defense, and the disgruntled ex-tester will find he has no audience and move on without further ado.

Other Preparations

Learn as much as you can from the best practices and mistakes of others. Talk to industry peers, obtain all the information (interviews, articles, post mortems) you can get your hands on, and, if necessary, work with consultants. CCP did this and we gained a wealth of knowledge about setting up a customer service support group for MMPs, and how to establish and motivate a volunteer/guide group. Before implementing the customer service group, we drew up a report outlining our vision and goals for it. The report was based on articles and interviews with people in the business. Finally, we also had consultants from an experienced team of former game masters who had worked on *Ultima Online*, *Anarchy Online*, and other games.

Start the customer support team during the beta phase. The beta period is a training period for both the dev team and the CS group. Although it will create additional cost overhead by assigning the CS team during the beta phase, you will more than make up for it with experienced game master support and streamlined operations upon your game's release. For *EVE*, we had the core CS group running eight months prior to release and supported the beta community in much the same way as we expected to support our customers post-release.

Alpha and beta testing periods are the time when you are allowed to make mistakes, so use that time wisely. Once the game is live, you won't find the players so forgiving and they will show their dissatisfaction with you by canceling their subscriptions. Don't be afraid to try things from many angles—both within the game and the Web community—and find what works best for you. Put as much effort as you can into testing prior to release, including software, people, business methods, game balancing, and so forth. Create software tools that will permit adequate server logging and database perusal. Make sure you can track the transfer of items from player to player, and ensure you give the game masters the tools and abilities to replace items, teleport around the game world instantaneously, and deal with troublemakers adequately and swiftly.

Even with all the information you might collect that will prepare you for the job, the goal of shipping a quality product can only be achieved with the right people who are smart and adaptive to a dynamic working environment. Establish a recruitment process with involved tests and interviews to ensure you obtain the best of the best. Dev team members should have played at least one MMP, and designers preferably more than one. Assign team leads who are organized, dedicated, and who can drive the team to milestone completion. At the end of the day, the whole team must keep the game's vision in sight—everyone should be building and creating to the same scope of product.

Negotiate deals with gaming sites to give away a certain number of player slots to the beta test. This is an easy way to obtain free exposure, as beta slots cost you nothing. Such contest announcements will be carried on gaming news sites and generate a high amount of chatter among the MMP community. We went a step beyond this and held numerous contests giving away limited edition concept artwork reproductions and other exclusive dev team memorabilia. *EVE*'s community manager was famous for popping into the official IRC channel and holding impromptu trivia contests for *EVE* goodies. Try it—it creates enormous positive vibes among the community.

Finally, be prepared for everything to change during and post-launch. No matter how much you prepare, things will change post-launch as the customers start playing the game. Their play path may also differ from the path your beta community took. Why? Well, beta and post-release are two different things, and now these are people paying to play and playing for keeps. However, with high caliber development and CS people, and experience from the beta test cycles, you should be able to endure any bumps in the road.

Launch day is approaching…

Post-Release

Now that the game is live, the team's main focus of communication shifts from raising awareness about the game to managing the game's community of players. By showing your presence to the customers, it will display dedication and respect by the team for the now-paying customers. Presence will go a long way toward retaining subscribers as the players see the dev team responding to their issues and needs. A visible, communicative dev team will generate positive goodwill with the players, which will in turn spawn helpful word-of-mouth advertising. We used five main outlets of communicating with the players: 1) official message boards, 2) in-game chats, 3) volunteer program, 4) dev blogs, and 5) other outlets such as IRC and interviews. Remember, you want players to ultimately decide to subscribe (and therefore pay).

The main communication medium should be the same as it was pre-release: the official message boards. Before release, trolls and flamers were tolerated to a degree; however, now you may want to take some steps to lock those troublemakers out. One thing you don't need right after release is a bunch of doomsayers and fanboys of other games bashing your brand new MMP. What we did with *EVE* was allow anybody to read the forums, but only subscribers were permitted to post. It is much easier to tolerate a message board troll if he's a paying customer.

You'll need to be prepared to be active in dealing with the multitude of questions that will hit the official forums. Organize the forums into specific channels in order to direct questions to the proper areas. Here you can count on players who participated in the beta test to answer questions because they'll want to be looked upon as knowledgeable members of the community. While fellow players will answer many questions, don't expect them to answer everything. You will need to monitor the forums and look for threads with a high number of responses or "bumps" that keep the thread at the top of the forums. These threads will often require a post from the OCR or a member of the dev team with an official answer. Answering even just one hot topic will go a long way in nurturing community spirit.

As the programmers and designers work to fix bugs and plug exploits, the CM should be collecting data on the biggest issues currently plaguing the players. Obtaining and relaying answers in a timely manner should be the highest priority for the CM. It is very important that your OCR staff has as much information as possible from the development team with clear indications of what may or may not be said publicly. This is your link to your player base and it's vital to ensure that your official representative appears knowledgeable about the current state of the game and what's on the agenda in the future.

Due to the nature of *EVE*'s single server (non-sharding) universe, we felt we had a unique opportunity to host in-game live chat sessions with the players. We set up a program that was called the Council of Stellar Management, or CSM, which was a program whereby we would select 12 players at a time to attend a dev chat held in-game. These player delegates were selected from various sizes of different corporations (*EVE*'s version of a guild) as well as independent or freelance players and were on the CSM for a period of six weeks. Membership revolved in order to give many corporations a chance to be represented. The council roster was posted publicly and players were encouraged to pass their questions to be asked during the meetings along to the delegates. This allowed other players to feel some form of belonging even if they were not actively participating in the meetings themselves. CSM meetings were held every two weeks, attended by the OCR and at least one member of the dev team, and lasted generally one hour. Logs of the CSM meetings were kept and posted to the message boards by either the OCR or a member in attendance. In all, CSM meetings were, and still are, a positive way to allow the players to communicate with the dev team, and they continue to this day.

Prior to release we established a volunteer program. This was a network of players who had a desire to learn more about the game in order to share their knowledge with others. During pre-release, the volunteers numbered around 80–100 active participants and we counted on those volunteers to help new players once we released the game. To ensure they would be able to contribute immediately, we provided them with a full copy of the gold master version of *EVE*, as well as a free account. The first priority of these in-game volunteers was to monitor the in-game "Help" channel, which was where players with questions would go for assistance. Later, as the volunteer group grew, we assigned volunteers to each of the new player starting areas to proactively go out and provide help as needed. *EVE* has a rather steep learning curve and we felt this direct, live aid went a long way in more expeditiously creating knowledgeable players who felt better about the game and who could also, if necessary, help one another. *Note: Many companies have removed volunteer programs due to legal issues; we encourage each company to do its own due diligence when seeking to institute a volunteer program.*

Developer diaries are the most popular form of communication for the dev team. These sometimes daily, but more often semi-weekly blogs are an outlet for each member of the team to post his or her thoughts on design methodologies, current and upcoming game features, and even to poll the players for their input on what they would like to see implemented. Blogs are an easy way for dev members to communicate with the players, thereby fueling the cohesive community feeling. Make sure that everyone on the team is aware of how to communicate effectively with the community—in other words, that they have gone through some form of "PR training." You don't want them revealing proprietary information or discussing features the team has no intention of implementing. It goes without saying that you also don't want your devs airing grievances or venting about internal political issues in a public forum.

Finally, we used IRC and other gaming sites as promotional informational outlets. IRC was eventually abandoned as an official communication channel several months after *EVE*'s release due its limited audience—we could only hit the very hardest core of the hardcore audience using IRC—and the effort involved with having to maintain yet another official communication outlet. While it was great for bringing early adaptors to *EVE*, it did virtually nothing post-release and the time invested was a losing proposition compared to the result gained. However, by using the gaming sites through exclusive dev team interviews, we were able to keep *EVE* on the main page of these gaming Web sites and, in turn, in the eyes of potential customers. Having a few members of the dev team take 10–20 minutes out of their day to answer some questions is more than worth the PR value derived from the time invested. Exclusive interviews will more than pay for themselves time and time again. Game sites love the exclusive content, and they have no problem flaunting the fact they are presenting such content that cannot be obtained anywhere else.

Newsletters

Hopefully, your registration process gathers valid e-mail addresses for players. This is a necessity not only for communicating critical information such as billing problems, but it is also a direct means for pushing information out to subscribers. Arguably, the most important time of a young MMOG's life is in the immediate 90 days following its release. During this span, we released a newsletter every six weeks to all subscribers in our database—active and inactive. These beautifully illustrated HTML e-mails detailed major fixes, outlined plans for upcoming patches, and thanked players for their continued support. Following that, every 90-day interval we sent out a newsletter to all beta testers and former subscribers (nonactive players) in our database and invited them back to the universe of *EVE*. We started off by offering a free 7-day trial, eventually raising that to 14 days free because we felt that would give them more time to become hooked. These newsletters covered major enhancements since release and gameplay changes significant to the player community. Each and every person in the database is a potential player. Use that vast collection of names and solicit them. The worst thing they can do is ignore you, but since they weren't players anyway, you have nothing to lose.

Newsletters are important for communicating both the recent changes to the game and for the long-term plans the dev team has in store for the game. Recent changes can bring back disenfranchised players who left due to issues they might have had with design or balancing. Long-term additions give players the fulfillment of knowing what's in store for the game down the road; everyone likes a little glimpse into the future. It should be noted that "long-term" can be anywhere from 90 days to one year out, as long as you clarify the plans to the best of your ability. Players will understand if a new feature takes longer to implement than originally planned. Keep these e-mails as short but informative as possible. You'll stand a better chance of having them read rather than being tossed immediately.

Promotional Programs

An MMP loses much of its momentum once it releases. To maintain momentum, marketing dollars are usually required to sustain the game's awareness among the MMP community. With a small developer, money for marketing is hard to come by. Therefore, we tried to structure win-win programs for the parties involved—the developer and either the subscriber, potential subscriber, or the Web site. By using this method, we were able to establish a number of highly successful programs that greatly expanded *EVE*'s active subscriber numbers.

Free Content Downloads

We essentially released "mini expansion packs" worth of content every three months following the game's deployment. This showed our players that the dev team was serious about adding to, expanding, and improving the feature set of *EVE*. We could have saved the content and released it all as a larger expansion pack for sale at retail, but knew players didn't want to wait, nor did they want to have to pay for added features. Our philosophy is that an MMP is ever-evolving; thus, we shouldn't make players pay for something when they've given us their loyalty (and money). In addition, we did a huge release, again for free, in late 2003. This was roughly six months following *EVE*'s release, and it was essentially a full expansion pack worth of features, graphics, and playability. We overhauled a good portion of the main parts of the game, which in retrospect went a long way to satisfy players and to even bring back a good percentage of those who had canceled their subscriptions. Plan and schedule free content download releases—the players will greatly appreciate it.

The Buddy Program

Everyone knows it's more fun to play with friends than without. Knowing that *EVE* players have friends, we set up the buddy program. This was a simple program by which an existing player could click on a link in the "Account Management" portion of the *EVE* Web site and invite a friend to join *EVE*. The friend would be able to download the client for free and would be given free game time. In the beginning, we offered three free days; that eventually evolved into 14 days, which we felt gave them more time to learn the game and decide they wanted to keep playing. The bonus in using the buddy program was the client was free, thereby saving the friend from having to buy *EVE* at retail. As an added benefit, to the initial inviting player, would be that if the friend ultimately signed up and became an active subscriber, the inviting player would be given free game time as well—a way to say "thank you" for referring a new *EVE* player. We made this process as easy to do as possible:

1. Having an individual page with instructions and buddy program details.
2. Clearly displaying multiple e-mail fields to enter the address of friends.
3. Showing the e-mail that will be sent, along with the opportunity to edit it.
4. Having a final confirmation link to send out the e-mails.
5. Displaying a sincere "Thank You" message from us to the inviting player.

The Free Trial Download

This method of promotion is an industry standard—allowing players to freely download the game client and giving them free game time in an effort to get them hooked. At first, we started by only offering three free days. This wasn't successful, as three days is hardly enough time to get one's feet wet in *EVE*. We boosted this to 10 and, eventually, the current 14 days, and it has been very successful for us. We learned a few things from this promotional program: 1) allow players to sign up without the need for a credit card—when we did away with that requirement, sign-ups rose significantly, and 2) give enough free game time that will allow players to become familiar with the game and want to stay. Finally, by offering this free trial download, it was picked up by nearly all of the gaming sites, thereby giving us a nice bump of free public relations.

Affiliate Program

By far the most successful program for us has been the affiliate program. It is a program by which we establish a type of profit sharing relationship with a gaming Web site. In this relationship, we provide eye-catching banner advertisements for *EVE* and they decide where and how many to show. When players click on the ad, they are taken to a page on the official *EVE* site where they can then download the game for $19.95 (30 days of game time included). Should these people then sign up and become monthly subscribers, the referring Web site will receive $7.00. We pay the referring sites for every referral that ultimately becomes an *EVE* subscriber. Therein lies the beauty—sites can earn more by giving us more exposure.

We make the affiliate process as simple and painless as possible. We require them to complete a quick form with all relevant contact information and then enter them into the program—nobody is denied participation. They are next sent a cluster of banner and flash advertisements of various shapes and sizes to fit every typical ad dimension. These are eye-catching, often animated ads. Along with the ads is an e-mail with all relevant information: login, password, how to check the number of referrals the site has generated, an important referral link, and instructions on how to set it all up. We even provide a tech support e-mail address for our affiliates. Seeing as how we have gained thousands of subscribers and paid out tens of thousands of dollars in referral awards, clearly this is a win-win promotional program for both sides.

Reactionary Moves

When Electronic Arts made an announcement in early 2004 that they would be shutting down the *Earth & Beyond* servers the following fall, CCP was presented with a unique opportunity to capitalize on the closure of one its MMP competitors. We were able to take advantage of that move by directing a marketing campaign targeted at *E&B* players who would eventually be without a game to play.

We instituted an outreach program specifically targeted at *E&B* players. We had marketing people go on to any and all accessible *E&B* sites and offer those players a free download of the client, as well as free trial period to play the game. By setting up a special jump page welcoming *E&B* players, a very easy to understand sign-up process, and by not requiring a credit card, we added thousands of subscribers to *EVE*. Granted, an opportunity such as this is infrequent, but it is a good example of how you can benefit from announcements by competitors—keep your eyes on what your competition is doing and look for creative ways to increase your subscription base should the opportunity present itself.

Team and Server Management—Post-Launch

In the few days following release, it may seem the plethora of issues is just too much. Keep your cool and don't panic! Make sure to filter out the noise and prioritize the important things. If necessary, roll back the game to a previously saved state to correct major holes such as exploits. During *EVE*'s launch, we had just such an issue. It happened exactly one week after launch and it required us to roll back the game state to 12 hours prior to plug a large exploit. As compensation for their lost time, we provided all players a decent amount of in-game currency and 12 hours of skill training, as well as a fair assessment of what had occurred and how we would fix it. Despite the negative implications of the rollback, our quick and honest handling of the situation and the resulting compensation was viewed favorably by the vast majority of players.

The real work has just begun. It's not time for vacations. Plan for at least two to three months of extensive work after launch; don't expect that anyone won't be needed. The team will probably be drained from intense crunch periods by this time, but, as previously noted, the first 90 days post-launch is generally regarded as the most critical time for a new MMP.

Finally, log everything and watch your server cluster carefully. If you don't log everything that's happening in your game world, you'll have a difficult time finding out whether something critical needs fixing and whether that something is a bug, exploit, hack, or even a bogus report. Having the extra logging enabled will keep you on top of everything and allow you to make the right decisions when your new business is starting up—at this early stage, every mistake is expensive in the long run. On the customer support side, we developed our backend *EVE* server pages to fit our needs and made extensive reports that enabled us to analyze core issues mounting in our customer support queues and to report problems quickly to the dev team.

Conclusion

A game will only be able to continue if it sustains profitability for the developer. As such, the overall goal is to increase the subscriber numbers. Whether your game uses a subscription-based model, charges exclusively for expansion packs or new content, or makes money by selling in-game items for real-world money, having more subscribers will enable you to have a larger revenue stream. Continue to promote your game in some manner, strive to lower the churn rate, and maintain positive community relations. The community is the backbone of your game—these core players will spread the word about your game to fellow players and potential players.

Play your own game. While dev team members know the nuances of the game and how it works at the base (theoretical) level, only by playing the game will they truly understand the problems the players are experiencing. These problems will usually be with balancing, but quirks with the UI, graphics, or other minor but annoying problems can frequently mount and decrease player satisfaction. Schedule a weekly session where your dev team plays together, and then meet to discuss their feelings and ideas about what is and isn't working well in the game.

Know your player base. Monitor trends in the game's economics to ensure balance, and plug any exploits. For example, if players are taking advantage of a particular weakness in the AI of an NPC enemy and "farming" the loot, re-tool that NPC's behavior. Watch the forums for hot topics—those will be the ones with hundreds of responses and thousands of views. If such a topic is related to something happening in-game, it is best to take notice of it and, if required, respond.

Talk to your customers. Strive for the best customer service. Don't try to hide major setbacks from the players—they are living in this universe you've created and they will know if you try to sweep problems under the rug. Be as honest as possible and let the players know of major changes before you implement them. Silent nerfs are always regarded with scorn. Posting news, using dev blogs, and forum posts by the live team do wonders for the community spirit, even if it seems as you just put oil on a fire. In the long run, it's a question of trust between the live team, developers, and the community that will give you the added patience you need while crunching those extra bugs out.

Finally, don't sweat the little stuff. Seeing the dream of a great game evolve from the imaginations of its creators into a fully-operational virtual world is exciting and rewarding. It can be unsettling to see negative reactions or criticism of your work on message boards or game sites, but if you are wise and learn to discern the legitimate complaints from the rumblings of the unfaithful, you'll be fine and your game will flourish. The bottom line is that it's all about making a game, and games are supposed to be fun. You are fortunate enough to be one of the lucky few who've managed to transform a hobby into a career. Allow yourself the opportunity to enjoy the ride.

3.4

Managing and Growing an MMOG as a Service

John Donham—Sony Online Entertainment

jdonham@soe.sony.com

Building, launching, and supporting a massively multiplayer online game (MMOG) is one of the hardest tasks within the game business. You, as one of the developers of the product, have a dramatic ability to affect the life of the service. Could your product live for five to ten years? It could live for many more, but along the way, you'll face many challenges, both from internal and external sources. Simply recognizing the challenge may be harder than you think, let alone having a plan to address it. Products that are able to change the most, and in ways that meet the expectations of a constantly changing marketplace, have the greatest chance of a long life.

This article delves into the basics of maintaining an online service and an online game—from defining the terms of the industry, to explaining what you need to understand and know about your customers, to methods of maximizing customer acquisition, converting retail customers into subscriptions, and retaining the greatest number of customers.

Why Make an Online Game?

Online games offer developers many unique personal and creative rewards. If you thrive on challenge, this sector of game development is for you. The scale of an online project can be dramatically greater than most single-player games, and it takes dedication, intelligence, and teamwork to make so many parts assemble into a satisfying whole. However, the nature of that "whole" is what is so thrilling. What other art forms give you the chance to literally create an entire world, from North Pole to South?

Still, making the game is only the beginning. (A *long* beginning, however—be prepared to spend two to four years getting your online steer to the rodeo.) When a team develops a single-player product, it's "fire and forget"; once they've handed off the gold master to the publisher, their job is done—not so with an online product. If you're lucky, your online game will be enjoyed by tens or even hundreds of thousands of players every day, and so the work never stops. Whether you're a designer, an artist, or a coder, you can count on an ever-replenishing "to do" list.

When you develop an online game, you aren't so much making a game as you are offering players an ongoing *service*, a place for people with wildly different backgrounds and interests to meet, hang out, and play. It's an amazing feeling to know that you've created something that brings people together. How often do two people meet and form enduring friendships by playing *Grand Theft Auto III,* or fall in love over *Super Mario 64* and get married? This sort of thing happens every day in online games and communities. Likewise, you will marvel at the passion and devotion your creation inspires in players. Thousands of people will play your game, and you can count on them to tell you everything they love and hate about the world you created for them. Sometimes this can be hard, but at least you'll never have to deal with an indifferent audience.

In addition to personal and creative rewards, the MMOG has another major appeal: profitability—250,000 box sales of a product at $20 profit per box results in $5 million in revenue. Add 100,000 average subscribers over three years, and revenue for this period of time rises to $48 million—almost 10 times the revenue from a standard retail model. Include expansions that will sell to nearly every subscriber of your product, and revenues could rise to nearly $65 million. A single-player game that sells 250,000 units is rarely considered a success, but an online product that sells that much, as long as it converts a substantial portion of purchasers into online subscribers, is dramatically profitable.

Over the life of an MMOG, each added source of revenue—retail box sales, subscriptions, expansions—is more profitable than the last. Once your service has launched, most of your month-to-month costs (such as bandwidth, server infrastructure, customer service, live team support, etc.) will stay constant. Your service might run at a 50% profit margin on a $10/month subscription, earning you $5/customer in profit per month. If you are able to find ways to raise the average revenue per customer by selling expansions, merchandise, or premium services or servers to play on, then these will be at a much higher profit margin, and your profits may double even if your revenue per customer rises by only 50%. Since costs do not rise proportionally with the revenue from each subsequent upsell, finding upsells that interest your customers is important to maximizing your profit.

Simply put, it isn't hard to understand the lure of this type of game. From the challenge of making such a difficult product, to the communities that your game will create, and the potential profitability, online games are an attractive product to create and run.

Things to Know Before You Launch

Understanding the structure of your business is vital to running a successful online service. In this section, we discuss two major topics: the general stages of a customer's life, and your service organization with a review of who is responsible for the customer at each stage as your customers move from one stage to another.

The Stages of a Customer's Life in Your Product

A customer's relationship to your game will proceed through four basic stages: acquisition, conversion, retention, and loss. Acquisition and conversion are how you "get" a customer; after that, your goal is to prevent loss by retaining that customer for as long as possible. Figure 3.4.1 shows how the stages play out.

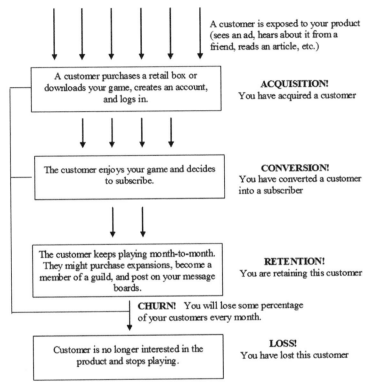

FIGURE 3.4.1 *Four basic stages of the online customer relationship.*

Essential Terms

The terms discussed in this section are not only stages of a customer's life in your product, but also specific data points that you should be prepared to track.

(Un)Entitled

You should define customers based on whether they currently have access to your product. Those who have access and can log in are *entitled* customers. Those who cannot log in are *unentitled*.

Unentitled, Initial

These customers have created an account and purchased the game, but have not yet provided adequate information to start playing. They are defined as being in the *initial* state. For example, they might not have entered billing information yet (and your product may require that in order to log in).

Entitled, Active, Trial

Customers who have created accounts, given you billing information, and have logged in to the game once are now entitled, active, *trial* customers. A common thing for many online games to provide is a 30-day free trial period after the purchase of the retail product—during this time, customers fall into this trial category.

Entitled, Active, Subscriber

After the trial period, many customers (hopefully) will decide to subscribe to your product on a monthly basis. These entitled customers are now active *subscribers*.

Entitled, Active, Pending Closed

If a customer decides to cancel his subscription it is likely that he will still have some amount of time on the subscription to provide continued access to the product (e.g., he's been billed for the month, but cancels half way through it—he retains access to the product until the end of the billing cycle). These customers are entitled, active, *pending closed*. Any time a customer's subscription has an "end date" without a viable method for billing to recur, he is a *pending closed* customer.

Tracking how many players are *pending closed* is valuable, because it gives you a forward-looking measure of people who are likely to exit your product. There are several ways to track pending players: look for those whose credit card expiration date has passed (so you won't be able to bill them again), those who used a pre-paid game card (and therefore have no recurring billing set up), and those who have cancelled their subscription but still have some active time left on their account.

You will recapture many of these players as they have second thoughts, or provide a credit card that isn't expired, or purchase a new game card, and so forth. However, if you want to know how many subscribers you'll have next month, a swift way to determine the worst-case scenario is by tracking how many pending closed customers you currently have.

Keep in mind that if your service offers long-term subscription options (such as a 12-month subscription), someone could be in this category for a long time! Therefore, in addition to knowing why players are in the pending category, it is also valuable to know how many are there for months to come (because the expiration of their subscription that they have decided not to renew is so far in the future).

Unentitled, Closed

People who have closed their accounts and no longer subscribe to your product.

With these categories defined, we can now define terms like *acquisition*, *conversion*, and *retention*.

Acquisition

Acquisition is bringing people to your storefront. They are interested in your product, and have decided to try it. You have acquired their interest.

Conversion

Conversion is converting an acquired person into a subscribing customer. Usually this occurs when your customers exit the free trial period and begin paying for the service.

Retention

Once you have a customer, you will want to keep him as long as you can. When customers continue to buy your service each month, you are retaining them.

One consistent theme throughout this article is that tracking customer behavior is critical so you can have the best possible feedback on how your game is doing. Here are a few (among many) statistics that you should keep a close eye on:

Lost acquisition: The percentage of customers who attempt to try your product but never become entitled because somewhere along the way they change their minds or give up. Your game can lose people at multiple points during the acquisition stage, the most common being when the customer is asked to enter billing information, or technical problems when the customer attempts to install or log on to the game.

Lost conversion: The percentage of customers who, having been acquired and after becoming entitled, fail to transition into the paying subscriber category. The most common examples of this category are customers who decide not to subscribe after exhausting a game's trial period or after a promotional offer. Methods to improve your conversion rate are mentioned later within this article.

Lost customer: This category refers to paying customers who close their accounts, transitioning from entitled to unentitled. Not all hope is lost, however; continue reading for hints on how to run successful win-back promotions.

Conversion rate: Customers converting to paying subscribers/total customers acquired—in a given period of time. For example, in one day, 4,000 people create accounts, and 1,000 become subscribers. Therefore, the conversion rate for this day is 25%.

Churn %:   The number of Lost Customers/Total Customers in some period of time. For example, in one month, 1,000 customers of 10,000 quit. Your churn for this month is 10%.

Potential loss: The number of people who move from active to pending closed in the paying subscriber category. This can be a leading indicator of people who are potentially going to exit the service; however, many customers will resubscribe when their subscription expires, as they have second thoughts about their cancellation.

Who Is Responsible for Success?

The answer to this question is simple. You—the development team—are responsible for the success or failure of your game. Everything the development team does has an impact. Once you realize the responsibility is yours, you will realize you are the one who is (or should be) empowered to run the service.

"But what about marketing?" you ask. It can help, but only with acquisition. Sure, this is valuable, but the fate of the service rests primarily in the hands of the development team. Counting on marketing to make your game succeeds is like spending vast sums on a wedding in the belief that it will make the marriage last.

An improved newbie experience can improve conversion. Bug fixes can address churn. New features can improve acquisition, conversion, *and* fight churn. When *Star Wars Galaxies* introduced player cities and mounts in a regular monthly patch, there was a 20% increase in acquisition. Publicity from positive additions to the game and word of mouth from happy customers will often lead to a significant improvement of all four as well.

Launch: The First Month

Launches can be painful, and the lessons to be learned through development and up through the first month of launch can (and probably do) fill this entire book. However, there are a few important lessons associated with running your live service to be aware of in your first month.

Managing Costs

What makes the first month so difficult—and so expensive—is the massive influx of customers your game will receive immediately after launch. Thousands of players are rushing home with a retail copy of your game in hand, loading it onto their computers, establishing accounts, and trying to enter the world you've created. It's a full-blown invasion, and your game's number of *simultaneous (or concurrent) users* skyrockets.

Players who are new to a product tend to use it the most. If they commit to a product for the long term, these players still enjoy it regularly, but often in a fewer amount of hours per week than they did when they first started playing. Since all users are new users when you first launch a service, this means the peak simultaneous usage of a product often occurs early in its life.

Figure 3.4.2 shows how this might play out for a typical online game. The product reaches maximum simultaneous use in its first several weeks. During this time, subscriptions are growing faster than the drop-off in simultaneous usage. Although subscription numbers are likely to rise in the first few weeks and months, your simultaneous usage percentage will likely drop, and the maximum number of simultaneous users will probably peak sometime in the first two months.

With the highest bandwidth usage, most customer service contacts, and the greatest server hardware requirements, your game's first month will likely incur higher costs than any other will. Thankfully, some of these costs scale downward: as peak simultaneous usage decreases, so do bandwidth costs. However, other costs do not scale downward at all. Of these, perhaps the most expensive example is server infrastructure.

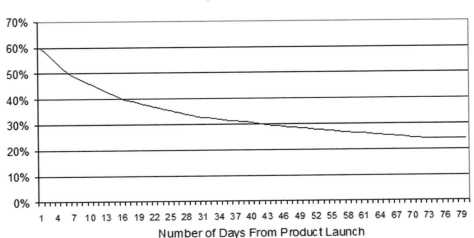

FIGURE 3.4.2   *Peak simultaneous users over time.*

A newly launched online product requires adequate server hardware to support the first few weeks of users; the problem is that this hardware may then go underutilized in the subsequent months when simultaneous usage has died down.

Therefore, gauging your needs before launch can be difficult. Guess wrong, and you either have much too much hardware on your hands, or you have tens of thousands of customers who have purchased your product and are unable to enjoy it.

Companies mitigate these risks in a variety of ways. For example, a strong presale program can help estimate what the first week of sales will be, and if started early enough (a couple of months before launch) allows a solid guess at how many users you will need to support immediately. You can also arrange with your server vendor ahead of time the purchase of additional hardware, with guarantees on swift delivery (in case you guess wrong on the low side). Put in place a plan to order this hardware at a specific threshold of capacity (say, 80%). As your service grows, you can purchase the additional hardware just in time.

There are other times when customers will spend more average time per week with your product, such as when a significant change takes place like the launch of an expansion or the patch of a major game system. You should expect and plan for these spikes in simultaneous usage, customer service contacts, and bandwidth costs over the entire life of your product.

Managing Your Team

It took months of hard work through a beta period that had tens of thousands of bugs, and now you've launched the product. Time to go on vacation?

Well, no. Developing the game was hard work, but the launch is harder still. The first month will see a host of unexpected problems. Many of these problems can be counted on to arise at 3 A.M. or 4 A.M.

Development teams have come up with several techniques to help manage this intense level of stress. Some teams, such as *The Matrix Online*, plan for a separate development team and live team. Their duties overlap in the few months before and after launch, but in theory, having a fresh live team ready to go and familiar with the product at launch allows the development team to get some rest.

Other products rotate the responsibility through the team, such as *Star Wars Galaxies*, where each programmer is knowledgeable enough to solve most problems, and being on-call for each team member lasts only a few days at a time. This requires many team members to be familiar with the infrastructure of the product and how to troubleshoot multiple problems, but the more you spread this knowledge around, the less you must rely on a small team to support your service.

Some products add a handful of additional support staff a couple of months before the ship of the game, and have them do nothing more than learn the details of the product. These people will be fresh when the game launches.

All of these techniques cost money, but unbridled team stress is a crucial issue that incurs serious risks. This is not the place to be pennywise and pound-foolish.

Customer Service

The first lesson of managing an online product is the recognition that you are not managing a game, you are managing a service. Developing a single-player game is akin to making a frozen dinner to be sold in a grocery store. An online game, in contrast, is like running a restaurant where you need to encourage people to come to your door, greet them the instant they arrive, provide them with whatever they ask for, make sure they have a good time, and invite them to return.

From week to week, the number and type of problems that a live game will encounter will change. A robust customer service (CS) department is your first line of defense. Unfortunately, it's a common mistake that if development time begins to run short before launch or after, a team will cut corners on customer service tools (there will be plenty of time to get to customer service tools when they actually have customers!). Don't make this mistake.

Be responsive. The development team needs to treat their CS department like a client and provide the tools and solutions requested. Again, these employees are the front line of your service, and they're the ones best equipped to identify the product's strengths, weaknesses, and what needs to be addressed most swiftly. Be flexible, and respond quickly.

Running a Live Service

You've made it past the first month, and your launch was not a crash. Congratulations. Now what?

After the first month, your game begins to mature and everyone in your service organization faces multiple challenges as the service grows and (hopefully) the team learns. You can expect problems such as difficulty in acquiring new customers, a community displeased with the current state of the product or service, increasing churn rates (either through competitive pressure, or customers losing interest), and, if you're lucky to last long enough, the problems of an aging customer base. Don't worry—strategies to meet all of these challenges are covered here. However, remember, it's essential to understand that your best bet for survival is tracking the behavior of your customers.

Tracking—Use Metrics

Metrics, metrics, metrics. How do you know if you are succeeding or failing unless you can measure this in some way? Subscription numbers are going down. Why? Unless you have strong metrics, you will have no idea. Once you have metrics, the next step is to understand how to use them.

How Metrics Can Track Your Success

Your service should track customers from each category based on where they came from. This results in having a further breakdown of customers into additional categories based on their source. As your service begins to gain customers from sources other than retail, tracking will become increasingly important.

If a product has gained customers from both retail and from a promotional program (such as a Web-based free trial), your service might track categories such as retail acquisition, retail conversion, and retail churn, and then Web promotion acquisition, Web promotion conversion, and Web promotion churn. Later, your service runs print ads, and now there are categories for print ad promotion acquisition, print ad promotion conversion, and print ad promotion churn. Having these metrics for an entire product, as well as on a per-source basis will be valuable.

Let's take an example where in a given month your service acquires 10,000 retail customers and 10,000 promotion customers. If 11,000 people convert to paid customers, which of the sources just discussed turned out to be more successful: the retail acquisition or the promotion acquisition? You don't have any idea, unless you've tracked these customers independently of each other.

Often, retail conversion is the highest conversion percentage of any type of customer. However, as you run multiple types of promotions it becomes increasingly important that you track each source independently so you can accurately measure which ones are your most successful source of customers. This segregation of customers may extend beyond which method was used to acquire them into from *where* they were acquired. Some companies rely heavily on Web-based acquisition. These customers can come from customer referrals, portal sites such as Yahoo!, or game sites such as Gamespot. Do the customers from Gamespot have a higher conversion rate than the customers from Yahoo!?

Table 3.4.1 shows an example of what you might see when tracking these subscribers from multiple sources.

Table 3.4.1   Tracking Subscribers from Multiple Sources (April 2001)

Customer Type	Acquired Customers	Conversion %	Number of Customers	Cost to Run Program	Cost/ Customer
Retail	10,000	90	9,000	variable	
Free Trial—Yahoo	50,000	10	5,000	$50,000	$10
Free Trial—Gamespot	25,000	15	3,750	$25,000	$6.67
Buddy Keys	15,000	40	6,000	0	0

In Table 3.4.1, what have we learned from the data? In terms of where to spend marketing money, did we learn that we want to go to Yahoo! (where we get more customers), or do we want to go to Gamespot (where each customer costs us less)? Now add in how long, on average, you retained a customer from each source, and you can generate total income per customer per source. Finally, by comparing both your total cost and your total revenue per customer, per source, you have determined where you want to spend more money—whichever location has the best return.

Usage Levels

Usage of your product is the first and best leading indicator of how much your customers are currently enjoying your service. If simultaneous usage drops significantly (so fewer people are interested in playing your game on a regular basis), then subscriptions are probably not far behind.

There are a few data points definitely worth tracking:

- Unique number of users per day, week, or month
- Average length of a typical play session
- Peak simultaneous usage

These numbers are your best forward-looking indicator of how good of a job your development team is doing at making features that are of interest to your subscribers.

This is an important measure of a product against itself—not against other products. If, historically, one product runs at 15% of its subscribers as the maximum simultaneous usage, and then rises to 17%, this is a big success because it means people are enjoying the product more. Even if this has greater bandwidth costs, you'd rather have more happy customers since they are more likely to subscribe the next month.

One common misconception is the belief that the perfect online game carries a high number of subscriptions but a low number of simultaneous users—this has the lowest bandwidth, hardware, and customer service costs. However, don't be fooled. You want users, and lots of them, to be playing your product. The more interested they are in the product, the more likely they are to keep their subscription, be interested in an upsell that you have to offer (such as the next expansion), tell their friends about your game and gain you some word-of-mouth customers, or stay with your product (because they are spending time with their friends in the game) rather than try a competitor's.

For many of your subscribers, there will come a point (and it may come very early on) where they aren't returning to play more of your game—instead, they are returning to see the friends they have made or simply be a part of the community. For this reason, and the others mentioned previously, you want to engage the interest of *all* subscribers and maintain their presence in your community as long as possible; losing one customer could lead to losing as many as dozens of others.

It's worth the time to invest effort in your tracking mechanisms. The only way you'll be able to make intelligent decisions later is if you are tracking the correct data now.

Maximizing Acquisition

It's tragically common for development teams to see acquisition as marketing's responsibility. This is a mistake. You can do more to bring customers to the virtual door of your online business than any marketer, and the type of efforts discussed next are also likely to improve your conversion and retention rates.

Expansions

The *EverQuest* live team attempts to produce two expansions per year—faster than most online games in the industry. Part of the reason for this quick pace of expansion development is the increased acquisition that EQ sees associated with every expansion release. This may be due to heightened visibility of the product, a new retail presence, or increased desire to play something "new" by the consumer. Perhaps due to all of these reasons, when compared to the prior month, EQ will often see a 300–400% increase in new customer acquisition in the month of an expansion release.

Expansions also generate additional retail and digital download revenue, higher subscription numbers, and generally if they have high-quality content, increased customer satisfaction among the user base.

The best part of an expansion is that retailers are likely interested in the product; therefore, having an ever-fresh product on the shelf keeps visibility and brand recognition among your demographic. Over the years, the value of this relationship is significant.

Adding New Styles of Gameplay

Expansions that add new styles of gameplay have been the most successful at garnering higher levels of acquisition. There are varying levels of this, from EQ's *Lost Dungeons of Norrath*, which added instanced dungeons to the adventuring world; to *City of Villains*, which adds PvP to the previously PvE game of *City of Heroes*; to *Jump to Light Speed (JTL)*, the first expansion from *Star Wars Galaxies (SWG)* that adds an action game on top of the existing role-playing game.

The most valuable expansions are those that add dramatically new forms of gameplay to the existing product. Not surprisingly, these expansions are also the hardest ones to do. Expansions are terrific for your business in general. Since you are likely to sell an expansion to 90%+ of your customer base, this makes it well worth the invested effort. Add on top of that a gain of 5–30% additional subscribers, and there's a clear case to make, that even though this type of expansion is especially difficult, it is the most valuable type to develop.

Business Approaches to Improving Acquisition

Your service can increase acquisition through launching in new territories, experimenting with alternate billing methods, or running new promotions to attract a broader audience. Some of the more common ideas are discussed briefly here.

Internationalization

One of the easiest and most effective ways to gain new customers is to begin selling your product to new territories. Localizing your product to European and Asian languages can add a tremendous number of users who may eventually become the core audience. For example, *Ultima Online,* which originally saw 100% of its user base from North America, now sees over 50% of its subscribers residing in Japan. *Dark Age of Camelot* sees a significant percentage of its user base in Europe.

Sometimes, localization of your product is as simple as changing the language of all the in-game text and launching servers local to the foreign territory. Other times, greater changes are required, such as altering the gameplay to appeal to the tastes of foreign gamers.

Internationalization should be one of the first opportunities you explore for acquiring new customers.

New Products and Free Trials

Keeping your product on the shelf can be particularly challenging, especially after several years. New SKUs are key to continuing to acquire retail customers, and these don't necessarily require much additional effort from your development team. If your development team is continually making new expansions, then rolling all your recent expansions into the base product, repackaging it, and selling it through retail channels is likely to see substantial success.

Retail subscribers are becoming harder and harder to acquire as competitors launch their new (and shinier) products. One potential way to combat this is with a free-trial program (discussed later) that requires a retail key to convert to a subscriber. *Star Wars Galaxies* has seen success in this area, where after a short free trial period of 14 days, trial members must obtain a retail copy of the product to continue playing.

There are both advantages and disadvantages to this method. By forcing customers to purchase your product at retail at the conclusion of the trial period, you are imposing a barrier to entry for them to become a subscriber (and gaining a subscriber is more important in the long term then gaining a retail sale). However, if your product is compelling and you see a high ratio of success of trial members purchasing the retail product, then the additional retail sales will encourage the retailers to stock your product for longer and at higher quantities, ever broadening the awareness of your product in the marketplace.

By forcing trial members to purchase the retail product, you are likely to keep a retail presence for much longer, and thereby gain more customers over the long term. The younger your product, the more likely this type of program is to be a success.

Promotions

There are a wide range of potential promotions you can run to improve acquisition. The effect on acquisition and conversion rates can vary dramatically between promotions; seeing a promotion reach tens of thousands of users with a 20–30% conversion rate is achievable, although this level of success is more often the exception rather than the rule.

Buddy Key Promotion

Sony Online and EA have seen success by sending free trial keys to customers to encourage them to bring their friends online. By sending an e-mail with a buddy key to every subscriber, your service is now attempting to double in size through new acquisition. These potential trial customers are more likely to convert to paying subscribers if they try the product because their friends are already online and can help them walk through the product.

Free Client Promotion

As a product ages and retail acquisition becomes more challenging, a service often wants to gain broader exposure by offering a free version of the game client. Although this can reduce retail sales, you gain much wider exposure. If you have a long list of expansions to lean on, as *EverQuest* does, your free downloadable client can be a smaller subset of your products while the retail product carries most or all of the recent expansions. In mid 2004, over five years after launch, *EverQuest* saw tens of thousands of downloads of its several-hundred-megabyte client in only a few short weeks. It's extremely difficult to gain this level of exposure (and acquisition) through other means.

Young Product Win-Back Promotions

Promotions can start one month after your launch, and a win-back program is a common place to start. These can be particularly effective ways of "winning back" subscribers who have closed their accounts in the first few months after launch (i.e., "young players"). An e-mail to every lost customer with the latest information on recent or upcoming additions to the game world often brings back a moderate percentage of those who have lost interest. Coupled with an offer to automatically re-entitle the player's closed account with a short free-trial period (thereby reducing the barrier to entry for him to come back to the game), you could win back as much as 5–10% of people who have exited the service in the first few months.

Older Product Win-Back Promotions

There comes a point in the life of your product when you have more customers who have canceled than the number of those who are currently active. This is especially true after a product has been open for years; a game's natural churn will cause the unentitled category to grow even though subscriptions will stay steady.

If a short-term win-back program is valuable, is a long-term win-back program equally valuable? There's a warning to be had in this category of promotion, which would otherwise seem like a good idea (and with the right data, it still can be).

Once a product is a couple of years old, a significant percentage (25% or more, depending on the product) of the people becoming subscribers on any given day are likely to be prior customers. For customers who are returning to a product, how long are they typically away from it before they return? The answer varies based on the product type. In the case of Sony Online's games, the median times for a customer to be unentitled before choosing to resubscribe are:

PlanetSide:	16 days
EverQuest:	4 days
EverQuest PS2:	3 days
Star Wars Galaxies:	7 days

It's also interesting to see the percentage of people at the extremes. In the case of *EverQuest* where the median time to be unentitled is just four days, there are nearly a third of resubscribers who had been unentitled for at least two weeks, and over 10% who had been unentitled for at least a month.

Your win-back program starts with an e-mail that hypes all the new things in the game and invites users to come back and try the product. You automatically re-entitle them for 30 days to give them a chance to get back into the game. However, if you re-entitle all of the people who canceled, then the number of subscribers you are gaining day to day is going to drop. In the case of a product that gains 25% of its resubscribers from people who had previously closed their account, this equates to a 25% drop in subscriber acquisition (or in this case, reacquisition) the day you started your win-back program. A previous subscriber who was already inclined to resubscribe and pay for your service no longer needs to pay for access, because you've just given it to him for free!

You can reduce the impact of this scenario by requiring customers to be unentitled for some length of time before they are eligible for this promotion; for example, choose only customers who have been unentitled for at least a month.

Even in this scenario, however, you see your resubscriber numbers drop immediately because there are still returning customers who receive the product for free when they would have been willing to pay for it. The longer the period of time you require a customer to have been unentitled in order to be eligible for a promotion, the less of a decline you'll see in resubscriber numbers when you initiate your win-back program. However, your promotion is less effective because the longer someone is away from the product, the less likely he is to return to it, and so you have excluded the people who are the most likely to be have been captured.

Successful win-back programs for older products have a few characteristics.

- Exclude those people who are likely to return to the product anyway (so you don't give away something for free that someone would be willing to pay for).
- Improve the chances that someone is inclined to resubscribe at the end of the re-trial period.
  - Offer an in-game benefit to resubscribe.
  - Target smaller sections of people who are more likely to return.

In *EverQuest*, an applicable win-back program might be seen when changes are made in profession balancing. If fighters are made more powerful in the game, run a win-back program for just those accounts that have fighter characters on them. If you can raise the conversion rates enough, it will more than offset the associated decline of resubscribers seen during the promotion period.

Whatever the method, be warned that this type of promotion (and this seems unintuitive, at least it was for us) can be negative for overall subscription levels. The method to making it a net gain is twofold: 1) attempt to exclude from the promotion ex-subscribers who are already inclined to return to your service (so that you avoid giving them something for free that they were prepared to pay for), and 2) target ex-subscribers who wouldn't otherwise be inclined to return, but are now, because you've provided them a hook and a free trial period.

Credit Card Required?

Most online game trials (whether a 30-day trial that comes "in the box" when a customer purchases the game, or a promotion) require players to enter credit card (or other billing) information in order to sample the product. By requiring billing information, the customer's option to start being billed month to month becomes a passive choice. In addition, customers who are willing to enter credit card information are more likely to be willing to purchase the product if they enjoy it (by entering the data they've proven they are a potential buyer).

However, a large percentage of customers who go through account registration will exit the process at the stage where they are forced to enter their billing information. By removing this barrier to entering the product, more people are likely to sample your service and determine if they are willing to purchase.

After a free-trial month, do you have more subscribers in the scenario where the customers entered billing information when they created the account (fewer raw acquisition numbers, but a higher conversion percentage), or do you have more subscribers in the scenario where the customer enters billing information only when he's prepared to purchase the game (greater acquisition, but a lower conversion percentage)?

There are other costs associated with not requiring billing information. This method likely puts additional strain on the customer service department because it becomes easier for disruptive players to make throwaway accounts to harass others anonymously. Greater acquisition can also mean higher customer service requirements, as there is a larger audience of new players who are the most likely to need help.

There are examples of products that have experimented with these two scenarios and saw the same number of new subscribers with both. Since there are greater customer service costs associated with not requiring billing information, the choice became requiring the billing data.

The results turn out to be different per product. How do you make this decision? Experiment with a small sample of your customers, and measure your success rate. Be willing to re-examine this several times as your product ages, since success may vary depending on the market, and the type of customers you are acquiring.

Marketing

Marketing comes last for a reason. All the strategies to maximize acquisition discussed so far are basically "free"—they require time from people already employed by your service. Marketing, however, is a strategy that actually requires you to spend dollars to acquire customers.

If you're going to spend money on acquisition, how and where should you spend it? This is quite different from marketing to increase brand awareness; your goal here is to bring in more subscribers and thus more revenue. Accordingly, you need to achieve this at the lowest cost per customer.

Advertising your product on the Web can be surprisingly successful. Simutronics, maker of the online games *GemStone* and *DragonRealms*, routinely runs Web ads on search engines under keywords of competitors' products. Search on Yahoo! for "dnd," or "online game," and don't be surprised to see an ad for "Accountant by day, Sorceress by night. Play *GemStone*."

Whatever the means of spending marketing dollars, the most important point to remember is to track the data closely. Spend a little money in a lot of places, find where the lowest cost per new subscriber comes from, and then push a lot of your marketing budget in that direction.

Maximizing Conversion

If your game's conversion rate is low, it's likely that its newbie experience is lacking. Improving a player's initial experience and getting him integrated into the game community sooner are the first solutions to consider.

Update the New and Low-Level Player Experience

Online games grow quickly. To keep players interested, the depth of the product increases dramatically, becoming increasingly more intricate and complex and generally harder to learn. In effect, you are trying to satisfy two increasingly divergent audiences: newbies who need the game to be easy to learn, and veteran players already familiar with the basics who want the game to reveal ever-greater intricacies and depth.

Update the newbie tutorial and constantly re-examine the low-level player experience. This helps avoid a gradual slide in conversion rates. In addition, the demographic of your new users may change over time (e.g., the average customer buying

EverQuest today is older than the average customer who purchased the game five years ago). If your demographic changes, your low-level player experience may need to change as well. If older people are coming to play the game more often, they're likely interested in shorter play cycles. Adjusting the game to meet a changing demographic can be difficult, but will be important to maintaining interest among your customers.

Introduce Newbies to Other Players Right Away

Getting potential customers engaged in the community dramatically increases the chance that they convert into subscribers. One of the primary reasons why your customers continue to enjoy your service is because their friends are online, and they want to be with their friends. How can this help you with conversion? Encourage newbies to make friends—right away.

GemStone IV has one of the best new player experiences of any online service. Once past the tutorial, new players are immediately introduced to experienced player "mentors" who will tour the new player around the game. These aren't employees— simply other players interested in meeting new people and helping others. However, *GemStone* goes the extra mile by specifically supporting them with special in-game commands, an in-game area just for them, and public recognition of their hard work. This new-player handoff to the world is a gradual one, where new customers are likely to make new friends, all for zero added cost to the company.

Improving Retention

Acquiring new customers costs more than retaining the ones you already have, so efforts in this area make financial sense. Retention will also improve customers' perception of your product, and can feed on itself: As long as a player's online friends keep playing, he is more likely to as well.

Identify Exit Points of Your Product

When do customers quit, and why? Finding this data out will be particular to your product, but in this case, we can use *EverQuest* as an example.

EQ tracks active users per level per class. In Figure 3.4.3, we see the distribution of active players in mage (top line) and bard (bottom line) classes across levels 5–50 on one live server (out of 46 live servers at the time of this writing).

One might expect a natural drop-off of active players when looking from the new player experience to the advanced game. For mages in EQ, we see a general decline as the player advances, but there are many spikes in the path.

EQ gives new spells and abilities at varying levels, and each arrow in Figure 3.4.3 points to a new level where players gain additional spells or abilities. To translate this, we can say, "More people are playing mages at the levels where they gain spells, or the level right afterward. The fewest relative number of people playing mages are at the level right before they gain new spells." You might also say, "The level where a mage gains spells, or the level right afterward, is the most fun—we know this because that's where people tend to be active players."

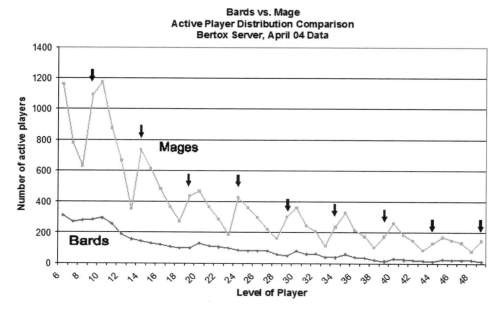

FIGURE 3.4.3   *Active users per level per class.*

The right-before-new-spells level is also the most difficult level, since characters have the same arsenal that they've had for the last three levels, but are struggling as they have to fight progressively more difficult creatures with the same weapons.

Bards, however, gain a new spell every level. This line is much more gradual, implying that there are fewer barriers in the progression of a bard class. While the bard profession appeals to fewer people than the mage profession, those who choose bard are more likely to have a gradual, more enjoyable play experience.

What conclusion can we draw from this data? In this case, we learned that players are more likely to stop playing the mage class when they stop getting rewards for a few levels in a row (and this situation occurs many times until level 50). EQ may choose to address that problem in multiple different ways (e.g., reducing the experience required to get through the level right before gaining new spells).

Does your game have professions and levels like EQ? If so, are there any professions that have levels at which the number of active users drops dramatically? Why?

An entire book could be written on this topic just for *EverQuest*. There are mountains of data for each profession, race, and groups of professions; for example, is a character more likely to keep playing a character class that has a pet? Or are they more likely to stick with a character that can increase their run speed? Through analysis of your character data, you should be able to identify exit points from your product, be able to determine why your product exhibits this behavior, and then find ways to improve the situation.

Message Boards and Community Management

A strong community is an extremely valuable asset to your service. The more interested the customer is in your product, the longer he is likely to subscribe to your service. Contact with your development team (through a community manager) is key to maintaining the interest level in the community. A large portion of online game subscribers are particularly interested in the content of future updates. In lieu of providing an update every week, simply discussing aspects of upcoming additions to the game will build anticipation and work in your favor. Subscribers are more likely to stay if they see a desired feature coming soon.

Valuable volumes have been written on the topic of community management. The author recommends Amy Jo Kim's book, *Community Building on the Web: Strategies for Successful Online Communities*.

Customer Service

Your customer service department is your front line of contact with the customer. Often, the first people to know what is upsetting the player base will be your customer service representatives. It is valuable to have a strong, constant relationship between the development team and the customer service department.

Here again, this topic could be dramatically larger in scope. This section touches on just a few of the areas to manage costs, track your successes, and areas on which to focus.

Methods of Contact, and Cost per Contact

Sony Online allows customers to contact them through in-game tools, e-mail, chat rooms, and telephone support. Allowing your customers to reach you through whatever means is most comfortable for them is valuable.

The cost of each method of feedback should be tracked; not only the total amount you have spent, but also the cost per contact. As your service recognizes where it spends most of its effort, and the areas where it is least efficient, you should work to provide solutions to these problems.

For example, Sony Online has discovered that most of its players want to submit feedback from within the game, and many of these questions have easy answers that experienced players already know.

Before reaching a customer service representative, Sony encourages users to scan a knowledge base of existing problems. For example, when a player requests help in game, he chooses a category and problem from a list of pre-made answers. One category and problem is "I'm stuck," with the problem, "I'm unable to move in the world." Up pops a knowledge base entry that reads, "Are you stuck in the world and unable to move? Have you tried these commands which are available for you to resolve this problem?" The user can still submit a formal request for help, but by attempting to answer the most common questions automatically, Sony is able to dramatically lower its costs.

Investing in Your Customer Service Tool

Invest in areas of the business where you can receive ongoing benefits for a one-time cost. One of the most obvious places for this investment is in your customer service tool. The faster you can respond to player concerns, the cheaper it is for you and the happier the customer becomes. Knowing how to invest in your CS tool is easy—just ask your CS department. As you streamline their ability to do their jobs, you lower your ongoing service costs by having invested a small amount of development effort.

Polling

A great way to determine what your players think and want is to ask them. Having a strong polling system within your game would be particularly valuable, since you'll frequently want to gauge the advantages and disadvantages of a particular decision.

Reaching Out to Community Leaders

Who are they and what do they think? These are leaders within your community, who run guilds of hundreds of other players, or manage Web sites with information specific to your game that attracts thousands of people, or they are simply opinion makers—the people whom others look to when they have questions.

Identify them. Invite them to your facility to talk with you. Learn what is on their minds and how you can address their concerns. By spending time with top community leaders and addressing some of their concerns, you are likely impacting the opinions of hundreds or even thousands of people.

The effects are far reaching and should not be underestimated. This type of community outreach is as key to your product as providing customer service.

The Aging Product: Changes to Your Customer Base

When your service launches, your target machine system requirements play a part in defining the size of your customer base and the life of your product. The higher your target system specs are (and presumably therefore the quality of the graphics), the longer your product will look fresh on the shelf. The lower your system specs are, the broader the audience of people that you can reach initially.

Raising your system specs with an existing player base forces some of your players out of the product—this suggests that you put this off as long as possible. However, looking graphically dated when compared to your competitors damages your ability to acquire customers, so therefore you want to constantly update your engine to stay as current as possible.

What about providing a new engine for those customers who can use it, and use the old engine (or older art) for customers with lower system specs? This is also fraught with difficulty. In this scenario, your development team (especially in art creation) needs to spend more time supporting a wide variety of system specs. More time and effort is required to produce new assets for an older game supporting multiple tiers of client machine specs than is required to produce spectacular assets for only the newest and latest computers.

Dealing with this problem isn't easy—and you should only leap off this bridge when you're forced to upgrade to keep the product looking competitive. Existing subscribers are the most important to serve, as gaining subscribers is more expensive then retaining the ones you already have (as discussed later).

Stable or Lower Subscribers Can Still Mean Higher Revenue

Even if your service is faced with declining subscribers, you may be in a position to maintain or even increase your revenue. As your subscriber base changes, you may find changes to things such as price sensitivity and penetration of upsells. You may have fewer customers, but they may be die-hard fans of your product interested in everything you can offer.

Raising or Lowering Prices

As sales decline in a typical retail product, a company frequently lowers the price in order to sell more units. This occurs throughout the video game industry, from console prices to games.

An online game also sees its retail product price decline, but the online subscription fee for the industry hasn't declined for nearly 10 years (since the shift from pay by the hour, to pay per month).

Could it be that the next breakout title is through some unique subscription model (as occurred in the 1990s)? Perhaps, but with existing online titles the subscription fee has tended to rise. We see this in a few other comparable industries as well, such as eBay raising the listing fee for auctions after it had established an industry-leading, large, captive audience.

Between $10 and $15 per month has become the industry standard, with the latest product launches generally landing closer to $15. Raising your subscription price on a live product can be a dangerous decision—certainly this provides an opportunity for every customer to reconsider this purchase (a decision you would much rather not present). However, the potential additional revenue is significant.

A 100,000-subscriber game that pulls in $10/month from each subscriber with a margin of 40% makes $400,000/month in profits. In raising the subscription fee to $12.95/month, the margins haven't changed (costs are still $6/customer), and profits rise to nearly $700,000/month. For this to be a profitable decision, the service must retain at least 60,000 customers. Would 40% of your service quit if you raised prices by $2.95 a month?

There are other factors to consider when raising the subscription fee. Choose a time when the development team is adding significant perceived value to the product, so that the community will respond more favorably. In addition, avoid raising prices in the face of direct competitive pressure. Raising prices potentially reduces acquisition, as a higher subscription fee may impose a new barrier to entry.

Increasing Revenue per Customer Through Upsells

If you need more revenue, raising prices isn't your only option. Increasing your revenue per subscriber is another potential avenue to explore by providing additional services that add perceived value at a low (or fixed) cost to you.

Each product is different, but some suggestions for potential upsells that may be well received by your customer are discussed in this section. The upsells that have thus far met with the most success include those that add perceived value for the purchaser, and do not provide the purchaser (what other customers consider) an "unfair" advantage as perceived by the rest of the customer base. A good example of this is expansions, because while they might provide new features that make the game easier for those who purchase it, those features are generally unlocked by achieving the content within the expansion. In other words, the purchaser of the upsell still has to "work for it."

Expansions

An expansion is valuable in many ways: it increases acquisition by generating positive buzz about additions to the game, it lengthens the life of the average subscriber by providing him more content, it increases your average revenue per subscriber significantly by selling through to a majority of your player base, and it keeps the product fresh and alive. Building expansions for your product, whatever the size of the subscriber base, is important to its longevity.

Selling an expansion, which reaches nearly the entire subscriber base, for $20 to $30 is a realistic goal.

Character Transfers, Name Changes

Many subscribers want to change data on their character that they do not have access to—such as changing their name, or changing the sever on which they play. While development effort goes into providing an easy mechanism for players to transfer their characters to another server (or change their name), this becomes a one-time cost of development effort that can pay off for years down the line. Sony Online charges a significant one-time fee to transfer characters from one server to another, and receives hundreds of requests for this per month.

Premium Servers

Premium servers are the equivalent of an exclusive club where a subscriber can play the same game, but among other exclusive club members. This may sound like a proposition of questionable value, but many subscribers look forward to playing with other people who can afford a higher subscription fee. Often, they are looking for a more intense role-playing environment, or to find other more mature players (as a higher subscription price deters a younger audience). Some companies provide higher levels of gamemaster interaction with the players by running specialized events.

Effective premium servers can be profitable while still providing a clear value addition for the subscriber. "Come to a more pure role-playing environment where unique events will be run by talented game developers, all for a slightly higher price."

Ticketed Events (Auctions, Weddings, etc.)

Some online games sell tickets (for as much as several hundred dollars for a single ticket) to online in-game events. Player weddings are a popular choice, where a gamemaster or developer helps arrange a unique setting, special scripted events, or wedding-oriented objects (such as dresses, veils, etc.) that can only be obtained through this ticketed event.

Extra Characters

Your product may have launched with a limited number of character slots available per server, and you can sell additional slots at a small cost per additional character.

Premium Subscription

Simutronics raises its average revenue per customer dramatically by offering a set of features packaged as a single "premium subscription" upsell. Access to special areas within the game, or extra inventory or bank space, or extra character slots are all examples of features that could be provided in a premium subscription.

These examples are just a few of your options. You might explore merchandising, creating a series of books based on your fictional universe with a popular author, creating a series of role-playing games, selling action figures, selling customized portraits of a subscriber's character . . . the list is endless, and is unique to your product.

Conclusion

How long will it last? The more you invest in your business, the more you track how your business evolves, and the more you learn from understanding how to change the product to meet the current challenges, the longer it will last. *GemStone III,* launched in 1990, and is now going into its 15th year. Is there any reason to believe it won't last another 15 years? *Ultima Online* is headed toward its eighth anniversary, and *EverQuest* to its sixth. These success stories have one thing in common—a constant reinvestment into the business to support continued growth of the product. There is every reason to believe that products like this are the norm for an online service, not the exception.

Therefore, expect the long term, and then begin planning for it. What challenges will your service be facing over the next few years? How will you address them? What do you expect will happen with your acquisition, retention, and conversion? What strategies will you plan now to meet the challenge that you can see coming in the future? In addition, how will you keep your product fresh and interesting such that you can keep your customers for years to come?

This article ends with a few recommendations: If you don't have the data, start getting it now. If you have the data, begin working on the area of the business that needs your help the most. Plan for what is to come, and be proactive about it. You, and your development team, can positively address every aspect of the service if you are able to make informed decisions.

3.5

Community Management: Do's and Don'ts from Those Who've Done Them

Graham Williams—UbiSoft

grahamw@rogers.com

Katie Postma—UbiSoft

guinevere4719@hotmail.com

This article is split into two major portions—one for project managers/developers, and one for Community Managers. If you're looking for a good reason to create a Community Management position for your MMO, or you'd like to know how to go about finding one, the first half of this article is for you. If you're a Community Manager and you're looking for some tips and inside info from some battle-worn Community Managers, the second half of this article is for you.

Nondisclosure Agreements

You don't go to battle without your armor. You don't raid a dungeon without a sword. You don't bring anyone onto your team in any capacity that may be exposed to sensitive material without the judicious application of a nondisclosure agreement (NDA). It doesn't exactly roll off your tongue, but the ramifications of unrestrained sensitive information being distributed can be catastrophic.

Blanket forms are good for people who may or may not come into contact with material they shouldn't see. They're your best defense against the casual leak. However, when you bring someone from the community into the inner sanctum (all software companies have an inner sanctum—where's yours?), a more detailed and individual NDA may be required.

Project Managers

Community management is important for any developer/producer in any type of genre. However, the dynamic nature of a massively multiplayer game changes more rapidly than traditional PR efforts can cope with. In an age when interest in games in general and MMORPGs in particular are at an all-time high, it is imperative that your offering to your community consists of more than just mere press releases and .plan files. It is essential to give your players a sense of ownership and participation beyond the world of your game, and that can spell the difference between a critically acclaimed success and a financial one.

A crucial aspect of any MMO, perhaps the most crucial, is the management of your customer base. There are examples of games whose technical sophistication was beyond measure, but despite the impressive nature of the project it failed. Sometimes, this is because the publisher was either unable or unwilling to heed the audience to which these games were marketed, and sometimes because they kept the game's community at arm's length. No one wants his or her project to end up as the next *Mythica*. As veterans who have sat on both sides of the table, we would like to present you with what we believe is a balanced approach to community management: one where you maintain creative control while preserving the relations with and the satisfaction of your customer base.

Investing time to attract and maintain your customer base is quite smart in today's marketplace. Whether you are selling gadgets or games, TVs, or toothpaste, the goal is the same: get someone to consume your product, and get the same someone to want to consume it again. In other words, once your marketing department has won over an online gamer, it's the job of the Community Manager to keep the gamer happy and comfortable, so that he or she will consume again. And again. And possibly again.

This goal of maintaining a customer is not just for the obvious reason (repeat sales = revenue base), but for many subtle gains as well. A happy customer will a) trust your company, and will begin to feel a glow of good will toward you, b) spread the great news to his or her friends that yours is the company to stick by, and c) likely start to look at your other offerings as products he or she will surely enjoy.

This trust creates loyalty; word of mouth creates positive hype, and curiosity creates new sales. Now we have a real win-win-win situation on our hands. What more could a business want?

One of the most difficult steps a company can take is recognizing just how valuable that single fan is. If you have a fan, you have someone loyal, trusting, and attentive. Think of a puppy—so full of enthusiasm and only has eyes for you! Feed him and pet him and reward him for his adoration, and he'll stick by your side for life. Kick him aside, ignore him, or neglect him, and he'll run away, find a nice neighbor, and likely bite you in the ankles any chance he gets.

Creating the position of Community Manager, therefore, isn't just something extra a company can do; it's crucial. To ignore the fact that the care and feeding of your fans is important is ignorant—it's bad business. Fans are the solid foundation on which MMOs can build their success. Sure, great hype, marketing, strong market share, good showing out of the gate, these are all important, too. Yet it will all fade away quickly and quietly if you do nothing to retain the good will and interest that fans are so eager to give.

The Community Manager's job is one of the most important jobs a company can support, and yet it's equally elusive to quantify. How can you measure a Community Manager's efforts? It isn't easy. Forum posts may be many and yet be ineffective. E-mails are numerous yet reach few. And Web site hits, while coveted are curiously cyclical. You never know just what it is that got those folks to click and hopefully rest on your precious community site. Were you "slashdotted?" Did someone with an enormous following post you in his latest blog? Or did your best friend's sister's boyfriend's brother's girlfriend hear from this guy who knows this kid who's going with a girl who saw Ferris pass out at 31 Flavors last night link there? Yes, it's pretty serious.

Wal-Mart Mentality

Think of the last time you went into a retail store; a real honest-to-goodness big box retail store. You walked in, looked around, desperately glanced up at the signs in between the aisle in the hopes that you'd glean some tidbit of information from them that would lead you to the product you were looking for. In vain, you searched for an employee to help you, red smock, blue smock—it really didn't matter. Dejected, you gave up, and headed to a smaller store; as soon as you walked in, there was your clerk with the information you needed! The parallels draw themselves; you need to be on the ball to provide good customer service.

It's Not My Job!

At any given point in the day, someone in the world is uttering the fatal words, "It's not my job!" It's a phrase we've become accustomed to hearing as well as using; it's a catch-all to describe the thing we can not, will not, and should not do. Community management should be recognized as an integral component of both of these departments; it will entail a great deal of hands-on interaction with both teams as well as your client base. There is a tendency for this positioning to be marginalized or underused. The benefits of an applied community management program outweigh the cost.

The job description may list nine to five, Monday through Friday as the hours involved. However, if you are going to have an employee pursue a successful tenure as a Community Manager, you might as well dispose of that idea right away. Your client base, your development teams, and your marketing managers will most likely span several time zones, and their work habits and hours are likely to be different.

We would strongly encourage anyone interested in taking on a community management position as a "second hat" to reconsider that course of action. Constant communication with such a vast audience and workgroup via Blackberry, IM, cell phone, telephone, and videoconferencing is not conducive to a secondary position. They will be communicating with their direct supervisor, teams in marketing and development, contacts in the media, fan sites, and your end users. These groups will most like be spread across the globe. If you are a team leader and you are tired of hearing "that's not in my job description!" it may be time to consider a coordinator who is interested in having it in his or hers.

Community as a Feature

A rapidly growing segment of the population no longer reads the boxes of any entertainment product at the retail level. Many hours of research, debate, and examination have already taken place by the time the customer arrives in a big box store or at an online site and either picks up the product or clicks it into his basket. Lush screenshots and taglines spread across glossy foldout covers are often ignored and unwanted; the twenty-first century digital entertainment consumer is informed, savvy, and likely to know your product just as well as you do.

Your first impression for most of your new customers will be your digital outpost and your online community. While "robust, involved, and meaningful interactions with others like you" does not make for a particularly elegant bullet, it is precisely that experience that the majority of MMORPG consumers are seeking. The environment you build outside your game is a companion of the world you are building inside it. Relationships forged on one side will cross over to the other. The more you can facilitate the creation and maintenance of these relationships, the more attractive you will be to new users and the more likely you are to retain your existing base.

Community as a Resource

The statement "they couldn't see the forest for the trees" has been the epitaph of many an online project; you can probably think of several examples of developers with vision, ambition, and a game that no one really wanted to play. While the development of any project should remain true to the vision and aspiration of its progenitors, tempering said vision with the desires and requests of its intended audience is appropriate. Think of your community as a creative SETI@Home supercomputer, mulling over your project and searching for those precious triplets. When a staccato burst erupts over the state, you don't want to miss it.

Building Support

Some online community managers maintain their brood entirely on a volunteer basis. While this would seem to be the ideal situation for any accounting department, there are many benefits to having your community manager on your payroll.

First and foremost, you have control. The official designation as "Company X's Community Manager for Product Y" is a source of pride for managers; the actual paycheck that accompanies it as well isn't anything to be scoffed at. Legal agreements, chains of command, and a position in the company are all valuable in keeping things in check. A formal structure to operate within will help you keep things organized. Professionalism begets professionalism.

Second, as mentioned earlier, the job is a demanding one. Wearing management as a second or third hat is something that can burn out even the most dedicated of fans. With the ability to concentrate on the job at hand, you're going to elevate the level of quality and the job satisfaction of all of those involved.

Part-Time Volunteer—Have Passion, Will Travel

That being said, it does stand to reason that, although you'd like to, you can't pay everyone who is going to work on making your community a better place. Your volunteers will help you for the good of your game and for the benefit of its audience; generally, though, most folks out there don't object to a little swag. It's amazing how far a promotional placard, a collector's mouse pad, or a one-of-a-kind signed by the dev team roach clip will go. We'll talk about how to find these people later.

There's Gold in Them Thar' Hills

Community Managers: This is where things start pertaining directly to you, so listen up! This section may seem redundant to those who have been members of the information industry; however, it is information that bears writing, reading, and remembering.

As a Community Manager, you will undoubtedly run a variety of initiatives, projects, and programs. A central aspect of all of these elements will be your ability to listen (metaphorically) to the influx of information and filter what is important to your community. At times, your role will include being a sympathetic ear, a disciplinarian, an educator, and a friend. Management of a community can be broken down as a science, but a great deal of it is intuitive—go with your gut. The skill of assigning the correct importance to each tidbit is difficult to acquire but worth developing. You will need to enjoy getting to know all kinds of people, have a natural gift for understanding many differences of opinion, and gain energy from surrounding yourselves with others.

Not Listening

We all have guidelines we cannot ignore. We are bound by the rules set forth in our contracts and the direction issued to us by marketing and occasionally by our developers. As a Community Manager, you will encounter situations where an adversarial environment develops—this can be especially noticeable if you've been hired from the community itself. You're going to establish relationships with a vast range of contacts; while many will be sincere, you must be aware that there will be the rare few who are not interested in the same vision that you are trying to promote. Whether they are digging for swag or actively trying to undermine your efforts, you will find that a percentage will over promise and under deliver on their promises, agreements, or efforts. Beware of those who seem too good to be true. Sometimes, it will feel right to break the rules; it isn't. There is a difference between a controlled leak (something your team knows about and has planned for) and spilling the beans to someone you think you can trust. When a conflict of interest arises, it is generally in your best interest to simply stop what you're doing. Take a breather, sit back, and let cooler heads prevail. Breaking a street date, leaking info, or allowing sneak peeks generally isn't worth your job. Think it through.

Fan Submissions and Copyright

As creators of intellectual property in our litigious society, we have great cause to be thankful for the laws in place to protect our hard work. It is vital to afford the same protection to submissions made by members of your client base. Many users will be pleased to be considered for inclusion in anything related to your project; it is essential to safeguard their rights and your right to use their submitted material in the manner you have outlined. Establish a protocol for user submissions; this should include an NDA as well as a standard release detailing the nature of any rights waived or retained by the user.

Community Managers

It's easy to find and conscript the ones who love you; generally, they're trying to find you. If you have a Web board or a listing of fan sites, the most active members are probably your best bet. There are a select few who go above and beyond and do their best to make your experience their experience.

The simplest and most effective thing you can do is ask. Be sure you have a clear idea of what you'd like these folks to do and communicate it to them. The Internet's most famous evangelist, Guy Kawasaki, has a few simple steps that translate well to this subject, as discussed in the following sections.

Sow Seeds with Individuals

Guy Kawasaki suggests that you evangelize your project to hone in on the creativity of individuals, not companies, because your most active members work on these things in their spare time, after their "day jobs."

You're making deposits with individuals; they, in turn, will help bring your message to others. This is a great example of taking care of the metaphorical pennies.

Blend Knowledge with Enthusiasm

Your game and its experience have had an impact. You want to take the feeling you get when talking about, demo-ing or playing your game, and impart that to others.

You Gotta Believe

No matter how tough the day gets, no matter what state the project is in, you are making it a little better just by being there. It's a very simple thing to do when things are going well. As with any true test of character, your determination is only put to the test when things really start to sour. Even through loss and failure, the maintenance of a positive countenance can do wonders for your fan base and your brand. Believe.

Making Friends of Enemies

We'll start this section with a caveat: You can't win 'em all.

You can, however, win some.

You'll find your biggest detractors in many of the same places that you will find your evangelists. They are generally trying your patience and that of the folks in your community. They flame, they troll, and they're generally ticking people off with reckless abandon.

What can you do? Try to make contact with these folks. Find out what's stuck in their craw. A few of these choice specimens of humanity are there just for the joy of the kill—they're fun spoilers. Others are there with a genuine complaint—these are the folks you can reach out to by making them part of the process. Be aware that this can backfire—the eternal chant of CYB (Cover your butt!) rings true. We'll discuss what to do when these yahoos strike later in this article.

Developing a Culture

As end users are becoming more difficult to impress, marketing campaigns have been spiraling into the realm of the extravagant and the ridiculous. However, for those who find the bombast and the excitability of conventional advertising irksome, a counter-culture has emerged; grassroots online movements have returned a subtlety to this segment of our work.

So what's the big deal? Why would you want to take this grassroots approach anyway? A grassroots approach can be used to take advantage of all of the resources the Internet has to offer. Tasks can include everything from coordinating a team to seed online reviews to forum campaigns to in-game fan-run games and quests. Your users will generally be more than happy to help: they make great reviewers on popular Web sites, they love building fan sites, and we've all seen how word of mouth can help a poorly advertised game reach its potential. Grass roots movements are inexpensive, almost free—done right, you're paying your Community Manager to coordinate your efforts, but everyone else participating is doing it for love of the game.

Coordinating with your evangelists on these efforts is not essential, but it is advisable.

With the online programs that ran, we used a central Web board to control the influx and outflow of information in our programs; reactions to forums, review runs, and online chats can be prepared and organized with ease. Make every effort not to limit your scope; reaching out in unique ways can yield unexpectedly positive results. The only group that will actively limit the demographic you're catering to is you. Our Guerilla Group made a concerted effort to list the facets of our lives that we didn't believe related to who we were as gamers. In turn, we used this data to create several archetypes of people who might not necessarily have been gamers, but due to their sharing elements of our personalities may have found our game to their liking. We were surprised to find that many of our hobbies, careers, and cultural elements were similar, leading us to new opportunities for promotion of our game. Take the time to analyze the more esoteric elements of your game; there may be user communities out there unaware that their skills in commerce, politics, or conflict resolution have a mirror image online that could be fun to explore. Reaching out to different social groups such as churches, parents groups, or boys and girls clubs may yield positive results from a demographic you would have not previously considered. We applied this to our program, and it in turn added an entirely new dynamic to our efforts and allowed us to expand the audience that we reached.

Leveraging this type of campaign can be done publicly or privately. In the past, we've had some fun playing it up as an exclusive "under the radar" program. We gave our user-reps code names, stressed the top-secret nature of our activities, and played with the idea that "this really isn't supposed to be happening." Promotion of a game should be a fun thing. Hold competitions to see who can draw the most traffic or who can come up with the most creative and outlandish idea to get your message across. Have fun with it—it can be a great stress reliever and really work to your advantage.

When discussing this issue in the past we have had several questions raised as to the ethical nature of an online campaign of this nature. When you "seed" a review (create the opportunity for one of your members to write a feedback review on a site like Amazon), is it unethical? Does it compromise the nature of the review? In our opinion, it does not. If the end users who propagate a campaign like this weren't passionate about the game, they wouldn't participate. There are few ethical quandaries to be found in simply organizing and harnessing enthusiasm and creative spirit.

The Inside Track—Everyone Wants In

If your project is successful, many very talented people will want to take part. This can create issues ranging from bruised egos to the frustration of being left out. One of the ways to solve the dilemma of "who can I give what job to" is to go to a small group in your community, a neighborhood or guild, for example, and simply *ask* who they feel would do the best job at whatever you need doing. So often, we simply find and ask an individual to join a team or to do a task for us, and it turns out that the team doesn't appreciate it, because they don't know the person or wouldn't consider them for the task. The act of asking others for a nominee does a couple of things. It gives the community members a sense of control over their own destiny, and ensures that the person or persons who are eventually in charge of the project will be more greatly appreciated and respected.

Now, instead of alienating all those who couldn't be asked to do something, you've made them an integral part of the process, which can be deemed as important as the jobs themselves. Recommending best candidates and then offering them support is a great way for all community members to be involved in the daily mechanism, which is, ultimately, their online home where they love to gather to support and enjoy *your* product. Make that home as comfortable as you can and they'll move in and live there forever.

Know When to Say No and How to Shut Up

You will undoubtedly have the services of many folks offered to you on a regular basis. If you've been paying attention, these fans and community members are yours to use to build the success of your community, and therefore your online marketing of your game. With the recruitment of others comes a quick recognition in all that you are asking for and accepting help. Also immediately evident will be the recognition that accompanies these kinds of voluntary roles. Why not ask everyone? Well, if the fact that your team will likely become unmanageable at best and collapse within itself and cease to function at all doesn't scare you, then perhaps the idea of working 24 hours a day to take care of the problems that will certainly arise will.

Don't invite chaos or create a larger amount of work for yourself. By keeping your volunteer moderators, project managers, and other community leaders to a select and trusted few, you will have a great way to delegate a lot of work without adding more. It's a wonderful thing, having folks around you who can do your bidding quickly, efficiently, and with a smile. It's quite another to have an entire army to mobilize, creating tensions and petty jealousies along the way.

Simply ask a few to join, thank them, tell them that if they have a recommendation for adding people to the team now and then to let you know, and then move along. When asked "why them and not me?" say, "Can't choose everyone, and these folks were recommended by others in the community. Please feel free to help by offering your services to those in the leadership positions, I'm sure they'd love that!" and that's that . . . no apologies, no regrets.

Oops! What to Do When the Wrong Message Gets Out

Now and then, no matter how good intentions may be or how vigilant you are, there will be a message that gets out that is detrimental to the popularity of the game, the developer, the publisher, or even the community manager or another member of the leadership team.

Oops, Now What?

The quickest way to fan the flames is to try to make an excuse or cover up the message that was received. The quickest way to put the fire out is to make an admission, give an apology, and promise to attempt to avoid the error in future.

1. Admit wrong.
2. Apologize for wrong.
3. Attempt to learn from wrong.

It may seem pretty simple, but ultimately you are dealing with human beings, and they will respond most kindly to honesty and a sense that you are committed to being forthcoming with information and acceptance of wrong.

The second thing you must do on these tough occasions is to ask someone in either the dev team or the PR department to read through any statement you prepare, just in case the message is at risk of being further distorted or ill will risks being exacerbated. Third-party credibility will help your position, and will also be a great way to reduce risk later if you need to try to explain what you were doing and why. It also tends to soothe your frayed nerves if you can lean on someone else a little. Don't try to be all things to all people. You are hired in this position to build and retain the community, but you also represent these developers and publishers. Let them come to your aid if need be. It will solidify your reputation as having the "official" word, and give you peace of mind if you know you aren't alone out there.

The third consideration is that many communities are "self-correcting." Be sure to read through *entire* threads, or follow whole conversations, or read *all* the e-mail generated on the subject, before you chime in. It may just be that your leaders or other community members have already corrected the message. Often, chiming in can make it worse or renew the debate, not the opposite. Ensure the desired outcome has not already been achieved before you step in to work for it. For example:

```
Troll: "This game SUX0rz"
Community Member 1: "No it doesn't."
Community Member 2: "No, you do."
Community Leader A: "That's your opinion, thanks for sharing it."
```
Can of worms closes
```
Community Manager: "Wow that Troll be nasty! Why do you think it sux?"
```
Can of worms opens

Know which messages need to be modified and when. Then, go and honestly tell people what the right message is. Good luck.

How to Keep It from Happening in the First Place

If success in real estate is location, location, location, then online communities' successes come from information, information, and information!

Keep your team leaders, your volunteer moderators, and your community at large well informed. As soon as a date change, a news item, or a product spec is announced internally, be sure to let those closest to you know and let that information trickle out. Even if some things are confidential internally, telling those closest to you that there will be news soon about this particular subject is a good idea, and it prepares everyone who will eventually need to get the word out.

The more information people have, the less they have to make up. Speculation comes from ignorance. Keep your community in the know and there won't be ignorant speculators having a field day in your members' circles. Have weekly team leader meetings, create a forum for moderators to discuss their issues and recommendations, and call up your fan site administrators now and then to check up. In the case of an online community, a lack of familiarity breeds contempt.

Do everything you can to avoid misinformation or lack of information. If your members can point to fact when answering newbies' questions, it will please and impress the potential new community members. Hearing "we have no idea, so we all assume it's going to be flying monkeys" isn't the most comforting to someone considering membership.

A time may come where someone in a position of relative privilege—perhaps a community leader or a user in whom you've placed your trust—may turn his back on your forward-facing vision. In our most recent effort, a user who had been randomly selected to participate and "report" on in-game developments managed to turn a fun diversion into a platform for a personal campaign against the game complete with out-of-context quotes and vicious diatribes. It hurt to watch that happen. We're all familiar with the fact that some people tend to doff their morals at the door when they jump online. Fame and fortune in the shape of their 15 minutes can shine brighter sooner than the nobility of aiding your cause in the long run. We'd like to say that there is a magical formula that would prevent this from happening, or in the event it does would rectify the situation—sadly, there is not. We won't offer you suggestions in the area of conflict resolution outside of the righteous application of an old axiom: "Fool me once, shame on you, fool me twice and I'm most likely out of a job."

Conclusion

Every game ever created has a fan. Whether it's a mainstream success or a total sleeper, there is somebody, somewhere who adores it. Knowing that this is the most available asset to build a strong foundation on which your game's success will rest is half the battle. Knowing how to *use* this asset is the other half.

Hopefully you've recognized that without the fans, there would be no word-of-mouth or online free support group, and more importantly, no demand for your supply. Once the game leaves your hands, it's not "over." It is just the beginning for those developers and publishers who want their title to become first known, then popular, and finally legendary.

Trust your allies. Use them. Thank them.

More importantly, give them the truth, find avenues to showcase their talents and contributions, and accept them with thanks and with grace. Your audience is not dumb or deaf or mute. Don't treat them as such. Open the door to a win-win-win situation!

Mo' Money, Fewer Problems

As a project leader, money can be your kryptonite. It's always in high demand yet in short supply.

This miracle lubricant comes in many forms, however, not just cold hard greenbacks. Given that you're working on an MMO, you've probably been steeped in countless different types of economic systems—so much so that you make the average tea bag look like the Sahara. We'll examine two issues here: compensating your community manager, and the strategic application of swag throughout the community.

Three magic letters govern the position we refer to as Community Manager: ROI—return on investment. It's notoriously difficult to categorize, but essential to determine whether the investment of time or money is valid. The following techniques can aid in quantifying the contributions being made to the community.

Ask that timelines be kept. These timelines should detail the flow of ideas from points of contact and how they have been acted upon. Couple this with quantifiable figures like sales penetration and Web traffic. If there is a correlation between the actions taken and positive feedback, it has been established that the team is on the right track.

You may ask to have work detailed in a blog. These are great for determining the status of a project, and depending on how public it is made, it can also be interesting reading for your installed base. Any CM will find a deluge of conference calls—notes should be taken and analyzed. Clear opportunities for a CM to do his job should stand out.

Earlier in this section, we mentioned that money could lubricate many sticky situations. Your position as a CM, while fun and entertaining, is also your job and you want to keep it. Throw your money—by which we mean your time—at this situation. You'll thank yourself in the long run.

Earlier we mentioned SWAG, stuff we all give away. It's a great way to make those deposits with your community that can really turn a sour situation around or liven up some dead air. Competitions for the silliest of things as well as salves to soothe some of the more savage breasts can really make your life a little easier. Talk to your merchandising department. Everything from T-shirts to shelf talkers to concept art will usually find their way into the hearts of your more rabid fans. Find a way to get it into their hands as well. A picture is worth a thousand words. A T-shirt? That's a thousand hours of community service.

You Have Your Finger on the Pulse of Your MMO Experience

As a CM or as the supervisor of a CM, you want to set yourself up for success. Assign the time, the personnel, and the budget that is reasonable in relation to your goals. Stay positive, shoot for the top, and you'll find yourself with your finger on the pulse of your MMOG.

Important Features to Attract and Retain Guilds

Sean "Dragons" Stalzer— The Syndicate

dragons@LLTS.org

Guilds play a vital role in the online gaming world by providing added value to players above and beyond the game itself. It is common for players to indicate that the reason they remain playing a game for many years is due to the quality of their guild or the friends they made within the guild more so than the game itself. Thus, attracting and retaining guilds is a key aspect of gaming that needs to be considered when games are designed.

The MMORPG landscape is becoming more crowded with game options, so competition for customers and guilds is ever increasing. A comprehensive list of game features is needed to attract guilds to a game and to entice them to remain playing the game for years. Games that do not take into account "guild needs" will not be able to retain those blocks of players and will lose them to games that do account for them. This article discusses features that should be included in a game to attract and retain guild support, and explains why those features are important for the guild or for the members of the guild.

Why Is It Important to Have Guilds Participate in and Remain Players of a Game?

A large number of players are involved with guilds, and even more players will join guilds in the future. As the gaming community matures and evolves, focus is shifting to "end game" content. That content often involves at least a group of players and often multiple groups, working together. Groups that can count on each other, know their roles, and know the encounter are becoming more critical to succeeding at the "end game." Since guilds, by their very nature, are groups of people with common interests who are often friends and work well together, guilds make succeeding in the end game easier, and sometimes succeeding at the end game means a player must be in a successful guild. Therefore, since many players are already in guilds and since MMORPGs have an increasing focus on end game content needing multiple players to complete, attracting guilds to a game is important for a game's success.

Additionally, it is common for players to express that the reason they stay with games for a long period of time is directly related to their membership in a guild of people with whom they enjoy playing the game. This indicates that content is important but guild membership is one of the key factors in retention. For example, one well-known gaming guild, The Syndicate, polled its members and found that more than half of the polled *Ultima Online* (UO) players would not still be playing UO if they were not members of the guild. Stable, successful guilds can build a community of which players enjoy being a part. Additionally, stable guilds serve as a model that other less-stable guilds aspire to achieve. Therefore, it stands to reason that games that offer guilds the most value and those that make running a guild and being successful as a guild within the game as fun and as low stress as possible will retain more players in the long run.

Finally, bad PR is a nightmare for a game in the current market that is brimming with options for players to choose. Organized, loud, recurring bad PR is a tool that guilds are increasingly aware that they possess. Large, well-known, organized guilds wield a good degree of sway in the player community, especially when they complain loudly and publicly. Fan sites are read by thousands of players and generate millions of hits in a month. Those sites offer the perfect, unrestricted forum to reach players by upset guilds. After its fifth year, *EverQuest* suffered a series of negative publicity hits that came from guild-driven player outcries. It reached a point where a special player conference was held that was intended to address the issues raised by players and guilds. By that point, a good deal of damage was done to the community and many players and guilds were lost, thereby illustrating the power of unhappy guilds. It also reinforces to guilds that they do hold some power. In the future, it will take fewer issues occurring over a shorter period of time to cause them to use that power, since it is clear that wielding it can and does achieve results. Games that make running a guild and being successful as a guild within the game as fun and as low stress as possible will keep the guilds happier. Those games will also retain players who aren't involved in guilds who might otherwise be driven off by large public outcry and the resulting bad press.

Key Features to Attract and Retain Guilds

There are a number of features that most players and guilds would agree that a game must have in order to meet the basic needs of a guild. Those same features are compared against other games when a decision is made as to which MMORPG to play. The list of features evolves over time, both as the gaming genre itself evolves and as player expectations rise in this results driven "what did you do for me today?" market.

Games that only include a bare minimum set of features or leave out key features will be less attractive to gamers. As such, it is wise to not only consider the following feature list, but also to remember the basic guiding premise of this article, which is: MMORPG is a business, and players are its customers. Businesses succeed only if they have a strong customer base that keeps coming back for more of it products. Guilds serve as a powerful tool to draw in customers and to keep those customers coming back far longer than they otherwise would. For the MMORPG business to succeed, the needs of the customer and the needs of the guild must be constantly assessed and addressed.

A list of features that a game needs to include to attract and retain guilds includes:

- A comprehensive guild management system
- Listening to guilds and reacting to that feedback
- Responsive customer service
- Continued and frequent game enhancements and new content
- Focus on end-game content
- Instanced content
- Eliminate the focus on items
- Optional PvP with a compelling, fun reason for players to participate
- Strict lore conformance isn't good—customer first
- Game mechanics that support player run events
- Ability to Alt-Tab out of a game or play in a window
- Internal guild competitions/stats

Comprehensive Guild Management System

Creating a guild is often a few simple mouse clicks in a very user-friendly GUI. Creating and managing a successful guild is not nearly so easy. The Syndicate performed a study of (UO guilds and found that approximately 100 guilds ceased to exist and approximately 100 more were created every day to replace them. The study also found that the average lifespan of guilds was three to six months. That study indicates that most guilds are going to fail. Since the retention of long-term players is affected by the stability of the guild a player is a member of, increasing a guild's chances for success is a worthwhile exercise. In *EverQuest* (EQ), nearly all guilds still failed eventually, with most guilds lasting 8 to 12 months on average. One of the key differences, from the guild perspective, between the two games is the guild management system. The EQ system evolved from an antiquated one into one that was more visual and offered easy-to-use menus with a lot of options and information available to guild leaders and guild members. The UO system has remained relatively static and retains bugs that have existed from day one. As newer MMORPGs were developed, the trend has been toward more GUI systems with many options to make management easier.

Article 1.7 in this book, "Guild Management Tools for a Successful MMP Game," outlines a number of features that players consider mandatory for a guild management system, such as a communications system and a detailed roster. The article also includes many optional but likely to become mandatory features such as guildhalls. Which features are included is a game-specific decision; however, the game that offers the more comprehensive guild management system will have an advantage over the game that does not.

Listening to Guilds and Reacting to That Feedback

The needs of gamers and guilds will change over time. Guilds need to be consulted and listened to, on a regular basis, to see how the changing MMORPG landscape is affecting them. That feedback should translate into new features or changes to existing ones that reduce stress on the guild and increase fun.

Players want to make a difference in the gaming world. Players want to feel that their opinions are heard and that they matter. Guilds, as they are player-created entities, share those same characteristics but are more focused on issues affecting the group. Those issues do not always manifest themselves in individual player comments, so they should be sought out when not readily offered up. When everything appears to be quiet and going well, take the time to go find out what problem is bubbling under the surface waiting to explode. One example of a problem that could have been headed off by more proactive developer involvement with guilds goes back to the early *EverQuest* days. Raid content was relatively new but already was becoming important to players. Guilds were increasingly focused on raiding. The cleric "epic" item was introduced, and it offered manaless resurrecting of dead players. The ability to rapidly resurrect a raid became a critical success factor. The cleric epic, however, had a developer-imposed bottleneck that resulted in a large amount of stress among players and a number of fights inside guilds and between guilds. Many customer service resources had to be invested, on a recurring basis, to deal with the fallout of that unintended consequence. Had there existed an established communication mechanism with guilds where the underlying problem could have been located, a solution could have been implemented months earlier and avoided the loss of some players, the downfall of some guilds, and an overall negative player feeling.

Establish a communication mechanism that is reviewed and acted on with regularity; this should help identify and aid in the elimination of guild issues. By catching and addressing guild issues earlier, guild stability is increased, and that means player retention is affected in a positive manner.

Responsive Customer Service

A common player complaint is having to wait for hours for a GM response to a critical issue. This is also an important issue to guilds. When a guild has key or vocal members who have had issues befall them or when the guild as a whole is having a major issue, rapid customer service responses are critical, and a lack of that is noticed by an entire guild. When two guilds come into conflict (e.g., when fighting over the same monster in games that don't use instanced content), involvement of a customer service representative who uses a standard, well-known, approved method of resolving the situation is needed. When bugs happen that affect guilds (e.g., corpses stuck in spots that cannot be looted or players stuck or members that cannot be added or removed), a rapid response from customer service with a solution, or with the ability to collect the information and escalate it to developers to correct, is needed.

Spending the time to develop a comprehensive set of GM tools that can resolve most issues and collect the necessary information for the issues that cannot be resolved is a worthwhile investment of time. Coming up with standard methods to resolve common guild issues, and requiring all customer service representatives to use the same method will eliminate the issue of subjective issue resolution, which only further inflames trouble situations between guilds.

Customer service, for guilds, is more than responding to pages in a queue. A comprehensive, rapid response with a consistently enforced set of customer service policies and tools needs to exist. Those tools and methods should be revised as the nature of the game changes over time, but the core focus should be on consistent, rapid, comprehensive support for common, major guild issues.

Continued and Frequent Game Enhancements and Content Additions

The MMORPGs of today need to offer content for single players, groups, and guilds all the way to and through the end game to fully capture the market. However, since guilds are organized and work as a team, they complete content more rapidly than solo players do. As such, new content is necessary. The "old" model was to make the content more difficult or artificially lengthy to slow players down. This resulted in smaller guilds and solo players being unable to progress past a certain point in the game. It also resulted in only the biggest guilds that had many hours of playtime per day being able to beat the end game. And that model disenfranchised gamers and guilds. The "new" model is more content driven. Give players and guilds many things to do solo, in groups, and in guilds all the way through the end game.

The positive side to this model is that it has wide player support and resolves all of the major issues that existed with the old model. The downside is that the burden is shifted from the player to the developer. The developer now has to create compelling, interesting, and fun content more rapidly. One expansion every 6 to 12 months is no longer sufficient. Much more frequent additions of new "zones" or new spells or new monsters or new quests are keys to success for this model. *World of Warcraft* is one example of the implementation of the new model. A "live team" is in place whose focus remains on adding new things on a frequent basis. The game itself is very content driven and can be played through the end game as a solo player or with a group of friends or as a guild. There is content that is most enjoyable when done solo, and content that can only be done as a guild, but there is something for all playing styles through the end game.

Guilds, having more power to put toward overcoming a goal than the individual player or group, will overcome content faster. Thus, new content, for guilds, needs to be a focus of the "live team." Guilds no longer accept the "make the content harder or add in artificial time delays (like long spawn times with limited drops)" model, and prefer the "make the content fun and give the players lots of it" model. Thus, having a team dedicated to new content and putting the design tools in place to allow rapid creation, testing, and deployment of new content is critical in the retention of guilds.

Focus on End-Game Content

Players and guilds spend the bulk of their time, within a specific game, at or near the end game. The journey from a new character to a powerful one may seem long at the beginning, but it represents only a small part of their total time within the game. Whether that journey takes one month or six months, when looked at across the multiyear lifespan of an MMORPG, it is clear that the main focus needs to be on the end game. When the *Shadowbane* beta test was nearing an end and the game was going live, there was a huge amount of focus on leveling a character and building a city and fighting other groups. Frequent posts on the beta boards, by guilds, asked the question, "what is the plan for the end game?" Guilds recognized that while the existing content was fun, more was needed over the long term. They were looking for a sign that it was on the radar and coming, as it was not yet implemented or discussed. The response was that end game content was not on the radar screen at that time. The result was a large percentage of the beta testers deciding not to pursue the game once it went live. Since the tempo of the game, once it goes live, is affected by the passion of the beta testers and the press that creates, *Shadowbane* was negatively affected. While that loss of tempo for *Shadowbane* didn't cause the game to fail, the game didn't, in our opinion, achieve anywhere near the success it could have with an increased end game focus.

Since then, development teams have been more vocal about their end game plans, and there seems to be industry recognition of the fact that players and guilds spend the bulk of their time at the end game. Thus, there needs to be a comprehensive plan for providing compelling, fun, end game content with frequent new additions (since the current player preferred gaming model is new, fast, and fun content driven). There is a general understanding of the need to avoid adding long spawn times for limited monsters with limited loot, and for making content harder simply to slow players down from completing it. It is not an issue of quality versus quantity; rather, players want quantity *and* quality, and they want it rapidly when it comes to end game content.

Instanced Content

Another major stress factor for guilds occurs when two guilds collide and compete for the same monster. The worst side of human nature can come to light under those circumstances, and that breeds unhappiness and stress within guilds. It is not an enjoyable contact by either group and often results in wasted customer service resources trying to sooth players and resolve the issue.

Recurring issues of that type result in players quitting the game and guilds disbanding. Guild disbanding undermines the premise that long-term, stable guilds provide a fun, enjoyable environment for players that results in them remaining customers of the MMORPG for longer than they would have without the guild.

The use of instanced zones can resolve that problem. Each guild or group that enters an area launches a private version of the content in which only they participate. The instanced area can be entered and exited at will, or the encounter can be repeated. There are no collisions between guilds. Customer service issues and costs are reduced. Player and guild stress decreases and happiness increases. Instance content resolves one of the largest stress factors guilds face.

Eliminate the Focus on Items

Players love to collect items even if they aren't worth much. *Ultima Online* is a great example of this behavior. Players stored so many items that server lag reached the point that a change was implemented to limit how many items could be stored. On the opposite extreme, items were critical to succeeding in end game content in *EverQuest*, yet so rare (a very few drops per monster, which had spawn times of three to seven days) that tension resulting from who would get to loot which item was very common.

Making items hard to get or making advancement through the game dependent on items is not a good thing. Doing so promotes infighting within guilds, which undermines the stability of a guild and in turn results in more guild failures and less retention of players. Added pressure is placed on the guild to "gear up" every member before the guild can advance to the next piece of content. This is an artificially imposed requirement on guilds that exists solely to slow a player's advancement through content. That design approach is the "old" model for an MMORPG and is no longer acceptable to most players. The "new" model is driven by frequent new content and being able to overcome that content and move to the next challenge without weeks or months of "gearing up."

Items should enhance a character but not make or break his ability to move forward in the game and to win the end game. Items should add value but not be impossible to obtain. There can be rare items, which players will desire to obtain, but those items should be nice enhancements to a character and not perceived as required to move forward in the game. The guiding principle for loot should be: it is fun to obtain, enhances your ability to play the game, but having "top end" gear for your level is not mandatory to move a guild or player forward.

Eliminating the loot stress on guilds will promote more stability among guilds and thus longer guild and player retention.

**Optional PvP with a Compelling,
Fun Reason to Participate**

While Player versus Player (PvP) is not for everyone, it is enjoyed by many players who are often very vocal about their support. While those players are a minority of gamers, they are a significant, active block of players. In addition, there is another much larger block of players who would enjoy the option to PvP when they feel like doing so.

Having optional PvP as a component of an MMORPG offers guilds another feature that they can offer their members. An organized, skilled group of friends to PvP with is both a tool to recruit members and a stabilizing force, since it is yet one more reason the guild is valuable to the player.

PvP without a purpose, however, does not hold a player's interest for long. That purpose cannot be "in order to survive you need to fight well," since the majority of gamers either do not PvP or prefer a game that offers them optional PvP, versus one that places them constantly at risk. Therefore, an enjoyable and compelling purpose for PvP needs to be included. That compelling purpose will keep PvP fun and serve to draw more players into it at least on a part-time basis.

Using instanced zones offers the ability to make PvP compelling and optional. Players who want to PvP enter the special zones and fight there. An instance can have a cap on the size to keep lag under control and more instances can open as needed. The instances themselves can have different themes. For example, a castle instance could exist with one side defending and another attacking. If the attackers breach the walls, they win. If the defenders hold them off for a period of time, they win. The first-person-shooter (FPS) game model is a good one to draw from given its popularity as what basically amounts to a PvP game. The FPS model is one that includes many servers (i.e., instances in the MMORPG world) with different missions (i.e., themes, purposes, goals) where scores are kept, winners are recognized, and possibly rewards are obtained for doing well.

Winning can have value, rather than penalizing the losers. Score can be kept. Titles can be awarded for high scores. Perhaps special PvP-specific items or skills can be obtained by spending points.

In summary, PvP offers guilds another outlet for fun within a game. PvP that is optional doesn't add stress to the guild entity. PvP that has a compelling, fun reason to participate adds value and enjoyment to being in a guild. All of that translates into more stable guilds that remain participants in the MMORPG for a longer period of time.

Strict Lore Conformance Isn't Good—Customer First

While it isn't a common occurrence, there have been cases where the relationship between developers and gamers becomes adversarial. If the developer takes a firm stand on an issue that doesn't conform to players' expectations, tension can arise. The tension can revolve around how an issue is presented and isn't due to the content of the issue itself. Conversely, it may represent a fundamental difference in beliefs. In those cases, the core principle that should come into play is, "The customer is always right."

The MMORPG is a business that needs customers. There is a lot of competition among games, and guilds are becoming increasingly organized and sophisticated. With that comes a willingness to pack up an entire guild and move to another game, since starting over is not that difficult for an organized group of friends. With competition at an all-time high, the fight for customers is fierce. When a dispute between developers and players arises, the players/customers need to prevail.

The most common example of where the tension between player and developer comes to light is when the reason of "because that is the Lore" is used to justify a decision. It is not a stretch to say that most players know very little of the lore and don't really care. They may know the overall vague concept and storyline, but very few know it well enough or care enough to agree with the "Lore" argument. For many players, the "Lore" justification is tantamount to saying, "it's my ball and you will play with it the way I tell you to." That leaves the player thinking, "wait a minute, I paid for the creation, use, and maintenance of that ball and the field we are playing on." The lesson of that semi-common example is, don't force players to conform to artificially created lore. A developer will never win the argument of "I'm sorry, since you are a dwarf you simply cannot play with your best friend who is a troll. Trolls eat dwarfs. So if you want to play with your friend, make a new character."

This manifests itself in guilds in a number of ways. Since an increasing number of guilds span gaming worlds and have migrated to one MMORPG from another, if a new game forces the guild to either fragment into pieces (since one race can't group with another or other such reasons) or forces players to choose a class or race or server that isn't their first choice, other game options will be considered and some customers will be lost. The market is very competitive, and to be a more successful MMORPG, guilds must be catered too and not driven to look for alternatives. An understanding that the guild bond is greater than the bond to the game itself should naturally lead to decisions that complement the guild bond and don't go against it. More often than not, the game will lose out when the player has to choose between the game and the guild or a game that allows him his first choice for play style and one that forces him to conform to developer-imposed play styles.

Game Mechanics That Support Player Run Events

Since many guilds exist not solely for the purpose of winning a specific game, games that also allow them to explore the social side of gaming offer more value than those that do not. Games that offer more value are more likely to be chosen to migrate to or to remain players of.

One of the things *Ultima Online* is famous for is the player-run event. Scavenger Hunts, PvP Tournaments, Lotteries, Crafting Days, Races, and all sorts of other events are common occurrences in UO. The fact that the game has the logistics within it to allow players to host those events is a powerful draw for guilds. That example shows that when given the framework within the game to host such events, many guilds will do so. That not only makes the guild itself more fun for its members, but also adds value to the whole gaming community. Player-run events complement the developer-created content, and the cost of that added value is basically free. Guilds feel like they have a positive and tangible impact on the gaming world, and in some cases they do, and thus they buy into the game more. Those efforts help guilds maintain stability and the whole community benefits.

Ability to Alt-Tab Out of a Game or Play in a Window

A common pet peeve among players is being forced to remain inside the game world for the duration of their gaming session. Those feelings develop because a significant amount of the guild experience takes place outside the game engine itself. Many guilds use chatzones/posting forums to communicate. Guilds use Internet Relay Chat (IRC) servers for additional real-time, more secure and flexible communications. E-mail is a very commonly used communications tool by guilds. Fan sites receive millions of hits a month from players since they contain strategies, guides, and their own forums in which players and guilds participate. Thus, locking players within the game itself for the duration of their play session either forces them to log out from the game to look things up and make use of those communications tools, or causes them to be less connected to their guilds. Strong guilds with strong connections among members can continue to add value and fun for a player long after the game itself has ceased to be fun. Allowing players to Alt-Tab out of the game, or to play the game in a window, allows players to make use of guild tools, thereby strengthening the guild's value to them, resulting in long-term game participation.

Internal Guild Competitions/Stats

Adding the ability for guilds to keep and optionally display statistics to the members or the ability to "purchase" and plug in new modules/games for their guild would be additional added value for gamers and a way to keep players in game. Competition to get into the top tier for a given metric could serve as motivators for some players or some types of guilds and increase the appeal of the game. It may not be as fun, after playing a game for some time, to hunt for gold. An optional guild-tracked metric for the biggest gold donator for the guild may keep that aspect of the game appealing, since it would become a challenge to some players to try to be the top dog on the list.

Additionally, another gold sink could be the creation of what modules/plug-ins that guilds could buy to offer to their members. They could be mini-games within the game itself or new metrics options. For example, basic games like chess and cards could be added in with the ability to track scores and winners within the guild. Alternatively, something like the ability to create and maintain a guild PvP ladder could be added where ladder scores are tracked and statistics kept. Games that really think outside the box could even go so far as to create in-game fantasy sports leagues to pull players into the game and guild for even more of their Internet uses. These types of features appeal to the social aspect of guilds and are not necessarily important to the lore and flow of the game itself. However, as said previously, many players remain playing a game long after the game itself ceases to be fun because of the social value the guild provides them.

Conclusion

MMORPGs are a business that exists to make money. While they are fun, an MMORPG that ceases to make money will cease to exist. Players are the customers of those businesses. Attracting and retaining players is key to making a successful game. Guild membership is one factor that determines if a player joins a specific game and whether he will remain a player of that game for the long term.

The MMORPG community has a variety of choices for players and guilds to consider. The competition for the pool of gamers that play MMORPGs is fierce. To attract more guilds, and thus attract and retain more players for the long term, a game needs to include a variety of features. Those features both entice guilds to choose one game over another, and provide reasons to keep playing a game for many years. Those features also promote guild stability, which in turn promotes player retention.

Guilds are becoming increasingly more aware of the power they wield to impact the bottom line for any game, both by using their unified, organized, relentless voices and via the dollars they bring to the game in which they choose to participate. A guild of 100 players participating in a game for multiple years pays the salary of a developer or for one or more of the servers to run the game. That is a significant amount of power for any one group, and when taken as a whole, guild support can have a large effect on the success of an MMORPG.

Guilds are becoming increasingly more discriminating in their choice of games, demand more features, and will tolerate fewer issues and problems than they did before. It behooves developers to include as many of the features discussed in this article as possible, and to continually focus on reassessing the changing MMORPG landscape. Being open to revisiting old features and revising or scrapping them is a helpful mindset to have. Being focused on adding new features to keep players interested is critical to long-term success. Maintaining a focus that players are customers, the customers are always right, and that players will remain active if their guild remains active will allow a development team to react to future changes in the gaming world.

Active guilds mean active, paying customers who play the game for much longer than if their guild dissolved or left the game.

3.7

Techniques for Providing Online Support for Massively Multiplayer Games

Tom Gordon—AlienPants

cro@alienpants.com

GMs are customer service specialists with expert knowledge of the game who will be present as characters within the game to provide assistance and guidance to players while also coordinating world functionality. In this capacity, GMs will serve as the direct link between the developer and its customers when the game goes live. Additionally, GMs will be responsible for in-game customer support, helping manage our online community, and assisting with the creation of content during the ongoing development of the game. The ideal candidate is a hardcore MMORPG player who is very organized, with excellent communication and customer service skills. GMs MUST be able to work full-time at our headquarters. Shift hours are initially scheduled as 9:00 am–6:00 pm, Monday–Friday.

Did you spot the deliberate mistake there? Yes, this is taken from a real job advertisement for a massively multiplayer (MMP) game, and unfortunately although you can probably guess which game this is in relation to, the reality is that it could be used for any of the current and upcoming generation of MMORPGs about to hit the market—the only real difference is in the location.

It strikes us as being incredibly illogical to provide in-game support for an MMP game during working hours. After all, during this time of the day, the majority of players are doing the same thing as the GMs—they're working at their own jobs. Wouldn't it make much more sense to provide in-game support during those times when people are playing the game?

However for any properly managed support service, there is a need for there to be some in-house resource to ensure there is a good interface between the customer support process (resolving customer problems), the ongoing game development process (adding new features), and the financial process (the parent company providing the game/service). This doesn't mean the entire team needs to be in-house, or that there needs to be someone managing the whole process in-house. It is the relationship between the two companies that is critical. Moving most of the Customer Support process online is simple, with numerous companies worldwide able to provide the necessary pure Customer Support service on a 24-hour basis.

The Case for Non-Centralized Customer Support

From my own practical experience over the past five years at AlienPants, we found it is entirely possible to find, interview, and employ people without a face-to-face meeting, and without requiring them to work in an office. We've had staff working in positions of absolute trust (e.g., having access to a live moderation interface for text to appear on UK satellite television, 24x7) where they are employees of the company and trusted to work unsupervised—and we've never met them in real life.

Call Center Customer Support

Something that seems ludicrous when you think about it logically is having people working to provide support to an online game required to work from a centralized call center. Yes, there are good reasons for having a centralized place of work in most environments, but in any venture where your customers can only access your product online, at random intervals and with varying levels of technical knowledge, you want to hire the best people you can to provide support.

On top of this, by making working from a fixed location a requirement, you immediately narrow your potential employment pool by around 99% of all potential applicants. This may be because of something as simple as not being able to relocate, or not being able to obtain the necessary work permits, or an unwillingness to move to another city or another country, leaving family and friends behind. None of these reasons has anything to do with the applicant's inherent ability to perform the work required of him.

It is entirely possible to run very large online games and game provision services without using a centralized office, with all people working from home over the Internet, and if the right people are employed, productivity actually increases rather than decreases. People working from home tend to be less stressed, especially when they don't have to deal with an often long commute to and from work. They can plan their lives better around the work they have to perform, have more free time, and tend to be more devoted to the job they are doing, often working longer hours than are required as part of their employment contract.

The Hidden Costs of Customer Support

In the Internet-enabled world, providing ongoing support for an Internet-based game requires looking at the way support is provided from a completely different perspective from traditional customer support. No longer are operating hours restricted to "normal" working hours. Moreover, with computer games being thought of as part of "leisure" time, most activity in relation to games occurs outside "normal working hours."

Looked at from a purely economic point of view, moving Customer Support online is a lot cheaper than providing the same level of support in-house. Providing an on-site team of customer support agents requires a certain level of financial commitment prior to the first customer support agent starting work in terms of office space, equipment, light, heat and administrative fees. On top of this, requiring all support personnel to be located at a central facility reduces the available pool of talent that can be drawn upon to those who are located within the local area, or who are willing to relocate.

However for any properly managed support service, there is a need for there to be some in-house resource to ensure there is a good interface between the customer support process (resolving customer problems), the ongoing game development process (adding new features), and the financial process (the parent company providing the game/service).

The issue, however, is not in finding the people to perform customer support, nor is it one of being able to provide the relevant tools to people who are not working from a central location. Rather, it is one of perception, control, and most importantly trust.

Case Study: The Cost of In-House versus Outsource (Online)

All companies have an internal employee cost, the total cost of employment of a single individual. This figure is never just the salary that person is paid, especially in the UK where each employer has to pay an additional 13% of each employee's salary to the Inland Revenue. This figure also includes provision for additional equipment costs, additional stationary, and office supplies, additional light, heat, power—in fact, everything that is needed to assist an employee with his job has a cost that may not have been incurred if that person was not employed.

One large company in the UK uses the figure £66,000 (~$106,000 US) as the average cost of employing one person for one year. This figure is worked out as the average of all salaries of all employees, and the indirect cost of supporting these employees (rent, light heat, etc.), divided by the number of employees. The figure has no actual relationship to any specific employee.

During the period when AlienPants provided Community Management and Customer Support to the online games community for this large company, the value of the labor provided in support of their customers could be accounted for in two ways: the cost of employing all the people who worked providing customer support in-house, or the price paid to have this support provided.

Using this company's own figure of the total cost of employment of one person, the cost of providing the level of support provided by the company worked out to more than £200,000 (~$320,000 US) per month.

The cost to outsource the service to the company was roughly 80–90% cheaper than if they had employed directly, for the same level of service and the same level of customer responsibility.

The Money Trail

So, why the reluctance to move Customer Support online? The only reason we can come up with is an inability to understand how anyone can work remotely and provide the same level of productivity as working from an office.

Numerous companies we have spoken to all give different reasons for why customer support is always provided from a call center, rather than in an online environment. The most common reasons given include:

- Security
- Cost
- Control
- Convenience

Local Language Support

The issue of providing customer support in a customer's local language is one that can be argued both for and against, especially when it comes to supporting massively multiplayer games, and is not one that can be easily quantified. Providing support in multiple languages is an expensive process; however, it can pay off by encouraging players to keep playing the game longer, and providing them with a familiar route for problems they may encounter. Providing the support in native languages can also help to reduce the burden on the support department, as less time is spent in deciphering the actual problem, and determining if there is an issue with concepts or problems being lost in poor translation.

> #### Case Study: Centralized Support Costs
> *Another European company recently recruited a number of GMs to work on the European support of a new MMO game. They recruited a group of people who spoke various European languages, and asked them all to move to the same city in Europe. The company provided free accommodation and a fixed salary per month.*
>
> *Here we're back to the relocation and centralized call center attitude displayed by most Customer Support managers, with (for the people providing support for this game) the chance to also live with the people with whom they work.*

We discussed outsourcing customer support in Europe with this company, and during these discussions we were told what salary levels were being offered. Interestingly, we calculated we could provide the same level of support as was being planned for Europe for the same cost as this company was paying in salary alone, which would have immediately saved them accommodation costs, relocation costs, equipment, heat, light, office supplies, Internet bandwidth costs, and so on.

In addition, we would have been able to deal with support staff churn much more quickly than is possible when dealing with a centralized support center location.

One of the primary complaints from customer support managers in these situations, especially in Europe, is the difficulty in getting people to relocate to another country just to work in a relatively low-paying job.

If this is the case, wouldn't it make better financial sense, and widen the talent pool that can be called upon, to manage the local language support issue remotely? In addition, this type of approach can be taken for translations. The last time we at AlienPants performed translation for another company, we outsourced the translation itself to the country in question. It made sense—why limit our choice of translators to those who happen to be nearby when we can call directly on native speakers? We also got a much better and more sympathetic translation of the text—an idiomatic translation rather than a literal translation.

Recruitment Techniques

There are many ways to find staff capable of working online, and most of them derive from standard recruitment and interviewing techniques. However, you can short-circuit most of the recruitment process by beginning your search within the online communities themselves, or by approaching existing staff.

Finding Staff in Online Communities

When trying to find support staff for an online game, searching within the communities is often a good step. Many companies already do this; however, they then require the support staff to relocate and work in a centralized office.

However, especially with large online communities and individuals who are easily identified as being suitable for support positions, their skill shows through in the way they provide support in an online environment, not in a structured, centralized environment. In these instances, there is no need to differentiate where the support staff is located, as long as suitable tools are provided.

Case Study: BarrysWorld

BarrysWorld was at one time the UK's largest games service provider, servicing a user base of more than 300,000 people. BarrysWorld was run by an extended team (all Community Management, Network Support, Customer Support, Development, and

Administrative staff) of 35 people. At no time did BarrysWorld have a central office that people worked from—every employee from the managing director, the finance director to the Web developers and the network managers worked from home, and communicated and managed the company purely online.

The company managed to grow from a small network of only a couple of game servers to its large size purely through the efforts of the people involved. There was no requirement for the customer support teams to work from a central location, as all tools were designed and developed to be used in an online environment.

Nepotism

It may seem odd, but when recruiting for online staff positions, nepotism is usually a very useful tool, especially if you trust your staff to suggest people whom they in turn trust.

Case Study: QuakeNet

QuakeNet is the world's largest Internet Relay Chat (IRC) network, and is a volunteer-run organization that has a registered user base of more than 400,000 people, and averages more than 200,000 concurrent connections every night of the week, eclipsing competing games-related networks, and even outstripping in size the more traditional IRC networks such as EFNet and IRCNet. Yet most of the 70 or so people who run this network have never met in real life, only in cyberspace, and each individual is personally known to at least one existing operator before he is recruited into the role.

Despite this, the network continues to grow, and has rapidly become the place where the vast majority of online games players throughout Europe, and increasingly through the rest of the world, meet to chat, meet new players, or organize matches.

Motivation

One of the biggest issues when dealing with online employees is motivation. Not everyone can find sufficient motivation to perform their work if they are working from home. This is a common problem in human resources; however, it is exacerbated when people are working remotely, as there may not be an immediate response

Burnout

Burnout is another common problem as people lose their routines, and work life bleeds into social life. This can lead to burnout among people who are not familiar with or used to working in an online environment.

Communication

Communication can often be seen as a big problem when it comes to managing online support teams, with most companies relying on things like Instant Messaging (IM) or in-game tools to provide communication channels.

However, communication even among physically separate staff can be facilitated by using technology such as IRC, which unlike IM is based on a one-to-many connection. By creating and maintaining a working environment where all support staff communicate in the same chat channel, problems can be quickly and easily shared, as can new instructions to staff and general management.

Many chat services also promote a company-wide communication channel, allowing everyone to communicate with everyone else at the same time. This type of communication has proven critical in running the support services for both BarrysWorld and QuakeNet at various times.

You also find that everyone is talking to everyone else at the same time, and more information is exchanged than through being in close physical proximity. This is mostly because people usually only talk to other staff within earshot, or may e-mail small groups. However, if you put them all in the same virtual space and require them to use it to communicate, they will quite happily discuss things as a group.

Support Tools

The Customer Support team, those people working directly with the game players, need to have access to tools that will allow them to resolve the vast majority of problems in-game and online. This includes access to character modification tools (such as names, inventory items, player location, and so forth), as well as giving them access to detailed game logs.

The developers need to give the Customer Support team the tools to help them assist players and resolve their problems quickly and efficiently. If there is such logging in place, it is only logical to take the next step and ensure there is proper logging of customer support activities as well. Moreover, when you have this in place, the location of the staff becomes essentially irrelevant.

Conclusion

In summation, let's review the pros and cons.

Onsite Pros

Physical access to CSRs, all CSRs in one place: This means you can meet one of your staff in person, or the entire staff can all work together in the same place providing support and encouragement.

Security of tools code: It's much easier to protect your game support software tools from external compromise if the applications are running within a secure, closed environment. Even so, it is entirely possible for a rogue employee to misuse these tools regardless of how secure the network is, as has been seen in a couple of instances with MMO games.

Security of internal tools: One common thread is in the security of staff, with the use of external staff perceived as being harder to control than internal staff. However, this is a disingenuous argument—if an employee is going to abuse the tools he is given, he will do it regardless of whether the tools are in-house or online. In addition, maybe, if the tools are used online, coding in-depth logging into the tools from the beginning will help mitigate these problems (see the earlier section, "Support Tools").

Onsite Cons

Expensive: When considering on-site staff, the actual cost of employing one person isn't his salary or even his salary and the employment taxes you may have to pay on his salary. However, it's often the only criteria used when determining the cost of customer support/community management. Office costs including heat, light, amenities, equipment costs, Internet access fees, and administration costs are often not considered, or are considered a cost center elsewhere in the business.

Limited pool of employees—can only get the best from your local area: We've never understood why any company would reject the most suitable person for a job based on his location, if the work he was required to do did not depend on physically being in a particular location. It seems counterproductive to running a successful business to place artificial limits on whom you can employ.

Online Pros

No office costs: There are no additional administration costs associated with facilities, although human resources costs still apply.

No equipment costs: Most online employees, especially those on freelance or part-time contracts, will provide their own equipment.

Expanded pool of potential employees (anywhere in the world, any time zone at daytime rates): It is simple to find staff to work any shift in any time zone, at local or daytime rates, simply by employing staff in one time zone to cover support in another.

3.8

Asian Game Markets and Game Development— Mass Market for MMP Games

Adi Gaash—Exci-TV

adigaash@yahoo.com

You may already know that MMP is a worldwide success story, but did you know that Asian MMP games and gamers propel those games and industry far beyond? Massively multiplayer games are the first truly mass market of interactive entertainment in greater China, with tens of millions of players, and with total revenues that already exceeded movie box office ticket sales in 2003.

If you are a producer, designer, business developer, or a game developer who considers developing an MMP, this is for you. What are the main differences between standard Western MMP game projects and Eastern ones? What do MMP games look like in the eyes of the players in the East? Here we will try to understand the Asian market: the facts, how to approach it, how to get to the local players, and how to make your game application succeed in Asia. After all, Asian-based companies like NCSoft and Webzen are some of the experts and leaders in the field, so we would do well to learn from them.

Market Overview

Unlike the rest of the world, and especially the Western part of it, the Asian market has a few big differences in major aspects. What are those differences and where do they exhibit themselves? Let's talk business.

The Asian Market

This article focuses on the Korean, Chinese, and Taiwanese markets. As it is, those places represent the direction and the edge of possibilities of gaming business development in the Far East. Other notable regions of the East include Japan, which is mostly outside the scope of this article, so whenever we refer to the Far East player, we're pointing more or less to those three main gaming regions.

Let's start by getting a better understanding of the general gaming market. Where developing markets are concerned, the Greater Chinese market is already huge, yet it is constantly evolving. With well over ten million gamers, China is the second largest Internet user base in the world, and the number of Internet users there is predicted to almost double by 2006. Moreover, the amount of broadband subscribers is forecasted to rise rapidly, improving access to prospective Chinese games. In addition, the cost of broadband access is decreasing rapidly, making online games even more affordable. The prospect of this market is huge, considering that China alone has hundreds of millions of people who are potential gamer end users. China is just one example and, as these figures show, not the most significant (yet) (see Figure 3.8.1).

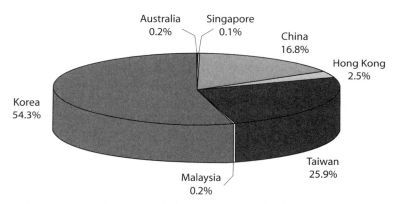

FIGURE 3.8.1   *Gamer breakdown by country in the Pacific region.*

If we look at China in more detail, we can see the Chinese market size by USD. Pay special attention to the estimation of the market's continuing growth until the end of 2007 (see Figure 3.8.2).

This market had already attracted 13 million players by 2003, and, as you can see, the prognosis for coming years is very bright.

Another report from the INQ7.net Web site [INQ7] states that sales of online games have made up 5% of total game software sales in 2001. This segment is expected to grow faster than the other segments, and revenue estimates from online games are 5.3 billion USD by 2005, and 131 million online gamers in 2006.

An important facet of the popularity of online games is the Eastern gaming culture, which underlies the way people in the East perceive and interact with multimedia applications. The average person is much more game-aware and gadget-aware,

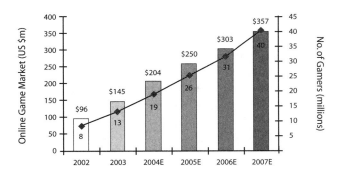

FIGURE 3.8.2 *Chinese online game market.*

and tends to adopt new technologies early and adapt to gaming interfaces easily. Therefore, the penetration of multimedia applications and games is quicker and stronger than in the West. For locals, it is very easy to get to the gaming marketplace and find a stockpile of new and old games for any type of computer or game console, be they in local or foreign language, used or new. Surprisingly enough, the cost of the content is not significantly lower than in the West; sometimes it is even higher, especially when taking into account the relatively low income of the average consumer.

The Main Players—Who Does What

First, we have the game developers: small, medium, and large-scale companies that design both graphics and story and program the games as well. The games are usually based on existing game engines and communication technology. The companies support the game product throughout its full life cycle: from the early stage of the game's development, to its final implementation, support (patches, etc.), and development of future versions.

Most of the successful developers are local companies. This is not surprising, since they cater to the preferences and tastes of the local end users much better than foreign companies do. The aesthetic differences are evident when you examine content and graphic design; for example, Manga titles vs. *Walt Disney* titles or *Shrek*. Games in China are based on local mythology and historical events (such as The Three Kingdoms), which have great appeal to the local gamer. There are a few hundred local companies that develop exclusively for this MMP industry. Some of them try to export their games, but most of them are meant to be sold inside the Asia market.

The central place for game studios is Korea. Some of the Korean studios also have branches in other Asian countries, but generally, most of the content comes from Korea. Some of the prominent companies in the local industry are NCSoft, Nexon, and Webzen.

Next, we have the service providers. Unlike the standard developer-publisher food chain, here the Internet service provider (ISP) takes the place of the traditional publisher. Business-wise, this makes a lot of sense, as promotion for new content can be easily carried out by online platforms. For example, Chinese companies SINA and NETEASE provide e-mail and Web hosting services, but by looking at their Web sites, one can see that those companies' main business is massively multiplayer role-playing games (MMP-RPGs).

The companies buying the local rights handle most of the service and support issues, and of course get most of the revenues. For funding, check NASDAQ for updates on some of the service providers. If this business is new to you, you will be surprised by the numbers and by the dramatic change this online Asian market has brought to the global market.

Last but not least, we have the Internet cafés. Unlike the common use of Internet café in the West, in the East an Internet café functions most of the time as a "gaming café," with most of the activities focused on games. One can say that they have replaced the 1980s' and the 1990s' arcades with regard to computer gaming.

As this option for online gaming use became easier to implement, chains of Internet-gaming cafés quickly gained in popularity. You can find a franchise as easily as you can find a fast food joint. In some cases, Internet café chains function as service providers with regard to publishing new games; our previous development firm negotiated directly with them for the rights to the game we have been developing. One of the major Internet café chains may be equivalent to a major service provider in helping a game become popular and achieve market penetration.

Communication Infrastructure to Support Your Game!

The fast Internet infrastructure situation is promising, as most of the houses in the main cities are already connected to broadband Internet—those not yet connected will most probably be connected in the near future. Funny as it may sound, a room in a cheap hotel in Seoul might not be equipped with towels and a bar of soap, but will have a PC and a broadband connection. Taiwan, for example, published a plan last year to build the infrastructure to provide full broadband access to the entire island.

As you know, other communication services are becoming increasingly popular, such as video on demand and videoconference calling. The demand for these services speeds up the building of the infrastructure. Thus, infrastructure and telecommunication firms like China Telecom, China Networks, and others promote this idea to provide their customers an attractively priced communication package consisting of telephone, TV, and Internet. Service providers have already contacted telecommunications companies to include online gaming services in their content packages.

According to a *DFC Intelligence* report, "[t]he rate of broadband penetration has grown even more rapidly in certain Asian markets, most notably China, Korea, Taiwan and Japan" [DFC04]. Their relatively optimistic estimate of 30.6 million households in Asia with broadband connection by the end of 2003 was exceeded by almost 18%. Since they also state, "the countries with the highest broadband penetration are some of the hottest markets for online games" [DFC04], we can conclude that the potential for online games in the Asian market is very high.

Defining the End User—The Player of Your Game

So far, we have discussed the market from the business, corporate, and infrastructure points of view. It's time to focus on those who really get things rolling—the users.

Internet Café vs. Playing from Home

We are already aware that Internet café play is extremely popular in Asia. As an example, in South Korea alone there are 22,000 such cafés, which are also known as "PC rooms" or "game cafés." So, why did the Asian market adopt this solution and what can we learn from it?

One of the main factors in preferring Internet café play to a home PC is the hardware issue. The buying power of Asian customers is low compared to the United States and Europe. Therefore, even though the cost of the hardware is cheaper, most of the households cannot afford a computer that meets a hardcore gamer's needs. The alternative is trivial: rent a computer by the hour with an Internet connection to play games—that is, go to the Internet café.

In spite of the fact that Internet cafés own much better computers than the ones most have at home, the hardware they use is still technologically inferior to that used in the United States. The standard is low-performance 3D cards and an older operation system, and Internet café owners will only update their hardware once every few years. For example, in 2003, with our company's MMP game still far from being finished, our Internet café customers requested that the game support older cards like NVIDIA's GeForce 2MX and Microsoft® Windows® 98. It turned out they planned *that* to be the main platform for our game, which was scheduled for release more than a year later! Therefore, should you choose to develop games for this market, be aware that cutting-edge PCs are uncommon. Make a product that is suitable for older operating systems, older 3D graphic cards, and sound cards. As a rule of thumb, target three years *back*.

Another factor in playing from an Internet café is its "community value." Socially speaking, computer gaming can be compared to going out to a movie; in some countries, like China, it has already become more profitable than movie box office ticket sales [Latitude1]. This is *the* social activity for youth with free (and sometimes not so free) time. The physical and social proximity of other players gives many levels of added value to a computer game. For example, it is much more rewarding to see the sad face of the opponent whose butt you just kicked in a game of *StarCraft*. From a gameplay point of view, it is easier to coordinate ramming a castle if all the fighters are in the same room. You can look at your friend's screen, understand his position, and call (verbally) other guild members for help. That's why most of the guilds of MMP-RPGs have their "home" Internet café, which is parallel to a local bar/playground in terms of socializing, a place where you can meet all of your friends and game together.

The last relevant issue is parents' disapproval of computer games. In most of the games, the content has a somewhat violent bent, as playing them usually involves action and fighting. This type of activity is of course frowned upon by parents, who would like to see their children studying or engaging in a more "productive" activity. Additionally, in a conservative society, any activity that has a chance to be related to gambling, porn, or violence is not condoned. There are also some stories of online gaming and game addiction (some examples are given later in this article) that perpetuate the disapproval of online games, and computer games in general. However, disapproval breeds rebellion, and if the young cannot play at home, they will play at the local Internet café.

The Player Drive—the Secrets of Success

There are of course many types of games, yet the MMP games still leave all the other types of games far behind. There are many technical and financial reasons for this, but the major reason is the gameplay possibilities that the game offers its players. Here we discuss the main elements and the benefits they bring to gameplay. These elements are by no means exclusively "Asian," but to understand Asian gaming, one must keep these firmly in mind.

First and foremost, playing with friends or against other people is much more exciting and rewarding than playing in single-player mode. This holds true even for simple games and casual gamers; in games like chess, the online alternative is much more popular than the traditional way and the player-versus-computer option. Through multiplayer, you can make new friends, find decent opponents (in both casual play and MMP games), receive praise and reward from others for your actions, and lead other players.

Therefore, most of the successful games in the MMP genre encourage "clan" play. This usually means that several players with the same game objectives team up to finish up hard task and quests, and when this gets boring they turn to fighting other clans. Most games also come with a built-in chat system to aid and promote the creation of an online community. The existence and development of such a community is central to the enjoyment of the game. To paraphrase the advertisements for *Lineage II*: "Become a hero," then "Become a leader or be a part of a clan," and finally, "Become a leader of an army" (which results in taking over other players' land).

Another appealing element is persistence. There are two components of persistence, and the combination of them maximizes what we call the MMP game's "addiction factor." One component is the continuity of the virtual world—it exists by itself, always progressing even when the player is offline—which is the same as in the real world, in the sense that even when the president is asleep, the war goes on. The player is always curious as to the development of game events, and this curiosity keeps him logging on to see the current answers: Is the castle still secure? Are the dragons still hunting the area? Who is the top-ranking player? Should I sell my magical ring now? Did I make a lasting effect on the world? The other component is the improvement and continuity of the character's actions—the idea that yesterday's achievements directly influence today's activities. Nothing that is gained is lost, and the character continues from the same place you left it. Thus, persistence makes the game more attractive than other online options and makes up the most of the game's "addiction factor."

Other types of games can fall into the *technical* term of MMP games other than RPG. One example is the MMP-RTS (real-time-strategy) game. Yet still, the RPG is more popular, as it is easier to control one character than command a full-size army. When compared to arcade games, RPGs provide much more versatility in directing the advancement of the character. Other popular types of games such as sports games and first person-shoot-'em-up games are more suitable for a scenario type of game. These games do not provide the continuity that is so central to MMP-RPGs. The format of the RPG game to this type of play is critical: the player has to feel that he is the character in the game, from the point of character creation and throughout the in-game advancement.

The last and perhaps most surprising element is money—*real* money. This money is made by buying and selling magical items and other stuff online. In this way, the virtual assets market becomes a way for the players to profit from their gaming hour investment. Players stay online trying to hunt monsters, steal treasure, and go back to the city to sell those goods to other players in return for other goods or virtual money, and for real money.

Some users take this issue much more seriously than others do. They invest hours in hunting down dragons and wizards for their treasure, and then sell this treasure to other players. The buyer might soon join the food chain as the powerful virtual item that he bought allows him to slay other monsters (or players) and get their treasure. The money obtained by the seller of the item will in turn be spent on playing the game. As you can see, this creates a system in which all the participants win, both the users and the game providers (and as we are dealing here with a market of millions, the virtual market, as small as it may still be, is significant).

In conclusion, the best game type to maximize all those elements is (of course) the MMP-RPG.

Content—West vs. East

Contrary to Western games, brand name is not the main issue here, as a player's interest is driven by curiosity. This means searching for new content: a new ability, new ways and situations to use old abilities, new fantastic wildernesses to explore and rule, new computer-generated type of opponents, and so forth. Thanks to this, the cost of a game's development is cheaper compared to MMP-RPGs such as the *Star Wars Galaxies* game, as there are no agents, studios, publishers, or brand owners (like LucasFilms in the previous example) to share with, or development costs to consider. As mentioned earlier, the majority of content development is done in Korea, which, having the most experience in the field has become the main place for online development. From a cultural point of view, the content produced there is more or less similar to other mass regions in Asia; you can see that lead games like *Lineage* and *Legend of Mir* (*1*, *2*, and *3*) that were originally developed in Korea are on the list of top MMP games in China. Therefore, it is not surprising that Korea's neighbors regularly choose Korea as their main source for imported online games.

As far as quality of content (graphics and features) is concerned, games in Asia are generally less graphically intensive and less complex in terms of functionality than those prevalent in the United States. This is largely the product of two factors: first is the need to support a wide range of hardware (not only the up-to-date hardware) and users; and second is the fact that the casual online game sector is growing (~45% by 2004), and casual gamers do not demand high-end graphics. This shortens the game development cycle, and therefore directly affects the number of games that can be released every year. Thus, players get a wider range of online games to choose from, and they will try many MMP games every year.

Revenue Models—Putting the Money Where Your Mouth Is

There are two main methods of payment in Asia. One is subscription, which is the standard in the rest of the world. The other and more common one is pay-per-play, or pay-by-the-hour. There is virtually no payment for the game software itself, as it can be easily downloaded from the game provider (via the fast broadband connection). If you really need the game software disk you can get it from 7–11 or other local shops for $1 USD at most.

How does pay-by-the-hour work in today's Asian market? It's quite simple actually. You can buy a pre-paid card in an Internet café, or in another store, and use it to log in to the game. When you use the card at the Internet café, you're actually paying both for game time and for Internet time. The idea is very appealing, as you can buy hour cards without committing to pay for a full month's use. You also don't need to have a credit card to use this method, which is a big plus as the majority of players do not own one.

The cost per use changes from country to country, but this solution is very affordable: for example, in China, the average cost is only 0.40 RMB (~$0.05 USD) per hour to be logged on to an online game server. Therefore, this should come as no surprise that leading online games attract between 400K–500K concurrent users. In China alone, the number of Internet cafés is over 200,000 [Latitude1], each of which houses dozens of computers.

Stories About MMP Games in the East

There are many stories to tell, and while some of them might sound outlandish or seem like an urban legend, we can assure you that some of them really happened. The following examples are presented here as they were presented to us.

The Addicted Player—Three Short Unhappy Cases

There are a few stories from the local news that have to do with health hazards to players of online games. Most of them have a sad ending, up to and including the player's death.

Poe News reports a 24-year-old South Korean man died after playing computer games nonstop for 86 hours in an Internet café. The story, which is eerily similar to a story from last year about another Korean Internet café patron dying after an extended play session, says, "the 'jobless' man had no decent sleep or meals for the duration of his three-plus day gaming marathon, and word is that an initial investigation has ruled out foul play" [Story1].

Another example comes from the *Sydney Morning Herald*, which reports on another gamer dying after a massive gaming binge. The report stated, "a 27-year-old Taiwanese man collapsed after playing computer games for 32 hours nonstop" in a cyber café in central Taiwan. According to the story, "a police spokesman stated that doctors believe Wen-cheng died from exhaustion, having remained in the same position for too long. The death highlights the danger of such intensive game-playing" [Manktelow03].

There are more sad stories about similar events that took place in Thailand and other regions in Asia. As you can see those games can and often do have a major impact on the player's life, and some players cross the boundary between game and real life.

Internet Café Kidnapping

In another case, a young player was boasting after killing a virtual warrior. This in itself is a very common occurrence with no dire consequences; however, in this case it turned out that this specific virtual warrior was played by a gangster. The gangster, offended by the defeat and humiliated by the boasting, asked the unsuspecting youngster to meet him in real life—a meeting that resulted in the kidnapping and roughing up of the poor player—to teach him a lesson that you simply cannot ignore the real world when playing.

Conquer the Castle—Matrix-Style

For some people, the trading in virtual MMP-RPG property discussed earlier has become an effective way to make a living. Some individuals choose to resign from their day jobs, and instead dedicate 10 or more hours per day to "work" in the virtual world, literally slaying dragons for a living. Some of them have also asked their gaming friends to do the same. In Korea, some people rented an apartment and started paying other people "salaries" to come to their place to "work" as a group/clan in the game.

As virtual property became increasingly expensive, it also became vital to guard it at all times, so one Internet café clan had assigned "guards" to protect a castle and some ruins that were both strategically located and contained lots of treasure. A specific group of the aforementioned "game workers" had repeatedly tried to take control of this castle to no avail. The defenders were much stronger, held a better position, and outnumbered the attackers. The only way to take control of the asset was to "hack" the defenders somehow, so after a few pings and communication tracing the attacking group of "workers" managed to find out where the Internet café of the castle defenders was based *in the real world*. Then, one of them went there and shut down the electricity of the Internet café, timing the attack from the office accordingly. As the defenders could not function offline, the castle easily fell into the attackers' hands. This attack bears striking resemblance to the *Matrix* scene in which Cypher unplugs part of the team from the *Matrix*.

Local Problems

Every rose has its thorn, and the Asian gaming market is no exception. However profitable it might be in the long run, there are hurdles to overcome, pitfalls to avoid, and potential problems to keep in mind before attempting to sell your game in this market.

The Government

Since the government's aim is to support the local industry, importing game consoles and games is severely hampered. The quantity of "foreign" games is therefore limited, and both their localization process and the procedure of content approval are slow. This has, of course, a very direct effect on the price of imported items. For example, in Beijing in mid 2004, a PS2 console was 150% of the price in the United States.

As far as content approval is concerned, games in the East sometimes count as a waste of time at best and as an activity that encourages violence and even porn or gambling at worst. Therefore, the rating of games is problematic. In Korea, only in the year 2003, 184 games (that's 27% of all of the games released in Korea that year) were rated "Over 18." The majority of them were related to "stirring up speculative spirit"; in 39 cases, the rating was due to excessive violence, and in 29 cases because of suggestive or sexual content [Government1]. Therefore, when you try to sell a game that has content considered acceptable in the West, you should be aware that the "standard" violence in your game will be approved, but only after an extended approval phase.

Local authorities also have a dim view of gaming activity and take steps to keep it in check. In China, Internet cafés are banned from operating less than 220 yards from public schools, because of the fear of the adverse effects that video games and Internet addiction might have on children. In 2003, the government of China shut down a significant number of Internet cafés near junior and high schools. The damage to the local online industry was extremely high. Things did not get better in 2004, either. From the local Beijing news of 5/2004: "China has shut down more than 8,600 Internet cafés in the last three months, many of them for illegally admitting juveniles. Any such place allowing juveniles to enter or allowing unhealthy information to spread through the Internet will face rigid, severe penalty" [Government2].

This particular cloud, however, has a silver lining. There is lots of support for the gaming market from the local governments, as the possibilities to export this specific industry are high. In Korea, as well as in Hong Kong and Taiwan, the trade and industry department fund marketing for this industry, support local development, and provide services for connecting providers to potential customers. Contacting your clients/partners through their offices is highly advisable. Sometimes, the government supports gamers; for example, see the world cyber games championship that took place in the Far East in the last couple of years. Another good example is China's government adopting pro-gaming policy initiatives, such as including online gaming in China's flagship project to enhance technology R&D, and adding "E-Athletics" (online sports games) to the government's overall sports program [Latitude1].

Software Piracy and Illegal Stuff

The Far East is a place where you can find every DVD quality movie for the cost of $1 USD (usually before it has the chance to be sold legally), so an "off-the-shelf" product does not have a real chance to be sold. This is one of the reasons why consoles and offline computer game products cannot become a real business option, despite the (seemingly) large market for them. People simply won't buy what they can download or burn nearly free of charge.

In the online MMP, this loss turns into opportunity—an opportunity for a free marketing campaign, as an installation disk of your game development product will move from one hand to another, one computer to the next in no time. As for charging money for your game, we've already shown how the payment/billing system is totally separate from the cost of the software.

Another local malady is illegal game servers, operated by hackers who provide them free of charge. This cuts quite deep into the source of the games' profits. Analysts say piracy in the industry is rampant, although it's difficult to quantify exactly how much knock-off sites hack into the sales of a market expected to be worth more than $400,000,000 USD this year.

Some private servers make money by selling advertisements. Others are run by fly-by-night hackers who have no interest in making money and believe they are helping their fellow gamers, but in the long run, they are causing real damage to the industry.

Evolving Business Models

Cooperation with the Locals

The best route to take is that of cooperation with players in the local industry. Assuming that you are not already a veteran player in the Asian market, whether this is your first or second step in this market or industry, we would highly advise you not to go alone.

Simply put, no article or advice can compare to experience. Try hooking up with local game operators, game developers, business development personnel, and, of course, content owners.

This approach yields numerous benefits, as it is better and easier to understand the local market through the eyes of the local industry. As you should realize by now, the majority of Asian gamers see gaming differently. That means that the "tried-and-true" Western game design, Western game features, Western game art, and Western marketing techniques will not automatically fit the local market. Another point is that the cost of local cooperation can be lower since the local cost of living is lower, especially when it comes to mainland China (excluding Hong Kong). You should also think about the implementation phase of the game; when it comes to marketing your product, it would be *much* easier to use local help (not to mention customer support issues), so why wait until the last minute?

For example, our company had a Taiwanese partner since the very first steps of developing. They helped us with adapting graphical design to the local players, and tried on our behalf to contact local Internet café chains and other major local publishers. This type of help is invaluable to anyone not familiar with the local industry.

Risk Factors

As you will be dealing with a different culture—different in both gaming culture and business culture—everything in your gaming plan needs to be carefully considered. You should ask yourself from the very early steps of game design, and up until the very last steps of implementation: "Will this game sell *in Asia*?" Not only "Is my content good," but especially, "Will my content 'work' *there*?" You must keep your finger firmly on the pulse of the latest game fashion, as your gamers are early adapters who are constantly looking for new and better games.

Understand your partners before you sign a deal. Sometimes, when game development is involved, your presentation might accidentally mislead your local clients/partners, not because it's badly done but because they see some things differently. This is generally good advice, but in this case, we strongly recommend to break everything down to details, and to re-check every point with your clients/partners. As much as you might think that everyone understands what was agreed upon, *never* base your cooperation on a verbal or informal agreement.

The Asian market is huge. Lead MMP developers already planted their feet here, not to mention the local game developers. Therefore, make sure that your product or offer is somehow better, special, or more attractive in some way than those already on the market. To put it bluntly, clones of already successful games might work, but will not make the breakthrough for new developers or publishers.

Conclusion

We strongly advise you to take advantage of the hunger for new games in Asia. If you do well here, the rest of the world will be a much easier task. The future of MMPs started here—even though Asia is expected to constitute only 23% of the worldwide online market in 2009 (55% U.S., 21% Europe), it has a great potential for dominating the entire MMP market and game development industry, as South Korean companies already aim to become the kings of network games.

Managers in lead MMP Asian firms hope that Western users will join this gaming sector, and that local U.S. developers like Blizzard and Sony Online Entertainment will help those gamers to "open their eyes" to the MMP experience. They strive toward a fully global industry and a worldwide game community, one that would ideally be controlled by Asian firms.

At mid-2004, after the release of *Lineage II* and *City of Heroes*, you can already see that NCSoft had taken the first step toward MMP Asia everywhere.

In summation:

Listen carefully.   Try to understand the players' needs and learn from the local developers, as many mistakes can be avoided this way.

Strive for excellence.   Always seek ways to improve your game's content, quality, and service.

Play local games.   Insist on trying as much as you can, even those that already achieved worldwide recognition.

Don't be late on early adapters!   Visit the target market often to keep up with the local industry.

References

[DFC04] DFCInt.com, "The Online Game Market Heats Up," available online at *www.dfcint.com/game_article/june04article.html*, June 30, 2004.

[INQ7] "131M Online Gamers Available in 2006," available online at *www.inq7.net*.

[Story1] "Another Korean Killed by Computer Games," available online at *www.poe-news.com/stories.php*.

[Manktelow03] Manktelow, Nicole "Health Hazard," *Sydney Morning Herald,* March 1, 2003, available online at *http://smh.com.au*.

[Latitude04] Latitude capital group, "LGC Market Perspectives—China Online Games Sector Review," March 2004, available online at *www. latitudecapitalgroup.com*.

[KGDI04] Korea Game Development & Promotion Institute (KGDI), "The Rise of Korean Games 2004," *Gameinfinity*, now available in PDF version at *www. gameinfinity.or.kr*.

[ABCNews04] ABC 7 news—"China Shuts More Than 8,600 Internet Cafes," available online at *www.wjla.com/headlines/0504/144885.html*.

INDEX